The Most Effective Official SAT Study Guide

The 717 pg All-in-One Solution for your Highest Possible Score

BOULEVARD BOOKS
The New Face of Publishing
www.BoulevardBooks.org
ISBN 13: 978-1-942500-65-0

The SAT remains an important aspect for most college admissions processes. Schools use it as one factor to determine a student's college readiness, and it can even help students qualify for merit scholarships.

We suggest that students take the SAT as early as possible in their junior year. That way, you can compare your score to the average scores of admitted students on your college list and see if you want to retake the test to improve your score.

Whether you've never taken the SAT or you're planning to retake it, you should definitely spend some time preparing for the test. But how much time should you spend? The answer, although you may not like it, is that it depends.

There is no wrong amount of time to spend preparing for the SAT. Some students spend months, while others cram their studying in to a couple of weeks. To gauge how long you need, it's a good idea to take practice tests so you can compare your scores—the total score and your section scores—to the scores of the schools you plan on applying to. The lower your score is compared to the school scores, the more time you should allot for studying and preparing.

Remember, as you go through the practice exams included in this book you are still learning about the world. The most effective mindset in preparation for any test is one that is eager for knowledge wherever it may be.

Evidence-Based Reading and Writing

The Evidence-Based Reading and Writing section is composed of 2 tests that assess different but related skills and knowledge. The Reading Test gives you a chance to show how well you understand what you read. The Writing and Language Test asks you to revise and edit text.

Reading Test Overview

- Total questions: 52 passage-based reading questions with multiple-choice responses.
- Time allotted: 65 minutes.
- Calculators may not be used or be on your desk.
- The questions often include references to direct you to the relevant part(s) of the passage(s).

What the Reading Test Is Like

When you take the Reading Test, you'll read passages and interpret informational graphics. Then you'll use what you've read to answer questions. Some questions ask you to locate a piece of information or an idea stated directly. But you'll also need to understand what the author's words or a graphic's data imply.

What You'll Read

Reading Test passages range in length from about 500 to 750 words and vary in complexity. The Reading Test includes:

- 1 passage from a classic or contemporary work of U.S. or world literature.
- 1 passage or a pair of passages from either a U.S. founding document (such as an essay by James Madison) or a text in the Great Global Conversation (such as a speech by Nelson Mandela).
- 1 passage on a social science topic from a field such as economics, psychology, or sociology.
- 2 science passages (or 1 passage and 1 passage pair) that examine foundational concepts or recent developments in Earth science, biology, chemistry, or physics.
- 2 passages accompanied by 1 or more informational graphics.

What the Reading Test Measures

To succeed in college and career, you'll need to apply reading skills in all sorts of subjects. You'll also need those skills to do well on the Reading Test.

The Reading Test measures skills and knowledge you'll need to apply when reading in college and workforce training programs. The test will ask you to find and interpret information and ideas, analyze how texts are put together and why they're written the way they are, work with data from informational graphics, and make connections between paired passages.

You'll be asked questions that require you to draw on the reading skills and knowledge needed most to succeed in the subjects the passages are drawn from. For instance, you might read about an experiment and then see questions that ask you to examine hypotheses, interpret data, or consider implications.

Answers are based only on the content stated in or implied by the passages and in any supplementary material, such as tables and graphs.

Command of Evidence

Some questions ask you to:

- Find evidence in a passage (or pair of passages) that best supports the answer to a previous question or serves as the basis for a reasonable conclusion.
- Identify how authors use (or fail to use) evidence to support their claims.
- Locate or interpret data in an informational graphic, or understand a relationship between a graphic and the passage it's paired with.

Words in Context

Some questions focus on important, widely used words and phrases that you'll find in texts in many different subjects. The words and phrases are ones that you'll use in college and the workplace long after test day.

These questions focus on your ability to:

- Figure out the meaning of words or phrases in context.
- Decide how an author's word choice shapes meaning, style, and tone.

Analysis in History/Social Studies and in Science

You'll be asked to read and analyze passages about topics in history/social studies and in science.

Tips for the Reading Test

To answer each question, consider what the passage or passages say directly, and use careful reasoning to draw supportable inferences and conclusions from the passage(s). The best answer to each question is derived from what is stated or implied in the passage(s) rather than from prior knowledge of the topics covered. All of the questions are passage based.

- Reading carefully is the key to finding the best answer to each question. The information you need to answer each Reading Test question is always in the passage(s). Don't be misled by an answer that looks correct but isn't supported by the actual text of the passage(s).

- The questions don't increase in difficulty from easy to hard. Instead, they are presented as logically as possible. Questions about central ideas and themes, point of view, and overall text structure generally come early in the sequence. After that come more specific questions about such matters as facts, details, and words in context.

- Stay with a passage until you have answered as many questions as you can before you proceed to the next passage. Don't jump from passage to passage.

- The questions often include references to help direct you to relevant part(s) of the passage(s). You may have to look elsewhere in the passage, however, to find the best answer to the question.

- In your test booklet, mark each question you skip so you can easily go back to it later if you have time.

- Remember that all questions are worth 1 point regardless of the type or difficulty. You don't lose points for guessing wrong, so you should try to answer each question as best you can.

Sample Reading Test Materials

Following are samples of the kinds of passages and questions that may appear on the Reading Test. For each set of sample materials:

- Read the passage(s) and any supplementary material carefully.

- Decide on the best answer to each question.

- Read the explanation for the best answer to each question and for the answer you chose (if they are different).

On the actual test, each passage will be followed by 10 or 11 questions. The directions that follow match the directions on the actual test.

Reading Test Questions

Directions

Each passage or pair of passages below is followed by a number of questions. After reading each passage or pair, choose the best answer to each question based on what is stated or implied in the passage or passages and in any accompanying graphics (such as a table or graph).

Questions 1-3 are based on the following passages.

Passage 1 is adapted from Susan Milius, "A Different Kind of Smart." ©2013 by Science News. Passage 2 is adapted from Bernd Heinrich, *Mind of the Raven: Investigations and Adventures with Wolf-Birds.* ©2007 by Bernd Heinrich.

Passage 1

In 1894, British psychologist C. Lloyd Morgan published what's called Morgan's canon, the principle that suggestions of humanlike mental processes behind
Line an animal's behavior should be rejected if a simpler
5   explanation will do.

Still, people seem to maintain certain expectations, especially when it comes to birds and mammals. "We somehow want to prove they are as 'smart' as people," zoologist Sara Shettleworth says. We want a
10   bird that masters a vexing problem to be employing human-style insight.

New Caledonian crows face the high end of these expectations, as possibly the second-best toolmakers on the planet. Their tools are hooked sticks or strips
15   made from spike-edged leaves, and they use them in the wild to winkle grubs out of crevices. Researcher Russell Gray first saw the process on a cold morning in a mountain forest in New Caledonia, an island chain east of Australia. Over the course of days, he and crow
20   researcher Gavin Hunt had gotten wild crows used to finding meat tidbits in holes in a log. Once the birds were checking the log reliably, the researchers placed a spiky tropical pandanus plant beside the log and hid behind a blind.

25   A crow arrived. It hopped onto the pandanus plant, grabbed the spiked edge of one of the long straplike leaves and began a series of ripping motions. Instead of just tearing away one long strip, the bird ripped and
30   nipped in a sequence to create a slanting stair-step edge on a leaf segment with a narrow point and a wide base. The process took only seconds. Then the bird dipped the narrow end of its leaf strip into a hole in the log, fished up the meat with the leaf-edge spikes, swallowed its prize and flew off.

35   "That was my 'oh wow' moment," Gray says. After the crow had vanished, he picked up the tool the bird

had left behind. "I had a go, and I couldn't do it," he recalls. Fishing the meat out was tricky. It turned out that Gray was moving the leaf shard too forcefully
40   instead of gently stroking the spines against the treat.

The crow's deft physical manipulation was what inspired Gray and Auckland colleague Alex Taylor to test other wild crows to see if they employed the seemingly insightful string-pulling solutions that some
45   ravens, kea parrots and other brainiac birds are known to employ. Three of four crows passed that test on the first try.

Passage 2

For one month after they left the nest, I led my four young ravens at least once and sometimes several times
50   a day on thirty-minute walks. During these walks, I wrote down everything in their environment they pecked at. In the first sessions, I tried to be teacher. I touched specific objects—sticks, moss, rocks—and nothing that I touched remained untouched by them.
55   They came to investigate what I had investigated, leading me to assume that young birds are aided in learning to identify food from the parents' example. They also, however, contacted almost everything else that lay directly in their own paths. They soon became
60   more independent by taking their own routes near mine. Even while walking along on their own, they pulled at leaves, grass stems, flowers, bark, pine needles, seeds, cones, clods of earth, and other objects they encountered. I wrote all this down, converting it to
65   numbers. After they were thoroughly familiar with the background objects in these woods and started to ignore them, I seeded the path we would later walk together with objects they had never before encountered. Some of these were conspicuous food items: raspberries, dead
70   meal worm beetles, and cooked corn kernels. Others were conspicuous and inedible: pebbles, glass chips, red winterberries. Still others were such highly cryptic foods as encased caddisfly larvae and moth cocoons. The results were dramatic.

75   The four young birds on our daily walks contacted all new objects preferentially. They picked them out at a rate of up to tens of thousands of times greater than background or previously contacted objects. The main initial criterion for pecking or picking anything up was
80   its novelty. In subsequent trials, when the previously novel items were edible, they became preferred and the inedible objects became "background" items, just like the leaves, grass, and pebbles, even if they were highly conspicuous. These experiments showed that ravens'
85   curiosity ensures exposure to all or almost all items in the environment.

1

Within Passage 1, the main purpose of the first two paragraphs (lines 1-11) is to

A) offer historical background in order to question the uniqueness of two researchers' findings.

B) offer interpretive context in order to frame the discussion of an experiment and its results.

C) introduce a scientific principle in order to show how an experiment's outcomes validated that principle.

D) present seemingly contradictory stances in order to show how they can be reconciled empirically.

Estimated Difficulty: Hard	**Key:** B

Choice B is the best answer. Passage 1 opens with an explanation of Morgan's canon and continues with a discussion of people's expectations regarding animal intelligence. Taken together, the first two paragraphs indicate that despite cautions to the contrary, people still tend to look for humanlike levels of intelligence in many animals, including birds. These two paragraphs provide a framework in which to assess the work of Gray and Hunt, presented in the rest of the passage. The passage's characterization of the experiment Gray and Hunt conduct, in which they observe a crow's tool-making ability and to which Gray responds by trying and failing to mimic the bird's behavior ("I had a go, and I couldn't do it," line 37), suggests that Shettleworth, quoted in the second paragraph, is at least partially correct in her assessment that "we somehow want to prove [birds] are as 'smart' as people" (lines 8-9).

Choice A is incorrect because while the reference to Morgan's canon in the first paragraph offers a sort of historical background (given that the canon was published in 1894), the second paragraph describes people's continuing expectations regarding animal intelligence. Furthermore, the fact that Gray and Hunt may share with other people the tendency to look for humanlike intelligence in many animals does not by itself establish that the main purpose of the first two paragraphs is to question the uniqueness of Gray and Hunt's findings.

Choice C is incorrect because while the reference to Morgan's canon in the first paragraph does introduce a scientific principle, the discussion in the second paragraph of people's expectations regarding animal intelligence, as well as the passage's characterization of Gray and Hunt's experiment and how the researchers interpret the results, primarily suggest that people tend to violate the canon by attributing humanlike levels of intelligence to many animals.

Choice D is incorrect because although the first two paragraphs do present different perspectives, they are not seemingly or genuinely contradictory. The second paragraph, particularly the quotation from Shettleworth, serves mainly to qualify (not contradict) the position staked out in the first paragraph by suggesting that while Morgan's canon is probably a sound principle, people still tend to project humanlike levels of intelligence onto many animals. Moreover, the experiment depicted in the rest of the passage primarily bears out Shettleworth's claim that "we somehow want to prove [birds] are as 'smart' as people" (lines 8-9) and thus does not reconcile the perspectives found in the opening paragraphs.

2

According to the experiment described in Passage 2, whether the author's ravens continued to show interest in a formerly new object was dictated primarily by whether that object was

A) edible.

B) plentiful.

C) conspicuous.

D) natural.

Estimated Difficulty: Easy	**Key:** A

Choice A is the best answer. The last paragraph of Passage 2 presents the results of an experiment in which the author scattered unfamiliar objects in the path of some ravens. According to the passage, the birds initially "contacted all new objects preferentially" but in "subsequent trials" only preferred those "previously novel items" that "were edible" (lines 75-81).

Choice B is incorrect because the ravens studied by the author only preferred those "previously novel items" that "were edible," whereas "the inedible objects became 'background' items, just like the leaves, grass, and pebbles" (lines 80-83). In other words, plentiful items did not continue to interest the ravens unless the items were edible.

Choice C is incorrect because the ravens studied by the author only preferred those "previously novel items" that "were edible," whereas "the inedible objects became 'background' items, just like the leaves, grass, and pebbles, even if they were highly conspicuous" (lines 80-84). In other words, conspicuous items did not continue to interest the ravens unless the items were edible.

Choice D is incorrect because the ravens studied by the author only preferred those "previously novel items" that "were edible," whereas "the inedible objects became 'background' items, just like the leaves, grass, and pebbles" (lines 80-83). In other words, natural items did not continue to interest the ravens unless the items were edible.

3

The crows in Passage 1 and the ravens in Passage 2 shared which trait?

A) They modified their behavior in response to changes in their environment.

B) They formed a strong bond with the humans who were observing them.

C) They manufactured useful tools for finding and accessing food.

D) They mimicked the actions they saw performed around them.

Estimated Difficulty: Medium	Key: A

Choice A is the best answer. Both bird species studied modified their behavior in response to changes in their environment. The researchers described in Passage 1 "had gotten wild crows used to finding meat tidbits in holes in a log" (lines 20-21). In other words, the researchers had repeatedly placed meat in the log—that is, changed the crows' environment—and the birds had responded by modifying their behavior, a point reinforced in line 22, which noted that the birds began "checking the log reliably." The ravens in Passage 2 act in analogous fashion, responding to the introduction of new objects in their environment by "pick[ing] them out at a rate of up to tens of thousands of times greater than background or previously contacted objects" (lines 76-78).

Choice B is incorrect because while there is some evidence that the ravens described in Passage 2 formed a bond with the author, going on walks with him and possibly viewing him as their "teacher," there is no evidence that a similar bond formed between the researchers described in Passage 1 and the crows they studied. Indeed, these researchers "hid behind a blind" (lines 23-24) in an effort to avoid contact with their subjects.

Choice C is incorrect because while crows' tool-making ability is the central focus of the experiment described in Passage 1, there is no evidence that the ravens in Passage 2 did anything similar. Passage 1 does mention that "some ravens" use "seemingly insightful string-pulling solutions" (lines 44-45), but nothing in Passage 2 suggests that the ravens in that particular study had or displayed tool-making abilities.

Choice D is incorrect because while there is some evidence that the ravens described in Passage 2 mimicked human behavior, going on walks with the author and possibly viewing him as their "teacher," there is no evidence that the crows in Passage 1 did any mimicking. Passage 1, in fact, suggests that the ability of the crow to produce the meat-fishing tool was innate rather than a skill it had acquired from either humans or other birds.

Questions 4-6 are based on the following passage and supplementary material.
This passage is adapted from Richard Florida, *The Great Reset*. ©2010 by Richard Florida.

In today's idea-driven economy, the cost of time is what really matters. With the constant pressure to innovate, it makes little sense to waste countless
Line collective hours commuting. So, the most efficient
5 and productive regions are those in which people are thinking and working—not sitting in traffic.

The auto-dependent transportation system has reached its limit in most major cities and megaregions. Commuting by car is among the least efficient of all
10 our activities—not to mention among the least enjoyable, according to detailed research by the Nobel Prize-winning economist Daniel Kahneman and his colleagues. Though one might think that the economic crisis beginning in 2007 would have reduced traffic (high
15 unemployment means fewer workers traveling to and from work), the opposite has been true. Average commutes have lengthened, and congestion has gotten worse, if anything. The average commute rose in 2008 to 25.5 minutes, "erasing years of decreases to stand at the
20 level of 2000, as people had to leave home earlier in the morning to pick up friends for their ride to work or to catch a bus or subway train," according to the U.S. Census Bureau, which collects the figures. And those are average figures. Commutes are far longer in the big
25 West Coast cities of Los Angeles and San Francisco and the East Coast cities of New York, Philadelphia, Baltimore, and Washington, D.C. In many of these cities, gridlock has become the norm, not just at rush hour but all day, every day.
30 The costs are astounding. In Los Angeles, congestion eats up more than 485 million working hours a year; that's seventy hours, or nearly two weeks, of full-time work per commuter. In D.C., the time cost of congestion is sixty-two hours per worker per year. In New York it's
35 forty-four hours. Average it out, and the time cost across America's thirteen biggest city-regions is fifty-one hours per worker per year. Across the country, commuting wastes 4.2 billion hours of work time annually—nearly a full workweek for every commuter. The overall cost
40 to the U.S. economy is nearly $90 billion when lost productivity and wasted fuel are taken into account.

At the Martin Prosperity Institute, we calculate that every minute shaved off America's commuting time is worth $19.5 billion in value added to the economy. The
45   numbers add up fast: five minutes is worth $97.7 billion; ten minutes, $195 billion; fifteen minutes, $292 billion.

It's ironic that so many people still believe the main remedy for traffic congestion is to build more roads and highways, which of course only makes the problem
50   worse. New roads generate higher levels of "induced traffic," that is, new roads just invite drivers to drive more and lure people who take mass transit back to their cars. Eventually, we end up with more clogged roads rather than a long-term improvement in traffic flow.
55   The coming decades will likely see more intense clustering of jobs, innovation, and productivity in a smaller number of bigger cities and city-regions. Some regions could end up bloated beyond the capacity of their infrastructure, while others struggle, their promise
60   stymied by inadequate human or other resources.

The Most Congested Cities in 2011
Yearly Hours of Delay per Automobile Commuter

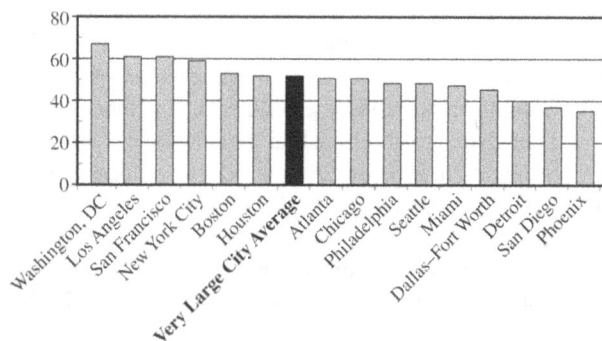

Adapted from Adam Werbach, "The American Commuter Spends 38 Hours a Year Stuck in Traffic." ©2013 by The Atlantic.

4

The passage most strongly suggests that researchers at the Martin Prosperity Institute share which assumption?

A) Employees who work from home are more valuable to their employers than employees who commute.

B) Employees whose commutes are shortened will use the time saved to do additional productive work for their employers.

C) Employees can conduct business activities, such as composing memos or joining conference calls, while commuting.

D) Employees who have lengthy commutes tend to make more money than employees who have shorter commutes.

Estimated Difficulty: Medium	**Key:** B

Choice B is the best answer because details in the third paragraph (lines 30-46) strongly suggest that researchers ("we") at the Martin Prosperity Institute assume that shorter commutes will lead to more productive time for workers. The author notes that "across the country, commuting wastes 4.2 billion hours of work time annually" and that "the overall cost to the U.S. economy is nearly $90 billion when lost productivity and wasted fuel are taken into account" (lines 37-41). Given also that those at the institute "calculate that every minute shaved off America's commuting time is worth $19.5 billion in value added to the economy" (lines 42-44), it can reasonably be concluded that some of that added value is from heightened worker productivity.

Choice A is incorrect because there is no evidence in the passage that researchers at the Martin Prosperity Institute assume that employees who work from home are more valuable to their employers than employees who commute. Although the passage does criticize long commutes, it does not propose working from home as a solution.

Choice C is incorrect because there is no evidence in the passage that researchers at the Martin Prosperity Institute assume that employees can conduct business activities, such as composing memos or joining conference calls, while commuting. The passage does discuss commuting in some detail, but it does not mention activities that commuters can or should be undertaking while commuting, and it generally portrays commuting time as lost or wasted time.

Choice D is incorrect because there is no evidence in the passage that researchers at the Martin Prosperity Institute assume that employees who have lengthy commutes tend to make more money than employees who have shorter commutes. The passage does not draw any clear links between the amount of money employees make and the commutes they have.

5

As used in line 55, "intense" most nearly means

A) emotional.
B) concentrated.
C) brilliant.
D) determined.

Estimated Difficulty: Easy	**Key:** B

Choice B is the best answer because the context makes clear that the clustering of jobs, innovation, and productivity will be more concentrated in, or more densely packed into, "a smaller number of bigger cities and city-regions" (lines 56-57).

Choice A is incorrect because although "intense" sometimes means "emotional," it would make no sense in context to say that the clustering of jobs, innovation, and productivity will be more emotional in "a smaller number of bigger cities and city-regions" (lines 56-57).

Choice C is incorrect because although "intense" sometimes means "brilliant," it would make no sense in context to say that the clustering of jobs, innovation, and productivity will be more brilliant in "a smaller number of bigger cities and city-regions" (lines 56-57).

Choice D is incorrect because although "intense" sometimes means "determined," it would make no sense in context to say that the clustering of jobs, innovation, and productivity will be more determined in "a smaller number of bigger cities and city-regions" (lines 56-57).

6

Which claim about traffic congestion is supported by the graph?

A) New York City commuters spend less time annually delayed by traffic congestion than the average for very large cities.
B) Los Angeles commuters are delayed more hours annually by traffic congestion than are commuters in Washington, D.C.
C) Commuters in Washington, D.C., face greater delays annually due to traffic congestion than do commuters in New York City.
D) Commuters in Detroit spend more time delayed annually by traffic congestion than do commuters in Houston, Atlanta, and Chicago.

Estimated Difficulty: Easy	**Key:** C

Choice C is the best answer. Higher bars on the graph represent longer annual commute delays than do lower bars; moreover, the number of hours of annual commute delay generally decreases as one moves from left to right on the graph. The bar for Washington, D.C., is higher than and to the left of that for New York City, meaning that D.C. automobile commuters experience greater amounts of delay each year.

Choice A is incorrect because the graph's bar for New York City is higher than and to the left of that for the average for very large cities, meaning that New York City automobile commuters experience greater, not lesser, amounts of delay each year.

Choice B is incorrect because the graph's bar for Los Angeles is lower than and to the right of that for Washington, D.C., meaning that Los Angeles automobile commuters experience lesser, not greater, amounts of delay each year.

Choice D is incorrect because the graph's bar for Detroit is lower than and to the right of those for Houston, Atlanta, and Chicago, meaning that Detroit automobile commuters experience lesser, not greater, amounts of delay each year.

Questions 7-9 are based on the following passage.
This passage is adapted from a speech delivered by Congresswoman Barbara Jordan of Texas on July 25, 1974, as a member of the Judiciary Committee of the United States House of Representatives. In the passage, Jordan discusses how and when a United States president may be impeached, or charged with serious offenses, while in office. Jordan's speech was delivered in the context of impeachment hearings against then president Richard M. Nixon.

Today, I am an inquisitor. An hyperbole would not be fictional and would not overstate the solemnness that I feel right now. My faith in the Constitution is whole; it is
Line complete; it is total. And I am not going to sit here and be
5 an idle spectator to the diminution, the subversion, the destruction, of the Constitution.

"Who can so properly be the inquisitors for the nation as the representatives of the nation themselves?" "The subjects of its jurisdiction are those offenses which
10 proceed from the misconduct of public men."* And that's what we're talking about. In other words, [the jurisdiction comes] from the abuse or violation of some public trust.

It is wrong, I suggest, it is a misreading of the Constitution for any member here to assert that for a
15 member to vote for an article of impeachment means that that member must be convinced that the President should be removed from office. The Constitution doesn't say that. The powers relating to impeachment are an essential check in the hands of the body of the legislature against
20 and upon the encroachments of the executive. The division between the two branches of the legislature, the House and the Senate, assigning to the one the right to accuse and to the other the right to judge—the framers

of this Constitution were very astute. They did not make
25 the accusers and the judges . . . the same person.

We know the nature of impeachment. We've been
talking about it a while now. It is chiefly designed for the
President and his high ministers to somehow be called
into account. It is designed to "bridle" the executive if he
30 engages in excesses. "It is designed as a method of
national inquest into the conduct of public men."* The
framers confided in the Congress the power, if need be,
to remove the President in order to strike a delicate
balance between a President swollen with power and
35 grown tyrannical, and preservation of the independence
of the executive.

The nature of impeachment: a narrowly channeled
exception to the separation of powers maxim. The Federal
40 Convention of 1787 said that. It limited impeachment to
high crimes and misdemeanors, and discounted and
opposed the term "maladministration." "It is to be used
only for great misdemeanors," so it was said in the North
Carolina ratification convention. And in the Virginia
ratification convention: "We do not trust our liberty to
45 a particular branch. We need one branch to check the
other."

. . . The North Carolina ratification convention: "No
one need be afraid that officers who commit oppression
will pass with immunity." "Prosecutions of impeachments
50 will seldom fail to agitate the passions of the whole
community," said Hamilton in the *Federalist* Papers,
number 65. "We divide into parties more or less friendly
or inimical to the accused."* I do not mean political
parties in that sense.
55 The drawing of political lines goes to the motivation
behind impeachment; but impeachment must proceed
within the confines of the constitutional term "high
crime[s] and misdemeanors." Of the impeachment
process, it was Woodrow Wilson who said that "Nothing
60 short of the grossest offenses against the plain law of the
land will suffice to give them speed and effectiveness.
Indignation so great as to overgrow party interest may
secure a conviction; but nothing else can."

Common sense would be revolted if we engaged
65 upon this process for petty reasons. Congress has a lot
to do: appropriations, tax reform, health insurance,
campaign finance reform, housing, environmental
protection, energy sufficiency, mass transportation.
Pettiness cannot be allowed to stand in the face of such
70 overwhelming problems. So today we're not being petty.
We're trying to be big, because the task we have before us
is a big one.

*Jordan quotes from *Federalist* No. 65, an essay by Alexander
Hamilton, published in 1788, on the powers of the United States
Senate, including the power to decide cases of impeachment
against a president of the United States.

7

The stance Jordan takes in the passage is best
described as that of

A) an idealist setting forth principles.

B) an advocate seeking a compromise position.

C) an observer striving for neutrality.

D) a scholar researching a historical controversy.

Estimated Difficulty: Hard	Key: A

Choice A is the best answer. Jordan helps establish
her idealism by declaring that she is an "inquisitor"
(line 1) and that her "faith in the Constitution is
whole; it is complete; it is total" (lines 3-4). At
numerous points in the passage, Jordan sets forth
principles (e.g., "The powers relating to impeachment
are an essential check in the hands of the body of the
legislature against and upon the encroachments of
the executive," in lines 18-20) and makes reference to
important documents that do the same, including the
U.S. Constitution and *Federalist* No. 65.

Choice B is incorrect because although Jordan is
advocating a position, there is no evidence in the
passage that she is seeking a compromise position.
Indeed, she notes that she is "not going to sit here and
be an idle spectator to the diminution, the subversion,
the destruction, of the Constitution" (lines 4-6),
indicating that she is not seeking compromise.

Choice C is incorrect because Jordan is a participant
("an inquisitor," line 1) in the proceedings, not a mere
observer. Indeed, she notes that she is "not going to
sit here and be an idle spectator to the diminution,
the subversion, the destruction, of the Constitution"
(lines 4-6).

Choice D is incorrect because Jordan is identified as
a congresswoman and an "inquisitor" (line 1), not
a scholar, and because she is primarily discussing
events happening at the moment, not researching
an unidentified historical controversy. Although she
refers to historical documents and individuals, her
main emphasis is on the (then) present impeachment
hearings.

8

In lines 49-54 ("Prosecutions . . . sense"), what is the most likely reason Jordan draws a distinction between two types of "parties"?

A) To counter the suggestion that impeachment is or should be about partisan politics

B) To disagree with Hamilton's claim that impeachment proceedings excite passions

C) To contend that Hamilton was too timid in his support for the concept of impeachment

D) To argue that impeachment cases are decided more on the basis of politics than on justice

Estimated Difficulty: Medium	**Key:** A

Choice A is the best answer. Jordan is making a distinction between two types of "parties": the informal associations to which Alexander Hamilton refers and formal, organized political parties such as the modern-day Republican and Democratic parties. Jordan anticipates that listeners to her speech might misinterpret her use of Hamilton's quotation as suggesting that she thinks impeachment is essentially a tool of organized political parties to achieve partisan ends, with one party attacking and another defending the president. Throughout the passage, and notably in the seventh paragraph (lines 55-63), Jordan makes clear that she thinks impeachment should be reserved only for the most serious of offenses—ones that should rankle people of any political affiliation.

Choice B is incorrect because Jordan offers no objection to Hamilton's notion that impeachment proceedings excite passions. Indeed, she quotes Hamilton extensively in a way that indicates that she fundamentally agrees with his view on impeachment. Moreover, she acknowledges that her own speech is impassioned—that she feels a "solemnness" (line 2) and a willingness to indulge in "hyperbole" (line 1).

Choice C is incorrect because Jordan offers no objection to Hamilton's level of support for the concept of impeachment. Indeed, she quotes Hamilton extensively in a way that indicates that she fundamentally agrees with his view on impeachment.

Choice D is incorrect because Jordan suggests that she and her fellow members of Congress are "trying to be big" (line 71), or high-minded, rather than decide the present case on the basis of politics. Indeed, throughout the last four paragraphs of the passage (lines 37-72), she elaborates on the principled, just basis on which impeachment should proceed. Moreover, throughout the passage, Jordan is focused on the present impeachment hearings, not on the justice or injustice of impeachments generally.

9

Which choice provides the best evidence for the answer to the previous question?

A) Lines 13-17 ("It . . . office")

B) Lines 20-24 ("The division . . . astute")

C) Lines 55-58 ("The drawing . . . misdemeanors'")

D) Lines 65-68 ("Congress . . . transportation")

Estimated Difficulty: Hard	**Key:** C

Choice C is the best answer because in lines 55-58, Jordan draws a contrast between political motivations and "high crime[s] and misdemeanors" as the basis for impeachment and argues that impeachment "must proceed within the confines" of the latter concept. These lines thus serve as the best evidence for the answer to the previous question.

Choice A is incorrect because lines 13-17 only address a misconception that Jordan contends some people have about what a vote for impeachment means. Therefore, these lines do not serve as the best evidence for the answer to the previous question.

Choice B is incorrect because lines 20-24 only speak to a division of responsibility between the two houses of the U.S. Congress. Therefore, these lines do not serve as the best evidence for the answer to the previous question.

Choice D is incorrect because lines 65-68 serve mainly to indicate that the U.S. Congress has an extensive and important agenda. Therefore, these lines do not serve as the best evidence for the answer to the previous question.

Writing and Language Test Overview

The Writing and Language Test asks you to be an editor and improve passages that were written especially for the test—and that include deliberate errors.

- Total questions: 44 passage-based questions with multiple-choice responses.
- Time allotted: 35 minutes.
- Calculators may not be used or be on your desk.

What the Writing and Language Test Is Like

When you take the Writing and Language Test, you'll do things that people do all the time when they edit: read, find mistakes and weaknesses, and fix them.

The good news: You do these things every time you revise your own schoolwork or workshop your writing with a friend.

You will revise the passages on the test for development, organization, and effective language use as well as edit the passages to ensure they follow the conventions of standard written English grammar, usage, and punctuation.

What You'll Read

Writing and Language passages range in length from about 400 to 450 words and vary in complexity. The passages you'll read will be informative/explanatory texts, nonfiction narratives, or arguments and will cover topics in the areas of careers, history/social studies, the humanities, and science. One or more passages will be accompanied by one or more informational graphics.

What the Writing and Language Test Measures

The Writing and Language Test measures the skills and knowledge you use to spot and fix problems in writing—the same skills and knowledge you've been acquiring in high school and that you'll need for success in college and career. All questions are multiple choice and based on passages and any supplementary material, such as tables and graphs.

Command of Evidence

Questions that test command of evidence ask you to improve the way passages develop information and ideas. For instance, you might choose an answer that sharpens an argumentative claim or adds a relevant supporting detail.

Words in Context

Some questions ask you to improve word choice. You'll need to choose the best words to use based on the text surrounding them. Your goal will be to make a passage more precise or concise or to improve syntax, style, or tone.

Analysis in History/Social Studies and in Science

You'll be asked to read and analyze passages about topics in history/social studies and in science and to make decisions that improve the passages (such as revising a paragraph to be more consistent with the data presented in an informational graphic).

Expression of Ideas

Some questions ask about a passage's topic development, organization, and language use. For instance, you may be asked which words or structural changes improve how a point is made or which phrase or sentence provides the most effective transition between ideas.

Standard English Conventions

Some questions relate to aspects of the mechanics of writing: sentence structure, usage, and punctuation. You'll be asked to edit text so that it conforms to the conventions of standard written English.

Tips for the Writing and Language Test

To answer some questions, you'll need to look closely at a single sentence. Others require thinking about the entire passage or interpreting a graphic. For instance, you might be asked to choose where a sentence should be placed or to correct a misinterpretation of a scientific table or graph.

- To make decisions that improve the passages, read the passages carefully.
- Rote recall of language rules isn't tested, nor are any questions based on short snippets of text taken out of context. The best answer to each question represents how a writer should develop, organize, and use language in a multiparagraph passage. You are demonstrating that you can make context-based improvements to the text.
- The most common format for the questions offers 3 alternatives to an underlined portion of the passage along with the option of not changing the passage's original wording. Remember to answer these questions in the context of the whole passage.

- Stay with a passage until you have answered as many questions as you can before you proceed to the next passage. Don't jump from passage to passage.

- In your test booklet, mark each question you skip so you can easily go back to it later if you have time.

- Remember that all questions are worth 1 point regardless of the type or difficulty. You don't lose points for guessing wrong, so you should try to answer each question as best you can.

Sample Writing and Language Test Materials

Following are samples of the kinds of passages and questions that may appear on the Writing and Language Test. For each set of sample materials:

- Read the passage carefully.
- Decide on the best answer to each question.
- Read the explanation for the best answer to each question and for the answer you chose (if they are different).

On the actual test, the passages and questions will be in side-by-side columns, with each passage (spread over multiple pages) in the left column and associated multiple-choice questions in the right column. The directions that follow match the directions on the actual test.

Writing and Language Test Questions

Questions 1-5 are based on the following passage.

Dong Kingman: Painter of Cities

A 1954 documentary about renowned watercolor painter Dong Kingman shows the artist sitting on a stool on Mott Street in New York City's Chinatown. A crowd of admiring spectators **1** watched as Kingman squeezes dollops of paint from several tubes into a tin watercolor **2** box, from just a few primary colors, Kingman creates dozens of beautiful hues as he layers the translucent paint onto the paper on his easel. Each stroke of the brush and dab of the sponge transforms thinly sketched outlines into buildings, shop signs, and streetlamps. The street scene Kingman begins composing in this short film is very much in keeping with the urban landscapes for which he is best known.

Kingman was keenly interested in landscape painting from an early age. His interest was so keen, in fact, that he was named after it. In Hong Kong, where Kingman completed his schooling, teachers at that time customarily assigned students a formal "school name." The young boy who had been Dong Moy Shu became Dong Kingman. The name Kingman was selected for its two **3** parts, "king" and "man"; Cantonese for "scenery" and "composition." As Kingman developed as a painter, his works were often compared to paintings by Chinese landscape artists dating back to CE 960, a time when a strong tradition of landscape painting emerged in Chinese art. Kingman, however, departed from that tradition in a number of ways, most notably in that he chose to focus not on natural landscapes, such as mountains and rivers, but on cities.

His fine brushwork conveys detailed street-level activity: a peanut vendor pushing his cart on the sidewalk, a pigeon pecking for crumbs around a fire hydrant, an old man tending to a baby outside a doorway. His broader brush strokes and sponge-painted shapes create majestic city skylines, with skyscrapers towering in the background, bridges connecting neighborhoods on either side of a river, and **4** delicately painted creatures, such as a tiny, barely visible cat prowling in the bushes of a park. To art critics and fans alike, these city scenes represent the innovative spirit of twentieth-century urban Modernism.

During his career, Kingman exhibited his work internationally, garnering much acclaim. In 1936, a critic described one of Kingman's solo exhibits as "twenty of the freshest, most satisfying watercolors that have been seen hereabouts in many a day." **5**

1

A) NO CHANGE
B) had watched
C) would watch
D) watches

Estimated Difficulty: Easy	Key: D

Choice D is the best answer because the simple present tense verb "watches" is consistent with the tense of the verbs in the rest of the sentence and paragraph.

Choice A is incorrect because "watched" creates an inappropriate shift to the past tense.

Choice B is incorrect because "had watched" creates an inappropriate shift to the past perfect tense.

Choice C is incorrect because "would watch" creates an inappropriate shift that suggests a habitual or hypothetical aspect when other verbs in the sentence and paragraph indicate that a specific, actual instance is being narrated.

2

A) NO CHANGE
B) box. From just a few primary colors,
C) box from just a few primary colors,
D) box, from just a few primary colors

Estimated Difficulty: Medium	Key: B

Choice B is the best answer because it provides punctuation that creates two grammatically complete and standard sentences.

Choice A is incorrect because it results in a comma splice as well as some confusion about what the prepositional phrase "from just a few primary colors" modifies.

Choice C is incorrect because it results in a run-on sentence as well as some confusion about what the prepositional phrase "from just a few primary colors" modifies.

Choice D is incorrect because it results in a comma splice.

3

A) NO CHANGE
B) parts: "king" and "man,"
C) parts "king" and "man";
D) parts; "king" and "man"

Estimated Difficulty: Hard	Key: B

Choice B is the best answer because the colon after "parts" effectively signals that what follows in the sentence further defines what the "two parts" of Kingman's name are and because the comma after "man" properly indicates that "'king' and 'man'" and "Cantonese for 'scenery' and 'composition'" are nonrestrictive appositives.

Choice A is incorrect because the semicolon after "man" incorrectly joins an independent clause and a phrase. Moreover, the comma after "parts" is arguably a weak form of punctuation to be signaling the strong break in the sentence indicated here.

Choice C is incorrect because the semicolon after "man" incorrectly joins an independent clause and a phrase and because the absence of appropriate punctuation after "parts" fails to indicate that "two parts" and "'king' and 'man'" are nonrestrictive appositives.

Choice D is incorrect because the semicolon after "parts" incorrectly joins an independent clause and two phrases and because the absence of appropriate punctuation after "man" fails to indicate that "'king' and 'man'" and "Cantonese for 'scenery' and 'composition'" are nonrestrictive appositives.

4

The writer wants to complete the sentence with a third example of a detail Kingman uses to create his majestic city skylines. Which choice best accomplishes this goal?

A) NO CHANGE
B) exquisitely lettered street and storefront signs.
C) other details that help define Kingman's urban landscapes.
D) enormous ships docking at busy urban ports.

Estimated Difficulty: Hard	Key: D

Choice D is the best answer because the phrase "enormous ships docking at busy urban ports" effectively continues the sentence's series of details ("skyscrapers towering in the background" and "bridges connecting neighborhoods") conveying the majesty of city skylines as depicted by Kingman.

Choice A is incorrect because the phrase "delicately painted creatures, such as a tiny, barely visible cat prowling in the bushes of a park" does not convey a sense of the majesty of city skylines as depicted by Kingman and thus does not effectively continue the sentence's series of details ("skyscrapers towering in the background" and "bridges connecting neighborhoods").

Choice B is incorrect because the phrase "exquisitely lettered street and storefront signs" does not convey a sense of the majesty of city skylines as depicted by Kingman and thus does not effectively continue the sentence's series of details ("skyscrapers towering in the background" and "bridges connecting neighborhoods").

Choice C is incorrect because the phrase "other details that help define Kingman's urban landscapes" is too vague and general to constitute a third example that conveys a sense of the majesty of city skylines as depicted by Kingman and thus does not effectively continue the sentence's series of details ("skyscrapers towering in the background" and "bridges connecting neighborhoods").

5

The writer wants to conclude the passage with a sentence that emphasizes an enduring legacy of Kingman's work. Which choice would best accomplish this goal?

A) Although Kingman's work might not be as famous as that of some other watercolor painters, such as Georgia O'Keeffe and Edward Hopper, it is well regarded by many people.
B) Since Kingman's death in 2000, museums across the United States and in China have continued to ensure that his now-iconic landscapes remain available for the public to enjoy.
C) The urban landscapes depicted in Kingman's body of work are a testament to the aptness of the name chosen for Kingman when he was just a boy.
D) Kingman's work was but one example of a long-lasting tradition refreshed by an innovative artist with a new perspective.

| **Estimated Difficulty:** Hard | **Key:** B |

Choice B is the best answer because it concludes the passage with a sentence that emphasizes the enduring legacy of Kingman's work by indicating that museums continue to make Kingman's iconic paintings accessible to the public.

Choice A is incorrect because it concludes the passage with a sentence that acknowledges that the works of other painters are more famous than Kingman's (which downplays, rather than emphasizes, the enduring legacy of Kingman's work) and offers only a general assertion that Kingman's work is "well regarded by many people."

Choice C is incorrect because instead of referring to the enduring legacy of Kingman's work, it concludes the passage with a sentence that recalls a detail the passage provides about Kingman's early life.

Choice D is incorrect because it concludes the passage with a sentence that is too vague and general to emphasize effectively an enduring legacy of Kingman's work. It is not clear what the idea of refreshing a long-lasting tradition is intended to mean or how (or even whether) this represents an enduring legacy. Moreover, referring to Kingman's work as "but one example" downplays the significance of any potential legacy that might be suggested.

Questions 6-10 are based on the following passage and supplementary material.

A Life in Traffic

A subway system is expanded to provide service to a growing suburb. A bike-sharing program is adopted to encourage nonmotorized transportation. Stoplight timing is coordinated to alleviate rush hour traffic jams in a congested downtown area. When any one of these changes **6** occur, it is likely the result of careful analysis conducted by transportation planners.

The work of transportation planners generally includes evaluating current transportation needs, assessing the effectiveness of existing facilities, and improving those facilities or designing new ones. Most transportation planners work in or near cities, **7** but some are employed in rural areas. Say, for example, a large factory is built on the outskirts of a small town. Traffic to and from that location would increase at the beginning and end of work shifts. The transportation planner's job might involve conducting a traffic count to determine the daily number of vehicles traveling on the road to the new factory. If analysis of the traffic count indicates that there is more traffic than the **8** current road as it is designed at this time can efficiently accommodate, the transportation planner might recommend widening the road to add another lane.

Transportation planners work closely with a number of community stakeholders, such as government officials and other interested organizations and individuals. For instance, representatives from the local public health department might provide input in designing a network of trails and sidewalks to encourage people to walk more. **9** According to the American Heart Association, walking provides numerous benefits related to health and well-being. Members of the Chamber of Commerce might share suggestions about designing transportation and parking facilities to support local businesses.

People who pursue careers in transportation planning have a wide variety of educational backgrounds. A two-year degree in transportation technology may be sufficient for some entry-level jobs in the field. Most jobs, however, require at least a bachelor's degree; majors of transportation planners are **10** varied, including fields such as urban studies, civil engineering, geography, or transportation and logistics management. For many positions in the field, a master's degree is required.

Transportation planners perform critical work within the broader field of urban and regional planning. As of 2010, there were approximately 40,300 urban and regional planners employed in the United States. The United States Bureau of Labor Statistics forecasts steady job growth in this field, predicting that employment of urban and regional planners will increase 16 percent between 2010 and 2020. Population growth and concerns about environmental sustainability are expected to spur the need for transportation planning professionals.

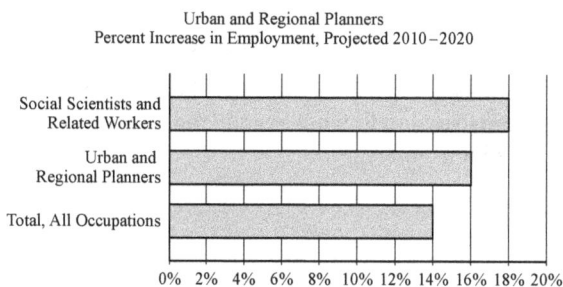

Urban and Regional Planners
Percent Increase in Employment, Projected 2010–2020

Adapted from United States Bureau of Labor Statistics, Employment Projections program. "All occupations" includes all occupations in the United States economy.

6

A) NO CHANGE
B) occur, they are
C) occurs, they are
D) occurs, it is

Estimated Difficulty: Hard	Key: D

Choice D is the best answer because it maintains agreement between the pronoun ("it") and the antecedent ("any one") and between the subject ("any one") and the verb ("occurs").

Choice A is incorrect because the plural verb "occur" does not agree with the singular subject "any one."

Choice B is incorrect because the plural verb "occur" does not agree with the singular subject "any one" and because the plural pronoun "they" does not agree with the singular antecedent "any one."

Choice C is incorrect because the plural pronoun "they" does not agree with the singular antecedent "any one."

7

Which choice results in the most effective transition to the information that follows in the paragraph?

A) NO CHANGE
B) where job opportunities are more plentiful.
C) and the majority are employed by government agencies.
D) DELETE the underlined portion and end the sentence with a period.

Estimated Difficulty: Medium	Key: A

Choice A is the best answer because it effectively signals the shift in the paragraph to the example of the work a transportation planner might perform if he or she were employed in a rural area and asked to consider the effects of a new factory built "on the outskirts of a small town."

Choice B is incorrect because noting that job opportunities are more plentiful in cities does not effectively signal the shift in the paragraph to the example of the work a transportation planner might perform if he or she were employed in a rural area.

Choice C is incorrect because noting that most transportation planners work for government agencies does not effectively signal the shift in the paragraph to the example of the work a transportation planner might perform if he or she were employed in a rural area.

Choice D is incorrect because the proposed deletion would create a jarring shift from the statement "Most transportation planners work in or near cities" to the example of the work a transportation planner might perform if he or she were employed in a rural area.

8

A) NO CHANGE
B) current design of the road right now
C) road as it is now currently designed
D) current design of the road

Estimated Difficulty: Medium	Key: D

Choice D is the best answer because it offers a clear and concise wording without redundancy or wordiness.

Choice A is incorrect because "current" is redundant with "at this time" and because "as it is designed" is unnecessarily wordy.

Choice B is incorrect because "current" is redundant with "right now."

Choice C is incorrect because "now" is redundant with "currently."

9

The writer is considering deleting the underlined sentence. Should the sentence be kept or deleted?

A) Kept, because it provides supporting evidence about the benefits of walking.
B) Kept, because it provides an additional example of a community stakeholder with whom transportation planners work.
C) Deleted, because it blurs the paragraph's focus on the community stakeholders with whom transportation planners work.
D) Deleted, because it doesn't provide specific examples of what the numerous benefits of walking are.

Estimated Difficulty: Medium	Key: C

Choice C is the best answer because it identifies the best reason the underlined sentence should not be kept. At this point in the passage and paragraph, a general statement about the benefits of walking only serves to interrupt the discussion of the community stakeholders with whom transportation planners work.

Choice A is incorrect because the underlined sentence should not be kept. Although the sentence theoretically provides supporting evidence about the benefits of walking, the passage has not made a claim that needs to be supported in this way, and including such a statement only serves to interrupt the discussion of the community stakeholders with whom transportation planners work.

Choice B is incorrect because the underlined sentence should not be kept. Although the American Heart Association could theoretically be an example of "other interested organizations" that transportation planners work with, the sentence does not suggest this is the case. Instead, the association is merely the source for the general statement about the benefits of walking, a statement that only serves to interrupt the discussion of the actual community stakeholders with whom transportation planners work.

Choice D is incorrect because, although the underlined sentence should be deleted, it is not because the sentence lacks specific examples of the numerous benefits of walking. Adding such examples would only serve to blur the focus of the paragraph further with general factual information, as the paragraph's main purpose is to discuss the community stakeholders with whom transportation planners work.

10

A) NO CHANGE
B) varied, and including
C) varied and which include
D) varied, which include

Estimated Difficulty: Hard	Key: A

Choice A is the best answer because it effectively uses a comma and "including" to set off the list of varied fields in which transportation planners major.

Choice B is incorrect because "and including" results in an ungrammatical sentence.

Choice C is incorrect because "and which include" results in an ungrammatical sentence.

Choice D is incorrect because is it unclear from this construction to what exactly the relative pronoun "which" refers.

Math

The SAT Math Test covers math practices, emphasizing problem solving, modeling, using tools strategically, and using algebraic structure. The questions test your ability to solve problems and use appropriate approaches and tools strategically.

Math Test Overview

The Math Test includes a portion that allows the use of a calculator and a portion that does not.

- Total questions: 58 (20 questions on the no-calculator portion; 38 questions on the calculator portion).
  - ◆ 45 standard multiple-choice questions.
  - ◆ 13 student-produced response questions.
- Time allotted for Math Test – No Calculator: 25 minutes; time allotted for Math Test – Calculator: 55 minutes.

What the Math Test Is Like

Instead of testing you on every math topic, the SAT asks you to use the math that you'll rely on most in all sorts of situations. Questions on the Math Test are designed to mirror the problem solving and modeling you'll do in:

- College math, science, and social science courses
- Jobs that you hold
- Your personal life

For instance, to answer some questions you'll need to use several steps because in the real world, a single calculation is rarely enough to get the job done.

- Most math questions will be multiple choice, but some—called student-produced responses—ask you to come up with the answer rather than select the answer.
- Some parts of the test include several questions about a single scenario.

What the Math Test Measures

Fluency
The Math Test is a chance to show that you:

- Carry out procedures flexibly, accurately, efficiently, and strategically.
- Solve problems quickly by identifying and using the most efficient solution approaches.

This might involve solving a problem by inspection, finding a shortcut, or reorganizing the information you've been given.

Conceptual Understanding
You'll demonstrate your grasp of math concepts, operations, and relations. For instance, you might be asked to make connections between properties of linear equations, their graphs, and the contexts they represent.

Applications
Some real-world problems ask you to analyze a situation, determine the essential elements required to solve the problem, represent the problem mathematically, and carry out a solution.

Calculator Use

Calculators are important tools, and to succeed after high school, you'll need to know how—and when—to use them. In the Math Test – Calculator portion of the test, you'll be able to focus on complex modeling and reasoning because your calculator can save you time.

However, using a calculator, like any tool, isn't always the best way to solve a problem. The Math Test includes some questions that it's better not to use a calculator for, even though you're allowed to. With these questions, you'll probably find that the structure of the problem or your reasoning skills will lead you to the answers more efficiently.

Calculator Smarts

- Bring your own calculator. You can't share one.
- Don't bring a calculator you've never used before. Bring one you know. Practice for the test using the same calculator you'll use on test day.
- It may help to do scratch work in the test book. Get your thoughts down before using your calculator.
- Make sure your calculator is in good working order with fresh batteries. The testing staff will not have batteries or extra calculators. If your calculator fails during testing and you have no backup, you can complete the test without it. All questions can be answered without a calculator.

Answering Student-Produced Response Questions

You'll see directions in the test book for answering student-produced response questions. (See page 35 for an example.) Take the time to be comfortable with the format before test day. Carefully read the directions for answering these questions. The directions explain what you can and can't do when entering your answers on the answer sheet.

Tips for the Math Test

- Familiarize yourself with the directions ahead of time.

- You don't have to memorize formulas. Commonly used formulas are provided with the test directions at the beginning of each Math Test portion. Other formulas that are needed are provided with the test questions themselves. It's up to you to decide which formula is appropriate to a question.

- Read the problem carefully. Look for key words that tell you what the problem is asking. Before you solve each problem, ask yourself these questions: What is the question asking? What do I know?

- With some problems, it may be useful to draw a sketch or diagram of the given information.

- Use the test booklet for scratch work. You're not expected to do all the reasoning and figuring in your head. You won't receive credit for anything written in the booklet, but you'll be able to check your work easily later.

- In the portion of the test that allows calculator use, be strategic when choosing to use your calculator.

- If you don't know the correct answer to a multiple-choice question, eliminate some of the choices. It's sometimes easier to find the wrong answers than the correct one. On some questions, you may even be able to eliminate all the incorrect choices. Remember that you won't lose points for incorrect answers, so plan to make your best guess if you don't know the answer.

- Check your answer to make sure it's a reasonable reply to the question asked. This is especially true for student-produced response questions, where no answer choices are given.

Sample Math Test Materials

The sample math questions that follow show the kinds of questions that may appear on both portions of the Math Test. For these sample materials:

- Review the notes at the beginning of each portion. They match the notes on the actual test.

- Decide on the correct answer to each multiple-choice question, then read the explanation for the correct answer to each question and for the answer you chose (if they are different).

- Follow the directions for the student-produced response questions shown later in this guide. The directions match the directions on the actual test.

Math Test – No Calculator Questions

Directions

For questions 1-5, solve each problem, choose the best answer from the choices provided, and fill in the corresponding bubble on your answer sheet. **For question 6**, solve the problem and enter your answer in the grid on the answer sheet. Please refer to the directions before question 6 on how to enter your answers in the grid. You may use any available space in your test booklet for scratch work.

Notes

1. The use of a calculator **is not permitted**.
2. All variables and expressions used represent real numbers unless otherwise indicated.
3. Figures provided in this test are drawn to scale unless otherwise indicated.
4. All figures lie in a plane unless otherwise indicated.
5. Unless otherwise indicated, the domain of a given function f is the set of all real numbers x for which $f(x)$ is a real number.

Reference

$A = \pi r^2$

$C = 2\pi r$

$A = \ell w$

$A = \dfrac{1}{2}bh$

$c^2 = a^2 + b^2$

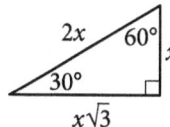

Special Right Triangles

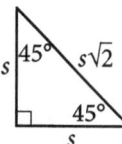

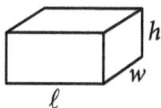

$V = \ell w h$

$V = \pi r^2 h$

$V = \dfrac{4}{3}\pi r^3$

$V = \dfrac{1}{3}\pi r^2 h$

$V = \dfrac{1}{3}\ell w h$

The number of degrees of arc in a circle is 360.

The number of radians of arc in a circle is 2π.

The sum of the measures in degrees of the angles of a triangle is 180.

1

Line ℓ is graphed in the *xy*-plane below.

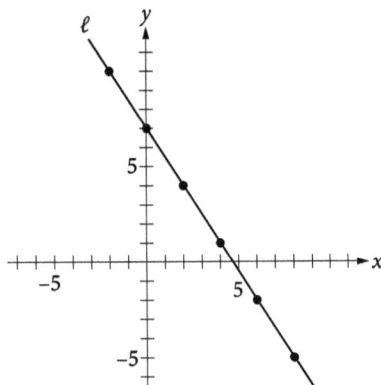

If line ℓ is translated up 5 units and right 7 units, then what is the slope of the new line?

A) $\dfrac{2}{5}$

B) $-\dfrac{3}{2}$

C) $-\dfrac{8}{9}$

D) $-\dfrac{11}{14}$

Estimated Difficulty: Easy	**Key:** B

Choice B is correct. The slope of a line can be determined by finding the difference in the *y*-coordinates divided by the difference in the *x*-coordinates for any two points on the line. Using the points indicated, the slope of line ℓ is $-\dfrac{3}{2}$. Translating line ℓ moves all the points on the line the same distance in the same direction, and the image will be a line parallel to ℓ. Therefore, the slope of the image is also $-\dfrac{3}{2}$.

Choice A is incorrect. This value may result from a combination of errors. You may have erroneously determined the slope of the new line by adding 5 to the numerator and adding 7 to the denominator in the slope of line ℓ and gotten the result $\dfrac{(-3+5)}{(-2+7)}$.

Choice C is incorrect. This value may result from a combination of errors. You may have erroneously determined the slope of the new line by subtracting 5 from the numerator and subtracting 7 from the denominator in the slope of line ℓ.

Choice D is incorrect and may result from adding $\dfrac{5}{7}$ to the slope of line ℓ.

2

The average number of students per classroom, *y*, at Central High School can be estimated using the equation $y = 0.8636x + 27.227$, where *x* represents the number of years since 2004 and $x \le 10$. Which of the following statements is the best interpretation of the number 0.8636 in the context of this problem?

A) The estimated average number of students per classroom in 2004

B) The estimated average number of students per classroom in 2014

C) The estimated yearly decrease in the average number of students per classroom

D) The estimated yearly increase in the average number of students per classroom

Estimated Difficulty: Easy	**Key:** D

Choice D is correct. When an equation is written in the form $y = mx + b$, the coefficient of the *x*-term (in this case 0.8636) is the slope of the graph of this equation in the *xy*-plane. The slope of the graph of this linear equation gives the amount that the mean number of students per classroom (represented by *y*) changes per year (represented by *x*).

Choice A is incorrect and may result from a misunderstanding of slope and *y*-intercept. The *y*-intercept of the graph of the equation represents the estimated average number of students per classroom in 2004.

Choice B is incorrect and may result from a misunderstanding of the limitations of the model. You may have seen that $x \le 10$ and erroneously used this statement to determine that the model finds the average number of students in 2014.

Choice C is incorrect and may result from a misunderstanding of slope. You may have recognized that slope models the rate of change but thought that a slope of less than 1 indicates a decreasing function.

3

The graph of $y = (2x - 4)(x - 4)$ is a parabola in the *xy*-plane. In which of the following equivalent equations do the *x*- and *y*-coordinates of the vertex of the parabola appear as constants or coefficients?

A) $y = 2x^2 - 12x + 16$

B) $y = 2x(x - 6) + 16$

C) $y = 2(x - 3)^2 + (-2)$

D) $y = (x - 2)(2x - 8)$

Estimated Difficulty: Medium	**Key:** C

Choice C is correct. The equation $y = (2x - 4)(x - 4)$ can be written in vertex form, $y = a(x - h)^2 + k$, to display the vertex, (h, k), of the parabola. To put the equation in vertex form, first multiply: $(2x - 4)(x - 4) = 2x^2 - 8x - 4x + 16$. Then, add like terms, $2x^2 - 8x - 4x + 16 = 2x^2 - 12x + 16$. The next step is completing the square.

$y = 2x^2 - 12x + 16$	
$y = 2(x^2 - 6x) + 16$	Isolate the x^2 term by factoring
$y = 2(x^2 - 6x + 9 - 9) + 16$	Make a perfect square in the parentheses
$y = 2(x^2 - 6x + 9) - 18 + 16$	Move the extra term out of the parentheses
$y = 2(x - 3)^2 - 18 + 16$	Factor inside the parentheses
$y = 2(x - 3)^2 - 2$	Simplify the remaining terms

Therefore, the coordinates of the vertex, $(3, -2)$, are both revealed only in choice C. Since you are told that all of the equations are equivalent, simply knowing the form that displays the coordinates of the vertex will save all of these steps—this is known as "seeing structure in the expression or equation."

Choice A is incorrect; it is in standard form, displaying the y-value of the y-intercept of the graph $(0, 16)$ as a constant.

Choice B is incorrect; it displays the y-value of the y-intercept of the graph $(0, 16)$ as a constant.

Choice D is incorrect; it displays the x-value of one of the x-intercepts of the graph $(2, 0)$ as a constant.

4

In the complex number system, which of the following is equal to $(14 - 2i)(7 + 12i)$? (Note: $i = \sqrt{-1}$)

A) 74

B) 122

C) 74 + 154i

D) 122 + 154i

Estimated Difficulty: Medium	**Key:** D

Choice D is correct. Applying the distributive property to multiply the binomials yields the expression $98 + 168i - 14i - 24i^2$. The note in the question reminds you that $i = \sqrt{-1}$, therefore, $i^2 = -1$. Substituting this value into the expression gives you $98 + 168i - 14i - (-24)$, and combining like terms results in $122 + 154i$.

Choice A is incorrect and may result from a combination of errors. You may not have correctly distributed when multiplying the binomials, multiplying only the first terms together and the second terms together. You may also have used the incorrect equality $i^2 = 1$.

Choice B is incorrect and may result from a combination of errors. You may not have correctly distributed when multiplying the binomials, multiplying only the first terms together and the second terms together.

Choice C is incorrect and results from misapplying the statement $i = \sqrt{-1}$.

5

Which of the following is equal to $\sin\left(\dfrac{\pi}{5}\right)$?

A) $-\cos\left(\dfrac{\pi}{5}\right)$

B) $-\sin\left(\dfrac{\pi}{5}\right)$

C) $\cos\left(\dfrac{3\pi}{10}\right)$

D) $\sin\left(\dfrac{7\pi}{10}\right)$

Estimated Difficulty: Hard	**Key:** C

Choice C is correct. Sine and cosine are cofunctions, or are related by the equation $\sin(x) = \cos\left(\dfrac{\pi}{2} - x\right)$.

Therefore, $\sin\left(\dfrac{\pi}{5}\right) = \cos\left(\dfrac{\pi}{2} - \dfrac{\pi}{5}\right)$, which reduces to $\cos\left(\dfrac{3\pi}{10}\right)$.

Choice A is incorrect and may result from a misunderstanding about trigonometric relationships. You may have thought that cosine is the inverse function of sine and therefore reasoned that the negative of the cosine of an angle is equivalent to the sine of that angle.

Choice B is incorrect and may result from a misunderstanding of the unit circle and how it relates to trigonometric expressions. You may have thought that, on a coordinate grid, the negative sign only changes the orientation of the triangle formed, not the value of the trigonometric expression.

Choice D is incorrect. You may have confused the relationship between sine and cosine and erroneously added $\dfrac{\pi}{2}$ to the given angle measure instead of subtracting the angle measure from $\dfrac{\pi}{2}$.

Student-Produced Response Math Questions

For some questions in the Math Tests, you will be asked to solve the problem and enter your answer in the grid, as described below, on the answer sheet.

1. Although not required, it is suggested that you write your answer in the boxes at the top of the columns to help you fill in the bubbles accurately. You will receive credit only if the bubbles are filled in correctly.

2. Mark no more than one bubble in any column.

3. No question has a negative answer.

4. Some problems may have more than one correct answer. In such cases, grid only one answer.

5. Mixed numbers such as $3\frac{1}{2}$ must be gridded as 3.5 or 7/2 (If [3 1 / 2] is entered into the grid, it will be interpreted as $\frac{31}{2}$, not $3\frac{1}{2}$.)

6. **Decimal answers:** If you obtain a decimal answer with more digits than the grid can accommodate, it may be either rounded or truncated, but it must fill the entire grid.

6

$$x^2 + y^2 - 6x + 8y = 144$$

The equation of a circle in the xy-plane is shown above. What is the diameter of the circle?

Estimated Difficulty: Hard	**Key:** 26

Completing the square yields the equation $(x - 3)^2 + (y + 4)^2 = 169$, the standard form of an equation of the circle. Understanding this form results in the equation $r^2 = 169$, which when solved for r gives the value of the radius as 13. Diameter is twice the value of the radius; therefore, the diameter is 26.

Answer: $\frac{7}{12}$

Write answer in boxes.

← Fraction line

Grid in result.

Answer: 2.5

← Decimal point

Acceptable ways to grid $\frac{2}{3}$ are:

Answer: 201– either position is correct

NOTE: You may start your answers in any column, space permitting. Columns you don't need to use should be left blank.

Math Test – Calculator Questions

Directions

For questions 1-8, solve each problem, choose the best answer from the choices provided, and fill in the corresponding bubble on your answer sheet. **For questions 9-10**, solve the problem and enter your answer in the grid on the answer sheet. Please refer to the directions before question 6 on page 35 on how to enter your answers in the grid. You may use any available space in your test booklet for scratch work.

Notes

1. The use of a calculator **is permitted**.

2. All variables and expressions used represent real numbers unless otherwise indicated.

3. Figures provided in this test are drawn to scale unless otherwise indicated.

4. All figures lie in a plane unless otherwise indicated.

5. Unless otherwise indicated, the domain of a given function f is the set of all real numbers x for which $f(x)$ is a real number.

Reference

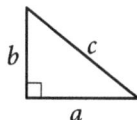
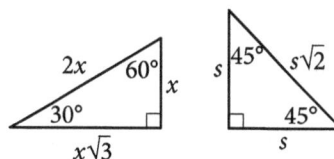

$A = \pi r^2$ $A = \ell w$ $A = \frac{1}{2}bh$ $c^2 = a^2 + b^2$ Special Right Triangles

$C = 2\pi r$

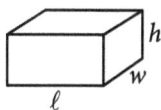
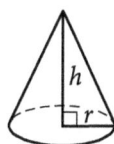
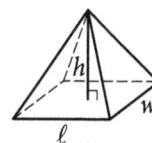

$V = \ell w h$ $V = \pi r^2 h$ $V = \frac{4}{3}\pi r^3$ $V = \frac{1}{3}\pi r^2 h$ $V = \frac{1}{3}\ell w h$

The number of degrees of arc in a circle is 360.

The number of radians of arc in a circle is 2π.

The sum of the measures in degrees of the angles of a triangle is 180.

1

The recommended daily calcium intake for a 20-year-old person is 1,000 milligrams (mg). One cup of milk contains 299 mg of calcium and one cup of juice contains 261 mg of calcium. Which of the following inequalities represents the possible number of cups of milk, m, and cups of juice, j, a 20-year-old person could drink in a day to meet or exceed the recommended daily calcium intake from these drinks alone?

A) $299m + 261j \geq 1,000$

B) $299m + 261j > 1,000$

C) $\dfrac{299}{m} + \dfrac{261}{j} \geq 1,000$

D) $\dfrac{299}{m} + \dfrac{261}{j} \geq 1,000$

Estimated Difficulty: Easy	**Key:** A

Choice A is correct. Multiplying the number of cups of milk by the amount of calcium each cup contains and multiplying the number of cups of juice by the amount of calcium each cup contains gives the total amount of calcium from each source. You must then find the sum of these two numbers to find the total amount of calcium. Because the question asks for the calcium from these two sources to meet or exceed the recommended daily intake, the sum of these two products must be greater than or equal to 1,000.

Choice B is incorrect and may result from a misunderstanding of the meaning of inequality symbols as they relate to real-life situations. This answer does not allow for the daily intake to meet the recommended daily amount.

Choice C is incorrect and may result from a misunderstanding of proportional relationships. Here the wrong operation is applied, with the total amount of calcium per cup divided by the number of cups of each type of drink. These values should be multiplied.

Choice D is incorrect and may result from a combination of mistakes. The inequality symbol used allows the option to exceed, but not to meet, the recommended daily value, and the wrong operation may have been applied when calculating the total amount of calcium intake from each drink.

2

A company's manager estimated that the cost C, in dollars, of producing n items is $C = 7n + 350$. The company sells each item for $12. The company makes a profit when the total income from selling a quantity of items is greater than the total cost of producing that quantity of items. Which of the following inequalities gives all possible values of n for which the manager estimates that the company will make a profit?

A) $n < 70$

B) $n < 84$

C) $n > 70$

D) $n > 84$

Estimated Difficulty: Medium	**Key:** C

Choice C is correct. One way to find the correct answer is to create an inequality. The income from sales of n items is $12n$. For the company to profit, $12n$ must be greater than the cost of producing n items; therefore, the inequality $12n > 7n + 350$ can be used to model the scenario. Solving this inequality yields $n > 70$.

Choice A is incorrect and may result from a misunderstanding of the properties of inequalities. You may have found the number of items of the break-even point as 70 and used the incorrect notation to express the answer, or you may have incorrectly modeled the scenario when setting up an inequality to solve.

Choice B is incorrect and may result from a misunderstanding of how the cost equation models the scenario. If you use the cost of $12 as the number of items n and evaluate the expression $7n$, you will find the value of 84. Misunderstanding how the inequality relates to the scenario might lead you to think n should be less than this value.

Choice D is incorrect and may result from a misunderstanding of how the cost equation models the scenario. If you use the cost of $12 as the number of items n and evaluate the expression $7n$, you will find the value of 84. Misunderstanding how the inequality relates to the scenario might lead you to think n should be greater than this value.

3

At a primate reserve, the mean age of all the male primates is 15 years, and the mean age of all female primates is 19 years. Which of the following must be true about the mean age m of the combined group of male and female primates at the primate reserve?

A) $m = 17$

B) $m > 17$

C) $m < 17$

D) $15 < m < 19$

Estimated Difficulty: Medium	**Key:** D

Choice D is correct. You must reason that because the mean of the males is lower than that of the females, the combined mean cannot be greater than or equal to that of the females, while also reasoning that because the mean of the females is greater than that of the males, the combined mean cannot be less than or equal to the mean of the males. Therefore, the combined mean must be between the two separate means.

Choice A is incorrect and results from finding the mean of the two means. This answer makes an unjustified assumption that there are an equal number of male and female primates.

Choice B is incorrect and results from finding the mean of the two means and misapplying an inequality to the scenario. This answer makes an unjustified assumption that there are more females than males.

Choice C is incorrect and results from finding the mean of the two means and misapplying an inequality to the scenario. This answer makes an unjustified assumption that there are more males than females.

4

A biology class at Central High School predicted that a local population of animals will double in size every 12 years. The population at the beginning of 2014 was estimated to be 50 animals. If P represents the population n years after 2014, then which of the following equations represents the class's model of the population over time?

A) $P = 12 + 50n$

B) $P = 50 + 12n$

C) $P = 50(2)^{12n}$

D) $P = 50(2)^{\frac{n}{12}}$

Estimated Difficulty: Medium	**Key:** D

Choice D is correct. A population that doubles in size over equal time periods is increasing at an exponential rate. In a doubling scenario, an exponential growth model can be written in the form $y = a(2)^{\frac{n}{b}}$, where a is the initial population (that is, the population when $n = 0$) and b is the number of years it takes for the population to double in size. In this case, the initial population is 50, the number of animals at the beginning of 2014. Therefore, $a = 50$. The text explains that the population will double in size every 12 years. Therefore, $b = 12$.

Choice A is incorrect and may result from a misunderstanding of exponential equations or of the context. This linear model indicates that the initial population is 12 animals and the population is increasing by 50 animals each year. However, this is not the case.

Choice B is incorrect and may result from a misunderstanding of exponential equations or of the context. This linear model indicates that the initial population is 50 animals and the population is increasing by 12 animals each year. However, this is not the case.

Choice C is incorrect. This exponential model indicates that the initial population is 50 animals and is doubling. However, the exponent $12n$ indicates that the population is doubling 12 times per year, not every 12 years.

5

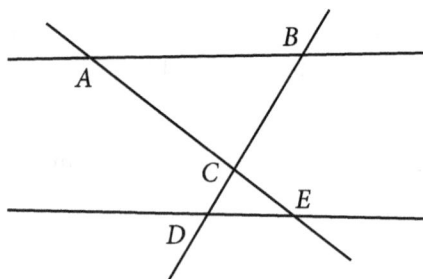

Note: Figure not drawn to scale.

In the figure above, $\triangle ABC$ is similar to $\triangle EDC$, with $\angle BAC$ corresponding to $\angle CED$ and $\angle ABC$ corresponding to $\angle CDE$. Which of the following must be true?

A) $\overline{AE} \parallel \overline{BD}$
B) $\overline{AE} \perp \overline{BD}$
C) $\overline{AB} \parallel \overline{DE}$
D) $\overline{AB} \perp \overline{DE}$

Estimated Difficulty: Medium	**Key:** C

Choice C is correct. Given that $\triangle ABC$ is similar to $\triangle EDC$ and $\angle BAC$ corresponds to $\angle CED$, you can determine that $\angle BAC$ is congruent to $\angle CED$. The converse of the alternate interior angle theorem tells us that $\overline{AB} \parallel \overline{DE}$. (You can also use the fact that $\angle ABC$ and $\angle CDE$ are congruent to make a similar argument.)

Choice A is incorrect and may result from multiple misconceptions. You may have misidentified the segments as perpendicular and used the wrong notation to express this statement.

Choice B is incorrect and may result from using only the diagram and not considering the given information. The line segments appear to be perpendicular, but need not be, given the information provided.

Choice D is incorrect and may result from misunderstanding either the notation or the vocabulary of parallel and perpendicular lines. You may have incorrectly identified parallel lines as perpendicular.

Questions 6-8 refer to the following information.

The first metacarpal bone is located in the hand. The scatterplot below shows the relationship between the length of the first metacarpal bone and height of 9 people. A line of best fit is also shown.

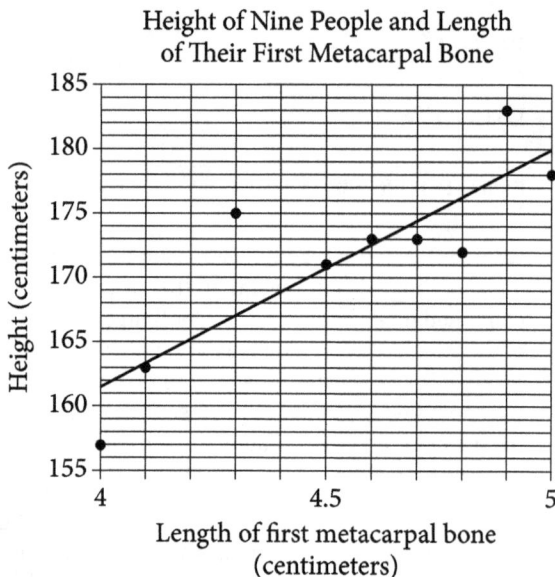

Height of Nine People and Length of Their First Metacarpal Bone

6

How many of the 9 people have an actual height that differs by more than 3 centimeters from the height predicted by the line of best fit?

A) 2
B) 4
C) 6
D) 9

Estimated Difficulty: Easy	**Key:** B

Choice B is correct. The people who have first metacarpal bones of length 4.0, 4.3, 4.8, and 4.9 centimeters have heights that differ by more than 3 centimeters from the height predicted by the line of best fit.

Choice A is incorrect. There are 2 people whose actual heights are more than 3 centimeters above the height predicted by the line of best fit. However, there are also 2 people whose actual heights are farther than 3 centimeters below the line of best fit.

Choice C is incorrect. There are 6 data points in which the absolute value between the actual height and the height predicted by the line of best fit is greater than 1 centimeter.

Choice D is incorrect. The data on the graph represents 9 different people; however, the absolute value of the difference between actual height and predicted height is not greater than 3 for all of the people.

7

Which of the following is the best interpretation of the slope of the line of best fit in the context of this problem?

A) The predicted height increase in centimeters for one centimeter increase in the first metacarpal bone

B) The predicted first metacarpal bone increase in centimeters for every centimeter increase in height

C) The predicted height in centimeters of a person with a first metacarpal bone length of 0 centimeters

D) The predicted first metacarpal bone length in centimeters for a person with a height of 0 centimeters

Estimated Difficulty: Easy	**Key:** A

Choice A is correct. The slope is the change in the vertical distance divided by the change in the horizontal distance between any two points on a line. In this context, the change in the vertical distance is the change in the predicted height of a person, and the change in the horizontal distance is the change in the length of his or her first metacarpal bone. The unit rate, or slope, is the increase in predicted height for each increase of one centimeter of the first metacarpal bone.

Choice B is incorrect. If you selected this answer, you may have interpreted the slope incorrectly as run over rise.

Choice C is incorrect. If you selected this answer, you may have mistaken the slope for the y-intercept.

Choice D is incorrect. If you selected this answer, you may have mistaken the slope for the x-intercept.

8

Based on the line of best fit, what is the predicted height for someone with a first metacarpal bone that has a length of 4.45 centimeters?

A) 168 centimeters

B) 169 centimeters

C) 170 centimeters

D) 171 centimeters

Estimated Difficulty: Easy	**Key:** C

Choice C is correct. First, notice that the scale of the x-axis is 0.1, and therefore the x-value of 4.45 is halfway between the unmarked value of 4.4 and the marked value of 4.5. Then find the y-value on the line of best fit that corresponds to an x-value of 4.45, which is 170.

Choice A is incorrect. If you mistakenly find the point on the line between the x-values of 4.3 and 4.4, you'll likely find a predicted metacarpal bone length of 168 centimeters.

Choice B is incorrect. If you mistakenly find the point on the line that corresponds to an x-value of 4.4 centimeters, you'll likely find a predicted height of approximately 169 centimeters.

Choice D is incorrect. If you mistakenly find the point on the line that corresponds to an x-value of 4.5 centimeters, you'll likely find a predicted height of approximately 171 centimeters. You might also choose this option if you mistakenly use the data point that has an x-value closest to 4.45 centimeters.

Student-Produced Response Math Questions

For questions 9 and 10, you are asked to solve the problem and enter your answer in the grid, as described on page 35 of this booklet.

9

The table shown classifies 103 elements as metal, metalloid, or nonmetal and as solid, liquid, or gas at standard temperature and pressure.

	Solids	Liquids	Gases	Total
Metals	77	1	0	78
Metalloids	7	0	0	7
Nonmetals	6	1	11	18
Total	90	2	11	103

What fraction of solids and liquids in the table are metalloids?

Estimated Difficulty: Easy	**Key:** $\dfrac{7}{92}$, .076

There are 7 metalloids that are solid or liquid, and there are 92 total solids and liquids. Therefore, the fraction of solids and liquids that are metalloids is 7/92 or .076.

10

An architect drew the sketch below while designing a house roof. The dimensions shown are for the interior of the triangle.

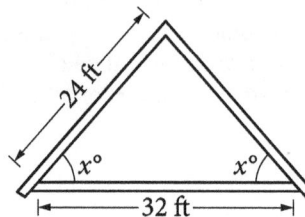

Note: Figure not drawn to scale.

What is the value of cos x?

Estimated Difficulty: Hard	**Key:** $\dfrac{2}{3}, \dfrac{4}{6},$ $\dfrac{6}{9}, \dfrac{8}{12},$ .666, .667

Because the triangle is isosceles, constructing a perpendicular from the top vertex to the opposite side will bisect the base and create two smaller right triangles. In a right triangle, the cosine of an acute angle is equal to the length of the side adjacent to the angle divided by the length of the hypotenuse. This gives cos $x = \dfrac{16}{24}$, which can be simplified to cos $x = \dfrac{2}{3}$. Note that $\dfrac{16}{24}$ cannot be entered into the answer grid, so this fraction must be reduced. Acceptable answers to grid are 2/3, 4/6, 6/9, 8/12, .666, and .667.

The SAT Essay

The SAT Essay is a lot like a typical college writing assignment that asks you to analyze a text. It shows colleges that you're able to read, analyze, and write at the college level.

IMPORTANT: *Do not write your name or any other personally identifying information on the lines on the answer sheet provided for your essay (for example, "by Jane Doe"). Doing so will delay the receipt of your essay results.*

SAT Essay Overview

- Total questions: 1 prompt, with points to consider and directions
- 1 passage
- Time allotted: 50 minutes to read and analyze the passage and to develop a written response

What the SAT Essay Is Like

The SAT Essay asks you to use your reading, analysis, and writing skills. You'll be asked to:

- Read a passage.
- Explain how the author builds an argument to persuade an audience.
- Support your explanation with evidence from the passage.

What the SAT Essay Measures

The SAT Essay shows how well you understand the passage and use it as the basis for a well-written, well-thought-out response. Your essay will be scored by 2 people on 3 dimensions, each with a score of 1–4. The scores are then added to create a scale of 2–8 for:

Reading: A successful essay shows that you understood the passage, including the interplay of central ideas and important details. It also shows effective use of textual evidence.

Analysis: A successful essay shows your understanding of how the author builds an argument by:

- Examining the author's use of evidence, reasoning, and/or stylistic and persuasive techniques (or other elements of your choosing)
- Supporting your claims and points effectively
- Focusing on those features of the passage that are most relevant for completing the task

Writing: A successful essay is cohesive, organized, and precise, uses an appropriate style and tone, has varied sentences, and observes the conventions of standard written English.

See The SAT Essay Scoring Guide later in this guide to learn more about how the essay is scored.

The Essay Prompt

The prompt (question) shown below is nearly identical to the one that will appear on the SAT.

As you read the passage below, consider how [the author] uses:

- Evidence, such as facts or examples, to support claims.
- Reasoning to develop ideas and to connect claims and evidence.
- Stylistic or persuasive elements, such as word choice or appeals to emotion, to add power to the ideas expressed.

Write an essay in which you explain how [the author] builds an argument to persuade [their] audience that [author's claim]. In your essay, analyze how [the author] uses one or more of the features listed above (or features of your own choice) to strengthen the logic and persuasiveness of [their] argument. Be sure that your analysis focuses on the most relevant features of the passage. Your essay should not explain whether you agree with [the author's] claims, but rather explain how [the author] builds an argument to persuade [their] audience.

The Essay Passage

All passages have these things in common:

- Written for a broad audience
- Argue a point
- Express subtle views on complex subjects
- Use logical reasoning and evidence to support claims
- Examine ideas, debates, or trends in the arts and sciences or in civic, cultural, or political life
- Always taken from published works

All the information you need to write your essay will be included in the passage or in notes about it.

Sample Essay Materials

The following student essays show you what kinds of attributes will be evaluated in the SAT Essay.

Each student essay is followed by an explanation of why it received the assigned score on each of the 3 dimensions. The directions on the next page match what you'll encounter on the actual test.

Sample Essay

Directions

The essay gives you an opportunity to show how effectively you can read and comprehend a passage and write an essay analyzing the passage. In your essay, you should demonstrate that you have read the passage carefully, present a clear and logical analysis, and use language precisely.

Your essay must be written on the lines provided in your answer booklet; except for the Planning Page of the answer booklet, you will receive no other paper on which to write. You will have enough space if you write on every line, avoid wide margins, and keep your handwriting to a reasonable size. Remember that people who are not familiar with your handwriting will read what you write. Try to write or print so that what you are writing is legible to those readers.

You have 50 minutes to read the passage and write an essay in response to the prompt provided inside this booklet.

Reminders:

- Do not write your essay in this booklet. Only what you write on the lined pages of your answer booklet will be evaluated.

- An off-topic essay will not be evaluated.

The following sample illustrates the general format of the essay task in the context of a specific prompt, this one related to a passage adapted from an article by Paul Bogard about the value of natural darkness.

As you read the passage below, consider how Paul Bogard uses

- evidence, such as facts or examples, to support claims.
- reasoning to develop ideas and to connect claims and evidence.
- stylistic or persuasive elements, such as word choice or appeals to emotion, to add power to the ideas expressed.

Adapted from Paul Bogard, "Let There Be Dark." ©2012 by Los Angeles Times. Originally published December 21, 2012.

1   At my family's cabin on a Minnesota lake, I knew woods so dark that my hands disappeared before my eyes. I knew night skies in which meteors left smoky trails across sugary spreads of stars. But now, when 8 of 10 children born in the United States will never know a sky dark enough for the Milky Way, I worry we are rapidly losing night's natural darkness before realizing its worth. This winter solstice, as we cheer the days' gradual movement back toward light, let us also remember the irreplaceable value of darkness.

2   All life evolved to the steady rhythm of bright days and dark nights. Today, though, when we feel the closeness of nightfall, we reach quickly for a light switch. And too little darkness, meaning too much artificial light at night, spells trouble for all.

3   Already the World Health Organization classifies working the night shift as a probable human carcinogen, and the American Medical Association has voiced its unanimous support for "light pollution reduction efforts and glare reduction efforts at both the national and state levels." Our bodies need darkness to produce the hormone melatonin, which keeps certain cancers from developing, and our bodies need darkness for sleep. Sleep disorders have been linked to diabetes, obesity, cardiovascular disease and depression, and recent research suggests one main cause of "short sleep" is "long light." Whether we work at night or simply take our tablets, notebooks and smartphones to bed, there isn't a place for this much artificial light in our lives.

4 The rest of the world depends on darkness as well, including nocturnal and crepuscular species of birds, insects, mammals, fish and reptiles. Some examples are well known—the 400 species of birds that migrate at night in North America, the sea turtles that come ashore to lay their eggs—and some are not, such as the bats that save American farmers billions in pest control and the moths that pollinate 80% of the world's flora. Ecological light pollution is like the bulldozer of the night, wrecking habitat and disrupting ecosystems several billion years in the making. Simply put, without darkness, Earth's ecology would collapse. . . .

5 In today's crowded, louder, more fast-paced world, night's darkness can provide solitude, quiet and stillness, qualities increasingly in short supply. Every religious tradition has considered darkness invaluable for a soulful life, and the chance to witness the universe has inspired artists, philosophers and everyday stargazers since time began. In a world awash with electric light . . . how would Van Gogh have given the world his "Starry Night"? Who knows what this vision of the night sky might inspire in each of us, in our children or grandchildren?

6 Yet all over the world, our nights are growing brighter. In the United States and Western Europe, the amount of light in the sky increases an average of about 6% every year. Computer images of the United States at night, based on NASA photographs, show that what was a very dark country as recently as the 1950s is now nearly covered with a blanket of light. Much of this light is wasted energy, which means wasted dollars. Those of us over 35 are perhaps among the last generation to have known truly dark nights. Even the northern lake where I was lucky to spend my summers has seen its darkness diminish.

7 It doesn't have to be this way. Light pollution is readily within our ability to solve, using new lighting technologies and shielding existing lights. Already, many cities and towns across North America and Europe are changing to LED streetlights, which offer dramatic possibilities for controlling wasted light. Other communities are finding success with simply turning off portions of their public lighting after midnight. Even Paris, the famed "city of light," which already turns off its monument lighting after 1 a.m., will this summer start to require its shops, offices and public buildings to turn off lights after 2 a.m. Though primarily designed to save energy, such reductions in light will also go far in addressing light pollution. But we will never truly address the problem of light pollution until we become aware of the irreplaceable value and beauty of the darkness we are losing.

Write an essay in which you explain how Paul Bogard builds an argument to persuade his audience that natural darkness should be preserved. In your essay, analyze how Bogard uses one or more of the features listed in the box above (or features of your own choice) to strengthen the logic and persuasiveness of his argument. Be sure that your analysis focuses on the most relevant features of the passage.

Your essay should not explain whether you agree with Bogard's claims, but rather explain how Bogard builds an argument to persuade his audience.

Sample Student Essays

The following student essays show you what kinds of attributes will be evaluated in the SAT Essay. Each essay is followed by an explanation of why it received the assigned score on each of the three dimensions.

SAMPLE 1

Bogard builds an argument to persuade his audience about what he is concering about and feels it important to take care about. His essay talks about so much facts about sleeping how so little can effect us health wise examples like getting sleep disorders, diabetes, obesity, cardiovascular disease and depression. This facts helps people persuade the audience he also say that the world health organization classifies working night shift is bad. In his argument is not all about how it bad for the body he also claims and have proof that light cost are expensive and really costing people because they have light all night long. He also claims light is messing with mother nature that animals need darkness to feed eat move around because there noctuaral creatures. He has details facts about human body, animals and about mother nature that he can use to support his idea of not using so much light at night and how we need darkness. With these features he can persuade the auidence because people dont know why darkness can be good for us. He was all of facts and examples that he claim is efficting us and there world.

This response scored a 2/1/1.

Reading—2: This response demonstrates some comprehension of the source text, although the writer's understanding of Bogard's central idea isn't conveyed until the latter part of the essay, where the writer indicates that Bogard includes *details facts about human body, animals and about mother nature that he can use to support his idea of not using so much light at night and how we need darkness.* Prior to this, the writer has included details from the text, but without contextualizing these details within Bogard's broader argument, suggesting that the writer is relaying ideas from the text without much understanding of how they contribute to the whole. For example, the writer mentions the health problems cited in the text, that working the night shift is classified as bad, and that light costs are high, but doesn't explain how these points relate to Bogard's main claim that we must preserve natural darkness. On the whole, this essay displays only a partial understanding of the source text.

Analysis—1: In this essay, the writer has merely identified aspects of Bogard's use of evidence without explaining how the evidence contributes to the argument. The writer notes that Bogard's text *talks about so much facts about sleeping how so little can effect us health wise examples like getting sleep disorders, diabetes, obesity, cardiovascular disease and depression. This facts helps people persuade the audience.* Other than identifying these as persuasive facts, however, the writer does nothing to indicate an understanding of the analytical task. The writer again mentions persuasion before the conclusion of the essay (*With these features he can persuade the auidence because people dont know why darkness can be good for us*), but once again, there is no explanation of how or why these features are persuasive. Thus, the essay offers inadequate analysis of Bogard's text.

Writing—1: This response demonstrates little cohesion and inadequate skill in the use and control of language. From the outset, problems with language control impede the writer's ability to establish a clear central claim (*Bogard builds an argument to persuade his audience about what he is concering about and feels it important to take care about*). The response also lacks a recognizable introduction and conclusion, and sentences are strung together without a clear progression of ideas (for much of the response, the writer merely lists claims Bogard makes). The response also lacks variety in sentence structures, in part because of repetitive transitions. (For example, *he also claims* is used two sentences in a row in this brief response). Weak control of the conventions of standard written English, coupled with vague word choice, undermines the quality of writing. Overall, this response demonstrates inadequate writing skill.

SAMPLE 2

Paul Bogard strongly believes that natural darkness should be preserved. In order to prove the need for natural darkness, Bogard divides his argument into three main topics, saying that natural darkness is beneficial to humans, essential to humans, and essential to ecosystems.

According to Bogard, natural darkness can be a positive help to humans. One of the ways it can accomplish this is by giving enjoyment to onlookers. To supplant this, Bogard gives a personal example of how he enjoyed seeing meteors dart across the night sky in Minnesota as a child. Also he states that natural darkness can be a source of solitude. Supporting this claim, Bogard states that darkness is invaluable to every religion. Additionally Bogard says that the night sky has inspired countless numbers of philosophers, artists, and stargazers for millennia. He then gives an appealing allusion by asking how Van Gogh could have painted "Starry Night" in the mist of electric light. One of Bogard's primary arguments for natural darkness shows how it can benefit humans.

Bogard then gives a scientific case that shows why natural darkness is essential to humans. He states a find of the World Health Organization that declares the night shift can be detrimental to one's health. He points to the necessity of darkness in producing melatonin, a hormone that helps prevent certain cancers from developing in the human body. Bogard then concludes his argument that darkness is essential to human well-being by analyzing sleep. He first makes the obvious claim that darkness is essential for sleep. Then, he talks about the negative health effects of sleep disorders.; these include "diabetes, obesity, cardiovascular disease and depression." To associate this with his argument for natural darkness, Bogard states the findings of recent research, which say that "long light" is one of the primary causes of "short sleep." Bogard uses scientific evidence to support his belief in the preservation of natural darkness.

Bogard's third primary defense of natural darkness declares that it is essential to nature. He notes that there are a variety of nocturnal and crepuscular species of birds, fish, mammals, insects, and reptiles worldwide. He gives two specific, well-known examples of these species; these discussed the 400 species of North American birds that migrate at night and the sea turtles that lay their eggs on the shore at night. He also gives a couple of lesser-known examples, involving bats and moths that show the positive actions that some nocturnal animals perform. He then concludes his argument for nocturnal darkness necessary to nature with persuasion, saying that removing natural darkness would essentially destroy an ecology that took billions of years to develop. Here, Bogard uses scientific fact to prove that natural darkness is a key to nature and ecology. Paul Bogard supports the preservation of natural darkness. He uses an argument to support his position that has three primary points—benefit to humans, need for humans and need for nature.

This response scored a 4/1/3.

Reading—4: This response demonstrates thorough comprehension of Bogard's text and a clear understanding of the interrelation between the central idea and important details. The writer briefly summarizes Bogard's central idea (*natural darkness should be preserved*) and aptly notes that Bogard's argument encompasses three main points: *that natural darkness is beneficial to humans, essential to humans, and essential to ecosystems*. The writer provides various details from the text that support these points. In the first body paragraph, for example, the writer demonstrates comprehension of how Bogard's *personal example of how he enjoyed seeing meteors dart across the night sky in Minnesota as a child* relates to his claim that natural darkness can give *enjoyment to onlookers*. The writer also sees the connection between darkness as a *source of solitude* and it inspiring *countless numbers of philosophers*, *artists*, and *stargazers for millennia*. Providing these details highlights the writer's understanding of Bogard's claim that natural darkness *can benefit humans*. The writer continues to demonstrate how details in Bogard's text relate to each other and to Bogard's central idea in the subsequent discussion of how darkness is essential to humans' health and to nature. Although little is directly quoted from the text, the writer's thorough paraphrasing of multiple details taken from across the passage indicates that the writer comprehensively understands Bogard's argument and is able to convey it in his own words.

Analysis—1: The response offers ineffective analysis of Bogard's text and demonstrates little understanding of the analytical task. Although clearly comprehending the entirety of Bogard's argument, the writer does not communicate how Bogard builds his argument with evidence, reasoning, or stylistic or persuasive elements, nor does the writer communicate what effect Bogard's argumentation has on his audience. Instead of providing effective analysis, the writer only identifies argumentative elements in Bogard's text, such as the *appealing allusion* Bogard offers regarding Van Gogh's *Starry Night* or the *scientific evidence* Bogard uses to *support his belief in the preservation of natural darkness*. The writer instead consistently lapses into summary. Overall, the response demonstrates inadequate analysis.

Writing—3: This mostly cohesive response demonstrates effective use and control of language. The writer presents an effective introduction with a clear central claim that lays out the three points discussed in the response (*In order to prove the need for natural darkness, Bogard divides his argument into three main topics, saying that natural darkness is beneficial to humans, essential to humans, and essential to the ecosystem*). The response also includes a generally effective conclusion that summarizes rather than advances the essay (*Paul Bogard supports the preservation of natural darkness. He uses an argument to support his position that has three primary points— benefit to humans, need for humans and need for nature*) although the conclusion is not marked off by a paragraph break. The response is organized clearly around the three points identified in the introduction, and each body paragraph stays on topic. The writer also demonstrates a clear progression of ideas both within paragraphs and throughout the essay. Sentence structure tends to be repetitive and simple, however. For example, at or near the end of each body paragraph, the writer restates the point that introduces that paragraph (*Bogard then gives a scientific case that shows why natural darkness is essential to humans. . . . Bogard uses scientific evidence to support his belief in the preservation of natural darkness*). Although the writing in this response is proficient, it does not demonstrate the sentence variety, precise word choice, or highly effective progression of ideas that is expected at the advanced level.

SAMPLE 3

In response to our world's growing reliance on artificial light, writer Paul Bogard argues that natural darkness should be preserved in his article "Let There be dark". He effectively builds his argument by using a personal anecdote, allusions to art and history, and rhetorical questions.

Bogard starts his article off by recounting a personal story – a summer spent on a Minnesota lake where there was "woods so dark that [his] hands disappeared before [his] eyes." In telling this brief anecdote, Bogard challenges the audience to remember a time where they could fully amass themselves in natural darkness void of artificial light. By drawing in his readers with a personal encounter about night darkness, the author means to establish the potential for beauty, glamour, and awe-inspiring mystery that genuine darkness can possess. He builds his argument for the preservation of natural darkness by reminiscing for his readers a first-hand encounter that proves the "irreplaceable value of darkness."

This anecdote provides a baseline of sorts for readers to find credence with the author's claims. Bogard's argument is also furthered by his use of allusion to art – Van Gogh's "Starry Night" – and modern history – Paris' reputation as "The City of Light". By first referencing "Starry Night", a painting generally considered to be undoubtedly beautiful, Bogard establishes that the natural magnificence of stars in a dark sky is definite. A world absent of excess artificial light could potentially hold the key to a grand, glorious night sky like Van Gogh's according to the writer. This urges the readers to weigh the disadvantages of our world consumed by unnatural, vapid lighting. Furthermore, Bogard's alludes to Paris as "the famed 'city of light'". He then goes on to state how Paris has taken steps to exercise more

sustainable lighting practices. By doing this, Bogard creates a dichotomy between Paris' traditionally alluded-to name and the reality of what Paris is becoming – no longer "the city of light", but moreso "the city of light...before 2 AM". This furthers his line of argumentation because it shows how steps can be and are being taken to preserve natural darkness. It shows that even a city that is literally famous for being constantly lit can practically address light pollution in a manner that preserves the beauty of both the city itself and the universe as a whole.

Finally, Bogard makes subtle yet efficient use of rhetorical questioning to persuade his audience that natural darkness preservation is essential. He asks the readers to consider "what the vision of the night sky might inspire in each of us, in our children or grandchildren?" in a way that brutally plays to each of our emotions. By asking this question, Bogard draws out heartfelt ponderance from his readers about the affecting power of an untainted night sky. This rhetorical question tugs at the readers' heartstrings; while the reader may have seen an unobscured night skyline before, the possibility that their child or grandchild will never get the chance sways them to see as Bogard sees. This strategy is definitively an appeal to pathos, forcing the audience to directly face an emotionally-charged inquiry that will surely spur some kind of response. By doing this, Bogard develops his argument, adding gutthral power to the idea that the issue of maintaining natural darkness is relevant and multifaceted.

Writing as a reaction to his disappointment that artificial light has largely permeated the prescence of natural darkness, Paul Bogard argues that we must preserve true, unaffected darkness. He builds this claim by making use of a personal anecdote, allusions, and rhetorical questioning.

This response scored a 4/4/4.

Reading—4: This response demonstrates thorough comprehension of the source text through skillful use of paraphrases and direct quotations. The writer briefly summarizes the central idea of Bogard's piece (*natural darkness should be preserved; we must preserve true, unaffected darkness*), and presents many details from the text, such as referring to the personal anecdote that opens the passage and citing Bogard's use of *Paris' reputation as "The City of Light."* There are few long direct quotations from the source text; instead, the response succinctly and accurately captures the entirety of Bogard's argument in the writer's own words, and the writer is able to articulate how details in the source text interrelate with Bogard's central claim. The response is also free of errors of fact or interpretation. Overall, the response demonstrates advanced reading comprehension.

Analysis—4: This response offers an insightful analysis of the source text and demonstrates a sophisticated understanding of the analytical task. In analyzing Bogard's use of *personal anecdote, allusions to art and history, and rhetorical questions,* the writer is able to explain carefully and thoroughly how Bogard builds his argument over the course of the passage. For example, the writer offers a possible reason for why Bogard chose to open his argument with a personal anecdote, and is also able to describe the overall effect of that choice on his audience (*In telling this brief anecdote, Bogard challenges the audience to remember a time where they could fully amass themselves in natural darkness void of artificial light. By drawing in his readers with a personal encounter … the author means to establish the potential for beauty, glamour, and awe-inspiring mystery that genuine darkness can possess. . . . This anecdote provides a baseline of sorts for readers to find credence with the author's claims*). The cogent chain of reasoning indicates an understanding of the overall effect of Bogard's personal narrative both in terms of its function in the passage and how it affects his audience. This type of insightful analysis is evident throughout the response and indicates advanced analytical skill.

Writing—4: The response is cohesive and demonstrates highly effective use and command of language. The response contains a precise central claim (*He effectively builds his argument by using personal anecdote, allusions to art and history, and rhetorical questions*), and the body paragraphs are tightly focused on those three elements of Bogard's text. There is a clear, deliberate progression of ideas within paragraphs and throughout the response. The writer's brief introduction and conclusion are skillfully written and encapsulate the main ideas of Bogard's piece as well as the overall structure of the writer's analysis. There is a consistent use of both precise word choice and well-chosen turns of phrase (*the natural magnificence of stars in a dark sky is definite, our world consumed by unnatural, vapid lighting, the affecting power of an untainted night sky*). Moreover, the response features a wide variety in sentence structure and many examples of sophisticated sentences (*By doing this, Bogard creates a dichotomy between Paris' traditionally alluded-to name and the reality of what Paris is becoming – no longer "the city of light", but more so "the city of light…before 2AM"*). The response demonstrates a strong command of the conventions of written English. Overall, the response exemplifies advanced writing proficiency.

The SAT Essay Scoring Guide

Score	Reading	Analysis	Writing
4	**Advanced:** The response demonstrates thorough comprehension of the source text. The response shows an understanding of the text's central idea(s) and of most important details and how they interrelate, demonstrating a comprehensive understanding of the text. The response is free of errors of fact or interpretation with regard to the text. The response makes skillful use of textual evidence (quotations, paraphrases, or both), demonstrating a complete understanding of the source text.	**Advanced:** The response offers an insightful analysis of the source text and demonstrates a sophisticated understanding of the analytical task. The response offers a thorough, well-considered evaluation of the author's use of evidence, reasoning, and/or stylistic and persuasive elements, and/or feature(s) of the student's own choosing. The response contains relevant, sufficient, and strategically chosen support for claim(s) or point(s) made. The response focuses consistently on those features of the text that are most relevant to addressing the task.	**Advanced:** The response is cohesive and demonstrates a highly effective use and command of language. The response includes a precise central claim. The response includes a skillful introduction and conclusion. The response demonstrates a deliberate and highly effective progression of ideas both within paragraphs and throughout the essay. The response has a wide variety in sentence structures. The response demonstrates a consistent use of precise word choice. The response maintains a formal style and objective tone. The response shows a strong command of the conventions of standard written English and is free or virtually free of errors.
3	**Proficient:** The response demonstrates effective comprehension of the source text. The response shows an understanding of the text's central idea(s) and important details. The response is free of substantive errors of fact and interpretation with regard to the text. The response makes appropriate use of textual evidence (quotations, paraphrases, or both), demonstrating an understanding of the source text.	**Proficient:** The response offers an effective analysis of the source text and demonstrates an understanding of the analytical task. The response competently evaluates the author's use of evidence, reasoning, and/or stylistic and persuasive elements, and/or feature(s) of the student's own choosing. The response contains relevant and sufficient support for claim(s) or point(s) made. The response focuses primarily on those features of the text that are most relevant to addressing the task.	**Proficient:** The response is mostly cohesive and demonstrates effective use and control of language. The response includes a central claim or implicit controlling idea. The response includes an effective introduction and conclusion. The response demonstrates a clear progression of ideas both within paragraphs and throughout the essay. The response has variety in sentence structures. The response demonstrates some precise word choice. The response maintains a formal style and objective tone. The response shows a good control of the conventions of standard written English and is free of significant errors that detract from the quality of writing.

Score	Reading	Analysis	Writing
2	**Partial:** The response demonstrates some comprehension of the source text. The response shows an understanding of the text's central idea(s) but not of important details. The response may contain errors of fact and/or interpretation with regard to the text. The response makes limited and/or haphazard use of textual evidence (quotations, paraphrases, or both), demonstrating some understanding of the source text.	**Partial:** The response offers limited analysis of the source text and demonstrates only partial understanding of the analytical task. The response identifies and attempts to describe the author's use of evidence, reasoning, and/or stylistic and persuasive elements, and/or feature(s) of the student's own choosing, but merely asserts rather than explains their importance. Or one or more aspects of the response's analysis are unwarranted based on the text. The response contains little or no support for claim(s) or point(s) made. The response may lack a clear focus on those features of the text that are most relevant to addressing the task.	**Partial:** The response demonstrates little or no cohesion and limited skill in the use and control of language. The response may lack a clear central claim or controlling idea or may deviate from the claim or idea over the course of the response. The response may include an ineffective introduction and/or conclusion. The response may demonstrate some progression of ideas within paragraphs but not throughout the response. The response has limited variety in sentence structures; sentence structures may be repetitive. The response demonstrates general or vague word choice; word choice may be repetitive. The response may deviate noticeably from a formal style and objective tone. The response shows a limited control of the conventions of standard written English and contains errors that detract from the quality of writing and may impede understanding.
1	**Inadequate:** The response demonstrates little or no comprehension of the source text. The response fails to show an understanding of the text's central idea(s), and may include only details without reference to central idea(s). The response may contain numerous errors of fact and/or interpretation with regard to the text. The response makes little or no use of textual evidence (quotations, paraphrases, or both), demonstrating little or no understanding of the source text.	**Inadequate:** The response offers little or no analysis or ineffective analysis of the source text and demonstrates little or no understanding of the analytic task. The response identifies without explanation some aspects of the author's use of evidence, reasoning, and/or stylistic and persuasive elements, and/or feature(s) of the student's choosing. Or numerous aspects of the response's analysis are unwarranted based on the text. The response contains little or no support for claim(s) or point(s) made, or support is largely irrelevant. The response may not focus on features of the text that are relevant to addressing the task. Or the response offers no discernible analysis (e.g., is largely or exclusively summary).	**Inadequate:** The response demonstrates little or no cohesion and inadequate skill in the use and control of language. The response may lack a clear central claim or controlling idea. The response lacks a recognizable introduction and conclusion. The response does not have a discernible progression of ideas. The response lacks variety in sentence structures; sentence structures may be repetitive. The response demonstrates general and vague word choice; word choice may be poor or inaccurate. The response may lack a formal style and objective tone. The response shows a weak control of the conventions of standard written English and may contain numerous errors that undermine the quality of writing.

General SAT Test Taking Strategies

- Read section directions before the test. ...
- Answer the questions you know first. ...
- Eliminate incorrect answers. ...
- Be neat. ...
- Use your test booklet. ...
- Avoid stray marks. ...
- Your first response is usually correct. ...
- There is only one correct answer.

SAT® Practice Test #1

IMPORTANT REMINDERS

1

A No. 2 pencil is required for the test. Do not use a mechanical pencil or pen.

2

Sharing any questions with anyone is a violation of Test Security and Fairness policies and may result in your scores being canceled.

This cover is representative of what you'll see on test day.

Reading Test

65 MINUTES, 52 QUESTIONS

Turn to Section 1 of your answer sheet to answer the questions in this section.

DIRECTIONS

Each passage or pair of passages below is followed by a number of questions. After reading each passage or pair, choose the best answer to each question based on what is stated or implied in the passage or passages and in any accompanying graphics (such as a table or graph).

Questions 1-10 are based on the following passage.

This passage is from Lydia Minatoya, *The Strangeness of Beauty*. ©1999 by Lydia Minatoya. The setting is Japan in 1920. Chie and her daughter Naomi are members of the House of Fuji, a noble family.

Akira came directly, breaking all tradition. Was that it? Had he followed form—had he asked his mother to speak to his father to approach a
Line go-between—would Chie have been more receptive?
5   He came on a winter's eve. He pounded on the door while a cold rain beat on the shuttered veranda, so at first Chie thought him only the wind. The maid knew better. Chie heard her soft scuttling footsteps, the creak of the door. Then the maid brought a
10 calling card to the drawing room, for Chie.
     Chie was reluctant to go to her guest; perhaps she was feeling too cozy. She and Naomi were reading at a low table set atop a charcoal brazier. A thick quilt spread over the sides of the table so their legs were
15 tucked inside with the heat.
     "Who is it at this hour, in this weather?" Chie questioned as she picked the name card off the maid's lacquer tray.
     "Shinoda, Akira. Kobe Dental College," she read.
20   Naomi recognized the name. Chie heard a soft intake of air.
     "I think you should go," said Naomi.

Akira was waiting in the entry. He was in his early twenties, slim and serious, wearing the black
25 military-style uniform of a student. As he bowed—his hands hanging straight down, a black cap in one, a yellow oil-paper umbrella in the other—Chie glanced beyond him. In the glistening surface of the courtyard's rain-drenched paving
30 stones, she saw his reflection like a dark double.
     "Madame," said Akira, "forgive my disruption, but I come with a matter of urgency."
     His voice was soft, refined. He straightened and stole a deferential peek at her face.
35   In the dim light his eyes shone with sincerity. Chie felt herself starting to like him.
     "Come inside, get out of this nasty night. Surely your business can wait for a moment or two."
     "I don't want to trouble you. Normally I would
40 approach you more properly but I've received word of a position. I've an opportunity to go to America, as dentist for Seattle's Japanese community."
     "Congratulations," Chie said with amusement. "That is an opportunity, I'm sure. But how am I
45 involved?"
     Even noting Naomi's breathless reaction to the name card, Chie had no idea. Akira's message, delivered like a formal speech, filled her with maternal amusement. You know how children speak
50 so earnestly, so hurriedly, so endearingly about things that have no importance in an adult's mind? That's how she viewed him, as a child.

CONTINUE

It was how she viewed Naomi. Even though Naomi was eighteen and training endlessly in the arts
55 needed to make a good marriage, Chie had made no effort to find her a husband.

Akira blushed.

"Depending on your response, I may stay in Japan. I've come to ask for Naomi's hand."
60 Suddenly Chie felt the dampness of the night.

"Does Naomi know anything of your . . . ambitions?"

"We have an understanding. Please don't judge my candidacy by the unseemliness of this proposal. I
65 ask directly because the use of a go-between takes much time. Either method comes down to the same thing: a matter of parental approval. If you give your consent, I become Naomi's yoshi.* We'll live in the House of Fuji. Without your consent, I must go to
70 America, to secure a new home for my bride."

Eager to make his point, he'd been looking her full in the face. Abruptly, his voice turned gentle. "I see I've startled you. My humble apologies. I'll take no more of your evening. My address is on my card. If
75 you don't wish to contact me, I'll reapproach you in two weeks' time. Until then, good night."

He bowed and left. Taking her ease, with effortless grace, like a cat making off with a fish.

"Mother?" Chie heard Naomi's low voice and
80 turned from the door. "He has asked you?"

The sight of Naomi's clear eyes, her dark brows gave Chie strength. Maybe his hopes were preposterous.

"Where did you meet such a fellow? Imagine! He
85 thinks he can marry the Fuji heir and take her to America all in the snap of his fingers!"

Chie waited for Naomi's ripe laughter.

Naomi was silent. She stood a full half minute looking straight into Chie's eyes. Finally, she spoke.
90 "I met him at my literary meeting."

Naomi turned to go back into the house, then stopped.

"Mother."

"Yes?"
95 "I mean to have him."

* a man who marries a woman of higher status and takes her family's name

1

Which choice best describes what happens in the passage?

A) One character argues with another character who intrudes on her home.

B) One character receives a surprising request from another character.

C) One character reminisces about choices she has made over the years.

D) One character criticizes another character for pursuing an unexpected course of action.

2

Which choice best describes the developmental pattern of the passage?

A) A careful analysis of a traditional practice

B) A detailed depiction of a meaningful encounter

C) A definitive response to a series of questions

D) A cheerful recounting of an amusing anecdote

3

As used in line 1 and line 65, "directly" most nearly means

A) frankly.

B) confidently.

C) without mediation.

D) with precision.

4

Which reaction does Akira most fear from Chie?

A) She will consider his proposal inappropriate.

B) She will mistake his earnestness for immaturity.

C) She will consider his unscheduled visit an imposition.

D) She will underestimate the sincerity of his emotions.

5

Which choice provides the best evidence for the answer to the previous question?

A) Line 33 ("His voice . . . refined")

B) Lines 49-51 ("You . . . mind")

C) Lines 63-64 ("Please . . . proposal")

D) Lines 71-72 ("Eager . . . face")

6

In the passage, Akira addresses Chie with

A) affection but not genuine love.

B) objectivity but not complete impartiality.

C) amusement but not mocking disparagement.

D) respect but not utter deference.

7

The main purpose of the first paragraph is to

A) describe a culture.

B) criticize a tradition.

C) question a suggestion.

D) analyze a reaction.

8

As used in line 2, "form" most nearly means

A) appearance.

B) custom.

C) structure.

D) nature.

9

Why does Akira say his meeting with Chie is "a matter of urgency" (line 32)?

A) He fears that his own parents will disapprove of Naomi.

B) He worries that Naomi will reject him and marry someone else.

C) He has been offered an attractive job in another country.

D) He knows that Chie is unaware of his feelings for Naomi.

10

Which choice provides the best evidence for the answer to the previous question?

A) Line 39 ("I don't . . . you")

B) Lines 39-42 ("Normally . . . community")

C) Lines 58-59 ("Depending . . . Japan")

D) Lines 72-73 ("I see . . . you")

4

CONTINUE

Questions 11-21 are based on the following passage and supplementary material.

This passage is adapted from Francis J. Flynn and Gabrielle S. Adams, "Money Can't Buy Love: Asymmetric Beliefs about Gift Price and Feelings of Appreciation." ©2008 by Elsevier Inc.

Every day, millions of shoppers hit the stores in full force—both online and on foot—searching frantically for the perfect gift. Last year, Americans spent over $30 billion at retail stores in the month of December alone. Aside from purchasing holiday gifts, most people regularly buy presents for other occasions throughout the year, including weddings, birthdays, anniversaries, graduations, and baby showers. This frequent experience of gift-giving can engender ambivalent feelings in gift-givers. Many relish the opportunity to buy presents because gift-giving offers a powerful means to build stronger bonds with one's closest peers. At the same time, many dread the thought of buying gifts; they worry that their purchases will disappoint rather than delight the intended recipients.

Anthropologists describe gift-giving as a positive social process, serving various political, religious, and psychological functions. Economists, however, offer a less favorable view. According to Waldfogel (1993), gift-giving represents an objective waste of resources. People buy gifts that recipients would not choose to buy on their own, or at least not spend as much money to purchase (a phenomenon referred to as "the deadweight loss of Christmas"). To wit, givers are likely to spend $100 to purchase a gift that receivers would spend only $80 to buy themselves. This "deadweight loss" suggests that gift-givers are not very good at predicting what gifts others will appreciate. That in itself is not surprising to social psychologists. Research has found that people often struggle to take account of others' perspectives— their insights are subject to egocentrism, social projection, and multiple attribution errors.

What is surprising is that gift-givers have considerable experience acting as both gift-givers and gift-recipients, but nevertheless tend to overspend each time they set out to purchase a meaningful gift. In the present research, we propose a unique psychological explanation for this overspending problem—i.e., that gift-givers equate how much they spend with how much recipients will appreciate the gift (the more expensive the gift, the stronger a gift-recipient's feelings of appreciation). Although a link between gift price and feelings of appreciation might seem intuitive to gift-givers, such an assumption may be unfounded. Indeed, we propose that gift-recipients will be less inclined to base their feelings of appreciation on the magnitude of a gift than givers assume.

Why do gift-givers assume that gift price is closely linked to gift-recipients' feelings of appreciation? Perhaps givers believe that bigger (i.e., more expensive) gifts convey stronger signals of thoughtfulness and consideration. According to Camerer (1988) and others, gift-giving represents a symbolic ritual, whereby gift-givers attempt to signal their positive attitudes toward the intended recipient and their willingness to invest resources in a future relationship. In this sense, gift-givers may be motivated to spend more money on a gift in order to send a "stronger signal" to their intended recipient. As for gift-recipients, they may not construe smaller and larger gifts as representing smaller and larger signals of thoughtfulness and consideration.

The notion of gift-givers and gift-recipients being unable to account for the other party's perspective seems puzzling because people slip in and out of these roles every day, and, in some cases, multiple times in the course of the same day. Yet, despite the extensive experience that people have as both givers and receivers, they often struggle to transfer information gained from one role (e.g., as a giver) and apply it in another, complementary role (e.g., as a receiver). In theoretical terms, people fail to utilize information about their own preferences and experiences in order to produce more efficient outcomes in their exchange relations. In practical terms, people spend hundreds of dollars each year on gifts, but somehow never learn to calibrate their gift expenditures according to personal insight.

Unauthorized copying or reuse of any part of this page is illegal.

5

CONTINUE

Givers' Perceived and Recipients' Actual Gift Appreciations

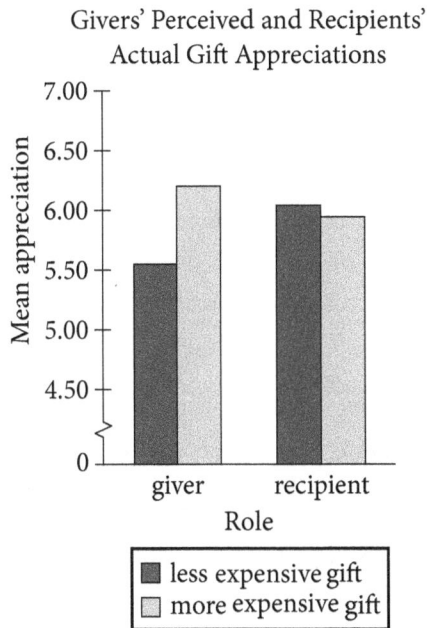

11

The authors most likely use the examples in lines 1-9 of the passage ("Every . . . showers") to highlight the

A) regularity with which people shop for gifts.

B) recent increase in the amount of money spent on gifts.

C) anxiety gift shopping causes for consumers.

D) number of special occasions involving gift-giving.

12

In line 10, the word "ambivalent" most nearly means

A) unrealistic.

B) conflicted.

C) apprehensive.

D) supportive.

13

The authors indicate that people value gift-giving because they feel it

A) functions as a form of self-expression.

B) is an inexpensive way to show appreciation.

C) requires the gift-recipient to reciprocate.

D) can serve to strengthen a relationship.

14

Which choice provides the best evidence for the answer to the previous question?

A) Lines 10-13 ("Many . . . peers")

B) Lines 22-23 ("People . . . own")

C) Lines 31-32 ("Research . . . perspectives")

D) Lines 44-47 ("Although . . . unfounded")

15

The "social psychologists" mentioned in paragraph 2 (lines 17-34) would likely describe the "deadweight loss" phenomenon as

A) predictable.

B) questionable.

C) disturbing.

D) unprecedented.

16

The passage indicates that the assumption made by gift-givers in lines 41-44 may be

A) insincere.

B) unreasonable.

C) incorrect.

D) substantiated.

Unauthorized copying or reuse of any part of this page is illegal.

6

CONTINUE

17

Which choice provides the best evidence for the answer to the previous question?

A) Lines 53-55 ("Perhaps . . . consideration")

B) Lines 55-60 ("According . . . relationship")

C) Lines 63-65 ("As . . . consideration")

D) Lines 75-78 ("In . . . relations")

18

As it is used in line 54, "convey" most nearly means

A) transport.

B) counteract.

C) exchange.

D) communicate.

19

The authors refer to work by Camerer and others (line 56) in order to

A) offer an explanation.

B) introduce an argument.

C) question a motive.

D) support a conclusion.

20

The graph following the passage offers evidence that gift-givers base their predictions of how much a gift will be appreciated on

A) the appreciation level of the gift-recipients.

B) the monetary value of the gift.

C) their own desires for the gifts they purchase.

D) their relationship with the gift-recipients.

21

The authors would likely attribute the differences in gift-giver and recipient mean appreciation as represented in the graph to

A) an inability to shift perspective.

B) an increasingly materialistic culture.

C) a growing opposition to gift-giving.

D) a misunderstanding of intentions.

Unauthorized copying or reuse of any part of this page is illegal.

7

CONTINUE

Questions 22-31 are based on the following passage and supplementary material.

This passage is adapted from J. D. Watson and F. H. C. Crick, "Genetical Implications of the Structure of Deoxyribonucleic Acid." ©1953 by Nature Publishing Group. Watson and Crick deduced the structure of DNA using evidence from Rosalind Franklin and R. G. Gosling's X-ray crystallography diagrams of DNA and from Erwin Chargaff's data on the base composition of DNA.

The chemical formula of deoxyribonucleic acid
(DNA) is now well established. The molecule is a
very long chain, the backbone of which consists of a
Line regular alternation of sugar and phosphate groups.
5 To each sugar is attached a nitrogenous base, which
can be of four different types. Two of the possible
bases—adenine and guanine—are purines, and the
other two—thymine and cytosine—are pyrimidines.
So far as is known, the sequence of bases along the
10 chain is irregular. The monomer unit, consisting of
phosphate, sugar and base, is known as a nucleotide.
    The first feature of our structure which is of
biological interest is that it consists not of one chain,
but of two. These two chains are both coiled around
15 a common fiber axis. It has often been assumed that
since there was only one chain in the chemical
formula there would only be one in the structural
unit. However, the density, taken with the X-ray
evidence, suggests very strongly that there are two.
20   The other biologically important feature is the
manner in which the two chains are held together.
This is done by hydrogen bonds between the bases.
The bases are joined together in pairs, a single base
from one chain being hydrogen-bonded to a single
25 base from the other. The important point is that only
certain pairs of bases will fit into the structure.
One member of a pair must be a purine and the other
a pyrimidine in order to bridge between the two
chains. If a pair consisted of two purines, for
30 example, there would not be room for it.
    We believe that the bases will be present almost
entirely in their most probable forms. If this is true,
the conditions for forming hydrogen bonds are more
restrictive, and the only pairs of bases possible are:
35 adenine with thymine, and guanine with cytosine.
Adenine, for example, can occur on either chain; but
when it does, its partner on the other chain must
always be thymine.
    The phosphate-sugar backbone of our model is
40 completely regular, but any sequence of the pairs of
bases can fit into the structure. It follows that in a
long molecule many different permutations are
possible, and it therefore seems likely that the precise
sequence of bases is the code which carries the
45 genetical information. If the actual order of the bases
on one of the pair of chains were given, one could
write down the exact order of the bases on the other
one, because of the specific pairing. Thus one chain
is, as it were, the complement of the other, and it is
50 this feature which suggests how the deoxyribonucleic
acid molecule might duplicate itself.

The table shows, for various organisms, the percentage of each of the four types of nitrogenous bases in that organism's DNA.

Base Composition of DNA				
Organism	Percentage of base in organism's DNA			
	adenine (%)	guanine (%)	cytosine (%)	thymine (%)
Maize	26.8	22.8	23.2	27.2
Octopus	33.2	17.6	17.6	31.6
Chicken	28.0	22.0	21.6	28.4
Rat	28.6	21.4	20.5	28.4
Human	29.3	20.7	20.0	30.0
Grasshopper	29.3	20.5	20.7	29.3
Sea urchin	32.8	17.7	17.3	32.1
Wheat	27.3	22.7	22.8	27.1
Yeast	31.3	18.7	17.1	32.9
E. coli	24.7	26.0	25.7	23.6

Adapted from Manju Bansal, "DNA Structure: Revisiting the Watson-Crick Double Helix." ©2003 by Current Science Association, Bangalore.

CONTINUE

22

The authors use the word "backbone" in lines 3 and 39 to indicate that

A) only very long chains of DNA can be taken from an organism with a spinal column.

B) the main structure of a chain in a DNA molecule is composed of repeating units.

C) a chain in a DNA molecule consists entirely of phosphate groups or of sugars.

D) nitrogenous bases form the main structural unit of DNA.

23

A student claims that nitrogenous bases pair randomly with one another. Which of the following statements in the passage contradicts the student's claim?

A) Lines 5-6 ("To each . . . types")

B) Lines 9-10 ("So far . . . irregular")

C) Lines 23-25 ("The bases . . . other")

D) Lines 27-29 ("One member . . . chains")

24

In the second paragraph (lines 12-19), what do the authors claim to be a feature of biological interest?

A) The chemical formula of DNA

B) The common fiber axis

C) The X-ray evidence

D) DNA consisting of two chains

25

The authors' main purpose of including the information about X-ray evidence and density is to

A) establish that DNA is the molecule that carries the genetic information.

B) present an alternate hypothesis about the composition of a nucleotide.

C) provide support for the authors' claim about the number of chains in a molecule of DNA.

D) confirm the relationship between the density of DNA and the known chemical formula of DNA.

26

Based on the passage, the authors' statement "If a pair consisted of two purines, for example, there would not be room for it" (lines 29-30) implies that a pair

A) of purines would be larger than the space between a sugar and a phosphate group.

B) of purines would be larger than a pair consisting of a purine and a pyrimidine.

C) of pyrimidines would be larger than a pair of purines.

D) consisting of a purine and a pyrimidine would be larger than a pair of pyrimidines.

27

The authors' use of the words "exact," "specific," and "complement" in lines 47-49 in the final paragraph functions mainly to

A) confirm that the nucleotide sequences are known for most molecules of DNA.

B) counter the claim that the sequences of bases along a chain can occur in any order.

C) support the claim that the phosphate-sugar backbone of the authors' model is completely regular.

D) emphasize how one chain of DNA may serve as a template to be copied during DNA replication.

28

Based on the table and passage, which choice gives the correct percentages of the purines in yeast DNA?

A) 17.1% and 18.7%

B) 17.1% and 32.9%

C) 18.7% and 31.3%

D) 31.3% and 32.9%

29

Do the data in the table support the authors' proposed pairing of bases in DNA?

A) Yes, because for each given organism, the percentage of adenine is closest to the percentage of thymine, and the percentage of guanine is closest to the percentage of cytosine.

B) Yes, because for each given organism, the percentage of adenine is closest to the percentage of guanine, and the percentage of cytosine is closest to the percentage of thymine.

C) No, because for each given organism, the percentage of adenine is closest to the percentage of thymine, and the percentage of guanine is closest to the percentage of cytosine.

D) No, because for each given organism, the percentage of adenine is closest to the percentage of guanine, and the percentage of cytosine is closest to the percentage of thymine.

30

According to the table, which of the following pairs of base percentages in sea urchin DNA provides evidence in support of the answer to the previous question?

A) 17.3% and 17.7%

B) 17.3% and 32.1%

C) 17.3% and 32.8%

D) 17.7% and 32.8%

31

Based on the table, is the percentage of adenine in each organism's DNA the same or does it vary, and which statement made by the authors is most consistent with that data?

A) The same; "Two of . . . pyrimidines" (lines 6-8)

B) The same; "The important . . . structure" (lines 25-26)

C) It varies; "Adenine . . . thymine" (lines 36-38)

D) It varies; "It follows . . . information" (lines 41-45)

10

CONTINUE

Questions 32-41 are based on the following passage.

This passage is adapted from Virginia Woolf, *Three Guineas*. ©1938 by Harcourt, Inc. Here, Woolf considers the situation of women in English society.

Close at hand is a bridge over the River Thames, an admirable vantage ground for us to make a survey. The river flows beneath; barges pass, laden
Line with timber, bursting with corn; there on one side are
5 the domes and spires of the city; on the other, Westminster and the Houses of Parliament. It is a place to stand on by the hour, dreaming. But not now. Now we are pressed for time. Now we are here to consider facts; now we must fix our eyes upon the
10 procession—the procession of the sons of educated men.
    There they go, our brothers who have been educated at public schools and universities, mounting those steps, passing in and out of those
15 doors, ascending those pulpits, preaching, teaching, administering justice, practising medicine, transacting business, making money. It is a solemn sight always—a procession, like a caravanserai crossing a desert. . . . But now, for the past twenty
20 years or so, it is no longer a sight merely, a photograph, or fresco scrawled upon the walls of time, at which we can look with merely an esthetic appreciation. For there, trapesing along at the tail end of the procession, we go ourselves. And that
25 makes a difference. We who have looked so long at the pageant in books, or from a curtained window watched educated men leaving the house at about nine-thirty to go to an office, returning to the house at about six-thirty from an office, need look passively
30 no longer. We too can leave the house, can mount those steps, pass in and out of those doors, . . . make money, administer justice. . . . We who now agitate these humble pens may in another century or two speak from a pulpit. Nobody will dare contradict us
35 then; we shall be the mouthpieces of the divine spirit—a solemn thought, is it not? Who can say whether, as time goes on, we may not dress in military uniform, with gold lace on our breasts, swords at our sides, and something like the old
40 family coal-scuttle on our heads, save that that venerable object was never decorated with plumes of white horsehair. You laugh—indeed the shadow of the private house still makes those dresses look a little queer. We have worn private clothes so
45 long. . . . But we have not come here to laugh, or to talk of fashions—men's and women's. We are here, on the bridge, to ask ourselves certain questions. And they are very important questions; and we have very little time in which to answer them. The
50 questions that we have to ask and to answer about that procession during this moment of transition are so important that they may well change the lives of all men and women for ever. For we have to ask ourselves, here and now, do we wish to join that
55 procession, or don't we? On what terms shall we join that procession? Above all, where is it leading us, the procession of educated men? The moment is short; it may last five years; ten years, or perhaps only a matter of a few months longer. . . . But, you will
60 object, you have no time to think; you have your battles to fight, your rent to pay, your bazaars to organize. That excuse shall not serve you, Madam. As you know from your own experience, and there are facts that prove it, the daughters of educated men
65 have always done their thinking from hand to mouth; not under green lamps at study tables in the cloisters of secluded colleges. They have thought while they stirred the pot, while they rocked the cradle. It was thus that they won us the right to our
70 brand-new sixpence. It falls to us now to go on thinking; how are we to spend that sixpence? Think we must. Let us think in offices; in omnibuses; while we are standing in the crowd watching Coronations and Lord Mayor's Shows; let us think . . . in the
75 gallery of the House of Commons; in the Law Courts; let us think at baptisms and marriages and funerals. Let us never cease from thinking—what is this "civilization" in which we find ourselves? What are these ceremonies and why should we take part in
80 them? What are these professions and why should we make money out of them? Where in short is it leading us, the procession of the sons of educated men?

32

The main purpose of the passage is to

A) emphasize the value of a tradition.

B) stress the urgency of an issue.

C) highlight the severity of social divisions.

D) question the feasibility of an undertaking.

33

The central claim of the passage is that

A) educated women face a decision about how to engage with existing institutions.

B) women can have positions of influence in English society only if they give up some of their traditional roles.

C) the male monopoly on power in English society has had grave and continuing effects.

D) the entry of educated women into positions of power traditionally held by men will transform those positions.

34

Woolf uses the word "we" throughout the passage mainly to

A) reflect the growing friendliness among a group of people.

B) advance the need for candor among a group of people.

C) establish a sense of solidarity among a group of people.

D) reinforce the need for respect among a group of people.

35

According to the passage, Woolf chooses the setting of the bridge because it

A) is conducive to a mood of fanciful reflection.

B) provides a good view of the procession of the sons of educated men.

C) is within sight of historic episodes to which she alludes.

D) is symbolic of the legacy of past and present sons of educated men.

36

Woolf indicates that the procession she describes in the passage

A) has come to have more practical influence in recent years.

B) has become a celebrated feature of English public life.

C) includes all of the richest and most powerful men in England.

D) has become less exclusionary in its membership in recent years.

37

Which choice provides the best evidence for the answer to the previous question?

A) Lines 12-17 ("There . . . money")

B) Lines 17-19 ("It . . . desert")

C) Lines 23-24 ("For . . . ourselves")

D) Lines 30-34 ("We . . . pulpit")

Unauthorized copying or reuse of any part of this page is illegal.

12

CONTINUE

38

Woolf characterizes the questions in lines 53-57 ("For we . . . men") as both

A) controversial and threatening.

B) weighty and unanswerable.

C) momentous and pressing.

D) provocative and mysterious.

39

Which choice provides the best evidence for the answer to the previous question?

A) Lines 46-47 ("We . . . questions")

B) Lines 48-49 ("And . . . them")

C) Line 57 ("The moment . . . short")

D) Line 62 ("That . . . Madam")

40

Which choice most closely captures the meaning of the figurative "sixpence" referred to in lines 70 and 71?

A) Tolerance

B) Knowledge

C) Opportunity

D) Perspective

41

The range of places and occasions listed in lines 72-76 ("Let us . . . funerals") mainly serves to emphasize how

A) novel the challenge faced by women is.

B) pervasive the need for critical reflection is.

C) complex the political and social issues of the day are.

D) enjoyable the career possibilities for women are.

Questions 42-52 are based on the following passages.

Passage 1 is adapted from Michael Slezak, "Space Mining: the Next Gold Rush?" ©2013 by New Scientist. Passage 2 is from the editors of New Scientist, "Taming the Final Frontier." ©2013 by New Scientist.

Passage 1

Follow the money and you will end up in space. That's the message from a first-of-its-kind forum on mining beyond Earth.

Line
5   Convened in Sydney by the Australian Centre for Space Engineering Research, the event brought together mining companies, robotics experts, lunar scientists, and government agencies that are all working to make space mining a reality.

The forum comes hot on the heels of the
10 2012 unveiling of two private asteroid-mining firms. Planetary Resources of Washington says it will launch its first prospecting telescopes in two years, while Deep Space Industries of Virginia hopes to be harvesting metals from asteroids by 2020. Another
15 commercial venture that sprung up in 2012, Golden Spike of Colorado, will be offering trips to the moon, including to potential lunar miners.

Within a few decades, these firms may be meeting earthly demands for precious metals, such as
20 platinum and gold, and the rare earth elements vital for personal electronics, such as yttrium and lanthanum. But like the gold rush pioneers who transformed the western United States, the first space miners won't just enrich themselves. They also hope
25 to build an off-planet economy free of any bonds with Earth, in which the materials extracted and processed from the moon and asteroids are delivered for space-based projects.

In this scenario, water mined from other
30 worlds could become the most desired commodity. "In the desert, what's worth more: a kilogram of gold or a kilogram of water?" asks Kris Zacny of HoneyBee Robotics in New York. "Gold is useless. Water will let you live."

35   Water ice from the moon's poles could be sent to astronauts on the International Space Station for drinking or as a radiation shield. Splitting water into oxygen and hydrogen makes spacecraft fuel, so ice-rich asteroids could become interplanetary
40 refuelling stations.

Companies are eyeing the iron, silicon, and aluminium in lunar soil and asteroids, which could be used in 3D printers to make spare parts or machinery. Others want to turn space dirt into
45 concrete for landing pads, shelters, and roads.

Passage 2

The motivation for deep-space travel is shifting from discovery to economics. The past year has seen a flurry of proposals aimed at bringing celestial riches down to Earth. No doubt this will make a few
50 billionaires even wealthier, but we all stand to gain: the mineral bounty and spin-off technologies could enrich us all.

But before the miners start firing up their rockets, we should pause for thought. At first glance, space
55 mining seems to sidestep most environmental concerns: there is (probably!) no life on asteroids, and thus no habitats to trash. But its consequences —both here on Earth and in space—merit careful consideration.

60   Part of this is about principles. Some will argue that space's "magnificent desolation" is not ours to despoil, just as they argue that our own planet's poles should remain pristine. Others will suggest that glutting ourselves on space's riches is not an
65 acceptable alternative to developing more sustainable ways of earthly life.

History suggests that those will be hard lines to hold, and it may be difficult to persuade the public that such barren environments are worth preserving.
70 After all, they exist in vast abundance, and even fewer people will experience them than have walked through Antarctica's icy landscapes.

There's also the emerging off-world economy to consider. The resources that are valuable in orbit and
75 beyond may be very different to those we prize on Earth. Questions of their stewardship have barely been broached—and the relevant legal and regulatory framework is fragmentary, to put it mildly.

Space miners, like their earthly counterparts, are
80 often reluctant to engage with such questions. One speaker at last week's space-mining forum in Sydney, Australia, concluded with a plea that regulation should be avoided. But miners have much to gain from a broad agreement on the for-profit
85 exploitation of space. Without consensus, claims will be disputed, investments risky, and the gains made insecure. It is in all of our long-term interests to seek one out.

42

In lines 9-17, the author of Passage 1 mentions several companies primarily to

A) note the technological advances that make space mining possible.

B) provide evidence of the growing interest in space mining.

C) emphasize the large profits to be made from space mining.

D) highlight the diverse ways to carry out space mining operations.

43

The author of Passage 1 indicates that space mining could have which positive effect?

A) It could yield materials important to Earth's economy.

B) It could raise the value of some precious metals on Earth.

C) It could create unanticipated technological innovations.

D) It could change scientists' understanding of space resources.

44

Which choice provides the best evidence for the answer to the previous question?

A) Lines 18-22 ("Within . . . lanthanum")

B) Lines 24-28 ("They . . . projects")

C) Lines 29-30 ("In this . . . commodity")

D) Lines 41-44 ("Companies . . . machinery")

45

As used in line 19, "demands" most nearly means

A) offers.

B) claims.

C) inquiries.

D) desires.

46

What function does the discussion of water in lines 35-40 serve in Passage 1?

A) It continues an extended comparison that begins in the previous paragraph.

B) It provides an unexpected answer to a question raised in the previous paragraph.

C) It offers hypothetical examples supporting a claim made in the previous paragraph.

D) It examines possible outcomes of a proposal put forth in the previous paragraph.

47

The central claim of Passage 2 is that space mining has positive potential but

A) it will end up encouraging humanity's reckless treatment of the environment.

B) its effects should be thoughtfully considered before it becomes a reality.

C) such potential may not include replenishing key resources that are disappearing on Earth.

D) experts disagree about the commercial viability of the discoveries it could yield.

48

As used in line 68, "hold" most nearly means

A) maintain.

B) grip.

C) restrain.

D) withstand.

CONTINUE

49

Which statement best describes the relationship between the passages?

A) Passage 2 refutes the central claim advanced in Passage 1.

B) Passage 2 illustrates the phenomenon described in more general terms in Passage 1.

C) Passage 2 argues against the practicality of the proposals put forth in Passage 1.

D) Passage 2 expresses reservations about developments discussed in Passage 1.

50

The author of Passage 2 would most likely respond to the discussion of the future of space mining in lines 18-28, Passage 1, by claiming that such a future

A) is inconsistent with the sustainable use of space resources.

B) will be difficult to bring about in the absence of regulations.

C) cannot be attained without technologies that do not yet exist.

D) seems certain to affect Earth's economy in a negative way.

51

Which choice provides the best evidence for the answer to the previous question?

A) Lines 60-63 ("Some . . . pristine")

B) Lines 74-76 ("The resources . . . Earth")

C) Lines 81-83 ("One . . . avoided")

D) Lines 85-87 ("Without . . . insecure")

52

Which point about the resources that will be highly valued in space is implicit in Passage 1 and explicit in Passage 2?

A) They may be different resources from those that are valuable on Earth.

B) They will be valuable only if they can be harvested cheaply.

C) They are likely to be primarily precious metals and rare earth elements.

D) They may increase in value as those same resources become rare on Earth.

STOP

If you finish before time is called, you may check your work on this section only.
Do not turn to any other section.

Writing and Language Test

35 MINUTES, 44 QUESTIONS

Turn to Section 2 of your answer sheet to answer the questions in this section.

DIRECTIONS

Each passage below is accompanied by a number of questions. For some questions, you will consider how the passage might be revised to improve the expression of ideas. For other questions, you will consider how the passage might be edited to correct errors in sentence structure, usage, or punctuation. A passage or a question may be accompanied by one or more graphics (such as a table or graph) that you will consider as you make revising and editing decisions.

Some questions will direct you to an underlined portion of a passage. Other questions will direct you to a location in a passage or ask you to think about the passage as a whole.

After reading each passage, choose the answer to each question that most effectively improves the quality of writing in the passage or that makes the passage conform to the conventions of standard written English. Many questions include a "NO CHANGE" option. Choose that option if you think the best choice is to leave the relevant portion of the passage as it is.

Questions 1-11 are based on the following passage.

Whey to Go

Greek yogurt—a strained form of cultured yogurt—has grown enormously in popularity in the United States since it was first introduced in the country in the late 1980s.

From 2011 to 2012 alone, sales of Greek yogurt in the US increased by 50 percent. The resulting increase in Greek yogurt production has forced those involved in the business to address the detrimental effects that the yogurt-making process may be having on the environment. Fortunately, farmers and others in the

Greek yogurt business have found many methods of controlling and eliminating most environmental threats. Given these solutions as well as the many health benefits of the food, the advantages of Greek yogurt **1** outdo the potential drawbacks of its production.

[1] The main environmental problem caused by the production of Greek yogurt is the creation of acid whey as a by-product. [2] Because it requires up to four times more milk to make than conventional yogurt does, Greek yogurt produces larger amounts of acid whey, which is difficult to dispose of. [3] To address the problem of disposal, farmers have found a number of uses for acid whey. [4] They can add it to livestock feed as a protein **2** supplement, and people can make their own Greek-style yogurt at home by straining regular yogurt. [5] If it is improperly introduced into the environment, acid-whey runoff **3** can pollute waterways, depleting the oxygen content of streams and rivers as it decomposes. [6] Yogurt manufacturers, food **4** scientists; and government officials are also working together to develop additional solutions for reusing whey. **5**

1
A) NO CHANGE
B) defeat
C) outperform
D) outweigh

2
Which choice provides the most relevant detail?
A) NO CHANGE
B) supplement and convert it into gas to use as fuel in electricity production.
C) supplement, while sweet whey is more desirable as a food additive for humans.
D) supplement, which provides an important element of their diet.

3
A) NO CHANGE
B) can pollute waterway's,
C) could have polluted waterways,
D) has polluted waterway's,

4
A) NO CHANGE
B) scientists: and
C) scientists, and
D) scientists, and,

5
To make this paragraph most logical, sentence 5 should be placed
A) where it is now.
B) after sentence 1.
C) after sentence 2.
D) after sentence 3.

[6] Though these conservation methods can be costly and time-consuming, they are well worth the effort. Nutritionists consider Greek yogurt to be a healthy food: it is an excellent source of calcium and protein, serves [7] to be a digestive aid, and [8] it contains few calories in its unsweetened low- and non-fat forms. Greek yogurt is slightly lower in sugar and carbohydrates than conventional yogurt is. [9] Also, because it is more concentrated, Greek yogurt contains slightly more protein per serving, thereby helping people stay

[6]

The writer is considering deleting the underlined sentence. Should the writer do this?

A) Yes, because it does not provide a transition from the previous paragraph.

B) Yes, because it fails to support the main argument of the passage as introduced in the first paragraph.

C) No, because it continues the explanation of how acid whey can be disposed of safely.

D) No, because it sets up the argument in the paragraph for the benefits of Greek yogurt.

[7]

A) NO CHANGE

B) as

C) like

D) for

[8]

A) NO CHANGE

B) containing

C) contains

D) will contain

[9]

A) NO CHANGE

B) In other words,

C) Therefore,

D) For instance,

Unauthorized copying or reuse of any part of this page is illegal.

20

CONTINUE ➤

[10] satiated for longer periods of time. These health benefits have prompted Greek yogurt's recent surge in popularity. In fact, Greek yogurt can be found in an increasing number of products such as snack food and frozen desserts. Because consumers reap the nutritional benefits of Greek yogurt and support those who make and sell [11] it, therefore farmers and businesses should continue finding safe and effective methods of producing the food.

10

A) NO CHANGE
B) fulfilled
C) complacent
D) sufficient

11

A) NO CHANGE
B) it, farmers
C) it, so farmers
D) it: farmers

CONTINUE

Questions 12-22 are based on the following passage and supplementary material.

Dark Snow

Most of Greenland's interior is covered by a thick layer of ice and compressed snow known as the Greenland Ice Sheet. The size of the ice sheet fluctuates seasonally: in summer, average daily high temperatures in Greenland can rise to slightly above 50 degrees Fahrenheit, partially melting the ice; in the winter, the sheet thickens as additional snow falls, and average daily low temperatures can drop 12 to as low as 20 degrees.

12

Which choice most accurately and effectively represents the information in the graph?
A) NO CHANGE
B) to 12 degrees Fahrenheit.
C) to their lowest point on December 13.
D) to 10 degrees Fahrenheit and stay there for months.

Average Daily High and Low Temperatures Recorded at Nuuk Weather Station, Greenland (1961—1990)

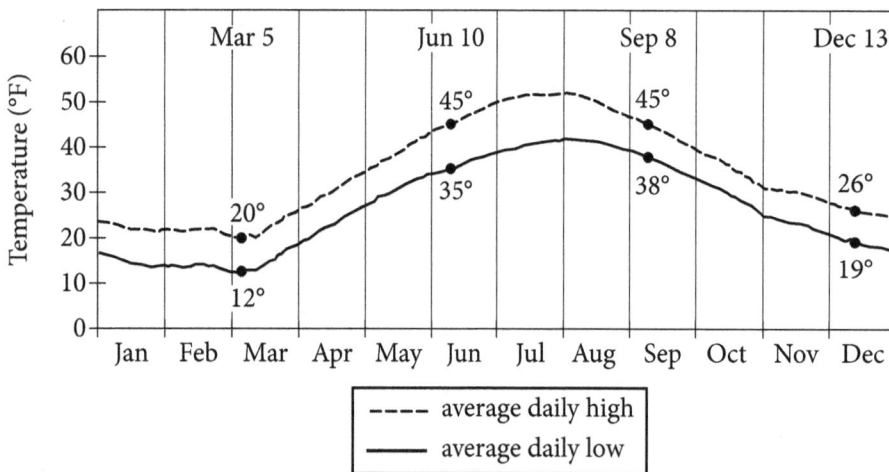

Adapted from WMO. ©2014 by World Meteorological Organization.

Unauthorized copying or reuse of any part of this page is illegal.

22

CONTINUE

Typically, the ice sheet begins to show evidence of thawing in late [13] summer. This follows several weeks of higher temperatures. [14] For example, in the summer of 2012, virtually the entire Greenland Ice Sheet underwent thawing at or near its surface by mid-July, the earliest date on record. Most scientists looking for the causes of the Great Melt of 2012 have focused exclusively on rising temperatures. The summer of 2012 was the warmest in 170 years, records show. But Jason [15] Box, an associate professor of geology at Ohio State believes that another factor added to the early [16] thaw; the "dark snow" problem.

[13]

Which choice most effectively combines the two sentences at the underlined portion?

A) summer, following

B) summer, and this thawing follows

C) summer, and such thawing follows

D) summer and this evidence follows

[14]

A) NO CHANGE

B) However,

C) As such,

D) Moreover,

[15]

A) NO CHANGE

B) Box an associate professor of geology at Ohio State,

C) Box, an associate professor of geology at Ohio State,

D) Box, an associate professor of geology, at Ohio State

[16]

A) NO CHANGE

B) thaw; and it was

C) thaw:

D) thaw: being

According to Box, a leading Greenland expert, tundra fires in 2012 from as far away as North America produced great amounts of soot, some [17] of it drifted over Greenland in giant plumes of smoke and then [18] fell as particles onto the ice sheet. Scientists have long known that soot particles facilitate melting by darkening snow and ice, limiting [19] it's ability to reflect the Sun's rays. As Box explains, "Soot is an extremely powerful light absorber. It settles over the ice and captures the Sun's heat." The result is a self-reinforcing cycle. As the ice melts, the land and water under the ice become exposed, and since land and water are darker than snow, the surface absorbs even more heat, which [20] is related to the rising temperatures.

[17]
A) NO CHANGE
B) soot
C) of which
D) DELETE the underlined portion.

[18]
A) NO CHANGE
B) falls
C) will fall
D) had fallen

[19]
A) NO CHANGE
B) its
C) there
D) their

[20]
Which choice best completes the description of a self-reinforcing cycle?
A) NO CHANGE
B) raises the surface temperature.
C) begins to cool at a certain point.
D) leads to additional melting.

[1] Box's research is important because the fires of 2012 may not be a one-time phenomenon. [2] According to scientists, rising Arctic temperatures are making northern latitudes greener and thus more fire prone. [3] The pattern Box observed in 2012 may repeat **21** itself again, with harmful effects on the Arctic ecosystem. [4] Box is currently organizing an expedition to gather this crucial information. [5] The next step for Box and his team is to travel to Greenland to perform direct sampling of the ice in order to determine just how much the soot is contributing to the melting of the ice sheet. [6] Members of the public will be able to track his team's progress—and even help fund the expedition—through a website Box has created. **22**

21

A) NO CHANGE
B) itself,
C) itself, with damage and
D) itself possibly,

22

To make this paragraph most logical, sentence 4 should be placed

A) where it is now.
B) after sentence 1.
C) after sentence 2.
D) after sentence 5.

CONTINUE

Questions 23-33 are based on the following passage.

Coworking: A Creative Solution

When I left my office job as a website developer at a small company for a position that allowed me to work full-time from home, I thought I had it made: I gleefully traded in my suits and dress shoes for sweatpants and slippers, my frantic early-morning bagged lunch packing for a leisurely midday trip to my refrigerator. The novelty of this comfortable work-from-home life, however, **23** soon got worn off quickly. Within a month, I found myself feeling isolated despite having frequent email and instant messaging contact with my colleagues. Having become frustrated trying to solve difficult problems, **24** no colleagues were nearby to share ideas. It was during this time that I read an article **25** into coworking spaces.

23
A) NO CHANGE
B) was promptly worn
C) promptly wore
D) wore

24
A) NO CHANGE
B) colleagues were important for sharing ideas.
C) ideas couldn't be shared with colleagues.
D) I missed having colleagues nearby to consult.

25
A) NO CHANGE
B) about
C) upon
D) for

The article, published by *Forbes* magazine, explained that coworking spaces are designated locations that, for a fee, individuals can use to conduct their work. The spaces are usually stocked with standard office [26] equipment, such as photocopiers, printers, and fax machines. [27] In these locations, however, the spaces often include small meeting areas and larger rooms for hosting presentations. [28] The cost of launching a new coworking business in the United States is estimated to be approximately $58,000.

26
A) NO CHANGE
B) equipment, such as:
C) equipment such as:
D) equipment, such as,

27
A) NO CHANGE
B) In addition to equipment,
C) For these reasons,
D) Likewise,

28
The writer is considering deleting the underlined sentence. Should the sentence be kept or deleted?
A) Kept, because it provides a detail that supports the main topic of the paragraph.
B) Kept, because it sets up the main topic of the paragraph that follows.
C) Deleted, because it blurs the paragraph's main focus with a loosely related detail.
D) Deleted, because it repeats information that has been provided in an earlier paragraph.

What most caught my interest, though, was a quotation from someone who described coworking spaces as "melting pots of creativity." The article refers to a 2012 survey in which [29] 64 percent of respondents noted that coworking spaces prevented them from completing tasks in a given time. The article goes on to suggest that the most valuable resources provided by coworking spaces are actually the people [30] whom use them.

[29]

At this point, the writer wants to add specific information that supports the main topic of the paragraph.

Perceived Effect of Coworking on Business Skills

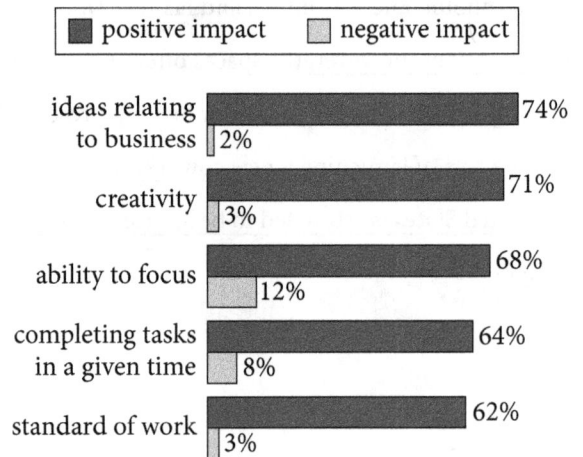

positive impact   negative impact

ideas relating to business	74%
	2%
creativity	71%
	3%
ability to focus	68%
	12%
completing tasks in a given time	64%
	8%
standard of work	62%
	3%

Adapted from "The 3rd Global Coworking Survey." ©2013 by Deskmag.

Which choice most effectively completes the sentence with relevant and accurate information based on the graph above?

A) NO CHANGE

B) 71 percent of respondents indicated that using a coworking space increased their creativity.

C) respondents credited coworking spaces with giving them 74 percent of their ideas relating to business.

D) respondents revealed that their ability to focus on their work improved by 12 percent in a coworking space.

[30]

A) NO CHANGE

B) whom uses

C) who uses

D) who use

[1] Thus, even though I already had all the equipment I needed in my home office, I decided to try using a coworking space in my city. [2] Because I was specifically interested in coworking's reported benefits related to creativity, I chose a facility that offered a bright, open work area where I wouldn't be isolated. [3] Throughout the morning, more people appeared. [4] Periods of quiet, during which everyone worked independently, were broken up occasionally with lively conversation. **31**

I liked the experience so much that I now go to the coworking space a few times a week. Over time, I've gotten to know several of my coworking **32** colleagues: another website developer, a graphic designer, a freelance writer, and several mobile app coders. Even those of us who work in disparate fields are able to **33** share advice and help each other brainstorm. In fact, it's the diversity of their talents and experiences that makes my coworking colleagues so valuable.

31

The writer wants to add the following sentence to the paragraph.

> After filling out a simple registration form and taking a quick tour of the facility, I took a seat at a table and got right to work on my laptop.

The best placement for the sentence is immediately

A) before sentence 1.

B) after sentence 1.

C) after sentence 2.

D) after sentence 3.

32

A) NO CHANGE

B) colleagues;

C) colleagues,

D) colleagues

33

A) NO CHANGE

B) give some wisdom

C) proclaim our opinions

D) opine

Questions 34-44 are based on the following passage.

The Consolations of Philosophy

   Long viewed by many as the stereotypical useless major, philosophy is now being seen by many students and prospective employers as in fact a very useful and practical major, offering students a host of transferable skills with relevance to the modern workplace. [34] In broad terms, philosophy is the study of meaning and the values underlying thought and behavior. But [35] more pragmatically, the discipline encourages students to analyze complex material, question conventional beliefs, and express thoughts in a concise manner.

   Because philosophy [36] teaching students not what to think but how to think, the age-old discipline offers consistently useful tools for academic and professional achievement. [37] A 1994 survey concluded that only 18 percent of American colleges required at least one philosophy course. [38] Therefore, between 1992 and 1996, more than 400 independent philosophy departments were eliminated from institutions.

34
A) NO CHANGE
B) For example,
C) In contrast,
D) Nevertheless,

35
A) NO CHANGE
B) speaking in a more pragmatic way,
C) speaking in a way more pragmatically,
D) in a more pragmatic-speaking way,

36
A) NO CHANGE
B) teaches
C) to teach
D) and teaching

37
Which choice most effectively sets up the information that follows?
A) Consequently, philosophy students have been receiving an increasing number of job offers.
B) Therefore, because of the evidence, colleges increased their offerings in philosophy.
C) Notwithstanding the attractiveness of this course of study, students have resisted majoring in philosophy.
D) However, despite its many utilitarian benefits, colleges have not always supported the study of philosophy.

38
A) NO CHANGE
B) Thus,
C) Moreover,
D) However,

Unauthorized copying or reuse of any part of this page is illegal.

30

CONTINUE

More recently, colleges have recognized the practicality and increasing popularity of studying philosophy and have markedly increased the number of philosophy programs offered. By 2008 there were 817 programs, up from 765 a decade before. In addition, the number of four-year graduates in philosophy has grown 46 percent in a decade. Also, studies have found that those students who major in philosophy often do better than students from other majors in both verbal reasoning and analytical **39** writing. These results can be measured by standardized test scores. On the Graduate Record Examination (GRE), for example, students intending to study philosophy in graduate school **40** has scored higher than students in all but four other majors.

These days, many **41** student's majoring in philosophy have no intention of becoming philosophers; instead they plan to apply those skills to other disciplines. Law and business specifically benefit from the complicated theoretical issues raised in the study of philosophy, but philosophy can be just as useful in engineering or any field requiring complex analytic skills. **42** That these skills are transferable across professions

39

Which choice most effectively combines the sentences at the underlined portion?

A) writing as

B) writing, and these results can be

C) writing, which can also be

D) writing when the results are

40

A) NO CHANGE

B) have scored

C) scores

D) scoring

41

A) NO CHANGE

B) students majoring

C) students major

D) student's majors

42

At this point, the writer is considering adding the following sentence.

> The ancient Greek philosopher Plato, for example, wrote many of his works in the form of dialogues.

Should the writer make this addition here?

A) Yes, because it reinforces the passage's main point about the employability of philosophy majors.

B) Yes, because it acknowledges a common counterargument to the passage's central claim.

C) No, because it blurs the paragraph's focus by introducing a new idea that goes unexplained.

D) No, because it undermines the passage's claim about the employability of philosophy majors.

[43] which makes them especially beneficial to twenty-first-century students. Because today's students can expect to hold multiple jobs—some of which may not even exist yet—during [44] our lifetime, studying philosophy allows them to be flexible and adaptable. High demand, advanced exam scores, and varied professional skills all argue for maintaining and enhancing philosophy courses and majors within academic institutions.

43

A) NO CHANGE

B) that

C) and

D) DELETE the underlined portion.

44

A) NO CHANGE

B) one's

C) his or her

D) their

STOP

If you finish before time is called, you may check your work on this section only.
Do not turn to any other section.

Math Test – No Calculator

25 MINUTES, 20 QUESTIONS

Turn to Section 3 of your answer sheet to answer the questions in this section.

DIRECTIONS

For questions 1-15, solve each problem, choose the best answer from the choices provided, and fill in the corresponding circle on your answer sheet. **For questions 16-20**, solve the problem and enter your answer in the grid on the answer sheet. Please refer to the directions before question 16 on how to enter your answers in the grid. You may use any available space in your test booklet for scratch work.

NOTES

1. The use of a calculator **is not permitted**.

2. All variables and expressions used represent real numbers unless otherwise indicated.

3. Figures provided in this test are drawn to scale unless otherwise indicated.

4. All figures lie in a plane unless otherwise indicated.

5. Unless otherwise indicated, the domain of a given function f is the set of all real numbers x for which $f(x)$ is a real number.

REFERENCE

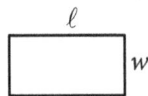 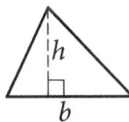 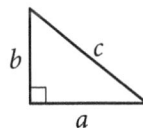 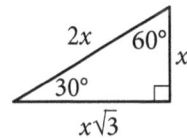 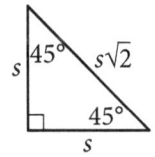

$A = \pi r^2$
$C = 2\pi r$

$A = \ell w$

$A = \frac{1}{2}bh$

$c^2 = a^2 + b^2$

Special Right Triangles

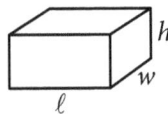 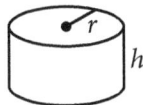  

$V = \ell w h$

$V = \pi r^2 h$

$V = \frac{4}{3}\pi r^3$

$V = \frac{1}{3}\pi r^2 h$

$V = \frac{1}{3}\ell w h$

The number of degrees of arc in a circle is 360.
The number of radians of arc in a circle is 2π.
The sum of the measures in degrees of the angles of a triangle is 180.

   CONTINUE ▶

1

If $\dfrac{x-1}{3} = k$ and $k = 3$, what is the value of x ?

A) 2

B) 4

C) 9

D) 10

2

For $i = \sqrt{-1}$, what is the sum $(7 + 3i) + (-8 + 9i)$?

A) $-1 + 12i$

B) $-1 - 6i$

C) $15 + 12i$

D) $15 - 6i$

3

On Saturday afternoon, Armand sent m text messages each hour for 5 hours, and Tyrone sent p text messages each hour for 4 hours. Which of the following represents the total number of messages sent by Armand and Tyrone on Saturday afternoon?

A) $9mp$

B) $20mp$

C) $5m + 4p$

D) $4m + 5p$

4

Kathy is a repair technician for a phone company. Each week, she receives a batch of phones that need repairs. The number of phones that she has left to fix at the end of each day can be estimated with the equation $P = 108 - 23d$, where P is the number of phones left and d is the number of days she has worked that week. What is the meaning of the value 108 in this equation?

A) Kathy will complete the repairs within 108 days.

B) Kathy starts each week with 108 phones to fix.

C) Kathy repairs phones at a rate of 108 per hour.

D) Kathy repairs phones at a rate of 108 per day.

5

$$(x^2y - 3y^2 + 5xy^2) - (-x^2y + 3xy^2 - 3y^2)$$

Which of the following is equivalent to the expression above?

A) $4x^2y^2$

B) $8xy^2 - 6y^2$

C) $2x^2y + 2xy^2$

D) $2x^2y + 8xy^2 - 6y^2$

6

$$h = 3a + 28.6$$

A pediatrician uses the model above to estimate the height h of a boy, in inches, in terms of the boy's age a, in years, between the ages of 2 and 5. Based on the model, what is the estimated increase, in inches, of a boy's height each year?

A)   3

B)   5.7

C)   9.5

D)   14.3

7

$$m = \frac{\left(\dfrac{r}{1,200}\right)\left(1 + \dfrac{r}{1,200}\right)^N}{\left(1 + \dfrac{r}{1,200}\right)^N - 1} P$$

The formula above gives the monthly payment m needed to pay off a loan of P dollars at r percent annual interest over N months. Which of the following gives P in terms of m, r, and N ?

A) $P = \dfrac{\left(\dfrac{r}{1,200}\right)\left(1 + \dfrac{r}{1,200}\right)^N}{\left(1 + \dfrac{r}{1,200}\right)^N - 1} m$

B) $P = \dfrac{\left(1 + \dfrac{r}{1,200}\right)^N - 1}{\left(\dfrac{r}{1,200}\right)\left(1 + \dfrac{r}{1,200}\right)^N} m$

C) $P = \left(\dfrac{r}{1,200}\right) m$

D) $P = \left(\dfrac{1,200}{r}\right) m$

CONTINUE ➤

8

If $\dfrac{a}{b} = 2$, what is the value of $\dfrac{4b}{a}$?

A) 0

B) 1

C) 2

D) 4

9

$$3x + 4y = -23$$
$$2y - x = -19$$

What is the solution (x, y) to the system of equations above?

A) $(-5, -2)$

B) $(3, -8)$

C) $(4, -6)$

D) $(9, -6)$

10

$$g(x) = ax^2 + 24$$

For the function g defined above, a is a constant and $g(4) = 8$. What is the value of $g(-4)$?

A) 8

B) 0

C) −1

D) −8

11

$$b = 2.35 + 0.25x$$
$$c = 1.75 + 0.40x$$

In the equations above, b and c represent the price per pound, in dollars, of beef and chicken, respectively, x weeks after July 1 during last summer. What was the price per pound of beef when it was equal to the price per pound of chicken?

A) $2.60

B) $2.85

C) $2.95

D) $3.35

12

A line in the xy-plane passes through the origin and has a slope of $\dfrac{1}{7}$. Which of the following points lies on the line?

A) $(0, 7)$

B) $(1, 7)$

C) $(7, 7)$

D) $(14, 2)$

13

If $x > 3$, which of the following is equivalent

to $\dfrac{1}{\dfrac{1}{x+2} + \dfrac{1}{x+3}}$?

A) $\dfrac{2x+5}{x^2+5x+6}$

B) $\dfrac{x^2+5x+6}{2x+5}$

C) $2x+5$

D) x^2+5x+6

14

If $3x - y = 12$, what is the value of $\dfrac{8^x}{2^y}$?

A) 2^{12}

B) 4^4

C) 8^2

D) The value cannot be determined from the information given.

15

If $(ax+2)(bx+7) = 15x^2 + cx + 14$ for all values of x, and $a + b = 8$, what are the two possible values for c ?

A) 3 and 5

B) 6 and 35

C) 10 and 21

D) 31 and 41

DIRECTIONS

For questions 16–20, solve the problem and enter your answer in the grid, as described below, on the answer sheet.

1. Although not required, it is suggested that you write your answer in the boxes at the top of the columns to help you fill in the circles accurately. You will receive credit only if the circles are filled in correctly.
2. Mark no more than one circle in any column.
3. No question has a negative answer.
4. Some problems may have more than one correct answer. In such cases, grid only one answer.
5. **Mixed numbers** such as $3\frac{1}{2}$ must be gridded as 3.5 or 7/2. (If $3|1|/|2$ is entered into the grid, it will be interpreted as $\frac{31}{2}$, not $3\frac{1}{2}$.)
6. **Decimal answers:** If you obtain a decimal answer with more digits than the grid can accommodate, it may be either rounded or truncated, but it must fill the entire grid.

Answer: $\frac{7}{12}$

Write answer in boxes. ← Fraction line

Grid in result.

Answer: 2.5 ← Decimal point

Acceptable ways to grid $\frac{2}{3}$ are:

Answer: 201 – either position is correct

NOTE: You may start your answers in any column, space permitting. Columns you don't need to use should be left blank.

CONTINUE

16

If $t > 0$ and $t^2 - 4 = 0$, what is the value of t ?

17

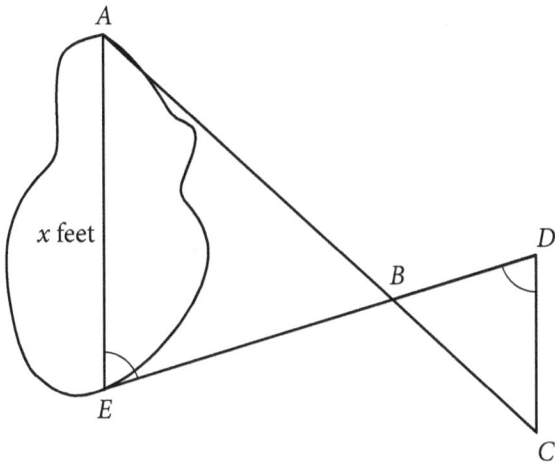

A summer camp counselor wants to find a length, x, in feet, across a lake as represented in the sketch above. The lengths represented by AB, EB, BD, and CD on the sketch were determined to be 1800 feet, 1400 feet, 700 feet, and 800 feet, respectively. Segments AC and DE intersect at B, and $\angle AEB$ and $\angle CDB$ have the same measure. What is the value of x ?

18

$$x + y = -9$$
$$x + 2y = -25$$

According to the system of equations above, what is the value of x ?

19

In a right triangle, one angle measures $x°$, where $\sin x° = \dfrac{4}{5}$. What is $\cos(90° - x°)$?

20

If $a = 5\sqrt{2}$ and $2a = \sqrt{2x}$, what is the value of x ?

STOP

If you finish before time is called, you may check your work on this section only.
Do not turn to any other section.

Math Test – Calculator

55 MINUTES, 38 QUESTIONS

Turn to Section 4 of your answer sheet to answer the questions in this section.

DIRECTIONS

For questions 1-30, solve each problem, choose the best answer from the choices provided, and fill in the corresponding circle on your answer sheet. **For questions 31-38**, solve the problem and enter your answer in the grid on the answer sheet. Please refer to the directions before question 31 on how to enter your answers in the grid. You may use any available space in your test booklet for scratch work.

NOTES

1. The use of a calculator **is permitted**.

2. All variables and expressions used represent real numbers unless otherwise indicated.

3. Figures provided in this test are drawn to scale unless otherwise indicated.

4. All figures lie in a plane unless otherwise indicated.

5. Unless otherwise indicated, the domain of a given function f is the set of all real numbers x for which $f(x)$ is a real number.

REFERENCE

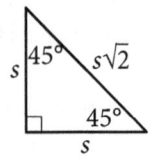

$A = \pi r^2$
$C = 2\pi r$

$A = \ell w$

$A = \frac{1}{2}bh$

$c^2 = a^2 + b^2$

Special Right Triangles

$V = \ell w h$

$V = \pi r^2 h$

$V = \frac{4}{3}\pi r^3$

$V = \frac{1}{3}\pi r^2 h$

$V = \frac{1}{3}\ell w h$

The number of degrees of arc in a circle is 360.
The number of radians of arc in a circle is 2π.
The sum of the measures in degrees of the angles of a triangle is 180.

CONTINUE ➡

1

John runs at different speeds as part of his training program. The graph shows his target heart rate at different times during his workout. On which interval is the target heart rate strictly increasing then strictly decreasing?

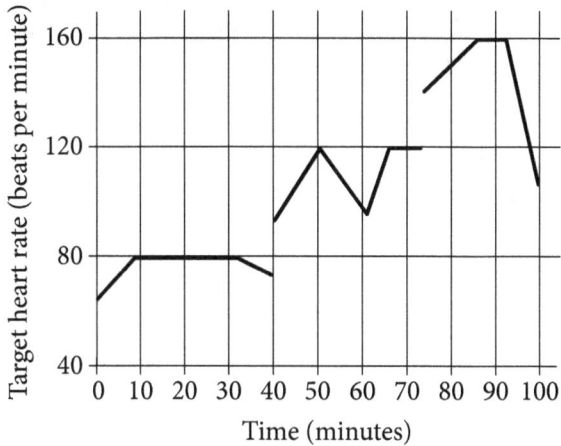

A) Between 0 and 30 minutes

B) Between 40 and 60 minutes

C) Between 50 and 65 minutes

D) Between 70 and 90 minutes

2

If $y = kx$, where k is a constant, and $y = 24$ when $x = 6$, what is the value of y when $x = 5$?

A) 6

B) 15

C) 20

D) 23

3

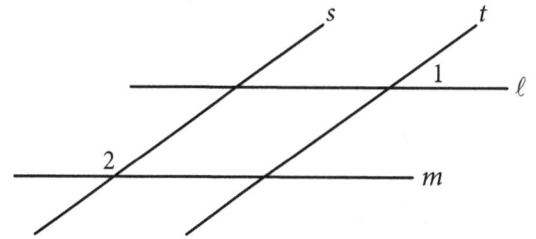

In the figure above, lines ℓ and m are parallel and lines s and t are parallel. If the measure of $\angle 1$ is 35°, what is the measure of $\angle 2$?

A) 35°

B) 55°

C) 70°

D) 145°

4

If $16 + 4x$ is 10 more than 14, what is the value of $8x$?

A) 2

B) 6

C) 16

D) 80

CONTINUE ▶

5

Which of the following graphs best shows a strong negative association between d and t ?

A)

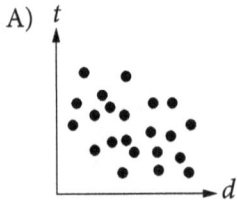

B)

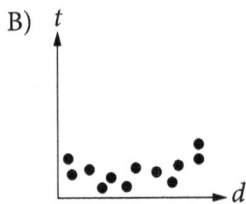

C)

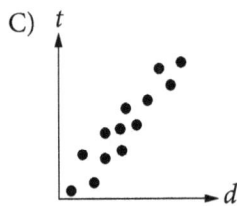

D)

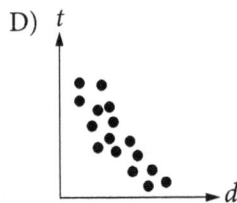

6

| 1 decagram = 10 grams |
| 1,000 milligrams = 1 gram |

A hospital stores one type of medicine in 2-decagram containers. Based on the information given in the box above, how many 1-milligram doses are there in one 2-decagram container?

A)   0.002

B)   200

C)   2,000

D)   20,000

CONTINUE

7

Rooftop Solar Panel
Installations in Five Cities

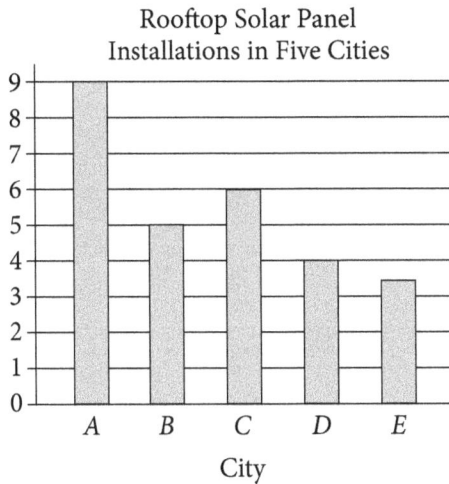

The number of rooftops with solar panel installations in 5 cities is shown in the graph above. If the total number of installations is 27,500, what is an appropriate label for the vertical axis of the graph?

A) Number of installations (in tens)

B) Number of installations (in hundreds)

C) Number of installations (in thousands)

D) Number of installations (in tens of thousands)

8

For what value of n is $|n - 1| + 1$ equal to 0 ?

A)   0

B)   1

C)   2

D)   There is no such value of n.

Questions 9 and 10 refer to the following information.

$$a = 1,052 + 1.08t$$

The speed of a sound wave in air depends on the air temperature. The formula above shows the relationship between a, the speed of a sound wave, in feet per second, and t, the air temperature, in degrees Fahrenheit (°F).

9

Which of the following expresses the air temperature in terms of the speed of a sound wave?

A) $t = \dfrac{a - 1,052}{1.08}$

B) $t = \dfrac{a + 1,052}{1.08}$

C) $t = \dfrac{1,052 - a}{1.08}$

D) $t = \dfrac{1.08}{a + 1,052}$

10

At which of the following air temperatures will the speed of a sound wave be closest to 1,000 feet per second?

A) -46°F

B) -48°F

C) -49°F

D) -50°F

11

Which of the following numbers is NOT a solution of the inequality $3x - 5 \geq 4x - 3$?

A) -1

B) -2

C) -3

D) -5

12

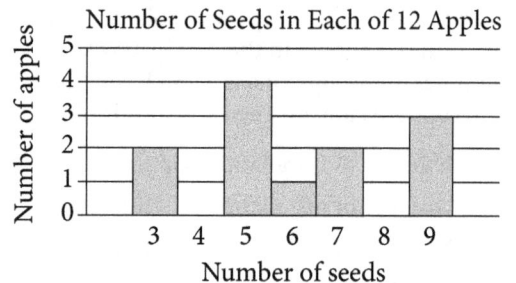

Number of Seeds in Each of 12 Apples

Based on the histogram above, of the following, which is closest to the average (arithmetic mean) number of seeds per apple?

A) 4

B) 5

C) 6

D) 7

CONTINUE

13

		Course			
		Algebra I	Geometry	Algebra II	Total
Gender	Female	35	53	62	150
	Male	44	59	57	160
	Total	79	112	119	310

A group of tenth-grade students responded to a survey that asked which math course they were currently enrolled in. The survey data were broken down as shown in the table above. Which of the following categories accounts for approximately 19 percent of all the survey respondents?

A) Females taking Geometry

B) Females taking Algebra II

C) Males taking Geometry

D) Males taking Algebra I

14

Lengths of Fish (in inches)						
8	9	9	9	10	10	11
11	12	12	12	12	13	13
13	14	14	15	15	16	24

The table above lists the lengths, to the nearest inch, of a random sample of 21 brown bullhead fish. The outlier measurement of 24 inches is an error. Of the mean, median, and range of the values listed, which will change the most if the 24-inch measurement is removed from the data?

A) Mean

B) Median

C) Range

D) They will all change by the same amount.

Questions 15 and 16 refer to the following information.

Total Cost of Renting
a Boat by the Hour

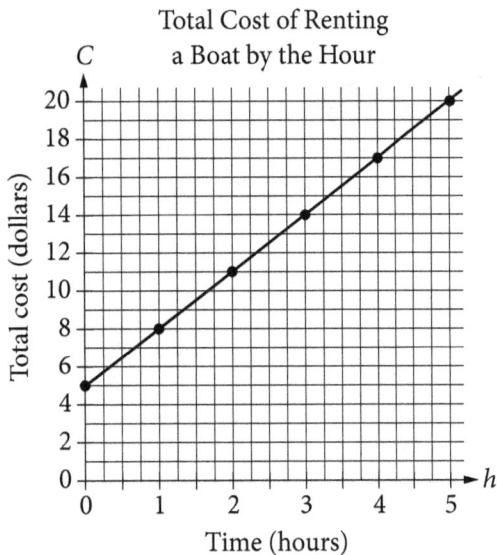

The graph above displays the total cost C, in dollars, of renting a boat for h hours.

15

What does the C-intercept represent in the graph?

A) The initial cost of renting the boat

B) The total number of boats rented

C) The total number of hours the boat is rented

D) The increase in cost to rent the boat for each additional hour

16

Which of the following represents the relationship between h and C ?

A) $C = 5h$

B) $C = \dfrac{3}{4}h + 5$

C) $C = 3h + 5$

D) $h = 3C$

17

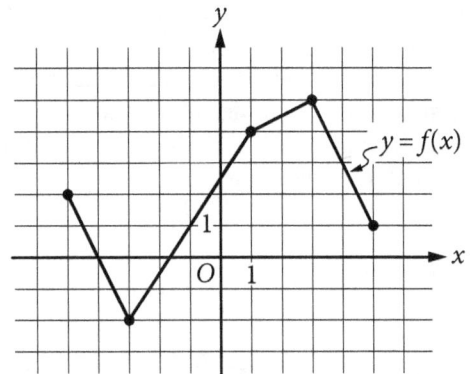

The complete graph of the function f is shown in the xy-plane above. For what value of x is the value of $f(x)$ at its minimum?

A) -5

B) -3

C) -2

D) 3

CONTINUE ➤

18

$$y < -x + a$$
$$y > x + b$$

In the *xy*-plane, if $(0, 0)$ is a solution to the system of inequalities above, which of the following relationships between a and b must be true?

A) $a > b$

B) $b > a$

C) $|a| > |b|$

D) $a = -b$

19

A food truck sells salads for $6.50 each and drinks for $2.00 each. The food truck's revenue from selling a total of 209 salads and drinks in one day was $836.50. How many salads were sold that day?

A) 77

B) 93

C) 99

D) 105

20

Alma bought a laptop computer at a store that gave a 20 percent discount off its original price. The total amount she paid to the cashier was p dollars, including an 8 percent sales tax on the discounted price. Which of the following represents the original price of the computer in terms of p ?

A) $0.88p$

B) $\dfrac{p}{0.88}$

C) $(0.8)(1.08)p$

D) $\dfrac{p}{(0.8)(1.08)}$

21

Dreams Recalled during One Week

	None	1 to 4	5 or more	Total
Group X	15	28	57	100
Group Y	21	11	68	100
Total	36	39	125	200

The data in the table above were produced by a sleep researcher studying the number of dreams people recall when asked to record their dreams for one week. Group X consisted of 100 people who observed early bedtimes, and Group Y consisted of 100 people who observed later bedtimes. If a person is chosen at random from those who recalled at least 1 dream, what is the probability that the person belonged to Group Y ?

A) $\dfrac{68}{100}$

B) $\dfrac{79}{100}$

C) $\dfrac{79}{164}$

D) $\dfrac{164}{200}$

Questions 22 and 23 refer to the following information.

Annual Budgets for Different Programs in Kansas, 2007 to 2010

Program	Year			
	2007	2008	2009	2010
Agriculture/natural resources	373,904	358,708	485,807	488,106
Education	2,164,607	2,413,984	2,274,514	3,008,036
General government	14,347,325	12,554,845	10,392,107	14,716,155
Highways and transportation	1,468,482	1,665,636	1,539,480	1,773,893
Human resources	4,051,050	4,099,067	4,618,444	5,921,379
Public safety	263,463	398,326	355,935	464,233

The table above lists the annual budget, in thousands of dollars, for each of six different state programs in Kansas from 2007 to 2010.

22

Which of the following best approximates the average rate of change in the annual budget for agriculture/natural resources in Kansas from 2008 to 2010 ?

A) $50,000,000 per year

B) $65,000,000 per year

C) $75,000,000 per year

D) $130,000,000 per year

23

Of the following, which program's ratio of its 2007 budget to its 2010 budget is closest to the human resources program's ratio of its 2007 budget to its 2010 budget?

A) Agriculture/natural resources

B) Education

C) Highways and transportation

D) Public safety

CONTINUE

24

Which of the following is an equation of a circle in

the xy-plane with center $(0, 4)$ and a radius with

endpoint $\left(\dfrac{4}{3}, 5\right)$?

A) $x^2 + (y - 4)^2 = \dfrac{25}{9}$

B) $x^2 + (y + 4)^2 = \dfrac{25}{9}$

C) $x^2 + (y - 4)^2 = \dfrac{5}{3}$

D) $x^2 + (y + 4)^2 = \dfrac{3}{5}$

25

$$h = -4.9t^2 + 25t$$

The equation above expresses the approximate height h, in meters, of a ball t seconds after it is launched vertically upward from the ground with an initial velocity of 25 meters per second. After approximately how many seconds will the ball hit the ground?

A) 3.5

B) 4.0

C) 4.5

D) 5.0

26

Katarina is a botanist studying the production of pears by two types of pear trees. She noticed that Type A trees produced 20 percent more pears than Type B trees did. Based on Katarina's observation, if the Type A trees produced 144 pears, how many pears did the Type B trees produce?

A) 115

B) 120

C) 124

D) 173

27

A square field measures 10 meters by 10 meters. Ten students each mark off a randomly selected region of the field; each region is square and has side lengths of 1 meter, and no two regions overlap. The students count the earthworms contained in the soil to a depth of 5 centimeters beneath the ground's surface in each region. The results are shown in the table below.

Region	Number of earthworms	Region	Number of earthworms
A	107	F	141
B	147	G	150
C	146	H	154
D	135	I	176
E	149	J	166

Which of the following is a reasonable approximation of the number of earthworms to a depth of 5 centimeters beneath the ground's surface in the entire field?

A) 150

B) 1,500

C) 15,000

D) 150,000

CONTINUE

28

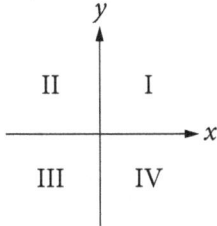

If the system of inequalities $y \geq 2x + 1$ and

$y > \dfrac{1}{2}x - 1$ is graphed in the xy-plane above, which

quadrant contains no solutions to the system?

A) Quadrant II

B) Quadrant III

C) Quadrant IV

D) There are solutions in all four quadrants.

29

For a polynomial $p(x)$, the value of $p(3)$ is -2. Which of the following must be true about $p(x)$?

A) $x - 5$ is a factor of $p(x)$.

B) $x - 2$ is a factor of $p(x)$.

C) $x + 2$ is a factor of $p(x)$.

D) The remainder when $p(x)$ is divided by $x - 3$ is -2.

30

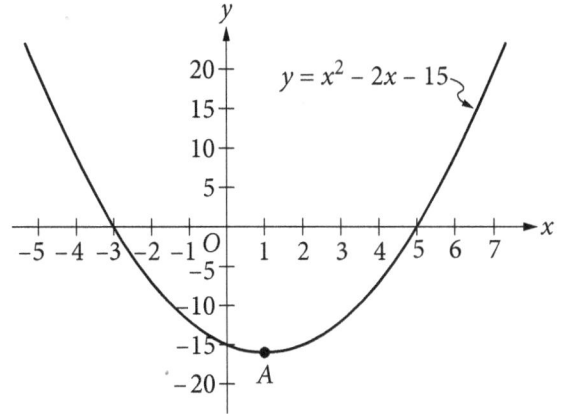

Which of the following is an equivalent form of the equation of the graph shown in the xy-plane above, from which the coordinates of vertex A can be identified as constants in the equation?

A) $y = (x + 3)(x - 5)$

B) $y = (x - 3)(x + 5)$

C) $y = x(x - 2) - 15$

D) $y = (x - 1)^2 - 16$

Unauthorized copying or reuse of any part of this page is illegal.

53

CONTINUE

DIRECTIONS

For questions 31–38, solve the problem and enter your answer in the grid, as described below, on the answer sheet.

1. Although not required, it is suggested that you write your answer in the boxes at the top of the columns to help you fill in the circles accurately. You will receive credit only if the circles are filled in correctly.
2. Mark no more than one circle in any column.
3. No question has a negative answer.
4. Some problems may have more than one correct answer. In such cases, grid only one answer.
5. **Mixed numbers** such as $3\frac{1}{2}$ must be gridded as 3.5 or 7/2. (If $3\,|\,1\,|\,/\,|\,2$ is entered into the grid, it will be interpreted as $\frac{31}{2}$, not $3\frac{1}{2}$.)
6. **Decimal answers:** If you obtain a decimal answer with more digits than the grid can accommodate, it may be either rounded or truncated, but it must fill the entire grid.

Answer: $\frac{7}{12}$

Write answer in boxes. → ← Fraction line

Grid in result.

Answer: 2.5

← Decimal point

Acceptable ways to grid $\frac{2}{3}$ are:

Answer: 201 – either position is correct

NOTE: You may start your answers in any column, space permitting. Columns you don't need to use should be left blank.

CONTINUE →

31

Wyatt can husk at least 12 dozen ears of corn per hour and at most 18 dozen ears of corn per hour. Based on this information, what is a possible amount of time, in hours, that it could take Wyatt to husk 72 dozen ears of corn?

32

The posted weight limit for a covered wooden bridge in Pennsylvania is 6000 pounds. A delivery truck that is carrying x identical boxes each weighing 14 pounds will pass over the bridge. If the combined weight of the empty delivery truck and its driver is 4500 pounds, what is the maximum possible value for x that will keep the combined weight of the truck, driver, and boxes below the bridge's posted weight limit?

33

Number of Portable Media Players
Sold Worldwide Each Year from 2006 to 2011

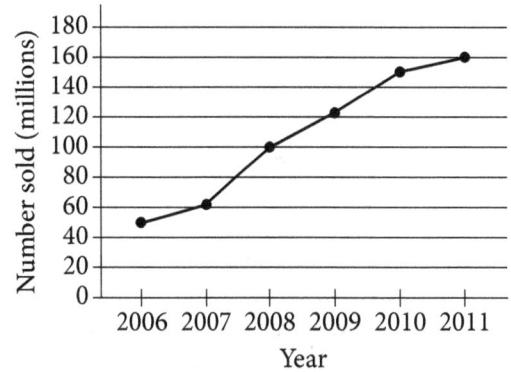

According to the line graph above, the number of portable media players sold in 2008 is what fraction of the number sold in 2011 ?

34

A local television station sells time slots for programs in 30-minute intervals. If the station operates 24 hours per day, every day of the week, what is the total number of 30-minute time slots the station can sell for Tuesday and Wednesday?

35

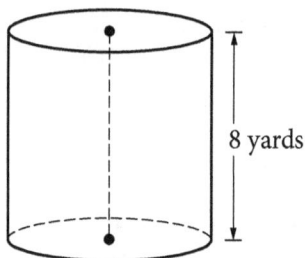

8 yards

A dairy farmer uses a storage silo that is in the shape of the right circular cylinder above. If the volume of the silo is 72π cubic yards, what is the <u>diameter</u> of the base of the cylinder, in yards?

36

$$h(x) = \frac{1}{(x - 5)^2 + 4(x - 5) + 4}$$

For what value of x is the function h above undefined?

Questions 37 and 38 refer to the following information.

Jessica opened a bank account that earns 2 percent interest compounded annually. Her initial deposit was $100, and she uses the expression $\$100(x)^t$ to find the value of the account after t years.

37

What is the value of x in the expression?

38

Jessica's friend Tyshaun found an account that earns 2.5 percent interest compounded annually. Tyshaun made an initial deposit of $100 into this account at the same time Jessica made a deposit of $100 into her account. After 10 years, how much more money will Tyshaun's initial deposit have earned than Jessica's initial deposit? (Round your answer to the nearest cent and ignore the dollar sign when gridding your response.)

STOP

If you finish before time is called, you may check your work on this section only.
Do not turn to any other section.

Unauthorized copying or reuse of any part of this page is illegal.

56

TEST TAKING TIP #1

Practice, Practice, Practice: Everyone knows that practice makes perfect. And it certainly is no different when preparing for the SAT exam. The more time you put into practice, the higher your final score will be. So just do it!

SAT® Practice Essay #1

ESSAY BOOK

DIRECTIONS

The essay gives you an opportunity to show how effectively you can read and comprehend a passage and write an essay analyzing the passage. In your essay, you should demonstrate that you have read the passage carefully, present a clear and logical analysis, and use language precisely.

Your essay must be written on the lines provided in your answer booklet; except for the Planning Page of the answer booklet, you will receive no other paper on which to write. You will have enough space if you write on every line, avoid wide margins, and keep your handwriting to a reasonable size. Remember that people who are not familiar with your handwriting will read what you write. Try to write or print so that what you are writing is legible to those readers.

You have 50 minutes to read the passage and write an essay in response to the prompt provided inside this booklet.

REMINDERS:

— Do not write your essay in this booklet. Only what you write on the lined pages of your answer booklet will be evaluated.

— An off-topic essay will not be evaluated.

Practice:
Follow this link for more information on scoring your test:
www.sat.org/scoring

This cover is representative of what you'll see on test day.

As you read the passage below, consider how Paul Bogard uses

- evidence, such as facts or examples, to support claims.
- reasoning to develop ideas and to connect claims and evidence.
- stylistic or persuasive elements, such as word choice or appeals to emotion, to add power to the ideas expressed.

Adapted from Paul Bogard, "Let There Be Dark." ©2012 by Los Angeles Times. Originally published December 21, 2012.

1 At my family's cabin on a Minnesota lake, I knew woods so dark that my hands disappeared before my eyes. I knew night skies in which meteors left smoky trails across sugary spreads of stars. But now, when 8 of 10 children born in the United States will never know a sky dark enough for the Milky Way, I worry we are rapidly losing night's natural darkness before realizing its worth. This winter solstice, as we cheer the days' gradual movement back toward light, let us also remember the irreplaceable value of darkness.

2 All life evolved to the steady rhythm of bright days and dark nights. Today, though, when we feel the closeness of nightfall, we reach quickly for a light switch. And too little darkness, meaning too much artificial light at night, spells trouble for all.

3 Already the World Health Organization classifies working the night shift as a probable human carcinogen, and the American Medical Association has voiced its unanimous support for "light pollution reduction efforts and glare reduction efforts at both the national and state levels." Our bodies need darkness to produce the hormone melatonin, which keeps certain cancers from developing, and our bodies need darkness for sleep. Sleep disorders have been linked to diabetes, obesity, cardiovascular disease and depression, and recent research suggests one main cause of "short sleep" is "long light." Whether we work at night or simply take our tablets, notebooks and smartphones to bed, there isn't a place for this much artificial light in our lives.

4 The rest of the world depends on darkness as well, including nocturnal and crepuscular species of birds, insects, mammals, fish and reptiles. Some examples are well known—the 400 species of birds that migrate at night in North America, the sea turtles that come ashore to lay their eggs—and some are not, such as the bats that save American farmers billions in pest control and the moths that pollinate 80% of the world's flora. Ecological light pollution is like the bulldozer of the night, wrecking habitat and disrupting ecosystems several billion years in the making. Simply put, without darkness, Earth's ecology would collapse. . . .

5   In today's crowded, louder, more fast-paced world, night's darkness can provide solitude, quiet and stillness, qualities increasingly in short supply. Every religious tradition has considered darkness invaluable for a soulful life, and the chance to witness the universe has inspired artists, philosophers and everyday stargazers since time began. In a world awash with electric light . . . how would Van Gogh have given the world his "Starry Night"? Who knows what this vision of the night sky might inspire in each of us, in our children or grandchildren?

6   Yet all over the world, our nights are growing brighter. In the United States and Western Europe, the amount of light in the sky increases an average of about 6% every year. Computer images of the United States at night, based on NASA photographs, show that what was a very dark country as recently as the 1950s is now nearly covered with a blanket of light. Much of this light is wasted energy, which means wasted dollars. Those of us over 35 are perhaps among the last generation to have known truly dark nights. Even the northern lake where I was lucky to spend my summers has seen its darkness diminish.

7   It doesn't have to be this way. Light pollution is readily within our ability to solve, using new lighting technologies and shielding existing lights. Already, many cities and towns across North America and Europe are changing to LED streetlights, which offer dramatic possibilities for controlling wasted light. Other communities are finding success with simply turning off portions of their public lighting after midnight. Even Paris, the famed "city of light," which already turns off its monument lighting after 1 a.m., will this summer start to require its shops, offices and public buildings to turn off lights after 2 a.m. Though primarily designed to save energy, such reductions in light will also go far in addressing light pollution. But we will never truly address the problem of light pollution until we become aware of the irreplaceable value and beauty of the darkness we are losing.

Write an essay in which you explain how Paul Bogard builds an argument to persuade his audience that natural darkness should be preserved. In your essay, analyze how Bogard uses one or more of the features listed in the box above (or features of your own choice) to strengthen the logic and persuasiveness of his argument. Be sure that your analysis focuses on the most relevant features of the passage.

Your essay should not explain whether you agree with Bogard's claims, but rather explain how Bogard builds an argument to persuade his audience.

Scoring Your SAT® Practice Test #1

Congratulations on completing an SAT® practice test. To score your test, use these instructions and the conversion tables and answer key at the end of this document.

Scores Overview

The redesigned SAT will provide more information about your learning by reporting more scores than ever before. Each of the redesigned assessments (SAT, PSAT/NMSQT®, PSAT™ 10, and PSAT™ 8/9) will report test scores and cross-test scores on a common scale. Additionally, subscores will be reported to provide additional diagnostic information to students, educators, and parents.

The practice test you completed was written by the College Board's Assessment Design & Development team using the same processes and review standards used when writing the actual SAT. Everything from the layout of the page to the construction of the questions accurately reflects what you'll see on test day.

How to Calculate Your Practice Test Scores

GET SET UP

❶ You'll need the answer sheet that you bubbled in while taking the practice test. You'll also need the conversion tables and answer key at the end of this document.

❷ Using the answer key, count up your total correct answers for each section. You may want to write the number of correct answers for each section at the bottom of that section in the answer key.

❸ Using your marked-up answer key and the conversion tables, follow the directions to get all of your scores.

GET SECTION AND TOTAL SCORES

Your total score on the SAT practice test is the sum of your Evidence-Based Reading and Writing Section score and your Math Section score. To get your total score, you will convert what we call the "raw score" for each section — the number of questions you got right in that section — into the "scaled score" for that section, then calculate the total score.

GET YOUR EVIDENCE-BASED READING AND WRITING SECTION SCORE

Calculate your SAT Evidence-Based Reading and Writing Section score (it's on a scale of 200–800) by first determining your Reading Test score and your Writing and Language Test score. Here's how:

1. Count the number of correct answers you got on Section 1 (the Reading Test). There is no penalty for wrong answers. The number of correct answers is your raw score.

2. Go to Raw Score Conversion Table 1: Section and Test Scores on page 7. Look in the "Raw Score" column for your raw score, and match it to the number in the "Reading Test Score" column.

3. Do the same with Section 2 to determine your Writing and Language Test score.

4. Add your Reading Test score to your Writing and Language Test score.

5. Multiply that number by 10. This is your Evidence-Based Reading and Writing Section score.

EXAMPLE: *Keisha answered 29 of the 52 questions correctly on the SAT Reading Test and 20 of the 44 questions correctly on the SAT Writing and Language Test. Using the table on page 7, she calculates that she received an SAT Reading Test score of 27 and an SAT Writing and Language Test score of 23. She adds 27 to 23 (gets 50) and then multiplies by 10 to determine her SAT Evidence-Based Reading and Writing Section score of 500.*

GET YOUR MATH SECTION SCORE

Calculate your SAT Math Section score (it's on a scale of 200–800).

1. Count the number of correct answers you got on Section 3 (Math Test — No Calculator) and Section 4 (Math Test — Calculator). There is no penalty for wrong answers.

2. Add the number of correct answers you got on Section 3 (Math Test — No Calculator) and Section 4 (Math Test — Calculator).

3. Use Raw Score Conversion Table 1: Section and Test Scores to turn your raw score into your Math Section score.

GET YOUR TOTAL SCORE

Add your Evidence-Based Reading and Writing Section score to your Math Section score. The result is your total score on the SAT Practice Test, on a scale of 400–1600.

GET SUBSCORES

Subscores provide more detailed information about your strengths in specific areas within literacy and math. They are reported on a scale of 1–15.

HEART OF ALGEBRA

The Heart of Algebra subscore is based on questions from the Math Test that focus on linear equations and inequalities.

① Add up your total correct answers from the following set of questions:

- ▶ Math Test – No Calculator: Questions 1; 3-4; 6; 9; 11-12; 18
- ▶ Math Test – Calculator: Questions 4; 8; 10-11; 15-16; 18-19; 28; 31-32

Your total correct answers from all of these questions is your raw score.

② Use Raw Score Conversion Table 2: Subscores on page 8 to determine your Heart of Algebra subscore.

PROBLEM SOLVING AND DATA ANALYSIS

The Problem Solving and Data Analysis subscore is based on questions from the Math Test that focus on quantitative reasoning, the interpretation and synthesis of data, and solving problems in rich and varied contexts.

① Add up your total correct answers from the following set of questions:

- ▶ Math Test – No Calculator: No Questions
- ▶ Math Test – Calculator: Questions 1-2; 5-7; 12-14; 17; 20-23; 26-27; 33-34

Your total correct answers from all of these questions is your raw score.

② Use Raw Score Conversion Table 2: Subscores to determine your Problem Solving and Data Analysis subscore.

PASSPORT TO ADVANCED MATH

The Passport to Advanced Math subscore is based on questions from the Math Test that focus on topics central to the ability of students to progress to more advanced mathematics, such as understanding the structure of expressions, reasoning with more complex equations, and interpreting and building functions.

① Add up your total correct answers from the following set of questions:

- ▶ Math Test – No Calculator: Questions 5; 7-8; 10; 13-16; 20
- ▶ Math Test – Calculator: Questions 9; 25; 29-30; 36-38

Your total correct answers from all of these questions is your raw score.

② Use Raw Score Conversion Table 2: Subscores to determine your Passport to Advanced Math subscore.

EXPRESSION OF IDEAS

The Expression of Ideas subscore is based on questions from the Writing and Language Test that focus on topic development, organization, and rhetorically effective use of language.

❶ Add up your total correct answers from the following set of questions:

▶ Writing and Language Test: Questions 1-2; 5-6; 9-10; 12-14; 20-23; 27-29; 31; 33-35; 37-39; 42

Your total correct answers from all of these questions is your raw score.

❷ Use Raw Score Conversion Table 2: Subscores to determine your Expression of Ideas subscore.

STANDARD ENGLISH CONVENTIONS

The Standard English Conventions subscore is based on questions from the Writing and Language Test that focus on sentence structure, usage, and punctuation.

❶ Add up your total correct answers from the following set of questions:

▶ Writing and Language Test: Questions 3-4; 7-8; 11; 15-19; 24-26; 30; 32; 36; 40-41; 43-44

Your total correct answers from all of these questions is your raw score.

❷ Use Raw Score Conversion Table 2: Subscores to determine your Standard English Conventions subscore.

WORDS IN CONTEXT

The Words in Context subscore is based on questions from both the Reading Test and the Writing and Language Test that address word/phrase meaning in context and rhetorical word choice.

❶ Add up your total correct answers from the following set of questions:

▶ Reading Test: Questions 3; 8; 12; 18; 22; 27; 34; 40; 45; 48

▶ Writing and Language Test: Questions 1; 10; 13; 21; 23; 33; 35; 39

Your total correct answers from all of these questions is your raw score.

❷ Use Raw Score Conversion Table 2: Subscores to determine your Words in Context subscore.

COMMAND OF EVIDENCE

The Command of Evidence subscore is based on questions from both the Reading Test and the Writing and Language Test that ask you to interpret and use evidence found in a wide range of passages and informational graphics, such as graphs, tables, and charts.

❶ Add up your total correct answers from the following set of questions:

▶ Reading Test: Questions 5; 10; 14; 17; 19; 23; 28-29; 37; 39

▶ Writing and Language Test: Questions 2; 6; 12; 20; 28-29; 37; 42

Your total correct answers from all of these questions is your raw score.

❷ Use Raw Score Conversion Table 2: Subscores to determine your Command of Evidence subscore.

GET CROSS-TEST SCORES

The new SAT also reports two cross-test scores: Analysis in History/Social Studies and Analysis in Science. These scores are based on questions in the Reading, Writing and Language, and Math Tests that ask students to think analytically about texts and questions in these subject areas. Cross-test scores are reported on a scale of 10–40.

ANALYSIS IN HISTORY/SOCIAL STUDIES

1. Add up your total correct answers from the following set of questions:

   ▶ Reading Test: Questions 11-21; 32-41

   ▶ Writing and Language Test: Questions 1-2; 5-6; 9-10

   ▶ Math Test – No Calculator: Questions 7, 11

   ▶ Math Test – Calculator: Questions 7; 22-23; 33; 37-38

   Your total correct answers from all of these questions is your raw score.

2. Use Raw Score Conversion Table 3: Cross-Test Scores on page 9 to determine your Analysis in History/Social Studies cross-test score.

ANALYSIS IN SCIENCE

1. Add up your total correct answers from the following set of questions:

   ▶ Reading Test: Questions 22-31; 42-52

   ▶ Writing and Language Test: Questions 12-14; 20-22

   ▶ Math Test – No Calculator: Question 6

   ▶ Math Test – Calculator: Questions 6; 9; 14; 21; 25-27

   Your total correct answers from all of these questions is your raw score.

2. Use Raw Score Conversion Table 3: Cross-Test Scores to determine your Analysis in Science cross-test score.

SAT Practice Test #1: Worksheets

ANSWER KEY

Reading Test Answers

1 B	12 B	23 D	34 C	45 D
2 B	13 D	24 D	35 B	46 C
3 C	14 A	25 C	36 D	47 B
4 A	15 A	26 B	37 C	48 A
5 C	16 C	27 D	38 C	49 D
6 D	17 C	28 C	39 B	50 B
7 D	18 D	29 A	40 C	51 D
8 B	19 A	30 A	41 B	52 A
9 C	20 B	31 D	42 B	
10 B	21 A	32 B	43 A	
11 A	22 B	33 A	44 A	

READING TEST
RAW SCORE
(NUMBER OF
CORRECT ANSWERS)

Writing and Language Test Answers

1 D	12 B	23 D	34 A
2 B	13 A	24 D	35 A
3 A	14 B	25 B	36 B
4 C	15 C	26 A	37 D
5 C	16 C	27 B	38 C
6 D	17 C	28 C	39 A
7 B	18 A	29 B	40 B
8 C	19 D	30 D	41 B
9 A	20 D	31 C	42 C
10 A	21 B	32 A	43 D
11 B	22 D	33 A	44 D

WRITING AND
LANGUAGE TEST
RAW SCORE
(NUMBER OF
CORRECT ANSWERS)

Math Test
No Calculator Answers

1 D	11 D
2 A	12 D
3 C	13 B
4 B	14 A
5 C	15 D
6 A	16 2
7 B	17 1600
8 C	18 7
9 B	19 4/5 or 0.8
10 A	20 100

MATH TEST
NO CALCULATOR
RAW SCORE
(NUMBER OF
CORRECT ANSWERS)

Math Test
Calculator Answers

1 B	11 A	21 C	31 Any number between 4-6, inclusive
2 C	12 C	22 B	32 107
3 D	13 C	23 B	33 5/8 or 0.625
4 C	14 C	24 A	34 96
5 D	15 A	25 D	35 6
6 D	16 C	26 B	36 3
7 C	17 B	27 C	37 1.02
8 D	18 A	28 C	38 6.11
9 A	19 B	29 D	
10 B	20 D	30 D	

MATH TEST
CALCULATOR
RAW SCORE
(NUMBER OF
CORRECT ANSWERS)

SAT Practice Test #1: Worksheets

RAW SCORE CONVERSION TABLE 1 — SECTION AND TEST SCORES

Raw Score (# of correct answers)	Math Section Score	Reading Test Score	Writing and Language Test Score	Raw Score (# of correct answers)	Math Section Score	Reading Test Score	Writing and Language Test Score
0	200	10	10	30	530	28	29
1	200	10	10	31	540	28	30
2	210	10	10	32	550	29	30
3	230	11	10	33	560	29	31
4	240	12	11	34	560	30	32
5	260	13	12	35	570	30	32
6	280	14	13	36	580	31	33
7	290	15	13	37	590	31	34
8	310	15	14	38	600	32	34
9	320	16	15	39	600	32	35
10	330	17	16	40	610	33	36
11	340	17	16	41	620	33	37
12	360	18	17	42	630	34	38
13	370	19	18	43	640	35	39
14	380	19	19	44	650	35	40
15	390	20	19	45	660	36	
16	410	20	20	46	670	37	
17	420	21	21	47	670	37	
18	430	21	21	48	680	38	
19	440	22	22	49	690	38	
20	450	22	23	50	700	39	
21	460	23	23	51	710	40	
22	470	23	24	52	730	40	
23	480	24	25	53	740		
24	480	24	25	54	750		
25	490	25	26	55	760		
26	500	25	26	56	780		
27	510	26	27	57	790		
28	520	26	28	58	800		
29	520	27	28				

CONVERSION EQUATION 1 — SECTION AND TEST SCORES

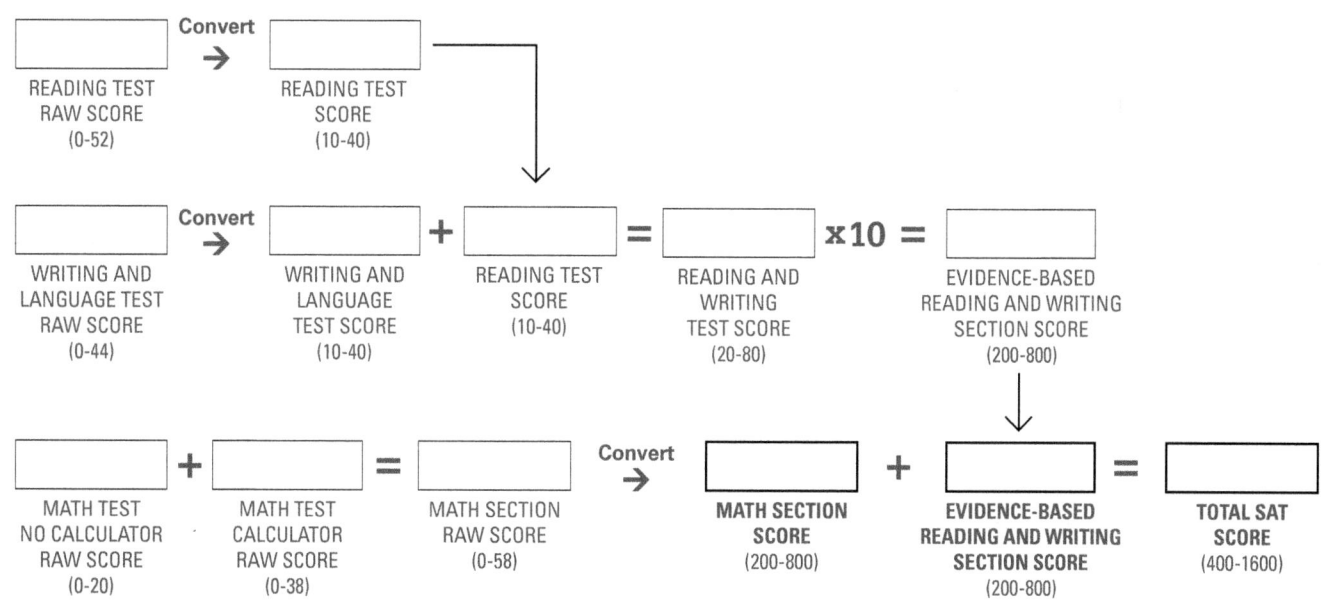

READING TEST RAW SCORE (0-52) **Convert →** READING TEST SCORE (10-40)

WRITING AND LANGUAGE TEST RAW SCORE (0-44) **Convert →** WRITING AND LANGUAGE TEST SCORE (10-40) **+** READING TEST SCORE (10-40) **=** READING AND WRITING TEST SCORE (20-80) **×10 =** EVIDENCE-BASED READING AND WRITING SECTION SCORE (200-800)

MATH TEST NO CALCULATOR RAW SCORE (0-20) **+** MATH TEST CALCULATOR RAW SCORE (0-38) **=** MATH SECTION RAW SCORE (0-58) **Convert →** MATH SECTION SCORE (200-800) **+** EVIDENCE-BASED READING AND WRITING SECTION SCORE (200-800) **=** TOTAL SAT SCORE (400-1600)

SAT Practice Test #1: Worksheets

Raw Score (# of correct answers)	Expression of Ideas	Standard English Conventions	Heart of Algebra	Problem Solving and Data Analysis	Passport to Advanced Math	Words in Context	Command of Evidence
0	1	1	1	1	1	1	1
1	1	1	1	1	3	1	1
2	1	1	2	2	5	2	2
3	2	2	3	3	6	3	3
4	3	2	4	4	7	4	4
5	4	3	5	5	8	5	5
6	5	4	6	6	9	6	6
7	6	5	6	7	10	6	7
8	6	6	7	8	11	7	8
9	7	6	8	8	11	8	8
10	7	7	8	9	12	8	9
11	8	7	9	10	12	9	10
12	8	8	9	10	13	9	10
13	9	8	9	11	13	10	11
14	9	9	10	12	14	11	12
15	10	10	10	13	14	12	13
16	10	10	11	14	15	13	14
17	11	11	12	15		14	15
18	11	12	13			15	15
19	12	13	15				
20	12	15					
21	13						
22	14						
23	14						
24	15						

CONVERSION EQUATION 2 SUBSCORES

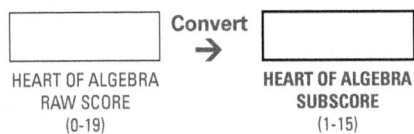

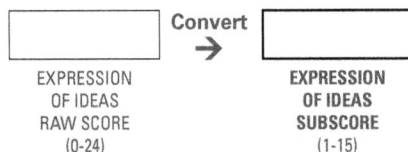

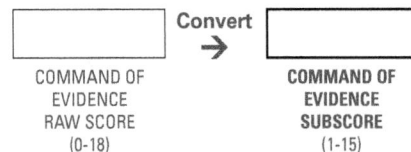

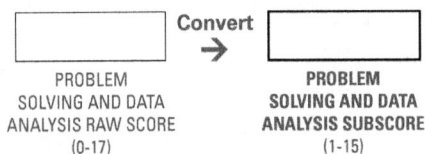

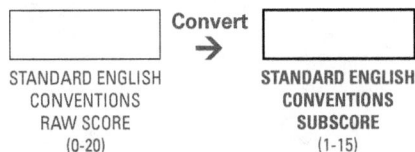

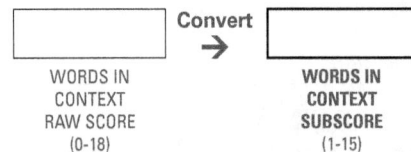

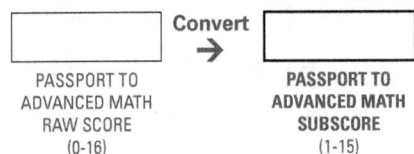

	Convert →	
HEART OF ALGEBRA RAW SCORE (0-19)		**HEART OF ALGEBRA SUBSCORE** (1-15)

	Convert →	
EXPRESSION OF IDEAS RAW SCORE (0-24)		**EXPRESSION OF IDEAS SUBSCORE** (1-15)

	Convert →	
COMMAND OF EVIDENCE RAW SCORE (0-18)		**COMMAND OF EVIDENCE SUBSCORE** (1-15)

	Convert →	
PROBLEM SOLVING AND DATA ANALYSIS RAW SCORE (0-17)		**PROBLEM SOLVING AND DATA ANALYSIS SUBSCORE** (1-15)

	Convert →	
STANDARD ENGLISH CONVENTIONS RAW SCORE (0-20)		**STANDARD ENGLISH CONVENTIONS SUBSCORE** (1-15)

	Convert →	
WORDS IN CONTEXT RAW SCORE (0-18)		**WORDS IN CONTEXT SUBSCORE** (1-15)

	Convert →	
PASSPORT TO ADVANCED MATH RAW SCORE (0-16)		**PASSPORT TO ADVANCED MATH SUBSCORE** (1-15)

SAT Practice Test #1: Worksheets

RAW SCORE CONVERSION TABLE 3 | CROSS-TEST SCORES

Raw Score (# of correct answers)	Analysis in History/ Social Studies Cross-Test Score	Analysis in Science Cross-Test Score	Raw Score (# of correct answers)	Analysis in History/ Social Studies Cross-Test Score	Analysis in Science Cross-Test Score
0	10	10	18	28	26
1	10	11	19	29	27
2	11	12	20	30	27
3	12	13	21	30	28
4	14	14	22	31	29
5	15	15	23	32	30
6	16	16	24	32	30
7	17	17	25	33	31
8	18	18	26	34	32
9	20	19	27	35	33
10	21	20	28	35	33
11	22	20	29	36	34
12	23	21	30	37	35
13	24	22	31	38	36
14	25	23	32	38	37
15	26	24	33	39	38
16	27	24	34	40	39
17	28	25	35	40	40

CONVERSION EQUATION 3 | CROSS-TEST SCORES

Test	Analysis in History/Social Studies		Analysis in Science	
	Questions	Raw Score	Questions	Raw Score
Reading Test	11-21; 32-41		22-31; 42-52	
Writing and Language Test	1-2; 5-6; 9-10		12-14; 20-22	
Math Test No Calculator	7, 11		6	
Math Test Calculator	7; 22-23; 33; 37-38		6; 9; 14; 21; 25-27	
Total				

	Convert →	
ANALYSIS IN HISTORY/ SOCIAL STUDIES RAW SCORE (0-35)		**ANALYSIS IN HISTORY/ SOCIAL STUDIES CROSS-TEST SCORE (10-40)**

	Convert →	
ANALYSIS IN SCIENCE RAW SCORE (0-35)		**ANALYSIS IN SCIENCE CROSS-TEST SCORE (10-40)**

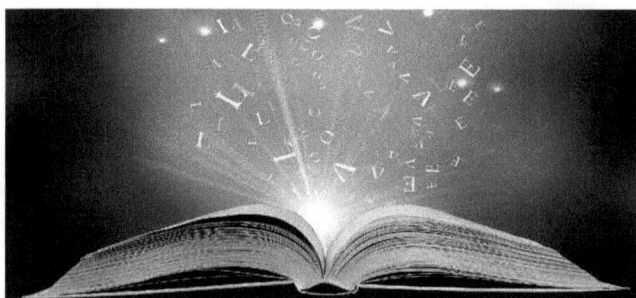

SAT® Practice Test #2

IMPORTANT REMINDERS

1

A No. 2 pencil is required for the test.
Do not use a mechanical pencil or pen.

2

Sharing any questions with anyone
is a violation of Test Security
and Fairness policies and may result
in your scores being canceled.

This cover is representative of what you'll see on test day.

TEST TAKING TIP #2

Take Breaks When You Need Them: Practicing for the SAT can sometimes be hard and strenuous. Taking breaks can help you cram more info into your brain and will allow you to study for longer periods. So don't feel bad when you make a quick snack run.

Reading Test

65 MINUTES, 52 QUESTIONS

Turn to Section 1 of your answer sheet to answer the questions in this section.

DIRECTIONS

Each passage or pair of passages below is followed by a number of questions. After reading each passage or pair, choose the best answer to each question based on what is stated or implied in the passage or passages and in any accompanying graphics (such as a table or graph).

Questions 1-10 are based on the following passage.

This passage is from Charlotte Brontë, *The Professor*, originally published in 1857.

No man likes to acknowledge that he has made a mistake in the choice of his profession, and every man, worthy of the name, will row long against wind
Line and tide before he allows himself to cry out, "I am
5 baffled!" and submits to be floated passively back to land. From the first week of my residence in X—— I felt my occupation irksome. The thing itself—the work of copying and translating business-letters—was a dry and tedious task enough, but had that been
10 all, I should long have borne with the nuisance; I am not of an impatient nature, and influenced by the double desire of getting my living and justifying to myself and others the resolution I had taken to become a tradesman, I should have endured in
15 silence the rust and cramp of my best faculties; I should not have whispered, even inwardly, that I longed for liberty; I should have pent in every sigh by which my heart might have ventured to intimate its distress under the closeness, smoke, monotony, and
20 joyless tumult of Bigben Close, and its panting desire for freer and fresher scenes; I should have set up the image of Duty, the fetish of Perseverance, in my small bedroom at Mrs. King's lodgings, and they two should have been my household gods, from which

25 my darling, my cherished-in-secret, Imagination, the tender and the mighty, should never, either by softness or strength, have severed me. But this was not all; the antipathy which had sprung up between myself and my employer striking deeper root and
30 spreading denser shade daily, excluded me from every glimpse of the sunshine of life; and I began to feel like a plant growing in humid darkness out of the slimy walls of a well.
Antipathy is the only word which can express the
35 feeling Edward Crimsworth had for me—a feeling, in a great measure, involuntary, and which was liable to be excited by every, the most trifling movement, look, or word of mine. My southern accent annoyed him; the degree of education evinced in my language
40 irritated him; my punctuality, industry, and accuracy, fixed his dislike, and gave it the high flavour and poignant relish of envy; he feared that I too should one day make a successful tradesman. Had I been in anything inferior to him, he would not
45 have hated me so thoroughly, but I knew all that he knew, and, what was worse, he suspected that I kept the padlock of silence on mental wealth in which he was no sharer. If he could have once placed me in a ridiculous or mortifying position, he would have
50 forgiven me much, but I was guarded by three faculties—Caution, Tact, Observation; and prowling and prying as was Edward's malignity, it could never baffle the lynx-eyes of these, my natural sentinels. Day by day did his malice watch my tact, hoping it
55 would sleep, and prepared to steal snake-like on its slumber; but tact, if it be genuine, never sleeps.

I had received my first quarter's wages, and was
returning to my lodgings, possessed heart and soul
with the pleasant feeling that the master who had
60 paid me grudged every penny of that hard-earned
pittance—(I had long ceased to regard
Mr. Crimsworth as my brother—he was a hard,
grinding master; he wished to be an inexorable
tyrant: that was all). Thoughts, not varied but strong,
65 occupied my mind; two voices spoke within me;
again and again they uttered the same monotonous
phrases. One said: "William, your life is intolerable."
The other: "What can you do to alter it?" I walked
fast, for it was a cold, frosty night in January; as I
70 approached my lodgings, I turned from a general
view of my affairs to the particular speculation as to
whether my fire would be out; looking towards the
window of my sitting-room, I saw no cheering red
gleam.

1

Which choice best summarizes the passage?

A) A character describes his dislike for his new job
and considers the reasons why.

B) Two characters employed in the same office
become increasingly competitive.

C) A young man regrets privately a choice that he
defends publicly.

D) A new employee experiences optimism, then
frustration, and finally despair.

2

The main purpose of the opening sentence of the
passage is to

A) establish the narrator's perspective on a
controversy.

B) provide context useful in understanding the
narrator's emotional state.

C) offer a symbolic representation of
Edward Crimsworth's plight.

D) contrast the narrator's good intentions with his
malicious conduct.

3

During the course of the first paragraph, the
narrator's focus shifts from

A) recollection of past confidence to
acknowledgment of present self-doubt.

B) reflection on his expectations of life as a
tradesman to his desire for another job.

C) generalization about job dissatisfaction to the
specifics of his own situation.

D) evaluation of factors making him unhappy to
identification of alternatives.

4

The references to "shade" and "darkness" at the end
of the first paragraph mainly have which effect?

A) They evoke the narrator's sense of dismay.

B) They reflect the narrator's sinister thoughts.

C) They capture the narrator's fear of confinement.

D) They reveal the narrator's longing for rest.

5

The passage indicates that Edward Crimsworth's
behavior was mainly caused by his

A) impatience with the narrator's high spirits.

B) scorn of the narrator's humble background.

C) indignation at the narrator's rash actions.

D) jealousy of the narrator's apparent superiority.

6

The passage indicates that when the narrator began
working for Edward Crimsworth, he viewed
Crimsworth as a

A) harmless rival.

B) sympathetic ally.

C) perceptive judge.

D) demanding mentor.

7

Which choice provides the best evidence for the answer to the previous question?

A) Lines 28-31 ("the antipathy . . . life")

B) Lines 38-40 ("My southern . . . irritated him")

C) Lines 54-56 ("Day . . . slumber")

D) Lines 61-62 ("I had . . . brother")

8

At the end of the second paragraph, the comparisons of abstract qualities to a lynx and a snake mainly have the effect of

A) contrasting two hypothetical courses of action.

B) conveying the ferocity of a resolution.

C) suggesting the likelihood of an altercation.

D) illustrating the nature of an adversarial relationship.

9

The passage indicates that, after a long day of work, the narrator sometimes found his living quarters to be

A) treacherous.

B) dreary.

C) predictable.

D) intolerable.

10

Which choice provides the best evidence for the answer to the previous question?

A) Lines 17-21 ("I should . . . scenes")

B) Lines 21-23 ("I should . . . lodgings")

C) Lines 64-67 ("Thoughts . . . phrases")

D) Lines 68-74 ("I walked . . . gleam")

Unauthorized copying or reuse of any part of this page is illegal.

4

CONTINUE

Questions 11-21 are based on the following passage and supplementary material.

This passage is adapted from Iain King, "Can Economics Be Ethical?" ©2013 by Prospect Publishing.

Recent debates about the economy have rediscovered the question, "is that right?", where "right" means more than just profits or efficiency.
Some argue that because the free markets allow
5 for personal choice, they are already ethical. Others have accepted the ethical critique and embraced corporate social responsibility. But before we can label any market outcome as "immoral," or sneer at economists who try to put a price on being ethical,
10 we need to be clear on what we are talking about.

There are different views on where ethics should apply when someone makes an economic decision. Consider Adam Smith, widely regarded as the founder of modern economics. He was a moral
15 philosopher who believed sympathy for others was the basis for ethics (we would call it empathy nowadays). But one of his key insights in *The Wealth of Nations* was that acting on this empathy could be counter-productive—he observed people becoming
20 better off when they put their own empathy aside, and interacted in a self-interested way. Smith justifies selfish behavior by the outcome. Whenever planners use cost-benefit analysis to justify a new railway line, or someone retrains to boost his or her earning
25 power, or a shopper buys one to get one free, they are using the same approach: empathizing with someone, and seeking an outcome that makes that person as well off as possible—although the person they are empathizing with may be themselves in the
30 future.

Instead of judging consequences, Aristotle said ethics was about having the right character—displaying virtues like courage and honesty. It is a view put into practice whenever
35 business leaders are chosen for their good character. But it is a hard philosophy to teach—just how much loyalty should you show to a manufacturer that keeps losing money? Show too little and you're a "greed is good" corporate raider; too much and you're wasting
40 money on unproductive capital. Aristotle thought there was a golden mean between the two extremes, and finding it was a matter of fine judgment. But if ethics is about character, it's not clear what those characteristics should be.

45 There is yet another approach: instead of rooting ethics in character or the consequences of actions, we can focus on our actions themselves. From this perspective some things are right, some wrong—we should buy fair trade goods, we shouldn't tell lies in
50 advertisements. Ethics becomes a list of commandments, a catalog of "dos" and "don'ts." When a finance official refuses to devalue a currency because they have promised not to, they are defining ethics this way. According to this approach
55 devaluation can still be bad, even if it would make everybody better off.

Many moral dilemmas arise when these three versions pull in different directions but clashes are not inevitable. Take fair trade coffee (coffee that is
60 sold with a certification that indicates the farmers and workers who produced it were paid a fair wage), for example: buying it might have good consequences, be virtuous, and also be the right way to act in a flawed market. Common ground like this
65 suggests that, even without agreement on where ethics applies, ethical economics is still possible.

Whenever we feel queasy about "perfect" competitive markets, the problem is often rooted in a phony conception of people. The model of man on
70 which classical economics is based—an entirely rational and selfish being—is a parody, as John Stuart Mill, the philosopher who pioneered the model, accepted. Most people—even economists— now accept that this "economic man" is a fiction.
75 We behave like a herd; we fear losses more than we hope for gains; rarely can our brains process all the relevant facts.

These human quirks mean we can never make purely "rational" decisions. A new wave of behavioral
80 economists, aided by neuroscientists, is trying to understand our psychology, both alone and in groups, so they can anticipate our decisions in the marketplace more accurately. But psychology can also help us understand why we react in disgust at
85 economic injustice, or accept a moral law as universal. Which means that the relatively new science of human behavior might also define ethics for us. Ethical economics would then emerge from one of the least likely places: economists themselves.

CONTINUE ➡

Regular Coffee Profits
Compared to Fair Trade Coffee
Profits in Tanzania

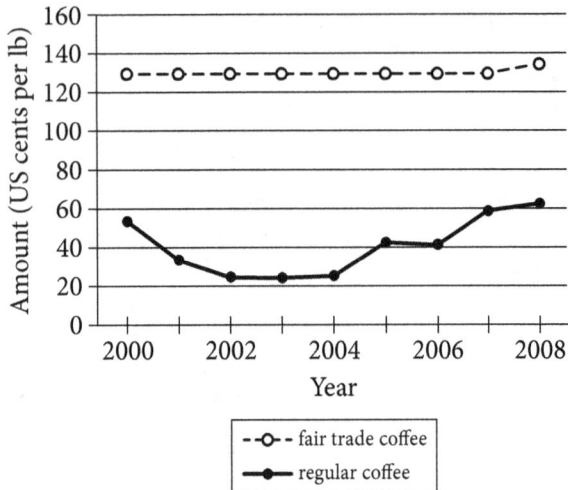

Adapted from the Fair Trade Vancouver website.

11

The main purpose of the passage is to

A) consider an ethical dilemma posed by cost-benefit analysis.

B) describe a psychology study of ethical economic behavior.

C) argue that the free market prohibits ethical economics.

D) examine ways of evaluating the ethics of economics.

12

In the passage, the author anticipates which of the following objections to criticizing the ethics of free markets?

A) Smith's association of free markets with ethical behavior still applies today.

B) Free markets are the best way to generate high profits, so ethics are a secondary consideration.

C) Free markets are ethical because they are made possible by devalued currency.

D) Free markets are ethical because they enable individuals to make choices.

13

Which choice provides the best evidence for the answer to the previous question?

A) Lines 4-5 ("Some . . . ethical")

B) Lines 7-10 ("But . . . about")

C) Lines 21-22 ("Smith . . . outcome")

D) Lines 52-54 ("When . . . way")

14

As used in line 6, "embraced" most nearly means

A) lovingly held.

B) readily adopted.

C) eagerly hugged.

D) reluctantly used.

15

The main purpose of the fifth paragraph (lines 45-56) is to

A) develop a counterargument to the claim that greed is good.

B) provide support for the idea that ethics is about character.

C) describe a third approach to defining ethical economics.

D) illustrate that one's actions are a result of one's character.

16

As used in line 58, "clashes" most nearly means

A) conflicts.

B) mismatches.

C) collisions.

D) brawls.

17

Which choice best supports the author's claim that there is common ground shared by the different approaches to ethics described in the passage?

A) Lines 11-12 ("There . . . decision")

B) Lines 47-50 ("From . . . advertisements")

C) Lines 59-64 ("Take . . . market")

D) Lines 75-77 ("We . . . facts")

18

The main idea of the final paragraph is that

A) human quirks make it difficult to predict people's ethical decisions accurately.

B) people universally react with disgust when faced with economic injustice.

C) understanding human psychology may help to define ethics in economics.

D) economists themselves will be responsible for reforming the free market.

19

Data in the graph about per-pound coffee profits in Tanzania most strongly support which of the following statements?

A) Fair trade coffee consistently earned greater profits than regular coffee earned.

B) The profits earned from regular coffee did not fluctuate.

C) Fair trade coffee profits increased between 2004 and 2006.

D) Fair trade and regular coffee were earning equal profits by 2008.

20

Data in the graph indicate that the greatest difference between per-pound profits from fair trade coffee and those from regular coffee occurred during which period?

A) 2000 to 2002

B) 2002 to 2004

C) 2004 to 2005

D) 2006 to 2008

21

21

Data in the graph provide most direct support for which idea in the passage?

A) Acting on empathy can be counterproductive.

B) Ethical economics is defined by character.

C) Ethical economics is still possible.

D) People fear losses more than they hope for gains.

Questions 22-32 are based on the following passages.

Passage 1 is adapted from Nicholas Carr, "Author Nicholas Carr: The Web Shatters Focus, Rewires Brains." ©2010 by Condé Nast. Passage 2 is from Steven Pinker, "Mind over Mass Media." ©2010 by The New York Times Company.

Passage 1

The mental consequences of our online info-crunching are not universally bad. Certain cognitive skills are strengthened by our use
Line of computers and the Net. These tend to involve
5 more primitive mental functions, such as hand-eye coordination, reflex response, and the processing of visual cues. One much-cited study of video gaming revealed that after just 10 days of playing action games on computers, a group of young people had
10 significantly boosted the speed with which they could shift their visual focus between various images and tasks.

It's likely that Web browsing also strengthens brain functions related to fast-paced problem
15 solving, particularly when it requires spotting patterns in a welter of data. A British study of the way women search for medical information online indicated that an experienced Internet user can, at least in some cases, assess the trustworthiness and
20 probable value of a Web page in a matter of seconds. The more we practice surfing and scanning, the more adept our brain becomes at those tasks.

But it would be a serious mistake to look narrowly at such benefits and conclude that the Web is making
25 us smarter. In a *Science* article published in early 2009, prominent developmental psychologist Patricia Greenfield reviewed more than 40 studies of the effects of various types of media on intelligence and learning ability. She concluded that "every medium
30 develops some cognitive skills at the expense of others." Our growing use of the Net and other screen-based technologies, she wrote, has led to the "widespread and sophisticated development of visual-spatial skills." But those gains go hand in hand
35 with a weakening of our capacity for the kind of "deep processing" that underpins "mindful knowledge acquisition, inductive analysis, critical thinking, imagination, and reflection."

We know that the human brain is highly
40 plastic; neurons and synapses change as circumstances change. When we adapt to a new cultural phenomenon, including the use of a new

Unauthorized copying or reuse of any part of this page is illegal.

8

CONTINUE

medium, we end up with a different brain, says
Michael Merzenich, a pioneer of the field of
45 neuroplasticity. That means our online habits
continue to reverberate in the workings of our brain
cells even when we're not at a computer. We're
exercising the neural circuits devoted to skimming
and multitasking while ignoring those used for
50 reading and thinking deeply.

Passage 2
    Critics of new media sometimes use science itself
to press their case, citing research that shows how
"experience can change the brain." But cognitive
neuroscientists roll their eyes at such talk. Yes, every
55 time we learn a fact or skill the wiring of the brain
changes; it's not as if the information is stored in the
pancreas. But the existence of neural plasticity does
not mean the brain is a blob of clay pounded into
shape by experience.
60   Experience does not revamp the basic
information-processing capacities of the brain.
Speed-reading programs have long claimed to do just
that, but the verdict was rendered by Woody Allen
after he read Leo Tolstoy's famously long novel
65 *War and Peace* in one sitting: "It was about Russia."
Genuine multitasking, too, has been exposed as a
myth, not just by laboratory studies but by the
familiar sight of an SUV undulating between lanes as
the driver cuts deals on his cell phone.
70   Moreover, the effects of experience are highly
specific to the experiences themselves. If you train
people to do one thing (recognize shapes, solve math
puzzles, find hidden words), they get better at doing
that thing, but almost nothing else. Music doesn't
75 make you better at math, conjugating Latin doesn't
make you more logical, brain-training games don't
make you smarter. Accomplished people don't bulk
up their brains with intellectual calisthenics; they
immerse themselves in their fields. Novelists read
80 lots of novels, scientists read lots of science.
    The effects of consuming electronic media are
likely to be far more limited than the panic implies.
Media critics write as if the brain takes on the
qualities of whatever it consumes, the informational
85 equivalent of "you are what you eat." As with ancient
peoples who believed that eating fierce animals made
them fierce, they assume that watching quick cuts in
rock videos turns your mental life into quick cuts or
that reading bullet points and online postings turns
90 your thoughts into bullet points and online postings.

22

The author of Passage 1 indicates which of the
following about the use of screen-based technologies?

A) It should be thoroughly studied.

B) It makes the brain increasingly rigid.

C) It has some positive effects.

D) It should be widely encouraged.

23

Which choice provides the best evidence for the
answer to the previous question?

A) Lines 3-4 ("Certain . . . Net")

B) Lines 23-25 ("But . . . smarter")

C) Lines 25-29 ("In a . . . ability")

D) Lines 29-31 ("She . . . others")

24

The author of Passage 1 indicates that becoming
adept at using the Internet can

A) make people complacent about their health.

B) undermine the ability to think deeply.

C) increase people's social contacts.

D) improve people's self-confidence.

25

As used in line 40, "plastic" most nearly means

A) creative.

B) artificial.

C) malleable.

D) sculptural.

26

The author of Passage 2 refers to the novel *War and Peace* primarily to suggest that Woody Allen

A) did not like Tolstoy's writing style.

B) could not comprehend the novel by speed-reading it.

C) had become quite skilled at multitasking.

D) regretted having read such a long novel.

27

According to the author of Passage 2, what do novelists and scientists have in common?

A) They take risks when they pursue knowledge.

B) They are eager to improve their minds.

C) They are curious about other subjects.

D) They become absorbed in their own fields.

28

The analogy in the final sentence of Passage 2 has primarily which effect?

A) It uses ornate language to illustrate a difficult concept.

B) It employs humor to soften a severe opinion of human behavior.

C) It alludes to the past to evoke a nostalgic response.

D) It criticizes the view of a particular group.

29

The main purpose of each passage is to

A) compare brain function in those who play games on the Internet and those who browse on it.

B) report on the problem-solving skills of individuals with varying levels of Internet experience.

C) take a position on increasing financial support for studies related to technology and intelligence.

D) make an argument about the effects of electronic media use on the brain.

30

Which choice best describes the relationship between the two passages?

A) Passage 2 relates first-hand experiences that contrast with the clinical approach in Passage 1.

B) Passage 2 critiques the conclusions drawn from the research discussed in Passage 1.

C) Passage 2 takes a high-level view of a result that Passage 1 examines in depth.

D) Passage 2 predicts the negative reactions that the findings discussed in Passage 1 might produce.

31

On which of the following points would the authors of both passages most likely agree?

A) Computer-savvy children tend to demonstrate better hand-eye coordination than do their parents.

B) Those who criticize consumers of electronic media tend to overreact in their criticism.

C) Improved visual-spatial skills do not generalize to improved skills in other areas.

D) Internet users are unlikely to prefer reading onscreen text to reading actual books.

32

Which choice provides the best evidence that the author of Passage 2 would agree to some extent with the claim attributed to Michael Merzenich in lines 41-43, Passage 1?

A) Lines 51-53 ("Critics . . . brain")

B) Lines 54-56 ("Yes . . . changes")

C) Lines 57-59 ("But . . . experience")

D) Lines 83-84 ("Media . . . consumes")

Questions 33-42 are based on the following passage.

This passage is adapted from Elizabeth Cady Stanton's address to the 1869 Woman Suffrage Convention in Washington, DC.

I urge a sixteenth amendment, because "manhood suffrage," or a man's government, is civil, religious, and social disorganization. The male element is a
Line destructive force, stern, selfish, aggrandizing, loving
5 war, violence, conquest, acquisition, breeding in the material and moral world alike discord, disorder, disease, and death. See what a record of blood and cruelty the pages of history reveal! Through what slavery, slaughter, and sacrifice, through what
10 inquisitions and imprisonments, pains and persecutions, black codes and gloomy creeds, the soul of humanity has struggled for the centuries, while mercy has veiled her face and all hearts have been dead alike to love and hope!
15 The male element has held high carnival thus far; it has fairly run riot from the beginning, overpowering the feminine element everywhere, crushing out all the diviner qualities in human nature, until we know but little of true manhood and
20 womanhood, of the latter comparatively nothing, for it has scarce been recognized as a power until within the last century. Society is but the reflection of man himself, untempered by woman's thought; the hard iron rule we feel alike in the church, the state, and the
25 home. No one need wonder at the disorganization, at the fragmentary condition of everything, when we remember that man, who represents but half a complete being, with but half an idea on every subject, has undertaken the absolute control of all
30 sublunary matters.

People object to the demands of those whom they choose to call the strong-minded, because they say "the right of suffrage will make the women masculine." That is just the difficulty in which we are
35 involved today. Though disfranchised, we have few women in the best sense; we have simply so many reflections, varieties, and dilutions of the masculine gender. The strong, natural characteristics of womanhood are repressed and ignored in

40 dependence, for so long as man feeds woman she will try to please the giver and adapt herself to his condition. To keep a foothold in society, woman must be as near like man as possible, reflect his ideas, opinions, virtues, motives, prejudices, and vices. She
45 must respect his statutes, though they strip her of every inalienable right, and conflict with that higher law written by the finger of God on her own soul. . . .

. . . [M]an has been molding woman to his ideas by direct and positive influences, while she, if not a
50 negation, has used indirect means to control him, and in most cases developed the very characteristics both in him and herself that needed repression. And now man himself stands appalled at the results of his own excesses, and mourns in bitterness that
55 falsehood, selfishness, and violence are the law of life. The need of this hour is not territory, gold mines, railroads, or specie payments but a new evangel of womanhood, to exalt purity, virtue, morality, true religion, to lift man up into the higher realms of
60 thought and action.

We ask woman's enfranchisement, as the first step toward the recognition of that essential element in government that can only secure the health, strength, and prosperity of the nation. Whatever is done to lift
65 woman to her true position will help to usher in a new day of peace and perfection for the race.

In speaking of the masculine element, I do not wish to be understood to say that all men are hard, selfish, and brutal, for many of the most beautiful
70 spirits the world has known have been clothed with manhood; but I refer to those characteristics, though often marked in woman, that distinguish what is called the stronger sex. For example, the love of acquisition and conquest, the very pioneers of
75 civilization, when expended on the earth, the sea, the elements, the riches and forces of nature, are powers of destruction when used to subjugate one man to another or to sacrifice nations to ambition.

Here that great conservator of woman's love, if
80 permitted to assert itself, as it naturally would in freedom against oppression, violence, and war, would hold all these destructive forces in check, for woman knows the cost of life better than man does, and not with her consent would one drop of blood
85 ever be shed, one life sacrificed in vain.

33

The central problem that Stanton describes in the passage is that women have been

A) denied equal educational opportunities, which has kept them from reaching their potential.

B) prevented from exerting their positive influence on men, which has led to societal breakdown.

C) prevented from voting, which has resulted in poor candidates winning important elections.

D) blocked by men from serving as legislators, which has allowed the creation of unjust laws.

34

Stanton uses the phrase "high carnival" (line 15) mainly to emphasize what she sees as the

A) utter domination of women by men.

B) freewheeling spirit of the age.

C) scandalous decline in moral values.

D) growing power of women in society.

35

Stanton claims that which of the following was a relatively recent historical development?

A) The control of society by men

B) The spread of war and injustice

C) The domination of domestic life by men

D) The acknowledgment of women's true character

36

Which choice provides the best evidence for the answer to the previous question?

A) Lines 3-7 ("The male . . . death")

B) Lines 15-22 ("The male . . . century")

C) Lines 22-25 ("Society . . . home")

D) Lines 48-52 ("[M]an . . . repression")

37

As used in line 24, "rule" most nearly refers to

A) a general guideline.

B) a controlling force.

C) an established habit.

D) a procedural method.

38

It can reasonably be inferred that "the strong-minded" (line 32) was a term generally intended to

A) praise women who fight for their long-denied rights.

B) identify women who demonstrate intellectual skill.

C) criticize women who enter male-dominated professions.

D) condemn women who agitate for the vote for their sex.

39

As used in line 36, "best" most nearly means

A) superior.

B) excellent.

C) genuine.

D) rarest.

40

Stanton contends that the situation she describes in the passage has become so dire that even men have begun to

A) lament the problems they have created.

B) join the call for woman suffrage.

C) consider women their social equals.

D) ask women how to improve civic life.

41

Which choice provides the best evidence for the answer to the previous question?

A) Lines 25-30 ("No one . . . matters")

B) Lines 53-55 ("And now . . . life")

C) Lines 56-60 ("The need . . . action")

D) Lines 61-64 ("We ask . . . nation")

42

The sixth paragraph (lines 67-78) is primarily concerned with establishing a contrast between

A) men and women.

B) the spiritual world and the material world.

C) bad men and good men.

D) men and masculine traits.

Questions 43-52 are based on the following passage and supplementary material.

This passage is adapted from Geoffrey Giller, "Long a Mystery, How 500-Meter-High Undersea Waves Form Is Revealed." ©2014 by Scientific American.

Some of the largest ocean waves in the world are nearly impossible to see. Unlike other large waves, these rollers, called internal waves, do not ride the
Line ocean surface. Instead, they move underwater,
5 undetectable without the use of satellite imagery or sophisticated monitoring equipment. Despite their hidden nature, internal waves are fundamental parts of ocean water dynamics, transferring heat to the ocean depths and bringing up cold water from below.
10 And they can reach staggering heights—some as tall as skyscrapers.

Because these waves are involved in ocean mixing and thus the transfer of heat, understanding them is crucial to global climate modeling, says Tom
15 Peacock, a researcher at the Massachusetts Institute of Technology. Most models fail to take internal waves into account. "If we want to have more and more accurate climate models, we have to be able to capture processes such as this," Peacock says.
20 Peacock and his colleagues tried to do just that. Their study, published in November in *Geophysical Research Letters*, focused on internal waves generated in the Luzon Strait, which separates Taiwan and the Philippines. Internal waves in this region, thought to
25 be some of the largest in the world, can reach about 500 meters high. "That's the same height as the Freedom Tower that's just been built in New York," Peacock says.

Although scientists knew of this phenomenon in
30 the South China Sea and beyond, they didn't know exactly how internal waves formed. To find out, Peacock and a team of researchers from M.I.T. and Woods Hole Oceanographic Institution worked with France's National Center for Scientific Research
35 using a giant facility there called the Coriolis Platform. The rotating platform, about 15 meters (49.2 feet) in diameter, turns at variable speeds and can simulate Earth's rotation. It also has walls, which means scientists can fill it with water and create
40 accurate, large-scale simulations of various oceanographic scenarios.

Peacock and his team built a carbon-fiber resin scale model of the Luzon Strait, including the islands and surrounding ocean floor topography. Then they
45 filled the platform with water of varying salinity to replicate the different densities found at the strait, with denser, saltier water below and lighter, less briny water above. Small particles were added to the solution and illuminated with lights from below in
50 order to track how the liquid moved. Finally, they re-created tides using two large plungers to see how the internal waves themselves formed.

The Luzon Strait's underwater topography, with a distinct double-ridge shape, turns out to be
55 responsible for generating the underwater waves. As the tide rises and falls and water moves through the strait, colder, denser water is pushed up over the ridges into warmer, less dense layers above it. This action results in bumps of colder water trailed
60 by warmer water that generate an internal wave. As these waves move toward land, they become steeper—much the same way waves at the beach become taller before they hit the shore—until they break on a continental shelf.
65 The researchers were also able to devise a mathematical model that describes the movement and formation of these waves. Whereas the model is specific to the Luzon Strait, it can still help researchers understand how internal waves are
70 generated in other places around the world. Eventually, this information will be incorporated into global climate models, making them more accurate. "It's very clear, within the context of these [global climate] models, that internal waves play a role in
75 driving ocean circulations," Peacock says.

CHANGES IN DEPTH OF ISOTHERMS*
IN AN INTERNAL WAVE OVER A 24-HOUR PERIOD

Time (hours)

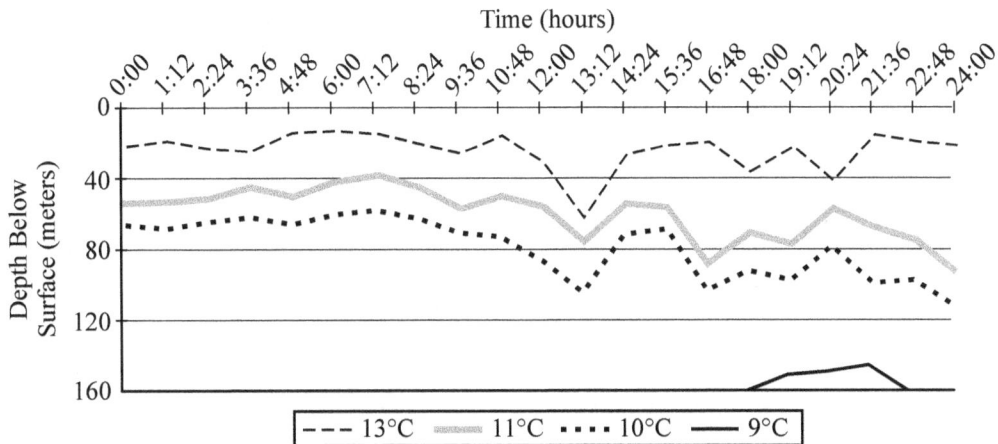

* Bands of water of constant temperatures

Adapted from Justin Small et al., "Internal Solitons in the Ocean: Prediction from SAR." ©1998 by Oceanography, Defence Evaluation and Research Agency.

43

The first paragraph serves mainly to

A) explain how a scientific device is used.

B) note a common misconception about an event.

C) describe a natural phenomenon and address its importance.

D) present a recent study and summarize its findings.

44

As used in line 19, "capture" is closest in meaning to

A) control.

B) record.

C) secure.

D) absorb.

45

According to Peacock, the ability to monitor internal waves is significant primarily because

A) it will allow scientists to verify the maximum height of such waves.

B) it will allow researchers to shift their focus to improving the quality of satellite images.

C) the study of wave patterns will enable regions to predict and prevent coastal damage.

D) the study of such waves will inform the development of key scientific models.

46

Which choice provides the best evidence for the answer to the previous question?

A) Lines 1-2 ("Some . . . see")

B) Lines 4-6 ("they . . . equipment")

C) Lines 17-19 ("If . . . this")

D) Lines 24-26 ("Internal . . . high")

47

As used in line 65, "devise" most nearly means

A) create.

B) solve.

C) imagine.

D) begin.

48

Based on information in the passage, it can reasonably be inferred that all internal waves

A) reach approximately the same height even though the locations and depths of continental shelves vary.

B) may be caused by similar factors but are influenced by the distinct topographies of different regions.

C) can be traced to inconsistencies in the tidal patterns of deep ocean water located near islands.

D) are generated by the movement of dense water over a relatively flat section of the ocean floor.

49

Which choice provides the best evidence for the answer to the previous question?

A) Lines 29-31 ("Although . . . formed")

B) Lines 56-58 ("As the . . . it")

C) Lines 61-64 ("As these . . . shelf")

D) Lines 67-70 ("Whereas . . . world")

50

In the graph, which isotherm displays an increase in depth below the surface during the period 19:12 to 20:24?

A) 9°C

B) 10°C

C) 11°C

D) 13°C

51

Which concept is supported by the passage and by the information in the graph?

A) Internal waves cause water of varying salinity to mix.

B) Internal waves push denser water above layers of less dense water.

C) Internal waves push bands of cold water above bands of warmer water.

D) Internal waves do not rise to break the ocean's surface.

52

How does the graph support the author's point that internal waves affect ocean water dynamics?

A) It demonstrates that wave movement forces warmer water down to depths that typically are colder.

B) It reveals the degree to which an internal wave affects the density of deep layers of cold water.

C) It illustrates the change in surface temperature that takes place during an isolated series of deep waves.

D) It shows that multiple waves rising near the surface of the ocean disrupt the flow of normal tides.

STOP

If you finish before time is called, you may check your work on this section only.
Do not turn to any other section.

Writing and Language Test

35 MINUTES, 44 QUESTIONS

Turn to Section 2 of your answer sheet to answer the questions in this section.

DIRECTIONS

Each passage below is accompanied by a number of questions. For some questions, you will consider how the passage might be revised to improve the expression of ideas. For other questions, you will consider how the passage might be edited to correct errors in sentence structure, usage, or punctuation. A passage or a question may be accompanied by one or more graphics (such as a table or graph) that you will consider as you make revising and editing decisions.

Some questions will direct you to an underlined portion of a passage. Other questions will direct you to a location in a passage or ask you to think about the passage as a whole.

After reading each passage, choose the answer to each question that most effectively improves the quality of writing in the passage or that makes the passage conform to the conventions of standard written English. Many questions include a "NO CHANGE" option. Choose that option if you think the best choice is to leave the relevant portion of the passage as it is.

Questions 1-11 are based on the following passage.

Librarians Help Navigate in the Digital Age

   In recent years, public libraries in the United States have experienced **1** reducing in their operating funds due to cuts imposed at the federal, state, and local government levels. **2** However, library staffing has been cut by almost four percent since 2008, and the demand for librarians continues to decrease, even though half of public libraries report that they have an insufficient number of staff to meet their patrons' needs. Employment in all job sectors in the United States is projected to grow by fourteen percent over the next

1
A) NO CHANGE
B) reductions
C) deducting
D) deducts

2
A) NO CHANGE
B) Consequently,
C) Nevertheless,
D) Previously,

decade, yet the expected growth rate for librarians is predicted to be only seven percent, or half of the overall rate. This trend, combined with the increasing accessibility of information via the Internet, [3] has led some to claim that librarianship is in decline as a profession. As public libraries adapt to rapid technological advances in information distribution, librarians' roles are actually expanding.

The share of library materials that is in nonprint formats [4] is increasing steadily; in 2010, at least 18.5 million e-books were available [5] for them to circulate. As a result, librarians must now be proficient curators of electronic information, compiling, [6] catalog, and updating these collections. But perhaps even more importantly, librarians function as first responders for their communities' computer needs. Since

[3]

A) NO CHANGE
B) have
C) which have
D) which has

[4]

At this point, the writer is considering adding the following information.

—e-books, audio and video materials, and online journals—

Should the writer make this addition here?

A) Yes, because it provides specific examples of the materials discussed in the sentence.
B) Yes, because it illustrates the reason for the increase mentioned later in the sentence.
C) No, because it interrupts the flow of the sentence by supplying irrelevant information.
D) No, because it weakens the focus of the passage by discussing a subject other than librarians.

[5]

A) NO CHANGE
B) to be circulated by them.
C) for their circulating.
D) for circulation.

[6]

A) NO CHANGE
B) librarians cataloging,
C) to catalog,
D) cataloging,

one of the fastest growing library services is public access computer use, there is great demand for computer instruction. **7** In fact, librarians' training now includes courses on research and Internet search methods. Many of whom teach classes in Internet navigation, database and software use, and digital information literacy. While these classes are particularly helpful to young students developing basic research skills, **8** but adult patrons can also benefit from librarian assistance in that they can acquire job-relevant computer skills. **9** Free to all who utilize their services, public libraries and librarians are especially valuable, because they offer free resources that may be difficult to find elsewhere, such as help with online job

7

Which choice most effectively combines the underlined sentences?

A) In fact, librarians' training now includes courses on research and Internet search methods; many librarians teach classes in Internet navigation, database and software use, and digital information literacy is taught by them.

B) In fact, many librarians, whose training now includes courses on research and Internet search methods, teach classes in Internet navigation, database and software use, and digital information literacy.

C) Training now includes courses on research and Internet search methods; many librarians, in fact, are teaching classes in Internet navigation, database and software use, and digital information literacy.

D) Including courses on research and Internet search methods in their training is, in fact, why many librarians teach classes in Internet navigation, database and software use, and digital information literacy.

8

A) NO CHANGE
B) and
C) for
D) DELETE the underlined portion.

9

Which choice most effectively sets up the examples given at the end of the sentence?

A) NO CHANGE
B) During periods of economic recession,
C) Although their value cannot be measured,
D) When it comes to the free services libraries provide,

searches as well as résumé and job material development. An overwhelming number of public libraries also report that they provide help with electronic government resources related to income taxes, **10** law troubles, and retirement programs.

In sum, the Internet does not replace the need for librarians, and librarians are hardly obsolete. **11** Like books, librarians have been around for a long time, but the Internet is extremely useful for many types of research.

10

A) NO CHANGE
B) legal issues,
C) concerns related to law courts,
D) matters for the law courts,

11

Which choice most clearly ends the passage with a restatement of the writer's primary claim?

A) NO CHANGE
B) Although their roles have diminished significantly, librarians will continue to be employed by public libraries for the foreseeable future.
C) The growth of electronic information has led to a diversification of librarians' skills and services, positioning them as savvy resource specialists for patrons.
D) However, given their extensive training and skills, librarians who have been displaced by budget cuts have many other possible avenues of employment.

Questions 12-22 are based on the following passage.

Tiny Exhibit, Big Impact

— 1 —

The first time I visited the Art Institute of Chicago, I expected to be impressed by its famous large paintings. **12** On one hand, I couldn't wait to view **13** painter, Georges Seurat's, 10-foot-wide *A Sunday Afternoon on the Island of La Grande Jatte* in its full size. It took me by surprise, then, when my favorite exhibit at the museum was one of **14** it's tiniest; the Thorne Miniature Rooms.

12

A) NO CHANGE
B) For instance,
C) However,
D) Similarly,

13

A) NO CHANGE
B) painter, Georges Seurat's
C) painter Georges Seurat's,
D) painter Georges Seurat's

14

A) NO CHANGE
B) its tiniest;
C) its tiniest:
D) it's tiniest,

Unauthorized copying or reuse of any part of this page is illegal.

22

CONTINUE

— 2 —

Viewing the exhibit, I was amazed by the intricate details of some of the more ornately decorated rooms. I marveled at a replica of a salon (a formal living room) dating back to the reign of French king Louis XV. [15] Built into the dark paneled walls are bookshelves stocked with leather-bound volumes. The couch and chairs, in keeping with the style of the time, are characterized by elegantly curved arms and [16] legs, they are covered in luxurious velvet. A dime-sized portrait of a French aristocratic woman hangs in a golden frame.

— 3 —

This exhibit showcases sixty-eight miniature rooms inserted into a wall at eye level. Each furnished room consists of three walls; the fourth wall is a glass pane through which museumgoers observe. The rooms and their furnishings were painstakingly created to scale at 1/12th their actual size, so that one inch in the exhibit correlates with one foot in real life. A couch, for example, is seven inches long, and [17] that is based on a seven-foot-long couch. Each room represents a distinctive style of European, American, or Asian interior design from the thirteenth to twentieth centuries.

[15]

At this point, the writer is considering adding the following sentence.

> Some scholars argue that the excesses of King Louis XV's reign contributed significantly to the conditions that resulted in the French Revolution.

Should the writer make this addition here?

A) Yes, because it provides historical context for the Thorne Miniature Rooms exhibit.

B) Yes, because it explains why salons are often ornately decorated.

C) No, because it interrupts the paragraph's description of the miniature salon.

D) No, because it implies that the interior designer of the salon had political motivations.

[16]

A) NO CHANGE

B) legs, the couch and chairs

C) legs and

D) legs,

[17]

Which choice gives a second supporting example that is most similar to the example already in the sentence?

A) NO CHANGE

B) a tea cup is about a quarter of an inch.

C) there are even tiny cushions on some.

D) household items are also on this scale.

— 4 —

The plainer rooms are more sparsely **18** furnished. Their architectural features, furnishings, and decorations are just as true to the periods they represent. One of my favorite rooms in the whole exhibit, in fact, is an 1885 summer kitchen. The room is simple but spacious, with a small sink and counter along one wall, a cast-iron wood stove and some hanging pots and pans against another wall, and **19** a small table under a window of the third wall. Aside from a few simple wooden chairs placed near the edges of the room, the floor is open and obviously well worn.

18

Which choice most effectively combines the sentences at the underlined portion?

A) furnished by their

B) furnished, but their

C) furnished: their

D) furnished, whereas

19

Which choice most closely matches the stylistic pattern established earlier in the sentence?

A) NO CHANGE

B) a small table is under the third wall's window.

C) the third wall has a window and small table.

D) the third wall has a small table against it and a window.

— 5 —

As I walked through the exhibit, I overheard a
20 visitors' remark, "You know, that grandfather clock
actually runs. Its glass door swings open, and the clock
can be wound up." **21** Dotted with pin-sized knobs,
another visitor noticed my fascination with a tiny writing
desk and its drawers. "All of those little drawers pull out.
And you see that hutch? Can you believe it has a secret
compartment?" Given the exquisite craftsmanship and
level of detail I'd already seen, I certainly could.

Question 22 asks about the previous passage as a whole.

A) NO CHANGE
B) visitors remarking,
C) visitor remarked,
D) visitor remark,

21

A) NO CHANGE
B) Another visitor, dotted with pin-sized knobs, noticed my fascination with a tiny writing desk and its drawers.
C) Another visitor dotted with pin-sized knobs noticed my fascination with a tiny writing desk and its drawers.
D) Another visitor noticed my fascination with a tiny writing desk and its drawers, dotted with pin-sized knobs.

Think about the previous passage as a whole as you answer question 22.

22

To make the passage most logical, paragraph 2 should be placed
A) where it is now.
B) after paragraph 3.
C) after paragraph 4.
D) after paragraph 5.

Questions 23-33 are based on the following passage and supplementary material.

Environmentalist Otters

It has long been known that the sea otters [23] living along the West Coast of North America help keep kelp forests in their habitat healthy and vital. They do this by feeding on sea urchins and other herbivorous invertebrates that graze voraciously on kelp. With sea otters to keep the population of sea urchins in check, kelp forests can flourish. In fact, [24] two years or less of sea otters can completely eliminate sea urchins in a coastal area (see chart).

Effects of Sea Otter Presence on Kelp
and Sea Urchin Density in Coastal Areas

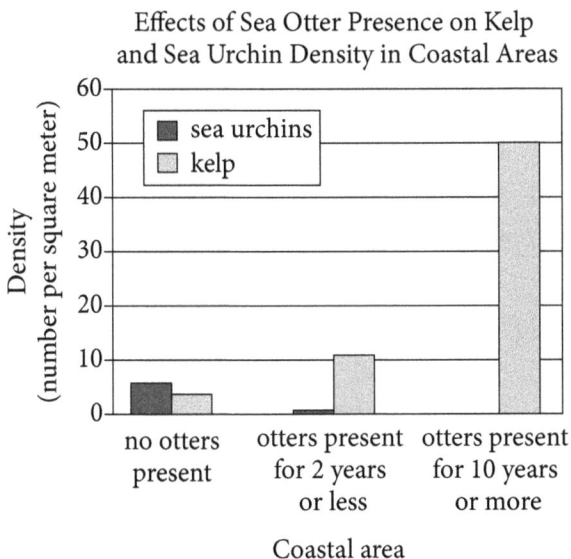

Adapted from David O. Duggins, "Kelp Beds and Sea Otters: An Experimental Approach." ©1980 by the Ecological Society of America.

Without sea otters present, [25] nevertheless, kelp forests run the danger of becoming barren stretches of coastal wasteland known as urchin barrens.

23

A) NO CHANGE

B) living along the West Coast of North America, they help

C) that live along the West Coast of North America and help to

D) that live along the West Coast of North America, where they help

24

Which choice offers an accurate interpretation of the data in the chart?

A) NO CHANGE

B) even two years or less of sea otter presence can reduce the sea urchin threat

C) kelp density increases proportionally as sea urchin density increases

D) even after sea otters were present for ten years or more, kelp density was still lower than sea urchin density

25

A) NO CHANGE

B) however,

C) hence,

D) likewise,

[1] What was less well-known, until recently at least, was how this relationship among sea otters, sea urchins, and kelp forests might help fight global warming. [2] The amount of carbon dioxide in the atmosphere has increased 40 percent 26 . [3] A recent study by two professors at the University of California, Santa Cruz, Chris Wilmers and James Estes, 27 suggests, that kelp forests protected by sea otters can absorb as much as twelve times the amount of carbon dioxide from the atmosphere as those where sea urchins are allowed to 28 devour the kelp. [4] Like 29 their terrestrial plant cousins, kelp removes carbon dioxide from the atmosphere, turning it into sugar fuel through photosynthesis, and releases oxygen back into the air.

26

At this point, the writer is considering adding the following information.

   since the start of the Industrial Revolution, resulting in a rise in global temperatures

Should the writer make this addition here?

A) Yes, because it establishes the relationship between the level of carbon dioxide in the atmosphere and global warming.

B) Yes, because it explains the key role sea otters, sea urchins, and kelp forests play in combating global warming.

C) No, because it contradicts the claim made in the previous paragraph that sea otters help keep kelp forests healthy.

D) No, because it mentions the Industrial Revolution, blurring the focus of the paragraph.

27

A) NO CHANGE
B) suggests—that
C) suggests, "that
D) suggests that

28

A) NO CHANGE
B) dispatch
C) overindulge on
D) dispose of

29

A) NO CHANGE
B) they're
C) its
D) it's

[5] Scientists knew this but did not recognize [30] how large a role they played in helping kelp forests to significantly decrease the amount of carbon dioxide in the atmosphere. [6] Far from making no difference to the ecosystem, the presence of otters was found to increase the carbon storage of kelp forests by 4.4 to 8.7 megatons annually, offsetting the amount of carbon dioxide emitted by three million to six million passenger cars each year. [31]

Wilmers and Estes caution, however, that [32] having more otters will not automatically solve the problem of higher levels of carbon dioxide in the air. But they suggest that the presence of otters provides a good model of how carbon can be sequestered, [33] or removed; from the atmosphere through the management of animal populations. If ecologists can better understand what kinds of impacts animals might have on the environment, Wilmers contends, "there might be opportunities for win-win conservation scenarios, whereby animal species are protected or enhanced, and carbon gets sequestered."

30

A) NO CHANGE
B) how large a role that it played
C) how large a role sea otters played
D) that they played such a large role

31

Where is the most logical place in this paragraph to add the following sentence?

What Wilmers and Estes discovered in their study, therefore, surprised them.

A) After sentence 1
B) After sentence 3
C) After sentence 4
D) After sentence 5

32

A) NO CHANGE
B) increasing the otter population
C) the otters multiplying
D) having more otters than other locations

33

A) NO CHANGE
B) or removed from,
C) or, removed from,
D) or removed, from

Questions 34-44 are based on the following passage.

A Quick Fix in a Throwaway Culture

Planned obsolescence, a practice [34] at which products are designed to have a limited period of [35] usefulness, has been a cornerstone of manufacturing strategy for the past 80 years. This approach increases sales, but it also stands in [36] austere contrast to a time when goods were produced to be durable. Planned obsolescence wastes materials as well as energy in making and shipping new products. It also reinforces the belief that it is easier to replace goods than to mend them, as repair shops are rare and [37] repair methods are often specialized. In 2009, an enterprising movement, the Repair Café, challenged this widely accepted belief.

[34]
A) NO CHANGE
B) from which
C) so that
D) whereby

[35]
A) NO CHANGE
B) usefulness—
C) usefulness;
D) usefulness

[36]
A) NO CHANGE
B) egregious
C) unmitigated
D) stark

[37]
Which choice provides information that best supports the claim made by this sentence?
A) NO CHANGE
B) obsolete goods can become collectible items.
C) no one knows whether something will fall into disrepair again.
D) new designs often have "bugs" that must be worked out.

[1] More like a 38 fair then an actual café, the first Repair Café took place in Amsterdam, the Netherlands. [2] It was the brainchild of former journalist Martine Postma, 39 wanting to take a practical stand in a throwaway culture. [3] Her goals were 40 straightforward, however: reduce waste, maintain and perpetuate knowledge and skills, and strengthen community. [4] Participants bring all manner of damaged articles—clothing, appliances, furniture, and more—to be repaired by a staff of volunteer specialists including tailors, electricians, and carpenters. [5] Since the inaugural Repair Café, others have been hosted in theater foyers, community centers, hotels, and auditoriums. [6] While 41 they await for service, patrons can enjoy coffee and snacks and mingle with their neighbors in need. 42

38

A) NO CHANGE
B) fair than
C) fare than
D) fair, then

39

A) NO CHANGE
B) whom wants
C) who wanted
D) she wanted

40

A) NO CHANGE
B) straightforward, therefore:
C) straightforward, nonetheless:
D) straightforward:

41

A) NO CHANGE
B) awaiting
C) they waited
D) waiting

42

To make this paragraph most logical, sentence 5 should be placed

A) where it is now.
B) before sentence 1.
C) after sentence 3.
D) after sentence 6.

Unauthorized copying or reuse of any part of this page is illegal.

30

CONTINUE

Though only about 3 percent of the Netherlands' municipal waste ends up in landfills, Repair Cafés still raise awareness about what may otherwise be mindless acts of waste by providing a venue for people to share and learn valuable skills that are in danger of being lost. **43** It is easy to classify old but fixable items as "junk" in an era that places great emphasis on the next big thing. In helping people consider how the goods they use on a daily basis work and are made, Repair Cafés restore a sense of relationship between human beings and material goods.

Though the concept remained a local trend at first, international Repair Cafés, all affiliated with the Dutch Repair Café via its website, have since arisen in France, Germany, South Africa, the United States, and other countries **44** on top of that. The original provides a central source for start-up tips and tools, as well as marketing advice to new Repair Cafés. As a result, the Repair Café has become a global network united by common ideals. Ironically, innovators are now looking back to old ways of doing things and applying them in today's cities in an effort to transform the way people relate to and think about the goods they consume.

43

At this point, the writer is considering adding the following sentence.

> As the number of corporate and service-based jobs has increased, the need for people who work with their hands has diminished.

Should the writer make this addition here?

A) Yes, because it provides an example of specific repair skills being lost.

B) Yes, because it elaborates on the statistic about the Netherlands' municipal waste.

C) No, because it blurs the paragraph's focus by introducing a topic that is not further explained.

D) No, because it contradicts the claims made in the rest of the paragraph.

44

A) NO CHANGE

B) in addition.

C) likewise.

D) DELETE the underlined portion, and end the sentence with a period.

STOP

If you finish before time is called, you may check your work on this section only.
Do not turn to any other section.

Math Test – No Calculator

25 MINUTES, 20 QUESTIONS

Turn to Section 3 of your answer sheet to answer the questions in this section.

For questions 1-15, solve each problem, choose the best answer from the choices provided, and fill in the corresponding circle on your answer sheet. **For questions 16-20**, solve the problem and enter your answer in the grid on the answer sheet. Please refer to the directions before question 16 on how to enter your answers in the grid. You may use any available space in your test booklet for scratch work.

NOTES

1. The use of a calculator **is not permitted**.

2. All variables and expressions used represent real numbers unless otherwise indicated.

3. Figures provided in this test are drawn to scale unless otherwise indicated.

4. All figures lie in a plane unless otherwise indicated.

5. Unless otherwise indicated, the domain of a given function f is the set of all real numbers x for which $f(x)$ is a real number.

REFERENCE

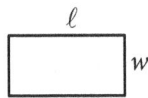
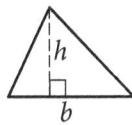
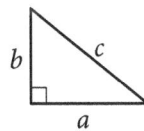
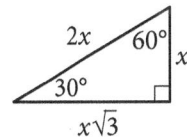
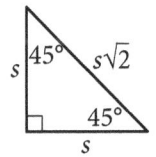

$A = \pi r^2$ $A = \ell w$ $A = \frac{1}{2}bh$ $c^2 = a^2 + b^2$ Special Right Triangles

$C = 2\pi r$

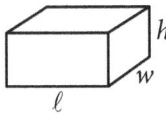

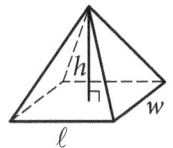

$V = \ell w h$ $V = \pi r^2 h$ $V = \frac{4}{3}\pi r^3$ $V = \frac{1}{3}\pi r^2 h$ $V = \frac{1}{3}\ell w h$

The number of degrees of arc in a circle is 360.

The number of radians of arc in a circle is 2π.

The sum of the measures in degrees of the angles of a triangle is 180.

1

If $5x + 6 = 10$, what is the value of $10x + 3$?

A) 4

B) 9

C) 11

D) 20

2

$$x + y = 0$$
$$3x - 2y = 10$$

Which of the following ordered pairs (x, y) satisfies the system of equations above?

A) $(3, -2)$

B) $(2, -2)$

C) $(-2, 2)$

D) $(-2, -2)$

3

A landscaping company estimates the price of a job, in dollars, using the expression $60 + 12nh$, where n is the number of landscapers who will be working and h is the total number of hours the job will take using n landscapers. Which of the following is the best interpretation of the number 12 in the expression?

A) The company charges $12 per hour for each landscaper.

B) A minimum of 12 landscapers will work on each job.

C) The price of every job increases by $12 every hour.

D) Each landscaper works 12 hours a day.

4

$$9a^4 + 12a^2b^2 + 4b^4$$

Which of the following is equivalent to the expression shown above?

A) $(3a^2 + 2b^2)^2$

B) $(3a + 2b)^4$

C) $(9a^2 + 4b^2)^2$

D) $(9a + 4b)^4$

5

$$\sqrt{2k^2 + 17} - x = 0$$

If $k > 0$ and $x = 7$ in the equation above, what is the value of k ?

A) 2

B) 3

C) 4

D) 5

6

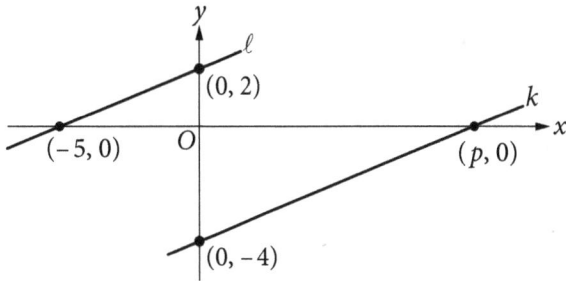

In the xy-plane above, line ℓ is parallel to line k. What is the value of p ?

A) 4

B) 5

C) 8

D) 10

7

If $\dfrac{x^{a^2}}{x^{b^2}} = x^{16}$, $x > 1$, and $a + b = 2$, what is the value of $a - b$?

A) 8

B) 14

C) 16

D) 18

8

$$nA = 360$$

The measure A, in degrees, of an exterior angle of a regular polygon is related to the number of sides, n, of the polygon by the formula above. If the measure of an exterior angle of a regular polygon is greater than $50°$, what is the greatest number of sides it can have?

A) 5

B) 6

C) 7

D) 8

9

The graph of a line in the xy-plane has slope 2 and contains the point $(1, 8)$. The graph of a second line passes through the points $(1, 2)$ and $(2, 1)$. If the two lines intersect at the point (a, b), what is the value of $a + b$?

A) 4

B) 3

C) −1

D) −4

10

Which of the following equations has a graph in the xy-plane for which y is always greater than or equal to −1 ?

A) $y = |x| - 2$

B) $y = x^2 - 2$

C) $y = (x - 2)^2$

D) $y = x^3 - 2$

11

Which of the following complex numbers is equivalent to $\dfrac{3 - 5i}{8 + 2i}$? (Note: $i = \sqrt{-1}$)

A) $\dfrac{3}{8} - \dfrac{5i}{2}$

B) $\dfrac{3}{8} + \dfrac{5i}{2}$

C) $\dfrac{7}{34} - \dfrac{23i}{34}$

D) $\dfrac{7}{34} + \dfrac{23i}{34}$

12

$$R = \frac{F}{N + F}$$

A website uses the formula above to calculate a seller's rating, R, based on the number of favorable reviews, F, and unfavorable reviews, N. Which of the following expresses the number of favorable reviews in terms of the other variables?

A) $F = \dfrac{RN}{R - 1}$

B) $F = \dfrac{RN}{1 - R}$

C) $F = \dfrac{N}{1 - R}$

D) $F = \dfrac{N}{R - 1}$

13

What is the sum of all values of m that satisfy
$2m^2 - 16m + 8 = 0$?

A) -8

B) $-4\sqrt{3}$

C) $4\sqrt{3}$

D) 8

14

A radioactive substance decays at an annual rate of 13 percent. If the initial amount of the substance is 325 grams, which of the following functions f models the remaining amount of the substance, in grams, t years later?

A) $f(t) = 325(0.87)^t$

B) $f(t) = 325(0.13)^t$

C) $f(t) = 0.87(325)^t$

D) $f(t) = 0.13(325)^t$

15

The expression $\dfrac{5x - 2}{x + 3}$ is equivalent to which of the following?

A) $\dfrac{5 - 2}{3}$

B) $5 - \dfrac{2}{3}$

C) $5 - \dfrac{2}{x + 3}$

D) $5 - \dfrac{17}{x + 3}$

DIRECTIONS

For questions 16 – 20, solve the problem and enter your answer in the grid, as described below, on the answer sheet.

1. Although not required, it is suggested that you write your answer in the boxes at the top of the columns to help you fill in the circles accurately. You will receive credit only if the circles are filled in correctly.

2. Mark no more than one circle in any column.

3. No question has a negative answer.

4. Some problems may have more than one correct answer. In such cases, grid only one answer.

5. **Mixed numbers** such as $3\frac{1}{2}$ must be gridded as 3.5 or 7/2. (If $\boxed{3\,1\,/\,2}$ is entered into the grid, it will be interpreted as $\frac{31}{2}$, not $3\frac{1}{2}$.)

6. **Decimal answers:** If you obtain a decimal answer with more digits than the grid can accommodate, it may be either rounded or truncated, but it must fill the entire grid.

Answer: $\frac{7}{12}$

Write answer in boxes. →   ← Fraction line

Grid in result.   ← Decimal point

Answer: 2.5

Acceptable ways to grid $\frac{2}{3}$ are:

2 / 3   .666   .667

Answer: 201 – either position is correct

201   201

NOTE: You may start your answers in any column, space permitting. Columns you don't need to use should be left blank.

16

The sales manager of a company awarded a total of $3000 in bonuses to the most productive salespeople. The bonuses were awarded in amounts of $250 or $750. If at least one $250 bonus and at least one $750 bonus were awarded, what is one possible number of $250 bonuses awarded?

17

$$2x(3x + 5) + 3(3x + 5) = ax^2 + bx + c$$

In the equation above, a, b, and c are constants. If the equation is true for all values of x, what is the value of b ?

18

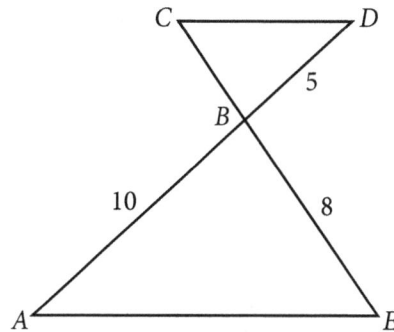

In the figure above, $\overline{AE} \parallel \overline{CD}$ and segment AD intersects segment CE at B. What is the length of segment CE ?

CONTINUE

19

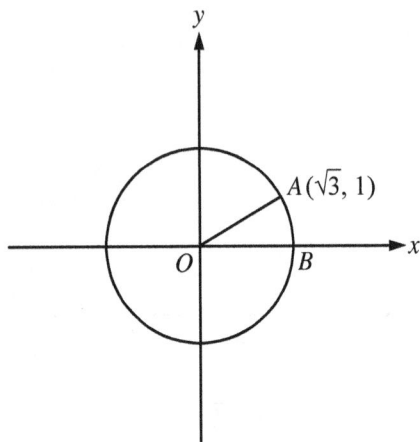

In the *xy*-plane above, O is the center of the circle, and the measure of $\angle AOB$ is $\dfrac{\pi}{a}$ radians. What is the value of a ?

20

$$ax + by = 12$$
$$2x + 8y = 60$$

In the system of equations above, a and b are constants. If the system has infinitely many solutions, what is the value of $\dfrac{a}{b}$?

STOP

If you finish before time is called, you may check your work on this section only.
Do not turn to any other section.

Math Test – Calculator

55 MINUTES, 38 QUESTIONS

Turn to Section 4 of your answer sheet to answer the questions in this section.

DIRECTIONS

For questions 1-30, solve each problem, choose the best answer from the choices provided, and fill in the corresponding circle on your answer sheet. **For questions 31-38,** solve the problem and enter your answer in the grid on the answer sheet. Please refer to the directions before question 31 on how to enter your answers in the grid. You may use any available space in your test booklet for scratch work.

NOTES

1. The use of a calculator **is permitted**.

2. All variables and expressions used represent real numbers unless otherwise indicated.

3. Figures provided in this test are drawn to scale unless otherwise indicated.

4. All figures lie in a plane unless otherwise indicated.

5. Unless otherwise indicated, the domain of a given function f is the set of all real numbers x for which $f(x)$ is a real number.

REFERENCE

$A = \pi r^2$
$C = 2\pi r$

$A = \ell w$

$A = \frac{1}{2}bh$

$c^2 = a^2 + b^2$

Special Right Triangles

$V = \ell wh$

$V = \pi r^2 h$

$V = \frac{4}{3}\pi r^3$

$V = \frac{1}{3}\pi r^2 h$

$V = \frac{1}{3}\ell wh$

The number of degrees of arc in a circle is 360.
The number of radians of arc in a circle is 2π.
The sum of the measures in degrees of the angles of a triangle is 180.

CONTINUE ➤

1

A musician has a new song available for downloading or streaming. The musician earns $0.09 each time the song is downloaded and $0.002 each time the song is streamed. Which of the following expressions represents the amount, in dollars, that the musician earns if the song is downloaded d times and streamed s times?

A) $0.002d + 0.09s$

B) $0.002d - 0.09s$

C) $0.09d + 0.002s$

D) $0.09d - 0.002s$

2

A quality control manager at a factory selects 7 lightbulbs at random for inspection out of every 400 lightbulbs produced. At this rate, how many lightbulbs will be inspected if the factory produces 20,000 lightbulbs?

A) 300

B) 350

C) 400

D) 450

3

$$\ell = 24 + 3.5m$$

One end of a spring is attached to a ceiling. When an object of mass m kilograms is attached to the other end of the spring, the spring stretches to a length of ℓ centimeters as shown in the equation above. What is m when ℓ is 73 ?

A) 14

B) 27.7

C) 73

D) 279.5

Questions 4 and 5 refer to the following information.

The amount of money a performer earns is directly proportional to the number of people attending the performance. The performer earns $120 at a performance where 8 people attend.

4

How much money will the performer earn when 20 people attend a performance?

A) $960

B) $480

C) $300

D) $240

5

The performer uses 43% of the money earned to pay the costs involved in putting on each performance. The rest of the money earned is the performer's profit. What is the profit the performer makes at a performance where 8 people attend?

A) $51.60

B) $57.00

C) $68.40

D) $77.00

6

When 4 times the number x is added to 12, the result is 8. What number results when 2 times x is added to 7 ?

A) -1

B) 5

C) 8

D) 9

7

$$y = x^2 - 6x + 8$$

The equation above represents a parabola in the xy-plane. Which of the following equivalent forms of the equation displays the x-intercepts of the parabola as constants or coefficients?

A) $y - 8 = x^2 - 6x$

B) $y + 1 = (x - 3)^2$

C) $y = x(x - 6) + 8$

D) $y = (x - 2)(x - 4)$

8

In a video game, each player starts the game with k points and loses 2 points each time a task is not completed. If a player who gains no additional points and fails to complete 100 tasks has a score of 200 points, what is the value of k ?

A)   0

B)   150

C)   250

D)   400

9

A worker uses a forklift to move boxes that weigh either 40 pounds or 65 pounds each. Let x be the number of 40-pound boxes and y be the number of 65-pound boxes. The forklift can carry up to either 45 boxes or a weight of 2,400 pounds. Which of the following systems of inequalities represents this relationship?

A) $\begin{cases} 40x + 65y \le 2{,}400 \\ x + y \le 45 \end{cases}$

B) $\begin{cases} \dfrac{x}{40} + \dfrac{y}{65} \le 2{,}400 \\ x + y \le 45 \end{cases}$

C) $\begin{cases} 40x + 65y \le 45 \\ x + y \le 2{,}400 \end{cases}$

D) $\begin{cases} x + y \le 2{,}400 \\ 40x + 65y \le 2{,}400 \end{cases}$

10

A function f satisfies $f(2) = 3$ and $f(3) = 5$. A function g satisfies $g(3) = 2$ and $g(5) = 6$. What is the value of $f(g(3))$?

A)   2

B)   3

C)   5

D)   6

11

Number of hours Tony plans to read the novel per day	3
Number of parts in the novel	8
Number of chapters in the novel	239
Number of words Tony reads per minute	250
Number of pages in the novel	1,078
Number of words in the novel	349,168

Tony is planning to read a novel. The table above shows information about the novel, Tony's reading speed, and the amount of time he plans to spend reading the novel each day. If Tony reads at the rates given in the table, which of the following is closest to the number of days it would take Tony to read the entire novel?

A)   6

B)   8

C)   23

D)   324

CONTINUE →

12

On January 1, 2000, there were 175,000 tons of trash in a landfill that had a capacity of 325,000 tons. Each year since then, the amount of trash in the landfill increased by 7,500 tons. If y represents the time, in years, after January 1, 2000, which of the following inequalities describes the set of years where the landfill is at or above capacity?

A) $325,000 - 7,500 \le y$

B) $325,000 \le 7,500y$

C) $150,000 \ge 7,500y$

D) $175,000 + 7,500y \ge 325,000$

13

A researcher conducted a survey to determine whether people in a certain large town prefer watching sports on television to attending the sporting event. The researcher asked 117 people who visited a local restaurant on a Saturday, and 7 people refused to respond. Which of the following factors makes it least likely that a reliable conclusion can be drawn about the sports-watching preferences of all people in the town?

A) Sample size

B) Population size

C) The number of people who refused to respond

D) Where the survey was given

14

Miles Traveled by Air Passengers in Country X, 1960 to 2005

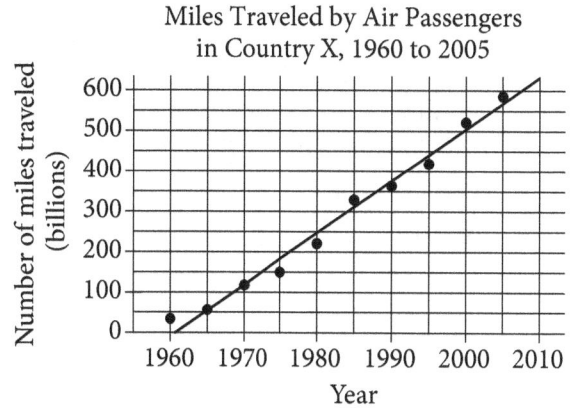

According to the line of best fit in the scatterplot above, which of the following best approximates the year in which the number of miles traveled by air passengers in Country X was estimated to be 550 billion?

A) 1997

B) 2000

C) 2003

D) 2008

15

The distance traveled by Earth in one orbit around the Sun is about 580,000,000 miles. Earth makes one complete orbit around the Sun in one year. Of the following, which is closest to the average speed of Earth, in miles per hour, as it orbits the Sun?

A) 66,000

B) 93,000

C) 210,000

D) 420,000

17

The atomic weight of an unknown element, in atomic mass units (amu), is approximately 20% less than that of calcium. The atomic weight of calcium is 40 amu. Which of the following best approximates the atomic weight, in amu, of the unknown element?

A) 8

B) 20

C) 32

D) 48

16

Results on the Bar Exam of Law School Graduates

	Passed bar exam	Did not pass bar exam
Took review course	18	82
Did not take review course	7	93

The table above summarizes the results of 200 law school graduates who took the bar exam. If one of the surveyed graduates who passed the bar exam is chosen at random for an interview, what is the probability that the person chosen did <u>not</u> take the review course?

A) $\dfrac{18}{25}$

B) $\dfrac{7}{25}$

C) $\dfrac{25}{200}$

D) $\dfrac{7}{200}$

18

A survey was taken of the value of homes in a county, and it was found that the mean home value was $165,000 and the median home value was $125,000. Which of the following situations could explain the difference between the mean and median home values in the county?

A) The homes have values that are close to each other.

B) There are a few homes that are valued much less than the rest.

C) There are a few homes that are valued much more than the rest.

D) Many of the homes have values between $125,000 and $165,000.

CONTINUE

Questions 19 and 20 refer to the following information.

A sociologist chose 300 students at random from each of two schools and asked each student how many siblings he or she has. The results are shown in the table below.

Students' Sibling Survey

Number of siblings	Lincoln School	Washington School
0	120	140
1	80	110
2	60	30
3	30	10
4	10	10

There are a total of 2,400 students at Lincoln School and 3,300 students at Washington School.

19

What is the median number of siblings for all the students surveyed?

A) 0

B) 1

C) 2

D) 3

20

Based on the survey data, which of the following most accurately compares the expected total number of students with 4 siblings at the two schools?

A) The total number of students with 4 siblings is expected to be equal at the two schools.

B) The total number of students with 4 siblings at Lincoln School is expected to be 30 more than at Washington School.

C) The total number of students with 4 siblings at Washington School is expected to be 30 more than at Lincoln School.

D) The total number of students with 4 siblings at Washington School is expected to be 900 more than at Lincoln School.

21

A project manager estimates that a project will take x hours to complete, where $x > 100$. The goal is for the estimate to be within 10 hours of the time it will actually take to complete the project. If the manager meets the goal and it takes y hours to complete the project, which of the following inequalities represents the relationship between the estimated time and the actual completion time?

A) $x + y < 10$

B) $y > x + 10$

C) $y < x - 10$

D) $-10 < y - x < 10$

Questions 22 and 23 refer to the following information.

$$I = \frac{P}{4\pi r^2}$$

At a large distance r from a radio antenna, the intensity of the radio signal I is related to the power of the signal P by the formula above.

22

Which of the following expresses the square of the distance from the radio antenna in terms of the intensity of the radio signal and the power of the signal?

A) $r^2 = \dfrac{IP}{4\pi}$

B) $r^2 = \dfrac{P}{4\pi I}$

C) $r^2 = \dfrac{4\pi I}{P}$

D) $r^2 = \dfrac{I}{4\pi P}$

23

For the same signal emitted by a radio antenna, Observer A measures its intensity to be 16 times the intensity measured by Observer B. The distance of Observer A from the radio antenna is what fraction of the distance of Observer B from the radio antenna?

A) $\dfrac{1}{4}$

B) $\dfrac{1}{16}$

C) $\dfrac{1}{64}$

D) $\dfrac{1}{256}$

▲

24

$$x^2 + y^2 + 4x - 2y = -1$$

The equation of a circle in the xy-plane is shown above. What is the radius of the circle?

A) 2

B) 3

C) 4

D) 9

25

The graph of the linear function f has intercepts at $(a, 0)$ and $(0, b)$ in the xy-plane. If $a + b = 0$ and $a \neq b$, which of the following is true about the slope of the graph of f ?

A) It is positive.

B) It is negative.

C) It equals zero.

D) It is undefined.

26

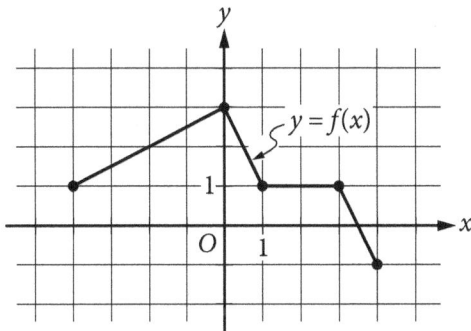

The complete graph of the function f is shown in the xy-plane above. Which of the following are equal to 1 ?

    I. $f(-4)$

    II. $f\left(\dfrac{3}{2}\right)$

    III. $f(3)$

A) III only

B) I and III only

C) II and III only

D) I, II, and III

27

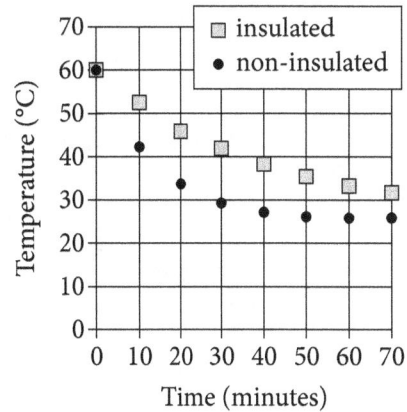

Two samples of water of equal mass are heated to 60 degrees Celsius (°C). One sample is poured into an insulated container, and the other sample is poured into a non-insulated container. The samples are then left for 70 minutes to cool in a room having a temperature of 25°C. The graph above shows the temperature of each sample at 10-minute intervals. Which of the following statements correctly compares the average rates at which the temperatures of the two samples change?

A) In every 10-minute interval, the magnitude of the rate of change of temperature of the insulated sample is greater than that of the non-insulated sample.

B) In every 10-minute interval, the magnitude of the rate of change of temperature of the non-insulated sample is greater than that of the insulated sample.

C) In the intervals from 0 to 10 minutes and from 10 to 20 minutes, the rates of change of temperature of the insulated sample are of greater magnitude, whereas in the intervals from 40 to 50 minutes and from 50 to 60 minutes, the rates of change of temperature of the non-insulated sample are of greater magnitude.

D) In the intervals from 0 to 10 minutes and from 10 to 20 minutes, the rates of change of temperature of the non-insulated sample are of greater magnitude, whereas in the intervals from 40 to 50 minutes and from 50 to 60 minutes, the rates of change of temperature of the insulated sample are of greater magnitude.

CONTINUE

28

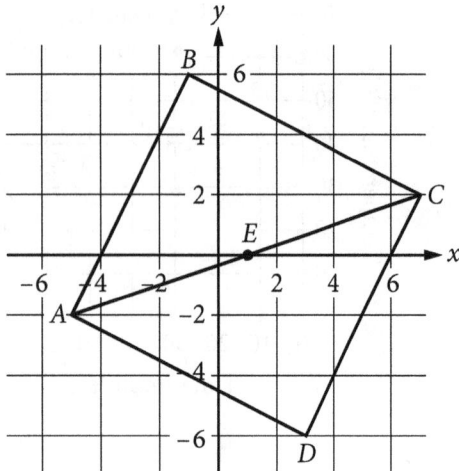

In the *xy*-plane above, *ABCD* is a square and point *E* is the center of the square. The coordinates of points *C* and *E* are $(7, 2)$ and $(1, 0)$, respectively. Which of the following is an equation of the line that passes through points *B* and *D* ?

A) $y = -3x - 1$

B) $y = -3(x - 1)$

C) $y = -\frac{1}{3}x + 4$

D) $y = -\frac{1}{3}x - 1$

29

$$y = 3$$
$$y = ax^2 + b$$

In the system of equations above, *a* and *b* are constants. For which of the following values of *a* and *b* does the system of equations have exactly two real solutions?

A) $a = -2, b = 2$

B) $a = -2, b = 4$

C) $a = 2, b = 4$

D) $a = 4, b = 3$

30

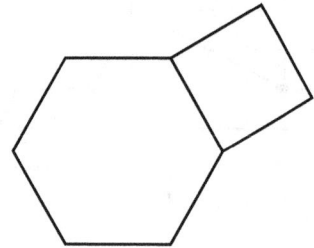

The figure above shows a regular hexagon with sides of length *a* and a square with sides of length *a*. If the area of the hexagon is $384\sqrt{3}$ square inches, what is the area, in square inches, of the square?

A) 256

B) 192

C) $64\sqrt{3}$

D) $16\sqrt{3}$

Unauthorized copying or reuse of any part of this page is illegal.

49

CONTINUE

DIRECTIONS

For questions 31-38, solve the problem and enter your answer in the grid, as described below, on the answer sheet.

1. Although not required, it is suggested that you write your answer in the boxes at the top of the columns to help you fill in the circles accurately. You will receive credit only if the circles are filled in correctly.

2. Mark no more than one circle in any column.

3. No question has a negative answer.

4. Some problems may have more than one correct answer. In such cases, grid only one answer.

5. **Mixed numbers** such as $3\frac{1}{2}$ must be gridded as 3.5 or 7/2. (If $\boxed{3\,|\,1\,|\,/\,|\,2}$ is entered into the grid, it will be interpreted as $\frac{31}{2}$, not $3\frac{1}{2}$.)

6. **Decimal answers:** If you obtain a decimal answer with more digits than the grid can accommodate, it may be either rounded or truncated, but it must fill the entire grid.

Answer: $\frac{7}{12}$ Answer: 2.5

Write answer in boxes. → Fraction line ← ← Decimal point

Grid in result.

Acceptable ways to grid $\frac{2}{3}$ are:

Answer: 201 – either position is correct

NOTE: You may start your answers in any column, space permitting. Columns you don't need to use should be left blank.

31

A coastal geologist estimates that a certain country's beaches are eroding at a rate of 1.5 feet per year. According to the geologist's estimate, how long will it take, in years, for the country's beaches to erode by 21 feet?

32

If h hours and 30 minutes is equal to 450 minutes, what is the value of h ?

33

In the xy-plane, the point $(3, 6)$ lies on the graph of the function $f(x) = 3x^2 - bx + 12$. What is the value of b ?

34

In one semester, Doug and Laura spent a combined 250 hours in the tutoring lab. If Doug spent 40 more hours in the lab than Laura did, how many hours did Laura spend in the lab?

35

$$a = 18t + 15$$

Jane made an initial deposit to a savings account. Each week thereafter she deposited a fixed amount to the account. The equation above models the amount a, in dollars, that Jane has deposited after t weekly deposits. According to the model, how many dollars was Jane's initial deposit? (Disregard the $ sign when gridding your answer.)

36

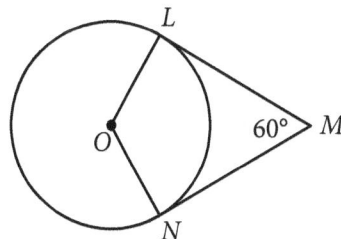

In the figure above, point O is the center of the circle, line segments LM and MN are tangent to the circle at points L and N, respectively, and the segments intersect at point M as shown. If the circumference of the circle is 96, what is the length of minor arc $\overparen{LN}$?

CONTINUE

Questions 37 and 38 refer to the following information.

A botanist is cultivating a rare species of plant in a controlled environment and currently has 3000 of these plants. The population of this species that the botanist expects to grow next year, $N_{\text{next year}}$, can be estimated from the number of plants this year, $N_{\text{this year}}$, by the equation below.

$$N_{\text{next year}} = N_{\text{this year}} + 0.2\left(N_{\text{this year}}\right)\left(1 - \frac{N_{\text{this year}}}{K}\right)$$

The constant K in this formula is the number of plants the environment is able to support.

37

According to the formula, what will be the number of plants two years from now if $K = 4000$? (Round your answer to the nearest whole number.)

38

The botanist would like to increase the number of plants that the environment can support so that the population of the species will increase more rapidly. If the botanist's goal is that the number of plants will increase from 3000 this year to 3360 next year, how many plants must the modified environment support?

STOP

If you finish before time is called, you may check your work on this section only.
Do not turn to any other section.

The SAT

GENERAL DIRECTIONS
- You may work on only one section at a time.
- If you finish a section before time is called, check your work on that section. You may NOT turn to any other section.

MARKING ANSWERS
- Be sure to mark your answer sheet properly.

COMPLETE MARK ●   EXAMPLES OF   Ⓐ Ⓧ ⊕ Ⓒ
                INCOMPLETE MARKS   Ⓐ Ⓑ Ⓒ Ⓓ

- You must use a No. 2 pencil.
- Carefully mark only one answer for each question.
- Make sure you fill the entire circle darkly and completely.
- Do not make any stray marks on your answer sheet.
- If you erase, do so completely. Incomplete erasures may be scored as intended answers.
- Use only the answer spaces that correspond to the question numbers.

USING YOUR TEST BOOK
- You may use the test book for scratch work, but you will not receive credit for anything that you write in your test book.
- After time has been called, you may not transfer answers from your test book to your answer sheet or fill in circles.
- You may not fold or remove pages or portions of a page from this book, or take the book or answer sheet from the testing room.

SCORING
- For each correct answer, you receive one point.
- You do not lose points for wrong answers; therefore, you should try to answer every question even if you are not sure of the correct answer.

IMPORTANT

**The codes below are unique to your test book.
Copy them on your answer sheet in boxes 8 and 9 and fill in the corresponding circles exactly as shown.**

9	TEST ID
	(Copy from back of test book.)

8	FORM CODE
	(Copy and grid as on back of test book.)

Follow this link for more information on scoring your practice test:
www.sat.org/scoring

DO NOT OPEN THIS BOOK UNTIL THE SUPERVISOR TELLS YOU TO DO SO.

SAT® Practice Essay #2

ESSAY BOOK

DIRECTIONS

The essay gives you an opportunity to show how effectively you can read and comprehend a passage and write an essay analyzing the passage. In your essay, you should demonstrate that you have read the passage carefully, present a clear and logical analysis, and use language precisely.

Your essay must be written on the lines provided in your answer booklet; except for the Planning Page of the answer booklet, you will receive no other paper on which to write. You will have enough space if you write on every line, avoid wide margins, and keep your handwriting to a reasonable size. Remember that people who are not familiar with your handwriting will read what you write. Try to write or print so that what you are writing is legible to those readers.

You have <u>50 minutes</u> to read the passage and write an essay in response to the prompt provided inside this booklet.

REMINDERS:

— Do not write your essay in this booklet. Only what you write on the lined pages of your answer booklet will be evaluated.

— An off-topic essay will not be evaluated.

Practice:
Follow this link for more information on scoring your test:
www.sat.org/scoring

This cover is representative of what you'll see on test day.

As you read the passage below, consider how Leo W. Gerard uses

- evidence, such as facts or examples, to support claims.
- reasoning to develop ideas and to connect claims and evidence.
- stylistic or persuasive elements, such as word choice or appeals to emotion, to add power to the ideas expressed.

Adapted from Leo W. Gerard, "Grading Colleges on Access to the American Dream." ©2013 by TheHuffingtonPost.com, Inc. Originally published August 26, 2013.

1   Right now, eager 18-year-olds from across the country are tweeting with bravado photos of their newly postered dorm rooms and scanning with private fear their freshmen class schedules. They're embarking on a journey to capture their piece of the American Dream. . . .

2   To expand access to the dream, President Obama announced . . . that he intends to grade colleges, just as colleges grade students. The U.S. Department of Education will evaluate the affordability of schools based on tuition, scholarships and financial aid. The department will look at outcomes including graduation rates, employment and salaries. Ultimately, Obama would like to reward colleges that earn good grades—those that graduate more students at lower costs. . . . The idea is to restore equal opportunity to attain the American Dream.

3   The parents and grandparents of today's 18-year-olds witnessed diminishing access to the dream. When they were teens, in the 1960s and 1970s, they could buy a year of college with three months' labor in a factory or mill. Also, a summer in a mill with good union wages and benefits persuaded some that this was the life for them, no college necessary.

4   But too many mills are gone now, lost to government's failure to enforce international trade regulations and to the corporate greed that swapped middle class wages for foreign sweatshop pittances. That means to attain the American Dream, even more youngsters now must get higher education or technical training.

5   And now, paying for that additional education is much more difficult. One of those old-time mill jobs—if it were still available—wouldn't cover a year's tuition now. Over the past three decades, the average tuition at a public four-year college increased more than 250 percent. Meanwhile, typical family income rose only 16 percent.

6   Tuition has risen even faster than health insurance costs. If the current trend continues through 2016, the cost of a public college diploma will have more than doubled in just 15 years.

7   Part of the reason for that is dubious expenditures by some schools, including paying coaches and college presidents multi-million dollar salaries and building fancy

dormitories and gymnasiums. But a crucial factor is the withdrawal of state and local support for public institutions—from community colleges and trade schools to state-owned colleges and land grant universities. It dropped 24 percent nationally from 2001 to 2011. Adjusted for inflation, it reached a 25-year low in 2012. . . .

8   The result of these cut backs is that governments shifted costs to the 70 percent of students who attend public colleges and universities as tuition skyrocketed.

9   For many teenagers, this foreclosed a college degree. It was too daunting to borrow tens of thousands of dollars then graduate into a shaky job market. For other young people, it has meant massive borrowing and debt.

10 Just a short time ago in the early 1990s, 45 percent of graduates borrowed money, including from family, banks and the government. Now, the figure is more than 66 percent, and that does not include students who borrow from family. . . .

11 Most student debt is to the federal government, which is now owed $1 trillion. Demos[1] calculates that to be a $4 trillion lifetime wealth loss for those students. That's significant both to them and to the economy. They won't be able to buy as many new cars or refrigerators or infant strollers. So no matter how hard they worked to graduate college and labor on the job, their American Dream is permanently encumbered. In addition, their non-spending impairs the economy. And that diminishes everyone's American Dream.

12 The United States has a long history of accepting education as a public responsibility. Publicly funded colleges and universities gave America teachers, engineers, architects, doctors and lawyers who helped build and care for a strong country. . . . These publicly supported institutions also provided scientists and researchers who discovered cures for dread diseases, put astronauts on the moon and invented the cell phone.

13 America cannot afford to return to the days when only the scions of the wealthiest could attend college. The nation is most prosperous when prosperity is most shared. The administration's plan to grade colleges and encourage resumed state support for public institutions will help restore equal access to the American Dream.

Write an essay in which you explain how Leo W. Gerard builds an argument to persuade his audience that American colleges and universities should be affordable for all students. In your essay, analyze how Gerard uses one or more of the features listed in the box above (or features of your own choice) to strengthen the logic and persuasiveness of his argument. Be sure that your analysis focuses on the most relevant features of the passage.

Your essay should not explain whether you agree with Gerard's claims, but rather explain how Gerard builds an argument to persuade his audience.

Scoring Your
SAT® Practice Test #2

Congratulations on completing an SAT® practice test. To score your test, use these instructions and the conversion tables and answer key at the end of this document.

Scores Overview

The redesigned SAT® will provide more information about your learning by reporting more scores than ever before. Each of the redesigned assessments (SAT, PSAT/NMSQT®, PSAT™ 10, and PSAT™ 8/9) will report test scores and cross-test scores on a common scale. Additionally, subscores will be reported to provide additional diagnostic information to students, educators, and parents.

The practice test you completed was written by the College Board's Assessment Design & Development team using the same processes and review standards used when writing the actual SAT. Everything from the layout of the page to the construction of the questions accurately reflects what you'll see on test day.

How to Calculate Your Practice Test Scores

GET SET UP

❶ You'll need the answer sheet that you bubbled in while taking the practice test. You'll also need the conversion tables and answer key at the end of this document.

❷ Using the answer key, count up your total correct answers for each section. You may want to write the number of correct answers for each section at the bottom of that section in the answer key.

❸ Using your marked-up answer key and the conversion tables, follow the directions to get all of your scores.

GET SECTION AND TOTAL SCORES

Your total score on the SAT practice test is the sum of your Evidence-Based Reading and Writing Section score and your Math Section score. To get your total score, you will convert what we call the "raw score" for each section — the number of questions you got right in that section — into the "scaled score" for that section, then calculate the total score.

GET YOUR EVIDENCE-BASED READING AND WRITING SECTION SCORE

Calculate your SAT Evidence-Based Reading and Writing Section score (it's on a scale of 200–800) by first determining your Reading Test score and your Writing and Language Test score. Here's how:

1. Count the number of correct answers you got on Section 1 (the Reading Test). There is no penalty for wrong answers. The number of correct answers is your raw score.

2. Go to Raw Score Conversion Table 1: Section and Test Scores on page 7. Look in the "Raw Score" column for your raw score, and match it to the number in the "Reading Test Score" column.

3. Do the same with Section 2 to determine your Writing and Language Test score.

4. Add your Reading Test Score to your Writing and Language Test score.

5. Multiply that number by 10. This is your Evidence-Based Reading and Writing Section score.

EXAMPLE: *Micah answered 29 of the 52 questions correctly on the SAT Reading Test and 20 of the 44 questions correctly on the SAT Writing and Language Test. Using the table on page 7, he calculates that he received an SAT Reading Test score of 27 and an SAT Writing and Language Test score of 23. He adds 27 to 23 (gets 50) and then multiplies by 10 to determine his SAT Evidence-Based Reading and Writing Section score of 500.*

GET YOUR MATH SECTION SCORE

Calculate your SAT Math Section score (it's on a scale of 200–800).

1. Count the number of correct answers you got on Section 3 (Math Test — No Calculator) and Section 4 (Math Test — Calculator). There is no penalty for wrong answers.

2. Add the number of correct answers you got on Section 3 (Math Test — No Calculator) and Section 4 (Math Test — Calculator).

3. Use Raw Score Conversion Table 1: Section and Test Scores to turn your raw score into your Math Section score.

GET YOUR TOTAL SCORE

Add your Evidence-Based Reading and Writing Section score to your Math Section score. The result is your total score on the SAT Practice Test, on a scale of 400–1600.

GET SUBSCORES

Subscores provide more detailed information about your strengths in specific areas within literacy and math. They are reported on a scale of 1–15.

HEART OF ALGEBRA

The Heart of Algebra subscore is based on questions from the Math Test that focus on linear equations and inequalities.

1. Add up your total correct answers from the following set of questions:

   ▶ Math Test – No Calculator: Questions 1-3; 6; 8-9; 16; 20

   ▶ Math Test – Calculator: Questions 1; 3; 6; 8-9; 12; 21; 25; 28; 34-35

   Your total correct answers from all of these questions is your raw score.

2. Use Raw Score Conversion Table 2: Subscores on page 8 to determine your Heart of Algebra subscore.

PROBLEM SOLVING AND DATA ANALYSIS

The Problem Solving and Data Analysis subscore is based on questions from the Math Test that focus on quantitative reasoning, the interpretation and synthesis of data, and solving problems in rich and varied contexts.

1. Add up your total correct answers from the following set of questions:

   ▶ Math Test – No Calculator: No Questions

   ▶ Math Test – Calculator: Questions 2; 4-5; 11; 13-20; 27; 31-32; 37-38

   Your total correct answers from all of these questions is your raw score.

2. Use Raw Score Conversion Table 2: Subscores to determine your Problem Solving and Data Analysis subscore.

PASSPORT TO ADVANCED MATH

The Passport to Advanced Math subscore is based on questions from the Math Test that focus on topics central to the ability of students to progress to more advanced mathematics, such as understanding the structure of expressions, reasoning with more complex equations, and interpreting and building functions.

1. Add up your total correct answers from the following set of questions:

   ▶ Math Test – No Calculator: Questions 4-5; 7; 10; 12-15; 17

   ▶ Math Test – Calculator: Questions 7; 10; 22-23; 26; 29; 33

   Your total correct answers from all of these questions is your raw score.

2. Use Raw Score Conversion Table 2: Subscores to determine your Passport to Advanced Math subscore.

EXPRESSION OF IDEAS

The Expression of Ideas subscore is based on questions from the Writing and Language Test that focus on topic development, organization, and rhetorically effective use of language.

① Add up your total correct answers from the following set of questions:

▶ Writing and Language Test: Questions 2; 4; 7; 9-12; 15; 17-19; 22; 24-26; 28; 31-32; 36-37; 40; 42-44

Your total correct answers from all of these questions is your raw score.

② Use Raw Score Conversion Table 2: Subscores to determine your Expression of Ideas subscore.

STANDARD ENGLISH CONVENTIONS

The Standard English Conventions subscore is based on questions from the Writing and Language Test that focus on sentence structure, usage, and punctuation.

① Add up your total correct answers from the following set of questions:

▶ Writing and Language Test: Questions 1; 3; 5-6; 8; 13-14; 16; 20-21; 23; 27; 29-30; 33-35; 38-39; 41

Your total correct answers from all of these questions is your raw score.

② Use Raw Score Conversion Table 2: Subscores to determine your Standard English Conventions subscore.

WORDS IN CONTEXT

The Words in Context subscore is based on questions from both the Reading Test and the Writing and Language Test that address word/phrase meaning in context and rhetorical word choice.

① Add up your total correct answers from the following set of questions:

▶ Reading Test: Questions 4; 8; 16; 25; 28; 34; 37; 39; 44; 47

▶ Writing and Language Test: Questions 7; 10; 18-19; 28; 32; 36; 44

Your total correct answers from all of these questions is your raw score.

② Use Raw Score Conversion Table 2: Subscores to determine your Words in Context subscore.

COMMAND OF EVIDENCE

The Command of Evidence subscore is based on questions from both the Reading Test and the Writing and Language Test that ask you to interpret and use evidence found in a wide range of passages and informational graphics, such as graphs, tables, and charts.

① Add up your total correct answers from the following set of questions:

▶ Reading Test: Questions 10; 13; 20-21; 23; 32; 36; 41; 46; 51

▶ Writing and Language Test: Questions 4; 9; 15; 17; 24; 26; 37; 43

Your total correct answers from all of these questions is your raw score.

② Use Raw Score Conversion Table 2: Subscores to determine your Command of Evidence subscore.

GET CROSS-TEST SCORES

The new SAT also reports two cross-test scores: Analysis in History/Social Studies and Analysis in Science. These scores are based on questions in the Reading, Writing and Language, and Math Tests that ask students to think analytically about texts and questions in these subject areas. Cross-test scores are reported on a scale of 10–40.

ANALYSIS IN HISTORY/SOCIAL STUDIES

① Add up your total correct answers from the following set of questions:

- ▶ Reading Test: Questions 11-21; 33-42
- ▶ Writing and Language Test: Questions 36-37; 40; 42-44
- ▶ Math Test – No Calculator: No Questions
- ▶ Math Test – Calculator: Questions 4-5; 11-13; 16; 18; 35

Your total correct answers from all of these questions is your raw score.

② Use Raw Score Conversion Table 3: Cross-Test Scores on page 9 to determine your Analysis in History/Social Studies cross-test score.

ANALYSIS IN SCIENCE

① Add up your total correct answers from the following set of questions:

- ▶ Reading Test: Questions 22-32; 43-52
- ▶ Writing and Language Test: Questions 24-26; 28; 31-32
- ▶ Math Test – No Calculator: Question 14
- ▶ Math Test – Calculator: Questions: 3; 15; 17; 22-23; 27; 31

Your total correct answers from all of these questions is your raw score.

② Use Raw Score Conversion Table 3: Cross-Test Scores to determine your Analysis in Science cross-test score.

SAT Practice Test #2: Worksheets

ANSWER KEY

Reading Test Answers

1 A	12 D	23 A	34 A	45 D
2 B	13 A	24 B	35 D	46 C
3 C	14 B	25 C	36 B	47 A
4 A	15 C	26 B	37 B	48 B
5 D	16 A	27 D	38 D	49 D
6 B	17 C	28 D	39 C	50 D
7 D	18 C	29 D	40 A	51 D
8 D	19 A	30 B	41 B	52 A
9 B	20 B	31 C	42 D	
10 D	21 C	32 B	43 C	
11 D	22 C	33 B	44 B	

READING TEST
RAW SCORE
(NUMBER OF
CORRECT ANSWERS)

Writing and Language Test Answers

1 B	12 B	23 A	34 D
2 B	13 D	24 B	35 A
3 A	14 C	25 B	36 D
4 A	15 C	26 A	37 A
5 D	16 C	27 D	38 B
6 D	17 B	28 A	39 C
7 B	18 B	29 C	40 D
8 D	19 A	30 C	41 D
9 B	20 D	31 D	42 C
10 B	21 D	32 B	43 C
11 C	22 B	33 D	44 D

WRITING AND
LANGUAGE TEST
RAW SCORE
(NUMBER OF
CORRECT ANSWERS)

Math Test
No Calculator Answers

1 C	11 C
2 B	12 B
3 A	13 D
4 A	14 A
5 C	15 D
6 D	16 3, 6, or 9
7 A	17 19
8 C	18 12
9 B	19 6
10 C	20 1/4 or .25

MATH TEST
NO CALCULATOR
RAW SCORE
(NUMBER OF
CORRECT ANSWERS)

Math Test
Calculator Answers

1 C	11 B	21 D	31 14
2 B	12 D	22 B	32 7
3 A	13 D	23 A	33 11
4 C	14 C	24 A	34 105
5 C	15 A	25 A	35 15
6 B	16 B	26 D	36 32
7 D	17 C	27 D	37 3284
8 D	18 C	28 B	38 7500
9 A	19 B	29 B	
10 B	20 C	30 A	

MATH TEST
CALCULATOR
RAW SCORE
(NUMBER OF
CORRECT ANSWERS)

SAT Practice Test #2: Worksheets

SECTION AND TEST SCORES

Raw Score (# of correct answers)	Math Section Score	Reading Test Score	Writing and Language Test Score	Raw Score (# of correct answers)	Math Section Score	Reading Test Score	Writing and Language Test Score
0	200	10	10	30	550	27	29
1	200	10	10	31	560	28	29
2	210	10	10	32	570	28	30
3	230	11	11	33	570	29	31
4	250	12	12	34	580	29	31
5	270	13	13	35	590	30	32
6	290	14	14	36	600	30	33
7	300	15	14	37	610	31	33
8	320	15	15	38	620	31	34
9	330	16	16	39	630	32	35
10	340	17	17	40	640	32	36
11	360	18	17	41	650	33	37
12	370	18	18	42	650	33	38
13	380	19	18	43	660	34	39
14	390	19	19	44	670	34	40
15	400	20	20	45	680	35	
16	420	20	20	46	690	35	
17	430	21	21	47	690	36	
18	440	21	22	48	700	37	
19	450	22	22	49	710	37	
20	460	22	23	50	720	38	
21	470	23	23	51	730	39	
22	480	23	24	52	740	40	
23	490	24	25	53	750		
24	500	24	25	54	760		
25	510	24	26	55	770		
26	510	25	26	56	780		
27	520	25	27	57	790		
28	530	26	27	58	800		
29	540	27	28				

SECTION AND TEST SCORES

[ ] READING TEST RAW SCORE (0-52) **Convert →** [ ] READING TEST SCORE (10-40)

[ ] WRITING AND LANGUAGE TEST RAW SCORE (0-44) **Convert →** [ ] WRITING AND LANGUAGE TEST SCORE (10-40) **+** [ ] READING TEST SCORE (10-40) **=** [ ] READING AND WRITING TEST SCORE (20-80) **x10 =** [ ] EVIDENCE-BASED READING AND WRITING SECTION SCORE (200-800)

[ ] MATH TEST NO CALCULATOR RAW SCORE (0-20) **+** [ ] MATH TEST CALCULATOR RAW SCORE (0-38) **=** [ ] MATH SECTION RAW SCORE (0-58) **Convert →** [ ] MATH SECTION SCORE (200-800) **+** [ ] EVIDENCE-BASED READING AND WRITING SECTION SCORE (200-800) **=** [ ] TOTAL SAT SCORE (400-1600)

SAT Practice Test #2: Worksheets

RAW SCORE CONVERSION TABLE 2 SUBSCORES

Raw Score (# of correct answers)	Expression of Ideas	Standard English Conventions	Heart of Algebra	Problem Solving and Data Analysis	Passport to Advanced Math	Words in Context	Command of Evidence
0	1	1	1	1	1	1	1
1	1	1	1	1	3	1	1
2	1	1	2	2	5	2	2
3	2	2	3	3	6	3	3
4	3	2	4	4	7	4	4
5	4	3	5	5	8	5	5
6	5	4	6	6	9	6	6
7	6	5	6	7	10	6	7
8	6	6	7	8	11	7	8
9	7	6	8	8	11	8	8
10	7	7	8	9	12	8	9
11	8	7	9	10	12	9	10
12	8	8	9	10	13	9	10
13	9	8	9	11	13	10	11
14	9	9	10	12	14	11	12
15	10	10	10	13	14	12	13
16	10	10	11	14	15	13	14
17	11	11	12	15		14	15
18	11	12	13			15	15
19	12	13	15				
20	12	15					
21	13						
22	14						
23	14						
24	15						

CONVERSION EQUATION 2 SUBSCORES

	Convert →	
HEART OF ALGEBRA RAW SCORE (0-19)		HEART OF ALGEBRA SUBSCORE (1-15)

	Convert →	
EXPRESSION OF IDEAS RAW SCORE (0-24)		EXPRESSION OF IDEAS SUBSCORE (1-15)

	Convert →	
COMMAND OF EVIDENCE RAW SCORE (0-18)		COMMAND OF EVIDENCE SUBSCORE (1-15)

	Convert →	
PROBLEM SOLVING AND DATA ANALYSIS RAW SCORE (0-17)		PROBLEM SOLVING AND DATA ANALYSIS SUBSCORE (1-15)

	Convert →	
STANDARD ENGLISH CONVENTIONS RAW SCORE (0-20)		STANDARD ENGLISH CONVENTIONS SUBSCORE (1-15)

	Convert →	
WORDS IN CONTEXT RAW SCORE (0-18)		WORDS IN CONTEXT SUBSCORE (1-15)

	Convert →	
PASSPORT TO ADVANCED MATH RAW SCORE (0-16)		PASSPORT TO ADVANCED MATH SUBSCORE (1-15)

SAT Practice Test #2: Worksheets

RAW SCORE CONVERSION TABLE 3 — CROSS-TEST SCORES

Raw Score (# of correct answers)	Analysis in History/ Social Studies Cross-Test Score	Analysis in Science Cross-Test Score	Raw Score (# of correct answers)	Analysis in History/ Social Studies Cross-Test Score	Analysis in Science Cross-Test Score
0	10	10	18	26	26
1	10	11	19	26	26
2	10	12	20	27	27
3	12	13	21	28	28
4	13	14	22	29	29
5	15	15	23	29	29
6	16	16	24	30	30
7	16	17	25	31	31
8	17	18	26	31	31
9	18	19	27	32	32
10	19	19	28	33	33
11	20	20	29	34	34
12	21	21	30	35	34
13	22	22	31	36	35
14	23	22	32	37	36
15	24	23	33	38	37
16	24	24	34	39	38
17	25	25	35	40	40

CONVERSION EQUATION 3 — CROSS-TEST SCORES

Test	Analysis in History/Social Studies		Analysis in Science	
	Questions	Raw Score	Questions	Raw Score
Reading Test	11-21; 33-42		22-32; 43-52	
Writing and Language Test	36-37; 40; 42-44		24-26; 28; 31-32	
Math Test No Calculator	None		3	
Math Test Calculator	4-5; 11-13; 16; 18; 35		15; 17; 22-23; 27; 31	
Total				

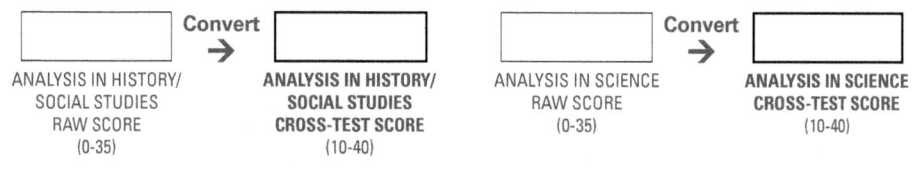

	Convert →			Convert →	
ANALYSIS IN HISTORY/ SOCIAL STUDIES RAW SCORE (0-35)		**ANALYSIS IN HISTORY/ SOCIAL STUDIES CROSS-TEST SCORE (10-40)**	ANALYSIS IN SCIENCE RAW SCORE (0-35)		**ANALYSIS IN SCIENCE CROSS-TEST SCORE (10-40)**

SAT® Practice Test #3

TEST TAKING TIP #3

Learn the Directions for the Sections: The directions for each section of the exam do not change from test to test (unless there is a major update). Knowing the directions for each section will allow you to skip reading them come test day. This will save you valuable time that can be used to answer questions.

Reading Test

65 MINUTES, 52 QUESTIONS

Turn to Section 1 of your answer sheet to answer the questions in this section.

DIRECTIONS

Each passage or pair of passages below is followed by a number of questions. After reading each passage or pair, choose the best answer to each question based on what is stated or implied in the passage or passages and in any accompanying graphics (such as a table or graph).

Questions 1-10 are based on the following passage.

This passage is adapted from Saki, "The Schartz-Metterklume Method." Originally published in 1911.

Lady Carlotta stepped out on to the platform of the small wayside station and took a turn or two up and down its uninteresting length, to kill time till the
Line train should be pleased to proceed on its way. Then,
5 in the roadway beyond, she saw a horse struggling with a more than ample load, and a carter of the sort that seems to bear a sullen hatred against the animal that helps him to earn a living. Lady Carlotta promptly betook her to the roadway, and put rather a
10 different complexion on the struggle. Certain of her acquaintances were wont to give her plentiful admonition as to the undesirability of interfering on behalf of a distressed animal, such interference being "none of her business." Only once had she put the
15 doctrine of non-interference into practice, when one of its most eloquent exponents had been besieged for nearly three hours in a small and extremely uncomfortable may-tree by an angry boar-pig, while Lady Carlotta, on the other side of the fence, had
20 proceeded with the water-colour sketch she was engaged on, and refused to interfere between the boar and his prisoner. It is to be feared that she lost the friendship of the ultimately rescued lady. On this occasion she merely lost the train, which gave way to
25 the first sign of impatience it had shown throughout the journey, and steamed off without her. She bore the desertion with philosophical indifference; her

friends and relations were thoroughly well used to the fact of her luggage arriving without her.
30 She wired a vague non-committal message to her destination to say that she was coming on "by another train." Before she had time to think what her next move might be she was confronted by an imposingly attired lady, who seemed to be taking a
35 prolonged mental inventory of her clothes and looks.
"You must be Miss Hope, the governess I've come to meet," said the apparition, in a tone that admitted of very little argument.
"Very well, if I must I must," said Lady Carlotta to
40 herself with dangerous meekness.
"I am Mrs. Quabarl," continued the lady; "and where, pray, is your luggage?"
"It's gone astray," said the alleged governess, falling in with the excellent rule of life that the absent
45 are always to blame; the luggage had, in point of fact, behaved with perfect correctitude. "I've just telegraphed about it," she added, with a nearer approach to truth.
"How provoking," said Mrs. Quabarl; "these
50 railway companies are so careless. However, my maid can lend you things for the night," and she led the way to her car.
During the drive to the Quabarl mansion Lady Carlotta was impressively introduced to the
55 nature of the charge that had been thrust upon her; she learned that Claude and Wilfrid were delicate, sensitive young people, that Irene had the artistic temperament highly developed, and that Viola was

Unauthorized copying or reuse of any part of this page is illegal.

2

CONTINUE →

something or other else of a mould equally
60 commonplace among children of that class and type
in the twentieth century.

"I wish them not only to be TAUGHT," said Mrs.
Quabarl, "but INTERESTED in what they learn. In
their history lessons, for instance, you must try to
65 make them feel that they are being introduced to the
life-stories of men and women who really lived, not
merely committing a mass of names and dates to
memory. French, of course, I shall expect you to talk
at meal-times several days in the week."

70 "I shall talk French four days of the week and
Russian in the remaining three."

"Russian? My dear Miss Hope, no one in the
house speaks or understands Russian."

"That will not embarrass me in the least," said
75 Lady Carlotta coldly.

Mrs. Quabarl, to use a colloquial expression, was
knocked off her perch. She was one of those
imperfectly self-assured individuals who are
magnificent and autocratic as long as they are not
80 seriously opposed. The least show of unexpected
resistance goes a long way towards rendering them
cowed and apologetic. When the new governess
failed to express wondering admiration of the large
newly-purchased and expensive car, and lightly
85 alluded to the superior advantages of one or two
makes which had just been put on the market, the
discomfiture of her patroness became almost abject.
Her feelings were those which might have animated a
general of ancient warfaring days, on beholding his
90 heaviest battle-elephant ignominiously driven off the
field by slingers and javelin throwers.

1

Which choice best summarizes the passage?

A) A woman weighs the positive and negative
   aspects of accepting a new job.

B) A woman does not correct a stranger who
   mistakes her for someone else.

C) A woman impersonates someone else to seek
   revenge on an acquaintance.

D) A woman takes an immediate dislike to her new
   employer.

2

In line 2, "turn" most nearly means

A) slight movement.

B) change in rotation.

C) short walk.

D) course correction.

3

The passage most clearly implies that other people
regarded Lady Carlotta as

A) outspoken.

B) tactful.

C) ambitious.

D) unfriendly.

4

Which choice provides the best evidence for the
answer to the previous question?

A) Lines 10-14 ("Certain . . . business")

B) Lines 22-23 ("It is . . . lady")

C) Lines 23-26 ("On this . . . her")

D) Lines 30-32 ("She . . . train")

CONTINUE

5

The description of how Lady Carlotta "put the doctrine of non-interference into practice" (lines 14-15) mainly serves to

A) foreshadow her capacity for deception.

B) illustrate the subtle cruelty in her nature.

C) provide a humorous insight into her character.

D) explain a surprising change in her behavior.

6

In line 55, "charge" most nearly means

A) responsibility.

B) attack.

C) fee.

D) expense.

7

The narrator indicates that Claude, Wilfrid, Irene, and Viola are

A) similar to many of their peers.

B) unusually creative and intelligent.

C) hostile to the idea of a governess.

D) more educated than others of their age.

8

The narrator implies that Mrs. Quabarl favors a form of education that emphasizes

A) traditional values.

B) active engagement.

C) artistic experimentation.

D) factual retention.

9

As presented in the passage, Mrs. Quabarl is best described as

A) superficially kind but actually selfish.

B) outwardly imposing but easily defied.

C) socially successful but irrationally bitter.

D) naturally generous but frequently imprudent.

10

Which choice provides the best evidence for the answer to the previous question?

A) Lines 49-50 ("How . . . careless")

B) Lines 62-68 ("I wish . . . memory")

C) Lines 70-73 ("I shall . . . Russian")

D) Lines 77-82 ("She was . . . apologetic")

Questions 11-20 are based on the following passage and supplementary material.

This passage is adapted from Taras Grescoe, *Straphanger: Saving Our Cities and Ourselves from the Automobile.* ©2012 by Taras Grescoe.

Though there are 600 million cars on the planet, and counting, there are also seven billion people, which means that for the vast majority of us getting
Line around involves taking buses, ferryboats, commuter
5 trains, streetcars, and subways. In other words, traveling to work, school, or the market means being a straphanger: somebody who, by choice or necessity, relies on public transport, rather than a privately owned automobile.
10 Half the population of New York, Toronto, and London do not own cars. Public transport is how most of the people of Asia and Africa, the world's most populous continents, travel. Every day, subway systems carry 155 million passengers, thirty-four
15 times the number carried by all the world's airplanes, and the global public transport market is now valued at $428 billion annually. A century and a half after the invention of the internal combustion engine, private car ownership is still an anomaly.
20 And yet public transportation, in many minds, is the opposite of glamour—a squalid last resort for those with one too many impaired driving charges, too poor to afford insurance, or too decrepit to get behind the wheel of a car. In much of North
25 America, they are right: taking transit is a depressing experience. Anybody who has waited far too long on a street corner for the privilege of boarding a lurching, overcrowded bus, or wrestled luggage onto subways and shuttles to get to a big city airport,
30 knows that transit on this continent tends to be underfunded, ill-maintained, and ill-planned. Given the opportunity, who wouldn't drive? Hopping in a car almost always gets you to your destination more quickly.
35 It doesn't have to be like this. Done right, public transport can be faster, more comfortable, and cheaper than the private automobile. In Shanghai, German-made magnetic levitation trains skim over elevated tracks at 266 miles an hour, whisking people
40 to the airport at a third of the speed of sound. In provincial French towns, electric-powered streetcars run silently on rubber tires, sliding through narrow streets along a single guide rail set into cobblestones. From Spain to Sweden, Wi-Fi equipped high-speed
45 trains seamlessly connect with highly ramified metro networks, allowing commuters to work on laptops as they prepare for same-day meetings in once distant capital cities. In Latin America, China, and India, working people board fast-loading buses that move
50 like subway trains along dedicated busways, leaving the sedans and SUVs of the rich mired in dawn-to-dusk traffic jams. And some cities have transformed their streets into cycle-path freeways, making giant strides in public health and safety and
55 the sheer livability of their neighborhoods—in the process turning the workaday bicycle into a viable form of mass transit.
If you credit the demographers, this transit trend has legs. The "Millenials," who reached adulthood
60 around the turn of the century and now outnumber baby boomers, tend to favor cities over suburbs, and are far more willing than their parents to ride buses and subways. Part of the reason is their ease with iPads, MP3 players, Kindles, and smartphones: you
65 can get some serious texting done when you're not driving, and earbuds offer effective insulation from all but the most extreme commuting annoyances. Even though there are more teenagers in the country than ever, only ten million have a driver's license
70 (versus twelve million a generation ago). Baby boomers may have been raised in Leave It to Beaver suburbs, but as they retire, a significant contingent is favoring older cities and compact towns where they have the option of walking and riding bikes. Seniors,
75 too, are more likely to use transit, and by 2025, there will be 64 million Americans over the age of sixty-five. Already, dwellings in older neighborhoods in Washington, D.C., Atlanta, and Denver, especially those near light-rail or subway stations, are
80 commanding enormous price premiums over suburban homes. The experience of European and Asian cities shows that if you make buses, subways, and trains convenient, comfortable, fast, and safe, a surprisingly large percentage of citizens will opt to
85 ride rather than drive.

Figure 1

Primary Occupation of Public
Transportation Passengers
in US Cities

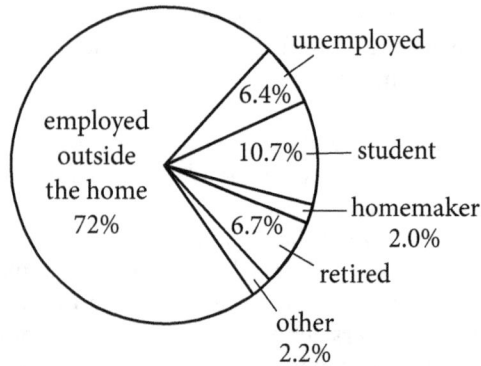

Figure 2

Purpose of Public Transportation
Trips in US Cities

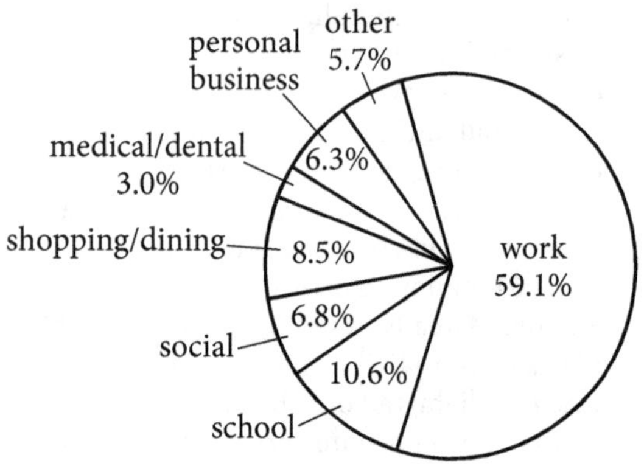

Figure 1 and figure 2 are adapted from the American Public
Transportation Association, "A Profile of Public Transportation
Passenger Demographics and Travel Characteristics Reported in
On-Board Surveys." ©2007 by American Public Transportation
Association.

11

What function does the third paragraph (lines 20-34)
serve in the passage as a whole?

A) It acknowledges that a practice favored by the
author of the passage has some limitations.

B) It illustrates with detail the arguments made in
the first two paragraphs of the passage.

C) It gives an overview of a problem that has not
been sufficiently addressed by the experts
mentioned in the passage.

D) It advocates for abandoning a practice for which
the passage as a whole provides mostly
favorable data.

12

Which choice does the author explicitly cite as
an advantage of automobile travel in North America?

A) Environmental impact

B) Convenience

C) Speed

D) Cost

13

Which choice provides the best evidence for the
answer to the previous question?

A) Lines 5-9 ("In . . . automobile")

B) Lines 20-24 ("And . . . car")

C) Lines 24-26 ("In . . . experience")

D) Lines 32-34 ("Hopping . . . quickly")

14

The central idea of the fourth paragraph (lines 35-57) is that

A) European countries excel at public transportation.

B) some public transportation systems are superior to travel by private automobile.

C) Americans should mimic foreign public transportation systems when possible.

D) much international public transportation is engineered for passengers to work while on board.

15

Which choice provides the best evidence for the answer to the previous question?

A) Line 35 ("It . . . this")

B) Lines 35-37 ("Done . . . automobile")

C) Lines 37-40 ("In . . . sound")

D) Lines 44-48 ("From . . . cities")

16

As used in line 58, "credit" most nearly means

A) endow.

B) attribute.

C) believe.

D) honor.

17

As used in line 61, "favor" most nearly means

A) indulge.

B) prefer.

C) resemble.

D) serve.

18

Which choice best supports the conclusion that public transportation is compatible with the use of personal electronic devices?

A) Lines 59-63 ("The . . . subways")

B) Lines 63-67 ("Part . . . annoyances")

C) Lines 68-70 ("Even . . . ago")

D) Lines 77-81 ("Already . . . homes")

19

Which choice is supported by the data in the first figure?

A) The number of students using public transportation is greater than the number of retirees using public transportation.

B) The number of employed people using public transportation and the number of unemployed people using public transportation is roughly the same.

C) People employed outside the home are less likely to use public transportation than are homemakers.

D) Unemployed people use public transportation less often than do people employed outside the home.

20

Taken together, the two figures suggest that most people who use public transportation

A) are employed outside the home and take public transportation to work.

B) are employed outside the home but take public transportation primarily in order to run errands.

C) use public transportation during the week but use their private cars on weekends.

D) use public transportation only until they are able to afford to buy a car.

Questions 21-30 are based on the following passage.

This passage is adapted from Thor Hanson, *Feathers*. ©2011 by Thor Hanson. Scientists have long debated how the ancestors of birds evolved the ability to fly. The ground-up theory assumes they were fleet-footed ground dwellers that captured prey by leaping and flapping their upper limbs. The tree-down theory assumes they were tree climbers that leapt and glided among branches.

At field sites around the world, Ken Dial saw a
pattern in how young pheasants, quail, tinamous,
and other ground birds ran along behind their
Line parents. "They jumped up like popcorn," he said,
5 describing how they would flap their half-formed
wings and take short hops into the air. So when a
group of graduate students challenged him
to come up with new data on the age-old
ground-up-tree-down debate, he designed a project
10 to see what clues might lie in how baby game birds
learned to fly.

Ken settled on the Chukar Partridge as a
model species, but he might not have made his
discovery without a key piece of advice from the local
15 rancher in Montana who was supplying him with
birds. When the cowboy stopped by to see how
things were going, Ken showed him his nice, tidy
laboratory setup and explained how the birds' first
hops and flights would be measured. The rancher
20 was incredulous. "He took one look and said, in
pretty colorful language, 'What are those birds doing
on the ground? They hate to be on the ground! Give
them something to climb on!' " At first it seemed
unnatural—ground birds don't like the ground? But
25 as he thought about it Ken realized that all the
species he'd watched in the wild preferred to rest on
ledges, low branches, or other elevated perches where
they were safe from predators. They really only used
the ground for feeding and traveling. So he brought
30 in some hay bales for the Chukars to perch on and
then left his son in charge of feeding and data
collection while he went away on a short work trip.

Barely a teenager at the time, young Terry Dial
was visibly upset when his father got back. "I asked
35 him how it went," Ken recalled, "and he said,

'Terrible! The birds are cheating!' " Instead of flying
up to their perches, the baby Chukars were using
their legs. Time and again Terry had watched them
run right up the side of a hay bale, flapping all the
40 while. Ken dashed out to see for himself, and that
was the "aha" moment. "The birds were using their
wings and legs cooperatively," he told me, and that
single observation opened up a world of possibilities.

Working together with Terry (who has since gone
45 on to study animal locomotion), Ken came up with a
series of ingenious experiments, filming the birds as
they raced up textured ramps tilted at increasing
angles. As the incline increased, the partridges began
to flap, but they angled their wings differently from
50 birds in flight. They aimed their flapping down and
backward, using the force not for lift but to keep
their feet firmly pressed against the ramp. "It's like
the spoiler on the back of a race car," he explained,
which is a very apt analogy. In Formula One racing,
55 spoilers are the big aerodynamic fins that push the
cars downward as they speed along, increasing
traction and handling. The birds were doing the very
same thing with their wings to help them scramble
up otherwise impossible slopes.
60 Ken called the technique WAIR, for wing-assisted
incline running, and went on to document it in a
wide range of species. It not only allowed young
birds to climb vertical surfaces within the first few
weeks of life but also gave adults an energy-efficient
65 alternative to flying. In the Chukar experiments,
adults regularly used WAIR to ascend ramps steeper
than 90 degrees, essentially running up the wall and
onto the ceiling.

In an evolutionary context, WAIR takes on
70 surprising explanatory powers. With one fell swoop,
the Dials came up with a viable origin for the
flapping flight stroke of birds (something gliding
animals don't do and thus a shortcoming of the
tree-down theory) and an aerodynamic function for
75 half-formed wings (one of the main drawbacks to the
ground-up hypothesis).

21

Which choice best reflects the overall sequence of events in the passage?

A) An experiment is proposed but proves unworkable; a less ambitious experiment is attempted, and it yields data that give rise to a new set of questions.

B) A new discovery leads to reconsideration of a theory; a classic study is adapted, and the results are summarized.

C) An anomaly is observed and simulated experimentally; the results are compared with previous findings, and a novel hypothesis is proposed.

D) An unexpected finding arises during the early phase of a study; the study is modified in response to this finding, and the results are interpreted and evaluated.

22

As used in line 7, "challenged" most nearly means

A) dared.

B) required.

C) disputed with.

D) competed with.

23

Which statement best captures Ken Dial's central assumption in setting up his research?

A) The acquisition of flight in young birds sheds light on the acquisition of flight in their evolutionary ancestors.

B) The tendency of certain young birds to jump erratically is a somewhat recent evolved behavior.

C) Young birds in a controlled research setting are less likely than birds in the wild to require perches when at rest.

D) Ground-dwelling and tree-climbing predecessors to birds evolved in parallel.

24

Which choice provides the best evidence for the answer to the previous question?

A) Lines 1-4 ("At field . . . parents")

B) Lines 6-11 ("So when . . . fly")

C) Lines 16-19 ("When . . . measured")

D) Lines 23-24 ("At first . . . the ground")

25

In the second paragraph (lines 12-32), the incident involving the local rancher mainly serves to

A) reveal Ken Dial's motivation for undertaking his project.

B) underscore certain differences between laboratory and field research.

C) show how an unanticipated piece of information influenced Ken Dial's research.

D) introduce a key contributor to the tree-down theory.

26

After Ken Dial had his "'aha' moment" (line 41), he

A) tried to train the birds to fly to their perches.

B) studied videos to determine why the birds no longer hopped.

C) observed how the birds dealt with gradually steeper inclines.

D) consulted with other researchers who had studied Chukar Partridges.

27

The passage identifies which of the following as a factor that facilitated the baby Chukars' traction on steep ramps?

A) The speed with which they climbed

B) The position of their flapping wings

C) The alternation of wing and foot movement

D) Their continual hopping motions

28

As used in line 61, "document" most nearly means

A) portray.

B) record.

C) publish.

D) process.

29

What can reasonably be inferred about gliding animals from the passage?

A) Their young tend to hop along beside their parents instead of flying beside them.

B) Their method of locomotion is similar to that of ground birds.

C) They use the ground for feeding more often than for perching.

D) They do not use a flapping stroke to aid in climbing slopes.

30

Which choice provides the best evidence for the answer to the previous question?

A) Lines 4-6 ("They jumped . . . air")

B) Lines 28-29 ("They really . . . traveling")

C) Lines 57-59 ("The birds . . . slopes")

D) Lines 72-74 ("something . . . theory")

Questions 31-41 are based on the following passages.

Passage 1 is adapted from Talleyrand et al., *Report on Public Instruction*. Originally published in 1791. Passage 2 is adapted from Mary Wollstonecraft, *A Vindication of the Rights of Woman*. Originally published in 1792. Talleyrand was a French diplomat; the *Report* was a plan for national education. Wollstonecraft, a British novelist and political writer, wrote *Vindication* in response to Talleyrand.

Passage 1

That half the human race is excluded by the other half from any participation in government; that they are native by birth but foreign by law in the very land
Line where they were born; and that they are
5 property-owners yet have no direct influence or representation: are all political phenomena apparently impossible to explain on abstract principle. But on another level of ideas, the question changes and may be easily resolved. The purpose of
10 all these institutions must be the happiness of the greatest number. Everything that leads us farther from this purpose is in error; everything that brings us closer is truth. If the exclusion from public employments decreed against women leads to a
15 greater sum of mutual happiness for the two sexes, then this becomes a law that all Societies have been compelled to acknowledge and sanction.

Any other ambition would be a reversal of our primary destinies; and it will never be in women's
20 interest to change the assignment they have received.

It seems to us incontestable that our common happiness, above all that of women, requires that they never aspire to the exercise of political rights and functions. Here we must seek their interests in
25 the wishes of nature. Is it not apparent, that their delicate constitutions, their peaceful inclinations, and the many duties of motherhood, set them apart from strenuous habits and onerous duties, and summon them to gentle occupations and the cares of the
30 home? And is it not evident that the great conserving principle of Societies, which makes the division of powers a source of harmony, has been expressed and revealed by nature itself, when it divided the functions of the two sexes in so obviously distinct a
35 manner? This is sufficient; we need not invoke principles that are inapplicable to the question. Let us not make rivals of life's companions. You must, you truly must allow the persistence of a union that no interest, no rivalry, can possibly undo. Understand
40 that the good of all demands this of you.

Passage 2

Contending for the rights of woman, my main
argument is built on this simple principle, that if she
be not prepared by education to become the
companion of man, she will stop the progress of
45 knowledge and virtue; for truth must be common to
all, or it will be inefficacious with respect to its
influence on general practice. And how can woman
be expected to co-operate unless she know why she
ought to be virtuous? unless freedom strengthen her
50 reason till she comprehend her duty, and see in what
manner it is connected with her real good? If
children are to be educated to understand the true
principle of patriotism, their mother must be a
patriot; and the love of mankind, from which an
55 orderly train of virtues spring, can only be produced
by considering the moral and civil interest of
mankind; but the education and situation of woman,
at present, shuts her out from such investigations. . . .

Consider, sir, dispassionately, these
60 observations—for a glimpse of this truth seemed to
open before you when you observed, "that to see one
half of the human race excluded by the other from all
participation of government, was a political
phenomenon that, according to abstract principles, it
65 was impossible to explain." If so, on what does your
constitution rest? If the abstract rights of man will
bear discussion and explanation, those of woman, by
a parity of reasoning, will not shrink from the same
test: though a different opinion prevails in this
70 country, built on the very arguments which you use
to justify the oppression of woman—prescription.

Consider—I address you as a legislator—
whether, when men contend for their freedom, and
to be allowed to judge for themselves respecting their
75 own happiness, it be not inconsistent and unjust to
subjugate women, even though you firmly believe
that you are acting in the manner best calculated to
promote their happiness? Who made man the
exclusive judge, if woman partake with him the gift
80 of reason?

In this style, argue tyrants of every
denomination, from the weak king to the weak
father of a family; they are all eager to crush reason;
yet always assert that they usurp its throne only to be
85 useful. Do you not act a similar part, when you force
all women, by denying them civil and political rights,
to remain immured in their families groping in
the dark?

31

As used in line 21, "common" most nearly means

A) average.

B) shared.

C) coarse.

D) similar.

32

It can be inferred that the authors of Passage 1
believe that running a household and raising
children

A) are rewarding for men as well as for women.

B) yield less value for society than do the roles
performed by men.

C) entail very few activities that are difficult or
unpleasant.

D) require skills similar to those needed to run a
country or a business.

33

Which choice provides the best evidence for the
answer to the previous question?

A) Lines 4-6 ("they are . . . representation")

B) Lines 13-17 ("If the . . . sanction")

C) Lines 25-30 ("Is it . . . home")

D) Lines 30-35 ("And . . . manner")

34

According to the author of Passage 2, in order for
society to progress, women must

A) enjoy personal happiness and financial security.

B) follow all currently prescribed social rules.

C) replace men as figures of power and authority.

D) receive an education comparable to that of men.

35

As used in line 50, "reason" most nearly means

A) motive.

B) sanity.

C) intellect.

D) explanation.

36

In Passage 2, the author claims that freedoms granted by society's leaders have

A) privileged one gender over the other.

B) resulted in a general reduction in individual virtue.

C) caused arguments about the nature of happiness.

D) ensured equality for all people.

37

Which choice provides the best evidence for the answer to the previous question?

A) Lines 41-45 ("Contending . . . virtue")

B) Lines 45-47 ("truth . . . practice")

C) Lines 65-66 ("If so . . . rest")

D) Lines 72-75 ("Consider . . . happiness")

38

In lines 61-65, the author of Passage 2 refers to a statement made in Passage 1 in order to

A) call into question the qualifications of the authors of Passage 1 regarding gender issues.

B) dispute the assertion made about women in the first sentence of Passage 1.

C) develop her argument by highlighting what she sees as flawed reasoning in Passage 1.

D) validate the concluding declarations made by the authors of Passage 1 about gender roles.

39

Which best describes the overall relationship between Passage 1 and Passage 2?

A) Passage 2 strongly challenges the point of view in Passage 1.

B) Passage 2 draws alternative conclusions from the evidence presented in Passage 1.

C) Passage 2 elaborates on the proposal presented in Passage 1.

D) Passage 2 restates in different terms the argument presented in Passage 1.

40

The authors of both passages would most likely agree with which of the following statements about women in the eighteenth century?

A) Their natural preferences were the same as those of men.

B) They needed a good education to be successful in society.

C) They were just as happy in life as men were.

D) They generally enjoyed fewer rights than men did.

41

How would the authors of Passage 1 most likely respond to the points made in the final paragraph of Passage 2?

A) Women are not naturally suited for the exercise of civil and political rights.

B) Men and women possess similar degrees of reasoning ability.

C) Women do not need to remain confined to their traditional family duties.

D) The principles of natural law should not be invoked when considering gender roles.

Questions 42-52 are based on the following passage and supplementary material.

This passage is adapted from Richard J. Sharpe and Lisa Heyden, "Honey Bee Colony Collapse Disorder is Possibly Caused by a Dietary Pyrethrum Deficiency." ©2009 by Elsevier Ltd. Colony collapse disorder is characterized by the disappearance of adult worker bees from hives.

Honey bees are hosts to the pathogenic large ectoparasitic mite *Varroa destructor* (Varroa mites). These mites feed on bee hemolymph (blood) and can
Line kill bees directly or by increasing their susceptibility
5 to secondary infection with fungi, bacteria or viruses. Little is known about the natural defenses that keep the mite infections under control.

Pyrethrums are a group of flowering plants which include *Chrysanthemum coccineum, Chrysanthemum*
10 *cinerariifolium, Chrysanthemum marschalli,* and related species. These plants produce potent insecticides with anti-mite activity. The naturally occurring insecticides are known as pyrethrums. A synonym for the naturally occurring pyrethrums is
15 pyrethrin and synthetic analogues of pyrethrums are known as pyrethroids. In fact, the human mite infestation known as scabies (*Sarcoptes scabiei*) is treated with a topical pyrethrum cream.

We suspect that the bees of commercial bee
20 colonies which are fed mono-crops are nutritionally deficient. In particular, we postulate that the problem is a diet deficient in anti-mite toxins: pyrethrums, and possibly other nutrients which are inherent in such plants. Without, at least, intermittent feeding on
25 the pyrethrum producing plants, bee colonies are susceptible to mite infestations which can become fatal either directly or due to a secondary infection of immunocompromised or nutritionally deficient bees. This secondary infection can be viral, bacterial or
30 fungal and may be due to one or more pathogens. In addition, immunocompromised or nutritionally deficient bees may be further weakened when commercially produced insecticides are introduced into their hives by bee keepers in an effort to fight
35 mite infestation. We further postulate that the proper dosage necessary to prevent mite infestation may be better left to the bees, who may seek out or avoid pyrethrum containing plants depending on the amount necessary to defend against mites and the
40 amount already consumed by the bees, which in higher doses could be potentially toxic to them.

This hypothesis can best be tested by a trial wherein a small number of commercial honey bee colonies are offered a number of pyrethrum
45 producing plants, as well as a typical bee food source such as clover, while controls are offered only the clover. Mites could then be introduced to each hive with note made as to the choice of the bees, and the effects of the mite parasites on the experimental
50 colonies versus control colonies.

It might be beneficial to test wild-type honey bee colonies in this manner as well, in case there could be some genetic difference between them that affects the bees' preferences for pyrethrum producing flowers.

Pathogen Occurence in Honey Bee Colonies With and Without Colony Collapse Disorder

Pathogen	Percent of colonies affected by pathogen	
	Colonies with colony collapse disorder (%)	Colonies without colony collapse disorder (%)
Viruses		
IAPV	83	5
KBV	100	76
Fungi		
Nosema apis	90	48
Nosema ceranae	100	81
All four pathogens	77	0

Adapted from Diana L. Cox-Foster et al., "A Metagenomic Survey of Microbes in Honey Bee Colony Collapse Disorder." ©2007 by American Association for the Advancement of Science.

The table above shows, for colonies with colony collapse disorder and for colonies without colony collapse disorder, the percent of colonies having honey bees infected by each of four pathogens and by all four pathogens together.

42

How do the words "can," "may," and "could" in the third paragraph (lines 19-41) help establish the tone of the paragraph?

A) They create an optimistic tone that makes clear the authors are hopeful about the effects of their research on colony collapse disorder.

B) They create a dubious tone that makes clear the authors do not have confidence in the usefulness of the research described.

C) They create a tentative tone that makes clear the authors suspect but do not know that their hypothesis is correct.

D) They create a critical tone that makes clear the authors are skeptical of claims that pyrethrums are inherent in mono-crops.

43

In line 42, the authors state that a certain hypothesis "can best be tested by a trial." Based on the passage, which of the following is a hypothesis the authors suggest be tested in a trial?

A) Honeybees that are exposed to both pyrethrums and mites are likely to develop a secondary infection by a virus, a bacterium, or a fungus.

B) Beekeepers who feed their honeybee colonies a diet of a single crop need to increase the use of insecticides to prevent mite infestations.

C) A honeybee diet that includes pyrethrums results in honeybee colonies that are more resistant to mite infestations.

D) Humans are more susceptible to varroa mites as a result of consuming nutritionally deficient food crops.

44

Which choice provides the best evidence for the answer to the previous question?

A) Lines 3-5 ("These mites . . . viruses")

B) Lines 16-18 ("In fact . . . cream")

C) Lines 19-21 ("We suspect . . . deficient")

D) Lines 24-28 ("Without . . . bees")

45

The passage most strongly suggests that beekeepers' attempts to fight mite infestations with commercially produced insecticides have what unintentional effect?

A) They increase certain mite populations.

B) They kill some beneficial forms of bacteria.

C) They destroy bees' primary food source.

D) They further harm the health of some bees.

46

Which choice provides the best evidence for the answer to the previous question?

A) Lines 1-2 ("Honey bees . . . mites")

B) Lines 6-7 ("Little . . . control")

C) Lines 31-35 ("In addition . . . infestation")

D) Lines 47-50 ("Mites . . . control colonies")

47

As used in line 35, "postulate" most nearly means to

A) make an unfounded assumption.

B) put forth an idea or claim.

C) question a belief or theory.

D) conclude based on firm evidence.

48

The main purpose of the fourth paragraph (lines 42-50) is to

A) summarize the results of an experiment that confirmed the authors' hypothesis about the role of clover in the diets of wild-type honeybees.

B) propose an experiment to investigate how different diets affect commercial honeybee colonies' susceptibility to mite infestations.

C) provide a comparative nutritional analysis of the honey produced by the experimental colonies and by the control colonies.

D) predict the most likely outcome of an unfinished experiment summarized in the third paragraph (lines 19-41).

49

An unstated assumption made by the authors about clover is that the plants

A) do not produce pyrethrums.

B) are members of the *Chrysanthemum* genus.

C) are usually located near wild-type honeybee colonies.

D) will not be a good food source for honeybees in the control colonies.

50

Based on data in the table, in what percent of colonies with colony collapse disorder were the honeybees infected by all four pathogens?

A)   0 percent

B)   77 percent

C)   83 percent

D) 100 percent

51

Based on data in the table, which of the four pathogens infected the highest percentage of honeybee colonies without colony collapse disorder?

A) IAPV

B) KBV

C) *Nosema apis*

D) *Nosema ceranae*

52

Do the data in the table provide support for the authors' claim that infection with varroa mites increases a honeybee's susceptibility to secondary infections?

A) Yes, because the data provide evidence that infection with a pathogen caused the colonies to undergo colony collapse disorder.

B) Yes, because for each pathogen, the percent of colonies infected is greater for colonies with colony collapse disorder than for colonies without colony collapse disorder.

C) No, because the data do not provide evidence about bacteria as a cause of colony collapse disorder.

D) No, because the data do not indicate whether the honeybees had been infected with mites.

STOP

If you finish before time is called, you may check your work on this section only.
Do not turn to any other section.

Writing and Language Test

35 MINUTES, 44 QUESTIONS

Turn to Section 2 of your answer sheet to answer the questions in this section.

DIRECTIONS

Each passage below is accompanied by a number of questions. For some questions, you will consider how the passage might be revised to improve the expression of ideas. For other questions, you will consider how the passage might be edited to correct errors in sentence structure, usage, or punctuation. A passage or a question may be accompanied by one or more graphics (such as a table or graph) that you will consider as you make revising and editing decisions.

Some questions will direct you to an underlined portion of a passage. Other questions will direct you to a location in a passage or ask you to think about the passage as a whole.

After reading each passage, choose the answer to each question that most effectively improves the quality of writing in the passage or that makes the passage conform to the conventions of standard written English. Many questions include a "NO CHANGE" option. Choose that option if you think the best choice is to leave the relevant portion of the passage as it is.

Questions 1-11 are based on the following passage.

Shed Some Light on the Workplace

Studies have shown that employees are happier, **1** healthier, and more productive when they work in an environment **2** in which temperatures are carefully controlled. New buildings may be designed with these studies in mind, but many older buildings were not, resulting in spaces that often depend primarily on artificial lighting. While employers may balk at the expense of reconfiguring such buildings to increase the amount of natural light, the investment has been shown to be well worth it in the long run—for both employees and employers.

1
A) NO CHANGE
B) healthy, and more
C) healthier, and they are
D) healthier, being more

2
Which choice provides the most appropriate introduction to the passage?
A) NO CHANGE
B) that affords them adequate amounts of natural light.
C) that is thoroughly sealed to prevent energy loss.
D) in which they feel comfortable asking managers for special accommodations.

For one thing, lack of exposure to natural light has a significant impact on employees' health. A study conducted in 2013 by Northwestern University in Chicago showed that inadequate natural light could result in eye strain, headaches, and fatigue, as well as interference with the body's circadian rhythms. [3] Circadian rhythms, which are controlled by the [4] bodies biological clocks, influence body temperature, hormone release, cycles of sleep and wakefulness, and other bodily functions. Disruptions of circadian rhythms have been linked to sleep disorders, diabetes, depression, and bipolar disorder. Like any other health problems, these ailments can increase employee absenteeism, which, in turn, [5] is costly for employers. Employees who feel less than 100 percent and are sleep deprived are also less prone to work at their maximal productivity. One company in California [6] gained a huge boost in its employees' morale when it moved from an artificially lit distribution facility to one with natural illumination.

---

[3]

At this point, the writer is considering adding the following sentence.

> Workers in offices with windows sleep an average of 46 minutes more per night than workers in offices without windows.

Should the writer make this addition here?

A) Yes, because it supplies quantitative data that will be examined in the rest of the paragraph.

B) Yes, because it explains the nature of the bodily functions referred to in the next sentence.

C) No, because it interrupts the discussion of circadian rhythms.

D) No, because it does not take into account whether workers were exposed to sunlight outside the office.

---

[4]

A) NO CHANGE

B) bodies' biological clocks',

C) body's biological clocks,

D) body's biological clock's,

---

[5]

A) NO CHANGE

B) are

C) is being

D) have been

---

[6]

Which choice best supports the statement made in the previous sentence?

A) NO CHANGE

B) saw a 5 percent increase in productivity

C) saved a great deal on its operational costs

D) invested large amounts of time and capital

[7] Artificial light sources are also costly aside from lowering worker productivity. They typically constitute anywhere from 25 to 50 percent of a building's energy use. When a plant in Seattle, Washington, was redesigned for more natural light, the company was able to enjoy annual electricity cost reductions of $500,000 [8] each year.

[7]

In context, which choice best combines the underlined sentences?

A) Aside from lowering worker productivity, artificial light sources are also costly, typically constituting anywhere from 25 to 50 percent of a building's energy use.

B) The cost of artificial light sources, aside from lowering worker productivity, typically constitutes anywhere from 25 to 50 percent of a building's energy use.

C) Typically constituting 25 to 50 percent of a building's energy use, artificial light sources lower worker productivity and are costly.

D) Artificial lights, which lower worker productivity and are costly, typically constitute anywhere from 25 to 50 percent of a building's energy use.

[8]

A) NO CHANGE

B) every year.

C) per year.

D) DELETE the underlined portion and end the sentence with a period.

Among the possibilities to reconfigure a building's lighting is the installation of full-pane windows to allow the greatest degree of sunlight to reach office interiors. [9] Thus, businesses can install light tubes, [10] these are pipes placed in workplace roofs to capture and funnel sunlight down into a building's interior. Glass walls and dividers can also be used to replace solid walls as a means [11] through distributing natural light more freely. Considering the enormous costs of artificial lighting, both in terms of money and productivity, investment in such improvements should be a natural choice for businesses.

9

A) NO CHANGE
B) Nevertheless,
C) Alternatively,
D) Finally,

10

A) NO CHANGE
B) they are
C) which are
D) those being

11

A) NO CHANGE
B) of
C) from
D) DELETE the underlined portion.

Questions 12-22 are based on the following passage.

Transforming the American West Through Food and Hospitality

Just as travelers taking road trips today may need to take a break for food at a rest area along the highway, settlers traversing the American West by train in the mid-1800s often found **12** themselves in need of refreshment. However, food available on rail lines was generally of terrible quality. **13** Despite having worked for railroad companies, Fred Harvey, an English-born **14** entrepreneur. He decided to open his own restaurant business to serve rail customers. Beginning in the 1870s, he opened dozens of restaurants in rail stations and dining cars. These Harvey Houses, which constituted the first restaurant chain in the United States, **15** was unique for its high standards of service and quality. The menu was modeled after those of fine restaurants, so the food was leagues beyond the **16** sinister fare travelers were accustomed to receiving in transit.

12
A) NO CHANGE
B) himself or herself
C) their selves
D) oneself

13
Which choice provides the most logical introduction to the sentence?
A) NO CHANGE
B) He had lived in New York and New Orleans, so
C) To capitalize on the demand for good food,
D) DELETE the underlined portion.

14
A) NO CHANGE
B) entrepreneur:
C) entrepreneur; he
D) entrepreneur,

15
A) NO CHANGE
B) were unique for their
C) was unique for their
D) were unique for its

16
Which choice best maintains the tone established in the passage?
A) NO CHANGE
B) surly
C) abysmal
D) icky

His restaurants were immediately successful, but Harvey was not content to follow conventional business practices. **17** Although women did not traditionally work in restaurants in the nineteenth century, Harvey decided to try employing women as waitstaff. In 1883, he placed an advertisement seeking educated, well-mannered, articulate young women between the ages of 18 and 30. **18** Response to the advertisement was overwhelming, even tremendous, and Harvey soon replaced the male servers at his restaurants with women. Those who were hired as "Harvey Girls" joined an elite group of workers, who were expected to complete a 30-day training program and follow a strict code of rules for conduct and curfews. In the workplace, the women donned identical black-and-white uniforms and carried out their duties with precision. Not only were such regulations meant to ensure the efficiency of the business and the safety of the workers, **19** but also helped to raise people's generally low opinion of the restaurant industry.

17

The writer is considering deleting the previous sentence. Should the writer make this change?

A) Yes, because it introduces information that is irrelevant at this point in the passage.

B) Yes, because it does not logically follow from the previous paragraph.

C) No, because it provides a logical introduction to the paragraph.

D) No, because it provides a specific example in support of arguments made elsewhere in the passage.

18

A) NO CHANGE

B) Response to the advertisement was overwhelming,

C) Overwhelming, even tremendous, was the response to the advertisement,

D) There was an overwhelming, even tremendous, response to the advertisement,

19

A) NO CHANGE

B) but also helping

C) also helping

D) but they also helped

In return for the servers' work, the position paid quite well for the time: $17.50 a month, plus tips, meals, room and board, laundry service, and travel expenses. 20

For as long as Harvey Houses served rail travelers through the mid-twentieth century, working there was a steady and lucrative position for women. Living independently and demonstrating an intense work 21 ethic; the Harvey Girls became known as a transformative force in the American 22 West. Advancing the roles of women in the restaurant industry and the American workforce as a whole, the Harvey Girls raised the standards for restaurants and blazed a trail in the fast-changing landscape of the western territories.

20

Which choice most logically follows the previous sentence?

A) The growth of Harvey's business coincided with the expansion of the Santa Fe Railway, which served large sections of the American West.

B) Harvey would end up opening dozens of restaurants and dining cars, plus 15 hotels, over his lucrative career.

C) These benefits enabled the Harvey Girls to save money and build new and exciting lives for themselves in the so-called Wild West.

D) The compensation was considered excellent at the time, though it may not seem like much money by today's standards.

21

A) NO CHANGE

B) ethic:

C) ethic, and

D) ethic,

22

The writer is considering revising the underlined portion of the sentence to read:

> West, inspiring books, documentaries, and even a musical.

Should the writer add this information here?

A) Yes, because it provides examples of the Harvey Girls' influence.

B) Yes, because it serves as a transitional point in the paragraph.

C) No, because it should be placed earlier in the passage.

D) No, because it contradicts the main claim of the passage.

 CONTINUE

Questions 23-33 are based on the following passage and supplementary material.

How Do You Like Those Apples?

Marketed as SmartFresh, the chemical 1-MCP (1-methylcyclopropene) has been used by fruit growers since 2002 in the United States and elsewhere to preserve the crispness and lengthen the storage life of apples and other fruit, which often must travel long distances before being eaten by consumers. **23** 1-MCP lengthens storage life by three to four times when applied to apples. This extended life allows producers to sell their apples in the off-season, months after the apples have been harvested. And at a cost of about one cent per pound of apples, 1-MCP is a highly cost-effective treatment. However, 1-MCP is not a panacea for fruit producers or sellers: there are problems and limitations associated with its use.

23

Which choice most effectively combines the underlined sentences?

A) When applied to apples, 1-MCP lengthens storage life by three to four times, allowing producers to sell their apples in the off-season, months after the apples have been harvested.

B) Producers are allowed to sell their apples months after they have been harvested—in the off-season—because 1-MCP, when applied to apples, lengthens their storage life by three to four times.

C) 1-MCP lengthens storage life, when applied to apples, by three to four times, allowing producers to sell their apples months after the apples have been harvested in the off-season.

D) Months after apples have been harvested, producers are allowed to sell their apples, in the off-season, because 1-MCP lengthens storage life when applied to apples by three to four times.

[1] 1-MCP works by limiting a fruit's production of ethylene, 24 it is a chemical that causes fruit to ripen and eventually rot. [2] While 1-MCP keeps apples 25 tight and crisp for months, it also limits 26 their scent production. [3] This may not be much of a problem with certain kinds of apples that are not naturally very fragrant, such as Granny Smith, but for apples that are prized for their fruity fragrance, such as McIntosh, this can be a problem with consumers, 27 that will reject apples lacking the expected aroma. [4] But some fruits do not respond as well to 1-MCP as others 28 did, and some even respond adversely. [5] Furthermore, some fruits, particularly those that naturally produce a large

24

A) NO CHANGE
B) being
C) that is
D) DELETE the underlined portion.

25

A) NO CHANGE
B) firm
C) stiff
D) taut

26

A) NO CHANGE
B) there
C) its
D) it's

27

A) NO CHANGE
B) they
C) which
D) who

28

A) NO CHANGE
B) do,
C) have,
D) will,

amount of ethylene, do not respond as well to 1-MCP treatment. [6] Take Bartlett 29 pears, for instance, unless they are treated with exactly the right amount of 1-MCP at exactly the right time, they will remain hard and green until they rot, and consumers who experience this will be unlikely to purchase them again. 30

29

A) NO CHANGE
B) pears, for instance:
C) pears for instance,
D) pears. For instance,

30

To make this paragraph most logical, sentence 4 should be placed

A) where it is now.
B) after sentence 1.
C) after sentence 2.
D) after sentence 5.

Finally, researchers have found that 1-MCP actually increases susceptibility to some pathologies in certain apple varieties. For example, Empire apples are prone to a condition that causes the flesh of the apple to turn brown. Traditionally, apple producers have dealt with this problem by leaving the apples in the open air for three weeks before storing them in a controlled atmosphere with tightly regulated temperature, humidity, and carbon dioxide levels. As the graph shows, the flesh of untreated Empire apples that are first stored in the open air undergoes [31] roughly five percent less browning than the flesh of untreated Empire apples that are immediately put into storage in a controlled environment. However, when Empire apples are treated with 1-MCP, [32] their flesh turns brown when the apples are first stored in the open air, though not under other conditions. Although

31

Which choice offers an accurate interpretation of the data in the graph?

A) NO CHANGE

B) slightly more browning than

C) twice as much browning as

D) substantially less browning than

32

Which choice offers an accurate interpretation of the data in the graph?

A) NO CHANGE

B) roughly half of their flesh turns brown, regardless of whether the apples are first stored in the open air.

C) their flesh browns when they are put directly into a controlled atmosphere but not when they are first stored in the open air.

D) their flesh turns brown when they are first stored in the open air, though not as quickly as the apple flesh in an untreated group does.

researchers continue to search for the right combination of factors that will keep fruits fresh and attractive, [33] the problem may be that consumers are overly concerned with superficial qualities rather than the actual freshness of the fruit.

Results of Treatment to Control Browning of Empire Apples

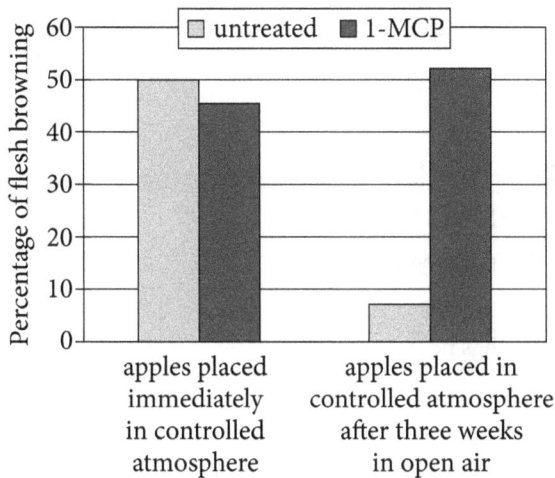

Adapted from Hannah J. James, Jacqueline F. Nock, and Chris B. Watkins, "The Failure of Postharvest Treatments to Control Firm Flesh Browning in Empire Apples." ©2010 by The New York State Horticultural Society.

[33]

The writer wants a conclusion that conveys how the shortcomings of 1-MCP presented in the passage affect the actions of people in the fruit industry. Which choice best accomplishes this goal?

A) NO CHANGE

B) many of the improvements to fruit quality they have discovered so far have required trade-offs in other properties of the fruit.

C) for now many fruit sellers must weigh the relative values of aroma, color, and freshness when deciding whether to use 1-MCP.

D) it must be acknowledged that 1-MCP, despite some inadequacies, has enabled the fruit industry to ship and store fruit in ways that were impossible before.

Questions 34-44 are based on the following passage.

More than One Way to Dress a Cat

From Michelangelo's *David* to Vincent van Gogh's series of self-portraits to Grant Wood's iconic image of a farming couple in *American* [34] *Gothic. These works* by human artists have favored representations of members of their own species to those of other species. Indeed, when we think about animals depicted in well-known works of art, the image of dogs playing poker—popularized in a series of paintings by American artist C. M. [35] Coolidge, may be the first and only one that comes to mind. Yet some of the earliest known works of art, including paintings and drawings tens of thousands of years old found on cave walls in Spain and France, [36] portrays animals. Nor has artistic homage to our fellow creatures entirely died out in the millennia since, [37] despite the many years that have passed between then and now.

34

A) NO CHANGE
B) *Gothic.* Works
C) *Gothic;* these works
D) *Gothic,* works

35

A) NO CHANGE
B) Coolidge—
C) Coolidge;
D) Coolidge

36

A) NO CHANGE
B) portraying
C) portray
D) has portrayed

37

The writer wants to link the first paragraph with the ideas that follow. Which choice best accomplishes this goal?

A) NO CHANGE
B) with special attention being paid to domestic animals such as cats.
C) even though most paintings in museums are of people, not animals.
D) as the example of one museum in Russia shows.

[1] The State Hermitage Museum in St. Petersburg, one of Russia's greatest art museums, has long had a productive partnership with a much loved animal: the cat. [2] For centuries, cats have guarded this famous museum, ridding it of mice, rats, and other rodents that could damage the art, not to mention 38 scared off visitors. [3] Peter the Great introduced the first cat to the Hermitage in the early eighteenth century. [4] Later Catherine the Great declared the cats to be official guardians of the galleries. [5] Continuing the tradition, Peter's daughter Elizaveta introduced the best and strongest cats in Russia to the Hermitage. [6] Today, the museum holds a yearly festival honoring these faithful workers. 39

38
A) NO CHANGE
B) scaring
C) scare
D) have scared

39
To make this paragraph most logical, sentence 5 should be placed
A) where it is now.
B) after sentence 1.
C) after sentence 3.
D) after sentence 6.

These cats are so cherished by the museum that officials recently **40** decreed original paintings to be made of six of them. In each, a cat is depicted upright in a humanlike pose and clothed in imperial-era Russian attire. The person chosen for this **41** task, digital artist, Eldar Zakirov painted the cats in the style traditionally used by portrait artists, in so doing **42** presenting the cats as noble individuals worthy of respect. One portrait, *The Hermitage Court Chamber Herald Cat*, includes an

40

A) NO CHANGE
B) commissioned
C) forced
D) licensed

41

A) NO CHANGE
B) task, digital artist, Eldar Zakirov,
C) task digital artist Eldar Zakirov,
D) task, digital artist Eldar Zakirov,

42

Which choice most effectively sets up the examples that follow?

A) NO CHANGE
B) managing to capture unique characteristics of each cat.
C) commenting on the absurdity of dressing up cats in royal robes.
D) indicating that the cats were very talented mouse catchers.

aristocratic tilt of feline ears as well as a stately sweep of tail emerging from the stiff scarlet and gold of royal court dress. The wise, thoughtful green eyes of the subject of *The Hermitage Court Outrunner Cat* mimic those of a trusted royal advisor. **43** Some may find it peculiar to observe cats portrayed in formal court poses, but these felines, by **44** mastering the art of killing mice and rats, are benefactors of the museum as important as any human.

43

At this point, the writer is considering adding the following sentence.

> The museum occupies six historic buildings, including the Winter Palace, a former residence of Russian emperors.

Should the writer make this addition here?

A) Yes, because it shows the link between Peter the Great and the cat paintings.

B) Yes, because it helps explain why Russian art celebrates animals.

C) No, because it fails to indicate why the Winter Palace became an art museum.

D) No, because it provides background information that is irrelevant to the paragraph.

44

A) NO CHANGE

B) acting as the lead predator in the museum's ecosystem,

C) hunting down and killing all the mice and rats one by one,

D) protecting the museum's priceless artworks from destructive rodents,

STOP

If you finish before time is called, you may check your work on this section only.
Do not turn to any other section.

Math Test – No Calculator

25 MINUTES, 20 QUESTIONS

Turn to Section 3 of your answer sheet to answer the questions in this section.

DIRECTIONS

For questions 1-15, solve each problem, choose the best answer from the choices provided, and fill in the corresponding circle on your answer sheet. **For questions 16-20**, solve the problem and enter your answer in the grid on the answer sheet. Please refer to the directions before question 16 on how to enter your answers in the grid. You may use any available space in your test booklet for scratch work.

NOTES

1. The use of a calculator **is not permitted**.

2. All variables and expressions used represent real numbers unless otherwise indicated.

3. Figures provided in this test are drawn to scale unless otherwise indicated.

4. All figures lie in a plane unless otherwise indicated.

5. Unless otherwise indicated, the domain of a given function f is the set of all real numbers x for which $f(x)$ is a real number.

REFERENCE

$A = \pi r^2$
$C = 2\pi r$

$A = \ell w$

$A = \frac{1}{2}bh$

$c^2 = a^2 + b^2$

Special Right Triangles

$V = \ell w h$

$V = \pi r^2 h$

$V = \frac{4}{3}\pi r^3$

$V = \frac{1}{3}\pi r^2 h$

$V = \frac{1}{3}\ell w h$

The number of degrees of arc in a circle is 360.
The number of radians of arc in a circle is 2π.
The sum of the measures in degrees of the angles of a triangle is 180.

CONTINUE ➡

1

A painter will paint n walls with the same size and shape in a building using a specific brand of paint. The painter's fee can be calculated by the expression $nK\ell h$, where n is the number of walls, K is a constant with units of dollars per square foot, ℓ is the length of each wall in feet, and h is the height of each wall in feet. If the customer asks the painter to use a more expensive brand of paint, which of the factors in the expression would change?

A) h

B) ℓ

C) K

D) n

2

If $3r = 18$, what is the value of $6r + 3$?

A)　6

B)　27

C)　36

D)　39

3

Which of the following is equal to $a^{\frac{2}{3}}$, for all values of a ?

A) $\sqrt{a^{\frac{1}{3}}}$

B) $\sqrt{a^3}$

C) $\sqrt[3]{a^{\frac{1}{2}}}$

D) $\sqrt[3]{a^2}$

4

The number of states that joined the United States between 1776 and 1849 is twice the number of states that joined between 1850 and 1900. If 30 states joined the United States between 1776 and 1849 and x states joined between 1850 and 1900, which of the following equations is true?

A) $30x = 2$

B) $2x = 30$

C) $\dfrac{x}{2} = 30$

D) $x + 30 = 2$

5

If $\dfrac{5}{x} = \dfrac{15}{x+20}$, what is the value of $\dfrac{x}{5}$?

A) 10

B) 5

C) 2

D) $\dfrac{1}{2}$

6

$$2x - 3y = -14$$
$$3x - 2y = -6$$

If (x, y) is a solution to the system of equations above, what is the value of $x - y$?

A) −20

B) −8

C) −4

D) 8

7

x	$f(x)$
0	3
2	1
4	0
5	−2

The function f is defined by a polynomial. Some values of x and $f(x)$ are shown in the table above. Which of the following must be a factor of $f(x)$?

A) $x - 2$

B) $x - 3$

C) $x - 4$

D) $x - 5$

8

The line $y = kx + 4$, where k is a constant, is graphed in the xy-plane. If the line contains the point (c, d), where $c \neq 0$ and $d \neq 0$, what is the slope of the line in terms of c and d ?

A) $\dfrac{d - 4}{c}$

B) $\dfrac{c - 4}{d}$

C) $\dfrac{4 - d}{c}$

D) $\dfrac{4 - c}{d}$

CONTINUE

9

$$kx - 3y = 4$$

$$4x - 5y = 7$$

In the system of equations above, k is a constant and x and y are variables. For what value of k will the system of equations have no solution?

A) $\dfrac{12}{5}$

B) $\dfrac{16}{7}$

C) $-\dfrac{16}{7}$

D) $-\dfrac{12}{5}$

10

In the xy-plane, the parabola with equation $y = (x - 11)^2$ intersects the line with equation $y = 25$ at two points, A and B. What is the length of $\overline{AB}$?

A) 10

B) 12

C) 14

D) 16

11

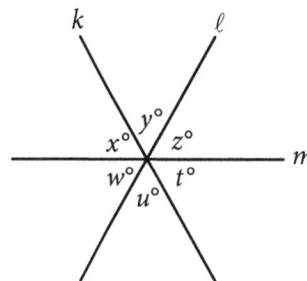

Note: Figure not drawn to scale.

In the figure above, lines k, ℓ, and m intersect at a point. If $x + y = u + w$, which of the following must be true?

I. $x = z$

II. $y = w$

III. $z = t$

A) I and II only

B) I and III only

C) II and III only

D) I, II, and III

12

$$y = a(x - 2)(x + 4)$$

In the quadratic equation above, a is a nonzero constant. The graph of the equation in the xy-plane is a parabola with vertex (c, d). Which of the following is equal to d ?

A) $-9a$

B) $-8a$

C) $-5a$

D) $-2a$

Unauthorized copying or reuse of any part of this page is illegal.

35

CONTINUE ▶

13

The equation $\dfrac{24x^2 + 25x - 47}{ax - 2} = -8x - 3 - \dfrac{53}{ax - 2}$ is

true for all values of $x \neq \dfrac{2}{a}$, where a is a constant.

What is the value of a ?

A) -16

B) -3

C) 3

D) 16

14

What are the solutions to $3x^2 + 12x + 6 = 0$?

A) $x = -2 \pm \sqrt{2}$

B) $x = -2 \pm \dfrac{\sqrt{30}}{3}$

C) $x = -6 \pm \sqrt{2}$

D) $x = -6 \pm 6\sqrt{2}$

15

$$C = \frac{5}{9}(F - 32)$$

The equation above shows how a temperature F, measured in degrees Fahrenheit, relates to a temperature C, measured in degrees Celsius. Based on the equation, which of the following must be true?

   I. A temperature increase of 1 degree Fahrenheit is equivalent to a temperature increase of $\dfrac{5}{9}$ degree Celsius.

  II. A temperature increase of 1 degree Celsius is equivalent to a temperature increase of 1.8 degrees Fahrenheit.

 III. A temperature increase of $\dfrac{5}{9}$ degree Fahrenheit is equivalent to a temperature increase of 1 degree Celsius.

A) I only

B) II only

C) III only

D) I and II only

CONTINUE

DIRECTIONS

For questions 16–20, solve the problem and enter your answer in the grid, as described below, on the answer sheet.

1. Although not required, it is suggested that you write your answer in the boxes at the top of the columns to help you fill in the circles accurately. You will receive credit only if the circles are filled in correctly.
2. Mark no more than one circle in any column.
3. No question has a negative answer.
4. Some problems may have more than one correct answer. In such cases, grid only one answer.
5. **Mixed numbers** such as $3\frac{1}{2}$ must be gridded as 3.5 or 7/2. (If 3 1 / 2 is entered into the grid, it will be interpreted as $\frac{31}{2}$, not $3\frac{1}{2}$.)
6. **Decimal answers:** If you obtain a decimal answer with more digits than the grid can accommodate, it may be either rounded or truncated, but it must fill the entire grid.

Answer: $\frac{7}{12}$

Write answer in boxes. ← Fraction line

Grid in result.

Answer: 2.5

← Decimal point

Acceptable ways to grid $\frac{2}{3}$ are:

Answer: 201 – either position is correct

NOTE: You may start your answers in any column, space permitting. Columns you don't need to use should be left blank.

16

$$x^3(x^2 - 5) = -4x$$

If $x > 0$, what is one possible solution to the equation above?

17

If $\dfrac{7}{9}x - \dfrac{4}{9}x = \dfrac{1}{4} + \dfrac{5}{12}$, what is the value of x ?

18

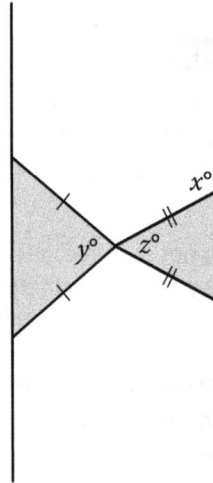

Note: Figure not drawn to scale.

Two isosceles triangles are shown above. If $180 - z = 2y$ and $y = 75$, what is the value of x ?

19

At a lunch stand, each hamburger has 50 more calories than each order of fries. If 2 hamburgers and 3 orders of fries have a total of 1700 calories, how many calories does a hamburger have?

20

In triangle ABC, the measure of $\angle B$ is $90°$, $BC = 16$, and $AC = 20$. Triangle DEF is similar to triangle ABC, where vertices D, E, and F correspond to vertices A, B, and C, respectively, and each side of triangle DEF is $\frac{1}{3}$ the length of the corresponding side of triangle ABC. What is the value of $\sin F$?

STOP

If you finish before time is called, you may check your work on this section only.
Do not turn to any other section.

Unauthorized copying or reuse of any part of this page is illegal.

39

Math Test – Calculator

55 MINUTES, 38 QUESTIONS

Turn to Section 4 of your answer sheet to answer the questions in this section.

DIRECTIONS

For questions 1-30, solve each problem, choose the best answer from the choices provided, and fill in the corresponding circle on your answer sheet. **For questions 31-38**, solve the problem and enter your answer in the grid on the answer sheet. Please refer to the directions before question 31 on how to enter your answers in the grid. You may use any available space in your test booklet for scratch work.

NOTES

1. The use of a calculator **is permitted**.

2. All variables and expressions used represent real numbers unless otherwise indicated.

3. Figures provided in this test are drawn to scale unless otherwise indicated.

4. All figures lie in a plane unless otherwise indicated.

5. Unless otherwise indicated, the domain of a given function f is the set of all real numbers x for which $f(x)$ is a real number.

REFERENCE

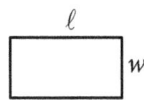 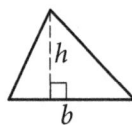 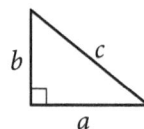 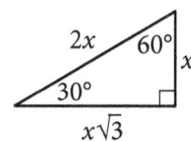 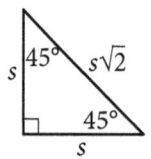

$A = \pi r^2$ $A = \ell w$ $A = \dfrac{1}{2}bh$ $c^2 = a^2 + b^2$ Special Right Triangles

$C = 2\pi r$

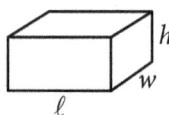 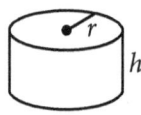 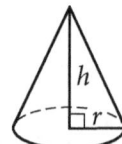 

$V = \ell wh$ $V = \pi r^2 h$ $V = \dfrac{4}{3}\pi r^3$ $V = \dfrac{1}{3}\pi r^2 h$ $V = \dfrac{1}{3}\ell wh$

The number of degrees of arc in a circle is 360.
The number of radians of arc in a circle is 2π.
The sum of the measures in degrees of the angles of a triangle is 180.

1

Marilyn's Hike

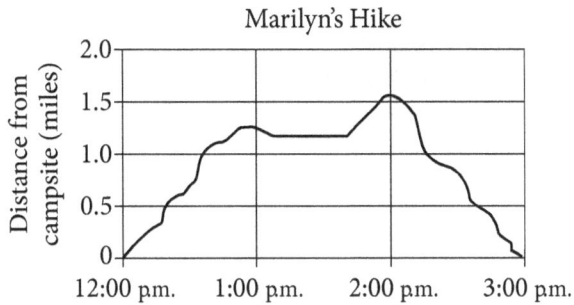

The graph above shows Marilyn's distance from her campsite during a 3-hour hike. She stopped for 30 minutes during her hike to have lunch. Based on the graph, which of the following is closest to the time she finished lunch and continued her hike?

A) 12:40 P.M.

B) 1:10 P.M.

C) 1:40 P.M.

D) 2:00 P.M.

2

Gender	Age		Total
	Under 40	40 or older	
Male	12	2	14
Female	8	3	11
Total	20	5	25

The table above shows the distribution of age and gender for 25 people who entered a contest. If the contest winner will be selected at random, what is the probability that the winner will be either a female under age 40 or a male age 40 or older?

A) $\frac{4}{25}$

B) $\frac{10}{25}$

C) $\frac{11}{25}$

D) $\frac{16}{25}$

3

The graph below shows the total number of music album sales, in millions, each year from 1997 through 2009.

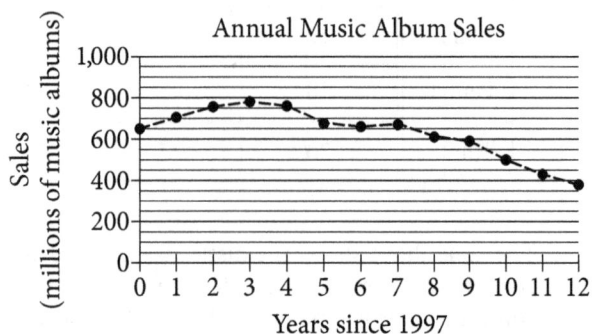

Annual Music Album Sales

Based on the graph, which of the following best describes the general trend in music album sales from 1997 through 2009 ?

A) Sales generally increased each year since 1997.

B) Sales generally decreased each year since 1997.

C) Sales increased until 2000 and then generally decreased.

D) Sales generally remained steady from 1997 through 2009.

4

n	1	2	3	4
$f(n)$	–2	1	4	7

The table above shows some values of the linear function f. Which of the following defines f ?

A) $f(n) = n - 3$

B) $f(n) = 2n - 4$

C) $f(n) = 3n - 5$

D) $f(n) = 4n - 6$

5

At Lincoln High School, approximately 7 percent of enrolled juniors and 5 percent of enrolled seniors were inducted into the National Honor Society last year. If there were 562 juniors and 602 seniors enrolled at Lincoln High School last year, which of the following is closest to the total number of juniors and seniors at Lincoln High School last year who were inducted into the National Honor Society?

A) 140

B) 69

C) 39

D) 30

6

$$3x^2 - 5x + 2$$
$$5x^2 - 2x - 6$$

Which of the following is the sum of the two polynomials shown above?

A) $8x^2 - 7x - 4$

B) $8x^2 + 7x - 4$

C) $8x^4 - 7x^2 - 4$

D) $8x^4 + 7x^2 - 4$

CONTINUE

7

If $\dfrac{3}{5} w = \dfrac{4}{3}$, what is the value of w ?

A) $\dfrac{9}{20}$

B) $\dfrac{4}{5}$

C) $\dfrac{5}{4}$

D) $\dfrac{20}{9}$

8

The average number of students per classroom at Central High School from 2000 to 2010 can be modeled by the equation $y = 0.56x + 27.2$, where x represents the number of years since 2000, and y represents the average number of students per classroom. Which of the following best describes the meaning of the number 0.56 in the equation?

A) The total number of students at the school in 2000

B) The average number of students per classroom in 2000

C) The estimated increase in the average number of students per classroom each year

D) The estimated difference between the average number of students per classroom in 2010 and in 2000

9

Nate walks 25 meters in 13.7 seconds. If he walks at this same rate, which of the following is closest to the distance he will walk in 4 minutes?

A) 150 meters

B) 450 meters

C) 700 meters

D) 1,400 meters

Questions 10 and 11 refer to the following information.

Planet	Acceleration due to gravity $\left(\dfrac{m}{sec^2}\right)$
Mercury	3.6
Venus	8.9
Earth	9.8
Mars	3.8
Jupiter	26.0
Saturn	11.1
Uranus	10.7
Neptune	14.1

The chart above shows approximations of the acceleration due to gravity in meters per second squared $\left(\dfrac{m}{sec^2}\right)$ for the eight planets in our solar system. The weight of an object on a given planet can be found by using the formula $W = mg$, where W is the weight of the object measured in newtons, m is the mass of the object measured in kilograms, and g is the acceleration due to gravity on the planet measured in $\dfrac{m}{sec^2}$.

10

What is the weight, in newtons, of an object on Mercury with a mass of 90 kilograms?

A) 25

B) 86

C) 101

D) 324

11

An object on Earth has a weight of 150 newtons. On which planet would the same object have an approximate weight of 170 newtons?

A) Venus

B) Saturn

C) Uranus

D) Neptune

Unauthorized copying or reuse of any part of this page is illegal.

44

CONTINUE

12

If the function f has five distinct zeros, which of the following could represent the complete graph of f in the xy-plane?

A)

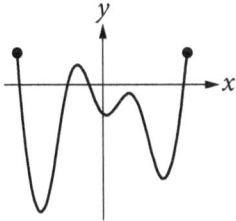

B)

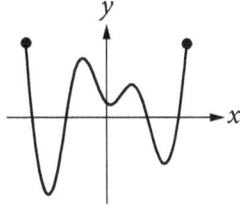

C)

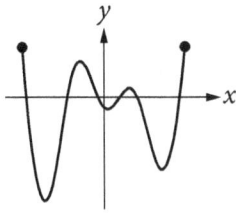

D)

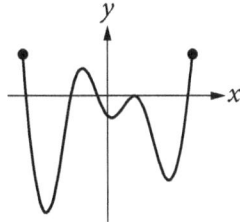

13

$$h = -16t^2 + vt + k$$

The equation above gives the height h, in feet, of a ball t seconds after it is thrown straight up with an initial speed of v feet per second from a height of k feet. Which of the following gives v in terms of h, t, and k ?

A) $v = h + k - 16t$

B) $v = \dfrac{h - k + 16}{t}$

C) $v = \dfrac{h + k}{t} - 16t$

D) $v = \dfrac{h - k}{t} + 16t$

14

The cost of using a telephone in a hotel meeting room is \$0.20 per minute. Which of the following equations represents the total cost c, in dollars, for h <u>hours</u> of phone use?

A) $c = 0.20(60h)$

B) $c = 0.20h + 60$

C) $c = \dfrac{60h}{0.20}$

D) $c = \dfrac{0.20h}{60}$

15

In order to determine if treatment X is successful in improving eyesight, a research study was conducted. From a large population of people with poor eyesight, 300 participants were selected at random. Half of the participants were randomly assigned to receive treatment X, and the other half did not receive treatment X. The resulting data showed that participants who received treatment X had significantly improved eyesight as compared to those who did not receive treatment X. Based on the design and results of the study, which of the following is an appropriate conclusion?

A) Treatment X is likely to improve the eyesight of people who have poor eyesight.

B) Treatment X improves eyesight better than all other available treatments.

C) Treatment X will improve the eyesight of anyone who takes it.

D) Treatment X will cause a substantial improvement in eyesight.

16

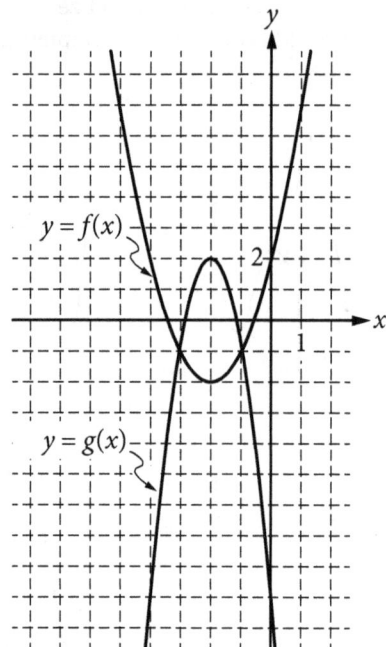

Graphs of the functions f and g are shown in the xy-plane above. For which of the following values of x does $f(x) + g(x) = 0$?

A) -3

B) -2

C) -1

D) 0

Questions 17 and 18 refer to the following information.

$$S(P) = \frac{1}{2}P + 40$$
$$D(P) = 220 - P$$

The quantity of a product supplied and the quantity of the product demanded in an economic market are functions of the price of the product. The functions above are the estimated supply and demand functions for a certain product. The function $S(P)$ gives the quantity of the product supplied to the market when the price is P dollars, and the function $D(P)$ gives the quantity of the product demanded by the market when the price is P dollars.

17

How will the quantity of the product supplied to the market change if the price of the product is increased by $10 ?

A) The quantity supplied will decrease by 5 units.

B) The quantity supplied will increase by 5 units.

C) The quantity supplied will increase by 10 units.

D) The quantity supplied will increase by 50 units.

18

At what price will the quantity of the product supplied to the market equal the quantity of the product demanded by the market?

A) $90

B) $120

C) $133

D) $155

▲

19

Graphene, which is used in the manufacture of integrated circuits, is so thin that a sheet weighing one ounce can cover up to 7 football fields. If a football field has an area of approximately $1\frac{1}{3}$ acres, about how many acres could 48 ounces of graphene cover?

A)   250

B)   350

C)   450

D) 1,350

20

Swimming Time versus Heart Rate

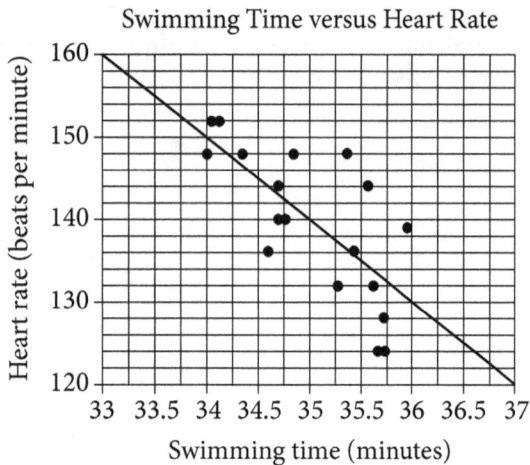

Michael swam 2,000 yards on each of eighteen days. The scatterplot above shows his swim time for and corresponding heart rate after each swim. The line of best fit for the data is also shown. For the swim that took 34 minutes, Michael's actual heart rate was about how many beats per minutes less than the rate predicted by the line of best fit?

A) 1

B) 2

C) 3

D) 4

21

Of the following four types of savings account plans, which option would yield exponential growth of the money in the account?

A) Each successive year, 2% of the initial savings is added to the value of the account.

B) Each successive year, 1.5% of the initial savings and $100 is added to the value of the account.

C) Each successive year, 1% of the current value is added to the value of the account.

D) Each successive year, $100 is added to the value of the account.

22

The sum of three numbers is 855. One of the numbers, x, is 50% more than the sum of the other two numbers. What is the value of x ?

A) 570

B) 513

C) 214

D) 155

23

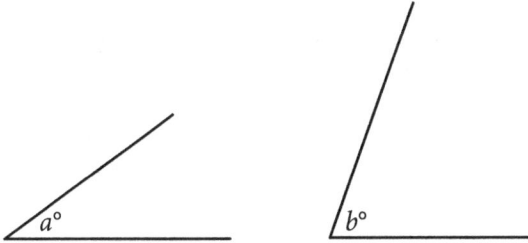

Note: Figures not drawn to scale.

The angles shown above are acute and $\sin(a°) = \cos(b°)$. If $a = 4k - 22$ and $b = 6k - 13$, what is the value of k ?

A) 4.5

B) 5.5

C) 12.5

D) 21.5

24

Mr. Kohl has a beaker containing n milliliters of solution to distribute to the students in his chemistry class. If he gives each student 3 milliliters of solution, he will have 5 milliliters left over. In order to give each student 4 milliliters of solution, he will need an additional 21 milliliters. How many students are in the class?

A) 16

B) 21

C) 23

D) 26

25

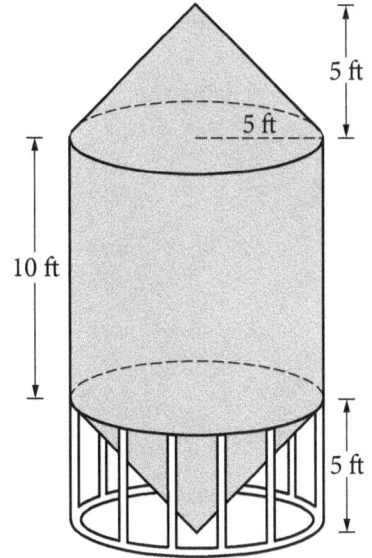

A grain silo is built from two right circular cones and a right circular cylinder with internal measurements represented by the figure above. Of the following, which is closest to the volume of the grain silo, in cubic feet?

A)   261.8

B)   785.4

C)   916.3

D) 1,047.2

26

In the xy-plane, the line determined by the points $(2, k)$ and $(k, 32)$ passes through the origin. Which of the following could be the value of k ?

A)   0

B)   4

C)   8

D) 16

28

In planning maintenance for a city's infrastructure, a civil engineer estimates that, starting from the present, the population of the city will decrease by 10 percent every 20 years. If the present population of the city is 50,000, which of the following expressions represents the engineer's estimate of the population of the city t years from now?

A) $50,000(0.1)^{20t}$

B) $50,000(0.1)^{\frac{t}{20}}$

C) $50,000(0.9)^{20t}$

D) $50,000(0.9)^{\frac{t}{20}}$

27

A rectangle was altered by increasing its length by 10 percent and decreasing its width by p percent. If these alterations decreased the area of the rectangle by 12 percent, what is the value of p ?

A) 12

B) 15

C) 20

D) 22

29

	Handedness	
Gender	Left	Right
Female		
Male		
Total	18	122

The incomplete table above summarizes the number of left-handed students and right-handed students by gender for the eighth-grade students at Keisel Middle School. There are 5 times as many right-handed female students as there are left-handed female students, and there are 9 times as many right-handed male students as there are left-handed male students. If there is a total of 18 left-handed students and 122 right-handed students in the school, which of the following is closest to the probability that a right-handed student selected at random is female? (Note: Assume that none of the eighth-grade students are both right-handed and left-handed.)

A) 0.410

B) 0.357

C) 0.333

D) 0.250

30

$$3x + b = 5x - 7$$
$$3y + c = 5y - 7$$

In the equations above, b and c are constants.

If b is c minus $\frac{1}{2}$, which of the following is true?

A) x is y minus $\frac{1}{4}$.

B) x is y minus $\frac{1}{2}$.

C) x is y minus 1.

D) x is y plus $\frac{1}{2}$.

DIRECTIONS

For questions 31-38, solve the problem and enter your answer in the grid, as described below, on the answer sheet.

1. Although not required, it is suggested that you write your answer in the boxes at the top of the columns to help you fill in the circles accurately. You will receive credit only if the circles are filled in correctly.
2. Mark no more than one circle in any column.
3. No question has a negative answer.
4. Some problems may have more than one correct answer. In such cases, grid only one answer.
5. **Mixed numbers** such as $3\frac{1}{2}$ must be gridded as 3.5 or 7/2. (If | 3 | 1 | / | 2 | is entered into the grid, it will be interpreted as $\frac{31}{2}$, not $3\frac{1}{2}$.)
6. **Decimal answers:** If you obtain a decimal answer with more digits than the grid can accommodate, it may be either rounded or truncated, but it must fill the entire grid.

Answer: $\frac{7}{12}$

Write answer in boxes. → ← Fraction line

Grid in result. →

Answer: 2.5

← Decimal point

Acceptable ways to grid $\frac{2}{3}$ are:

Answer: 201 – either position is correct

NOTE: You may start your answers in any column, space permitting. Columns you don't need to use should be left blank.

31

Tickets for a school talent show cost $2 for students and $3 for adults. If Chris spends at least $11 but no more than $14 on x student tickets and 1 adult ticket, what is one possible value of x ?

33

$$(-3x^2 + 5x - 2) - 2(x^2 - 2x - 1)$$

If the expression above is rewritten in the form $ax^2 + bx + c$, where a, b, and c are constants, what is the value of b ?

32

Ages of the First 12 United States Presidents
at the Beginning of Their Terms in Office

President	Age (years)	President	Age (years)
Washington	57	Jackson	62
Adams	62	Van Buren	55
Jefferson	58	Harrison	68
Madison	58	Tyler	51
Monroe	59	Polk	50
Adams	58	Taylor	65

The table above lists the ages of the first 12 United States presidents when they began their terms in office. According to the table, what was the mean age, in years, of these presidents at the beginning of their terms? (Round your answer to the nearest tenth.)

34

In a circle with center O, central angle AOB has a measure of $\dfrac{5\pi}{4}$ radians. The area of the sector formed by central angle AOB is what fraction of the area of the circle?

35

An online store receives customer satisfaction ratings between 0 and 100, inclusive. In the first 10 ratings the store received, the average (arithmetic mean) of the ratings was 75. What is the least value the store can receive for the 11th rating and still be able to have an average of at least 85 for the first 20 ratings?

36

$$y \leq -15x + 3000$$
$$y \leq 5x$$

In the xy-plane, if a point with coordinates (a, b) lies in the solution set of the system of inequalities above, what is the maximum possible value of b ?

Unauthorized copying or reuse of any part of this page is illegal.

54

CONTINUE

Questions 37 and 38 refer to the following information.

If shoppers enter a store at an average rate of r shoppers per minute and each stays in the store for an average time of T minutes, the average number of shoppers in the store, N, at any one time is given by the formula $N = rT$. This relationship is known as Little's law.

The owner of the Good Deals Store estimates that during business hours, an average of 3 shoppers per minute enter the store and that each of them stays an average of 15 minutes. The store owner uses Little's law to estimate that there are 45 shoppers in the store at any time.

37

Little's law can be applied to any part of the store, such as a particular department or the checkout lines. The store owner determines that, during business hours, approximately 84 shoppers per hour make a purchase and each of these shoppers spend an average of 5 minutes in the checkout line. At any time during business hours, about how many shoppers, on average, are waiting in the checkout line to make a purchase at the Good Deals Store?

38

The owner of the Good Deals Store opens a new store across town. For the new store, the owner estimates that, during business hours, an average of 90 shoppers per <u>hour</u> enter the store and each of them stays an average of 12 minutes. The average number of shoppers in the new store at any time is what percent less than the average number of shoppers in the original store at any time? (Note: Ignore the percent symbol when entering your answer. For example, if the answer is 42.1%, enter 42.1)

STOP

If you finish before time is called, you may check your work on this section only.

Do not turn to any other section.

SAT Practice Essay #3

ESSAY BOOK

DIRECTIONS

The essay gives you an opportunity to show how effectively you can read and comprehend a passage and write an essay analyzing the passage. In your essay, you should demonstrate that you have read the passage carefully, present a clear and logical analysis, and use language precisely.

Your essay must be written on the lines provided in your answer booklet; except for the Planning Page of the answer booklet, you will receive no other paper on which to write. You will have enough space if you write on every line, avoid wide margins, and keep your handwriting to a reasonable size. Remember that people who are not familiar with your handwriting will read what you write. Try to write or print so that what you are writing is legible to those readers.

You have <u>50 minutes</u> to read the passage and write an essay in response to the prompt provided inside this booklet.

REMINDERS:

— Do not write your essay in this booklet. Only what you write on the lined pages of your answer booklet will be evaluated.

— An off-topic essay will not be evaluated.

Practice:
Follow this link for more information on scoring your test:
www.sat.org/scoring

This cover is representative of what you'll see on test day.

As you read the passage below, consider how Adam B. Summers uses

- evidence, such as facts or examples, to support claims.
- reasoning to develop ideas and to connect claims and evidence.
- stylistic or persuasive elements, such as word choice or appeals to emotion, to add power to the ideas expressed.

Adapted from Adam B. Summers, "Bag Ban Bad for Freedom and Environment." ©2013 by The San Diego Union-Tribune, LLC. Originally published June 13, 2013.

1   Californians dodged yet another nanny-state regulation recently when the state Senate narrowly voted down a bill to ban plastic bags statewide, but the reprieve might only be temporary. Not content to tell us how much our toilets can flush or what type of light bulb to use to brighten our homes, some politicians and environmentalists are now focused on deciding for us what kind of container we can use to carry our groceries.

2   The bill . . . would have prohibited grocery stores and convenience stores with at least $2 million in gross annual sales and 10,000 square feet of retail space from providing single-use plastic or paper bags, although stores would have been allowed to sell recycled paper bags for an unspecified amount. The bill fell just three votes short of passage in the Senate . . . and Sen. Alex Padilla, D-Los Angeles, who sponsored the measure, has indicated that he would like to bring it up again, so expect this fight to be recycled rather than trashed.

3   While public debate over plastic bag bans often devolves into emotional pleas to save the planet or preserve marine life (and, believe me, I love sea turtles as much as the next guy), a little reason and perspective is in order.

4   According to the U.S. Environmental Protection Agency, plastic bags, sacks, and wraps of all kinds (not just grocery bags) make up only about 1.6 percent of all municipal solid waste materials. High-density polyethylene (HDPE) bags, which are the most common kind of plastic grocery bags, make up just 0.3 percent of this total.

5   The claims that plastic bags are worse for the environment than paper bags or cotton reusable bags are dubious at best. In fact, compared to paper bags, plastic grocery bags produce fewer greenhouse gas emissions, require 70 percent less energy to make, generate 80 percent less waste, and utilize less than 4 percent of the amount of water needed to manufacture them. This makes sense because plastic bags are lighter and take up less space than paper bags.

6 Reusable bags come with their own set of problems. They, too, have a larger carbon footprint than plastic bags. Even more disconcerting are the findings of several studies that plastic bag bans lead to increased health problems due to food contamination from bacteria that remain in the reusable bags. A November 2012 statistical analysis by University of Pennsylvania law professor Jonathan Klick and George Mason University law professor and economist Joshua D. Wright found that San Francisco's plastic bag ban in 2007 resulted in a subsequent spike in hospital emergency room visits due to E. coli, salmonella, and campylobacter-related intestinal infectious diseases. The authors conclude that the ban even accounts for several additional deaths in the city each year from such infections.

7 The description of plastic grocery bags as "single-use" bags is another misnomer. The vast majority of people use them more than once, whether for lining trash bins or picking up after their dogs. (And still other bags are recycled.) Since banning plastic bags also means preventing their additional uses as trash bags and pooper scoopers, one unintended consequence of the plastic bag ban would likely be an increase in plastic bag purchases for these other purposes. This is just what happened in Ireland in 2002 when a 15 Euro cent ($0.20) tax imposed on plastic shopping bags led to a 77 percent increase in the sale of plastic trash can liner bags.

8 And then there are the economic costs. The plastic bag ban would threaten the roughly 2,000 California jobs in the plastic bag manufacturing and recycling industry, although, as noted in the Irish example above, they might be able to weather the storm if they can successfully switch to producing other types of plastic bags. In addition, taxpayers will have to pony up for the added bureaucracy, and the higher regulatory costs foisted upon bag manufacturers and retailers will ultimately be borne by consumers in the form of price increases.

9 Notwithstanding the aforementioned reasons why plastic bags are not, in fact, evil incarnate, environmentalists have every right to try to convince people to adopt certain beliefs or lifestyles, but they do not have the right to use government force to compel people to live the way they think best. In a free society, we are able to live our lives as we please, so long as we do not infringe upon the rights of others. That includes the right to make such fundamental decisions as "Paper or plastic?"

Write an essay in which you explain how Adam B. Summers builds an argument to persuade his audience that plastic shopping bags should not be banned. In your essay, analyze how Summers uses one or more of the features listed in the box above (or features of your own choice) to strengthen the logic and persuasiveness of his argument. Be sure that your analysis focuses on the most relevant features of the passage.

Your essay should not explain whether you agree with Summers's claims, but rather explain how Summers builds an argument to persuade his audience.

Scoring Your SAT® Practice Test #3

Congratulations on completing an SAT® practice test. To score your test, use these instructions and the conversion tables and answer key at the end of this document.

Scores Overview

The redesigned SAT will provide more information about your learning by reporting more scores than ever before. Each of the redesigned assessments (SAT, PSAT/NMSQT®, PSAT™ 10, and PSAT™ 8/9) will report test scores and cross-test scores on a common scale. Additionally, subscores will be reported to provide additional diagnostic information to students, educators, and parents. For more details about scores, visit **collegereadiness.collegeboard.org/sat/scores**.

The practice test you completed was written by the College Board's Assessment Design & Development team using the same processes and review standards used when writing the actual SAT. Everything from the layout of the page to the construction of the questions accurately reflects what you'll see on test day.

How to Calculate Your Practice Test Scores

GET SET UP

❶ You'll need the answer sheet that you bubbled in while taking the practice test. You'll also need the conversion tables and answer key at the end of this document.

❷ Using the answer key, count up your total correct answers for each section. You may want to write the number of correct answers for each section at the bottom of that section in the answer key.

❸ Using your marked-up answer key and the conversion tables, follow the directions to get all of your scores.

GET SECTION AND TOTAL SCORES

Your total score on the SAT practice test is the sum of your Evidence-Based Reading and Writing Section score and your Math Section score. To get your total score, you will convert what we call the "raw score" for each section — the number of questions you got right in that section — into the "scaled score" for that section, then calculate the total score.

GET YOUR EVIDENCE-BASED READING AND WRITING SECTION SCORE

Calculate your SAT Evidence-Based Reading and Writing Section score (it's on a scale of 200–800) by first determining your Reading Test score and your Writing and Language Test score. Here's how:

1. Count the number of correct answers you got on Section 1 (the Reading Test). There is no penalty for wrong answers. The number of correct answers is your raw score.

2. Go to Raw Score Conversion Table 1: Section and Test Scores on page 7. Look in the "Raw Score" column for your raw score, and match it to the number in the "Reading Test Score" column.

3. Do the same with Section 2 to determine your Writing and Language Test score.

4. Add your Reading Test score to your Writing and Language Test score.

5. Multiply that number by 10. This is your Evidence-Based Reading and Writing Section score.

EXAMPLE: *Ada answered 28 of the 52 questions correctly on the SAT Reading Test and 18 of the 44 questions correctly on the SAT Writing and Language Test. Using the table on page 7, she calculates that she received an SAT Reading Test score of 27 and an SAT Writing and Language Test score of 23. She adds 27 to 23 (gets 50) and then multiplies by 10 to determine her SAT Evidence-Based Reading and Writing Section score of 500.*

GET YOUR MATH SECTION SCORE

Calculate your SAT Math Section score (it's on a scale of 200–800).

1. Count the number of correct answers you got on Section 3 (Math Test — No Calculator) and Section 4 (Math Test — Calculator). There is no penalty for wrong answers.

2. Add the number of correct answers you got on Section 3 (Math Test — No Calculator) and Section 4 (Math Test — Calculator).

3. Use Raw Score Conversion Table 1: Section and Test Scores to turn your raw score into your Math Section score.

GET YOUR TOTAL SCORE

Add your Evidence-Based Reading and Writing Section score to your Math Section score. The result is your total score on the SAT Practice Test, on a scale of 400–1600.

GET SUBSCORES

Subscores provide more detailed information about your strengths in specific areas within literacy and math. They are reported on a scale of 1–15.

HEART OF ALGEBRA

The Heart of Algebra subscore is based on questions from the Math Test that focus on linear equations and inequalities.

1. Add up your total correct answers from the following set of questions:

    ▸ Math Test – No Calculator: Questions 2; 4; 6; 8-9; 15; 17; 19

    ▸ Math Test – Calculator: Questions 4; 7-8; 14; 18; 22; 24; 26; 30-31; 36

    Your total correct answers from all of these questions is your raw score.

2. Use Raw Score Conversion Table 2: Subscores on page 8 to determine your Heart of Algebra subscore.

PROBLEM SOLVING AND DATA ANALYSIS

The Problem Solving and Data Analysis subscore is based on questions from the Math Test that focus on quantitative reasoning, the interpretation and synthesis of data, and solving problems in rich and varied contexts.

1. Add up your total correct answers from the following set of questions:

    ▸ Math Test – No Calculator: No Questions

    ▸ Math Test – Calculator: Questions 1-3; 5; 9-11; 15; 19-21; 27; 29; 32; 35; 37-38

    Your total correct answers from all of these questions is your raw score.

2. Use Raw Score Conversion Table 2: Subscores to determine your Problem Solving and Data Analysis subscore.

PASSPORT TO ADVANCED MATH

The Passport to Advanced Math subscore is based on questions from the Math Test that focus on topics central to the ability of students to progress to more advanced mathematics, such as understanding the structure of expressions, reasoning with more complex equations, and interpreting and building functions.

1. Add up your total correct answers from the following set of questions:

    ▸ Math Test – No Calculator: Questions 1; 3; 5; 7; 10; 12-14; 16

    ▸ Math Test – Calculator: Questions 6; 12-13; 16-17; 28; 33

    Your total correct answers from all of these questions is your raw score.

2. Use Raw Score Conversion Table 2: Subscores to determine your Passport to Advanced Math subscore.

EXPRESSION OF IDEAS

The Expression of Ideas subscore is based on questions from the Writing and Language Test that focus on topic development, organization, and rhetorically effective use of language.

① Add up your total correct answers from the following set of questions:

▸ Writing and Language Test: Questions 2-3; 6-9; 13; 16-18; 20; 22-23; 25; 30-33; 37; 39-40; 42-44

▸ Your total correct answers from all of these questions is your raw score.

② Use Raw Score Conversion Table 2: Subscores to determine your Expression of Ideas subscore.

STANDARD ENGLISH CONVENTIONS

The Standard English Conventions subscore is based on questions from the Writing and Language Test that focus on sentence structure, usage, and punctuation.

① Add up your total correct answers from the following set of questions:

▸ Writing and Language Test: Questions 1; 4-5; 10-12; 14-15; 19; 21; 24; 26-29; 34-36; 38; 41

Your total correct answers from all of these questions is your raw score.

② Use Raw Score Conversion Table 2: Subscores to determine your Standard English Conventions subscore.

WORDS IN CONTEXT

The Words in Context subscore is based on questions from both the Reading Test and the Writing and Language Test that address word/phrase meaning in context and rhetorical word choice.

① Add up your total correct answers from the following set of questions:

▸ Reading Test: Questions 2; 6; 16-17; 22; 28; 31; 35; 42; 47

▸ Writing and Language Test: Questions 7-8; 16; 18; 23; 25; 40; 44

Your total correct answers from all of these questions is your raw score.

② Use Raw Score Conversion Table 2: Subscores to determine your Words in Context subscore.

COMMAND OF EVIDENCE

The Command of Evidence subscore is based on questions from both the Reading Test and the Writing and Language Test that ask you to interpret and use evidence found in a wide range of passages and informational graphics, such as graphs, tables, and charts.

① Add up your total correct answers from the following set of questions:

▸ Reading Test: Questions 4; 10; 15; 19; 24; 30; 37; 44; 50; 52

▸ Writing and Language Test: Questions 3; 6; 13; 22; 31-32; 42-43

Your total correct answers from all of these questions is your raw score.

② Use Raw Score Conversion Table 2: Subscores to determine your Command of Evidence subscore.

GET CROSS-TEST SCORES

The new SAT also reports two cross-test scores: Analysis in History/Social Studies and Analysis in Science. These scores are based on questions in the Reading, Writing and Language, and Math Tests that ask students to think analytically about texts and questions in these subject areas. Cross-test scores are reported on a scale of 10–40.

ANALYSIS IN HISTORY/SOCIAL STUDIES

1. Add up your total correct answers from the following set of questions:

   ▶ Reading Test: Questions 11-20; 31-41

   ▶ Writing and Language Test: Questions 13; 16-18; 20; 22

   ▶ Math Test – No Calculator: No Questions

   ▶ Math Test – Calculator: Questions 3; 8; 17-18; 21; 28; 32; 37

   Your total correct answers from all of these questions is your raw score.

2. Use Raw Score Conversion Table 3: Cross-Test Scores on page 9 to determine your Analysis in History/Social Studies cross-test score.

ANALYSIS IN SCIENCE

1. Add up your total correct answers from the following set of questions:

   ▶ Reading Test: Questions 21-30; 42-52

   ▶ Writing and Language Test: Questions 23; 25; 30-33

   ▶ Math Test – No Calculator: Question 15

   ▶ Math Test – Calculator: Questions 9-10; 13; 15; 19-20; 25

   Your total correct answers from all of these questions is your raw score.

2. Use Raw Score Conversion Table 3: Cross-Test Scores to determine your Analysis in Science cross-test score.

SAT Practice Test #3: Worksheets

ANSWER KEY

Reading Test Answers

1 B	12 C	23 A	34 D	45 D
2 C	13 D	24 B	35 C	46 C
3 A	14 B	25 C	36 A	47 B
4 A	15 B	26 C	37 D	48 B
5 C	16 C	27 B	38 C	49 A
6 A	17 B	28 B	39 A	50 B
7 A	18 B	29 D	40 D	51 D
8 B	19 A	30 D	41 A	52 D
9 B	20 A	31 B	42 C	
10 D	21 D	32 C	43 C	
11 A	22 A	33 C	44 D	

READING TEST
RAW SCORE
(NUMBER OF
CORRECT ANSWERS)

Writing and Language Test Answers

1 A	12 A	23 A	34 D
2 B	13 C	24 D	35 B
3 C	14 D	25 B	36 C
4 C	15 B	26 A	37 D
5 A	16 C	27 D	38 C
6 B	17 C	28 B	39 C
7 A	18 B	29 B	40 B
8 D	19 D	30 B	41 D
9 C	20 C	31 D	42 A
10 C	21 D	32 B	43 D
11 B	22 A	33 C	44 D

WRITING AND
LANGUAGE TEST
RAW SCORE
(NUMBER OF
CORRECT ANSWERS)

Math Test
No Calculator Answers

1 C	11 B
2 D	12 A
3 D	13 B
4 B	14 A
5 C	15 D
6 C	16 1 or 2
7 C	17 2
8 A	18 105
9 A	19 370
10 A	20 3/5 or 0.6

MATH TEST
NO CALCULATOR
RAW SCORE
(NUMBER OF
CORRECT ANSWERS)

Math Test
Calculator Answers

1 C	11 B	21 C	31 4 or 5
2 B	12 D	22 B	32 58.6
3 C	13 D	23 C	33 9
4 C	14 A	24 D	34 5/8 or 0.625
5 B	15 A	25 D	35 50
6 A	16 B	26 C	36 750
7 D	17 B	27 C	37 7
8 C	18 B	28 D	38 60
9 B	19 C	29 A	
10 D	20 B	30 A	

MATH TEST
CALCULATOR
RAW SCORE
(NUMBER OF
CORRECT ANSWERS)

SAT Practice Test #3: Worksheets

RAW SCORE CONVERSION TABLE 1 SECTION AND TEST SCORES

Raw Score (# of correct answers)	Math Section Score	Reading Test Score	Writing and Language Test Score	Raw Score (# of correct answers)	Math Section Score	Reading Test Score	Writing and Language Test Score
0	200	10	10	30	570	28	30
1	200	10	10	31	580	29	30
2	210	10	10	32	580	29	31
3	230	11	11	33	590	29	32
4	250	12	12	34	600	30	33
5	270	13	13	35	610	30	33
6	290	14	14	36	620	31	34
7	300	14	15	37	630	31	34
8	320	15	15	38	630	32	35
9	330	16	16	39	640	32	35
10	340	17	17	40	650	33	36
11	360	17	18	41	660	33	37
12	370	18	19	42	660	34	38
13	380	19	19	43	670	34	39
14	390	19	20	44	680	35	40
15	410	20	21	45	680	36	
16	420	21	22	46	690	36	
17	430	21	22	47	690	37	
18	440	22	23	48	700	38	
19	450	22	24	49	710	38	
20	460	23	24	50	710	39	
21	470	24	25	51	720	40	
22	480	24	25	52	730	40	
23	490	25	26	53	740		
24	500	25	26	54	750		
25	510	26	27	55	770		
26	530	26	27	56	780		
27	540	27	28	57	790		
28	550	27	29	58	800		
29	560	28	29				

CONVERSION EQUATION 1 SECTION AND TEST SCORES

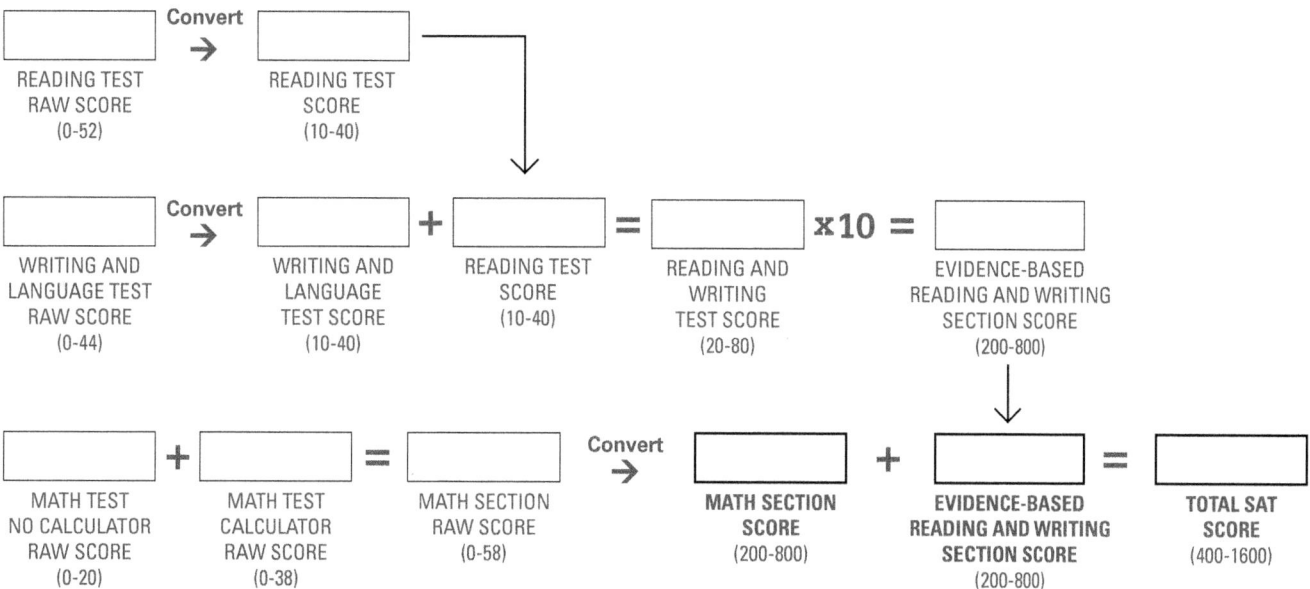

SAT Practice Test #3: Worksheets

Raw Score (# of correct answers)	Expression of Ideas	Standard English Conventions	Heart of Algebra	Problem Solving and Data Analysis	Passport to Advanced Math	Words in Context	Command of Evidence
0	1	1	1	1	1	1	1
1	1	1	1	2	2	1	2
2	2	1	2	3	3	1	3
3	3	2	3	4	5	3	4
4	4	4	5	5	6	4	5
5	5	4	6	6	7	5	6
6	6	5	6	7	8	6	7
7	6	6	7	8	9	6	8
8	7	6	8	8	9	7	8
9	8	7	9	9	10	8	9
10	8	7	9	10	11	8	10
11	8	8	10	10	11	9	10
12	9	8	11	11	12	10	11
13	9	9	11	12	13	10	12
14	10	9	12	13	13	11	12
15	10	10	13	13	14	12	13
16	11	11	13	14	15	13	14
17	11	11	14	15		14	15
18	12	12	15			15	15
19	12	13	15				
20	13	15					
21	13						
22	14						
23	14						
24	15						

	Convert →	
HEART OF ALGEBRA RAW SCORE (0-19)		**HEART OF ALGEBRA SUBSCORE** (1-15)

	Convert →	
EXPRESSION OF IDEAS RAW SCORE (0-24)		**EXPRESSION OF IDEAS SUBSCORE** (1-15)

	Convert →	
COMMAND OF EVIDENCE RAW SCORE (0-18)		**COMMAND OF EVIDENCE SUBSCORE** (1-15)

	Convert →	
PROBLEM SOLVING AND DATA ANALYSIS RAW SCORE (0-17)		**PROBLEM SOLVING AND DATA ANALYSIS SUBSCORE** (1-15)

	Convert →	
STANDARD ENGLISH CONVENTIONS RAW SCORE (0-20)		**STANDARD ENGLISH CONVENTIONS SUBSCORE** (1-15)

	Convert →	
WORDS IN CONTEXT RAW SCORE (0-18)		**WORDS IN CONTEXT SUBSCORE** (1-15)

	Convert →	
PASSPORT TO ADVANCED MATH RAW SCORE (0-16)		**PASSPORT TO ADVANCED MATH SUBSCORE** (1-15)

SAT Practice Test #3: Worksheets

CROSS-TEST SCORES

Raw Score (# of correct answers)	Analysis in History/ Social Studies Cross-Test Score	Analysis in Science Cross-Test Score	Raw Score (# of correct answers)	Analysis in History/ Social Studies Cross-Test Score	Analysis in Science Cross-Test Score
0	10	10	18	27	27
1	10	11	19	28	27
2	11	12	20	29	28
3	12	13	21	29	29
4	14	14	22	30	29
5	15	15	23	30	30
6	16	16	24	31	31
7	17	17	25	32	31
8	18	18	26	33	32
9	19	19	27	33	32
10	20	20	28	34	33
11	21	21	29	35	34
12	22	22	30	36	34
13	23	23	31	36	35
14	24	23	32	37	36
15	25	24	33	38	37
16	25	25	34	39	38
17	26	26	35	40	40

CONVERSION EQUATION 3 CROSS-TEST SCORES

Test	Analysis in History/Social Studies		Analysis in Science	
	Questions	Raw Score	Questions	Raw Score
Reading Test	11-20; 31-41		21-30; 42-52	
Writing and Language Test	13; 16-18; 20; 22		23; 25; 30-33	
Math Test No Calculator	None		15	
Math Test Calculator	3; 8; 17-18; 21; 28; 32; 37		9-10; 13; 15; 19-20; 25	
Total				

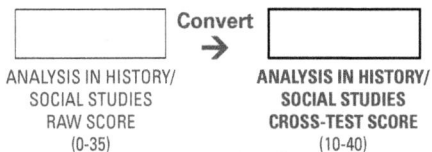

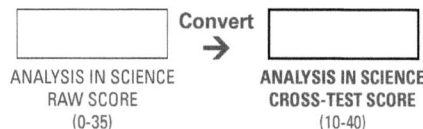

	Convert →			Convert →	
ANALYSIS IN HISTORY/ SOCIAL STUDIES RAW SCORE (0-35)		**ANALYSIS IN HISTORY/ SOCIAL STUDIES CROSS-TEST SCORE (10-40)**	ANALYSIS IN SCIENCE RAW SCORE (0-35)		**ANALYSIS IN SCIENCE CROSS-TEST SCORE (10-40)**

SAT® Practice Test #4

IMPORTANT REMINDERS

1

A No. 2 pencil is required for the test.
Do not use a mechanical pencil or pen.

2

Sharing any questions with anyone
is a violation of Test Security
and Fairness policies and may result
in your scores being canceled.

This cover is representative of what you'll see on test day.

TEST TAKING TIP #4

Know the Different Questions Types That Might Be Asked:
Knowledge is power and that certainly is no different for the SAT.
Being aware of the types of questions you might be asked allows
you to gear your study towards those questions. It also helps to
alleviate nerves on exam day because you know what is coming.

Reading Test

65 MINUTES, 52 QUESTIONS

Turn to Section 1 of your answer sheet to answer the questions in this section.

DIRECTIONS

Each passage or pair of passages below is followed by a number of questions. After reading each passage or pair, choose the best answer to each question based on what is stated or implied in the passage or passages and in any accompanying graphics (such as a table or graph).

Questions 1-10 are based on the following passage.

This passage is adapted from MacDonald Harris, *The Balloonist*. ©2011 by The Estate of Donald Heiney. During the summer of 1897, the narrator of this story, a fictional Swedish scientist, has set out for the North Pole in a hydrogen-powered balloon.

My emotions are complicated and not readily verifiable. I feel a vast yearning that is simultaneously a pleasure and a pain. I am certain
Line of the consummation of this yearning, but I don't
5 know yet what form it will take, since I do not understand quite what it is that the yearning desires. For the first time there is borne in upon me the full truth of what I myself said to the doctor only an hour ago: that my motives in this undertaking are not
10 entirely clear. For years, for a lifetime, the machinery of my destiny has worked in secret to prepare for this moment; its clockwork has moved exactly toward this time and place and no other. Rising slowly from the earth that bore me and gave me sustenance, I am
15 carried helplessly toward an uninhabited and hostile, or at best indifferent, part of the earth, littered with the bones of explorers and the wrecks of ships, frozen supply caches, messages scrawled with chilled fingers and hidden in cairns that no eye will ever see.
20 Nobody has succeeded in this thing, and many have died. Yet in freely willing this enterprise, in choosing this moment and no other when the south wind will carry me exactly northward at a velocity of eight knots, I have converted the machinery of my

25 fate into the servant of my will. All this I understand, as I understand each detail of the technique by which this is carried out. What I don't understand is why I am so intent on going to this particular place. Who wants the North Pole! What good is it! Can you eat
30 it? Will it carry you from Gothenburg to Malmö like a railway? The Danish ministers have declared from their pulpits that participation in polar expeditions is beneficial to the soul's eternal well-being, or so I read in a newspaper. It isn't clear how this doctrine is to
35 be interpreted, except that the Pole is something difficult or impossible to attain which must nevertheless be sought for, because man is condemned to seek out and know everything whether or not the knowledge gives him pleasure. In
40 short, it is the same unthinking lust for knowledge that drove our First Parents out of the garden.
And suppose you were to find it in spite of all, this wonderful place that everybody is so anxious to stand on! *What* would you find? Exactly nothing.
45 A point precisely identical to all the others in a completely featureless wasteland stretching around it for hundreds of miles. It is an abstraction, a mathematical fiction. No one but a Swedish madman could take the slightest interest in it. Here I am. The
50 wind is still from the south, bearing us steadily northward at the speed of a trotting dog. Behind us, perhaps forever, lie the Cities of Men with their

2

CONTINUE →

teacups and their brass bedsteads. I am going forth of
my own volition to join the ghosts of Bering and
55 poor Franklin, of frozen De Long and his men.
What I am on the brink of knowing, I now see, is not
an ephemeral mathematical spot but myself. The
doctor was right, even though I dislike him.
Fundamentally I am a dangerous madman, and what
60 I do is both a challenge to my egotism and a
surrender to it.

1

Over the course of the passage, the narrator's attitude
shifts from

A) fear about the expedition to excitement about it.

B) doubt about his abilities to confidence in them.

C) uncertainty of his motives to recognition of
them.

D) disdain for the North Pole to appreciation of it.

2

Which choice provides the best evidence for the
answer to the previous question?

A) Lines 10-12 ("For . . . moment")

B) Lines 21-25 ("Yet . . . will")

C) Lines 42-44 ("And . . . stand on")

D) Lines 56-57 ("What . . . myself")

3

As used in lines 1-2, "not readily verifiable" most
nearly means

A) unable to be authenticated.

B) likely to be contradicted.

C) without empirical support.

D) not completely understood.

4

The sentence in lines 10-13 ("For years . . . other")
mainly serves to

A) expose a side of the narrator that he prefers to
keep hidden.

B) demonstrate that the narrator thinks in a
methodical and scientific manner.

C) show that the narrator feels himself to be
influenced by powerful and independent forces.

D) emphasize the length of time during which the
narrator has prepared for his expedition.

5

The narrator indicates that many previous explorers
seeking the North Pole have

A) perished in the attempt.

B) made surprising discoveries.

C) failed to determine its exact location.

D) had different motivations than his own.

6

Which choice provides the best evidence for the
answer to the previous question?

A) Lines 20-21 ("Nobody . . . died")

B) Lines 25-27 ("All . . . out")

C) Lines 31-34 ("The . . . newspaper")

D) Lines 51-53 ("Behind . . . bedsteads")

7

Which choice best describes the narrator's view of
his expedition to the North Pole?

A) Immoral but inevitable

B) Absurd but necessary

C) Socially beneficial but misunderstood

D) Scientifically important but hazardous

8

The question the narrator asks in lines 30-31 ("Will it . . . railway") most nearly implies that

A) balloons will never replace other modes of transportation.

B) the North Pole is farther away than the cities usually reached by train.

C) people often travel from one city to another without considering the implications.

D) reaching the North Pole has no foreseeable benefit to humanity.

9

As used in line 49, "take the slightest interest in" most nearly means

A) accept responsibility for.

B) possess little regard for.

C) pay no attention to.

D) have curiosity about.

10

As used in line 50, "bearing" most nearly means

A) carrying.

B) affecting.

C) yielding.

D) enduring.

Questions 11-21 are based on the following passage and supplementary material.

This passage is adapted from Alan Ehrenhalt, *The Great Inversion and the Future of the American City.* ©2013 by Vintage. Ehrenhalt is an urbanologist—a scholar of cities and their development. Demographic inversion is a phenomenon that describes the rearrangement of living patterns throughout a metropolitan area.

We are not witnessing the abandonment of the suburbs, or a movement of millions of people back to the city all at once. The 2010 census certainly did not

Line turn up evidence of a middle-class stampede to the
5 nation's cities. The news was mixed: Some of the larger cities on the East Coast tended to gain population, albeit in small increments. Those in the Midwest, including Chicago, tended to lose substantial numbers. The cities that showed gains in
10 overall population during the entire decade tended to be in the South and Southwest. But when it comes to measuring demographic inversion, raw census numbers are an ineffective blunt instrument. A closer look at the results shows that the most powerful
15 demographic events of the past decade were the movement of African Americans out of central cities (180,000 of them in Chicago alone) and the settlement of immigrant groups in suburbs, often ones many miles distant from downtown.
20 Central-city areas that gained affluent residents in the first part of the decade maintained that population in the recession years from 2007 to 2009. They also, according to a 2011 study by Brookings, suffered considerably less from increased
25 unemployment than the suburbs did. Not many young professionals moved to new downtown condos in the recession years because few such residences were being built. But there is no reason to believe that the demographic trends prevailing prior
30 to the construction bust will not resume once that bust is over. It is important to remember that demographic inversion is not a proxy for population growth; it can occur in cities that are growing, those whose numbers are flat, and even in those
35 undergoing a modest decline in size.

America's major cities face enormous fiscal problems, many of them the result of public pension obligations they incurred in the more prosperous years of the past two decades. Some, Chicago

40 prominent among them, simply are not producing enough revenue to support the level of public services to which most of the citizens have grown to feel entitled. How the cities are going to solve this problem, I do not know. What I do know is that if

45 fiscal crisis were going to drive affluent professionals out of central cities, it would have done so by now. There is no evidence that it has.

The truth is that we are living at a moment in which the massive outward migration of the affluent

50 that characterized the second half of the twentieth century is coming to an end. And we need to adjust our perceptions of cities, suburbs, and urban mobility as a result.

Much of our perspective on the process of

55 metropolitan settlement dates, whether we realize it or not, from a paper written in 1925 by the University of Chicago sociologist Ernest W. Burgess. It was Burgess who defined four urban/suburban zones of settlement: a central business district; an

60 area of manufacturing just beyond it; then a residential area inhabited by the industrial and immigrant working class; and finally an outer enclave of single-family dwellings.

Burgess was right about the urban America of

65 1925; he was right about the urban America of 1974. Virtually every city in the country had a downtown, where the commercial life of the metropolis was conducted; it had a factory district just beyond; it had districts of working-class residences just beyond that;

70 and it had residential suburbs for the wealthy and the upper middle class at the far end of the continuum. As a family moved up the economic ladder, it also moved outward from crowded working-class districts to more spacious apartments and,

75 eventually, to a suburban home. The suburbs of Burgess's time bore little resemblance to those at the end of the twentieth century, but the theory still essentially worked. People moved ahead in life by moving farther out.

80 But in the past decade, in quite a few places, this model has ceased to describe reality. There are still downtown commercial districts, but there are no factory districts lying next to them. There are scarcely any factories at all. These close-in parts of

85 the city, whose few residents Burgess described as dwelling in "submerged regions of poverty, degradation and disease," are increasingly the preserve of the affluent who work in the commercial core. And just as crucially newcomers to America are

90 not settling on the inside and accumulating the resources to move out; they are living in the suburbs from day one.

United States Population by Metropolitan Size/Status, 1980–2010

Chart 1

2010 Population Shares
by Metro Size (%)

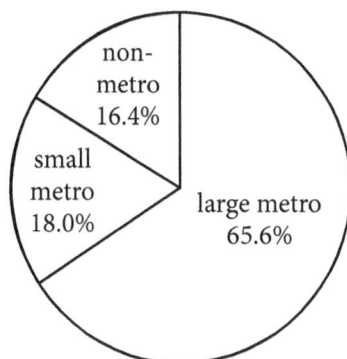

non-metro 16.4%
small metro 18.0%
large metro 65.6%

Chart 2

Growth Rates by Metro Size

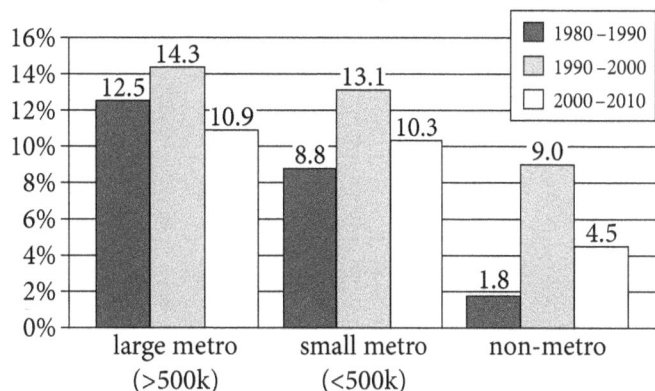

Legend: 1980–1990, 1990–2000, 2000–2010

large metro (>500k): 12.5, 14.3, 10.9
small metro (<500k): 8.8, 13.1, 10.3
non-metro: 1.8, 9.0, 4.5

Adapted from William H. Frey, "Population Growth in Metro America since 1980: Putting the Volatile 2000s in Perspective." Published 2012 by Metropolitan Policy Program, Brookings Institution.

CONTINUE

11

Which choice best summarizes the first paragraph of the passage (lines 1-35)?

A) The 2010 census demonstrated a sizeable growth in the number of middle-class families moving into inner cities.

B) The 2010 census is not a reliable instrument for measuring population trends in American cities.

C) Population growth and demographic inversion are distinct phenomena, and demographic inversion is evident in many American cities.

D) Population growth in American cities has been increasing since roughly 2000, while suburban populations have decreased.

12

According to the passage, members of which group moved away from central-city areas in large numbers in the early 2000s?

A) The unemployed

B) Immigrants

C) Young professionals

D) African Americans

13

In line 34, "flat" is closest in meaning to

A) static.

B) deflated.

C) featureless.

D) obscure.

14

According to the passage, which choice best describes the current financial situation in many major American cities?

A) Expected tax increases due to demand for public works

B) Economic hardship due to promises made in past years

C) Greater overall prosperity due to an increased inner-city tax base

D) Insufficient revenues due to a decrease in manufacturing

15

Which choice provides the best evidence for the answer to the previous question?

A) Lines 36-39 ("America's . . . decades")

B) Lines 43-44 ("How . . . not know")

C) Lines 44-46 ("What . . . now")

D) Lines 48-51 ("The truth . . . end")

16

The passage implies that American cities in 1974

A) were witnessing the flight of minority populations to the suburbs.

B) had begun to lose their manufacturing sectors.

C) had a traditional four-zone structure.

D) were already experiencing demographic inversion.

17

Which choice provides the best evidence for the answer to the previous question?

A) Lines 54-57 ("Much . . . Ernest W. Burgess")

B) Lines 58-59 ("It was . . . settlement")

C) Lines 66-71 ("Virtually . . . continuum")

D) Lines 72-75 ("As . . . home")

18

As used in line 68, "conducted" is closest in meaning to

A) carried out.

B) supervised.

C) regulated.

D) inhibited.

19

The author of the passage would most likely consider the information in chart 1 to be

A) excellent evidence for the arguments made in the passage.

B) possibly accurate but too crude to be truly informative.

C) compelling but lacking in historical information.

D) representative of a perspective with which the author disagrees.

20

According to chart 2, the years 2000–2010 were characterized by

A) less growth in metropolitan areas of all sizes than had taken place in the 1990s.

B) more growth in small metropolitan areas than in large metropolitan areas.

C) a significant decline in the population of small metropolitan areas compared to the 1980s.

D) roughly equal growth in large metropolitan areas and nonmetropolitan areas.

21

Chart 2 suggests which of the following about population change in the 1990s?

A) Large numbers of people moved from suburban areas to urban areas in the 1990s.

B) Growth rates fell in smaller metropolitan areas in the 1990s.

C) Large numbers of people moved from metropolitan areas to nonmetropolitan areas in the 1990s.

D) The US population as a whole grew more in the 1990s than in the 1980s.

Questions 22-31 are based on the following passage.

This passage is adapted from Emily Anthes, *Frankenstein's Cat.* ©2013 by Emily Anthes.

When scientists first learned how to edit the genomes of animals, they began to imagine all the ways they could use this new power. Creating
Line brightly colored novelty pets was not a high priority.
5 Instead, most researchers envisioned far more consequential applications, hoping to create genetically engineered animals that saved human lives. One enterprise is now delivering on this dream. Welcome to the world of "pharming," in which
10 simple genetic tweaks turn animals into living pharmaceutical factories.

Many of the proteins that our cells crank out naturally make for good medicine. Our bodies' own enzymes, hormones, clotting factors, and antibodies
15 are commonly used to treat cancer, diabetes, autoimmune diseases, and more. The trouble is that it's difficult and expensive to make these compounds on an industrial scale, and as a result, patients can face shortages of the medicines they need. Dairy
20 animals, on the other hand, are expert protein producers, their udders swollen with milk. So the creation of the first transgenic animals—first mice, then other species—in the 1980s gave scientists an idea: What if they put the gene for a human antibody
25 or enzyme into a cow, goat, or sheep? If they put the gene in just the right place, under the control of the right molecular switch, maybe they could engineer animals that produced healing human proteins in their milk. Then doctors could collect medicine by
30 the bucketful.

Throughout the 1980s and '90s, studies provided proof of principle, as scientists created transgenic mice, sheep, goats, pigs, cattle, and rabbits that did in fact make therapeutic compounds in their milk.
35 At first, this work was merely gee-whiz, scientific geekery, lab-bound thought experiments come true. That all changed with ATryn, a drug produced by the Massachusetts firm GTC Biotherapeutics. ATryn is antithrombin, an anticoagulant that can be used to
40 prevent life-threatening blood clots. The compound, made by our liver cells, plays a key role in keeping our bodies clot-free. It acts as a molecular bouncer, sidling up to clot-forming compounds and escorting them out of the bloodstream. But as many as 1 in

45 2,000 Americans are born with a genetic mutation that prevents them from making antithrombin. These patients are prone to clots, especially in their legs and lungs, and they are at elevated risk of suffering from fatal complications during surgery
50 and childbirth. Supplemental antithrombin can reduce this risk, and GTC decided to try to manufacture the compound using genetically engineered goats.

To create its special herd of goats, GTC used
55 microinjection, the same technique that produced GloFish and AquAdvantage salmon. The company's scientists took the gene for human antithrombin and injected it directly into fertilized goat eggs. Then they implanted the eggs in the wombs of female goats.
60 When the kids were born, some of them proved to be transgenic, the human gene nestled safely in their cells. The researchers paired the antithrombin gene with a promoter (which is a sequence of DNA that controls gene activity) that is normally active in the
65 goat's mammary glands during milk production. When the transgenic females lactated, the promoter turned the transgene on and the goats' udders filled with milk containing antithrombin. All that was left to do was to collect the milk, and extract and purify
70 the protein. *Et voilà*—human medicine! And, for GTC, liquid gold. ATryn hit the market in 2006, becoming the world's first transgenic animal drug. Over the course of a year, the "milking parlors" on GTC's 300-acre farm in Massachusetts can collect
75 more than a kilogram of medicine from a single animal.

22

The primary purpose of the passage is to

A) present the background of a medical breakthrough.

B) evaluate the research that led to a scientific discovery.

C) summarize the findings of a long-term research project.

D) explain the development of a branch of scientific study.

23

The author's attitude toward pharming is best described as one of

A) apprehension.

B) ambivalence.

C) appreciation.

D) astonishment.

24

As used in line 20, "expert" most nearly means

A) knowledgeable.

B) professional.

C) capable.

D) trained.

25

What does the author suggest about the transgenic studies done in the 1980s and 1990s?

A) They were limited by the expensive nature of animal research.

B) They were not expected to yield products ready for human use.

C) They were completed when an anticoagulant compound was identified.

D) They focused only on the molecular properties of cows, goats, and sheep.

26

Which choice provides the best evidence for the answer to the previous question?

A) Lines 16-19 ("The trouble . . . need")

B) Lines 25-29 ("If they . . . milk")

C) Lines 35-36 ("At first . . . true")

D) Lines 37-40 ("That all . . . clots")

27

According to the passage, which of the following is true of antithrombin?

A) It reduces compounds that lead to blood clots.

B) It stems from a genetic mutation that is rare in humans.

C) It is a sequence of DNA known as a promoter.

D) It occurs naturally in goats' mammary glands.

28

Which choice provides the best evidence for the answer to the previous question?

A) Lines 12-16 ("Many . . . more")

B) Lines 42-44 ("It acts . . . bloodstream")

C) Lines 44-46 ("But as . . . antithrombin")

D) Lines 62-65 ("The researchers . . . production")

29

Which of the following does the author suggest about the "female goats" mentioned in line 59?

A) They secreted antithrombin in their milk after giving birth.

B) Some of their kids were not born with the antithrombin gene.

C) They were the first animals to receive microinjections.

D) Their cells already contained genes usually found in humans.

30

The most likely purpose of the parenthetical information in lines 63-64 is to

A) illustrate an abstract concept.

B) describe a new hypothesis.

C) clarify a claim.

D) define a term.

31

The phrase "liquid gold" (line 71) most directly suggests that

A) GTC has invested a great deal of money in the microinjection technique.

B) GTC's milking parlors have significantly increased milk production.

C) transgenic goats will soon be a valuable asset for dairy farmers.

D) ATryn has proved to be a financially beneficial product for GTC.

Questions 32-41 are based on the following passages.

Passage 1 is adapted from Edmund Burke, *Reflections on the Revolution in France*. Originally published in 1790. Passage 2 is adapted from Thomas Paine, *Rights of Man*. Originally published in 1791.

Passage 1

To avoid . . . the evils of inconstancy and versatility, ten thousand times worse than those of obstinacy and the blindest prejudice, we have
Line consecrated the state, that no man should approach
5 to look into its defects or corruptions but with due caution; that he should never dream of beginning its reformation by its subversion; that he should approach to the faults of the state as to the wounds of a father, with pious awe and trembling solicitude. By
10 this wise prejudice we are taught to look with horror on those children of their country who are prompt rashly to hack that aged parent in pieces, and put him into the kettle of magicians, in hopes that by their poisonous weeds, and wild incantations, they may
15 regenerate the paternal constitution, and renovate their father's life.

Society is indeed a contract. Subordinate contracts for objects of mere occasional interest may be dissolved at pleasure—but the state ought not to be
20 considered as nothing better than a partnership agreement in a trade of pepper and coffee, calico or tobacco, or some other such low concern, to be taken up for a little temporary interest, and to be dissolved by the fancy of the parties. It is to be looked on with
25 other reverence; because it is not a partnership in things subservient only to the gross animal existence of a temporary and perishable nature. It is a partnership in all science; a partnership in all art; a partnership in every virtue, and in all perfection.
30 As the ends of such a partnership cannot be obtained in many generations, it becomes a partnership not only between those who are living, but between those who are living, those who are dead, and those who are to be born. . . . The municipal corporations of
35 that universal kingdom are not morally at liberty at their pleasure, and on their speculations of a contingent improvement, wholly to separate and tear asunder the bands of their subordinate community, and to dissolve it into an unsocial, uncivil,
40 unconnected chaos of elementary principles.

CONTINUE

Passage 2

Every age and generation must be as free to act for itself, *in all cases*, as the ages and generations which preceded it. The vanity and presumption of governing beyond the grave, is the most ridiculous
45 and insolent of all tyrannies.

Man has no property in man; neither has any generation a property in the generations which are to follow. The Parliament or the people of 1688, or of any other period, had no more right to dispose of the
50 people of the present day, or to bind or to control them in any shape whatever, than the parliament or the people of the present day have to dispose of, bind, or control those who are to live a hundred or a thousand years hence.

55 Every generation is, and must be, competent to all the purposes which its occasions require. It is the living, and not the dead, that are to be accommodated. When man ceases to be, his power and his wants cease with him; and having no longer
60 any participation in the concerns of this world, he has no longer any authority in directing who shall be its governors, or how its government shall be organized, or how administered. . . .

Those who have quitted the world, and those who
65 are not yet arrived at it, are as remote from each other, as the utmost stretch of mortal imagination can conceive. What possible obligation, then, can exist between them; what rule or principle can be laid down, that two nonentities, the one out of existence,
70 and the other not in, and who never can meet in this world, that the one should control the other to the end of time? . . .

The circumstances of the world are continually changing, and the opinions of men change also; and
75 as government is for the living, and not for the dead, it is the living only that has any right in it. That which may be thought right and found convenient in one age, may be thought wrong and found inconvenient in another. In such cases, who is to
80 decide, the living, or the dead?

32

In Passage 1, Burke indicates that a contract between a person and society differs from other contracts mainly in its

A) brevity and prominence.

B) complexity and rigidity.

C) precision and usefulness.

D) seriousness and permanence.

33

As used in line 4, "state" most nearly refers to a

A) style of living.

B) position in life.

C) temporary condition.

D) political entity.

34

As used in line 22, "low" most nearly means

A) petty.

B) weak.

C) inadequate.

D) depleted.

35

It can most reasonably be inferred from Passage 2 that Paine views historical precedents as

A) generally helpful to those who want to change society.

B) surprisingly difficult for many people to comprehend.

C) frequently responsible for human progress.

D) largely irrelevant to current political decisions.

36

How would Paine most likely respond to Burke's statement in lines 30-34, Passage 1 ("As the . . . born")?

A) He would assert that the notion of a partnership across generations is less plausible to people of his era than it was to people in the past.

B) He would argue that there are no politically meaningful links between the dead, the living, and the unborn.

C) He would question the possibility that significant changes to a political system could be accomplished within a single generation.

D) He would point out that we cannot know what judgments the dead would make about contemporary issues.

37

Which choice provides the best evidence for the answer to the previous question?

A) Lines 41-43 ("Every . . . it")

B) Lines 43-45 ("The vanity . . . tyrannies")

C) Lines 56-58 ("It is . . . accommodated")

D) Lines 67-72 ("What . . . time")

38

Which choice best describes how Burke would most likely have reacted to Paine's remarks in the final paragraph of Passage 2?

A) With approval, because adapting to new events may enhance existing partnerships.

B) With resignation, because changing circumstances are an inevitable aspect of life.

C) With skepticism, because Paine does not substantiate his claim with examples of governments changed for the better.

D) With disapproval, because changing conditions are insufficient justification for changing the form of government.

39

Which choice provides the best evidence for the answer to the previous question?

A) Lines 1-4 ("To avoid . . . state")

B) Lines 7-9 ("he should . . . solicitude")

C) Lines 27-29 ("It is . . . perfection")

D) Lines 34-38 ("The municipal . . . community")

40

Which choice best states the relationship between the two passages?

A) Passage 2 challenges the primary argument of Passage 1.

B) Passage 2 advocates an alternative approach to a problem discussed in Passage 1.

C) Passage 2 provides further evidence to support an idea introduced in Passage 1.

D) Passage 2 exemplifies an attitude promoted in Passage 1.

41

The main purpose of both passages is to

A) suggest a way to resolve a particular political struggle.

B) discuss the relationship between people and their government.

C) evaluate the consequences of rapid political change.

D) describe the duties that governments have to their citizens.

CONTINUE

Questions 42-52 are based on the following passage and supplementary material.

This passage is adapted from Carolyn Gramling, "Source of Mysterious Medieval Eruption Identified." ©2013 by American Association for the Advancement of Science.

About 750 years ago, a powerful volcano erupted somewhere on Earth, kicking off a centuries-long cold snap known as the Little Ice Age. Identifying the
Line volcano responsible has been tricky.
5   That a powerful volcano erupted somewhere in the world, sometime in the Middle Ages, is written in polar ice cores in the form of layers of sulfate deposits and tiny shards of volcanic glass. These cores suggest that the amount of sulfur the mystery
10 volcano sent into the stratosphere put it firmly among the ranks of the strongest climate-perturbing eruptions of the current geological epoch, the Holocene, a period that stretches from 10,000 years ago to the present. A haze of stratospheric sulfur
15 cools the climate by reflecting solar energy back into space.
       In 2012, a team of scientists led by geochemist Gifford Miller strengthened the link between the mystery eruption and the onset of the Little Ice Age
20 by using radiocarbon dating of dead plant material from beneath the ice caps on Baffin Island and Iceland, as well as ice and sediment core data, to determine that the cold summers and ice growth began abruptly between 1275 and 1300 C.E. (and
25 became intensified between 1430 and 1455 C.E.). Such a sudden onset pointed to a huge volcanic eruption injecting sulfur into the stratosphere and starting the cooling. Subsequent, unusually large and frequent eruptions of other volcanoes, as well as
30 sea-ice/ocean feedbacks persisting long after the aerosols have been removed from the atmosphere, may have prolonged the cooling through the 1700s.
       Volcanologist Franck Lavigne and colleagues now think they've identified the volcano in question:
35 Indonesia's Samalas. One line of evidence, they note, is historical records. According to Babad Lombok, records of the island written on palm leaves in Old Javanese, Samalas erupted catastrophically before the end of the 13th century, devastating surrounding
40 villages—including Lombok's capital at the time, Pamatan—with ash and fast-moving sweeps of hot rock and gas called pyroclastic flows.
       The researchers then began to reconstruct the formation of the large, 800-meter-deep caldera [a
45 basin-shaped volcanic crater] that now sits atop the volcano. They examined 130 outcrops on the flanks of the volcano, exposing sequences of pumice—ash hardened into rock—and other pyroclastic material. The volume of ash deposited, and the estimated
50 height of the eruption plume (43 kilometers above sea level) put the eruption's magnitude at a minimum of 7 on the volcanic explosivity index (which has a scale of 1 to 8)—making it one of the largest known in the Holocene.
55   The team also performed radiocarbon analyses on carbonized tree trunks and branches buried within the pyroclastic deposits to confirm the date of the eruption; it could not, they concluded, have happened before 1257 C.E., and certainly happened
60 in the 13th century.
       It's not a total surprise that an Indonesian volcano might be the source of the eruption, Miller says. "An equatorial eruption is more consistent with the apparent climate impacts." And, he adds, with sulfate
65 appearing in both polar ice caps—Arctic and Antarctic—there is "a strong consensus" that this also supports an equatorial source.
       Another possible candidate—both in terms of timing and geographical location—is Ecuador's
70 Quilotoa, estimated to have last erupted between 1147 and 1320 C.E. But when Lavigne's team examined shards of volcanic glass from this volcano, they found that they didn't match the chemical composition of the glass found in polar ice cores,
75 whereas the Samalas glass is a much closer match. That, they suggest, further strengthens the case that Samalas was responsible for the medieval "year without summer" in 1258 C.E.

Estimated Temperature in Central England 1000 CE to 2000 CE

*Variation from the 1961-1990 average temperature, in °C, represented at 0.

Adapted from John P. Rafferty, "Little Ice Age." Originally published in 2011. ©2014 by Encyclopedia Britannica, Inc.

42

The main purpose of the passage is to

A) describe periods in Earth's recent geologic history.

B) explain the methods scientists use in radiocarbon analysis.

C) describe evidence linking the volcano Samalas to the Little Ice Age.

D) explain how volcanic glass forms during volcanic eruptions.

43

Over the course of the passage, the focus shifts from

A) a criticism of a scientific model to a new theory.

B) a description of a recorded event to its likely cause.

C) the use of ice core samples to a new method of measuring sulfates.

D) the use of radiocarbon dating to an examination of volcanic glass.

44

Which choice provides the best evidence for the answer to the previous question?

A) Lines 17-25 ("In 2012 . . . 1455 C.E.")

B) Lines 43-46 ("The researchers . . . atop the volcano")

C) Lines 46-48 ("They examined . . . material")

D) Lines 55-60 ("The team . . . 13th century")

45

The author uses the phrase "is written in" (line 6) most likely to

A) demonstrate the concept of the hands-on nature of the work done by scientists.

B) highlight the fact that scientists often write about their discoveries.

C) underscore the sense of importance that scientists have regarding their work.

D) reinforce the idea that the evidence is there and can be interpreted by scientists.

46

Where does the author indicate the medieval volcanic eruption most probably was located?

A) Near the equator, in Indonesia

B) In the Arctic region

C) In the Antarctic region

D) Near the equator, in Ecuador

47

Which choice provides the best evidence for the answer to the previous question?

A) Lines 1-3 ("About 750 . . . Ice Age")

B) Lines 26-28 ("Such a . . . the cooling")

C) Lines 49-54 ("The volume . . . the Holocene")

D) Lines 61-64 ("It's not . . . climate impacts")

48

As used in line 68, the phrase "Another possible candidate" implies that

A) powerful volcanic eruptions occur frequently.

B) the effects of volcanic eruptions can last for centuries.

C) scientists know of other volcanoes that erupted during the Middle Ages.

D) other volcanoes have calderas that are very large.

49

Which choice best supports the claim that Quilotoa was not responsible for the Little Ice Age?

A) Lines 3-4 ("Identifying . . . tricky")

B) Lines 26-28 ("Such a . . . cooling")

C) Lines 43-46 ("The researchers . . . atop the volcano")

D) Lines 71-75 ("But . . . closer match")

50

According to the data in the figure, the greatest below-average temperature variation occurred around what year?

A) 1200 CE

B) 1375 CE

C) 1675 CE

D) 1750 CE

51

The passage and the figure are in agreement that the onset of the Little Ice Age began

A) around 1150 CE.

B) just before 1300 CE.

C) just before 1500 CE.

D) around 1650 CE.

52

What statement is best supported by the data presented in the figure?

A) The greatest cooling during the Little Ice Age occurred hundreds of years after the temperature peaks of the Medieval Warm Period.

B) The sharp decline in temperature supports the hypothesis of an equatorial volcanic eruption in the Middle Ages.

C) Pyroclastic flows from volcanic eruptions continued for hundreds of years after the eruptions had ended.

D) Radiocarbon analysis is the best tool scientists have to determine the temperature variations after volcanic eruptions.

STOP

If you finish before time is called, you may check your work on this section only.

Do not turn to any other section.

Writing and Language Test

35 MINUTES, 44 QUESTIONS

Turn to Section 2 of your answer sheet to answer the questions in this section.

DIRECTIONS

Each passage below is accompanied by a number of questions. For some questions, you will consider how the passage might be revised to improve the expression of ideas. For other questions, you will consider how the passage might be edited to correct errors in sentence structure, usage, or punctuation. A passage or a question may be accompanied by one or more graphics (such as a table or graph) that you will consider as you make revising and editing decisions.

Some questions will direct you to an underlined portion of a passage. Other questions will direct you to a location in a passage or ask you to think about the passage as a whole.

After reading each passage, choose the answer to each question that most effectively improves the quality of writing in the passage or that makes the passage conform to the conventions of standard written English. Many questions include a "NO CHANGE" option. Choose that option if you think the best choice is to leave the relevant portion of the passage as it is.

Questions 1-11 are based on the following passage.

Ghost Mural

In 1932 the well-known Mexican muralist David Alfaro Siqueiros was commissioned to paint a mural on the second-story exterior wall of a historic building in downtown Los Angeles. Siqueiros was asked to celebrate tropical America in his work, **1** he accordingly titled it "América Tropical." He painted the mural's first two sections, featuring images of a tropical rainforest and a Maya pyramid, during the day. **2** Also, to avoid

1
A) NO CHANGE
B) which he accordingly titled
C) accordingly he titled it
D) it was titled accordingly

2
A) NO CHANGE
B) However,
C) Although,
D) Moreover,

scrutiny, Siqueiros painted the final section of the mural, the **3** centerpiece at night.

   4 The reason for Siqueiros's secrecy became clear when the mural was **5** confided. The centerpiece of the work was dominated by images of native people being oppressed and **6** including an eagle symbolizing the United States. Siqueiros's political message did not please the wealthy citizens who had commissioned his work. They eventually ordered the mural to be literally whitewashed, or painted over with white paint.

   However, by the 1970s, the white paint had begun to fade, and the bright colors of the mural were beginning to show through. At the same time, a social and civil rights movement for Mexican Americans was working to raise awareness of Mexican American cultural identity. Artists associated with **7** this began to rediscover and promote the work of the Mexican muralists, particularly Siqueiros. To them, "América Tropical" was an example of how art in public spaces could be used to celebrate Mexican American heritage while at the same time making a political statement. Inspired by Siqueiros and the other muralists, this new generation of artists strove to emulate the old mural masters.

3

A) NO CHANGE
B) centerpiece,
C) centerpiece;
D) centerpiece—

4

Which choice best connects the sentence with the previous paragraph?
A) NO CHANGE
B) All three sections of the mural were on display
C) The community turned out in large numbers
D) Siqueiros was informed of people's reactions

5

A) NO CHANGE
B) promulgated.
C) imparted.
D) unveiled.

6

A) NO CHANGE
B) included
C) includes
D) had included

7

A) NO CHANGE
B) it
C) them
D) this movement

CONTINUE

[8] The result was an explosion of mural painting that spread throughout California and the southwestern United States in the 1970s. It was the Chicano mural movement. Hundreds of large, colorful new murals depicting elements of Mexican American life and history appeared during this period, some in designated cultural locations but many more in abandoned lots, on unused buildings, or [9] painted on infrastructure such as highways and bridges. Many of these murals can still be seen today, although some have not been well maintained.

8

Which choice most effectively combines the underlined sentences?

A) The result was an explosion, the Chicano mural movement, of mural painting that spread throughout California and the southwestern United States in the 1970s.

B) The result was the Chicano mural movement, an explosion of mural painting that spread throughout California and the southwestern United States in the 1970s.

C) The explosion of mural painting that spread throughout California and the southwestern United States in the 1970s was the resulting Chicano mural movement.

D) An explosion of mural painting resulted and it spread throughout California and the southwestern United States in the 1970s; it was the Chicano mural movement.

9

A) NO CHANGE
B) they were painted on
C) on
D) DELETE the underlined portion.

Fortunately, a new group of artists has discovered the murals, and efforts are underway to clean, restore, and repaint them. Once again, Siqueiros's "América Tropical" is [10] leading the way. After a lengthy and complex restoration process, this powerful work is now a tourist attraction, complete with a visitor center and a rooftop viewing platform. [11] Advocates hope that Siqueiros's mural will once more serve as an inspiration, this time inspiring viewers to save and restore an important cultural and artistic legacy.

10

Which choice most effectively sets up the information that follows?

A) NO CHANGE

B) being cleaned and restored.

C) at risk of destruction.

D) awaiting its moment of appreciation.

11

At this point, the writer is considering adding the following sentence.

> When it was painted in 1932, Siqueiros's mural was considered offensive, but now it is acclaimed.

Should the writer make this addition here?

A) Yes, because it provides historical context for the changes discussed in the passage.

B) Yes, because it provides a useful reminder of how people once viewed Siqueiros's work.

C) No, because it unnecessarily repeats information from earlier in the passage.

D) No, because it makes a claim about Siqueiros's work that is not supported by the passage.

Questions 12-22 are based on the following passage.

The Hype of Healthier Organic Food

Some people buy organic food because they believe organically grown crops are more nutritious and safer for consumption than [12] the people who purchase their conventionally grown counterparts, which are usually produced with pesticides and synthetic fertilizers. In the name of health, [13] spending $1.60 for every dollar they would have spent on food that is [14] grown in a manner that is considered conventional. Scientific evidence, [15] therefore, suggests that consumers do not reap significant benefits, in terms of either nutritional value or safety, from organic food.

[12]
A) NO CHANGE
B) the purchase of
C) purchasing
D) DELETE the underlined portion.

[13]
A) NO CHANGE
B) these consumers spend
C) having spent
D) to spend

[14]
A) NO CHANGE
B) grown with conventional methods, using pesticides and synthetic fertilizers.
C) conventionally and therefore not organically grown.
D) conventionally grown.

[15]
A) NO CHANGE
B) furthermore,
C) however,
D) subsequently,

Although advocates of organic food [16] preserve that organic produce is healthier than conventionally grown produce because it has more vitamins and minerals, this assertion is not supported by scientific research. [17] For instance, one review published in *The American Journal of Clinical Nutrition* provided analysis of the results of comparative studies conducted over a span of 50 years; researchers consistently found no evidence that organic crops are more nutritious than conventionally grown ones in terms of their vitamin and mineral content. [18] Similarly, Stanford University researchers who examined almost 250 studies comparing the nutritional content of different kinds of organic foods with that of their nonorganic counterparts found very little difference between the two.

[16]

A) NO CHANGE
B) carry on
C) maintain
D) sustain

[17]

A) NO CHANGE
B) However,
C) In addition,
D) Likewise,

[18]

At this point, the writer is considering adding the following sentence.

> The United States Department of Agriculture (USDA) reports that organic agricultural products are now available in approximately 20,000 markets specializing in natural foods.

Should the writer make this addition here?

A) Yes, because it adds a relevant research finding from a government agency.
B) Yes, because it supports the passage's argument that organic food is less nutritious than conventionally grown food.
C) No, because it is not relevant to the paragraph's discussion of scientific evidence.
D) No, because it introduces a term that has not been defined in the passage.

Evidence also undermines the claim that organic food is safer to eat. While researchers have found lower levels of pesticide residue in organic produce than in nonorganic produce, the pesticide residue detected in conventional produce falls within acceptable safety limits. According to such organizations as the US Environmental Protection Agency, the minute amounts of residue falling within such limits **19** have no negative impact on human health. **20**

19

A) NO CHANGE
B) is having
C) has had
D) has

20

At this point, the writer wants to further reinforce the paragraph's claim about the safety of nonorganic food. Which choice most effectively accomplishes this goal?

A) To be labeled organic, a product must meet certain standards determined and monitored by the US Department of Agriculture.

B) Organic food, however, is regulated to eliminate artificial ingredients that include certain types of preservatives, sweeteners, colorings, and flavors.

C) Moreover, consumers who are concerned about ingesting pesticide residue can eliminate much of it by simply washing or peeling produce before eating it.

D) In fact, the Environmental Protection Agency estimates that about one-fifth of the pesticides used worldwide are applied to crops in the United States.

Based on scientific evidence, organic food offers neither significant nutritional nor safety benefits for consumers. Proponents of organic food, of course, are quick to add that **21** their are numerous other reasons to buy organic **22** food, such as, a desire to protect the environment from potentially damaging pesticides or a preference for the taste of organically grown foods. Research regarding these issues is less conclusive than the findings regarding nutritional content and pesticide residue safety limits. What is clear, though, is this: if a consumer's goal is to buy the healthiest and safest food to eat, the increased cost of organic food is a waste of money.

21

A) NO CHANGE
B) there are
C) there is
D) their is

22

A) NO CHANGE
B) food such as:
C) food such as,
D) food, such as

Questions 23-33 are based on the following passage and supplementary material.

You Are Where You Say

Research on regional variations in English-language use has not only yielded answers to such **23** life-altering questions as how people in different parts of the United States refer to carbonated beverages ("soda"? "pop"? "coke"?) **24** it also illustrates how technology can change the very nature of research. While traditional, human-intensive data collection **25** has all but disappeared in language studies, the explosion of social media has opened new avenues for investigation.

[1] Perhaps the epitome of traditional methodology is the *Dictionary of American Regional English*, colloquially known as *DARE*. [2] Its fifth and final alphabetical volume—ending with "zydeco"—released in 2012, the dictionary represents decades of arduous work. [3] Over a six-year period from 1965 to 1970, university graduate students conducted interviews in more than a thousand communities across the nation. [4] Their goal was to determine what names people used for such everyday objects and concepts as a submarine sandwich

---

23

The writer wants to convey an attitude of genuine interest and to avoid the appearance of mockery. Which choice best accomplishes this goal?
A) NO CHANGE
B) galvanizing
C) intriguing
D) weird

24

A) NO CHANGE
B) and also illustrates
C) but also illustrates
D) illustrating

25

Which choice most effectively sets up the contrast in the sentence and is consistent with the information in the rest of the passage?
A) NO CHANGE
B) still has an important place
C) remains the only option
D) yields questionable results

(a "hero" in New York City but a "dagwood" in many parts of Minnesota, Iowa, and Colorado) and a heavy rainstorm (variously a "gully washer," "pour-down," or "stump mover"). [5] The work that dictionary founder Frederic G. Cassidy had expected to be finished by 1976 was not, in fact, completed in his lifetime. [6] The wait did not dampen enthusiasm among 26 scholars. Scholars consider the work a signal achievement in linguistics. 27

Not all research into regional English varieties 28 requires such time, effort, and resources, however. Today's researchers have found that the veritable army of trained volunteers traveling the country conducting face-to-face interviews can sometimes be 29 replaced by another army the vast array of individuals volunteering details about their lives—and, inadvertently, their language—through social media. Brice Russ of Ohio State University, for example, has employed software to sort through postings on one social media 30 cite in search of particular words and phrases of interest as well as the location from which users are posting. From these data,

26
A) NO CHANGE
B) scholars, and these scholars
C) scholars, but scholars
D) scholars, who

27

To improve the cohesion and flow of this paragraph, the writer wants to add the following sentence.

> Data gathering proved to be the quick part of the project.

The sentence would most logically be placed after

A) sentence 2.
B) sentence 3.
C) sentence 4.
D) sentence 5.

28
A) NO CHANGE
B) are requiring
C) have required
D) require

29
A) NO CHANGE
B) replaced—by another army,
C) replaced by another army;
D) replaced by another army:

30
A) NO CHANGE
B) site in search of
C) sight in search for
D) cite in search for

he was able, among other things, to confirm regional variations in people's terms for soft drinks. As the map shows, "soda" is commonly heard in the middle and western portions of the United States; "pop" is frequently used in many southern states; and "coke" is predominant in the northeastern and southwest regions but used elsewhere as well. **31** As interesting as Russ's findings are, though, **32** they're true value lies in their reminder that the Internet is not merely a sophisticated tool for collecting data but is also **33** itself a rich source of data.

Soft Drink Descriptions by State
Highest Percentage Reported

- pop
- coke
- soda

Adapted from Jennifer M. Smith, Department of Geography, The Pennsylvania State University, with data from www.popvssoda.com

---

31

The writer wants the information in the passage to correspond as closely as possible with the information in the map. Given that goal and assuming that the rest of the previous sentence would remain unchanged, in which sequence should the three terms for soft drinks be discussed?

A) NO CHANGE

B) "pop," "soda," "coke"

C) "pop," "coke," "soda"

D) "soda," "coke," "pop"

32

A) NO CHANGE

B) their true value lies in their

C) there true value lies in they're

D) their true value lies in there

33

Which choice most effectively concludes the sentence and paragraph?

A) NO CHANGE

B) where we can learn what terms people use to refer to soft drinks.

C) a useful way to stay connected to friends, family, and colleagues.

D) helpful to researchers.

Questions 34-44 are based on the following passage.

Creating Worlds: A Career in Game Design

If you love video games and have thought about how the games you play might be changed or improved, or if you've imagined creating a video game of your own, you might want to consider a career as a video game designer. There [34] were a number of steps you can take to determine whether game design is the right field for you and, if it is, to prepare yourself for such a career.

Before making the choice, you should have some sense of what a video game designer does. Every video game, whether for a console, computer, or mobile device, starts with a concept that originates in the mind of a designer. The designer envisions the game's fundamental [35] elements: the settings, characters, and plots that make each game unique, and is thus a primary creative force behind a video game.

Conceptualizing a game is only the beginning of a video game designer's [36] job, however, no matter how good a concept is, it will never be translated into a video game unless it is communicated effectively to all the other members of the video game development team. [37] A designer must generate extensive documentation and

34

A) NO CHANGE
B) has been
C) are
D) was

35

A) NO CHANGE
B) elements: the settings, characters, and plots that make each game unique—
C) elements—the settings, characters, and plots that make each game unique—
D) elements; the settings, characters, and plots that make each game unique;

36

A) NO CHANGE
B) job, however. No
C) job—however, no
D) job however no

37

At this point, the writer is considering adding the following sentence.

> Successful communication is essential if a designer's idea is to become a reality.

Should the writer make this addition here?

A) Yes, because it supports the conclusion drawn in the following sentence.
B) Yes, because it illustrates a general principle discussed in the paragraph.
C) No, because it distracts from the focus of the paragraph by introducing irrelevant material.
D) No, because it merely reformulates the thought expressed in the preceding sentence.

38 explain his or her ideas clearly in order to ensure that the programmers, artists, and others on the team all share the same vision. 39 Likewise, anyone considering a career as a video game designer must be 40 skilled writers and speakers. In addition, because video game development is a collaborative effort and because the development of any one game may take months or even years, a designer must be an effective team player as well as detail oriented.

[1] A basic understanding of computer programming is essential. [2] In fact, many designers 41 initially begin their pursuits as programmers. [3] Consider taking some general computer science courses as well as courses in artificial intelligence and graphics in order to increase your understanding of the technical challenges involved in developing a video game. [4] Courses in psychology and human behavior may help you develop 42 emphatic collaboration skills, while courses in the humanities, such as in literature and film, should give you the background necessary to develop effective narrative structures. [5] A

38

Which choice results in a sentence that best supports the point developed in this paragraph?

A) NO CHANGE

B) possess a vivid imagination

C) assess his or her motivations carefully

D) learn to accept constructive criticism

39

A) NO CHANGE

B) Nevertheless,

C) Consequently,

D) However,

40

A) NO CHANGE

B) a skilled writer and speaker.

C) skilled both as writers and speakers.

D) both skilled writers and speakers.

41

A) NO CHANGE

B) start to begin their work

C) initiate their progression

D) begin their careers

42

A) NO CHANGE

B) paramount

C) eminent

D) important

designer also needs careful educational preparation. [6] Finally, because a designer should understand the business aspects of the video game industry, such as budgeting and marketing, you may want to consider taking some business courses. [7] Although demanding and deadline driven, 43 video game design can be a lucrative and rewarding field for people who love gaming and have prepared themselves with the necessary skills and knowledge. 44

43

A) NO CHANGE
B) the choice of video game design
C) you should choose video game design because it
D) choosing to design video games

44

To make this paragraph most logical, sentence 5 should be
A) placed where it is now.
B) placed before sentence 1.
C) placed after sentence 3.
D) DELETED from the paragraph.

STOP

If you finish before time is called, you may check your work on this section only.
Do not turn to any other section.

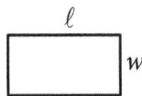

Math Test – No Calculator

25 MINUTES, 20 QUESTIONS

Turn to Section 3 of your answer sheet to answer the questions in this section.

DIRECTIONS

For questions 1-15, solve each problem, choose the best answer from the choices provided, and fill in the corresponding circle on your answer sheet. **For questions 16-20**, solve the problem and enter your answer in the grid on the answer sheet. Please refer to the directions before question 16 on how to enter your answers in the grid. You may use any available space in your test booklet for scratch work.

NOTES

1. The use of a calculator **is not permitted**.

2. All variables and expressions used represent real numbers unless otherwise indicated.

3. Figures provided in this test are drawn to scale unless otherwise indicated.

4. All figures lie in a plane unless otherwise indicated.

5. Unless otherwise indicated, the domain of a given function f is the set of all real numbers x for which $f(x)$ is a real number.

REFERENCE

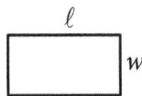 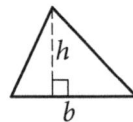 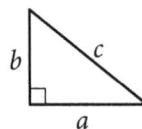 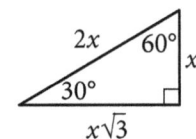 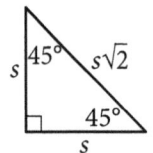

$A = \pi r^2$ $A = \ell w$ $A = \frac{1}{2}bh$ $c^2 = a^2 + b^2$ Special Right Triangles
$C = 2\pi r$

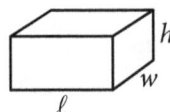 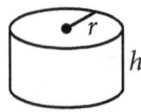 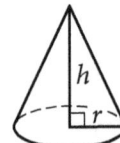 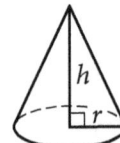 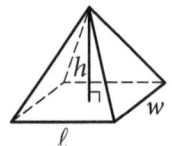

$V = \ell wh$ $V = \pi r^2 h$ $V = \frac{4}{3}\pi r^3$ $V = \frac{1}{3}\pi r^2 h$ $V = \frac{1}{3}\ell wh$

The number of degrees of arc in a circle is 360.
The number of radians of arc in a circle is 2π.
The sum of the measures in degrees of the angles of a triangle is 180.

        CONTINUE ➡

1

Which of the following expressions is equal to 0 for some value of x ?

A) $|x - 1| - 1$

B) $|x + 1| + 1$

C) $|1 - x| + 1$

D) $|x - 1| + 1$

2

$$f(x) = \frac{3}{2}x + b$$

In the function above, b is a constant. If $f(6) = 7$, what is the value of $f(-2)$?

A) -5

B) -2

C) 1

D) 7

3

$$\frac{x}{y} = 6$$
$$4(y + 1) = x$$

If (x, y) is the solution to the system of equations above, what is the value of y ?

A) 2

B) 4

C) 12

D) 24

4

If $f(x) = -2x + 5$, what is $f(-3x)$ equal to?

A) $-6x - 5$

B) $6x + 5$

C) $6x - 5$

D) $6x^2 - 15x$

CONTINUE

5

$$3(2x + 1)(4x + 1)$$

Which of the following is equivalent to the expression above?

A) $45x$

B) $24x^2 + 3$

C) $24x^2 + 18x + 3$

D) $18x^2 + 6$

6

If $\dfrac{a - b}{b} = \dfrac{3}{7}$, which of the following must also be true?

A) $\dfrac{a}{b} = -\dfrac{4}{7}$

B) $\dfrac{a}{b} = \dfrac{10}{7}$

C) $\dfrac{a + b}{b} = \dfrac{10}{7}$

D) $\dfrac{a - 2b}{b} = -\dfrac{11}{7}$

7

While preparing to run a marathon, Amelia created a training schedule in which the distance of her longest run every week increased by a constant amount. If Amelia's training schedule requires that her longest run in week 4 is a distance of 8 miles and her longest run in week 16 is a distance of 26 miles, which of the following best describes how the distance Amelia runs changes between week 4 and week 16 of her training schedule?

A) Amelia increases the distance of her longest run by 0.5 miles each week.

B) Amelia increases the distance of her longest run by 2 miles each week.

C) Amelia increases the distance of her longest run by 2 miles every 3 weeks.

D) Amelia increases the distance of her longest run by 1.5 miles each week.

8

Which of the following equations represents a line that is parallel to the line with equation $y = -3x + 4$?

A) $6x + 2y = 15$

B) $3x - y = 7$

C) $2x - 3y = 6$

D) $x + 3y = 1$

9

$$\sqrt{x - a} = x - 4$$

If $a = 2$, what is the solution set of the equation above?

A) $\{3, 6\}$

B) $\{2\}$

C) $\{3\}$

D) $\{6\}$

10

If $\dfrac{t + 5}{t - 5} = 10$, what is the value of t ?

A) $\dfrac{45}{11}$

B) 5

C) $\dfrac{11}{2}$

D) $\dfrac{55}{9}$

11

$$x = 2y + 5$$
$$y = (2x - 3)(x + 9)$$

How many ordered pairs (x, y) satisfy the system of equations shown above?

A) 0

B) 1

C) 2

D) Infinitely many

CONTINUE ➡

12

Ken and Paul each ordered a sandwich at a restaurant. The price of Ken's sandwich was x dollars, and the price of Paul's sandwich was \$1 more than the price of Ken's sandwich. If Ken and Paul split the cost of the sandwiches evenly and each paid a 20% tip, which of the following expressions represents the amount, in dollars, each of them paid? (Assume there is no sales tax.)

A) $0.2x + 0.2$

B) $0.5x + 0.1$

C) $1.2x + 0.6$

D) $2.4x + 1.2$

13

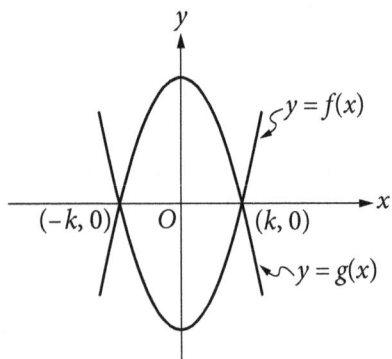

The functions f and g, defined by $f(x) = 8x^2 - 2$ and $g(x) = -8x^2 + 2$, are graphed in the xy-plane above. The graphs of f and g intersect at the points $(k, 0)$ and $(-k, 0)$. What is the value of k ?

A) $\dfrac{1}{4}$

B) $\dfrac{1}{2}$

C) 1

D) 2

14

$$\frac{8 - i}{3 - 2i}$$

If the expression above is rewritten in the form $a + bi$, where a and b are real numbers, what is the value of a ? (Note: $i = \sqrt{-1}$)

A) 2

B) $\dfrac{8}{3}$

C) 3

D) $\dfrac{11}{3}$

15

$$x^2 - \frac{k}{2}x = 2p$$

In the quadratic equation above, k and p are constants. What are the solutions for x ?

A) $x = \dfrac{k}{4} \pm \dfrac{\sqrt{k^2 + 2p}}{4}$

B) $x = \dfrac{k}{4} \pm \dfrac{\sqrt{k^2 + 32p}}{4}$

C) $x = \dfrac{k}{2} \pm \dfrac{\sqrt{k^2 + 2p}}{2}$

D) $x = \dfrac{k}{2} \pm \dfrac{\sqrt{k^2 + 32p}}{4}$

DIRECTIONS

For questions 16–20, solve the problem and enter your answer in the grid, as described below, on the answer sheet.

1. Although not required, it is suggested that you write your answer in the boxes at the top of the columns to help you fill in the circles accurately. You will receive credit only if the circles are filled in correctly.
2. Mark no more than one circle in any column.
3. No question has a negative answer.
4. Some problems may have more than one correct answer. In such cases, grid only one answer.
5. **Mixed numbers** such as $3\frac{1}{2}$ must be gridded as 3.5 or 7/2. (If 3 1 / 2 is entered into the grid, it will be interpreted as $\frac{31}{2}$, not $3\frac{1}{2}$.)
6. **Decimal answers:** If you obtain a decimal answer with more digits than the grid can accommodate, it may be either rounded or truncated, but it must fill the entire grid.

Answer: $\frac{7}{12}$

Write answer in boxes.

← Fraction line

Grid in result.

Answer: 2.5

← Decimal point

Acceptable ways to grid $\frac{2}{3}$ are:

Answer: 201 – either position is correct

NOTE: You may start your answers in any column, space permitting. Columns you don't need to use should be left blank.

CONTINUE

16

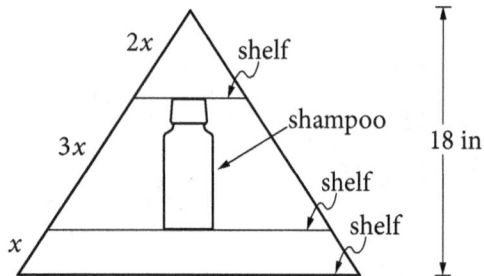

Jim has a triangular shelf system that attaches to his showerhead. The total height of the system is 18 inches, and there are three parallel shelves as shown above. What is the maximum height, in inches, of a shampoo bottle that can stand upright on the middle shelf?

17

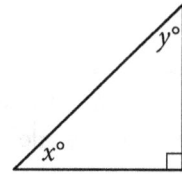

In the triangle above, the sine of $x°$ is 0.6. What is the cosine of $y°$?

18

$$x^3 - 5x^2 + 2x - 10 = 0$$

For what real value of x is the equation above true?

19

$$-3x + 4y = 20$$
$$6x + 3y = 15$$

If (x, y) is the solution to the system of equations above, what is the value of x ?

20

The mesosphere is the layer of Earth's atmosphere between 50 kilometers and 85 kilometers above Earth's surface. At a distance of 50 kilometers from Earth's surface, the temperature in the mesosphere is $-5°$ Celsius, and at a distance of 80 kilometers from Earth's surface, the temperature in the mesosphere is $-80°$ Celsius. For every additional 10 kilometers from Earth's surface, the temperature in the mesosphere decreases by $k°$ Celsius, where k is a constant. What is the value of k ?

STOP

If you finish before time is called, you may check your work on this section only.
Do not turn to any other section.

Math Test – Calculator

55 MINUTES, 38 QUESTIONS

Turn to Section 4 of your answer sheet to answer the questions in this section.

DIRECTIONS

For questions 1-30, solve each problem, choose the best answer from the choices provided, and fill in the corresponding circle on your answer sheet. **For questions 31-38**, solve the problem and enter your answer in the grid on the answer sheet. Please refer to the directions before question 31 on how to enter your answers in the grid. You may use any available space in your test booklet for scratch work.

NOTES

1. The use of a calculator **is permitted**.

2. All variables and expressions used represent real numbers unless otherwise indicated.

3. Figures provided in this test are drawn to scale unless otherwise indicated.

4. All figures lie in a plane unless otherwise indicated.

5. Unless otherwise indicated, the domain of a given function f is the set of all real numbers x for which $f(x)$ is a real number.

REFERENCE

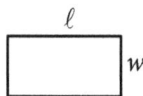

$A = \pi r^2$
$C = 2\pi r$

$A = \ell w$

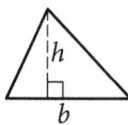

$A = \frac{1}{2}bh$

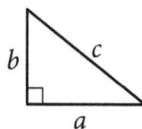

$c^2 = a^2 + b^2$

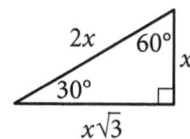

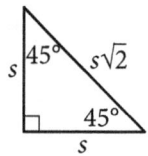

Special Right Triangles

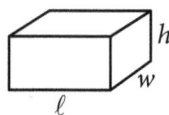

$V = \ell wh$

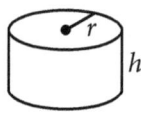

$V = \pi r^2 h$

$V = \frac{4}{3}\pi r^3$

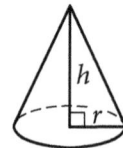

$V = \frac{1}{3}\pi r^2 h$

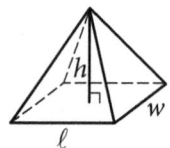

$V = \frac{1}{3}\ell wh$

The number of degrees of arc in a circle is 360.
The number of radians of arc in a circle is 2π.
The sum of the measures in degrees of the angles of a triangle is 180.

CONTINUE ➤

1

The monthly membership fee for an online television and movie service is $9.80. The cost of viewing television shows online is included in the membership fee, but there is an additional fee of $1.50 to rent each movie online. For one month, Jill's membership and movie rental fees were $12.80. How many movies did Jill rent online that month?

A) 1
B) 2
C) 3
D) 4

2

One of the requirements for becoming a court reporter is the ability to type 225 words per minute. Donald can currently type 180 words per minute, and believes that with practice he can increase his typing speed by 5 words per minute each month. Which of the following represents the number of words per minute that Donald believes he will be able to type m months from now?

A) $5 + 180m$
B) $225 + 5m$
C) $180 + 5m$
D) $180 - 5m$

3

If a 3-pound pizza is sliced in half and each half is sliced into thirds, what is the weight, in ounces, of each of the slices? (1 pound = 16 ounces)

A) 4
B) 6
C) 8
D) 16

4

Nick surveyed a random sample of the freshman class of his high school to determine whether the Fall Festival should be held in October or November. Of the 90 students surveyed, 25.6% preferred October. Based on this information, about how many students in the entire 225-person class would be expected to prefer having the Fall Festival in October?

A) 50
B) 60
C) 75
D) 80

5

The density of an object is equal to the mass of the object divided by the volume of the object. What is the volume, in milliliters, of an object with a mass of 24 grams and a density of 3 grams per milliliter?

A) 0.125

B) 8

C) 21

D) 72

6

Last week Raul worked 11 more hours than Angelica. If they worked a combined total of 59 hours, how many hours did Angelica work last week?

A) 24

B) 35

C) 40

D) 48

7

Movies with Greatest Ticket Sales in 2012

MPAA rating	Type of movie				
	Action	Animated	Comedy	Drama	Total
PG	2	7	0	2	11
PG-13	10	0	4	8	22
R	6	0	5	6	17
Total	18	7	9	16	50

The table above represents the 50 movies that had the greatest ticket sales in 2012, categorized by movie type and Motion Picture Association of America (MPAA) rating. What proportion of the movies are comedies with a PG-13 rating?

A) $\dfrac{2}{25}$

B) $\dfrac{9}{50}$

C) $\dfrac{2}{11}$

D) $\dfrac{11}{25}$

8

Line ℓ in the xy-plane contains points from each of Quadrants II, III, and IV, but no points from Quadrant I. Which of the following must be true?

A) The slope of line ℓ is undefined.

B) The slope of line ℓ is zero.

C) The slope of line ℓ is positive.

D) The slope of line ℓ is negative.

Number of Registered Voters
in the United States in 2012, in Thousands

| Region | Age, in years | | | | | Total |
	18 to 24	25 to 44	45 to 64	65 to 74	75 and older	
Northeast	2,713	8,159	10,986	3,342	2,775	27,975
Midwest	3,453	11,237	13,865	4,221	3,350	36,126
South	5,210	18,072	21,346	7,272	4,969	56,869
West	3,390	10,428	11,598	3,785	2,986	32,187
Total	14,766	47,896	57,795	18,620	14,080	153,157

The table above shows the number of registered voters in 2012, in thousands, in four geographic regions and five age groups. Based on the table, if a registered voter who was 18 to 44 years old in 2012 is chosen at random, which of the following is closest to the probability that the registered voter was from the Midwest region?

A) 0.10

B) 0.25

C) 0.40

D) 0.75

Questions 10 and 11 refer to the following information.

Gestation Period versus Life Expectancy

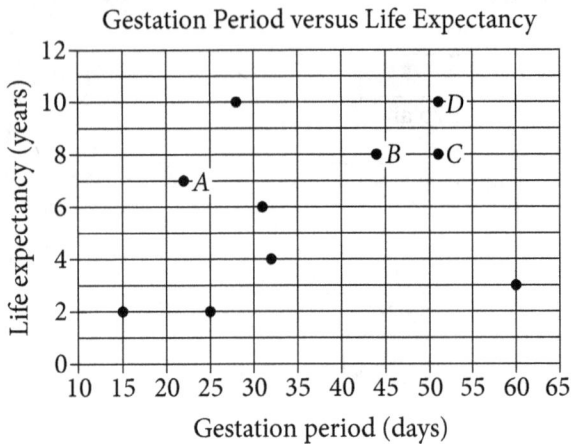

A curator at a wildlife society created the scatterplot above to examine the relationship between the gestation period and life expectancy of 10 species of animals.

10

What is the life expectancy, in years, of the animal that has the longest gestation period?

A) 3

B) 4

C) 8

D) 10

11

Of the labeled points, which represents the animal for which the ratio of life expectancy to gestation period is greatest?

A) A

B) B

C) C

D) D

12

In the xy-plane, the graph of function f has x-intercepts at -3, -1, and 1. Which of the following could define f ?

A) $f(x) = (x - 3)(x - 1)(x + 1)$

B) $f(x) = (x - 3)(x - 1)^2$

C) $f(x) = (x - 1)(x + 1)(x + 3)$

D) $f(x) = (x + 1)^2(x + 3)$

13

The population of mosquitoes in a swamp is estimated over the course of twenty weeks, as shown in the table.

Time (weeks)	Population
0	100
5	1,000
10	10,000
15	100,000
20	1,000,000

Which of the following best describes the relationship between time and the estimated population of mosquitoes during the twenty weeks?

A) Increasing linear

B) Decreasing linear

C) Exponential growth

D) Exponential decay

14

$$1{,}000\left(1 + \frac{r}{1{,}200}\right)^{12}$$

The expression above gives the amount of money, in dollars, generated in a year by a $1,000 deposit in a bank account that pays an annual interest rate of $r\%$, compounded monthly. Which of the following expressions shows how much additional money is generated at an interest rate of 5% than at an interest rate of 3% ?

A) $1{,}000\left(1 + \dfrac{5 - 3}{1{,}200}\right)^{12}$

B) $1{,}000\left(1 + \dfrac{\frac{5}{3}}{1{,}200}\right)^{12}$

C) $\dfrac{1{,}000\left(1 + \dfrac{5}{1{,}200}\right)^{12}}{1{,}000\left(1 + \dfrac{3}{1{,}200}\right)^{12}}$

D) $1{,}000\left(1 + \dfrac{5}{1{,}200}\right)^{12} - 1{,}000\left(1 + \dfrac{3}{1{,}200}\right)^{12}$

15

Which of the following scatterplots shows a relationship that is appropriately modeled with the equation $y = ax^b$, where a is positive and b is negative?

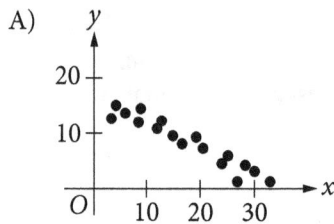

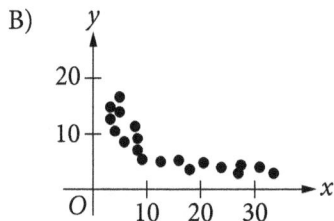

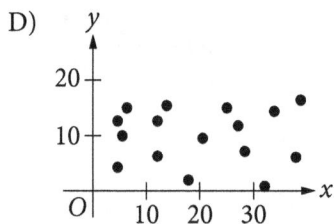

A)

B)

C)

D)

Questions 16 and 17 refer to the following information.

Mr. Martinson is building a concrete patio in his backyard and deciding where to buy the materials and rent the tools needed for the project. The table below shows the materials' cost and daily rental costs for three different stores.

Store	Materials' Cost, M (dollars)	Rental cost of wheelbarrow, W (dollars per day)	Rental cost of concrete mixer, K (dollars per day)
A	750	15	65
B	600	25	80
C	700	20	70

The total cost, y, for buying the materials and renting the tools in terms of the number of days, x, is given by $y = M + (W + K)x$.

16

For what number of days, x, will the total cost of buying the materials and renting the tools from Store B be less than or equal to the total cost of buying the materials and renting the tools from Store A ?

A) $x \leq 6$

B) $x \geq 6$

C) $x \leq 7.3$

D) $x \geq 7.3$

Unauthorized copying or reuse of any part of this page is illegal.

44

CONTINUE ➔

17

If the relationship between the total cost, y, of buying the materials and renting the tools at Store C and the number of days, x, for which the tools are rented is graphed in the xy-plane, what does the slope of the line represent?

A) The total cost of the project

B) The total cost of the materials

C) The total daily cost of the project

D) The total daily rental costs of the tools

18

Jim has identical drinking glasses each in the shape of a right circular cylinder with internal diameter of 3 inches. He pours milk from a gallon jug into each glass until it is full. If the height of milk in each glass is about 6 inches, what is the largest number of full milk glasses that he can pour from one gallon of milk? (Note: There are 231 cubic inches in 1 gallon.)

A) 2

B) 4

C) 5

D) 6

19

If $3p - 2 \geq 1$, what is the least possible value of $3p + 2$?

A) 5

B) 3

C) 2

D) 1

20

The mass of living organisms in a lake is defined to be the biomass of the lake. If the biomass in a lake doubles each year, which of the following graphs could model the biomass in the lake as a function of time? (Note: In each graph below, O represents $(0,0)$.)

A)

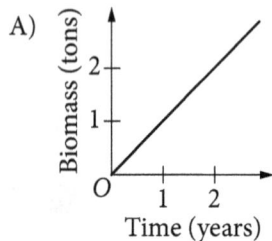

B)

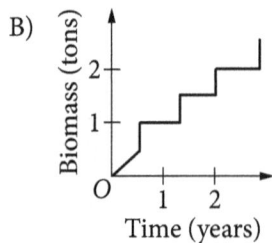

C)

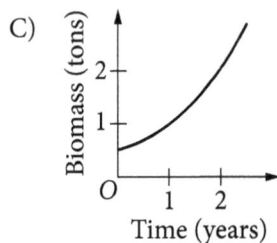

D)

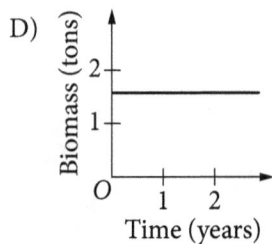

Questions 21 and 22 refer to the following information.

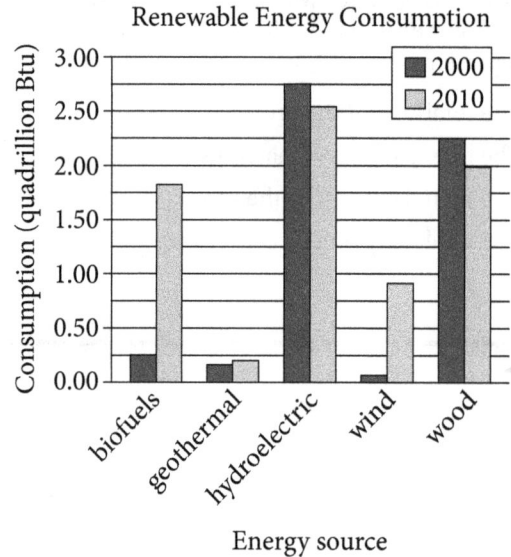

The bar graph above shows renewable energy consumption in quadrillions of British thermal units (Btu) in the United States, by energy source, for several energy sources in the years 2000 and 2010.

21

In a scatterplot of this data, where renewable energy consumption in the year 2000 is plotted along the x-axis and renewable energy consumption in the year 2010 is plotted along the y-axis for each of the given energy sources, how many data points would be above the line $y = x$?

A) 1

B) 2

C) 3

D) 4

CONTINUE ➡

22

Of the following, which best approximates the percent decrease in consumption of wood power in the United States from 2000 to 2010 ?

A)   6%

B)   11%

C)   21%

D)   26%

▲

23

The tables below give the distribution of high temperatures in degrees Fahrenheit (°F) for City A and City B over the same 21 days in March.

City A

Temperature (°F)	Frequency
80	3
79	14
78	2
77	1
76	1

City B

Temperature (°F)	Frequency
80	6
79	3
78	2
77	4
76	6

Which of the following is true about the data shown for these 21 days?

A)   The standard deviation of temperatures in City A is larger.

B)   The standard deviation of temperatures in City B is larger.

C)   The standard deviation of temperatures in City A is the same as that of City B.

D)   The standard deviation of temperatures in these cities cannot be calculated with the data provided.

24

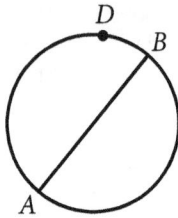

In the circle above, segment AB is a diameter. If the length of arc $\overset{\frown}{ADB}$ is 8π, what is the length of the radius of the circle?

A) 2

B) 4

C) 8

D) 16

25

$$f(x) = 2x^3 + 6x^2 + 4x$$
$$g(x) = x^2 + 3x + 2$$

The polynomials $f(x)$ and $g(x)$ are defined above. Which of the following polynomials is divisible by $2x + 3$?

A) $h(x) = f(x) + g(x)$

B) $p(x) = f(x) + 3g(x)$

C) $r(x) = 2f(x) + 3g(x)$

D) $s(x) = 3f(x) + 2g(x)$

26

Let x and y be numbers such that $-y < x < y$. Which of the following must be true?

　　I. $|x| < y$

　　II. $x > 0$

　　III. $y > 0$

A) I only

B) I and II only

C) I and III only

D) I, II, and III

27

The relative housing cost for a US city is defined to be the ratio $\dfrac{\text{average housing cost for the city}}{\text{national average housing cost}}$, expressed as a percent.

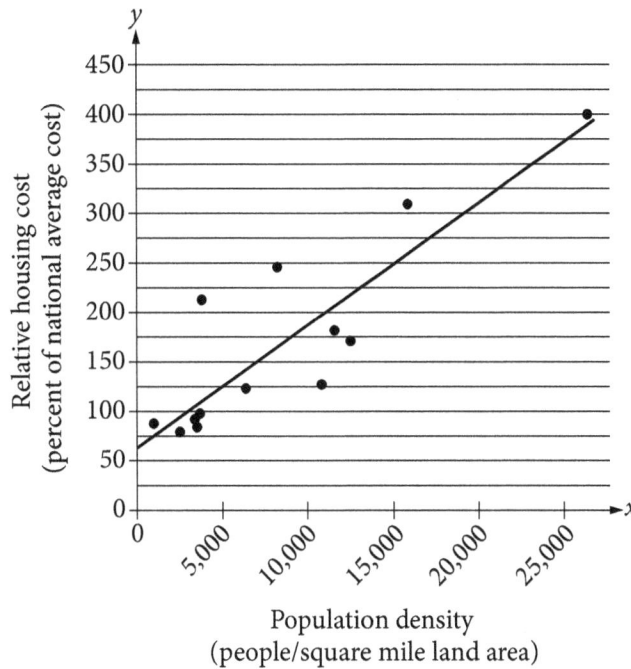

The scatterplot above shows the relative housing cost and the population density for several large US cities in the year 2005. The line of best fit is also shown and has equation $y = 0.0125x + 61$. Which of the following best explains how the number 61 in the equation relates to the scatterplot?

A) In 2005, the lowest housing cost in the United States was about $61 per month.

B) In 2005, the lowest housing cost in the United States was about 61% of the highest housing cost.

C) In 2005, even in cities with low population densities, housing costs were never below 61% of the national average.

D) In 2005, even in cities with low population densities, housing costs were likely at least 61% of the national average.

28

$$f(x) = (x + 6)(x - 4)$$

Which of the following is an equivalent form of the function f above in which the minimum value of f appears as a constant or coefficient?

A) $f(x) = x^2 - 24$

B) $f(x) = x^2 + 2x - 24$

C) $f(x) = (x - 1)^2 - 21$

D) $f(x) = (x + 1)^2 - 25$

29

If x is the average (arithmetic mean) of m and 9, y is the average of $2m$ and 15, and z is the average of $3m$ and 18, what is the average of x, y, and z in terms of m ?

A) $m + 6$

B) $m + 7$

C) $2m + 14$

D) $3m + 21$

30

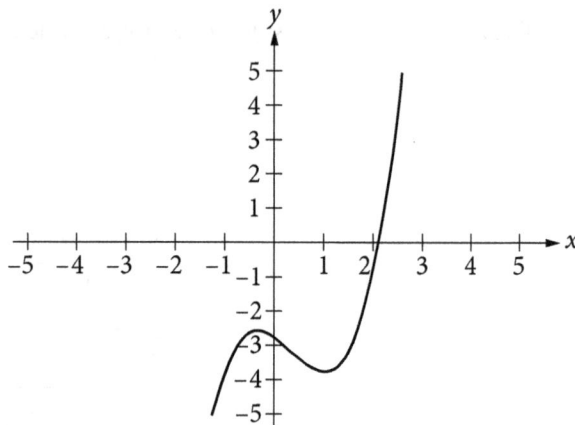

The function $f(x) = x^3 - x^2 - x - \dfrac{11}{4}$ is graphed in the xy-plane above. If k is a constant such that the equation $f(x) = k$ has three real solutions, which of the following could be the value of k ?

A)   2

B)   0

C) −2

D) −3

50

CONTINUE

DIRECTIONS

For questions 31–38, solve the problem and enter your answer in the grid, as described below, on the answer sheet.

1. Although not required, it is suggested that you write your answer in the boxes at the top of the columns to help you fill in the circles accurately. You will receive credit only if the circles are filled in correctly.

2. Mark no more than one circle in any column.

3. No question has a negative answer.

4. Some problems may have more than one correct answer. In such cases, grid only one answer.

5. **Mixed numbers** such as $3\frac{1}{2}$ must be gridded as 3.5 or 7/2. (If [3 1 / 2] is entered into the grid, it will be interpreted as $\frac{31}{2}$, not $3\frac{1}{2}$.)

6. **Decimal answers:** If you obtain a decimal answer with more digits than the grid can accommodate, it may be either rounded or truncated, but it must fill the entire grid.

Answer: $\frac{7}{12}$

Write answer in boxes. → Fraction line

Grid in result. ← Decimal point

Answer: 2.5

Acceptable ways to grid $\frac{2}{3}$ are:

Answer: 201 – either position is correct

NOTE: You may start your answers in any column, space permitting. Columns you don't need to use should be left blank.

31

A partially filled pool contains 600 gallons of water. A hose is turned on, and water flows into the pool at the rate of 8 gallons per minute. How many gallons of water will be in the pool after 70 minutes?

32

The normal systolic blood pressure P, in millimeters of mercury, for an adult male x years old can be modeled by the equation $P = \dfrac{x + 220}{2}$. According to the model, for every increase of 1 year in age, by how many millimeters of mercury will the normal systolic blood pressure for an adult male increase?

33

The *pes*, a Roman measure of length, is approximately equal to 11.65 inches. It is also equivalent to 16 smaller Roman units called digits. Based on these relationships, 75 Roman digits is equivalent to how many <u>feet</u>, to the nearest hundredth? (12 inches = 1 foot)

34

In a study of bat migration habits, 240 male bats and 160 female bats have been tagged. If 100 more female bats are tagged, how many more male bats must be tagged so that $\dfrac{3}{5}$ of the total number of bats in the study are male?

35

$$q = \frac{1}{2} n v^2$$

The dynamic pressure q generated by a fluid moving with velocity v can be found using the formula above, where n is the constant density of the fluid. An aeronautical engineer uses the formula to find the dynamic pressure of a fluid moving with velocity v and the same fluid moving with velocity $1.5v$. What is the ratio of the dynamic pressure of the faster fluid to the dynamic pressure of the slower fluid?

36

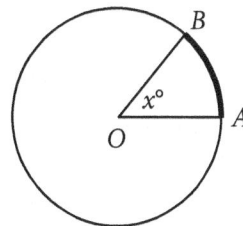

Note: Figure not drawn to scale.

In the figure above, the circle has center O and has radius 10. If the length of arc $\overparen{AB}$ (shown in bold) is between 5 and 6, what is one possible <u>integer</u> value of x ?

---

53 CONTINUE ➤

Questions 37 and 38 refer to the following information.

The stock price of one share in a certain company is worth $360 today. A stock analyst believes that the stock will lose 28 percent of its value each week for the next three weeks. The analyst uses the equation $V = 360(r)^t$ to model the value, V, of the stock after t weeks.

37

What value should the analyst use for r ?

38

To the nearest dollar, what does the analyst believe the value of the stock will be at the end of three weeks? (Note: Disregard the $ sign when gridding your answer.)

STOP

If you finish before time is called, you may check your work on this section only.
Do not turn to any other section.

SAT Practice Essay #4

ESSAY BOOK

DIRECTIONS

The essay gives you an opportunity to show how effectively you can read and comprehend a passage and write an essay analyzing the passage. In your essay, you should demonstrate that you have read the passage carefully, present a clear and logical analysis, and use language precisely.

Your essay must be written on the lines provided in your answer booklet; except for the Planning Page of the answer booklet, you will receive no other paper on which to write. You will have enough space if you write on every line, avoid wide margins, and keep your handwriting to a reasonable size. Remember that people who are not familiar with your handwriting will read what you write. Try to write or print so that what you are writing is legible to those readers.

You have 50 minutes to read the passage and write an essay in response to the prompt provided inside this booklet.

REMINDERS:

— Do not write your essay in this booklet. Only what you write on the lined pages of your answer booklet will be evaluated.

— An off-topic essay will not be evaluated.

As you read the passage below, consider how Peter S. Goodman uses

- evidence, such as facts or examples, to support claims.
- reasoning to develop ideas and to connect claims and evidence.
- stylistic or persuasive elements, such as word choice or appeals to emotion, to add power to the ideas expressed.

Adapted from Peter S. Goodman, "Foreign News at a Crisis Point." ©2013 by TheHuffingtonPost.com, Inc. Originally published September 25, 2013. Peter Goodman is the executive business and global news editor at TheHuffingtonPost.com.

1 Back in 2003, American Journalism Review produced a census of foreign correspondents then employed by newspapers based in the United States, and found 307 full-time people. When AJR repeated the exercise in the summer of 2011, the count had dropped to 234. And even that number was significantly inflated by the inclusion of contract writers who had replaced full-time staffers.

2 In the intervening eight years, 20 American news organizations had entirely eliminated their foreign bureaus.

3 The same AJR survey zeroed in on a representative sampling of American papers from across the country and found that the space devoted to foreign news had shrunk by 53 percent over the previous quarter-century.

4 All of this decline was playing out at a time when the U.S. was embroiled in two overseas wars, with hundreds of thousands of Americans deployed in Iraq and Afghanistan. It was happening as domestic politics grappled with the merits and consequences of a global war on terror, as a Great Recession was blamed in part on global imbalances in savings, and as world leaders debated a global trade treaty and pacts aimed at addressing climate change. It unfolded as American workers heard increasingly that their wages and job security were under assault by competition from counterparts on the other side of oceans.

5 In short, news of the world is becoming palpably more relevant to the day-to-day experiences of American readers, and it is rapidly disappearing.

6 Yet the same forces that have assailed print media, eroding foreign news along the way, may be fashioning a useful response. Several nonprofit outlets have popped up to finance foreign reporting, and a for-profit outfit, GlobalPost, has dispatched a team of 18 senior correspondents into the field, supplemented by dozens of stringers and freelancers. . . .

7 We are intent on forging fresh platforms for user-generated content: testimonials, snapshots and video clips from readers documenting issues in need of attention. Too often these sorts of efforts wind up feeling marginal or even patronizing: "Dear peasant, here's your chance to speak to the pros about what's happening in your tiny little corner of the world." We see user-generated content as a genuine reporting tool,

one that operates on the premise that we can only be in so many places at once. Crowd-sourcing is a fundamental advantage of the web, so why not embrace it as a means of piecing together a broader and more textured understanding of events?

8   We all know the power of Twitter, Facebook and other forms of social media to connect readers in one place with images and impressions from situations unfolding far away. We know the force of social media during the Arab Spring, as activists convened and reacted to changing circumstances. . . . Facts and insights reside on social media, waiting to be harvested by the digitally literate contemporary correspondent.

9   And yet those of us who have been engaged in foreign reporting for many years will confess to unease over many of the developments unfolding online, even as we recognize the trends are as unstoppable as globalization or the weather. Too often it seems as if professional foreign correspondents, the people paid to use their expertise while serving as informational filters, are being replaced by citizen journalists who function largely as funnels, pouring insight along with speculation, propaganda and other white noise into the mix.

10   We can celebrate the democratization of media, the breakdown of monopolies, the rise of innovative means of telling stories, and the inclusion of a diversity of voices, and still ask whether the results are making us better informed. Indeed, we have a professional responsibility to continually ask that question while seeking to engineer new models that can channel the web in the interest of better informing readers. . . .

11   We need to embrace the present and gear for the future. These are days in which newsrooms simply must be entrepreneurial and creative in pursuit of new means of reporting and paying for it. That makes this a particularly interesting time to be doing the work, but it also requires forthright attention to a central demand: We need to put back what the Internet has taken away. We need to turn the void into something fresh and compelling. We need to re-examine and update how we gather information and how we engage readers, while retaining the core values of serious-minded journalism.

12   This will not be easy. . . . But the alternative—accepting ignorance and parochialism—is simply not an option.

Write an essay in which you explain how Peter S. Goodman builds an argument to persuade his audience that news organizations should increase the amount of professional foreign news coverage provided to Americans. In your essay, analyze how Goodman uses one or more of the features listed in the box above (or features of your own choice) to strengthen the logic and persuasiveness of his argument. Be sure that your analysis focuses on the most relevant features of the passage.

Your essay should not explain whether you agree with Goodman's claims, but rather explain how Goodman builds an argument to persuade his audience.

YOUR NAME (PRINT) ....

LAST   FIRST   MI

TEST CENTER ....

NUMBER   NAME OF TEST CENTER   ROOM NUMBER

5LS04E

DO NOT OPEN THIS BOOK UNTIL THE TEST ADMINISTRATOR TELLS YOU TO DO SO.

Scoring Your
SAT® Practice Test #4

Congratulations on completing an SAT® practice test. To score your test, use these instructions and the conversion tables and answer key at the end of this document.

Scores Overview

The redesigned SAT will provide more information about your learning by reporting more scores than ever before. Each of the redesigned assessments (SAT, PSAT/NMSQT®, PSAT™ 10, and PSAT™ 8/9) will report test scores and cross-test scores on a common scale. Additionally, subscores will be reported to provide additional diagnostic information to students, educators, and parents. For more details about scores, visit **collegereadiness.collegeboard.org/sat/scores**.

The practice test you completed was written by the College Board's Assessment Design & Development team using the same processes and review standards used when writing the actual SAT. Everything from the layout of the page to the construction of the questions accurately reflects what you'll see on test day.

How to Calculate Your Practice Test Scores

GET SET UP

❶ You'll need the answer sheet that you bubbled in while taking the practice test. You'll also need the conversion tables and answer key at the end of this document.

❷ Using the answer key, count up your total correct answers for each section. You may want to write the number of correct answers for each section at the bottom of that section in the answer key.

❸ Using your marked-up answer key and the conversion tables, follow the directions to get all of your scores.

GET SECTION AND TOTAL SCORES

Your total score on the SAT practice test is the sum of your Evidence-Based Reading and Writing Section score and your Math Section score. To get your total score, you will convert what we call the "raw score" for each section — the number of questions you got right in that section — into the "scaled score" for that section, then calculate the total score.

GET YOUR EVIDENCE-BASED READING AND WRITING SECTION SCORE

Calculate your SAT Evidence-Based Reading and Writing Section score (it's on a scale of 200–800) by first determining your Reading Test score and your Writing and Language Test score. Here's how:

1. Count the number of correct answers you got on Section 1 (the Reading Test). There is no penalty for wrong answers. The number of correct answers is your raw score.

2. Go to Raw Score Conversion Table 1: Section and Test Scores on page 7. Look in the "Raw Score" column for your raw score, and match it to the number in the "Reading Test Score" column.

3. Do the same with Section 2 to determine your Writing and Language Test score.

4. Add your Reading Test score to your Writing and Language Test score.

5. Multiply that number by 10. This is your Evidence-Based Reading and Writing Section score.

EXAMPLE: *Sofia answered 29 of the 52 questions correctly on the SAT Reading Test and 19 of the 44 questions correctly on the SAT Writing and Language Test. Using the table on page 7, she calculates that she received an SAT Reading Test score of 27 and an SAT Writing and Language Test score of 23. She adds 27 to 23 (gets 50) and then multiplies by 10 to determine her SAT Evidence-Based Reading and Writing Section score of 500.*

GET YOUR MATH SECTION SCORE

Calculate your SAT Math Section score (it's on a scale of 200–800).

1. Count the number of correct answers you got on Section 3 (Math Test — No Calculator) and Section 4 (Math Test — Calculator). There is no penalty for wrong answers.

2. Add the number of correct answers you got on Section 3 (Math Test — No Calculator) and Section 4 (Math Test — Calculator).

3. Use Raw Score Conversion Table 1: Section and Test Scores to turn your raw score into your Math Section score.

GET YOUR TOTAL SCORE

Add your Evidence-Based Reading and Writing Section score to your Math Section score. The result is your total score on the SAT Practice Test, on a scale of 400–1600.

GET SUBSCORES

Subscores provide more detailed information about your strengths in specific areas within literacy and math. They are reported on a scale of 1–15.

HEART OF ALGEBRA

The Heart of Algebra subscore is based on questions from the Math Test that focus on linear equations and inequalities.

1. Add up your total correct answers from the following set of questions:

   ▶ Math Test – No Calculator: Questions 1-3; 7-8; 12; 19-20

   ▶ Math Test – Calculator: Questions 1-2; 6; 8; 16-17; 19; 26; 29; 32; 34

   Your total correct answers from all of these questions is your raw score.

2. Use Raw Score Conversion Table 2: Subscores on page 8 to determine your Heart of Algebra subscore.

PROBLEM SOLVING AND DATA ANALYSIS

The Problem Solving and Data Analysis subscore is based on questions from the Math Test that focus on quantitative reasoning, the interpretation and synthesis of data, and solving problems in rich and varied contexts.

1. Add up your total correct answers from the following set of questions:

   ▶ Math Test – No Calculator: No Questions

   ▶ Math Test – Calculator: Questions 3-5; 7; 9-11; 13-15; 20-23; 27; 31; 33

   Your total correct answers from all of these questions is your raw score.

2. Use Raw Score Conversion Table 2: Subscores to determine your Problem Solving and Data Analysis subscore.

PASSPORT TO ADVANCED MATH

The Passport to Advanced Math subscore is based on questions from the Math Test that focus on topics central to the ability of students to progress to more advanced mathematics, such as understanding the structure of expressions, reasoning with more complex equations, and interpreting and building functions.

1. Add up your total correct answers from the following set of questions:

   ▶ Math Test – No Calculator: Questions 4-6; 9-11; 13; 15; 18

   ▶ Math Test – Calculator: Questions 12; 25; 28; 30; 35; 37-38

   Your total correct answers from all of these questions is your raw score.

2. Use Raw Score Conversion Table 2: Subscores to determine your Passport to Advanced Math subscore.

EXPRESSION OF IDEAS

The Expression of Ideas subscore is based on questions from the Writing and Language Test that focus on topic development, organization, and rhetorically effective use of language.

1. Add up your total correct answers from the following set of questions:

   ▸ Writing and Language Test: Questions 2; 4-5; 8; 10-11; 14-18; 20; 23; 25-27; 31; 33; 37-39; 41-42; 44

   Your total correct answers from all of these questions is your raw score.

2. Use Raw Score Conversion Table 2: Subscores to determine your Expression of Ideas subscore.

STANDARD ENGLISH CONVENTIONS

The Standard English Conventions subscore is based on questions from the Writing and Language Test that focus on sentence structure, usage, and punctuation.

1. Add up your total correct answers from the following set of questions:

   ▸ Writing and Language Test: Questions 1; 3; 6-7; 9; 12-13; 19; 21-22; 24; 28-30; 32; 34-36; 40; 43

   Your total correct answers from all of these questions is your raw score.

2. Use Raw Score Conversion Table 2: Subscores to determine your Standard English Conventions subscore.

WORDS IN CONTEXT

The Words in Context subscore is based on questions from both the Reading Test and the Writing and Language Test that address word/phrase meaning in context and rhetorical word choice.

1. Add up your total correct answers from the following set of questions:

   ▸ Reading Test: Questions 3; 9; 13; 18; 24; 31; 33-34; 45; 48

   ▸ Writing and Language Test: Questions 5; 8; 14; 16; 23; 26; 41-42

   Your total correct answers from all of these questions is your raw score.

2. Use Raw Score Conversion Table 2: Subscores to determine your Words in Context subscore.

COMMAND OF EVIDENCE

The Command of Evidence subscore is based on questions from both the Reading Test and the Writing and Language Test that ask you to interpret and use evidence found in a wide range of passages and informational graphics, such as graphs, tables, and charts.

1. Add up your total correct answers from the following set of questions:

   ▸ Reading Test: Questions 2; 6; 15; 20; 28; 39; 44; 47; 50; 52

   ▸ Writing and Language Test: Questions 10-11; 18; 20; 25; 31; 37-38

   Your total correct answers from all of these questions is your raw score.

2. Use Raw Score Conversion Table 2: Subscores to determine your Command of Evidence subscore.

GET CROSS-TEST SCORES

The new SAT also reports two cross-test scores: Analysis in History/Social Studies and Analysis in Science. These scores are based on questions in the Reading, Writing and Language, and Math Tests that ask students to think analytically about texts and questions in these subject areas. Cross-test scores are reported on a scale of 10–40.

ANALYSIS IN HISTORY/SOCIAL STUDIES

1. Add up your total correct answers from the following set of questions:

   ▶ Reading Test: Questions 11-21; 32-41

   ▶ Writing and Language Test: Questions 23; 25-27; 31; 33

   ▶ Math Test – No Calculator: Question 12

   ▶ Math Test – Calculator: Questions 9; 14; 16-17; 27; 33; 37

   Your total correct answers from all of these questions is your raw score.

2. Use Raw Score Conversion Table 3: Cross-Test Scores on page 9 to determine your Analysis in History/Social Studies cross-test score.

ANALYSIS IN SCIENCE

1. Add up your total correct answers from the following set of questions:

   ▶ Reading Test: Questions 22-31; 42-52

   ▶ Writing and Language Test: Questions 14-18; 20

   ▶ Math Test – No Calculator: Question 20

   ▶ Math Test – Calculator: Questions 5; 10-11; 13; 21-22; 32

   Your total correct answers from all of these questions is your raw score.

2. Use Raw Score Conversion Table 3: Cross-Test Scores to determine your Analysis in Science cross-test score.

SAT Practice Test #4: Worksheets

ANSWER KEY

Reading Test Answers

1 C	12 D	23 C	34 A	45 D
2 D	13 A	24 C	35 D	46 A
3 D	14 B	25 B	36 B	47 D
4 C	15 A	26 C	37 D	48 C
5 A	16 C	27 A	38 D	49 D
6 A	17 C	28 B	39 D	50 C
7 B	18 A	29 B	40 A	51 B
8 D	19 B	30 D	41 B	52 A
9 D	20 A	31 D	42 C	
10 A	21 D	32 D	43 B	
11 C	22 A	33 D	44 A	

READING TEST
RAW SCORE
(NUMBER OF
CORRECT ANSWERS)

Writing and Language Test Answers

1 B	12 D	23 C	34 C
2 B	13 B	24 C	35 C
3 B	14 D	25 B	36 B
4 A	15 C	26 D	37 D
5 D	16 C	27 C	38 A
6 B	17 A	28 A	39 C
7 D	18 C	29 D	40 B
8 B	19 A	30 B	41 D
9 C	20 C	31 C	42 D
10 A	21 B	32 B	43 A
11 C	22 D	33 A	44 B

WRITING AND
LANGUAGE TEST
RAW SCORE
(NUMBER OF
CORRECT ANSWERS)

Math Test
No Calculator Answers

1 A	11 C
2 A	12 C
3 A	13 B
4 B	14 A
5 C	15 B
6 B	16 9
7 D	17 3/5 or 0.6
8 A	18 5
9 D	19 0
10 D	20 25

MATH TEST
NO CALCULATOR
RAW SCORE
(NUMBER OF
CORRECT ANSWERS)

Math Test
Calculator Answers

1 B	11 A	21 C	31 1160
2 C	12 C	22 B	32 1/2 or 0.5
3 C	13 C	23 B	33 4.55
4 B	14 D	24 C	34 150
5 B	15 B	25 B	35 9/4 or 2.25
6 A	16 A	26 C	36 29, 30, 31, 32, 33, or 34
7 A	17 D	27 D	37 0.72
8 D	18 C	28 D	38 134
9 B	19 A	29 B	
10 A	20 C	30 D	

MATH TEST
CALCULATOR
RAW SCORE
(NUMBER OF
CORRECT ANSWERS)

SAT Practice Test #4: Worksheets

RAW SCORE CONVERSION TABLE 1 SECTION AND TEST SCORES

Raw Score (# of correct answers)	Math Section Score	Reading Test Score	Writing and Language Test Score	Raw Score (# of correct answers)	Math Section Score	Reading Test Score	Writing and Language Test Score
0	200	10	10	30	580	27	30
1	200	10	10	31	590	28	31
2	210	10	10	32	600	28	31
3	230	11	10	33	600	28	32
4	250	12	11	34	610	29	32
5	270	13	12	35	620	29	33
6	280	14	13	36	630	30	33
7	300	15	14	37	640	30	34
8	320	16	15	38	650	31	35
9	340	16	16	39	660	31	36
10	350	17	16	40	670	32	37
11	360	18	17	41	680	32	37
12	370	18	18	42	690	33	38
13	390	19	19	43	700	33	39
14	410	20	19	44	710	34	40
15	420	20	20	45	710	35	
16	430	21	21	46	720	35	
17	450	21	22	47	730	36	
18	460	22	23	48	730	37	
19	470	22	23	49	740	38	
20	480	23	24	50	750	39	
21	490	23	24	51	750	39	
22	500	23	25	52	760	40	
23	510	24	26	53	770		
24	520	24	26	54	780		
25	530	25	27	55	790		
26	540	25	27	56	790		
27	550	26	28	57	800		
28	560	26	29	58	800		
29	570	27	29				

CONVERSION EQUATION 1 SECTION AND TEST SCORES

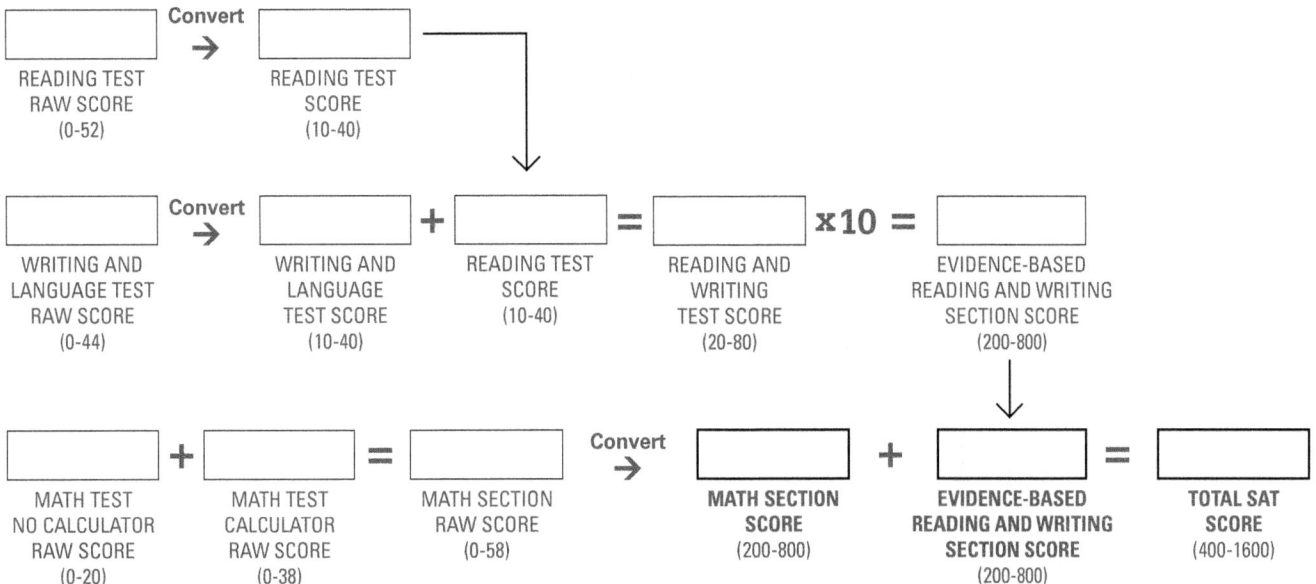

[ ] **Convert →** [ ]
READING TEST RAW SCORE (0-52) → READING TEST SCORE (10-40)

[ ] **Convert →** [ ] + [ ] = [ ] **x10 =** [ ]
WRITING AND LANGUAGE TEST RAW SCORE (0-44) → WRITING AND LANGUAGE TEST SCORE (10-40) + READING TEST SCORE (10-40) = READING AND WRITING TEST SCORE (20-80) x10 = EVIDENCE-BASED READING AND WRITING SECTION SCORE (200-800)

[ ] + [ ] = [ ] **Convert →** [ ] + [ ] = [ ]
MATH TEST NO CALCULATOR RAW SCORE (0-20) + MATH TEST CALCULATOR RAW SCORE (0-38) = MATH SECTION RAW SCORE (0-58) → MATH SECTION SCORE (200-800) + EVIDENCE-BASED READING AND WRITING SECTION SCORE (200-800) = TOTAL SAT SCORE (400-1600)

SAT Practice Test #4: Worksheets

Raw Score (# of correct answers)	Expression of Ideas	Standard English Conventions	Heart of Algebra	Problem Solving and Data Analysis	Passport to Advanced Math	Words in Context	Command of Evidence
0	1	1	1	1	2	1	1
1	1	1	1	1	3	1	1
2	1	1	2	2	5	2	2
3	2	2	4	4	6	3	3
4	3	3	5	5	7	4	4
5	4	5	6	6	8	5	5
6	5	5	7	7	9	6	6
7	5	6	8	8	10	6	7
8	6	7	8	8	11	7	8
9	7	7	9	9	12	7	9
10	7	8	9	9	12	8	9
11	8	8	10	10	13	9	10
12	8	9	11	11	13	9	10
13	9	9	11	12	14	10	11
14	9	10	12	13	14	10	12
15	9	11	13	13	15	11	13
16	10	12	14	14	15	12	14
17	11	12	14	15		13	15
18	11	13	15			15	15
19	12	14	15				
20	12	15					
21	13						
22	13						
23	14						
24	15						

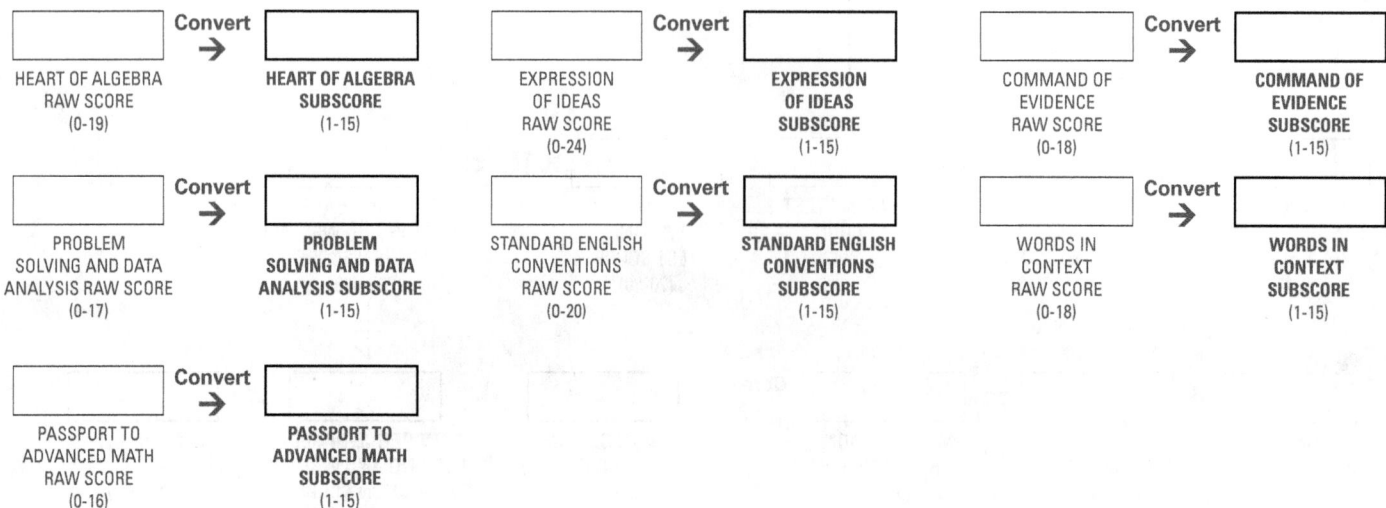

| HEART OF ALGEBRA RAW SCORE (0-19) | Convert → | HEART OF ALGEBRA SUBSCORE (1-15) | EXPRESSION OF IDEAS RAW SCORE (0-24) | Convert → | EXPRESSION OF IDEAS SUBSCORE (1-15) | COMMAND OF EVIDENCE RAW SCORE (0-18) | Convert → | COMMAND OF EVIDENCE SUBSCORE (1-15) |

PROBLEM SOLVING AND DATA ANALYSIS RAW SCORE (0-17) → PROBLEM SOLVING AND DATA ANALYSIS SUBSCORE (1-15)

STANDARD ENGLISH CONVENTIONS RAW SCORE (0-20) → STANDARD ENGLISH CONVENTIONS SUBSCORE (1-15)

WORDS IN CONTEXT RAW SCORE (0-18) → WORDS IN CONTEXT SUBSCORE (1-15)

PASSPORT TO ADVANCED MATH RAW SCORE (0-16) → PASSPORT TO ADVANCED MATH SUBSCORE (1-15)

SAT Practice Test #4: Worksheets

Raw Score (# of correct answers)	Analysis in History/ Social Studies Cross-Test Score	Analysis in Science Cross-Test Score	Raw Score (# of correct answers)	Analysis in History/ Social Studies Cross-Test Score	Analysis in Science Cross-Test Score
0	10	10	18	28	26
1	10	11	19	29	26
2	11	13	20	29	27
3	13	14	21	30	28
4	15	15	22	31	28
5	16	16	23	31	29
6	17	17	24	32	30
7	18	18	25	33	30
8	19	18	26	34	31
9	20	19	27	34	32
10	21	20	28	35	33
11	22	21	29	36	34
12	23	22	30	37	35
13	24	22	31	38	36
14	25	23	32	38	37
15	26	24	33	39	38
16	27	24	34	40	39
17	28	25	35	40	40

CONVERSION EQUATION 3   CROSS-TEST SCORES

Test	Analysis in History/Social Studies		Analysis in Science	
	Questions	Raw Score	Questions	Raw Score
Reading Test	11-21; 32-41		22-31; 42-52	
Writing and Language Test	3; 25-27; 31; 33		14-18; 20	
Math Test No Calculator	12		20	
Math Test Calculator	9; 14; 16-17; 27; 33; 37		5; 10-11; 13; 21-22; 32	
Total				

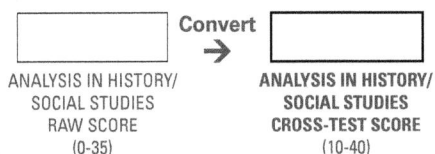

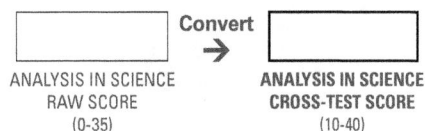

	Convert			**Convert**	
ANALYSIS IN HISTORY/ SOCIAL STUDIES RAW SCORE (0-35)	→	**ANALYSIS IN HISTORY/ SOCIAL STUDIES CROSS-TEST SCORE (10-40)**	ANALYSIS IN SCIENCE RAW SCORE (0-35)	→	**ANALYSIS IN SCIENCE CROSS-TEST SCORE (10-40)**

The SAT

Practice Test #5

Make time to take the practice test. It's one of the best ways to get ready for the SAT.

After you've taken the practice test, score it right away at **sat.org/scoring**.

TEST TAKING TIP #5

Practice with Problems at the Edge of Your Ability: Practicing with problems that are too easy does not allow you to grow your skill. And practicing with questions that are too hard is frustrating and wastes your time. Find that middle ground where you get the best bang for your studying buck.

Reading Test

65 MINUTES, 52 QUESTIONS

Turn to Section 1 of your answer sheet to answer the questions in this section.

DIRECTIONS

Each passage or pair of passages below is followed by a number of questions. After reading each passage or pair, choose the best answer to each question based on what is stated or implied in the passage or passages and in any accompanying graphics (such as a table or graph).

Questions 1-10 are based on the following passage.

This passage is adapted from William Maxwell, *The Folded Leaf*. ©1959 by William Maxwell. Originally published in 1945.

The Alcazar Restaurant was on Sheridan Road near Devon Avenue. It was long and narrow, with tables for two along the walls and tables for four
Line down the middle. The decoration was *art moderne*,
5 except for the series of murals depicting the four seasons, and the sick ferns in the front window. Lymie sat down at the second table from the cash register, and ordered his dinner. The history book, which he propped against the catsup and the glass
10 sugar bowl, had been used by others before him. Blank pages front and back were filled in with maps, drawings, dates, comic cartoons, and organs of the body; also with names and messages no longer clear and never absolutely legible. On nearly every other
15 page there was some marginal notation, either in ink or in very hard pencil. And unless someone had upset a glass of water, the marks on page 177 were from tears.
    While Lymie read about the Peace of Paris, signed
20 on the thirtieth of May, 1814, between France and the Allied powers, his right hand managed again and again to bring food up to his mouth. Sometimes he chewed, sometimes he swallowed whole the food that he had no idea he was eating. The Congress of
25 Vienna met, with some allowance for delays, early in November of the same year, and all the powers engaged in the war on either side sent

plenipotentiaries. It was by far the most splendid and important assembly ever convoked to discuss and
30 determine the affairs of Europe. The Emperor of Russia, the King of Prussia, the Kings of Bavaria, Denmark, and Wurttemberg, all were present in person at the court of the Emperor Francis I in the Austrian capital. When Lymie put down his fork and
35 began to count them off, one by one, on the fingers of his left hand, the waitress, whose name was Irma, thought he was through eating and tried to take his plate away. He stopped her. Prince Metternich (his right thumb) presided over the Congress, and
40 Prince Talleyrand (the index finger) represented France.
    A party of four, two men and two women, came into the restaurant, all talking at once, and took possession of the center table nearest Lymie.
45 The women had shingled hair and short tight skirts which exposed the underside of their knees when they sat down. One of the women had the face of a young boy but disguised by one trick or another (rouge, lipstick, powder, wet bangs plastered against
50 the high forehead, and a pair of long pendent earrings) to look like a woman of thirty-five, which as a matter of fact she was. The men were older. They laughed more than there seemed any occasion for, while they were deciding between soup and shrimp
55 cocktail, and their laughter was too loud. But it was the women's voices, the terrible not quite sober pitch of the women's voices which caused Lymie to skim over two whole pages without knowing what was on them. Fortunately he realized this and went back.
60 Otherwise he might never have known about the

---

secret treaty concluded between England, France, and Austria, when the pretensions of Prussia and Russia, acting in concert, seemed to threaten a renewal of the attack. The results of the Congress
65 were stated clearly at the bottom of page 67 and at the top of page 68, but before Lymie got halfway through them, a coat that he recognized as his father's was hung on the hook next to his chair. Lymie closed the book and said, "I didn't think you
70 were coming."

Time is probably no more unkind to sporting characters than it is to other people, but physical decay unsustained by respectability is somehow more noticeable. Mr. Peters' hair was turning gray and his
75 scalp showed through on top. He had lost weight also; he no longer filled out his clothes the way he used to. His color was poor, and the flower had disappeared from his buttonhole. In its place was an American Legion button.
80 Apparently he himself was not aware that there had been any change. He straightened his tie self-consciously and when Irma handed him a menu, he gestured with it so that the two women at the next table would notice the diamond ring on the fourth
85 finger of his right hand. Both of these things, and also the fact that his hands showed signs of the manicurist, one can blame on the young man who had his picture taken with a derby hat on the back of his head, and also sitting with a girl in the curve of
90 the moon. The young man had never for one second deserted Mr. Peters. He was always there, tugging at Mr. Peters' elbow, making him do things that were not becoming in a man of forty-five.

1

Over the course of the passage, the primary focus shifts from

A) Lymie's inner thoughts to observations made by the other characters.

B) an exchange between strangers to a satisfying personal relationship.

C) the physical setting of the scene to the different characters' personality traits.

D) Lymie's experience reading a book to descriptions of people in the restaurant.

2

The main purpose of the first paragraph is to

A) introduce the passage's main character by showing his nightly habits.

B) indicate the date the passage takes place by presenting period details.

C) convey the passage's setting by describing a place and an object.

D) foreshadow an event that is described in detail later in the passage.

3

It can reasonably be inferred that Irma, the waitress, thinks Lymie is "through eating" (line 37) because

A) he has begun reading his book.

B) his plate is empty.

C) he is no longer holding his fork.

D) he has asked her to clear the table.

4

Lymie's primary impression of the "party of four" (line 42) is that they

A) are noisy and distracting.

B) are a refreshing change from the other customers.

C) resemble characters from his history book.

D) represent glamour and youth.

5

Which choice provides the best evidence for the answer to the previous question?

A) Lines 45-47 ("The women . . . down")

B) Lines 47-52 ("One . . . was")

C) Lines 55-59 ("But . . . them")

D) Line 69 ("Lymie . . . book")

CONTINUE

6

The narrator indicates that Lymie finally closes the history book because

A) his father has joined him at the table.

B) the people at the other table are too disruptive.

C) he has finished the chapter about the Congress.

D) he is preparing to leave the restaurant.

7

The primary impression created by the narrator's description of Mr. Peters in lines 74-79 is that he is

A) healthy and fit.

B) angry and menacing.

C) nervous and hesitant.

D) aging and shriveled.

8

The main idea of the last paragraph is that Mr. Peters

A) neglects to spend any time with his family members.

B) behaves as if he is a younger version of himself.

C) is very conscious of symbols of wealth and power.

D) is preoccupied with the knowledge that he is growing old.

9

Which choice best supports the conclusion that Mr. Peters wants to attract attention?

A) Lines 80-81 ("Apparently . . . change")

B) Lines 81-85 ("He straightened . . . hand")

C) Lines 90-91 ("The young . . . Mr. Peters")

D) Lines 91-93 ("He was . . . forty-five")

10

As used in line 93, "becoming" most nearly means

A) emerging.

B) fitting.

C) developing.

D) happening.

Unauthorized copying or reuse of any part of this page is illegal.

5

CONTINUE

Questions 11-21 are based on the following passages.

Passage 1 is adapted from Catharine Beecher, *Essay on Slavery and Abolitionism*. Originally published in 1837. Passage 2 is adapted from Angelina E. Grimké, *Letters to Catharine Beecher*. Originally published in 1838. Grimké encouraged Southern women to oppose slavery publicly. Passage 1 is Beecher's response to Grimké's views. Passage 2 is Grimké's response to Beecher.

Passage 1

Heaven has appointed to one sex the superior, and to the other the subordinate station, and this without any reference to the character or conduct of
Line either. It is therefore as much for the dignity as it is
5 for the interest of females, in all respects to conform to the duties of this relation. . . . But while woman holds a subordinate relation in society to the other sex, it is not because it was designed that her duties or her influence should be any the less important, or
10 all-pervading. But it was designed that the mode of gaining influence and of exercising power should be altogether different and peculiar. . . .
A man may act on society by the collision of intellect, in public debate; he may urge his measures
15 by a sense of shame, by fear and by personal interest; he may coerce by the combination of public sentiment; he may drive by physical force, and he does not outstep the boundaries of his sphere. But all the power, and all the conquests that are lawful to
20 woman, are those only which appeal to the kindly, generous, peaceful and benevolent principles.
Woman is to win every thing by peace and love; by making herself so much respected, esteemed and loved, that to yield to her opinions and to gratify her
25 wishes, will be the free-will offering of the heart. But this is to be all accomplished in the domestic and social circle. There let every woman become so cultivated and refined in intellect, that her taste and judgment will be respected; so benevolent in feeling
30 and action; that her motives will be reverenced;—so unassuming and unambitious, that collision and competition will be banished;—so "gentle and easy to be entreated," as that every heart will repose in her presence; then, the fathers, the husbands, and the
35 sons, will find an influence thrown around them, to which they will yield not only willingly but proudly. . . .
A woman may seek the aid of co-operation and combination among her own sex, to assist her in her
40 appropriate offices of piety, charity, maternal and domestic duty; but whatever, in any measure, throws a woman into the attitude of a combatant, either for herself or others—whatever binds her in a party conflict—whatever obliges her in any way to exert
45 coercive influences, throws her out of her appropriate sphere. If these general principles are correct, they are entirely opposed to the plan of arraying females in any Abolition movement.

Passage 2

The investigation of the rights of the slave has led
50 me to a better understanding of my own. I have found the Anti-Slavery cause to be the high school of morals in our land—the school in which *human rights* are more fully investigated, and better understood and taught, than in any other. Here a
55 great fundamental principle is uplifted and illuminated, and from this central light, rays innumerable stream all around.
Human beings have *rights*, because they are *moral* beings: the rights of *all* men grow out of their moral
60 nature; and as all men have the same moral nature, they have essentially the same rights. These rights may be wrested from the slave, but they cannot be alienated: his title to himself is as perfect now, as is that of Lyman Beecher:[1] it is stamped on his moral
65 being, and is, like it, imperishable. Now if rights are founded in the nature of our moral being, then the *mere circumstance of sex* does not give to man higher rights and responsibilities, than to woman. To suppose that it does, would be to deny the
70 self-evident truth, that the "physical constitution is the mere instrument of the moral nature." To suppose that it does, would be to break up utterly the relations, of the two natures, and to reverse their functions, exalting the animal nature into a monarch,
75 and humbling the moral into a slave; making the former a proprietor, and the latter its property.
When human beings are regarded as *moral* beings, *sex*, instead of being enthroned upon the summit, administering upon rights and
80 responsibilities, sinks into insignificance and nothingness. My doctrine then is, that whatever it is morally right for man to do, it is morally right for woman to do. Our duties originate, not from difference of sex, but from the diversity of our
85 relations in life, the various gifts and talents committed to our care, and the different eras in which we live.

[1] Lyman Beecher was a famous minister and the father of Catharine Beecher.

11

In Passage 1, Beecher makes which point about the status of women relative to that of men?

A) Women depend on men for their safety and security, but men are largely independent of women.

B) Women are inferior to men, but women play a role as significant as that played by men.

C) Women have fewer rights than men do, but women also have fewer responsibilities.

D) Women are superior to men, but tradition requires women to obey men.

12

Which choice provides the best evidence for the answer to the previous question?

A) Lines 6-10 ("But . . . all-pervading")

B) Lines 13-14 ("A man . . . debate")

C) Lines 16-18 ("he may coerce . . . sphere")

D) Lines 41-46 ("but whatever . . . sphere")

13

In Passage 1, Beecher implies that women's effect on public life is largely

A) overlooked, because few men are interested in women's thoughts about politics.

B) indirect, because women exert their influence within the home and family life.

C) unnecessary, because men are able to govern society themselves.

D) symbolic, because women tend to be more idealistic about politics than men are.

14

As used in line 2, "station" most nearly means

A) region.

B) studio.

C) district.

D) rank.

15

As used in line 12, "peculiar" most nearly means

A) eccentric.

B) surprising.

C) distinctive.

D) infrequent.

16

What is Grimké's central claim in Passage 2?

A) The rights of individuals are not determined by race or gender.

B) Men and women must learn to work together to improve society.

C) Moral rights are the most important distinction between human beings and animals.

D) Men and women should have equal opportunities to flourish.

17

In Passage 2, Grimké makes which point about human rights?

A) They are viewed differently in various cultures around the world.

B) They retain their moral authority regardless of whether they are recognized by law.

C) They are sometimes at odds with moral responsibilities.

D) They have become more advanced and refined throughout history.

18

Which choice provides the best evidence for the answer to the previous question?

A) Lines 58-61 ("Human . . . same rights")

B) Lines 61-65 ("These . . . imperishable")

C) Lines 71-76 ("To suppose . . . property")

D) Lines 77-81 ("When . . . nothingness")

19

Which choice best states the relationship between the two passages?

A) Passage 2 illustrates the practical difficulties of a proposal made in Passage 1.

B) Passage 2 takes issue with the primary argument of Passage 1.

C) Passage 2 provides a historical context for the perspective offered in Passage 1.

D) Passage 2 elaborates upon several ideas implied in Passage 1.

20

Based on the passages, both authors would agree with which of the following claims?

A) Women have moral duties and responsibilities.

B) Men often work selflessly for political change.

C) The ethical obligations of women are often undervalued.

D) Political activism is as important for women as it is for men.

21

Beecher would most likely have reacted to lines 65-68 ("Now . . . woman") of Passage 2 with

A) sympathy, because she feels that human beings owe each other a debt to work together in the world.

B) agreement, because she feels that human responsibilities are a natural product of human rights.

C) dismay, because she feels that women actually have a more difficult role to play in society than men do.

D) disagreement, because she feels that the natures of men and women are fundamentally different.

Questions 22-31 are based on the following passage and supplementary material.

This passage is adapted from Bryan Walsh, "Whole Food Blues: Why Organic Agriculture May Not Be So Sustainable." ©2012 by Time Inc.

When it comes to energy, everyone loves efficiency. Cutting energy waste is one of those goals that both sides of the political divide can agree on,
Line even if they sometimes diverge on how best to get
5 there. Energy efficiency allows us to get more out of our given resources, which is good for the economy and (mostly) good for the environment as well. In an increasingly hot and crowded world, the only sustainable way to live is to get more out of less.
10 Every environmentalist would agree.

But change the conversation to food, and suddenly efficiency doesn't look so good. Conventional industrial agriculture has become incredibly efficient on a simple land to food basis.
15 Thanks to fertilizers, mechanization and irrigation, each American farmer feeds over 155 people worldwide. Conventional farming gets more and more crop per square foot of cultivated land— over 170 bushels of corn per acre in Iowa, for
20 example—which can mean less territory needs to be converted from wilderness to farmland. And since a third of the planet is already used for agriculture—destroying forests and other wild habitats along the way—anything that could help us
25 produce more food on less land would seem to be good for the environment.

Of course, that's not how most environmentalists regard their arugula [a leafy green]. They have embraced organic food as better for the planet—and
30 healthier and tastier, too—than the stuff produced by agricultural corporations. Environmentalists disdain the enormous amounts of energy needed and waste created by conventional farming, while organic practices—forgoing artificial fertilizers and chemical
35 pesticides—are considered far more sustainable. Sales of organic food rose 7.7% in 2010, up to $26.7 billion—and people are making those purchases for their consciences as much as their taste buds.

Yet a new meta-analysis in *Nature* does the math
40 and comes to a hard conclusion: organic farming yields 25% fewer crops on average than conventional agriculture. More land is therefore needed to produce fewer crops—and that means organic farming may not be as good for the planet as
45 we think.

In the *Nature* analysis, scientists from McGill University in Montreal and the University of Minnesota performed an analysis of 66 studies comparing conventional and organic methods across
50 34 different crop species, from fruits to grains to legumes. They found that organic farming delivered a lower yield for every crop type, though the disparity varied widely. For rain-watered legume crops like beans or perennial crops like fruit trees, organic
55 trailed conventional agriculture by just 5%. Yet for major cereal crops like corn or wheat, as well as most vegetables—all of which provide the bulk of the world's calories—conventional agriculture outperformed organics by more than 25%.
60 The main difference is nitrogen, the chemical key to plant growth. Conventional agriculture makes use of 171 million metric tons of synthetic fertilizer each year, and all that nitrogen enables much faster plant growth than the slower release of nitrogen from the
65 compost or cover crops used in organic farming. When we talk about a Green Revolution, we really mean a nitrogen revolution—along with a lot of water.

But not all the nitrogen used in conventional
70 fertilizer ends up in crops—much of it ends up running off the soil and into the oceans, creating vast polluted dead zones. We're already putting more nitrogen into the soil than the planet can stand over the long term. And conventional agriculture also
75 depends heavily on chemical pesticides, which can have unintended side effects.

What that means is that while conventional agriculture is more efficient—sometimes much more efficient—than organic farming, there are trade-offs
80 with each. So an ideal global agriculture system, in the views of the study's authors, may borrow the best from both systems, as Jonathan Foley of the University of Minnesota explained:

The bottom line? Today's organic farming
85 practices are probably best deployed in fruit and vegetable farms, where growing nutrition (not just bulk calories) is the primary goal. But for delivering sheer calories, especially in our staple crops of wheat, rice, maize, soybeans and so on,
90 conventional farms have the advantage right now.

Looking forward, I think we will need to deploy different kinds of practices (especially new, mixed approaches that take the best of organic
95 and conventional farming systems) where they are best suited—geographically, economically, socially, etc.

Figure 1

Organic Yield as a Percentage of
Conventional Yield, by Crop Type

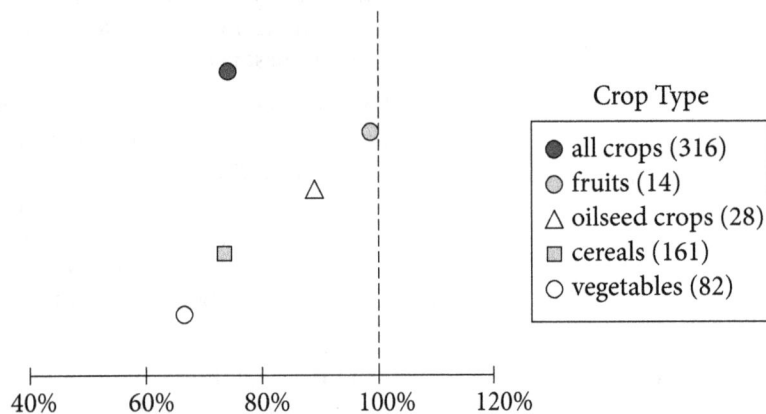

Crop Type

- ● all crops (316)
- ○ fruits (14)
- △ oilseed crops (28)
- ▢ cereals (161)
- ○ vegetables (82)

40%　60%　80%　100%　120%

At 100%, the organic yield is the same as
the conventional yield. The number of
observations for each crop type is shown
in parentheses.

Figure 2

Organic Yield as a Percentage of
Conventional Yield, by Species

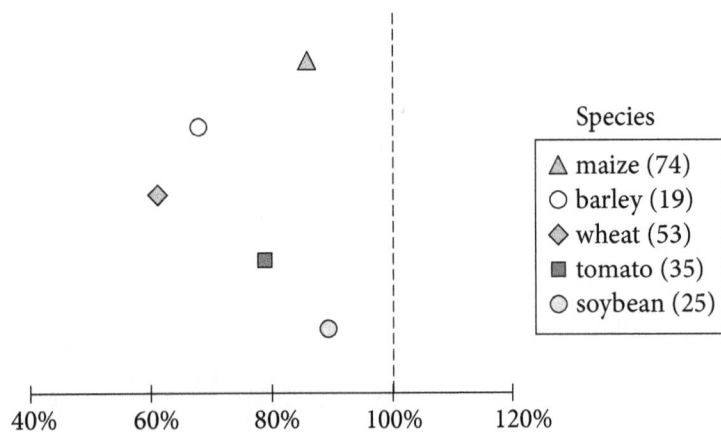

Species

- △ maize (74)
- ○ barley (19)
- ◇ wheat (53)
- ▪ tomato (35)
- ○ soybean (25)

40%　60%　80%　100%　120%

At 100%, the organic yield is the same as
the conventional yield. The number of
observations for each species is shown in
parentheses.

Figures adapted from Verena Seufert, Navin Ramankutty, and Jonathan A. Foley,
"Comparing the Yields of Organic and Conventional Agriculture." ©2012
by Nature Publishing Group.

22

As used in line 14, "simple" most nearly means

A) straightforward.

B) modest.

C) unadorned.

D) easy.

23

According to the passage, a significant attribute of conventional agriculture is its ability to

A) produce a wide variety of fruits and vegetables.

B) maximize the output of cultivated land.

C) satisfy the dietary needs of the world's population.

D) lessen the necessity of nitrogen in plant growth.

24

Which choice best reflects the perspective of the "environmentalists" (line 27) on conventional agriculture?

A) It produces inferior fruits and vegetables and is detrimental to the environment.

B) It is energy efficient and reduces the need to convert wilderness to farmland.

C) It is good for the environment only in the short run.

D) It depletes critical resources but protects wildlife habitats.

25

Which choice provides the best evidence for the answer to the previous question?

A) Lines 27-28 ("Of course . . . green")

B) Lines 28-31 ("They . . . corporations")

C) Lines 31-35 ("Environmentalists . . . sustainable")

D) Lines 42-45 ("More . . . think")

26

Which statement best expresses a relationship between organic farming and conventional farming that is presented in the passage?

A) Both are equally sustainable, but they differ dramatically in the amount of land they require to produce equivalent yields.

B) Both rely on artificial chemicals for pest control, but organic farmers use the chemicals sparingly in conjunction with natural remedies.

C) Both use nitrogen to encourage plant growth, but the nitrogen used in conventional farming comes from synthetic sources.

D) Both create a substantial amount of nitrogen runoff, but only the type of nitrogen found in fertilizers used in conventional farming can be dangerous.

27

Which choice provides the best evidence for the answer to the previous question?

A) Lines 13-14 ("Conventional . . . basis")

B) Lines 22-26 ("And since . . . environment")

C) Lines 51-53 ("They . . . widely")

D) Lines 61-65 ("Conventional . . . farming")

28

According to Foley, an "ideal global agriculture system" (line 80)

A) focuses primarily on yield percentages and global markets.

B) considers multiple factors in the selection of farming techniques.

C) weighs the economic interests of farmers against the needs of consumers.

D) puts the nutritional value of produce first and foremost.

29

In line 88, "sheer" most nearly means

A) transparent.

B) abrupt.

C) steep.

D) pure.

30

Which statement is best supported by the information provided in figure 1?

A) The organic yield as a percentage of conventional yield is greater for vegetables than for fruits.

B) The organic yield as a percentage of conventional yield is similar for cereals and all crops.

C) The reported number of observations for each crop type exceeds 82.

D) The organic yield as a percentage of conventional yield is greater for vegetable crops than it is for oilseed crops.

31

Which of the following claims is supported by figure 2?

A) Of the organically grown species represented, soybeans have the lowest yield.

B) The organically grown maize and barley represented are comparable in their yields to conventionally grown maize and barley.

C) Of the organically grown species represented, tomatoes have the highest yield.

D) The organically grown species represented have lower yields than their conventionally grown counterparts do.

Questions 32-41 are based on the following passage and supplementary material.

This passage is adapted from John Bohannon, "Why You Shouldn't Trust Internet Comments." ©2013 by American Association for the Advancement of Science.

The "wisdom of crowds" has become a mantra of the Internet age. Need to choose a new vacuum cleaner? Check out the reviews on online merchant
Line Amazon. But a new study suggests that such online
5 scores don't always reveal the best choice. A massive controlled experiment of Web users finds that such ratings are highly susceptible to irrational "herd behavior"—and that the herd can be manipulated.

Sometimes the crowd really is wiser than you. The
10 classic examples are guessing the weight of a bull or the number of gumballs in a jar. Your guess is probably going to be far from the mark, whereas the average of many people's choices is remarkably close to the true number.
15 But what happens when the goal is to judge something less tangible, such as the quality or worth of a product? According to one theory, the wisdom of the crowd still holds—measuring the aggregate of people's opinions produces a stable, reliable
20 value. Skeptics, however, argue that people's opinions are easily swayed by those of others. So nudging a crowd early on by presenting contrary opinions—for example, exposing them to some very good or very bad attitudes—will steer the crowd in a
25 different direction. To test which hypothesis is true, you would need to manipulate huge numbers of people, exposing them to false information and determining how it affects their opinions.

A team led by Sinan Aral, a network scientist at
30 the Massachusetts Institute of Technology in Cambridge, did exactly that. Aral has been secretly working with a popular website that aggregates news stories. The website allows users to make comments about news stories and vote each other's comments
35 up or down. The vote tallies are visible as a number next to each comment, and the position of the comments is chronological. (Stories on the site get an average of about ten comments and about three votes per comment.) It's a follow-up to his experiment
40 using people's ratings of movies to measure how much individual people influence each other online (answer: a lot). This time, he wanted to know how much the crowd influences the individual, and whether it can be controlled from outside.

45 For five months, every comment submitted by a user randomly received an "up" vote (positive); a "down" vote (negative); or as a control, no vote at all. The team then observed how users rated those comments. The users generated more than
50 100,000 comments that were viewed more than 10 million times and rated more than 300,000 times by other users.

At least when it comes to comments on news sites, the crowd is more herdlike than wise.
55 Comments that received fake positive votes from the researchers were 32% more likely to receive more positive votes compared with a control, the team reports. And those comments were no more likely than the control to be down-voted by the next viewer
60 to see them. By the end of the study, positively manipulated comments got an overall boost of about 25%. However, the same did not hold true for negative manipulation. The ratings of comments that got a fake down vote were usually negated by an up
65 vote by the next user to see them.

"Our experiment does not reveal the psychology behind people's decisions," Aral says, "but an intuitive explanation is that people are more skeptical of negative social influence. They're more
70 willing to go along with positive opinions from other people."

Duncan Watts, a network scientist at Microsoft Research in New York City, agrees with that conclusion. "[But] one question is whether the
75 positive [herding] bias is specific to this site" or true in general, Watts says. He points out that the category of the news items in the experiment had a strong effect on how much people could be manipulated. "I would have thought that 'business' is
80 pretty similar to 'economics,' yet they find a much stronger effect (almost 50% stronger) for the former than the latter. What explains this difference? If we're going to apply these findings in the real world, we'll need to know the answers."

85 Will companies be able to boost their products by manipulating online ratings on a massive scale? "That is easier said than done," Watts says. If people detect—or learn—that comments on a website are being manipulated, the herd may spook and leave
90 entirely.

CONTINUE

Artificially Up-Voted Comments versus Control Comments

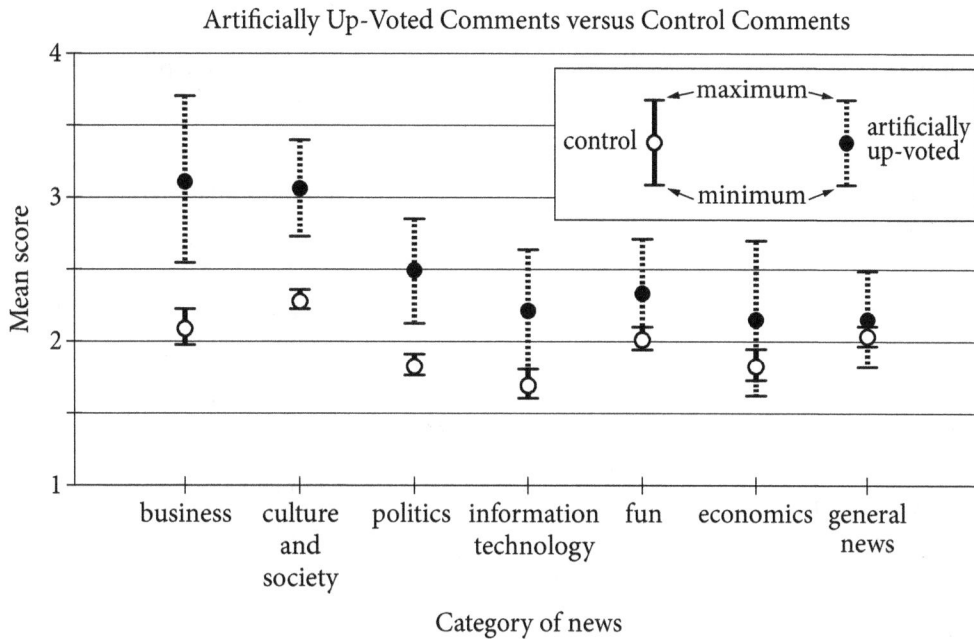

Mean score: mean of scores for the comments in each category, with the score for each comment being determined by the number of positive votes from website users minus the number of negative votes

Adapted from Lev Muchnik, Sinan Aral, and Sean J. Taylor, "Social Influence Bias: A Randomized Experiment." ©2013 by American Association for the Advancement of Science.

32

Over the course of the passage, the main focus shifts from a discussion of an experiment and its results to

A) an explanation of the practical applications of the results.

B) a consideration of the questions prompted by the results.

C) an analysis of the defects undermining the results.

D) a conversation with a scientist who disputes the results.

33

The author of the passage suggests that crowds may be more effective at

A) creating controversy than examining an issue in depth.

B) reinforcing members' ideas than challenging those ideas.

C) arriving at accurate quantitative answers than producing valid qualitative judgments.

D) ranking others' opinions than developing genuinely original positions.

34

Which choice provides the best evidence for the answer to the previous question?

A) Line 9 ("Sometimes . . . you")

B) Lines 11-14 ("Your . . . number")

C) Lines 17-20 ("According . . . value")

D) Lines 25-28 ("To test . . . opinions")

35

Which choice best supports the view of the "skeptics" (line 20)?

A) Lines 55-58 ("Comments . . . reports")

B) Lines 58-60 ("And . . . them")

C) Lines 63-65 ("The ratings . . . them")

D) Lines 76-79 ("He . . . manipulated")

36

Which action would best address a question Watts raises about the study?

A) Providing fewer fake positive comments

B) Using multiple websites to collect ratings

C) Requiring users to register on the website before voting

D) Informing users that voting data are being analyzed

37

As used in line 85, "boost" most nearly means

A) increase.

B) accelerate.

C) promote.

D) protect.

38

As used in line 86, "scale" most nearly means

A) level.

B) wage.

C) interval.

D) scheme.

39

In the figure, which category of news has an artificially up-voted mean score of 2.5?

A) Business

B) Politics

C) Fun

D) General news

40

According to the figure, which category of news showed the smallest difference in mean score between artificially up-voted comments and control comments?

A) Culture and society

B) Information technology

C) Fun

D) General news

41

Data presented in the figure most directly support which idea from the passage?

A) The mean score of artificially down-voted comments is similar to that of the control.

B) The patterns observed in the experiment suggest that people are suspicious of negative social influence.

C) The positive bias observed in users of the news site may not apply to human behavior in other contexts.

D) The type of story being commented on has an impact on the degree to which people can be influenced.

Questions 42-52 are based on the following passage.

This passage is adapted from Joshua Foer, *Moonwalking with Einstein: The Art and Science of Remembering Everything*. ©2011 by Joshua Foer.

In 2000, a neuroscientist at University College London named Eleanor Maguire wanted to find out what effect, if any, all that driving around the
Line labyrinthine streets of London might have on
5 cabbies' brains. When she brought sixteen taxi drivers into her lab and examined their brains in an MRI scanner, she found one surprising and important difference. The right posterior hippocampus, a part of the brain known to be
10 involved in spatial navigation, was 7 percent larger than normal in the cabbies—a small but very significant difference. Maguire concluded that all of that way-finding around London had physically altered the gross structure of their brains. The more
15 years a cabbie had been on the road, the more pronounced the effect.

The brain is a mutable organ, capable—within limits—of reorganizing itself and readapting to new kinds of sensory input, a phenomenon known as
20 neuroplasticity. It had long been thought that the adult brain was incapable of spawning new neurons—that while learning caused synapses to rearrange themselves and new links between brain cells to form, the brain's basic anatomical structure
25 was more or less static. Maguire's study suggested the old inherited wisdom was simply not true.

After her groundbreaking study of London cabbies, Maguire decided to turn her attention to mental athletes. She teamed up with Elizabeth
30 Valentine and John Wilding, authors of the academic monograph *Superior Memory*, to study ten individuals who had finished near the top of the World Memory Championship. They wanted to find out if the memorizers' brains were—like the London
35 cabbies'—structurally different from the rest of ours, or if they were somehow just making better use of memory abilities that we all possess.

The researchers put both the mental athletes and a group of matched control subjects into MRI scanners
40 and asked them to memorize three-digit numbers, black-and-white photographs of people's faces, and magnified images of snowflakes, while their brains were being scanned. Maguire and her team thought it was possible that they might discover anatomical
45 differences in the brains of the memory champs,

evidence that their brains had somehow reorganized themselves in the process of doing all that intensive remembering. But when the researchers reviewed the imaging data, not a single significant structural
50 difference turned up. The brains of the mental athletes appeared to be indistinguishable from those of the control subjects. What's more, on every single test of general cognitive ability, the mental athletes' scores came back well within the normal range. The
55 memory champs weren't smarter, and they didn't have special brains.

But there was one telling difference between the brains of the mental athletes and the control subjects: When the researchers looked at which parts of the
60 brain were lighting up when the mental athletes were memorizing, they found that they were activating entirely different circuitry. According to the functional MRIs [fMRIs], regions of the brain that were less active in the control subjects seemed to be
65 working in overdrive for the mental athletes.

Surprisingly, when the mental athletes were learning new information, they were engaging several regions of the brain known to be involved in two specific tasks: visual memory and spatial
70 navigation, including the same right posterior hippocampal region that the London cabbies had enlarged with all their daily way-finding. At first glance, this wouldn't seem to make any sense. Why would mental athletes be conjuring images in
75 their mind's eye when they were trying to learn three-digit numbers? Why should they be navigating like London cabbies when they're supposed to be remembering the shapes of snowflakes?

Maguire and her team asked the mental athletes
80 to describe exactly what was going through their minds as they memorized. The mental athletes said they were consciously converting the information they were being asked to memorize into images, and distributing those images along familiar spatial
85 journeys. They weren't doing this automatically, or because it was an inborn talent they'd nurtured since childhood. Rather, the unexpected patterns of neural activity that Maguire's fMRIs turned up were the result of training and practice.

18

CONTINUE

42

According to the passage, Maguire's findings regarding taxi drivers are significant because they

A) demonstrate the validity of a new method.

B) provide evidence for a popular viewpoint.

C) call into question an earlier consensus.

D) challenge the authenticity of previous data.

43

Which choice provides the best evidence for the answer to the previous question?

A) Lines 8-12 ("The right . . . difference")

B) Lines 12-16 ("Maguire . . . effect")

C) Lines 17-20 ("The brain . . . neuroplasticity")

D) Lines 20-26 ("It had . . . true")

44

As used in line 24, "basic" most nearly means

A) initial.

B) simple.

C) necessary.

D) fundamental.

45

Which question was Maguire's study of mental athletes primarily intended to answer?

A) Does the act of memorization make use of different brain structures than does the act of navigation?

B) Do mental athletes inherit their unusual brain structures, or do the structures develop as a result of specific activities?

C) Does heightened memorization ability reflect abnormal brain structure or an unusual use of normal brain structure?

D) What is the relationship between general cognitive ability and the unusual brain structures of mental athletes?

46

Which choice provides the best evidence for the answer to the previous question?

A) Lines 27-29 ("After . . . athletes")

B) Lines 33-37 ("They . . . possess")

C) Lines 38-43 ("The researchers . . . scanned")

D) Lines 52-54 ("What's . . . range")

Unauthorized copying or reuse of any part of this page is illegal.

19

CONTINUE

47

As used in line 39, "matched" most nearly means

A) comparable.

B) identical.

C) distinguishable.

D) competing.

48

The main purpose of the fifth paragraph
(lines 57-65) is to

A) relate Maguire's study of mental athletes to her study of taxi drivers.

B) speculate on the reason for Maguire's unexpected results.

C) identify an important finding of Maguire's study of mental athletes.

D) transition from a summary of Maguire's findings to a description of her methods.

49

According to the passage, when compared to mental athletes, the individuals in the control group in Maguire's second study

A) showed less brain activity overall.

B) demonstrated a wider range of cognitive ability.

C) exhibited different patterns of brain activity.

D) displayed noticeably smaller hippocampal regions.

50

The passage most strongly suggests that mental athletes are successful at memorization because they

A) exploit parts of the brain not normally used in routine memorization.

B) convert information they are trying to memorize into abstract symbols.

C) organize information into numerical lists prior to memorization.

D) exercise their brains regularly through puzzles and other mental challenges.

Which choice provides the best evidence for the answer to the previous question?

A) Lines 66-72 ("Surprisingly . . . way-finding")

B) Lines 72-73 ("At first . . . sense")

C) Lines 79-81 ("Maguire . . . memorized")

D) Lines 85-87 ("They . . . childhood")

The questions in lines 74-78 primarily serve to

A) raise doubts about the reliability of the conclusions reached by Maguire.

B) emphasize and elaborate on an initially puzzling result of Maguire's study of mental athletes.

C) imply that Maguire's findings undermine earlier studies of the same phenomenon.

D) introduce and explain a connection between Maguire's two studies and her earlier work.

STOP

If you finish before time is called, you may check your work on this section only.
Do not turn to any other section.

Writing and Language Test

35 MINUTES, 44 QUESTIONS

Turn to Section 2 of your answer sheet to answer the questions in this section.

DIRECTIONS

Each passage below is accompanied by a number of questions. For some questions, you will consider how the passage might be revised to improve the expression of ideas. For other questions, you will consider how the passage might be edited to correct errors in sentence structure, usage, or punctuation. A passage or a question may be accompanied by one or more graphics (such as a table or graph) that you will consider as you make revising and editing decisions.

Some questions will direct you to an underlined portion of a passage. Other questions will direct you to a location in a passage or ask you to think about the passage as a whole.

After reading each passage, choose the answer to each question that most effectively improves the quality of writing in the passage or that makes the passage conform to the conventions of standard written English. Many questions include a "NO CHANGE" option. Choose that option if you think the best choice is to leave the relevant portion of the passage as it is.

Questions 1-11 are based on the following passage.

Prehistoric Printing

Paleontologists are using modern technology to gain a greater understanding of the distant past. With the aid of computed tomography (CT) scanning and 3-D printing, researchers are able to create accurate models of prehistoric fossils. **1** These models have expanded

1

At this point, the writer is considering adding the following sentence.

> Fossils provide paleontologists with a convenient way of estimating the age of the rock in which the fossils are found.

Should the writer make this addition here?

A) Yes, because it supports the paragraph's argument with an important detail.

B) Yes, because it provides a logical transition from the preceding sentence.

C) No, because it is not directly related to the main point of the paragraph.

D) No, because it undermines the main claim of the paragraph.

researchers' knowledge of ancient species and [2] swear to advance the field of paleontology in the years to come.

CT scanners use X-rays to map the surface of a fossil in minute detail, recording as many as one million data points to create a digital blueprint. A 3-D printer then builds a polymer model based on this blueprint, much as a regular computer printer reproduces digital documents on paper. [3] Whereas the head of an ordinary computer printer moves back and forth while printing ink onto paper, the corresponding part of a 3-D printer moves in multiple dimensions while squirting out thin layers of melted polymer plastic. The plastic hardens quickly, [4] it allows the printer to build the layers of the final model. Compared with older ways of modeling fossils, scanning and printing in this way is extremely versatile.

[2]

A) NO CHANGE
B) subscribe
C) vow
D) promise

[3]

The writer is considering deleting the underlined sentence. Should the sentence be kept or deleted?

A) Kept, because it helps explain why X-rays are used in CT scanners.
B) Kept, because it provides details to illustrate how a 3-D printer works.
C) Deleted, because it contradicts the passage's information about digital blueprints.
D) Deleted, because it creates confusion about how researchers gather data.

[4]

A) NO CHANGE
B) this
C) which
D) that

[1] One significant benefit of 3-D printing technology is its ability to create scale reproductions of fossils. [2] But now 3-D scale models can be rearranged with ease, which is a huge boon to scientists. [3] A team led by Drexel University professor Kenneth Lacovara is making models of dinosaur bones one-tenth the bones' original sizes [5] in order to learn how they fit together when the animals were alive. [4] In the past, such research was limited by the weight and bulk of the fossils as well as [6] its preciousness and fragility. [5] In many cases, scientists had to rearrange bones virtually, using artists' renderings. [7]

Because CT scanners can map objects that are impossible to excavate, CT scanning and 3-D printing can also be used to reproduce fossils that scientists cannot observe firsthand. [8] By contrast, researchers

5

A) NO CHANGE
B) in order for learning
C) so that one is learning
D) so to learn

6

A) NO CHANGE
B) it's
C) their
D) there

7

To make this paragraph most logical, sentence 2 should be placed

A) where it is now.
B) before sentence 1.
C) after sentence 4.
D) after sentence 5.

8

A) NO CHANGE
B) Nonetheless,
C) Besides,
D) For example,

from the National Museum of Brazil **9** has relied on this technique to study a fossilized skeleton that was discovered protruding from a rock at an old São Paulo railroad site. **10** The fossil was too delicate to be removed from the rock. Because of the fossil's delicate nature, the team dug up a block of stone around the fossil and brought it to their lab. With the aid of a CT scanner and a 3-D printer, they were able to produce a resin model of the fossil. Examining the model, the researchers determined that **11** one had found a new species, a 75-million-year-old crocodile. While not every discovery will be as dramatic as this one, paleontologists anticipate further expanding their knowledge of ancient life-forms as CT scanning and 3-D printing continue to make fossils more accessible.

9

A) NO CHANGE
B) relied
C) will rely
D) is relying

10

Which choice most effectively combines the underlined sentences?

A) The fossil could not be removed from the rock on account of it being too delicate; moreover, the team dug up a block of stone around it and brought it to their lab.

B) The team thought the fossil was too delicate to remove from the rock, and their next decision was to dig up a block of stone around the fossil and bring it to their lab.

C) The fossil was too delicate to be removed from the rock, so the team dug up a block of stone around the fossil and brought it to their lab.

D) In removing the fossil from the rock, the team found it was too delicate; then they dug up a block of stone around the fossil and brought it to their lab.

11

A) NO CHANGE
B) he or she
C) they
D) it

Questions 12-22 are based on the following passage.

Thomas Nast, the Crusading Cartoonist

"Stop them pictures!" Legend has it that the corrupt politician William "Boss" Tweed once used those words when ordering someone to offer a bribe to Thomas Nast, an artist who had become famous for cartoons that called for reforms to end corruption. **12** As a result, Tweed's attempt to silence the artist failed, and Nast's cartoons, published in magazines like *Harper's Weekly*, actually played a key role in bringing Boss Tweed and his cronies to justice.

13 There were powerful political organizations in the 1860s and the 1870s. The organizations were known as "political machines" and started taking control of city governments. These political machines were able to pack legislatures and courts with hand-picked supporters by purchasing **14** votes, a form of election fraud involving the exchange of money or favors for votes. Once a political machine had control of enough important positions, its members were able to use public funds to enrich themselves and their friends. Boss Tweed's Tammany Hall group, which controlled New York **15** City in the 1860s—stole more than $30 million,

12
A) NO CHANGE
B) Therefore,
C) Furthermore,
D) DELETE the underlined portion.

13
Which choice most effectively combines the underlined sentences?
A) Powerful political organizations in the 1860s and the 1870s started taking control of city governments, and they were known as "political machines."
B) Known as "political machines," in the 1860s and the 1870s, political organizations that were powerful started taking control of city governments.
C) City governments were taken control of in the 1860s and the 1870s, and powerful political organizations known as "political machines" did so.
D) In the 1860s and the 1870s, powerful political organizations known as "political machines" started taking control of city governments.

14
A) NO CHANGE
B) votes, being
C) votes, that is
D) votes, which it is

15
A) NO CHANGE
B) City in the 1860s,
C) City, in the 1860s,
D) City in the 1860s

the equivalent of more than $365 million today.

16 Tweed had been elected to a single two-year term in Congress in 1852. Tammany Hall was so powerful and **17** corrupt that, the *New York Times*, commented "There is absolutely nothing . . . in the city which is beyond the reach of the insatiable gang."

Given the extent of Tweed's power, it is remarkable that a single cartoonist could have played such a significant role in bringing about his downfall. Nast's cartoons depicted Tweed as a great big bloated thief. One of the artist's most **18** famous images showed Tweed with a bag of money in place of his **19** head. Another featured Tweed leaning against a ballot box with the caption "As long as I count the votes, what are you going to do about it?" These cartoons were so effective in part because many of the citizens who supported Tweed were illiterate and thus could not read the newspaper accounts of his criminal activities. Nast's cartoons, though, widely exposed the public to the injustice of Tweed's political machine.

16

The writer is considering deleting the underlined sentence. Should the sentence be kept or deleted?

A) Kept, because it introduces the quote from the *New York Times* in the next sentence.

B) Kept, because it adds a vital detail about Tweed that is necessary to understand his power.

C) Deleted, because it blurs the focus of the paragraph by introducing loosely related information.

D) Deleted, because it contains information that undermines the main claim of the passage.

17

A) NO CHANGE

B) corrupt, that the *New York Times* commented,

C) corrupt that the *New York Times* commented,

D) corrupt that the *New York Times*, commented

18

A) NO CHANGE

B) famous and well-known

C) famous and commonly known

D) famous, commonly known

19

Which choice adds the most relevant supporting information to the paragraph?

A) head; like many other Nast cartoons, that one was published in *Harper's Weekly*.

B) head; Nast would later illustrate Tweed's escape from prison.

C) head, one depiction that omits Tweed's signature hat.

D) head, an image that perfectly captured Tweed's greedy nature.

Nast's campaign to bring down Tweed and the Tammany Hall gang was ultimately successful. In the elections of 1871, the public voted against most of the Tammany Hall candidates, greatly weakening Tweed's power. Eventually, Tweed and his gang were [20] persecuted for a number of charges, including fraud and larceny, and many of them were sent to jail. In 1875 Tweed escaped from jail and fled to Spain and unwittingly [21] brought about one final [22] pinnacle for the power of political cartoons: A Spanish police officer recognized Tweed from one of Nast's cartoons. Consequently, Tweed was sent back to jail, and Nast was hailed as the man who toppled the great Tammany Hall machine.

20
A) NO CHANGE
B) persecuted on
C) persecuted with
D) prosecuted on

21
A) NO CHANGE
B) bringing
C) brings
D) has brought

22
A) NO CHANGE
B) triumph
C) culmination
D) apex

Questions 23-33 are based on the following passage and supplementary material.

Rethinking Crowdfunding in the Arts

Crowdfunding is a popular way to raise money using the Internet. The process sounds simple: an artist, entrepreneur, or other innovator takes his or her ideas straight to the public via a crowdfunding website. The innovator creates a video about the project and offers, in exchange for donations, a series of "perks," from acknowledgment on a social media site to a small piece of art. Many crowdfunding programs are all-or-nothing; in other words, the innovator must garner 100 percent funding for the project or the money is refunded to the donors. At **23** it's best, the system can give creators direct access to millions of potential backers.

The home page of one leading crowdfunding site features a project to manufacture pinhole cameras on a 3-D printer. **24** The idea is obviously very attractive. An obscure method of photography may be made available to many with little expense. Within weeks, the project was 621 percent funded. In contrast, on the same page, a small Brooklyn performance venue is attempting to raise money for its current season. The venue features works of performance art showcased in a storefront window. Those who have seen the space consider it vital. **25** However, that group may not be large enough; with just fourteen days to go in the fund-raising period, the campaign is only 46 percent funded.

23

A) NO CHANGE
B) its
C) its'
D) their

24

Which choice most effectively combines the underlined sentences?

A) With the idea being obviously very attractive, an obscure method of photography may be made available to many at little expense.
B) The idea is obviously very attractive: an obscure method of photography may be made available to many at little expense.
C) An obscure method of photography may be made available to many at little expense, and the idea is obviously very attractive.
D) An obscure method of photography, an idea that is obviously very attractive, may be made available to many at little expense.

25

A) NO CHANGE
B) Therefore,
C) In effect,
D) As a rule,

Artists such as these Brooklyn performers find that crowdfunding exacerbates problems that already exist. **26** Work, that is easily understood and appreciated, is supported, while more complex work goes unnoticed. **27** Time that could be used creating art is spent devising clever perks to draw the attention of potential contributors. **28** In addition, audiences may contain many "free **29** riders," they did not make contributions.

26

A) NO CHANGE

B) Work that is easily understood and appreciated is supported,

C) Work that is easily understood, and appreciated is supported

D) Work—that is easily understood and appreciated—is supported,

27

At this point, the writer is considering adding the following sentence.

> Crowdfunding tends to attract contributors from a wide variety of professional fields.

Should the writer make this addition here?

A) Yes, because it gives more information about the people who donate to crowdfunding campaigns.

B) Yes, because it reinforces the writer's point about the funding of artistic projects.

C) No, because it fails to take into account project funding received from public institutions.

D) No, because it blurs the focus of the paragraph by introducing a poorly integrated piece of information.

28

A) NO CHANGE

B) Conversely,

C) However,

D) Thus,

29

A) NO CHANGE

B) riders," not making

C) riders," who did not make

D) riders" to not make

Ironically, the success of crowdfunding may weaken overall funding for the arts if people begin to feel that paying for the art **30** loved by them is someone else's responsibility.

[1] One innovative playwright has woven the deficiencies of the system into her crowdfunding model. [2] Though the price for her tickets was higher than that of tickets for comparable shows, it was still affordable to most theatergoers—and reflected the real cost of the performance. [3] She presented the total cost for producing her play on a crowdfunding site. [4] Then she divided the total cost by the number of people she expected to attend the performance. [5] The result of the calculation was the minimum donor price, and only donors who paid at least the minimum ticket price were allowed to attend the performance. [6] By subverting the presumption that money used for her project is an altruistic donation, the playwright showed that **31** our work has monetary value to those who enjoy it. **32**

30

A) NO CHANGE
B) they love
C) loved by him or her
D) he or she loves

31

A) NO CHANGE
B) their
C) her
D) its

32

To make this paragraph most logical, sentence 2 should be placed

A) where it is now.
B) after sentence 3.
C) after sentence 4.
D) after sentence 5.

Unauthorized copying or reuse of any part of this page is illegal.

31

CONTINUE

Crowdfunded Projects on Kickstarter in 2012

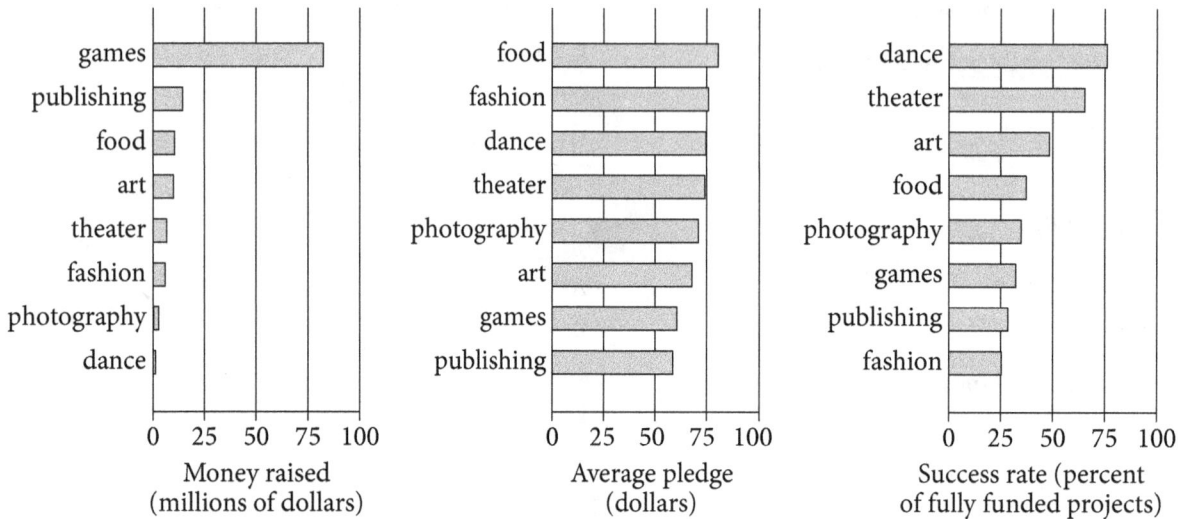

Money raised
(millions of dollars)

Average pledge
(dollars)

Success rate (percent
of fully funded projects)

Adapted from "These Were the Most Successful Projects on Kickstarter Last Year." ©2013 by The Economist Newspaper Limited.

Question 33 asks about the graphic.

33

Which choice offers an accurate interpretation of the data in the graphs?

A) The project category with the lowest amount of money raised was also the most successfully funded project category.

B) The project category with the highest average pledge amount was also the most successfully funded project category.

C) The project category with the lowest average pledge amount was also the project category that raised the most money.

D) The project category with the highest average pledge amount was also the project category with the most money raised.

Questions 34-44 are based on the following passage.

Investigative Journalism: An Evolving American Tradition

[1] The recent precipitous decline of print journalism as a viable profession has exacerbated long-held concerns about the state of investigative reporting in the United States. [2] Facing lower print circulation and diminished advertising revenue, many major newspapers have reduced or eliminated investigative resources. [3] Newspapers, the traditional nurturing ground for investigative journalism, have been hit especially hard by the widespread availability of free news online. [4] To survive, investigative journalism must continue to adapt to the digital age. 34

It is not difficult to understand why a cash-strapped, understaffed publication might feel pressure to cut teams of investigative 35 reporter's—their work is expensive and time-consuming. 36 Taking on the public interest, investigative journalism involves original, often long-form reporting on such topics as 37 illegal activities, street crime, corporate wrongdoing, and political corruption. An investigative story involves one or more experienced journalists dedicating their full energy and the resources of the publisher to a piece for a prolonged period of time. Expensive legal battles may ensue. The results of this work, though costly, have

34

For the sake of the logic and cohesion of the paragraph, sentence 3 should be

A) placed where it is now.
B) placed before sentence 1.
C) placed after sentence 1.
D) DELETED from the paragraph.

35

A) NO CHANGE
B) reporters:
C) reporters,
D) reporter's;

36

A) NO CHANGE
B) Undertaken in
C) Overtaking
D) Taking off from

37

A) NO CHANGE
B) business scandals,
C) abuse of government power,
D) DELETE the underlined portion.

helped keep those in power accountable. The exposure by *Washington Post* reporters Bob Woodward and Carl Bernstein of government misconduct in the Watergate scandal resulted in the resignation of President Richard Nixon in 1974. More recently, Seymour Hersh, reporting for the *New Yorker* in 2004, helped publicize the mistreatment of Iraqi prisoners by US personnel at Abu Ghraib during the Iraq War. **38** In these and other cases, exposure from reporters has served as an important **39** blockade to or scolding of malfeasance.

38

At this point, the writer is considering adding the following sentence.

> In 1954, Edward R. Murrow and Fred Friendly produced episodes of the CBS television show *See It Now* that contributed to the end of US senator Joseph McCarthy's anticommunist "witch hunts."

Should the writer make this addition here?

A) Yes, because it helps clarify that the passage's main focus is on investigations of political corruption.

B) Yes, because it offers an important counterpoint to the other cases previously described in the paragraph.

C) No, because it gives an example that is both chronologically and substantively out of place in the paragraph.

D) No, because it provides an example that is inconsistent with the passage's definition of investigative journalism.

39

A) NO CHANGE

B) interference to or condemnation of

C) drag on or reproof of

D) deterrent or rebuke to

While worrisome, the decline of traditional print media **40** could not entail the end of investigative journalism. **41** Although many newsrooms have reduced their staff, some still employ investigative reporters. Nonprofit **42** enterprises such as the Organized Crime and Corruption Reporting Project have begun to fill the void created by staff losses at newspapers and magazines. Enterprising freelance reporters, newly funded by nonprofits, make extensive use of social media,

40

Which choice most effectively suggests that the "end of investigative journalism" is a real possibility but one that can be prevented?

A) NO CHANGE

B) need

C) will

D) must

41

Which choice most effectively sets up the examples in the following sentences?

A) NO CHANGE

B) Investigative journalism also declined between the 1930s and 1950s, only to be revived in the 1960s.

C) According to the Pew Research Center, more people get their national and international news from the Internet than from newspapers.

D) Indeed, recent years have witnessed innovative adjustments to changing times.

42

A) NO CHANGE

B) enterprises: such as

C) enterprises such as:

D) enterprises, such as

including blogs and Twitter, to foster a public conversation about key issues. The Help Me Investigate project, **43** for example, solicited readers to submit tips and information related to ongoing stories to its website. Far from marking the end of investigative journalism, **44** cooperation among journalists and ordinary citizens has been facilitated by the advent of the digital age through an increase in the number of potential investigators.

43

A) NO CHANGE
B) therefore,
C) however,
D) in any case,

44

A) NO CHANGE
B) the number of potential investigators has increased since the advent of the digital age owing to the facilitation of cooperation among journalists and ordinary citizens.
C) the advent of the digital age has increased the number of potential investigators by facilitating cooperation among journalists and ordinary citizens.
D) by facilitating cooperation among journalists and ordinary citizens the advent of the digital age has increased the number of potential investigators.

STOP

If you finish before time is called, you may check your work on this section only.
Do not turn to any other section.

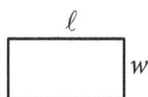

Math Test – No Calculator

25 MINUTES, 20 QUESTIONS

Turn to Section 3 of your answer sheet to answer the questions in this section.

For questions **1-15**, solve each problem, choose the best answer from the choices provided, and fill in the corresponding circle on your answer sheet. **For questions 16-20**, solve the problem and enter your answer in the grid on the answer sheet. Please refer to the directions before question 16 on how to enter your answers in the grid. You may use any available space in your test booklet for scratch work.

NOTES

1. The use of a calculator **is not permitted**.

2. All variables and expressions used represent real numbers unless otherwise indicated.

3. Figures provided in this test are drawn to scale unless otherwise indicated.

4. All figures lie in a plane unless otherwise indicated.

5. Unless otherwise indicated, the domain of a given function f is the set of all real numbers x for which $f(x)$ is a real number.

REFERENCE

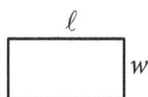 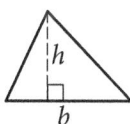 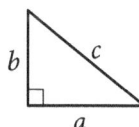 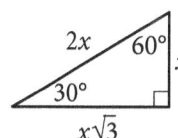 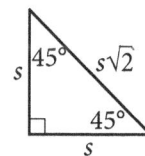

$A = \pi r^2$
$C = 2\pi r$

$A = \ell w$

$A = \frac{1}{2} bh$

$c^2 = a^2 + b^2$

Special Right Triangles

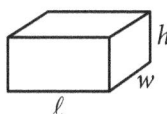 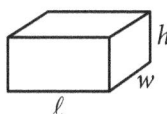 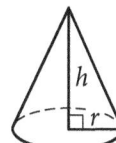 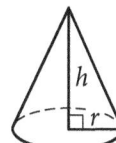 

$V = \ell wh$

$V = \pi r^2 h$

$V = \frac{4}{3}\pi r^3$

$V = \frac{1}{3}\pi r^2 h$

$V = \frac{1}{3}\ell wh$

The number of degrees of arc in a circle is 360.
The number of radians of arc in a circle is 2π.
The sum of the measures in degrees of the angles of a triangle is 180.

1

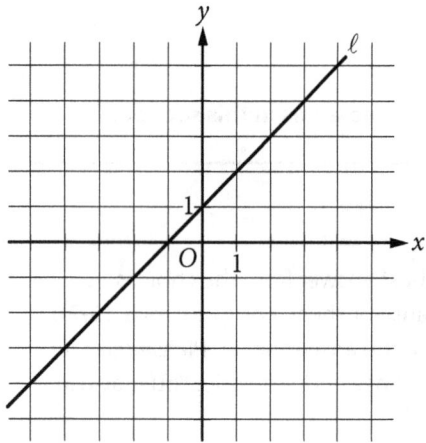

Which of the following is an equation of line ℓ in the *xy*-plane above?

A) $x = 1$

B) $y = 1$

C) $y = x$

D) $y = x + 1$

2

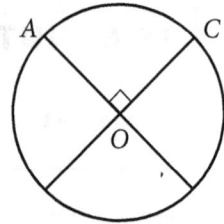

The circle above with center O has a circumference of 36. What is the length of minor arc $\overset{\frown}{AC}$?

A) 9

B) 12

C) 18

D) 36

3

What are the solutions of the quadratic equation $4x^2 - 8x - 12 = 0$?

A) $x = -1$ and $x = -3$

B) $x = -1$ and $x = 3$

C) $x = 1$ and $x = -3$

D) $x = 1$ and $x = 3$

4

Which of the following is an example of a function whose graph in the xy-plane has no x-intercepts?

A) A linear function whose rate of change is not zero

B) A quadratic function with real zeros

C) A quadratic function with no real zeros

D) A cubic polynomial with at least one real zero

5

$$\sqrt{k+2} - x = 0$$

In the equation above, k is a constant. If $x = 9$, what is the value of k ?

A) 1

B) 7

C) 16

D) 79

6

Which of the following is equivalent to the sum of the expressions $a^2 - 1$ and $a + 1$?

A) $a^2 + a$

B) $a^3 - 1$

C) $2a^2$

D) a^3

7

Jackie has two summer jobs. She works as a tutor, which pays \$12 per hour, and she works as a lifeguard, which pays \$9.50 per hour. She can work no more than 20 hours per week, but she wants to earn at least \$220 per week. Which of the following systems of inequalities represents this situation in terms of x and y, where x is the number of hours she tutors and y is the number of hours she works as a lifeguard?

A) $12x + 9.5y \leq 220$
$\quad x + y \geq 20$

B) $12x + 9.5y \leq 220$
$\quad x + y \leq 20$

C) $12x + 9.5y \geq 220$
$\quad x + y \leq 20$

D) $12x + 9.5y \geq 220$
$\quad x + y \geq 20$

8

In air, the speed of sound S, in meters per second, is a linear function of the air temperature T, in degrees Celsius, and is given by $S(T) = 0.6T + 331.4$. Which of the following statements is the best interpretation of the number 331.4 in this context?

A) The speed of sound, in meters per second, at 0°C

B) The speed of sound, in meters per second, at 0.6°C

C) The increase in the speed of sound, in meters per second, that corresponds to an increase of 1°C

D) The increase in the speed of sound, in meters per second, that corresponds to an increase of 0.6°C

9

$$y = x^2$$
$$2y + 6 = 2(x + 3)$$

If (x, y) is a solution of the system of equations above and $x > 0$, what is the value of xy ?

A) 1

B) 2

C) 3

D) 9

10

If $a^2 + b^2 = z$ and $ab = y$, which of the following is equivalent to $4z + 8y$?

A) $(a + 2b)^2$

B) $(2a + 2b)^2$

C) $(4a + 4b)^2$

D) $(4a + 8b)^2$

11

The volume of right circular cylinder A is 22 cubic centimeters. What is the volume, in cubic centimeters, of a right circular cylinder with twice the radius and half the height of cylinder A?

A) 11

B) 22

C) 44

D) 66

12

Which of the following is equivalent to $9^{\frac{3}{4}}$?

A) $\sqrt[3]{9}$

B) $\sqrt[4]{9}$

C) $\sqrt{3}$

D) $3\sqrt{3}$

13

At a restaurant, n cups of tea are made by adding t tea bags to hot water. If $t = n + 2$, how many additional tea bags are needed to make each additional cup of tea?

A) None

B) One

C) Two

D) Three

CONTINUE

14

$$f(x) = 2^x + 1$$

The function f is defined by the equation above. Which of the following is the graph of $y = -f(x)$ in the xy-plane?

A)

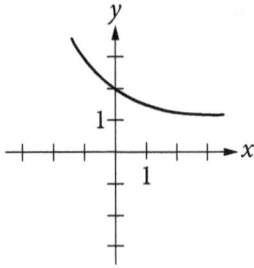

B)

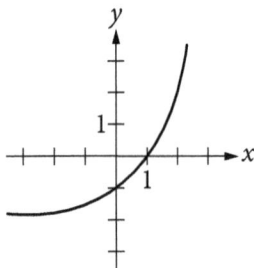

C)

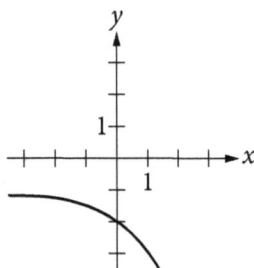

D)

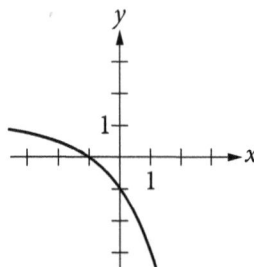

15

Alan drives an average of 100 miles each week. His car can travel an average of 25 miles per gallon of gasoline. Alan would like to reduce his weekly expenditure on gasoline by $5. Assuming gasoline costs $4 per gallon, which equation can Alan use to determine how many fewer average miles, m, he should drive each week?

A) $\dfrac{25}{4} m = 95$

B) $\dfrac{25}{4} m = 5$

C) $\dfrac{4}{25} m = 95$

D) $\dfrac{4}{25} m = 5$

DIRECTIONS

For questions 16-20, solve the problem and enter your answer in the grid, as described below, on the answer sheet.

1. Although not required, it is suggested that you write your answer in the boxes at the top of the columns to help you fill in the circles accurately. You will receive credit only if the circles are filled in correctly.

2. Mark no more than one circle in any column.

3. No question has a negative answer.

4. Some problems may have more than one correct answer. In such cases, grid only one answer.

5. **Mixed numbers** such as $3\frac{1}{2}$ must be gridded as 3.5 or 7/2. (If 3 1 / 2 is entered into the grid, it will be interpreted as $\frac{31}{2}$, not $3\frac{1}{2}$.)

6. **Decimal answers:** If you obtain a decimal answer with more digits than the grid can accommodate, it may be either rounded or truncated, but it must fill the entire grid.

Answer: $\frac{7}{12}$

Write answer in boxes.
← Fraction line
Grid in result.

Answer: 2.5
← Decimal point

Acceptable ways to grid $\frac{2}{3}$ are:

Answer: 201 – either position is correct

NOTE: You may start your answers in any column, space permitting. Columns you don't need to use should be left blank.

CONTINUE

16

Maria plans to rent a boat. The boat rental costs $60 per hour, and she will also have to pay for a water safety course that costs $10. Maria wants to spend no more than $280 for the rental and the course. If the boat rental is available only for a whole number of hours, what is the maximum number of hours for which Maria can rent the boat?

17

$$2(p + 1) + 8(p - 1) = 5p$$

What value of p is the solution of the equation above?

18

$$\frac{1}{2}(2x + y) = \frac{21}{2}$$
$$y = 2x$$

The system of equations above has solution (x, y). What is the value of x ?

CONTINUE →

19

$$\frac{2x+6}{(x+2)^2} - \frac{2}{x+2}$$

The expression above is equivalent to $\dfrac{a}{(x+2)^2}$,

where a is a positive constant and $x \neq -2$.

What is the value of a ?

20

Intersecting lines r, s, and t are shown below.

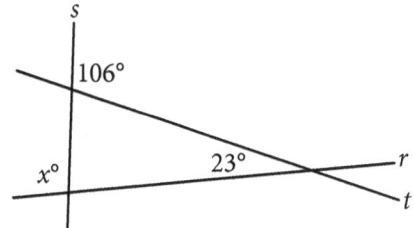

What is the value of x ?

STOP

If you finish before time is called, you may check your work on this section only.
Do not turn to any other section.

Math Test – Calculator

55 MINUTES, 38 QUESTIONS

Turn to Section 4 of your answer sheet to answer the questions in this section.

DIRECTIONS

For questions 1-30, solve each problem, choose the best answer from the choices provided, and fill in the corresponding circle on your answer sheet. **For questions 31-38**, solve the problem and enter your answer in the grid on the answer sheet. Please refer to the directions before question 31 on how to enter your answers in the grid. You may use any available space in your test booklet for scratch work.

NOTES

1. The use of a calculator **is permitted**.

2. All variables and expressions used represent real numbers unless otherwise indicated.

3. Figures provided in this test are drawn to scale unless otherwise indicated.

4. All figures lie in a plane unless otherwise indicated.

5. Unless otherwise indicated, the domain of a given function f is the set of all real numbers x for which $f(x)$ is a real number.

REFERENCE

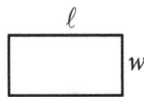
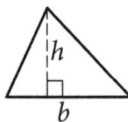
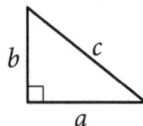
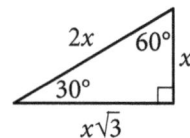
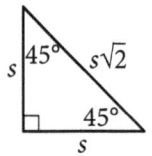

$A = \pi r^2$
$C = 2\pi r$

$A = \ell w$

$A = \frac{1}{2}bh$

$c^2 = a^2 + b^2$

Special Right Triangles

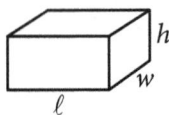
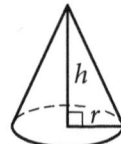

$V = \ell wh$

$V = \pi r^2 h$

$V = \frac{4}{3}\pi r^3$

$V = \frac{1}{3}\pi r^2 h$

$V = \frac{1}{3}\ell wh$

The number of degrees of arc in a circle is 360.
The number of radians of arc in a circle is 2π.
The sum of the measures in degrees of the angles of a triangle is 180.

CONTINUE ➡

1

Number of 3-D Movies Released by Year

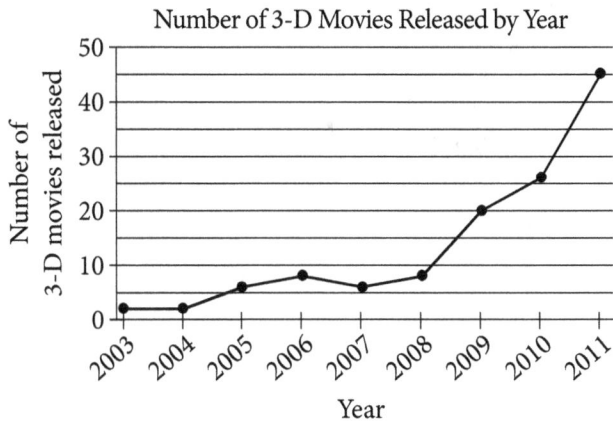

According to the line graph above, between which two consecutive years was there the greatest change in the number of 3-D movies released?

A) 2003–2004

B) 2008–2009

C) 2009–2010

D) 2010–2011

2

x	$f(x)$
1	5
3	13
5	21

Some values of the linear function f are shown in the table above. Which of the following defines f ?

A) $f(x) = 2x + 3$

B) $f(x) = 3x + 2$

C) $f(x) = 4x + 1$

D) $f(x) = 5x$

3

To make a bakery's signature chocolate muffins, a baker needs 2.5 ounces of chocolate for each muffin. How many pounds of chocolate are needed to make 48 signature chocolate muffins?
(1 pound = 16 ounces)

A)   7.5

B)   10

C)   50.5

D) 120

4

If $3(c + d) = 5$, what is the value of $c + d$?

A) $\dfrac{3}{5}$

B) $\dfrac{5}{3}$

C) 3

D) 5

6

An online bookstore sells novels and magazines. Each novel sells for \$4, and each magazine sells for \$1. If Sadie purchased a total of 11 novels and magazines that have a combined selling price of \$20, how many novels did she purchase?

A) 2

B) 3

C) 4

D) 5

5

The weight of an object on Venus is approximately $\dfrac{9}{10}$ of its weight on Earth. The weight of an object on Jupiter is approximately $\dfrac{23}{10}$ of its weight on Earth. If an object weighs 100 pounds on Earth, approximately how many more pounds does it weigh on Jupiter than it weighs on Venus?

A)   90

B)   111

C)   140

D)   230

7

The Downtown Business Association (DBA) in a certain city plans to increase its membership by a total of n businesses per year. There were b businesses in the DBA at the beginning of this year. Which function best models the total number of businesses, y, the DBA plans to have as members x years from now?

A) $y = nx + b$

B) $y = nx - b$

C) $y = b(n)^x$

D) $y = n(b)^x$

9

In the 1908 Olympic Games, the Olympic marathon was lengthened from 40 kilometers to approximately 42 kilometers. Of the following, which is closest to the increase in the distance of the Olympic marathon, in miles? (1 mile is approximately 1.6 kilometers.)

A) 1.00

B) 1.25

C) 1.50

D) 1.75

8

Which of the following is an equivalent form of $(1.5x - 2.4)^2 - (5.2x^2 - 6.4)$?

A) $-2.2x^2 + 1.6$

B) $-2.2x^2 + 11.2$

C) $-2.95x^2 - 7.2x + 12.16$

D) $-2.95x^2 - 7.2x + 0.64$

10

The density d of an object is found by dividing the mass m of the object by its volume V. Which of the following equations gives the mass m in terms of d and V ?

A) $m = dV$

B) $m = \dfrac{d}{V}$

C) $m = \dfrac{V}{d}$

D) $m = V + d$

11

$$-2x + 3y = 6$$

In the xy-plane, the graph of which of the following equations is perpendicular to the graph of the equation above?

A) $3x + 2y = 6$

B) $3x + 4y = 6$

C) $2x + 4y = 6$

D) $2x + 6y = 3$

12

$$\frac{1}{2}y = 4$$
$$x - \frac{1}{2}y = 2$$

The system of equations above has solution (x, y). What is the value of x ?

A) 3

B) $\dfrac{7}{2}$

C) 4

D) 6

13

$$y \le 3x + 1$$
$$x - y > 1$$

Which of the following ordered pairs (x, y) satisfies the system of inequalities above?

A) $(-2, -1)$

B) $(-1, 3)$

C) $(1, 5)$

D) $(2, -1)$

CONTINUE

14

Type of surgeon	Major professional activity		Total
	Teaching	Research	
General	258	156	414
Orthopedic	119	74	193
Total	377	230	607

In a survey, 607 general surgeons and orthopedic surgeons indicated their major professional activity. The results are summarized in the table above. If one of the surgeons is selected at random, which of the following is closest to the probability that the selected surgeon is an orthopedic surgeon whose indicated professional activity is research?

A) 0.122

B) 0.196

C) 0.318

D) 0.379

15

A polling agency recently surveyed 1,000 adults who were selected at random from a large city and asked each of the adults, "Are you satisfied with the quality of air in the city?" Of those surveyed, 78 percent responded that they were satisfied with the quality of air in the city. Based on the results of the survey, which of the following statements must be true?

    I. Of all adults in the city, 78 percent are satisfied with the quality of air in the city.

    II. If another 1,000 adults selected at random from the city were surveyed, 78 percent of them would report they are satisfied with the quality of air in the city.

    III. If 1,000 adults selected at random from a different city were surveyed, 78 percent of them would report they are satisfied with the quality of air in the city.

A) None

B) II only

C) I and II only

D) I and III only

Questions 16-18 refer to the following information.

Species of tree	Growth factor
Red maple	4.5
River birch	3.5
Cottonwood	2.0
Black walnut	4.5
White birch	5.0
American elm	4.0
Pin oak	3.0
Shagbark hickory	7.5

One method of calculating the approximate age, in years, of a tree of a particular species is to multiply the diameter of the tree, in inches, by a constant called the growth factor for that species. The table above gives the growth factors for eight species of trees.

16

According to the information in the table, what is the approximate age of an American elm tree with a diameter of 12 inches?

A) 24 years

B) 36 years

C) 40 years

D) 48 years

17

Tree Diameter versus Age

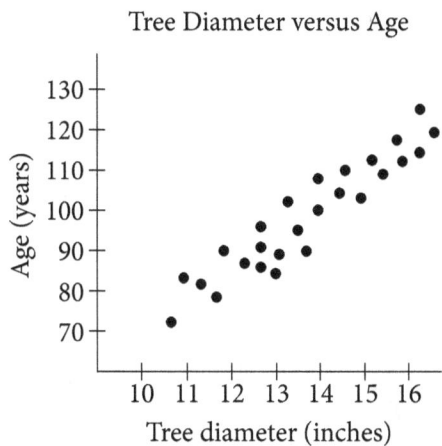

Tree diameter (inches)

The scatterplot above gives the tree diameter plotted against age for 26 trees of a single species. The growth factor of this species is closest to that of which of the following species of tree?

A) Red maple

B) Cottonwood

C) White birch

D) Shagbark hickory

18

If a white birch tree and a pin oak tree each now have a diameter of 1 foot, which of the following will be closest to the difference, in inches, of their diameters 10 years from now? (1 foot = 12 inches)

A) 1.0

B) 1.2

C) 1.3

D) 1.4

19

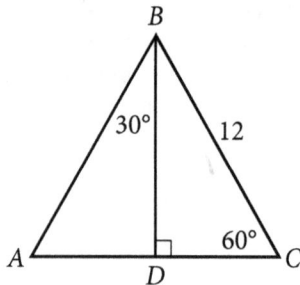

In $\triangle ABC$ above, what is the length of $\overline{AD}$?

A) 4

B) 6

C) $6\sqrt{2}$

D) $6\sqrt{3}$

20

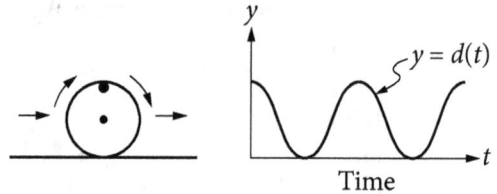

The figure on the left above shows a wheel with a mark on its rim. The wheel is rolling on the ground at a constant rate along a level straight path from a starting point to an ending point. The graph of $y = d(t)$ on the right could represent which of the following as a function of time from when the wheel began to roll?

A) The speed at which the wheel is rolling

B) The distance of the wheel from its starting point

C) The distance of the mark on the rim from the center of the wheel

D) The distance of the mark on the rim from the ground

21

$$\frac{a - b}{a} = c$$

In the equation above, if a is negative and b is positive, which of the following must be true?

A) $c > 1$

B) $c = 1$

C) $c = -1$

D) $c < -1$

22

In State X, Mr. Camp's eighth-grade class consisting of 26 students was surveyed and 34.6 percent of the students reported that they had at least two siblings. The average eighth-grade class size in the state is 26. If the students in Mr. Camp's class are representative of students in the state's eighth-grade classes and there are 1,800 eighth-grade classes in the state, which of the following best estimates the number of eighth-grade students in the state who have fewer than two siblings?

A) 16,200

B) 23,400

C) 30,600

D) 46,800

Questions 23 and 24 refer to the following information.

Townsend Realty Group Investments		
Property address	Purchase price (dollars)	Monthly rental price (dollars)
Clearwater Lane	128,000	950
Driftwood Drive	176,000	1,310
Edgemont Street	70,000	515
Glenview Street	140,000	1,040
Hamilton Circle	450,000	3,365

The Townsend Realty Group invested in the five different properties listed in the table above. The table shows the amount, in dollars, the company paid for each property and the corresponding monthly rental price, in dollars, the company charges for the property at each of the five locations.

23

The relationship between the monthly rental price r, in dollars, and the property's purchase price p, in thousands of dollars, can be represented by a linear function. Which of the following functions represents the relationship?

A) $r(p) = 2.5p - 870$

B) $r(p) = 5p + 165$

C) $r(p) = 6.5p + 440$

D) $r(p) = 7.5p - 10$

24

Townsend Realty purchased the Glenview Street property and received a 40% discount off the original price along with an additional 20% off the discounted price for purchasing the property in cash. Which of the following best approximates the original price, in dollars, of the Glenview Street property?

A) $350,000

B) $291,700

C) $233,300

D) $175,000

CONTINUE

25

A psychologist set up an experiment to study the tendency of a person to select the first item when presented with a series of items. In the experiment, 300 people were presented with a set of five pictures arranged in random order. Each person was asked to choose the most appealing picture. Of the first 150 participants, 36 chose the first picture in the set. Among the remaining 150 participants, p people chose the first picture in the set. If more than 20% of all participants chose the first picture in the set, which of the following inequalities best describes the possible values of p ?

A) $p > 0.20(300 - 36)$, where $p \le 150$

B) $p > 0.20(300 + 36)$, where $p \le 150$

C) $p - 36 > 0.20(300)$, where $p \le 150$

D) $p + 36 > 0.20(300)$, where $p \le 150$

26

The surface area of a cube is $6\left(\dfrac{a}{4}\right)^2$, where a is a positive constant. Which of the following gives the perimeter of one face of the cube?

A) $\dfrac{a}{4}$

B) a

C) $4a$

D) $6a$

27

The mean score of 8 players in a basketball game was 14.5 points. If the highest individual score is removed, the mean score of the remaining 7 players becomes 12 points. What was the highest score?

A) 20

B) 24

C) 32

D) 36

28

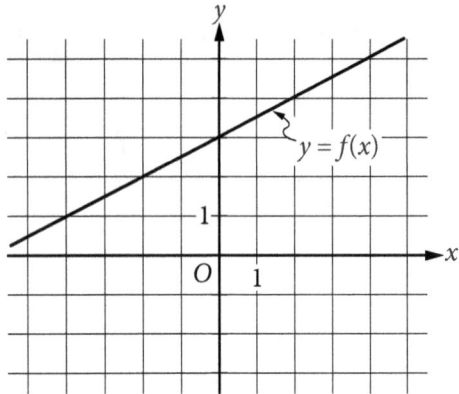

The graph of the linear function f is shown in the xy-plane above. The slope of the graph of the linear function g is 4 times the slope of the graph of f. If the graph of g passes through the point $(0, -4)$, what is the value of $g(9)$?

A) 5

B) 9

C) 14

D) 18

29

$$x^2 + 20x + y^2 + 16y = -20$$

The equation above defines a circle in the xy-plane. What are the coordinates of the center of the circle?

A) $(-20, -16)$

B) $(-10, -8)$

C) $(10, 8)$

D) $(20, 16)$

30

$$y = x^2 - a$$

In the equation above, a is a positive constant and the graph of the equation in the xy-plane is a parabola. Which of the following is an equivalent form of the equation?

A) $y = (x + a)(x - a)$

B) $y = (x + \sqrt{a})(x - \sqrt{a})$

C) $y = \left(x + \dfrac{a}{2}\right)\left(x - \dfrac{a}{2}\right)$

D) $y = (x + a)^2$

DIRECTIONS

For questions 31-38, solve the problem and enter your answer in the grid, as described below, on the answer sheet.

1. Although not required, it is suggested that you write your answer in the boxes at the top of the columns to help you fill in the circles accurately. You will receive credit only if the circles are filled in correctly.
2. Mark no more than one circle in any column.
3. No question has a negative answer.
4. Some problems may have more than one correct answer. In such cases, grid only one answer.
5. **Mixed numbers** such as $3\frac{1}{2}$ must be gridded as 3.5 or 7/2. (If $\boxed{3|1|/|2}$ is entered into the grid, it will be interpreted as $\frac{31}{2}$, not $3\frac{1}{2}$.)
6. **Decimal answers:** If you obtain a decimal answer with more digits than the grid can accommodate, it may be either rounded or truncated, but it must fill the entire grid.

Answer: $\frac{7}{12}$ Answer: 2.5

Write answer in boxes.

← Fraction line

← Decimal point

Grid in result.

Acceptable ways to grid $\frac{2}{3}$ are:

Answer: 201 – either position is correct

NOTE: You may start your answers in any column, space permitting. Columns you don't need to use should be left blank.

CONTINUE ➤

31

Horsepower and watts are units of measure of power. They are directly proportional such that 5 horsepower is equal to 3730 watts. How much power, in watts, is equal to 2 horsepower?

32

The painting *The Starry Night* by Vincent van Gogh is rectangular in shape with height 29 inches and width 36.25 inches. If a reproduction was made where each dimension is $\frac{1}{3}$ the corresponding original dimension, what is the height of the reproduction, in inches?

33

$$P \overset{\overset{\displaystyle x-1}{\Large\bullet}}{} \overset{\overset{\displaystyle}{\Large\bullet}}{} Q \quad \overset{\overset{\displaystyle x}{\Large\bullet}}{} R \quad \overset{\overset{\displaystyle 3x-7}{\Large\bullet}}{} S$$

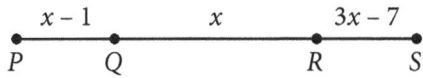

Note: Figure not drawn to scale.

On $\overline{PS}$ above, $PQ = RS$. What is the length of $\overline{PS}$?

34

In the xy-plane, the point $(2, 5)$ lies on the graph of the function f. If $f(x) = k - x^2$, where k is a constant, what is the value of k ?

35

A landscaper is designing a rectangular garden. The length of the garden is to be 5 feet longer than the width. If the area of the garden will be 104 square feet, what will be the length, in feet, of the garden?

36

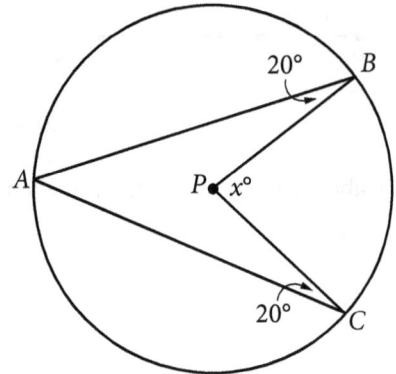

Point P is the center of the circle in the figure above. What is the value of x ?

Questions 37 and 38 refer to the following information.

Ms. Simon's Workday Morning Drive

Segment of drive	Distance (miles)	Average driving speed with no traffic delay (mph)
From home to freeway entrance	0.6	25
From freeway entrance to freeway exit	15.4	50
From freeway exit to workplace	1.4	35

Ms. Simon drives her car from her home to her workplace every workday morning. The table above shows the distance, in miles, and her average driving speed, in miles per hour (mph), when there is no traffic delay, for each segment of her drive.

37

One morning, Ms. Simon drove directly from her home to her workplace in 24 minutes. What was her average speed, in miles per hour, during her drive that morning?

38

If Ms. Simon starts her drive at 6:30 a.m., she can drive at her average driving speed with no traffic delay for each segment of the drive. If she starts her drive at 7:00 a.m., the travel time from the freeway entrance to the freeway exit increases by 33% due to slower traffic, but the travel time for each of the other two segments of her drive does not change. Based on the table, how many more <u>minutes</u> does Ms. Simon take to arrive at her workplace if she starts her drive at 7:00 a.m. than if she starts her drive at 6:30 a.m.? (Round your answer to the nearest minute.)

STOP

If you finish before time is called, you may check your work on this section only.

Do not turn to any other section.

The SAT® with Essay

Practice Essay #5

Make time to take the practice Essay.
It is one of the best ways to get ready
for the SAT Essay.

For information on scoring your essay, view
the SAT Essay scoring rubric at **sat.org/essay**.

As you read the passage below, consider how Todd Davidson uses

- evidence, such as facts or examples, to support claims.
- reasoning to develop ideas and to connect claims and evidence.
- stylistic or persuasive elements, such as word choice or appeals to emotion, to add power to the ideas expressed.

Adapted from Todd Davidson, "Government Must Preserve National Parks." ©2014 by Capitol Hill Publishing Corp. Originally published in the *Hill*, September 18, 2013.

1 The world has an enduring love affair with America's national parks. Conceived nearly 100 years ago, national parks connect us with our shared heritage and tell our nation's stories. Who among us has stared into the deep blue caldera of Crater Lake, looked up at Half Dome as the special time of winter approaches in the Yosemite Valley, or witnessed the spectacular October fall colors of red maples, oaks and hickories in the forests of the Great Smoky Mountains and not been overcome by the incredible, almost magical grandeur that has been preserved for us and future generations?

2 Collectively, our national parks, monuments, seashores, recreation areas, historic sites, military parks, battlefields and heritage areas represent the very best our nation has to offer. Along with their intrepid and iconic Park Rangers, they embody the true spirit of our country, bringing our nation's history to life.

3 In addition to being stunning and educational, national parks are immensely affordable destinations for American families and are top U.S. tourist attractions. Each year, nearly 300 million people visit one or more of America's 401 national parks, ranging from educational Civil War battlefields to awe-inspiring places like Yellowstone, Acadia National Park and the Grand Canyon. These park visitors are a significant component of the U.S. tourism economy. They stay in nearby hotels, rent cars, dine at local restaurants, buy at retail shops and visit other neighboring attractions, generating more than $30 billion in spending and supporting a quarter-million jobs. National parks are clearly a winning economic scenario for visitors, the economies of nearby towns and communities and ultimately our nation.

4 But now, these prolific economic engines are at risk. Over the last decade, national park budgets have seen a steady decline in funding, and currently suffer from an annual operations shortfall of more than $500 million. The National Park Service budget for construction and maintenance is only half of the amount necessary to maintain park sewer systems, roofs, foundations and road surfaces.

5   The sequester[1] cut another $153 million to national park budgets. Before Congress left for recess, each chamber shared a funding proposal with completely opposite visions for our national parks: one that cuts even deeper, affecting rangers, visitor centers and campgrounds, and another that would get our parks on the road to recovery. Through the across-the-board sequester cuts, parks have fewer rangers to protect and maintain historic sites and greet visitors, minimized visitor center hours, closed campgrounds, restrooms and picnic areas and reduced road and trail maintenance that is essential for park accessibility and enjoyment.

6   There is an irony to all this, because national parks are one of the best investments this country has ever made. In addition to supporting the U.S. travel and tourism industry, which is a cornerstone of the U.S. economy that represents $1.8 trillion in economic output and supports 14 million American jobs, every dollar invested in the National Park Service generates $10 in economic activity. National parks are veritable economic engines critical to supporting the livelihood of businesses and communities across the country.

7   Last year, President Obama called for a national travel and tourism strategy to make the United States the world's top travel and tourism destination, as part of a comprehensive effort to spur job creation. The White House released the strategy just over a year ago—an important step that officially elevates the travel and tourism industry to what it should be: a national priority. It also recognizes the industry for its fundamental contribution to our economy, national security and public diplomacy.

8   Our national parks can play an important role in making the U.S. a top travel destination. As the National Park System approaches its centennial in 2016, there should be a robust national park centennial initiative to help attract international visitors and provide needed support for our national parks to flourish into the next century.

> Write an essay in which you explain how Todd Davidson builds an argument to persuade his audience that the US government must continue to fund national parks. In your essay, analyze how Davidson uses one or more of the features listed in the box above (or features of your own choice) to strengthen the logic and persuasiveness of his argument. Be sure that your analysis focuses on the most relevant features of the passage.
>
> Your essay should not explain whether you agree with Davidson's claims, but rather explain how Davidson builds an argument to persuade his audience.

---

[1] A cut in spending by the federal government

Directions

The essay gives you an opportunity to show how effectively you can read and comprehend a passage and write an essay analyzing the passage. In your essay, you should demonstrate that you have read the passage carefully, present a clear and logical analysis, and use language precisely.

Your essay must be written on the lines provided in your answer booklet; except for the Planning Page of the answer booklet, you will receive no other paper on which to write. You will have enough space if you write on every line, avoid wide margins, and keep your handwriting to a reasonable size. Remember that people who are not familiar with your handwriting will read what you write. Try to write or print so that what you are writing is legible to those readers.

You have 50 minutes to read the passage and write an essay in response to the prompt provided inside this booklet.

⊙ **REMINDERS**
- Do not write your essay in this booklet. Only what you write on the lined pages of your answer booklet will be evaluated.

- An off-topic essay will not be evaluated.

⏱ **STANDARD TIME**
Essay: **50 minutes**

For information on scoring your essay, view the SAT Essay scoring rubric at **sat.org/essay**.

Scoring Your
SAT® Practice Test #5

Congratulations on completing an SAT® practice test. To score your test, use these instructions and the conversion tables and answer key at the end of this document.

Scores Overview

The redesigned SAT will provide more information about your learning by reporting more scores than ever before. Each of the redesigned assessments (SAT, PSAT/NMSQT®, PSAT™ 10, and PSAT™ 8/9) will report test scores and cross-test scores on a common scale. Additionally, subscores will be reported to provide more diagnostic information to students, educators, and parents.

The practice test you completed was written by the College Board's Assessment Design & Development team using the same processes and review standards used when writing the actual SAT. Everything from the layout of the page to the construction of the questions accurately reflects what you'll see on test day.

How to Calculate Your Practice Test Scores

GET SET UP

❶ You'll need the answer sheet that you bubbled in while taking the practice test. You'll also need the conversion tables and answer key at the end of this document.

❷ Using the answer key, count up your total correct answers for each section. You may want to write the number of correct answers for each section at the bottom of that section in the answer key.

❸ Using your marked-up answer key and the conversion tables, follow the directions to get all of your scores.

GET SECTION AND TOTAL SCORES

Your total score on the SAT practice test is the sum of your Evidence-Based Reading and Writing Section score and your Math Section score. To get your total score, you will convert what we call the "raw score" for each section — the number of questions you got right in that section — into the "scaled score" for that section, then calculate the total score.

GET YOUR EVIDENCE-BASED READING AND WRITING SECTION SCORE

Calculate your SAT Evidence-Based Reading and Writing Section score (it's on a scale of 200–800) by first determining your Reading Test score and your Writing and Language Test score. Here's how:

1. Count the number of correct answers you got on Section 1 (the Reading Test). There is no penalty for wrong answers. The number of correct answers is your raw score.

2. Go to Raw Score Conversion Table 1: Section and Test Scores on page 7. Look in the "Raw Score" column for your raw score, and match it to the number in the "Reading Test Score" column.

3. Do the same with Section 2 to determine your Writing and Language Test score.

4. Add your Reading Test score to your Writing and Language Test score.

5. Multiply that number by 10. This is your Evidence-Based Reading and Writing Section score.

EXAMPLE: *Sofia answered 29 of the 52 questions correctly on the SAT Reading Test and 19 of the 44 questions correctly on the SAT Writing and Language Test. Using the table on page 7, she calculates that she received an SAT Reading Test score of 27 and an SAT Writing and Language Test score of 23. She adds 27 to 23 (gets 50) and then multiplies by 10 to determine her SAT Evidence-Based Reading and Writing Section score of 500.*

GET YOUR MATH SECTION SCORE

Calculate your SAT Math Section score (it's on a scale of 200–800).

1. Count the number of correct answers you got on Section 3 (Math Test — No Calculator) and Section 4 (Math Test — Calculator). There is no penalty for wrong answers.

2. Add the number of correct answers you got on Section 3 (Math Test — No Calculator) and Section 4 (Math Test — Calculator).

3. Use Raw Score Conversion Table 1: Section and Test Scores to turn your raw score into your Math Section score.

GET YOUR TOTAL SCORE

Add your Evidence-Based Reading and Writing Section score to your Math Section score. The result is your total score on the SAT Practice Test, on a scale of 400–1600.

GET SUBSCORES

Subscores provide more detailed information about your strengths in specific areas within literacy and math. They are reported on a scale of 1–15.

HEART OF ALGEBRA

The Heart of Algebra subscore is based on questions from the Math Test that focus on linear equations and inequalities.

1. Add up your total correct answers from the following set of questions:
   - ▸ Math Test – No Calculator: Questions 1; 7–8; 13; 15–18
   - ▸ Math Test – Calculator: Questions 2; 4; 6; 11–13; 23–25; 28; 33

   Your total correct answers from all of these questions is your raw score.

2. Use Raw Score Conversion Table 2: Subscores on page 8 to determine your Heart of Algebra subscore.

PROBLEM SOLVING AND DATA ANALYSIS

The Problem Solving and Data Analysis subscore is based on questions from the Math Test that focus on quantitative reasoning, the interpretation and synthesis of data, and solving problems in rich and varied contexts.

1. Add up your total correct answers from the following set of questions:
   - ▸ Math Test – No Calculator: No Questions
   - ▸ Math Test – Calculator: Questions 1; 3; 5; 7; 9; 14–18; 20; 22; 27; 31–32; 37–38

   Your total correct answers from all of these questions is your raw score.

2. Use Raw Score Conversion Table 2: Subscores to determine your Problem Solving and Data Analysis subscore.

PASSPORT TO ADVANCED MATH

The Passport to Advanced Math subscore is based on questions from the Math Test that focus on topics central to the ability of students to progress to more advanced mathematics, such as understanding the structure of expressions, reasoning with more complex equations, and interpreting and building functions.

1. Add up your total correct answers from the following set of questions:
   - ▸ Math Test – No Calculator: Questions 3–6; 9–10; 12; 14; 19
   - ▸ Math Test – Calculator: Questions 8; 10; 21; 26; 30; 34; 35

   Your total correct answers from all of these questions is your raw score.

2. Use Raw Score Conversion Table 2: Subscores to determine your Passport to Advanced Math subscore.

EXPRESSION OF IDEAS

The Expression of Ideas subscore is based on questions from the Writing and Language Test that focus on topic development, organization, and rhetorically effective use of language.

1. Add up your total correct answers from the following set of questions:

   ▸ Writing and Language Test: Questions 1–3; 7–8; 10; 12–13; 16; 18–19; 22; 24–25; 27–28; 32–34; 37–39; 41; 43

   Your total correct answers from all of these questions is your raw score.

2. Use Raw Score Conversion Table 2: Subscores to determine your Expression of Ideas subscore.

STANDARD ENGLISH CONVENTIONS

The Standard English Conventions subscore is based on questions from the Writing and Language Test that focus on sentence structure, usage, and punctuation.

1. Add up your total correct answers from the following set of questions:

   ▸ Writing and Language Test: Questions 4–6; 9; 11; 14–15; 17; 20–21; 23; 26; 29–31; 35–36; 40; 42; 44

   Your total correct answers from all of these questions is your raw score.

2. Use Raw Score Conversion Table 2: Subscores to determine your Standard English Conventions subscore.

WORDS IN CONTEXT

The Words in Context subscore is based on questions from both the Reading Test and the Writing and Language Test that address word/phrase meaning in context and rhetorical word choice.

1. Add up your total correct answers from the following set of questions:

   ▸ Reading Test: Questions 7; 10; 14–15; 22; 29; 37–38; 44; 47

   ▸ Writing and Language Test: Questions 2; 10; 13; 18; 22; 24; 37; 39

   Your total correct answers from all of these questions is your raw score.

2. Use Raw Score Conversion Table 2: Subscores to determine your Words in Context subscore.

COMMAND OF EVIDENCE

The Command of Evidence subscore is based on questions from both the Reading Test and the Writing and Language Test that ask you to interpret and use evidence found in a wide range of passages and informational graphics, such as graphs, tables, and charts.

1. Add up your total correct answers from the following set of questions:

   ▸ Reading Test: Questions 5; 9; 12; 18; 30–31; 34; 39; 43; 46

   ▸ Writing and Language Test: Questions 1; 3; 16; 19; 27; 33; 38; 41

   Your total correct answers from all of these questions is your raw score.

2. Use Raw Score Conversion Table 2: Subscores to determine your Command of Evidence subscore.

GET CROSS-TEST SCORES

The new SAT also reports two cross-test scores: Analysis in History/Social Studies and Analysis in Science. These scores are based on questions in the Reading, Writing and Language, and Math Tests that ask students to think analytically about texts and questions in these subject areas. Cross-test scores are reported on a scale of 10–40.

ANALYSIS IN HISTORY/SOCIAL STUDIES

1. Add up your total correct answers from the following set of questions:

   ▶ Reading Test: Questions 11–21; 32–41

   ▶ Writing and Language Test: Questions 12–13; 16; 18; 19; 22

   ▶ Math Test – No Calculator: No Questions

   ▶ Math Test – Calculator: Questions 7; 9; 14–15; 23–25; 32

   Your total correct answers from all of these questions is your raw score.

2. Use Raw Score Conversion Table 3: Cross-Test Scores on page 9 to determine your Analysis in History/Social Studies cross-test score.

ANALYSIS IN SCIENCE

1. Add up your total correct answers from the following set of questions:

   ▶ Reading Test: Questions 22–31; 42–52

   ▶ Writing and Language Test: Questions 1–3; 7–8; 10

   ▶ Math Test – No Calculator: Question 8

   ▶ Math Test – Calculator: Questions 5; 10; 16–18; 20; 31

   Your total correct answers from all of these questions is your raw score.

2. Use Raw Score Conversion Table 3: Cross-Test Scores on page 9 to determine your Analysis in Science cross-test score.

SAT Practice Test #5: Worksheets

Reading Test Answers

1 D	12 A	23 B	34 B	45 C
2 C	13 B	24 A	35 A	46 B
3 C	14 D	25 B	36 B	47 A
4 A	15 C	26 C	37 C	48 C
5 C	16 A	27 D	38 A	49 C
6 A	17 B	28 B	39 B	50 A
7 D	18 B	29 D	40 D	51 A
8 B	19 B	30 B	41 D	52 B
9 B	20 A	31 D	42 C	
10 B	21 D	32 B	43 D	
11 B	22 A	33 C	44 D	

READING TEST
RAW SCORE
(NUMBER OF
CORRECT ANSWERS)

Writing and Language Test Answers

1 C	12 D	23 B	34 C
2 D	13 D	24 B	35 B
3 B	14 A	25 A	36 B
4 C	15 B	26 B	37 D
5 A	16 C	27 D	38 C
6 C	17 C	28 A	39 D
7 D	18 A	29 C	40 B
8 D	19 D	30 B	41 D
9 B	20 D	31 C	42 A
10 C	21 A	32 D	43 A
11 C	22 B	33 A	44 C

WRITING AND
LANGUAGE TEST
RAW SCORE
(NUMBER OF
CORRECT ANSWERS)

Math Test
No Calculator Answers

1 D	11 C
2 A	12 D
3 B	13 B
4 C	14 C
5 D	15 D
6 A	16 4
7 C	17 6/5, 1.2
8 A	18 21/4, 5.25
9 A	19 2
10 B	20 97

MATH TEST
NO CALCULATOR
RAW SCORE
(NUMBER OF
CORRECT ANSWERS)

Math Test
Calculator Answers

1 D	11 A	21 A	31 1492
2 C	12 D	22 C	32 29/3, 9.66, 9.67
3 A	13 D	23 D	33 7
4 B	14 A	24 B	34 9
5 C	15 A	25 D	35 13
6 B	16 D	26 B	36 80
7 A	17 D	27 C	37 43, 43.5, 44, 87/2
8 C	18 C	28 C	38 6
9 B	19 B	29 B	
10 A	20 D	30 B	

MATH TEST
CALCULATOR
RAW SCORE
(NUMBER OF
CORRECT ANSWERS)

SAT Practice Test #5: Worksheets

RAW SCORE CONVERSION TABLE 1 — SECTION AND TEST SCORES

Raw Score (# of correct answers)	Math Section Score	Reading Test Score	Writing and Language Test Score	Raw Score (# of correct answers)	Math Section Score	Reading Test Score	Writing and Language Test Score
0	200	10	10	30	540	26	30
1	200	10	10	31	540	27	30
2	210	10	10	32	550	28	31
3	230	10	10	33	560	28	32
4	250	11	11	34	570	29	32
5	260	11	12	35	580	29	33
6	270	12	13	36	590	29	34
7	290	13	13	37	600	30	34
8	300	14	14	38	600	30	35
9	320	14	15	39	610	31	36
10	330	15	16	40	620	31	37
11	340	16	16	41	630	32	38
12	360	16	17	42	640	32	39
13	370	17	18	43	650	33	40
14	390	17	18	44	660	33	40
15	400	18	19	45	660	34	
16	410	18	20	46	670	35	
17	420	19	20	47	680	35	
18	430	20	21	48	690	36	
19	440	20	22	49	700	37	
20	450	21	23	50	710	37	
21	460	21	23	51	710	39	
22	470	22	24	52	720	40	
23	480	23	25	53	730		
24	490	23	25	54	750		
25	500	24	26	55	760		
26	510	24	27	56	770		
27	510	25	28	57	790		
28	520	25	28	58	800		
29	530	26	29				

CONVERSION EQUATION 1 — SECTION AND TEST SCORES

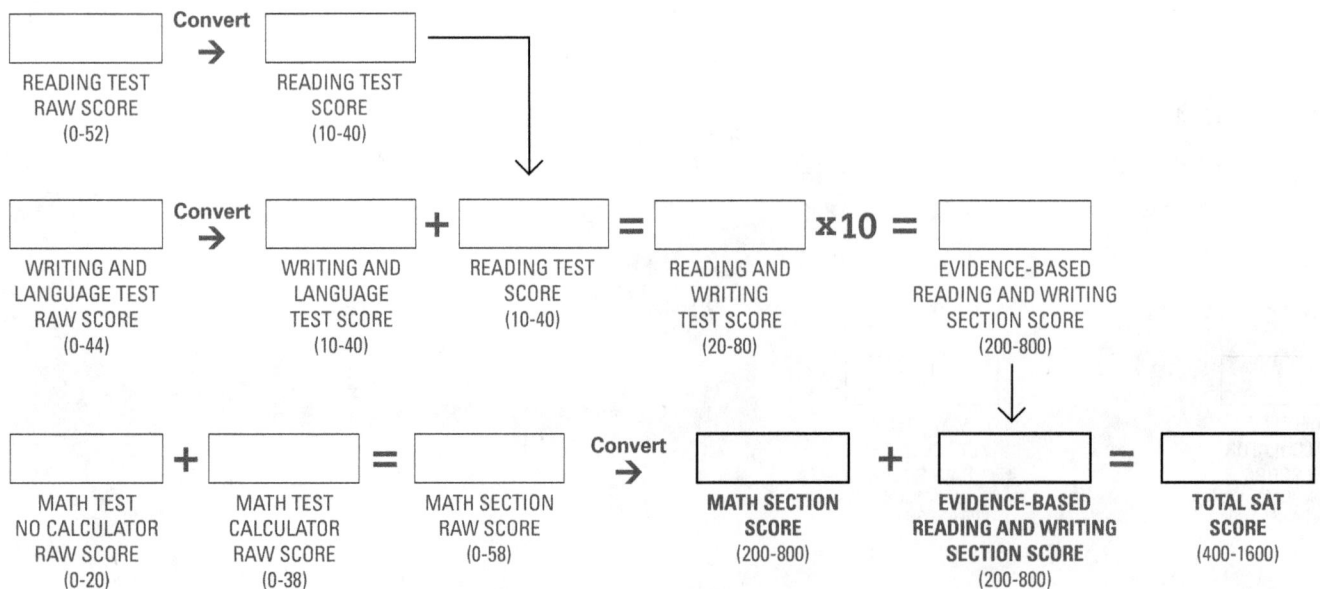

Convert →

READING TEST RAW SCORE (0-52) → READING TEST SCORE (10-40)

Convert →

WRITING AND LANGUAGE TEST RAW SCORE (0-44) → WRITING AND LANGUAGE TEST SCORE (10-40)

WRITING AND LANGUAGE TEST SCORE (10-40) + READING TEST SCORE (10-40) = READING AND WRITING TEST SCORE (20-80) ×10 = EVIDENCE-BASED READING AND WRITING SECTION SCORE (200-800)

MATH TEST NO CALCULATOR RAW SCORE (0-20) + MATH TEST CALCULATOR RAW SCORE (0-38) = MATH SECTION RAW SCORE (0-58)

Convert → MATH SECTION SCORE (200-800) + EVIDENCE-BASED READING AND WRITING SECTION SCORE (200-800) = TOTAL SAT SCORE (400-1600)

SAT Practice Test #5: Worksheets

RAW SCORE CONVERSION TABLE 2 SUBSCORES

Raw Score (# of correct answers)	Expression of Ideas	Standard English Conventions	Heart of Algebra	Problem Solving and Data Analysis	Passport to Advanced Math	Words in Context	Command of Evidence
0	1	1	1	1	1	1	1
1	1	1	2	1	3	1	2
2	1	1	3	1	4	1	3
3	2	1	4	2	5	2	4
4	3	2	5	3	6	3	4
5	4	3	6	4	7	4	5
6	4	4	7	5	8	5	6
7	5	4	7	6	9	6	6
8	6	5	8	7	9	7	7
9	6	6	9	8	10	7	8
10	7	7	9	9	11	8	8
11	8	7	10	10	11	9	9
12	8	8	10	10	12	10	10
13	9	9	11	11	13	11	10
14	9	10	11	12	14	11	11
15	10	11	12	13	14	12	12
16	10	12	13	14	15	13	13
17	11	13	13	15		14	14
18	12	14	14			15	15
19	12	15	15				
20	13	15					
21	14						
22	14						
23	15						
24	15						

CONVERSION EQUATION 2 SUBSCORES

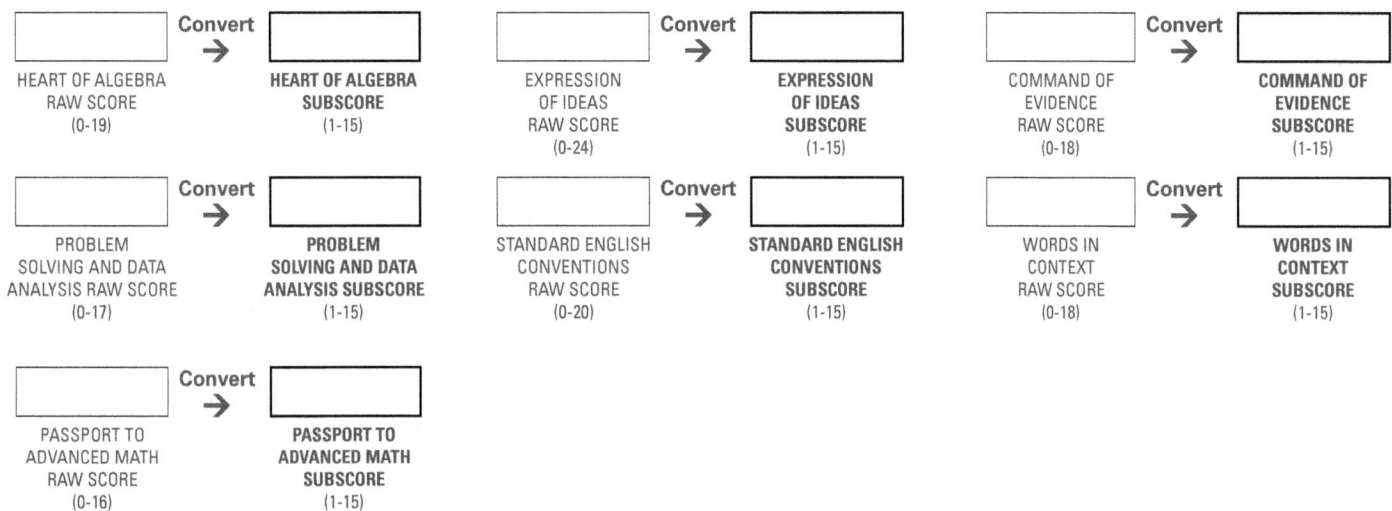

	Convert →	
HEART OF ALGEBRA RAW SCORE (0-19)		**HEART OF ALGEBRA SUBSCORE** (1-15)

	Convert →	
EXPRESSION OF IDEAS RAW SCORE (0-24)		**EXPRESSION OF IDEAS SUBSCORE** (1-15)

	Convert →	
COMMAND OF EVIDENCE RAW SCORE (0-18)		**COMMAND OF EVIDENCE SUBSCORE** (1-15)

	Convert →	
PROBLEM SOLVING AND DATA ANALYSIS RAW SCORE (0-17)		**PROBLEM SOLVING AND DATA ANALYSIS SUBSCORE** (1-15)

	Convert →	
STANDARD ENGLISH CONVENTIONS RAW SCORE (0-20)		**STANDARD ENGLISH CONVENTIONS SUBSCORE** (1-15)

	Convert →	
WORDS IN CONTEXT RAW SCORE (0-18)		**WORDS IN CONTEXT SUBSCORE** (1-15)

	Convert →	
PASSPORT TO ADVANCED MATH RAW SCORE (0-16)		**PASSPORT TO ADVANCED MATH SUBSCORE** (1-15)

SAT Practice Test #5: Worksheets

Raw Score (# of correct answers)	Analysis in History/ Social Studies Cross-Test Score	Analysis in Science Cross-Test Score	Raw Score (# of correct answers)	Analysis in History/ Social Studies Cross-Test Score	Analysis in Science Cross-Test Score
0	10	10	18	26	26
1	10	10	19	27	26
2	10	12	20	27	27
3	11	13	21	28	28
4	13	14	22	29	28
5	14	15	23	29	29
6	15	16	24	30	30
7	16	17	25	30	30
8	17	18	26	31	31
9	18	19	27	32	31
10	19	20	28	33	32
11	20	21	29	33	33
12	21	21	30	34	34
13	22	22	31	35	34
14	23	23	32	36	35
15	24	24	33	37	36
16	24	24	34	38	38
17	25	25	35	40	40

CONVERSION EQUATION 3 CROSS-TEST SCORES

Test	Analysis in History/Social Studies		Analysis in Science	
	Questions	Raw Score	Questions	Raw Score
Reading Test	11–21; 32–41		22–31; 42–52	
Writing and Language Test	12–13; 16; 18–19; 22		1–3; 7–8; 10	
Math Test No Calculator	No Questions		8	
Math Test Calculator	7; 9; 14–15; 23–25; 32		5; 10; 16–18; 20; 31	
Total				

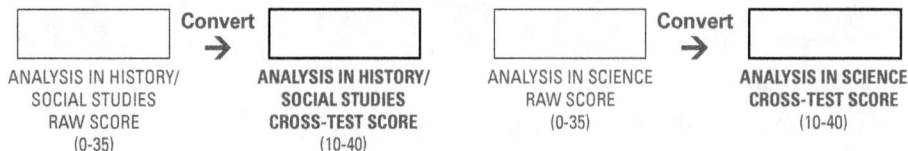

	Convert			Convert	
ANALYSIS IN HISTORY/ SOCIAL STUDIES RAW SCORE (0-35)	→	**ANALYSIS IN HISTORY/ SOCIAL STUDIES CROSS-TEST SCORE (10-40)**	ANALYSIS IN SCIENCE RAW SCORE (0-35)	→	**ANALYSIS IN SCIENCE CROSS-TEST SCORE (10-40)**

The SAT

Practice Test #6

Make time to take the practice test.
It's one of the best ways to get ready
for the SAT.

TEST TAKING TIPS #6

- Simulate Correct Testing Conditions: To be prepared for exam day, you have to know exactly what you will be facing. The best way to do this is to take practice tests under the exact conditions that you will see on test day. This will allow you to see where you really need to improve.

- Up Your Studying With an SAT Prep Course: To take their studying to the next level, some students take SAT prep courses with experienced tutors. These courses structure themselves to help students increase their scores rapidly. Luckily for you, we have created a page reviewing the best SAT tutors at www.BoulevardBooks.org

Reading Test

65 MINUTES, 52 QUESTIONS

Turn to Section 1 of your answer sheet to answer the questions in this section.

DIRECTIONS

Each passage or pair of passages below is followed by a number of questions. After reading each passage or pair, choose the best answer to each question based on what is stated or implied in the passage or passages and in any accompanying graphics (such as a table or graph).

Questions 1-10 are based on the following passage.

This passage is adapted from Daniyal Mueenuddin, "Nawabdin Electrician." ©2009 by Daniyal Mueenuddin.

Another man might have thrown up his
hands—but not Nawabdin. His twelve daughters
acted as a spur to his genius, and he looked with
Line satisfaction in the mirror each morning at the face of
5   a warrior going out to do battle. Nawab of course
knew that he must proliferate his sources of
revenue—the salary he received from K. K. Harouni
for tending the tube wells would not even begin to
suffice. He set up a little one-room flour mill, run off
10 a condemned electric motor—condemned by him.
He tried his hand at fish-farming in a little pond at
the edge of his master's fields. He bought broken
radios, fixed them, and resold them. He did not
demur even when asked to fix watches, though that
15 enterprise did spectacularly badly, and in fact earned
him more kicks than kudos, for no watch he took
apart ever kept time again.
    K. K. Harouni rarely went to his farms, but lived
mostly in Lahore. Whenever the old man visited,
20 Nawab would place himself night and day at the door
leading from the servants' sitting area into the walled
grove of ancient banyan trees where the old
farmhouse stood. Grizzled, his peculiar aviator

glasses bent and smudged, Nawab tended the
25 household machinery, the air conditioners, water
heaters, refrigerators, and water pumps, like an
engineer tending the boilers on a foundering steamer
in an Atlantic gale. By his superhuman efforts he
almost managed to maintain K. K. Harouni in the
30 same mechanical cocoon, cooled and bathed and
lighted and fed, that the landowner enjoyed in
Lahore.
    Harouni of course became familiar with this
ubiquitous man, who not only accompanied him on
35 his tours of inspection, but morning and night could
be found standing on the master bed rewiring the
light fixture or in the bathroom poking at the water
heater. Finally, one evening at teatime, gauging the
psychological moment, Nawab asked if he might say
40 a word. The landowner, who was cheerfully filing his
nails in front of a crackling rosewood fire, told him
to go ahead.
    "Sir, as you know, your lands stretch from here to
the Indus, and on these lands are fully seventeen tube
45 wells, and to tend these seventeen tube wells there is
but one man, me, your servant. In your service I have
earned these gray hairs"—here he bowed his head to
show the gray—"and now I cannot fulfill my duties
as I should. Enough, sir, enough. I beg you, forgive
50 me my weakness. Better a darkened house and proud
hunger within than disgrace in the light of day.
Release me, I ask you, I beg you."
    The old man, well accustomed to these sorts of
speeches, though not usually this florid, filed away at
55 his nails and waited for the breeze to stop.
    "What's the matter, Nawabdin?"

"Matter, sir? O what could be the matter in your
service. I've eaten your salt for all my years. But sir,
on the bicycle now, with my old legs, and with the
60 many injuries I've received when heavy machinery
fell on me—I cannot any longer bicycle about like a
bridegroom from farm to farm, as I could when I
first had the good fortune to enter your employment.
I beg you, sir, let me go."

65   "And what's the solution?" asked Harouni, seeing
that they had come to the crux. He didn't particularly
care one way or the other, except that it touched on
his comfort—a matter of great interest to him.

    "Well, sir, if I had a motorcycle, then I could
70 somehow limp along, at least until I train up some
younger man."

    The crops that year had been good, Harouni felt
expansive in front of the fire, and so, much to the
disgust of the farm managers, Nawab received a
75 brand-new motorcycle, a Honda 70. He even
managed to extract an allowance for gasoline.

    The motorcycle increased his status, gave him
weight, so that people began calling him "Uncle," and
asking his opinion on world affairs, about which he
80 knew absolutely nothing. He could now range
further, doing a much wider business. Best of all,
now he could spend every night with his wife, who
had begged to live not on the farm but near her
family in Firoza, where also they could educate at
85 least the two eldest daughters. A long straight road
ran from the canal headworks near Firoza all the way
to the Indus, through the heart of the K. K. Harouni
lands. Nawab would fly down this road on his new
machine, with bags and cloths hanging from every
90 knob and brace, so that the bike, when he hit a bump,
seemed to be flapping numerous small vestigial
wings; and with his grinning face, as he rolled up to
whichever tube well needed servicing, with his ears
almost blown off, he shone with the speed of his
95 arrival.

CONTINUE →

1

The main purpose of the first paragraph is to

A) characterize Nawab as a loving father.

B) outline the schedule of a typical day in
Nawab's life.

C) describe Nawab's various moneymaking
ventures.

D) contrast Nawab's and Harouni's lifestyles.

2

As used in line 16, "kicks" most nearly means

A) thrills.

B) complaints.

C) jolts.

D) interests.

3

The author uses the image of an engineer at sea
(lines 23-28) most likely to

A) suggest that Nawab often dreams of having a
more exciting profession.

B) highlight the fact that Nawab's primary job is to
tend to Harouni's tube wells.

C) reinforce the idea that Nawab has had many
different occupations in his life.

D) emphasize how demanding Nawab's work for
Harouni is.

4

Which choice best supports the claim that Nawab performs his duties for Harouni well?

A) Lines 28-32 ("By his . . . Lahore")

B) Lines 40-42 ("The landowner . . . ahead")

C) Lines 46-49 ("In your . . . should")

D) Line 58 ("I've . . . years")

5

In the context of the conversation between Nawab and Harouni, Nawab's comments in lines 43-52 ("Sir . . . beg you") mainly serve to

A) flatter Harouni by mentioning how vast his lands are.

B) boast to Harouni about how competent and reliable Nawab is.

C) emphasize Nawab's diligence and loyalty to Harouni.

D) notify Harouni that Nawab intends to quit his job tending the tube wells.

6

Nawab uses the word "bridegroom" (line 62) mainly to emphasize that he's no longer

A) in love.

B) naive.

C) busy.

D) young.

7

It can reasonably be inferred from the passage that Harouni provides Nawab with a motorcycle mainly because

A) Harouni appreciates that Nawab has to work hard to support his family.

B) Harouni sees benefit to himself from giving Nawab a motorcycle.

C) Nawab's speech is the most eloquent that Harouni has ever heard.

D) Nawab threatens to quit if Harouni doesn't agree to give him a motorcycle.

8

Which choice provides the best evidence for the answer to the previous question?

A) Lines 65-66 ("And . . . crux")

B) Lines 66-68 ("He didn't . . . him")

C) Lines 75-76 ("He even . . . gasoline")

D) Lines 80-81 ("He could . . . business")

9

The passage states that the farm managers react to Nawab receiving a motorcycle with

A) disgust.

B) happiness.

C) envy.

D) indifference.

10

According to the passage, what does Nawab consider to be the best result of getting the motorcycle?

A) People start calling him "Uncle."

B) He's able to expand his business.

C) He's able to educate his daughters.

D) He can spend more time with his wife.

Questions 11-21 are based on the following passage and supplementary material.

This passage is adapted from Stephen Coleman, Scott Anthony, and David E. Morrison, "Public Trust in the News." ©2009 by Stephen Coleman.

The news is a form of public knowledge. Unlike personal or private knowledge (such as the health of one's friends and family; the conduct of a private hobby; a secret liaison), public knowledge increases in value as it is shared by more people. The date of an election and the claims of rival candidates; the causes and consequences of an environmental disaster; a debate about how to frame a particular law; the latest reports from a war zone—these are all examples of public knowledge that people are generally expected to know in order to be considered informed citizens. Thus, in contrast to personal or private knowledge, which is generally left to individuals to pursue or ignore, public knowledge is promoted even to those who might not think it matters to them. In short, the circulation of public knowledge, including the news, is generally regarded as a public good which cannot be solely demand-driven.

The production, circulation, and reception of public knowledge is a complex process. It is generally accepted that public knowledge should be authoritative, but there is not always common agreement about what the public needs to know, who is best placed to relate and explain it, and how authoritative reputations should be determined and evaluated. Historically, newspapers such as *The Times* and broadcasters such as the BBC were widely regarded as the trusted shapers of authoritative agendas and conventional wisdom. They embodied the *Oxford English Dictionary's* definition of authority as the "power over, or title to influence, the opinions of others." As part of the general process of the transformation of authority whereby there has been a reluctance to uncritically accept traditional sources of public knowledge, the demand has been for all authority to make explicit the frames of value which determine their decisions. Centres of news production, as our focus groups show, have not been exempt from this process. Not surprisingly perhaps some news journalists feel uneasy about this renegotiation of their authority:

Editors are increasingly casting a glance at the "most read" lists on their own and other websites to work out which stories matter to readers and viewers. And now the audience—which used to know its place—is being asked to act as a kind of journalistic ombudsman, ruling on our credibility (broadcast journalist, 2008).

The result of democratising access to TV news could be political disengagement by the majority and a dumbing down through a popularity contest of stories (online news editor, 2007).

Despite the rhetorical bluster of these statements, they amount to more than straightforward professional defensiveness. In their reference to an audience "which used to know its place" and conflation between democratisation and "dumbing down," they are seeking to argue for a particular mode of public knowledge: one which is shaped by experts, immune from populist pressures; and disseminated to attentive, but mainly passive recipients. It is a view of citizenship that closes down opportunities for popular involvement in the making of public knowledge by reinforcing the professional claims of experts. The journalists quoted above are right to feel uneasy, for there is, at almost every institutional level in contemporary society, scepticism towards the epistemological authority of expert elites. There is a growing feeling, as expressed by several of our focus group participants, that the news media should be "informative rather than authoritative"; the job of journalists should be to "give the news as raw as it is, without putting their slant on it"; and people should be given "sufficient information" from which "we would be able to form opinions of our own."

At stake here are two distinct conceptions of authority. The journalists we have quoted are resistant to the democratisation of news: the supremacy of the clickstream (according to which editors raise or lower the profile of stories according to the number of readers clicking on them online); the parity of popular culture with "serious" news; the demands of some audience members for raw news rather than constructed narratives.

CONTINUE

Percentage of Respondents Seeing News Stories
as Inaccurate or Favoring One Side

	1985	1992	2003	2007	2011
News organizations...					
• Get the facts straight	55	49	36	39	25
• Often have inaccurate stories	34	44	56	53	66
• Don't know	11	7	8	8	9
• Are pretty independent	37	35	23	23	15
• Are often influenced by powerful people and organizations	53	58	70	69	80
• Don't know	10	7	7	8	5
On political and social issues, news organizations...					
• Deal fairly with all sides	34	31	26	26	16
• Tend to favor one side	53	63	66	66	77
• Don't know	13	6	8	8	7

Adapted from "Pew Research Center for the People & the Press Report on Views of the News Media, 1985–2011." ©2011 by Pew Research Center.

CONTINUE

11

The main purpose of the passage is to

A) analyze the technological developments that have affected the production, circulation, and reception of news stories.

B) discuss changes in the perception of the news media as a source of public knowledge.

C) show how journalists' frames of value influence the production of news stories.

D) challenge the conventional view that news is a form of public knowledge.

12

According to the passage, which expectation do traditional authorities now face?

A) They should be uninfluenced by commercial considerations.

B) They should be committed to bringing about positive social change.

C) They should be respectful of the difference between public and private knowledge.

D) They should be transparent about their beliefs and assumptions.

13

Which choice provides the best evidence for the answer to the previous question?

A) Lines 2-5 ("Unlike . . . people")

B) Lines 20-21 ("The production . . . process")

C) Lines 33-38 ("As part . . . decisions")

D) Lines 43-46 ("Editors . . . viewers")

14

As used in line 24, "common" most nearly means

A) numerous.

B) familiar.

C) widespread.

D) ordinary.

15

The authors most likely include the extended quotations in lines 43-53 to

A) present contradictory examples.

B) cite representative opinions.

C) criticize typical viewpoints.

D) suggest viable alternatives.

16

The authors indicate that the public is coming to believe that journalists' reports should avoid

A) personal judgments about the events reported.

B) more information than is absolutely necessary.

C) quotations from authorities on the subject matter.

D) details that the subjects of news reports wish to keep private.

Unauthorized copying or reuse of any part of this page is illegal.

8

CONTINUE

17

Which choice provides the best evidence for the answer to the previous question?

A) Lines 12-16 ("Thus . . . them")

B) Lines 30-33 ("They . . . others")

C) Lines 40-42 ("Not surprisingly . . . authority")

D) Lines 70-77 ("There . . . own")

18

As used in line 74, "raw" most nearly means

A) unfiltered.

B) exposed.

C) harsh.

D) inexperienced.

19

Based on the table, in which year were people the most trusting of the news media?

A) 1985

B) 1992

C) 2003

D) 2011

20

Which statement is best supported by information presented in the table?

A) Between 1985 and 2011, the proportion of inaccurate news stories rose dramatically.

B) Between 1992 and 2003, the proportion of people who believed that news organizations were biased almost doubled.

C) Between 2003 and 2007, people's views of the accuracy, independence, and fairness of news organizations changed very little.

D) Between 2007 and 2011, people's perception that news organizations are accurate increased, but people's perception that news organizations are fair diminished.

21

The 2011 data in the table best serve as evidence of

A) "political disengagement by the majority" (line 51).

B) "the professional claims of experts" (lines 65-66).

C) "scepticism towards the epistemological authority of expert elites" (lines 69-70).

D) "the supremacy of the clickstream" (line 81).

Unauthorized copying or reuse of any part of this page is illegal.

9

CONTINUE

Questions 22-32 are based on the following passage.

This passage is adapted from Elsa Youngsteadt, "Decoding a Flower's Message." ©2012 by Sigma Xi, The Scientific Research Society.

Texas gourd vines unfurl their large, flared blossoms in the dim hours before sunrise. Until they close at noon, their yellow petals and mild, squashy
Line aroma attract bees that gather nectar and shuttle
5 pollen from flower to flower. But "when you advertise [to pollinators], you advertise in an open communication network," says chemical ecologist Ian Baldwin of the Max Planck Institute for Chemical Ecology in Germany. "You attract not just
10 the good guys, but you also attract the bad guys." For a Texas gourd plant, striped cucumber beetles are among the very bad guys. They chew up pollen and petals, defecate in the flowers and transmit the dreaded bacterial wilt disease, an infection that can
15 reduce an entire plant to a heap of collapsed tissue in mere days.

In one recent study, Nina Theis and Lynn Adler took on the specific problem of the Texas gourd—how to attract enough pollinators but not
20 too many beetles. The Texas gourd vine's main pollinators are honey bees and specialized squash bees, which respond to its floral scent. The aroma includes 10 compounds, but the most abundant—and the only one that lures squash bees
25 into traps—is 1,4-dimethoxybenzene.

Intuition suggests that more of that aroma should be even more appealing to bees. "We have this assumption that a really fragrant flower is going to attract a lot of pollinators," says Theis, a chemical
30 ecologist at Elms College in Chicopee, Massachusetts. But, she adds, that idea hasn't really been tested—and extra scent could well call in more beetles, too. To find out, she and Adler planted 168 Texas gourd vines in an Iowa field and,
35 throughout the August flowering season, made half the plants more fragrant by tucking dimethoxybenzene-treated swabs deep inside their flowers. Each treated flower emitted about 45 times more fragrance than a normal one; the other half of
40 the plants got swabs without fragrance.

The researchers also wanted to know whether extra beetles would impose a double cost by both damaging flowers and deterring bees, which might not bother to visit (and pollinate) a flower laden with
45 other insects and their feces. So every half hour throughout the experiments, the team plucked all the beetles off of half the fragrance-enhanced flowers and half the control flowers, allowing bees to respond to the blossoms with and without interference by
50 beetles.

Finally, they pollinated by hand half of the female flowers in each of the four combinations of fragrance and beetles. Hand-pollinated flowers should develop into fruits with the maximum number of seeds,
55 providing a benchmark to see whether the fragrance-related activities of bees and beetles resulted in reduced pollination.

"It was very labor intensive," says Theis. "We would be out there at four in the morning, three
60 in the morning, to try and set up before these flowers open." As soon as they did, the team spent the next several hours walking from flower to flower, observing each for two-minute intervals "and writing down everything we saw."

65 What they saw was double the normal number of beetles on fragrance-enhanced blossoms. Pollinators, to their surprise, did not prefer the highly scented flowers. Squash bees were indifferent, and honey bees visited enhanced flowers less often
70 than normal ones. Theis thinks the bees were repelled not by the fragrance itself, but by the abundance of beetles: The data showed that the more beetles on a flower, the less likely a honey bee was to visit it.

75 That added up to less reproduction for fragrance-enhanced flowers. Gourds that developed from those blossoms weighed 9 percent less and had, on average, 20 fewer seeds than those from normal flowers. Hand pollination didn't rescue the seed set,
80 indicating that beetles damaged flowers directly —regardless of whether they also repelled pollinators. (Hand pollination did rescue fruit weight, a hard-to-interpret result that suggests that lost bee visits did somehow harm fruit development.)

CONTINUE →

85 The new results provide a reason that Texas gourd plants never evolved to produce a stronger scent: "If you really ramp up the odor, you don't get more pollinators, but you can really get ripped apart by your enemies," says Rob Raguso, a chemical ecologist
90 at Cornell University who was not involved in the Texas gourd study.

22

The primary purpose of the passage is to

A) discuss the assumptions and reasoning behind a theory.

B) describe the aim, method, and results of an experiment.

C) present and analyze conflicting data about a phenomenon.

D) show the innovative nature of a procedure used in a study.

23

As presented in the passage, Theis and Adler's research primarily relied on which type of evidence?

A) Direct observation

B) Historical data

C) Expert testimony

D) Random sampling

24

Which statement about striped cucumber beetles can most reasonably be inferred from the passage?

A) They feed primarily on Texas gourd plants.

B) They are less attracted to dimethoxybenzene than honey bees are.

C) They experience only minor negative effects as a result of carrying bacterial wilt disease.

D) They are attracted to the same compound in Texas gourd scent that squash bees are.

25

The author indicates that it seems initially plausible that Texas gourd plants could attract more pollinators if they

A) did not have aromatic flowers.

B) targeted insects other than bees.

C) increased their floral scent.

D) emitted more varied fragrant compounds.

26

As used in line 38, "treated" most nearly means

A) altered.

B) restored.

C) provided.

D) preserved.

27

What did Theis and Adler do as part of their study that most directly allowed Theis to reason that "bees were repelled not by the fragrance itself" (lines 70-71)?

A) They observed the behavior of bees and beetles both before and after the flowers opened in the morning.

B) They increased the presence of 1,4-dimethoxybenzene only during the August flowering season.

C) They compared the gourds that developed from naturally pollinated flowers to the gourds that developed from hand-pollinated flowers.

D) They gave bees a chance to choose between beetle-free enhanced flowers and beetle-free normal flowers.

28

Which choice provides the best evidence for the answer to the previous question?

A) Lines 45-50 ("So every . . . beetles")

B) Lines 51-53 ("Finally . . . beetles")

C) Lines 59-61 ("We would . . . open")

D) Lines 76-79 ("Gourds . . . flowers")

29

The primary function of the seventh and eighth paragraphs (lines 65-84) is to

A) summarize Theis and Adler's findings.

B) describe Theis and Adler's hypotheses.

C) illustrate Theis and Adler's methods.

D) explain Theis and Adler's reasoning.

30

In describing squash bees as "indifferent" (line 68), the author most likely means that they

A) could not distinguish enhanced flowers from normal flowers.

B) visited enhanced flowers and normal flowers at an equal rate.

C) largely preferred normal flowers to enhanced flowers.

D) were as likely to visit beetle-infested enhanced flowers as to visit beetle-free enhanced flowers.

31

According to the passage, Theis and Adler's research offers an answer to which of the following questions?

A) How can Texas gourd plants increase the number of visits they receive from pollinators?

B) Why is there an upper limit on the intensity of the aroma emitted by Texas gourd plants?

C) Why does hand pollination rescue the fruit weight of beetle-infested Texas gourd plants?

D) Why do Texas gourd plants stop producing fragrance attractive to pollinators when beetles are present?

32

Which choice provides the best evidence for the answer to the previous question?

A) Lines 17-20 ("In one . . . beetles")

B) Lines 22-25 ("The aroma . . . 1,4-dimethoxybenzene")

C) Lines 79-84 ("Hand . . . development")

D) Lines 85-86 ("The new . . . scent")

Questions 33-42 are based on the following passages.

Passage 1 is adapted from Abraham Lincoln, "Address to the Young Men's Lyceum of Springfield, Illinois." Originally delivered in 1838. Passage 2 is from Henry David Thoreau, "Resistance to Civil Government." Originally published in 1849.

Passage 1

Let every American, every lover of liberty, every well wisher to his posterity, swear by the blood of the Revolution, never to violate in the least particular,
Line the laws of the country; and never to tolerate their
5   violation by others. As the patriots of seventy-six did to the support of the Declaration of Independence, so to the support of the Constitution and Laws, let every American pledge his life, his property, and his sacred honor;—let every man remember that to violate the
10   law, is to trample on the blood of his father, and to tear the character of his own, and his children's liberty. Let reverence for the laws, be breathed by every American mother, to the lisping babe, that prattles on her lap—let it be taught in schools, in
15   seminaries, and in colleges;—let it be written in Primers, spelling books, and in Almanacs;—let it be preached from the pulpit, proclaimed in legislative halls, and enforced in courts of justice. And, in short, let it become the *political religion* of the nation;
20   and let the old and the young, the rich and the poor, the grave and the gay, of all sexes and tongues, and colors and conditions, sacrifice unceasingly upon its altars. . . .

When I so pressingly urge a strict observance of
25   all the laws, let me not be understood as saying there are no bad laws, nor that grievances may not arise, for the redress of which, no legal provisions have been made. I mean to say no such thing. But I do mean to say, that, although bad laws, if they exist,
30   should be repealed as soon as possible, still while they continue in force, for the sake of example, they should be religiously observed. So also in unprovided cases. If such arise, let proper legal provisions be made for them with the least possible delay; but, till
35   then, let them if not too intolerable, be borne with.

There is no grievance that is a fit object of redress by mob law. In any case that arises, as for instance, the promulgation of abolitionism, one of two positions is necessarily true; that is, the thing is right
40   within itself, and therefore deserves the protection of all law and all good citizens; or, it is wrong, and therefore proper to be prohibited by legal enactments; and in neither case, is the interposition of mob law, either necessary, justifiable, or excusable.

Passage 2

45   Unjust laws exist; shall we be content to obey them, or shall we endeavor to amend them, and obey them until we have succeeded, or shall we transgress them at once? Men generally, under such a government as this, think that they ought to wait
50   until they have persuaded the majority to alter them. They think that, if they should resist, the remedy would be worse than the evil. But it is the fault of the government itself that the remedy is worse than the evil. It makes it worse. Why is it not more apt to
55   anticipate and provide for reform? Why does it not cherish its wise minority? Why does it cry and resist before it is hurt? . . .

If the injustice is part of the necessary friction of the machine of government, let it go, let it go;
60   perchance it will wear smooth—certainly the machine will wear out. If the injustice has a spring, or a pulley, or a rope, or a crank, exclusively for itself, then perhaps you may consider whether the remedy will not be worse than the evil; but if it is of such a
65   nature that it requires you to be the agent of injustice to another, then, I say, break the law. Let your life be a counter friction to stop the machine. What I have to do is to see, at any rate, that I do not lend myself to the wrong which I condemn.
70   As for adopting the ways which the State has provided for remedying the evil, I know not of such ways. They take too much time, and a man's life will be gone. I have other affairs to attend to. I came into this world, not chiefly to make this a good place to
75   live in, but to live in it, be it good or bad. A man has not everything to do, but something; and because he cannot do everything, it is not necessary that he should do something wrong. . . .

CONTINUE

I do not hesitate to say, that those who call
80 themselves Abolitionists should at once effectually
withdraw their support, both in person and property,
from the government . . . and not wait till they
constitute a majority of one, before they suffer the
right to prevail through them. I think that it is
85 enough if they have God on their side, without
waiting for that other one. Moreover, any man more
right than his neighbors constitutes a majority of one
already.

33

In Passage 1, Lincoln contends that breaking the law
has which consequence?

A) It slows the repeal of bad laws.

B) It undermines and repudiates the nation's values.

C) It leads slowly but inexorably to rule by the mob.

D) It creates divisions between social groups.

34

Which choice provides the best evidence for the
answer to the previous question?

A) Lines 9-12 ("let every man . . . liberty")

B) Lines 20-23 ("and let . . . altars")

C) Lines 33-35 ("If such . . . borne with")

D) Lines 36-37 ("There . . . law")

35

As used in line 24, "urge" most nearly means

A) hasten.

B) stimulate.

C) require.

D) advocate.

36

The sentence in lines 24-28 ("When . . . made")
primarily serves which function in Passage 1?

A) It raises and refutes a potential counterargument
to Lincoln's argument.

B) It identifies and concedes a crucial shortcoming
of Lincoln's argument.

C) It acknowledges and substantiates a central
assumption of Lincoln's argument.

D) It anticipates and corrects a possible
misinterpretation of Lincoln's argument.

37

As used in line 32, "observed" most nearly means

A) followed.

B) scrutinized.

C) contemplated.

D) noticed.

38

In Passage 2, Thoreau indicates that some unjust aspects of government are

A) superficial and can be fixed easily.

B) subtle and must be studied carefully.

C) self-correcting and may be beneficial.

D) inevitable and should be endured.

39

Which choice provides the best evidence for the answer to the previous question?

A) Lines 45-48 ("Unjust . . . once")

B) Lines 51-52 ("They . . . evil")

C) Lines 58-59 ("If the injustice . . . go")

D) Lines 75-78 ("A man . . . wrong")

40

The primary purpose of each passage is to

A) make an argument about the difference between legal duties and moral imperatives.

B) discuss how laws ought to be enacted and changed in a democracy.

C) advance a view regarding whether individuals should follow all of the country's laws.

D) articulate standards by which laws can be evaluated as just or unjust.

41

Based on the passages, Lincoln would most likely describe the behavior that Thoreau recommends in lines 64-66 ("if it . . . law") as

A) an excusable reaction to an intolerable situation.

B) a rejection of the country's proper forms of remedy.

C) an honorable response to an unjust law.

D) a misapplication of a core principle of the Constitution.

42

Based on the passages, one commonality in the stances Lincoln and Thoreau take toward abolitionism is that

A) both authors see the cause as warranting drastic action.

B) both authors view the cause as central to their argument.

C) neither author expects the cause to win widespread acceptance.

D) neither author embraces the cause as his own.

Unauthorized copying or reuse of any part of this page is illegal.

17

CONTINUE

Questions 43-52 are based on the following passage and supplementary material.

This passage is adapted from Kevin Bullis, "What Tech Is Next for the Solar Industry?" ©2013 by MIT Technology Review.

Solar panel installations continue to grow quickly, but the solar panel manufacturing industry is in the doldrums because supply far exceeds demand. The
Line poor market may be slowing innovation, but
5 advances continue; judging by the mood this week at the IEEE Photovoltaics Specialists Conference in Tampa, Florida, people in the industry remain optimistic about its long-term prospects.

The technology that's surprised almost everyone
10 is conventional crystalline silicon. A few years ago, silicon solar panels cost $4 per watt, and Martin Green, professor at the University of New South Wales and one of the leading silicon solar panel researchers, declared that they'd never go
15 below $1 a watt. "Now it's down to something like 50 cents a watt, and there's talk of hitting 36 cents per watt," he says.

The U.S. Department of Energy has set a goal of reaching less than $1 a watt—not just for the solar
20 panels, but for complete, installed systems—by 2020. Green thinks the solar industry will hit that target even sooner than that. If so, that would bring the direct cost of solar power to six cents per kilowatt-hour, which is cheaper than the average cost
25 expected for power from new natural gas power plants.

All parts of the silicon solar panel industry have been looking for ways to cut costs and improve the power output of solar panels, and that's led to steady
30 cost reductions. Green points to something as mundane as the pastes used to screen-print some of the features on solar panels. Green's lab built a solar cell in the 1990s that set a record efficiency for silicon solar cells—a record that stands to this day. To
35 achieve that record, he had to use expensive lithography techniques to make fine wires for collecting current from the solar cell. But gradual improvements have made it possible to use screen printing to produce ever-finer lines. Recent research
40 suggests that screen-printing techniques can produce lines as thin as 30 micrometers—about the width of the lines Green used for his record solar cells, but at costs far lower than his lithography techniques.

Meanwhile, researchers at the National Renewable
45 Energy Laboratory have made flexible solar cells on a new type of glass from Corning called Willow Glass, which is thin and can be rolled up. The type of solar cell they made is the only current challenger to silicon in terms of large-scale production—thin-film
50 cadmium telluride. Flexible solar cells could lower the cost of installing solar cells, making solar power cheaper.

One of Green's former students and colleagues, Jianhua Zhao, cofounder of solar panel manufacturer
55 China Sunergy, announced this week that he is building a pilot manufacturing line for a two-sided solar cell that can absorb light from both the front and back. The basic idea, which isn't new, is that during some parts of the day, sunlight falls on the
60 land between rows of solar panels in a solar power plant. That light reflects onto the back of the panels and could be harvested to increase the power output. This works particularly well when the solar panels are built on sand, which is highly reflective. Where a
65 one-sided solar panel might generate 340 watts, a two-sided one might generate up to 400 watts. He expects the panels to generate 10 to 20 percent more electricity over the course of a year.

Even longer-term, Green is betting on silicon,
70 aiming to take advantage of the huge reductions in cost already seen with the technology. He hopes to greatly increase the efficiency of silicon solar panels by combining silicon with one or two other semiconductors, each selected to efficiently convert a
75 part of the solar spectrum that silicon doesn't convert efficiently. Adding one semiconductor could boost efficiencies from the 20 to 25 percent range to around 40 percent. Adding another could make efficiencies as high as 50 percent feasible, which
80 would cut in half the number of solar panels needed for a given installation. The challenge is to produce good connections between these semiconductors, something made challenging by the arrangement of silicon atoms in crystalline silicon.

CONTINUE

Figure 1

Projected Energy Cost
per Megawatt-Hour in 2017

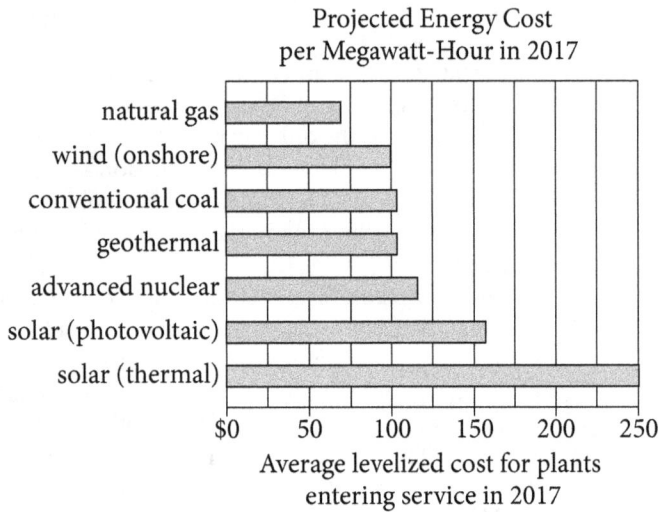

Average levelized cost for plants
entering service in 2017

Adapted from Peter Schwartz, "Abundant Natural Gas and Oil Are Putting the Kibosh on Clean Energy." ©2012 by Condé Nast.

Figure 2

Solar Photovoltaic Cost per Megawatt-Hour (MWh)
(Projected beyond 2009. All data in 2009 dollars.)

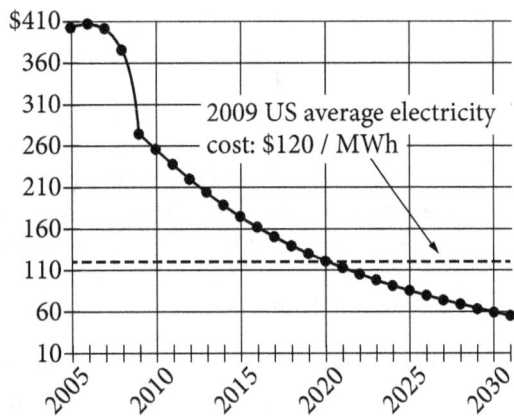

2009 US average electricity cost: $120 / MWh

Adapted from Ramez Naam, "Smaller, Cheaper, Faster: Does Moore's Law Apply to Solar Cells?" ©2011 by Scientific American.

19

CONTINUE

43

The passage is written from the point of view of a

A) consumer evaluating a variety of options.

B) scientist comparing competing research methods.

C) journalist enumerating changes in a field.

D) hobbyist explaining the capabilities of new technology.

44

As used in line 4, "poor" most nearly means

A) weak.

B) humble.

C) pitiable.

D) obsolete.

45

It can most reasonably be inferred from the passage that many people in the solar panel industry believe that

A) consumers don't understand how solar panels work.

B) two-sided cells have weaknesses that have not yet been discovered.

C) the cost of solar panels is too high and their power output too low.

D) Willow Glass is too inefficient to be marketable.

46

Which choice provides the best evidence for the answer to the previous question?

A) Lines 1-3 ("Solar . . . demand")

B) Lines 10-15 ("A few . . . a watt")

C) Lines 22-26 ("If so . . . plants")

D) Lines 27-30 ("All . . . reductions")

47

According to the passage, two-sided solar panels will likely raise efficiency by

A) requiring little energy to operate.

B) absorbing reflected light.

C) being reasonably inexpensive to manufacture.

D) preventing light from reaching the ground.

48

Which choice provides the best evidence for the answer to the previous question?

A) Lines 58-61 ("The basic . . . plant")

B) Lines 61-62 ("That . . . output")

C) Lines 63-64 ("This . . . reflective")

D) Lines 64-66 ("Where . . . 400 watts")

49

As used in line 69, "betting on" most nearly means

A) dabbling in.

B) gambling with.

C) switching from.

D) optimistic about.

50

The last sentence of the passage mainly serves to

A) express concern about the limitations of a material.

B) identify a hurdle that must be overcome.

C) make a prediction about the effective use of certain devices.

D) introduce a potential new area of study.

51

According to figure 1, in 2017, the cost of which of the following fuels is projected to be closest to the 2009 US average electricity cost shown in figure 2?

A) Natural gas

B) Wind (onshore)

C) Conventional coal

D) Advanced nuclear

52

According to figure 2, in what year is the average cost of solar photovoltaic power projected to be equal to the 2009 US average electricity cost?

A) 2018

B) 2020

C) 2025

D) 2027

STOP

If you finish before time is called, you may check your work on this section only.
Do not turn to any other section.

Writing and Language Test

35 MINUTES, 44 QUESTIONS

Turn to Section 2 of your answer sheet to answer the questions in this section.

DIRECTIONS

Each passage below is accompanied by a number of questions. For some questions, you will consider how the passage might be revised to improve the expression of ideas. For other questions, you will consider how the passage might be edited to correct errors in sentence structure, usage, or punctuation. A passage or a question may be accompanied by one or more graphics (such as a table or graph) that you will consider as you make revising and editing decisions.

Some questions will direct you to an underlined portion of a passage. Other questions will direct you to a location in a passage or ask you to think about the passage as a whole.

After reading each passage, choose the answer to each question that most effectively improves the quality of writing in the passage or that makes the passage conform to the conventions of standard written English. Many questions include a "NO CHANGE" option. Choose that option if you think the best choice is to leave the relevant portion of the passage as it is.

Questions 1-11 are based on the following passage.

A Necessary Resource for Science

In the winter of 1968, scientists David Schindler and Gregg Brunskill poured nitrates and phosphates into Lake **1** 227, this is one of the 58 freshwater bodies that compose Canada's remotely located Experimental Lakes Area. Schindler and Brunskill were contaminating the water not out of malice but in the name of research. While deliberately adding chemical compounds to a lake may seem **2** destructive and irresponsible, this method of experimenting is sometimes the most effective way to influence policy and save the environment from even more damaging pollution.

1

A) NO CHANGE
B) 227. Which is one
C) 227. One
D) 227, one

2

A) NO CHANGE
B) destructive, and irresponsible this method
C) destructive and, irresponsible, this method
D) destructive and irresponsible this method,

Schindler and Brunskill were investigating possible causes for the large blooms of blue-green algae, or cyanobacteria, that had been affecting bodies of water such as Lake Erie. **3** In addition to being unsightly and odorous, these algal blooms cause oxygen depletion. Oxygen depletion kills fish and other wildlife in the lakes. Just weeks after the scientists added the nitrates and phosphates, the water in Lake 227 turned bright **4** green. It was thick with: the same type of algal blooms that had plagued Lake Erie.

3

Which choice most effectively combines the underlined sentences?

A) In addition to being unsightly and odorous, these algal blooms cause oxygen depletion: the result being that it kills fish and other wildlife in the lakes.

B) In addition to being unsightly and odorous, these algal blooms cause oxygen depletion; the algal blooms cause oxygen depletion that kills fish and other wildlife in the lakes.

C) In addition to being unsightly and odorous, these algal blooms cause oxygen depletion, and oxygen depletion caused by the algal blooms kills fish and other wildlife in the lakes.

D) In addition to being unsightly and odorous, these algal blooms cause oxygen depletion, which kills fish and other wildlife in the lakes.

4

A) NO CHANGE

B) green: it was thick with

C) green. It was thick with—

D) green, it was thick with

[5] One mission of the Experimental Lakes Area is to conduct research that helps people better understand threats to the environment. The scientists divided the lake in half by placing a nylon barrier through the narrowest part of its figure-eight shape. In one half of Lake 226, they added phosphates, nitrates, and a source of carbon; in the other, they added just nitrates [6] and a source of carbon was added. Schindler and Brunskill hypothesized that phosphates were responsible for the growth of cyanobacteria. The experiment confirmed their suspicions when the half of the lake containing the phosphates [7] was teeming with blue-green algae.

5

Which choice provides the best transition from the previous paragraph to this one?

A) NO CHANGE

B) The Experimental Lakes Area is located in a sparsely inhabited region that experiences few effects of human and industrial activity.

C) To isolate the cause of the algae, Schindler and Brunskill performed another experiment, this time using Lake 226.

D) The process by which water becomes enriched by dissolved nutrients, such as phosphates, is called eutrophication.

6

A) NO CHANGE

B) and a source of carbon.

C) plus also a source of carbon.

D) but also adding a source of carbon.

7

A) NO CHANGE

B) were teeming

C) are teeming

D) teems

Schindler and Brunskill's findings were 8 <u>shown off by</u> the journal *Science*. The research demonstrated a clear correlation between introducing phosphates and the growth of blue-green algae. 9 <u>For example,</u> legislators in Canada passed laws banning phosphates in laundry detergents, which had been entering the water supply. 10

8

A) NO CHANGE
B) put in the spotlight of
C) published in
D) put into

9

A) NO CHANGE
B) Similarly,
C) However,
D) Subsequently,

10

At this point, the writer wants to add a second policy outcome of the research described. Which choice best accomplishes this goal?

A) Lake 226 continued to develop blooms of blue-green algae for eight consecutive years after the experiment took place.

B) In the United States, many individual states have also adopted legislation to eliminate, or at least reduce, phosphorous content in laundry detergents.

C) In 1974, Schindler initiated a study of the effects of acid rain, using Lake 223 to examine how sulfuric acid altered aquatic ecosystems.

D) Aerial photos of the lakes taken before and during algal blooms helped convey the effects of phosphates in water to the public.

Experiments like these can help people understand the unintended consequences of using certain household products. **11** Of course, regulating the use of certain chemical compounds can be a controversial issue. Selectively establishing remote study locations, such as the Experimental Lakes Area, can provide scientists with opportunities to safely conduct controlled research. This research can generate evidence solid enough to persuade policy makers to take action in favor of protecting the larger environment.

11

Which choice most effectively anticipates and addresses a relevant counterargument to the argument in favor of the types of experiments described in the passage?

A) NO CHANGE

B) Many companies now offer phosphate-free alternatives for household cleaning products.

C) Obviously, scientists should not be allowed to randomly perform experiments on just any body of water.

D) Phosphates are sometimes used in agricultural fertilizers, in addition to being used in cleaning products.

Questions 12-22 are based on the following passage.

A Little to the Left, but Not Too Much!

Italy's Tower of Pisa has been leaning southward since the initial [12] stages of it's construction over 800 years ago. [13] Indeed, if the tower's construction had not taken two centuries and involved significant breaks due to war and civil unrest, which allowed the ground beneath the tower to settle, the tower would likely have collapsed before it was completed.

[12]

A) NO CHANGE
B) stage's of its'
C) stage's of it's
D) stages of its

[13]

A) NO CHANGE
B) Therefore,
C) Nevertheless,
D) However,

Luckily, the tower survived, and its tilt has made it an Italian [14] icon, it attracts visitors from all over who flock to Pisa to see one of the greatest architectural [15] weirdnesses in the world. [16] By the late twentieth century, the angle of the tower's tilt had reached an astonishing 5.5 degrees; in [17] 1990, Italy's government closed the tower to visitors and appointed a committee to find a way to save it.

[14]

A) NO CHANGE
B) icon, attracting
C) icon, its attracting
D) icon; attracting

[15]

A) NO CHANGE
B) deviations
C) oddities
D) abnormalities

[16]

At this point, the writer is considering adding the following sentence.

> Unfortunately, the tower's tilt has steadily increased over the centuries, placing the structure in danger of collapse.

Should the writer make this addition here?

A) Yes, because it provides an important restatement of the main claim in the previous sentence.
B) Yes, because it establishes an important shift in emphasis in the paragraph's discussion about the tower's tilt.
C) No, because it interrupts the paragraph's discussion with irrelevant information.
D) No, because it repeats information that is already presented in the first paragraph.

[17]

A) NO CHANGE
B) 1990, Italy's government, closed
C) 1990 Italy's government, closed,
D) 1990: Italy's government closed

The committee was charged with saving the tower without ruining its aesthetic, **18** which no one had yet managed to achieve. The committee's first attempt to reduce the angle of the tower's tilt—placing 600 tons of iron ingots (molded pieces of metal) on the tower's north side to create a counterweight—was derided because the bulky weights ruined the tower's appearance. The attempt at a less visible solution—sinking anchors into the ground below the tower—almost caused the tower to fall.

18

Which choice best supports the main point of the paragraph?

A) NO CHANGE

B) although not everyone on the committee agreed completely about what that aesthetic was.

C) which meant somehow preserving the tower's tilt while preventing that tilt from increasing and toppling the tower.

D) which included the pristine white marble finish that has come to be widely associated with the tower's beauty.

CONTINUE

[1] Enter committee member John Burland, [19] he is a geotechnical engineer from England who saved London's clock tower Big Ben from collapse. [2] Burland began a years-long process of drilling out small amounts of soil from under the tower [20] that took several years to complete and then monitoring the tower's resulting movement. [3] Twice daily, Burland evaluated these movements and made recommendations as to how much soil should be removed in the next drilling. [4] By 2001, almost 77 tons of soil had been removed, and the tower's tilt had decreased by over 1.5 degrees; the ugly iron weights were removed, and the tower was reopened to visitors. [5] Burland [21] advocated using soil extraction: removing small amounts of soil from under the tower's north side, opposite its tilt, to enable gravity to straighten the tower. [22]

The tower's tilt has not increased since, and the committee is confident that the tower will be safe for another 200 years. Burland is now working on a more permanent solution for keeping the tower upright, but he is adamant that the tower never be completely straightened. In an interview with PBS's *Nova*, Burland explained that it is very important "that we don't really change the character of the monument. That would be quite wrong and quite inappropriate."

19

A) NO CHANGE
B) Burland is
C) his being
D) DELETE the underlined portion.

20

A) NO CHANGE
B) —taking several years to complete—
C) that took him several years to complete
D) DELETE the underlined portion.

21

A) NO CHANGE
B) advocated to use
C) advocated the using of
D) advocating to use

22

To make this paragraph most logical, sentence 5 should be

A) placed after sentence 1.
B) placed after sentence 2.
C) placed after sentence 3.
D) DELETED from the paragraph.

Questions 23-33 are based on the following passage and supplementary material.

The Physician Assistant Will See You Now

[23] The term "paramedics" refers to health care workers who provide routine and clinical services. While the pressures of an aging population, insurance reforms, and health epidemics have increased demand for care, the supply of physicians is not expected to [24] keep pace. The Association of American Medical Colleges predicts a shortage of over 90,000 physicians by 2020; by 2025, that number could climb to more than 130,000. In some parts of the country, shortages are already a sad fact of life. A 2009 report by the Bureau of Health Professions notes that although a fifth of the US population lives in rural areas, less than a tenth of US physicians serves that population. Because a traditionalist response to the crisis—[25] amping up medical-college enrollments and expanding physician training programs—is too slow and costly to address the near-term problem, alternatives are being explored. One promising avenue has been greater reliance on physician assistants (PAs).

23

Which choice is the best introduction to the paragraph?

A) NO CHANGE

B) For many Americans, finding a physician is likely to become a growing challenge.

C) Getting treatment for an illness usually requires seeing either a general practitioner or a specialist.

D) Worldwide the costs of health care are increasing at an alarming rate.

24

A) NO CHANGE

B) maintain the tempo.

C) get in line.

D) move along.

25

A) NO CHANGE

B) bolstering

C) arousing

D) revving up

[26] By virtue of [27] <u>there</u> medical training, PAs can perform many of the jobs traditionally done by doctors, including treating chronic and acute conditions, performing minor [28] <u>surgeries: and</u> prescribing some medications. However, although well [29] <u>compensated earning in 2012 a median annual salary of $90,930,</u> PAs cost health care providers less than do the physicians who

[26]

At this point, the writer is considering adding the following sentence.

> Several factors argue in favor of such an expanded role.

Should the writer make this addition here?

A) Yes, because it introduces a counterargument for balance.

B) Yes, because it frames the points that the paragraph will examine.

C) No, because it does not specify the education required to be a PA.

D) No, because it presents information that is only tangential to the main argument.

[27]

A) NO CHANGE

B) they're

C) their

D) his or her

[28]

A) NO CHANGE

B) surgeries; and

C) surgeries, and,

D) surgeries, and

[29]

A) NO CHANGE

B) compensated (earning in 2012 a median annual salary of $90,930),

C) compensated, earning in 2012 a median annual salary of $90,930

D) compensated: earning in 2012 a median annual salary of $90,930,

might otherwise undertake these tasks. Moreover, the training period for PAs is markedly shorter than [30] those for physicians—two to three years versus the seven to eleven required for physicians.

Physician assistants already offer vital primary care in many locations. Some 90,000 PAs were employed nationwide in 2012. Over and above their value in partially compensating for the general physician shortage has been their extraordinary contribution to rural health care. A recent review of the scholarly literature by Texas researchers found that PAs lend cost-efficient, widely appreciated services in underserved areas. [31] In addition, rural-based PAs often provide a broader spectrum of such services than do their urban and suburban counterparts, possibly as a consequence of the limited pool of rural-based physicians.

30

A) NO CHANGE
B) that compared with
C) that for
D) DELETE the underlined portion.

31

A) NO CHANGE
B) Thus,
C) Despite this,
D) On the other hand,

Increasingly, PAs and other such medical practitioners have become a critical complement to physicians. A 2013 RAND Corporation report estimates that while the number of primary care physicians will increase slowly from 2010 to 2025, the number of physician assistants and nurse-practitioners in primary care will grow at much faster rates. [32] Both by merit and from necessity, PAs are likely to greet more [33] patience than ever before.

Supply of Physicians, Physician Assistants,
and Nurse-Practitioners in Primary Care
Clinical Practice in 2010 and 2025

| Provider type | 2010 | | 2025 (predicted) | |
	Number	Percent of total	Number	Percent of total
Physicians	210,000	71	216,000	60
Physician assistants	30,000	10	42,000	12
Nurse-practitioners	56,000	19	103,000	28
Total	296,000	100	361,000	100

Adapted from David I. Auerbach et al., "Nurse-Managed Health Centers and Patient-Centered Medical Homes Could Mitigate Expected Primary Care Physician Shortage." ©2013 by Project HOPE: The People-to-People Health Foundation, Inc.

32

At this point, the writer is considering adding the following sentence.

> In fact, according to the data presented in the table, physician assistants will likely outnumber physicians by 2025.

Should the writer make this addition here?

A) Yes, because it provides additional support for the main point of the paragraph.

B) Yes, because it addresses a possible counterargument to the writer's main claim.

C) No, because it is not an accurate interpretation of the data.

D) No, because it introduces irrelevant information that interrupts the flow of the passage.

33

A) NO CHANGE

B) patience, than

C) patients then

D) patients than

Questions 34-44 are based on the following passage.

Gold into Silver: The "Reverse Alchemy" of Superhero Comics History

[34] Popular film franchises are often "rebooted" in an effort to make their characters and stories fresh and relevant for new audiences. Superhero comic books are periodically reworked to try to increase their appeal to contemporary readers. This practice is almost as [35] elderly as the medium itself and has in large part established the "ages" that compose comic book history. The shift from the Golden to the Silver Age is probably the most successful [36] example: of publishers responding to changing times and tastes.

34

Which choice most effectively combines the underlined sentences?

A) In an effort to make their characters and stories fresh and relevant for new audiences, popular film franchises, which are often "rebooted," are similar to superhero comic books, which are periodically reworked to try to increase their appeal to contemporary readers.

B) Just as popular film franchises are often "rebooted" in an effort to make their characters and stories fresh and relevant for new audiences, superhero comic books are periodically reworked to try to increase their appeal to contemporary readers.

C) Superhero comic books are periodically reworked to try to increase their appeal to contemporary readers, while popular film franchises are often "rebooted" in an effort to make their characters and stories fresh and relevant for new audiences.

D) Superhero comic books are much like popular film franchises in being often "rebooted" in an effort to make their characters and stories fresh and relevant for new audiences and periodically reworked to try to increase their appeal to contemporary readers.

35

A) NO CHANGE
B) old
C) mature
D) geriatric

36

A) NO CHANGE
B) example, of publishers
C) example of publishers,
D) example of publishers

The start of the first ("Golden") age of comic books is often dated to 1938 with the debut of Superman in *Action Comics* #1. Besides beginning the age, Superman in many respects defined it, becoming the model on which many later superheroes were based. His characterization, as established in *Superman* #1 (1939), was relatively simple. He could "hurdle skyscrapers" and "leap an eighth of a mile"; "run faster than a streamline train"; withstand anything less than a "bursting shell"; and [37] lift a car over his head. Sent to Earth from the "doomed planet" Krypton, he was raised by human foster parents, whose love helped infuse him with an unapologetic desire to "benefit mankind." Admirable but aloof, the Golden Age Superman was arguably more paragon than character, a problem only partially solved by giving him a human alter ego. Other Golden Age superheroes were similarly archetypal: Batman was a crime-fighting millionaire, Wonder Woman a warrior princess from a mythical island.

[37]

Which choice is most consistent with the previous examples in the sentence?

A) NO CHANGE

B) hold down a regular job as a newspaper reporter.

C) wear a bright blue costume with a flowing red cape.

D) live in the big city of Metropolis instead of the small town where he grew up.

By contrast, the second ("Silver") age of comics was marked by characters that, though somewhat simplistic by today's standards, [38] were provided with origin stories often involving scientific experiments gone wrong. In addition to super villains, the new, soon-to-be-iconic characters of the [39] age: Spider-Man, the Fantastic Four, and the Hulk among them—had to cope with mundane, real-life problems, including paying the rent, dealing with family squabbles, and facing anger, loneliness, and ostracism. Their interior lives were richer and their motivations more complex. Although sales remained strong for Golden Age stalwarts Superman and, to a lesser extent, Batman, [40] subsequent decades would show the enduring appeal of these characters.

[38]

Which choice most effectively sets up the main idea of the following two sentences?

A) NO CHANGE

B) reflected the increasing conservatism of the United States in the 1950s.

C) engaged in bizarre adventures frequently inspired by science fiction.

D) were more "realistic" than their Golden Age counterparts.

[39]

A) NO CHANGE

B) age;

C) age,

D) age—

[40]

The writer wants a conclusion to the sentence and paragraph that logically completes the discussion of the Silver Age and provides an effective transition into the next paragraph. Which choice best accomplishes these goals?

A) NO CHANGE

B) the distinctions between later stages of comic book history are less well defined than the one between the Golden and Silver Ages.

C) readers increasingly gravitated to the upstarts as the 1960s and the Silver Age drew to a close.

D) these characters themselves underwent significant changes over the course of the Silver Age.

Unauthorized copying or reuse of any part of this page is illegal.

37

CONTINUE

More transformations would take place in the medium as the Silver Age gave way to the Bronze and Modern (and possibly Postmodern) Ages. Such efforts 41 have yielded diminishing returns, as even the complete relaunch of DC 42 Comics' superhero's, line in 2011 has failed to arrest the steep two-decade decline of comic book sales. For both commercial and, arguably, creative reasons, 43 then, no transition was more successful than 44 those from the Golden to Silver Age.

41

A) NO CHANGE
B) would have yielded
C) were yielding
D) will yield

42

A) NO CHANGE
B) Comic's superhero's
C) Comics superhero's
D) Comics' superhero

43

A) NO CHANGE
B) however,
C) nevertheless,
D) yet,

44

A) NO CHANGE
B) these
C) that
D) DELETE the underlined portion.

STOP

**If you finish before time is called, you may check your work on this section only.
Do not turn to any other section.**

Math Test – No Calculator

25 MINUTES, 20 QUESTIONS

Turn to Section 3 of your answer sheet to answer the questions in this section.

For questions 1-15, solve each problem, choose the best answer from the choices provided, and fill in the corresponding circle on your answer sheet. **For questions 16-20,** solve the problem and enter your answer in the grid on the answer sheet. Please refer to the directions before question 16 on how to enter your answers in the grid. You may use any available space in your test booklet for scratch work.

NOTES

1. The use of a calculator **is not permitted**.

2. All variables and expressions used represent real numbers unless otherwise indicated.

3. Figures provided in this test are drawn to scale unless otherwise indicated.

4. All figures lie in a plane unless otherwise indicated.

5. Unless otherwise indicated, the domain of a given function f is the set of all real numbers x for which $f(x)$ is a real number.

REFERENCE

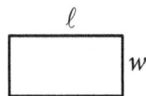

$A = \pi r^2$
$C = 2\pi r$

$A = \ell w$

$A = \frac{1}{2} bh$

$c^2 = a^2 + b^2$

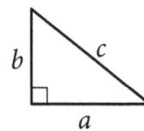 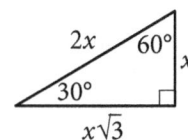

Special Right Triangles

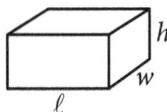

$V = \ell w h$

$V = \pi r^2 h$

$V = \frac{4}{3}\pi r^3$

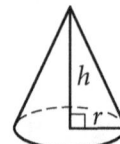

$V = \frac{1}{3}\pi r^2 h$

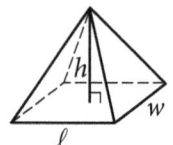

$V = \frac{1}{3}\ell w h$

The number of degrees of arc in a circle is 360.
The number of radians of arc in a circle is 2π.
The sum of the measures in degrees of the angles of a triangle is 180.

CONTINUE

1

Salim wants to purchase tickets from a vendor to watch a tennis match. The vendor charges a one-time service fee for processing the purchase of the tickets. The equation $T = 15n + 12$ represents the total amount T, in dollars, Salim will pay for n tickets. What does 12 represent in the equation?

A) The price of one ticket, in dollars

B) The amount of the service fee, in dollars

C) The total amount, in dollars, Salim will pay for one ticket

D) The total amount, in dollars, Salim will pay for any number of tickets

2

A gardener buys two kinds of fertilizer. Fertilizer A contains 60% filler materials by weight and Fertilizer B contains 40% filler materials by weight. Together, the fertilizers bought by the gardener contain a total of 240 pounds of filler materials. Which equation models this relationship, where x is the number of pounds of Fertilizer A and y is the number of pounds of Fertilizer B?

A) $0.4x + 0.6y = 240$

B) $0.6x + 0.4y = 240$

C) $40x + 60y = 240$

D) $60x + 40y = 240$

3

What is the sum of the complex numbers $2 + 3i$ and $4 + 8i$, where $i = \sqrt{-1}$?

A) 17

B) $17i$

C) $6 + 11i$

D) $8 + 24i$

4

$$4x^2 - 9 = (px + t)(px - t)$$

In the equation above, p and t are constants. Which of the following could be the value of p ?

A) 2

B) 3

C) 4

D) 9

5

Which of the following is the graph of the equation $y = 2x - 5$ in the *xy*-plane?

A)
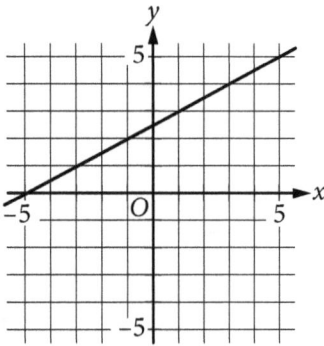

B)
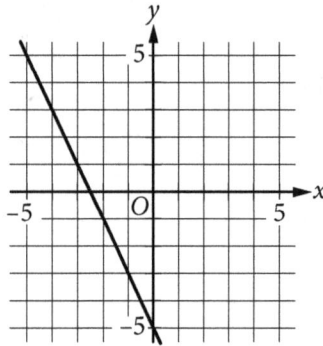

C)
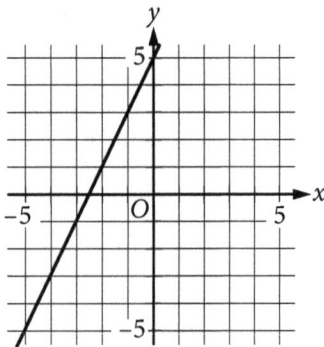

D)
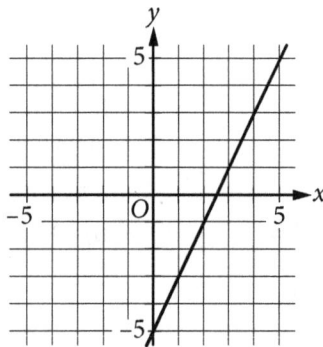

Unauthorized copying or reuse of any part of this page is illegal.

42

CONTINUE

6

If $x = \dfrac{2}{3}y$ and $y = 18$, what is the value of $2x - 3$?

A) 21

B) 15

C) 12

D) 10

7

A bricklayer uses the formula $n = 7\ell h$ to estimate the number of bricks, n, needed to build a wall that is ℓ feet long and h feet high. Which of the following correctly expresses ℓ in terms of n and h ?

A) $\ell = \dfrac{7}{nh}$

B) $\ell = \dfrac{h}{7n}$

C) $\ell = \dfrac{n}{7h}$

D) $\ell = \dfrac{n}{7+h}$

8

x	$w(x)$	$t(x)$
1	−1	−3
2	3	−1
3	4	1
4	3	3
5	−1	5

The table above shows some values of the functions w and t. For which value of x is $w(x) + t(x) = x$?

A) 1

B) 2

C) 3

D) 4

9

If $\sqrt{x} + \sqrt{9} = \sqrt{64}$, what is the value of x ?

A) $\sqrt{5}$

B) 5

C) 25

D) 55

10

Jaime is preparing for a bicycle race. His goal is to bicycle an average of at least 280 miles per week for 4 weeks. He bicycled 240 miles the first week, 310 miles the second week, and 320 miles the third week. Which inequality can be used to represent the number of miles, x, Jaime could bicycle on the 4th week to meet his goal?

A) $\dfrac{240 + 310 + 320}{3} + x \geq 280$

B) $240 + 310 + 320 \geq x(280)$

C) $\dfrac{240}{4} + \dfrac{310}{4} + \dfrac{320}{4} + x \geq 280$

D) $240 + 310 + 320 + x \geq 4(280)$

11

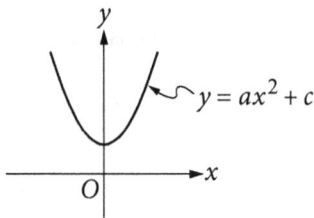

The vertex of the parabola in the xy-plane above is $(0, c)$. Which of the following is true about the parabola with the equation $y = -a(x - b)^2 + c$?

A) The vertex is (b, c) and the graph opens upward.

B) The vertex is (b, c) and the graph opens downward.

C) The vertex is $(-b, c)$ and the graph opens upward.

D) The vertex is $(-b, c)$ and the graph opens downward.

12

Which of the following is equivalent to $\dfrac{4x^2 + 6x}{4x + 2}$?

A) x

B) $x + 4$

C) $x - \dfrac{2}{4x + 2}$

D) $x + 1 - \dfrac{2}{4x + 2}$

13

$$2x^2 - 4x = t$$

In the equation above, t is a constant. If the equation has no real solutions, which of the following could be the value of t ?

A) -3

B) -1

C) 1

D) 3

14

A laundry service is buying detergent and fabric softener from its supplier. The supplier will deliver no more than 300 pounds in a shipment. Each container of detergent weighs 7.35 pounds, and each container of fabric softener weighs 6.2 pounds. The service wants to buy at least twice as many containers of detergent as containers of fabric softener. Let d represent the number of containers of detergent, and let s represent the number of containers of fabric softener, where d and s are nonnegative integers. Which of the following systems of inequalities best represents this situation?

A) $7.35d + 6.2s \le 300$
$\quad d \ge 2s$

B) $7.35d + 6.2s \le 300$
$\quad 2d \ge s$

C) $14.7d + 6.2s \le 300$
$\quad d \ge 2s$

D) $14.7d + 6.2s \le 300$
$\quad 2d \ge s$

15

Which of the following is equivalent to $\left(a + \dfrac{b}{2}\right)^2$?

A) $a^2 + \dfrac{b^2}{2}$

B) $a^2 + \dfrac{b^2}{4}$

C) $a^2 + \dfrac{ab}{2} + \dfrac{b^2}{2}$

D) $a^2 + ab + \dfrac{b^2}{4}$

DIRECTIONS

For questions 16-20, solve the problem and enter your answer in the grid, as described below, on the answer sheet.

1. Although not required, it is suggested that you write your answer in the boxes at the top of the columns to help you fill in the circles accurately. You will receive credit only if the circles are filled in correctly.
2. Mark no more than one circle in any column.
3. No question has a negative answer.
4. Some problems may have more than one correct answer. In such cases, grid only one answer.
5. **Mixed numbers** such as $3\frac{1}{2}$ must be gridded as 3.5 or 7/2. (If [3|1|/|2] is entered into the grid, it will be interpreted as $\frac{31}{2}$, not $3\frac{1}{2}$.)
6. **Decimal answers:** If you obtain a decimal answer with more digits than the grid can accommodate, it may be either rounded or truncated, but it must fill the entire grid.

Answer: $\frac{7}{12}$

Write answer in boxes.

← Fraction line

Grid in result.

Answer: 2.5

← Decimal point

Acceptable ways to grid $\frac{2}{3}$ are:

Answer: 201 – either position is correct

NOTE: You may start your answers in any column, space permitting. Columns you don't need to use should be left blank.

16

If $a^{\frac{b}{4}} = 16$ for positive integers a and b, what is one

possible value of b ?

17

$$\frac{2}{3}t = \frac{5}{2}$$

What value of t is the solution of the equation above?

18

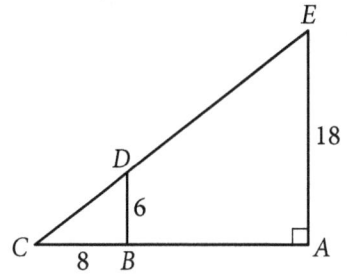

In the figure above, $\overline{BD}$ is parallel to $\overline{AE}$. What is the length of $\overline{CE}$?

CONTINUE ➡

19

How many liters of a 25% saline solution must be added to 3 liters of a 10% saline solution to obtain a 15% saline solution?

20

Points A and B lie on a circle with radius 1, and arc $\overset{\frown}{AB}$ has length $\dfrac{\pi}{3}$. What fraction of the circumference of the circle is the length of arc $\overset{\frown}{AB}$?

STOP

If you finish before time is called, you may check your work on this section only.
Do not turn to any other section.

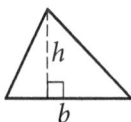
Math Test – Calculator

55 MINUTES, 38 QUESTIONS

Turn to Section 4 of your answer sheet to answer the questions in this section.

DIRECTIONS

For questions 1-30, solve each problem, choose the best answer from the choices provided, and fill in the corresponding circle on your answer sheet. **For questions 31-38**, solve the problem and enter your answer in the grid on the answer sheet. Please refer to the directions before question 31 on how to enter your answers in the grid. You may use any available space in your test booklet for scratch work.

NOTES

1. The use of a calculator **is permitted**.

2. All variables and expressions used represent real numbers unless otherwise indicated.

3. Figures provided in this test are drawn to scale unless otherwise indicated.

4. All figures lie in a plane unless otherwise indicated.

5. Unless otherwise indicated, the domain of a given function f is the set of all real numbers x for which $f(x)$ is a real number.

REFERENCE

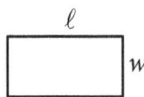 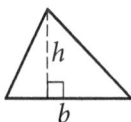 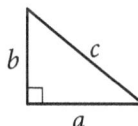 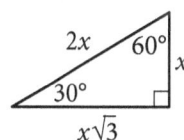 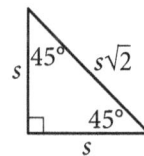

$A = \pi r^2$ $A = \ell w$ $A = \frac{1}{2}bh$ $c^2 = a^2 + b^2$ Special Right Triangles
$C = 2\pi r$

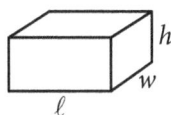 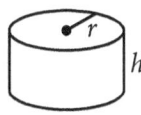 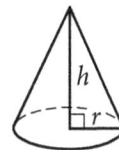 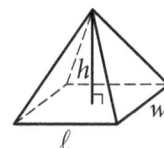

$V = \ell wh$ $V = \pi r^2 h$ $V = \frac{4}{3}\pi r^3$ $V = \frac{1}{3}\pi r^2 h$ $V = \frac{1}{3}\ell wh$

The number of degrees of arc in a circle is 360.
The number of radians of arc in a circle is 2π.
The sum of the measures in degrees of the angles of a triangle is 180.

CONTINUE

1

Which expression is equivalent to

$(2x^2 - 4) - (-3x^2 + 2x - 7)$?

A) $5x^2 - 2x + 3$

B) $5x^2 + 2x - 3$

C) $-x^2 - 2x - 11$

D) $-x^2 + 2x - 11$

2

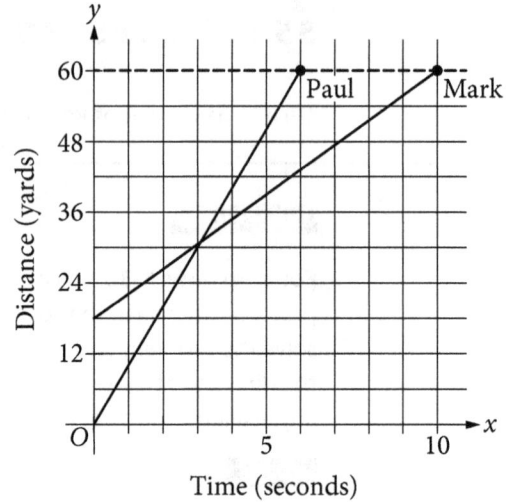

The graph above shows the positions of Paul and Mark during a race. Paul and Mark each ran at a constant rate, and Mark was given a head start to shorten the distance he needed to run. Paul finished the race in 6 seconds, and Mark finished the race in 10 seconds. According to the graph, Mark was given a head start of how many yards?

A)   3

B)   12

C)   18

D)   24

3

Snow fell and then stopped for a time. When the snow began to fall again, it fell at a faster rate than it had initially. Assuming that none of the snow melted during the time indicated, which of the following graphs could model the total accumulation of snow versus time?

A)

B)

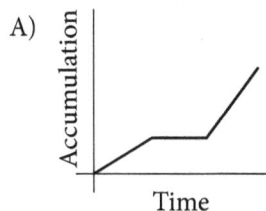

C)

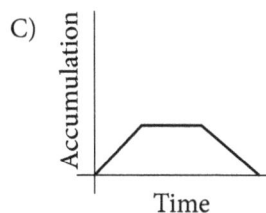

D)

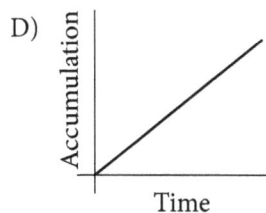

4

A website-hosting service charges businesses a onetime setup fee of \$350 plus d dollars for each month. If a business owner paid \$1,010 for the first 12 months, including the setup fee, what is the value of d ?

A) 25

B) 35

C) 45

D) 55

5

$$6x - 9y > 12$$

Which of the following inequalities is equivalent to the inequality above?

A) $x - y > 2$

B) $2x - 3y > 4$

C) $3x - 2y > 4$

D) $3y - 2x > 2$

Unauthorized copying or reuse of any part of this page is illegal.

52

CONTINUE

6

Where Do People Get Most of
Their Medical Information?

Source	Percent of those surveyed
Doctor	63%
Internet	13%
Magazines/brochures	9%
Pharmacy	6%
Television	2%
Other/none of the above	7%

The table above shows a summary of 1,200 responses to a survey question. Based on the table, how many of those surveyed get most of their medical information from either a doctor or the Internet?

A) 865

B) 887

C) 912

D) 926

7

The members of a city council wanted to assess the opinions of all city residents about converting an open field into a dog park. The council surveyed a sample of 500 city residents who own dogs. The survey showed that the majority of those sampled were in favor of the dog park. Which of the following is true about the city council's survey?

A) It shows that the majority of city residents are in favor of the dog park.

B) The survey sample should have included more residents who are dog owners.

C) The survey sample should have consisted entirely of residents who do not own dogs.

D) The survey sample is biased because it is not representative of all city residents.

8

Ice Cream and Topping Selections

		Flavor	
		Vanilla	Chocolate
Topping	Hot fudge	8	6
	Caramel	5	6

The table above shows the flavors of ice cream and the toppings chosen by the people at a party. Each person chose one flavor of ice cream and one topping. Of the people who chose vanilla ice cream, what fraction chose hot fudge as a topping?

A) $\dfrac{8}{25}$

B) $\dfrac{5}{13}$

C) $\dfrac{13}{25}$

D) $\dfrac{8}{13}$

9

The total area of a coastal city is 92.1 square miles, of which 11.3 square miles is water. If the city had a population of 621,000 people in the year 2010, which of the following is closest to the population density, in people per square mile of land area, of the city at that time?

A) 6,740

B) 7,690

C) 55,000

D) 76,000

10

Between 1497 and 1500, Amerigo Vespucci embarked on two voyages to the New World. According to Vespucci's letters, the first voyage lasted 43 days longer than the second voyage, and the two voyages combined lasted a total of 1,003 days. How many days did the second voyage last?

A) 460

B) 480

C) 520

D) 540

11

$$7x + 3y = 8$$
$$6x - 3y = 5$$

For the solution (x, y) to the system of equations above, what is the value of $x - y$?

A) $-\dfrac{4}{3}$

B) $\dfrac{2}{3}$

C) $\dfrac{4}{3}$

D) $\dfrac{22}{3}$

Questions 12-14 refer to the following information.

Sunflower Growth

Day	Height (cm)
0	0.00
7	17.93
14	36.36
21	67.76
28	98.10
35	131.00
42	169.50
49	205.50
56	228.30
63	247.10
70	250.50
77	253.80
84	254.50

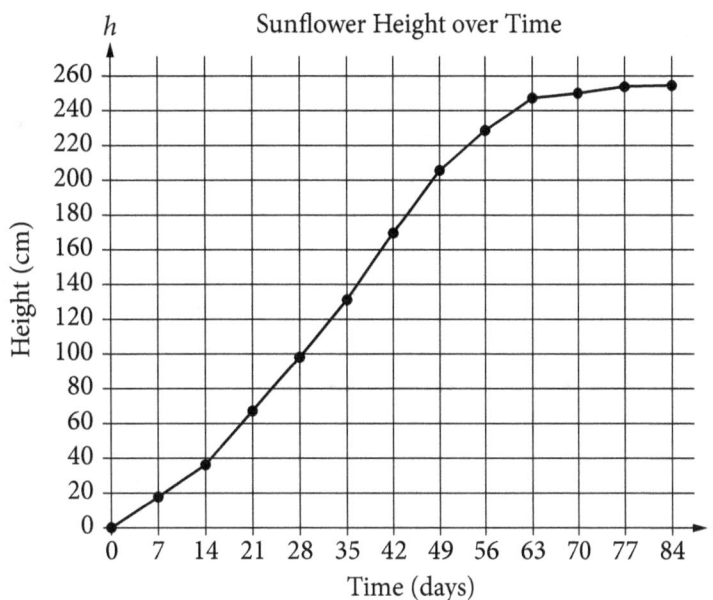

Sunflower Height over Time

In 1919, H. S. Reed and R. H. Holland published a paper on the growth of sunflowers. Included in the paper were the table and graph above, which show the height h, in centimeters, of a sunflower t days after the sunflower begins to grow.

12

Over which of the following time periods is the average growth rate of the sunflower least?

A) Day 0 to Day 21

B) Day 21 to Day 42

C) Day 42 to Day 63

D) Day 63 to Day 84

13

The function h, defined by $h(t) = at + b$, where a and b are constants, models the height, in centimeters, of the sunflower after t days of growth during a time period in which the growth is approximately linear. What does a represent?

A) The predicted number of centimeters the sunflower grows each day during the period

B) The predicted height, in centimeters, of the sunflower at the beginning of the period

C) The predicted height, in centimeters, of the sunflower at the end of the period

D) The predicted total increase in the height of the sunflower, in centimeters, during the period

14

The growth rate of the sunflower from day 14 to day 35 is nearly constant. On this interval, which of the following equations best models the height h, in centimeters, of the sunflower t days after it begins to grow?

A) $h = 2.1t - 15$

B) $h = 4.5t - 27$

C) $h = 6.8t - 12$

D) $h = 13.2t - 18$

15

x	1	2	3	4	5
y	$\dfrac{11}{4}$	$\dfrac{25}{4}$	$\dfrac{39}{4}$	$\dfrac{53}{4}$	$\dfrac{67}{4}$

Which of the following equations relates y to x for the values in the table above?

A) $y = \dfrac{1}{2} \cdot \left(\dfrac{5}{2}\right)^x$

B) $y = 2 \cdot \left(\dfrac{3}{4}\right)^x$

C) $y = \dfrac{3}{4}x + 2$

D) $y = \dfrac{7}{2}x - \dfrac{3}{4}$

16

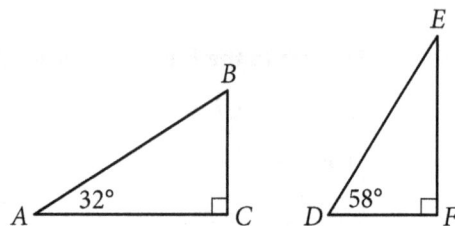

Triangles ABC and DEF are shown above. Which of the following is equal to the ratio $\dfrac{BC}{AB}$?

A) $\dfrac{DE}{DF}$

B) $\dfrac{DF}{DE}$

C) $\dfrac{DF}{EF}$

D) $\dfrac{EF}{DE}$

CONTINUE

Questions 17-19 refer to the following information.

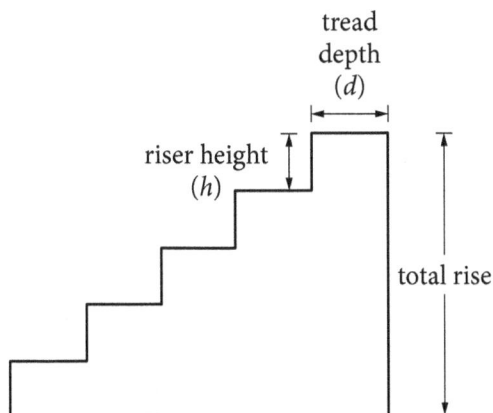

Note: Figure not drawn to scale.

When designing a stairway, an architect can use the riser-tread formula $2h + d = 25$, where h is the riser height, in inches, and d is the tread depth, in inches. For any given stairway, the riser heights are the same and the tread depths are the same for all steps in that stairway.

The number of steps in a stairway is the number of its risers. For example, there are 5 steps in the stairway in the figure above. The total rise of a stairway is the sum of the riser heights as shown in the figure.

17

Which of the following expresses the riser height in terms of the tread depth?

A) $h = \dfrac{1}{2}(25 + d)$

B) $h = \dfrac{1}{2}(25 - d)$

C) $h = -\dfrac{1}{2}(25 + d)$

D) $h = -\dfrac{1}{2}(25 - d)$

18

Some building codes require that, for indoor stairways, the tread depth must be at least 9 inches and the riser height must be at least 5 inches. According to the riser-tread formula, which of the following inequalities represents the set of all possible values for the riser height that meets this code requirement?

A) $0 \le h \le 5$

B) $h \ge 5$

C) $5 \le h \le 8$

D) $8 \le h \le 16$

19

An architect wants to use the riser-tread formula to design a stairway with a total rise of 9 feet, a riser height between 7 and 8 inches, and an odd number of steps. With the architect's constraints, which of the following must be the tread depth, in inches, of the stairway? (1 foot = 12 inches)

A)   7.2

B)   9.5

C)   10.6

D)   15

20

What is the sum of the solutions to
$(x-6)(x+0.7) = 0$?

A) −6.7

B) −5.3

C) 5.3

D) 6.7

21

A study was done on the weights of different types of fish in a pond. A random sample of fish were caught and marked in order to ensure that none were weighed more than once. The sample contained 150 largemouth bass, of which 30% weighed more than 2 pounds. Which of the following conclusions is best supported by the sample data?

A) The majority of all fish in the pond weigh less than 2 pounds.

B) The average weight of all fish in the pond is approximately 2 pounds.

C) Approximately 30% of all fish in the pond weigh more than 2 pounds.

D) Approximately 30% of all largemouth bass in the pond weigh more than 2 pounds.

22

Number of States with 10 or More
Electoral Votes in 2008

Electoral votes	Frequency
10	4
11	4
12	1
13	1
15	3
17	1
20	1
21	2
27	1
31	1
34	1
55	1

In 2008, there were 21 states with 10 or more electoral votes, as shown in the table above. Based on the table, what was the median number of electoral votes for the 21 states?

A) 13

B) 15

C) 17

D) 20

23

Height versus Time for a Bouncing Ball

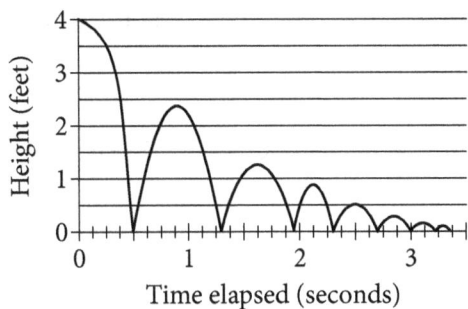

As part of an experiment, a ball was dropped and allowed to bounce repeatedly off the ground until it came to rest. The graph above represents the relationship between the time elapsed after the ball was dropped and the height of the ball above the ground. After it was dropped, how many times was the ball at a height of 2 feet?

A) One

B) Two

C) Three

D) Four

24

A customer's monthly water bill was $75.74. Due to a rate increase, her monthly bill is now $79.86. To the nearest tenth of a percent, by what percent did the amount of the customer's water bill increase?

A) 4.1%

B) 5.1%

C) 5.2%

D) 5.4%

25

x	$f(x)$
0	–2
2	4
6	16

Some values of the linear function f are shown in the table above. What is the value of $f(3)$?

A) 6

B) 7

C) 8

D) 9

26

A gear ratio *r:s* is the ratio of the number of teeth of two connected gears. The ratio of the number of revolutions per minute (rpm) of two gear wheels is *s:r*. In the diagram below, Gear A is turned by a motor. The turning of Gear A causes Gears B and C to turn as well.

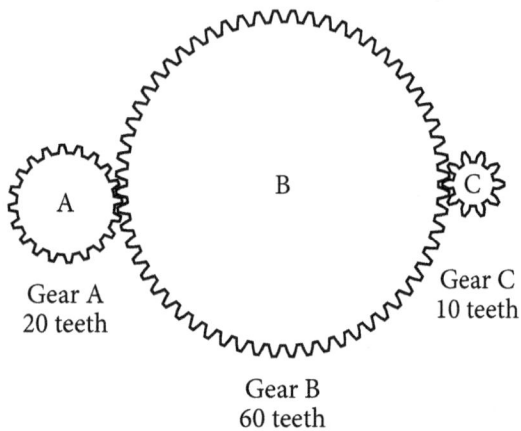

Gear A
20 teeth

Gear B
60 teeth

Gear C
10 teeth

If Gear A is rotated by the motor at a rate of 100 rpm, what is the number of revolutions per minute for Gear C?

A)　　50

B)　　110

C)　　200

D)　1,000

27

In the *xy*-plane, the graph of
$2x^2 - 6x + 2y^2 + 2y = 45$ is a circle. What is the radius of the circle?

A)　5

B)　6.5

C)　$\sqrt{40}$

D)　$\sqrt{50}$

28

Two different points on a number line are both 3 units from the point with coordinate −4. The solution to which of the following equations gives the coordinates of both points?

A)　$|x + 4| = 3$

B)　$|x - 4| = 3$

C)　$|x + 3| = 4$

D)　$|x - 3| = 4$

29

A motor powers a model car so that after starting from rest, the car travels s inches in t seconds, where $s = 16t\sqrt{t}$. Which of the following gives the average speed of the car, in inches per second, over the first t seconds after it starts?

A) $4\sqrt{t}$

B) $16\sqrt{t}$

C) $\dfrac{16}{\sqrt{t}}$

D) $16t$

30

The scatterplot below shows the amount of electric energy generated, in millions of megawatt-hours, by nuclear sources over a 10-year period.

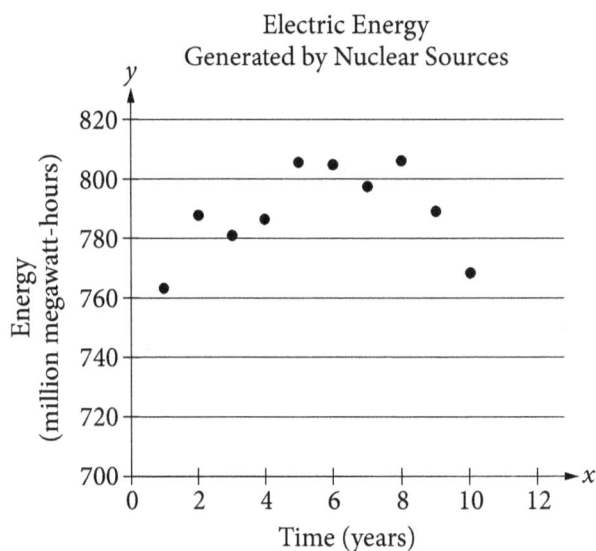

Electric Energy
Generated by Nuclear Sources

Of the following equations, which best models the data in the scatterplot?

A) $y = 1.674x^2 + 19.76x - 745.73$

B) $y = -1.674x^2 - 19.76x - 745.73$

C) $y = 1.674x^2 + 19.76x + 745.73$

D) $y = -1.674x^2 + 19.76x + 745.73$

DIRECTIONS

For questions 31-38, solve the problem and enter your answer in the grid, as described below, on the answer sheet.

1. Although not required, it is suggested that you write your answer in the boxes at the top of the columns to help you fill in the circles accurately. You will receive credit only if the circles are filled in correctly.

2. Mark no more than one circle in any column.

3. No question has a negative answer.

4. Some problems may have more than one correct answer. In such cases, grid only one answer.

5. **Mixed numbers** such as $3\frac{1}{2}$ must be gridded as 3.5 or 7/2. (If $\boxed{3|1|/|2}$ is entered into the grid, it will be interpreted as $\frac{31}{2}$, not $3\frac{1}{2}$.)

6. **Decimal answers:** If you obtain a decimal answer with more digits than the grid can accommodate, it may be either rounded or truncated, but it must fill the entire grid.

Answer: $\frac{7}{12}$ Answer: 2.5

Write answer in boxes. ← Fraction line

Grid in result. ← Decimal point

Acceptable ways to grid $\frac{2}{3}$ are:

Answer: 201 – either position is correct

NOTE: You may start your answers in any column, space permitting. Columns you don't need to use should be left blank.

31

A group of friends decided to divide the $800 cost of a trip equally among themselves. When two of the friends decided not to go on the trip, those remaining still divided the $800 cost equally, but each friend's share of the cost increased by $20. How many friends were in the group originally?

32

$$2(5x - 20) - (15 + 8x) = 7$$

What value of x satisfies the equation above?

33

A laboratory supply company produces graduated cylinders, each with an internal radius of 2 inches and an internal height between 7.75 inches and 8 inches. What is one possible volume, rounded to the nearest cubic inch, of a graduated cylinder produced by this company?

34

In the xy-plane, the graph of $y = 3x^2 - 14x$ intersects the graph of $y = x$ at the points $(0,0)$ and (a,a). What is the value of a ?

CONTINUE ▶

35

The line with the equation $\frac{4}{5}x + \frac{1}{3}y = 1$ is graphed

in the xy-plane. What is the x-coordinate of the

x-intercept of the line?

36

	Masses (kilograms)					
Andrew	2.4	2.5	3.6	3.1	2.5	2.7
Maria	x	3.1	2.7	2.9	3.3	2.8

Andrew and Maria each collected six rocks, and the masses of the rocks are shown in the table above. The mean of the masses of the rocks Maria collected is 0.1 kilogram greater than the mean of the masses of the rocks Andrew collected. What is the value of x ?

37

Jeremy deposited x dollars in his investment account on January 1, 2001. The amount of money in the account doubled each year until Jeremy had 480 dollars in his investment account on January 1, 2005. What is the value of x ?

38

A school district is forming a committee to discuss plans for the construction of a new high school. Of those invited to join the committee, 15% are parents of students, 45% are teachers from the current high school, 25% are school and district administrators, and the remaining 6 individuals are students. How many more teachers were invited to join the committee than school and district administrators?

STOP

If you finish before time is called, you may check your work on this section only.
Do not turn to any other section.

The SAT®

Practice Essay #6

Make time to take the practice Essay.
It's one of the best ways to get ready
for the SAT Essay.

As you read the passage below, consider how Christopher Hitchens uses

- evidence, such as facts or examples, to support claims.
- reasoning to develop ideas and to connect claims and evidence.
- stylistic or persuasive elements, such as word choice or appeals to emotion, to add power to the ideas expressed.

Adapted from Christopher Hitchens, "The Lovely Stones." ©2009 by Condé Nast Digital. Originally published July 2009.

1   The great classicist A. W. Lawrence . . . once remarked of the Parthenon[1] that it is "the one building in the world which may be assessed as absolutely *right*." . . .

2   Not that the beauty and symmetry of the Parthenon have not been abused and perverted and mutilated. Five centuries after the birth of Christianity the Parthenon was closed and desolated. . . . Turkish forces also used it for centuries as a garrison[2] and an arsenal, with the tragic result that in 1687 . . . a powder magazine was detonated and huge damage inflicted on the structure. Most horrible of all, perhaps, the Acropolis was made to fly a Nazi flag during the German occupation of Athens. . . .

3   The damage done by the ages to the building, and by past empires and occupations, cannot all be put right. But there is one desecration and dilapidation that can at least be partially undone. Early in the 19th century, Britain's ambassador to the Ottoman Empire, Lord Elgin, sent a wrecking crew to the Turkish-occupied territory of Greece, where it sawed off approximately half of the adornment of the Parthenon and carried it away. As with all things Greek, there were three elements to this, the most lavish and beautiful sculptural treasury in human history. Under the direction of the artistic genius Phidias, the temple had two massive pediments decorated with the figures of Pallas Athena, Poseidon, and the gods of the sun and the moon. It then had a series of 92 high-relief panels, or metopes, depicting a succession of mythical and historical battles. The most intricate element was the frieze, carved in bas-relief,[3] which showed the gods, humans, and animals that made up the annual Pan-Athens procession: there were 192 equestrian warriors and auxiliaries featured, which happens to be the exact number of the city's heroes who fell at the Battle of Marathon. Experts differ on precisely what story is being told here, but the frieze was quite clearly carved as a continuous narrative. Except that half the cast of the tale is still in Bloomsbury, in London, having been sold well below cost by Elgin to the British government in 1816 for $2.2 million in today's currency to pay off his many debts. . . .

---

[1] An ancient Greek temple located on the grounds of the ancient citadel, the Acropolis of Athens

[2] A military fort or base

[3] Raised carvings made of stone

4   . . . [T]here has been a bitter argument about the legitimacy of the British Museum's deal. I've written a whole book about this controversy and won't oppress you with all the details, but would just make this one point. If the *Mona Lisa* had been sawed in two during the Napoleonic Wars and the separated halves had been acquired by different museums in, say, St. Petersburg and Lisbon, would there not be a general wish to see what they might look like if re-united? If you think my analogy is overdrawn, consider this: the body of the goddess Iris is at present in London, while her head is in Athens. The front part of the torso of Poseidon is in London, and the rear part is in Athens. And so on. This is grotesque. . . .

5   It is unfortunately true that [Athens] allowed itself to become very dirty and polluted in the 20th century, and as a result the remaining sculptures and statues on the Parthenon were nastily eroded by "acid rain." . . . But gradually and now impressively, the Greeks have been living up to their responsibilities. Beginning in 1992, the endangered marbles were removed from the temple, given careful cleaning with ultraviolet and infra-red lasers, and placed in a climate-controlled interior. . . .

6   About a thousand feet southeast of the temple [is] the astonishing new Acropolis Museum. . . . With 10 times the space of the old repository, it display[s] all the marvels that go with the temples on top of the hill. Most important, it show[s], for the first time in centuries, how the Parthenon sculptures looked to the citizens of old. . . .

7   The British may continue in their constipated fashion to cling to what they have so crudely amputated, but . . . the Acropolis Museum has hit on the happy idea of exhibiting . . . its own original sculptures with the London-held pieces represented by beautifully copied casts. This creates a natural thirst to see the actual re-assembly completed. So, far from emptying or weakening a museum, this controversy has created another [museum], which is destined to be among Europe's finest galleries. And one day, surely, there will be an agreement to do the right thing by the world's most "right" structure.

Write an essay in which you explain how Christopher Hitchens builds an argument to persuade his audience that the original Parthenon sculptures should be returned to Greece. In your essay, analyze how Hitchens uses one or more of the features listed in the box above (or features of your own choice) to strengthen the logic and persuasiveness of his argument. Be sure that your analysis focuses on the most relevant features of the passage.

Your essay should not explain whether you agree with Hitchens's claims, but rather explain how Hitchens builds an argument to persuade his audience.

SAT Practice Test #1

Section 1: Reading Test

QUESTION 1

Choice B is the best answer. In the passage, a young man (Akira) asks a mother (Chie) for permission to marry her daughter (Naomi). The request was certainly surprising to the mother, as can be seen from line 47, which states that prior to Akira's question Chie "had no idea" the request was coming.

Choice A is incorrect because the passage depicts two characters engaged in a civil conversation, with Chie being impressed with Akira's "sincerity" and finding herself "starting to like him." Choice C is incorrect because the passage is focused on the idea of Akira's and Naomi's present lives and possible futures. Choice D is incorrect because the interactions between Chie and Akira are polite, not critical; for example, Chie views Akira with "amusement," not animosity.

QUESTION 2

Choice B is the best answer. The passage centers on a night when a young man tries to get approval to marry a woman's daughter. The passage includes detailed descriptions of setting (a "winter's eve" and a "cold rain," lines 5-6); character (Akira's "soft, refined" voice, line 33; Akira's eyes "sh[ining] with sincerity," line 35); and plot ("Naomi was silent. She stood a full half minute looking straight into Chie's eyes. Finally, she spoke," lines 88-89).

Choice A is incorrect because the passage focuses on a nontraditional marriage proposal. Choice C is incorrect because the passage concludes without resolution to the question of whether Akira and Naomi will receive permission to marry. Choice D is incorrect because the passage repeatedly makes clear that for Chie, her encounter with Akira is momentous and unsettling, as when Akira acknowledges in line 73 that he has "startled" her.

QUESTION 3

Choice C is the best answer. Akira "came directly, breaking all tradition," (line 1) when he approached Chie and asked to marry her daughter, and he "ask[ed] directly," without "a go-between" (line 65) or "mediation," because doing otherwise would have taken too much time.

Choices A, B, and D are incorrect because in these contexts, "directly" does not mean in a frank, confident, or precise manner.

QUESTION 4

Choice A is the best answer. Akira is very concerned Chie will find his marriage proposal inappropriate because he did not follow traditional protocol and use a "go-between" (line 65). This is clear in lines 63-64, when Akira says to Chie "Please don't judge my candidacy by the unseemliness of this proposal."

Choice B is incorrect because there is no evidence in the passage that Akira worries that Chie will mistake his earnestness for immaturity. Choice C is incorrect because while Akira recognizes that his unscheduled visit is a nuisance, his larger concern is that Chie will reject him due to the inappropriateness of his proposal. Choice D is incorrect because there is no evidence in the passage that Akira worries Chie will underestimate the sincerity of his emotions.

QUESTION 5

Choice C is the best answer. In lines 63-64, Akira says to Chie, "Please don't judge my candidacy by the unseemliness of this proposal." This reveals Akira's concern that Chie may say no to the proposal simply because Akira did not follow traditional practices.

Choices A, B, and D do not provide the best evidence for the answer to the previous question. Choice A is incorrect because line 33 merely describes Akira's voice as "soft, refined." Choice B is incorrect because lines 49-51 reflect Chie's perspective, not Akira's. Choice D is incorrect because lines 71-72 indicate only that Akira was speaking in an eager and forthright matter.

QUESTION 6

Choice D is the best answer because Akira clearly treats Chie with respect, including "bow[ing]" (line 26) to her, calling her "Madame" (line 31), and looking at her with "a deferential peek" (line 34). Akira does not offer Chie utter deference, though, as he asks to marry Naomi after he concedes that he is not following protocol and admits to being a "disruption" (line 31).

Choice A is incorrect because while Akira conveys respect to Chie, there is no evidence in the passage that he feels affection for her. Choice B is incorrect because neither objectivity nor impartiality accurately describes how Akira addresses Chie. Choice C is incorrect because Akira conveys respect to Chie and takes the conversation seriously.

QUESTION 7

Choice D is the best answer. The first paragraph (lines 1-4) reflects on how Akira approached Chie to ask for her daughter's hand in marriage. In these lines, the narrator is wondering whether Chie would have been more likely to say yes to Akira's proposal if Akira had followed tradition: "Akira came directly, breaking all tradition. Was that it? Had he followed form — had he asked his mother to speak to his father to approach a go-between — would Chie have been more receptive?" Thus, the main purpose of the first paragraph is to examine why Chie reacted a certain way to Akira's proposal.

Choice A is incorrect because the first paragraph describes only one aspect of Japanese culture (marriage proposals) but not the culture as a whole. Choice B is incorrect because the first paragraph implies a criticism of Akira's individual marriage proposal but not the entire tradition of Japanese marriage proposals. Choice C is incorrect because the narrator does not question a suggestion.

QUESTION 8

Choice B is the best answer. In line 1, the narrator suggests that Akira's direct approach broke "all tradition." The narrator then wonders if Akira had "followed form," or the tradition expected of him, would Chie have been more receptive to his proposal. In this context, following "form" thus means following a certain tradition or custom.

Choices A, C, and D are incorrect because in this context "form" does not mean the way something looks (appearance), the way it is built (structure), or its essence (nature).

QUESTION 9

Choice C is the best answer. Akira states that his unexpected meeting with Chie occurred only because of a "matter of urgency," which he explains as "an opportunity to go to America, as dentist for Seattle's Japanese community" (lines 41-42). Akira decides to directly speak to Chie because Chie's response to his marriage proposal affects whether Akira accepts the job offer.

Choice A is incorrect because there is no evidence in the passage that Akira is worried his parents will not approve of Naomi. Choice B is incorrect because Akira has "an understanding" with Naomi (line 63). Choice D is incorrect; while Akira may know that Chie is unaware of his feelings for Naomi, this is not what he is referring to when he mentions "a matter of urgency."

QUESTION 10

Choice B is the best answer. In lines 39-42, Akira clarifies that the "matter of urgency" is that he has "an opportunity to go to America, as dentist for Seattle's Japanese community." Akira needs Chie's answer to his marriage proposal so he can decide whether to accept the job in Seattle.

Choices A, C, and D do not provide the best evidence for the answer to the previous question. Choice A is incorrect because in line 39 Akira apologizes for interrupting Chie's quiet evening. Choice C is incorrect because lines 58-59 address the seriousness of Akira's request, not its urgency. Choice D is incorrect because line 73 shows only that Akira's proposal has "startled" Chie and does not explain why his request is time-sensitive.

QUESTION 11

Choice A is the best answer. Lines 1-9 include examples of how many people shop ("millions of shoppers"), how much money they spend ("over $30 billion at retail stores in the month of December alone"), and the many occasions that lead to shopping for gifts ("including weddings, birthdays, anniversaries, graduations, and baby showers."). Combined, these examples show how frequently people in the US shop for gifts.

Choice B is incorrect because even though the authors mention that "$30 billion" had been spent in retail stores in one month, that figure is never discussed as an increase (or a decrease). Choice C is incorrect because lines 1-9 provide a context for the amount of shopping that occurs in the US, but the anxiety (or "dread") it might cause is not introduced until later in the passage. Choice D is incorrect because lines 1-9 do more than highlight the number of different occasions that lead to gift-giving.

QUESTION 12

Choice B is the best answer. Lines 9-10 state "This frequent experience of gift-giving can engender ambivalent feelings in gift-givers." In the subsequent sentences, those "ambivalent" feelings are further exemplified as conflicted feelings, as shopping is said to be something that "[m]any relish" (lines 10-11) and "many dread" (line 14).

Choices A, C, and D are incorrect because in this context, "ambivalent" does not mean feelings that are unrealistic, apprehensive, or supportive.

QUESTION 13

Choice D is the best answer. In lines 10-13, the authors clearly state that some people believe gift-giving can help a relationship because it "offers a powerful means to build stronger bonds with one's closest peers."

Choice A is incorrect because even though the authors state that some shoppers make their choices based on "egocentrism," (line 33) there is no evidence in the passage that people view shopping as a form of self-expression. Choice B is incorrect because the passage implies that shopping is an expensive habit. Choice C is incorrect because the passage states that most people have purchased and received gifts, but it never implies that people are *required* to reciprocate the gift-giving process.

QUESTION 14

Choice A is the best answer. In lines 10-13, the authors suggest that people value gift-giving because it may strengthen their relationships with others: "Many relish the opportunity to buy presents because gift-giving offers a powerful means to build stronger bonds with one's closest peers."

Choices B, C, and D do not provide the best evidence for the answer to the previous question. Choice B is incorrect because lines 22-23 discuss how people often buy gifts that the recipients would not purchase. Choice C is incorrect because lines 31-32 explain how gift-givers often fail to consider the recipients' preferences. Choice D is incorrect because lines 44-47 suggest that the cost of a gift may not correlate to a recipient's appreciation of it.

QUESTION 15

Choice A is the best answer. The "deadweight loss" mentioned in the second paragraph is the significant monetary difference between what a gift-giver would pay for something and what a gift-recipient would pay for the same item. That difference would be predictable to social psychologists, whose research "has found that people often struggle to take account of others' perspectives — their insights are subject to egocentrism, social projection, and multiple attribution errors" lines 31-34).

Choices B, C, and D are all incorrect because lines 31-34 make clear that social psychologists would expect a disconnect between gift-givers and gift-recipients, not that they would question it, be disturbed by it, or find it surprising or unprecedented.

QUESTION 16

Choice C is the best answer. Lines 41-44 suggest that gift-givers assume a correlation between the cost of a gift and how well-received it will be: ". . . gift-givers equate how much they spend with how much recipients will appreciate the gift (the more expensive the gift, the stronger a gift-recipient's feelings of appreciation)." However, the authors suggest this assumption may be incorrect or "unfounded" (line 47), as gift-recipients "may not construe smaller and larger gifts as representing smaller and larger signals of thoughtfulness and consideration" (lines 63-65).

Choices A, B, and D are all incorrect because the passage neither states nor implies that the gift-givers' assumption is insincere, unreasonable, or substantiated.

QUESTION 17

Choice C is the best answer. Lines 63-65 suggest that the assumption made by gift-givers in lines 41-44 may be incorrect. The gift-givers assume that recipients will have a greater appreciation for costly gifts than for less costly gifts, but the authors suggest this relationship may be incorrect, as gift-recipients "may not construe smaller and larger gifts as representing smaller and larger signals of thoughtfulness and consideration" (lines 63-65).

Choices A and D are incorrect because lines 53-55 and 75-78 address the question of "why" gift-givers make specific assumptions rather than addressing the validity of these assumptions. Choice B is incorrect because lines 55-60 focus on the reasons people give gifts to others.

QUESTION 18

Choice D is the best answer. Lines 53-55 state that "Perhaps givers believe that bigger (i.e., more expensive) gifts convey stronger signals of thoughtfulness and consideration." In this context, saying that more expensive gifts "convey" stronger signals means the gifts send, or communicate, stronger signals to the recipients.

Choices A, B, and C are incorrect because in this context, to "convey" something does not mean to transport it (physically move something), counteract it (act in opposition to something), or exchange it (trade one thing for another).

QUESTION 19

Choice A is the best answer. The paragraph examines how gift-givers believe expensive gifts are more thoughtful than less expensive gifts and will be more valued by recipients. The work of Camerer and others offers an explanation for the gift-givers' reasoning: "gift-givers attempt to signal their positive attitudes toward the intended recipient and their willingness to invest resources in a future relationship" lines 57-60).

Choices B, C, and D are incorrect because the theory articulated by Camerer and others is used to explain an idea put forward by the authors ("givers believe that bigger . . . gifts convey stronger signals"), not to introduce an argument, question a motive, or support a conclusion.

QUESTION 20

Choice B is the best answer. The graph clearly shows that gift-givers believe that a "more valuable" gift will be more appreciated than a "less valuable gift." According to the graph, gift-givers believe the monetary value of a gift will determine whether that gift is well received or not.

Choice A is incorrect because the graph does not suggest that gift-givers are aware of gift-recipients' appreciation levels. Choices C and D are incorrect because neither the gift-givers' desire for the gifts they purchase nor the gift-givers' relationship with the gift-recipients is addressed in the graph.

QUESTION 21

Choice A is the best answer. Lines 69-75 explain that while people are often both gift-givers and gift-receivers, they struggle to apply information they learned as a gift-giver to a time when they were a gift-receiver: "Yet, despite the extensive experience that people have as both givers and receivers, they often struggle to transfer information gained from one role (e.g., as a giver) and apply it in another, complementary role (e.g., as a receiver)." The authors suggest that the disconnect between how much appreciation a gift-giver thinks a gift merits and how much appreciation a gift-recipient displays for the gift may be caused by both individuals' inability to comprehend the other's perspective.

Choices B and C are incorrect because neither the passage nor the graph addresses the idea that society has become more materialistic or that there is a growing opposition to gift-giving. Choice D is incorrect because the passage emphasizes that gift-givers and gift-recipients fail to understand each other's perspective, but it offers no evidence that the disconnect results only from a failure to understand the other's intentions.

QUESTION 22

Choice B is the best answer. Lines 2-4 of the passage describe DNA as "a very long chain, the backbone of which consists of a regular alternation of sugar and phosphate groups." The backbone of DNA, in other words, is the main structure of a chain made up of repeating units of sugar and phosphate.

Choice A is incorrect because the passage describes DNA on the molecular level only and never mentions the spinal column of organisms. Choice C is incorrect because the passage describes the backbone of the molecule as having "a regular alternation" of sugar and phosphate, not one or the other. Choice D is incorrect because the nitrogenous bases are not the main structural unit of DNA; rather, they are attached only to the repeating units of sugar.

QUESTION 23

Choice D is the best answer. The authors explain that hydrogen bonds join together pairs of nitrogenous bases, and that these bases have a specific structure that leads to the pairing: "One member of a pair must be a purine and the other a pyrimidine in order to bridge between the two chains" (lines 27-29). Given the specific chemical properties of a nitrogenous base, it would be inaccurate to call the process random.

Choice A is incorrect because lines 5-6 describe how nitrogenous bases attach to sugar but not how those bases pair with one another. Choice B is incorrect because lines 9-10 do not contradict the student's claim. Choice C is incorrect because lines 23-25 describe how the two molecules' chains are linked, not what the specific pairing between nitrogenous bases is.

QUESTION 24

Choice D is the best answer. In lines 12-14 the authors state: "the first feature of our structure which is of biological interest is that it consists not of one chain, but of two."

Choices A and B are incorrect because lines 12-14 explicitly state that it is the two chains of DNA that are of "biological interest," not the chemical formula of DNA, nor the common fiber axis those two chains are wrapped around. Choice C is incorrect because, while the X-ray evidence did help Watson and Crick to discover that DNA consists of two chains, it was not claimed to be the feature of biological interest.

QUESTION 25

Choice C is the best answer. In lines 12-14 the authors claim that DNA molecules appear to be comprised of two chains, even though "it has often been assumed . . . there would be only one" (lines 15-17). The authors support this claim with evidence compiled from an X-ray: "the density, taken with the X-ray evidence, suggests very strongly that there are two [chains]" (lines 18-19).

Choices A, B, and D are incorrect because the authors mention density and X-ray evidence to support a claim, not to establish that DNA carries genetic information, present a hypothesis about the composition of a nucleotide, or confirm a relationship between the density and chemical formula of DNA.

QUESTION 26

Choice B is the best answer. The authors explain that "only certain pairs of bases will fit into the structure" (lines 25-26) of the DNA molecule. These pairs must contain "a purine and the other a pyrimidine in order to bridge between the two chains" (lines 27-29), which implies that any other pairing would not "fit into the structure" of the DNA molecule. Therefore, a pair of purines would be larger than the required purine/pyrimidine pair and would not fit into the structure of the DNA molecule.

Choice A is incorrect because this section is not discussing the distance between a sugar and phosphate group. Choice C is incorrect because the passage never makes clear the size of the pyrimidines or purines in relation to each other, only in relation to the space needed to bond the chains of the DNA molecule. Choice D is incorrect because the lines do not make an implication about the size of a pair of pyrimidines in relation to the size of a pair consisting of a purine and a pyrimidine.

QUESTION 27

Choice D is the best answer. The authors explain how the DNA molecule contains a "precise sequence of bases" (lines 43-44), and that the authors can use the order of bases on one chain to determine the order of bases on the other chain: "If the actual order of the bases on one of the pair of chains were given, one could write down the exact order of the bases on the other one, because of the specific pairing. Thus one chain is, as it were, the complement of the other, and it is this feature which suggests how the deoxyribonucleic acid molecule might duplicate itself" (lines 45-51). The authors use the words "exact," "specific," and "complement" in these lines to suggest that the base pairings along a DNA chain is understood and predictable, and may explain how DNA "duplicate[s] itself" (line 51).

Choice A is incorrect because the passage does not suggest that most nucleotide sequences are known. Choice B is incorrect because these lines are not discussing the random nature of the base sequence along one chain of DNA. Choice C is incorrect because the authors are describing the bases attached only to the sugar, not to the sugar-phosphate backbone.

QUESTION 28

Choice C is the best answer. Lines 6-7 state that "Two of the possible bases — adenine and guanine — are purines," and on the table the percentages of adenine and guanine in yeast DNA are listed as 31.3% and 18.7% respectively.

Choices A, B, and D are incorrect because they do not state the percentages of both purines, adenine and guanine, in yeast DNA.

QUESTION 29

Choice A is the best answer. The authors state: "We believe that the bases will be present almost entirely in their most probable forms. If this is true, the conditions for forming hydrogen bonds are more restrictive, and the only pairs of bases possible are: adenine with thymine, and guanine with cytosine" (lines 31-35). The table shows that the pairs adenine/thymine and guanine/cytosine have notably similar percentages in DNA for all organisms listed.

Choice B is incorrect. Although the choice of "Yes" is correct, the explanation for that choice misrepresents the data in the table. Choices C and D are incorrect because the table does support the authors' proposed pairing of nitrogenous bases in DNA molecules.

QUESTION 30

Choice A is the best answer because it gives the percentage of cytosine (17.3%) in sea urchin DNA and the percentage of guanine (17.7%) in sea urchin DNA. Their near similar pairing supports the authors' proposal that possible pairings of nitrogenous bases are "adenine with thymine, and guanine with cytosine" (line 35).

Choices B, C, and D do not provide the best evidence for the answer to the previous question. Choice B (cytosine and thymine), Choice C (cytosine and adenine), and Choice D (guanine and adenine) are incorrect because they show pairings of nitrogenous bases that do not compose a similar percentage of the bases in sea urchin DNA.

QUESTION 31

Choice D is the best answer. The table clearly shows that the percentage of adenine in each organism's DNA is different, ranging from 24.7% in *E.coli* to 33.2% in the octopus. That such a variability would exist is predicted in lines 41-43, which states that "in a long molecule many different permutations are possible."

Choices A and B are incorrect because the table shows that the percentage of adenine varies between 24.7% and 33.2% in different organisms. Choice C is incorrect because lines 36-38 state that adenine pairs with thymine but does not mention the variability of the base composition of DNA.

QUESTION 32

Choice B is the best answer. In this passage, Woolf asks women a series of questions. Woolf wants women to consider joining "the procession of educated men" (lines 56-57) by becoming members of the workforce. Woolf stresses that this issue is urgent, as women "have very little time in which to answer [these questions]" (lines 48-49).

Choice A is incorrect because Woolf argues against the tradition of only "the sons of educated men" (lines 82-83) joining the workforce. Choice C is incorrect because Woolf is not highlighting the severity of social divisions as much as she is explaining how those divisions might be reduced (with women joining the workforce). Choice D is incorrect because Woolf does not question the feasibility of changing the workforce dynamic.

QUESTION 33

Choice A is the best answer. Throughout the passage, Woolf advocates for more women to engage with existing institutions by joining the workforce: "We too can leave the house, can mount those steps [to an office], pass in and out of those doors, . . . make money, administer justice . . ." (lines 30-32). Woolf tells educated women that they are at a "moment of transition" (line 51) where they must consider their future role in the workforce.

Choice B is incorrect because even though Woolf mentions women's traditional roles (lines 68-69: "while they stirred the pot, while they rocked the cradle"), she does not suggest that women will have to give up these traditional roles to gain positions of influence. Choice C is incorrect because though Woolf wonders how "the procession of the sons of educated men" impacts women's roles, she does not argue that this male-dominated society has had grave and continuing effects. Choice D is incorrect because while Woolf suggests educated women can hold positions currently held by men, she does not suggest that women's entry into positions of power will change those positions.

QUESTION 34

Choice C is the best answer. Woolf uses the word "we" to refer to herself and educated women in English society, the "daughters of educated men" (line 64). Woolf wants these women to consider participating in a changing workforce: "For there, trapesing along at the tail end of the procession [to and from work], we go ourselves" (lines 23-24). In using the word "we" throughout the passage, Woolf establishes a sense of solidarity among educated women.

Choice A is incorrect because Woolf does not use "we" to reflect on whether people in a group are friendly to one another; she is concerned with generating solidarity among women. Choice B is incorrect because though Woolf admits women have predominantly "done their thinking" within traditional female roles (lines 64-69), she does not use "we" to advocate for more candor among women. Choice D is incorrect because Woolf does not use "we" to emphasize a need for people in a group to respect one other; rather, she wants to establish a sense of solidarity among women.

QUESTION 35

Choice B is the best answer. Woolf argues that the "bridge over the River Thames, [has] an admirable vantage ground for us to make a survey" (lines 1-3). The phrase "make a survey" means to carefully examine an event or activity. Woolf wants educated women to "fix [their] eyes upon the procession — the procession of the sons of educated men" (lines 9-11) walking to work.

Choice A is incorrect because while Woolf states the bridge "is a place to stand on by the hour dreaming," she states that she is using the bridge "to consider the facts" (lines 6-9). Woolf is not using the bridge for fanciful reflection; she is analyzing "the procession of the sons of educated men" (lines 10-11). Choice C is incorrect because Woolf does not compare the bridge to historic episodes. Choice D is incorrect because Woolf does not suggest that the bridge is a symbol of a male-dominated past, but rather that it serves as a good place to watch men proceed to work.

QUESTION 36

Choice D is the best answer. Woolf writes that the men who conduct the affairs of the nation (lines 15-17: "ascending those pulpits, preaching, teaching, administering justice, practising medicine, transacting business, making money") are the same men who go to and from work in a "procession" (line 10). Woolf notes that women are joining this procession, an act that suggests the workforce has become less exclusionary: "For there, trapesing along at the tail end of the procession, we go ourselves" (lines 23-24).

Choice A is incorrect because the procession is described as "a solemn sight always" (lines 17-18), which indicates that it has always been influential. Choice B is incorrect because the passage does not indicate that this procession has become a celebrated feature of English life. Choice C is incorrect because the passage states only that the procession is made up of "the sons of educated men" (lines 10-11).

QUESTION 37

Choice C is the best answer, as lines 23-24 suggest that the workforce has become less exclusionary. In these lines Woolf describes how women are joining the male-dominated procession that travels to and from the work place: "For there, trapesing along at the tail end of the procession, we go ourselves."

Choices A, B, and D are incorrect because they do not provide the best evidence for the answer to the previous question. Choice A is incorrect because lines 12-17 describe the positions predominantly held by men. Choice B is incorrect because lines 17-19 use a metaphor to describe how the procession physically looks. Choice D is incorrect because lines 30-34 hypothesize about future jobs for women.

QUESTION 38

Choice C is the best answer. Woolf characterizes the questions she asks in lines 53-57 as significant ("so important that they may well change the lives of all men and women for ever," lines 52-53) and urgent ("we have very little time in which to answer them," lines 48-49). Therefore, Woolf considers the questions posed in lines 53-57 as both momentous (significant) and pressing (urgent).

Choice A is incorrect because Woolf characterizes the questions as urgent and important, not as something that would cause controversy or fear. Choice B is incorrect because though Woolf considers the questions to be weighty (or "important"), she implies that they can be answered. Choice D is incorrect because Woolf does not imply that the questions are mysterious.

QUESTION 39

Choice B is the best answer. The answer to the previous question shows how Woolf characterizes the questions posed in lines 53-57 as momentous and pressing. In lines 48-49, Woolf describes these questions as "important," or momentous, and states that women "have very little time in which to answer them," which shows their urgency.

Choices A, C, and D do not provide the best evidence for the answer to the previous question. Choices A and D are incorrect because lines 46-47 and line 62 suggest that women need to think about these questions and not offer trivial objections to them. Choice C is incorrect because line 57 characterizes only the need for urgency and does not mention the significance of the questions.

QUESTION 40

Choice C is the best answer. Woolf writes that women "have thought" while performing traditional roles such as cooking and caring for children (lines 67-69). Woolf argues that this "thought" has shifted women's roles in society and earned them a "brand-new sixpence" that they need to learn how to "spend" (lines 70-71). The "sixpence" mentioned in these lines is not a literal coin. Woolf is using the "sixpence" as a metaphor, as she is suggesting women take advantage of the opportunity to join the male-dominated workforce.

Choices A, B, and D are incorrect because in this context, "sixpence" does not refer to tolerance, knowledge, or perspective.

QUESTION 41

Choice B is the best answer. In lines 72-76, Woolf repeats the phrase "let us think" to emphasize how important it is for women to critically reflect on their role in society. Woolf states this reflection can occur at any time: "Let us think in offices; in omnibuses; while we are standing in the crowd watching Coronations and Lord Mayor's Shows; let us think . . . in the gallery of the House of Commons; in the Law Courts; let us think at baptisms and marriages and funerals."

Choices A, C, and D are incorrect because in lines 72-76 Woolf is not emphasizing the novelty of the challenge faced by women, the complexity of social and political issues, or the enjoyable aspect of women's career possibilities.

QUESTION 42

Choice B is the best answer. The author of Passage 1 identifies specific companies such as the "Planetary Resources of Washington," "Deep Space Industries of Virginia," and "Golden Spike of Colorado" to support his earlier assertion that there are many interested groups "working to make space mining a reality" (line 8).

Choices A, C, and D are incorrect because the author of Passage 1 does not mention these companies to profile the technological advances in space mining, the profit margins from space mining, or the diverse approaches to space mining.

QUESTION 43

Choice A is the best answer. The author of Passage 1 explicitly states that one benefit to space mining is access to precious metals and earth elements: "within a few decades, [space mining] may be meeting earthly demands for precious metals, such as platinum and gold, and the rare earth elements vital for personal electronics, such as yttrium and lanthanum" (lines 18-22).

Choice B is incorrect because Passage 1 does not suggest that precious metals extracted from space may make metals more valuable on Earth. Choice C and Choice D are incorrect because Passage 1 never mentions how space mining could create unanticipated technological innovations or change scientists' understanding of space resources.

QUESTION 44

Choice A is the best answer. Lines 18-22 suggest that space mining may help meet "earthly demands for precious metals . . . and the rare earth elements vital for personal electronics." In this statement, the author is stating materials ("metals," "earth elements") that may be gathered as a result of space mining, and that these materials may be important to Earth's economy.

Choices B, C, and D do not provide the best evidence for the answer to the previous question. Choice B is incorrect because lines 24-28 focus on an "off-planet economy" but never address positive effects of space mining. Choice C is incorrect because lines 29-30 suggest the relative value of water found in space. Choice D is incorrect because lines 41-44 state that space mining companies hope to find specific resources in lunar soil and asteroids but do not address how these resources are important to Earth's economy.

QUESTION 45

Choice D is the best answer. The author suggests in lines 19-22 that space mining may meet "earthly demands for precious metals, such as platinum and gold, and the rare earth elements vital for personal electronics." In this sentence, "earthly demands" suggests that people want, or desire, these precious metals and rare earth elements.

Choices A, B, and C are incorrect because in this context "demands" does not mean offers, claims, or inquiries.

QUESTION 46

Choice C is the best answer. Lines 29-30 introduce the idea that water mined in space may be very valuable: "water mined from other worlds could become the most desired commodity." Lines 35-40 support this assertion by suggesting how mined space water could be used "for drinking or as a radiation shield" (lines 36-37) or to make "spacecraft fuel" (line 38).

Choice A is incorrect because the comparison in the previous paragraph (the relative value of gold and water to someone in the desert) is not expanded upon in lines 35-40. Choice B is incorrect because the question asked in the previous paragraph is also answered in that paragraph. Choice D is incorrect because no specific proposals are made in the previous paragraph; rather, an assertion is made and a question is posed.

QUESTION 47

Choice B is the best answer. The author of Passage 2 recognizes that space mining may prove beneficial to humanity, stating that "we all stand to gain: the mineral bounty and spin-off technologies could enrich us all" (lines 50-52). The author also repeatedly mentions that space mining should be carefully considered before it is implemented: "But before the miners start firing up their rockets, we should pause for thought" (lines 53-54); "But [space mining's] consequences — both here on Earth and in space — merit careful consideration" (lines 57-59).

Choice A is incorrect because the author of Passage 2 concedes that "space mining seems to sidestep most environmental concerns" (lines 55-56) but does not imply that space mining will recklessly harm the environment, either on Earth or in space. Choice C is incorrect because the author of Passage 2 does not address any key resources that may be disappearing on Earth. Choice D is incorrect because the author of Passage 2 admits that "resources that are valuable in orbit and beyond may be very different to those we prize on Earth" (lines 74-76) but does not mention any disagreement about the commercial viabilities of space mining discoveries.

QUESTION 48

Choice A is the best answer. In lines 60-66, the author presents some environmental arguments against space mining: "[space] is not ours to despoil" and we should not "[glut] ourselves on space's riches." The author then suggests that these environmental arguments will be hard to "hold," or maintain, when faced with the possible monetary rewards of space mining: "History suggests that those will be hard lines to hold . . ." (line 68).

Choices B, C, and D are incorrect because in this context, "hold" does not mean grip, restrain, or withstand.

QUESTION 49

Choice D is the best answer. The author of Passage 1 is excited about the possibilities of space mining and how it can yield valuable materials, such as metals and elements (lines 19-20 and lines 41-42), water ice (line 35), and space dirt (line 44). The author of Passage 2, on the other hand, recognizes the possible benefits of space mining but also states that space mining should be thoughtfully considered before being implemented. Therefore, the author of Passage 2 expresses some concerns about a concept discussed in Passage 1.

Choice A is incorrect because the author of Passage 2 does not refute the central claim of Passage 1; both authors agree there are possible benefits to space mining. Choice B is incorrect because the author of Passage 1 does not describe space mining in more general terms than does the author of Passage 2. Choice C is incorrect because the author of Passage 2 is not suggesting that the space mining proposals stated in Passage 1 are impractical.

QUESTION 50

Choice B is the best answer. In lines 18-28, the author of Passage 1 describes many of the possible economic benefits of space mining, including the building of "an off-planet economy" (line 25). The author of Passage 2 warns that there may be ramifications to implementing space mining and building an "emerging off-world economy" (line 73) without regulation: "But miners have much to gain from a broad agreement on the for-profit exploitation of space. Without consensus, claims will be disputed, investments risky, and the gains made insecure" (lines 83-87).

Choices A, C, and D are incorrect because the author of Passage 2 does not suggest that the benefits to space mining mentioned in lines 18-28 of Passage 1 are unsustainable, unachievable, or will negatively affect Earth's economy. Rather, the author recognizes the benefits of space mining but advocates for the development of regulation procedures.

QUESTION 51

Choice D is the best answer. In lines 85-87, the author of Passage 2 states that the future of space mining will prove difficult without regulations because "claims will be disputed, investments risky, and the gains made insecure."

Choices A, B, and C are incorrect because they do not provide the best evidence for the answer to the previous question. Choice A is incorrect because lines 60-63 present some environmental concerns toward space mining. Choice B is incorrect because lines 74-76 focus on how space mining may discover valuable resources that are different from the ones found on Earth. Choice C is incorrect because lines 81-83 simply describe one person's objections to the regulation of the space mining industry.

QUESTION 52

Choice A is the best answer because both Passage 1 and Passage 2 indicate a belief that the resources most valued in space may differ from those most valued on our planet. Passage 2 says this explicitly in lines 74-76: "The resources that are valuable in orbit and beyond may be very different to those we prize on Earth." Meanwhile Passage 1 suggests that water mined from space may be more valuable than metals or other earth elements when creating an "off-plant economy" lines 25-30).

Choice B is incorrect because neither passage discusses, either implicitly or explicitly, the need for space mining to be inexpensive. Choice C is incorrect because Passage 2 does not specifically identify precious metals or rare earth elements but instead focuses on theoretical problems with space mining. Choice D is incorrect because diminishing resources on Earth is not discussed in Passage 2.

Section 2: Writing and Language Test

QUESTION 1

Choice D is the best answer because "outweigh" is the only choice that appropriately reflects the relationship the sentence sets up between "advantages" and "drawbacks."

Choices A, B, and C are incorrect because each implies a competitive relationship that is inappropriate in this context.

QUESTION 2

Choice B is the best answer because it offers a second action that farmers can undertake to address the problem of acid whey disposal, thus supporting the claim made in the previous sentence ("To address the problem of disposal, farmers have found a *number of uses* for acid whey").

Choices A, C, and D are incorrect because they do not offer examples of how farmers could make use of acid whey.

QUESTION 3

Choice A is the best answer because it results in a sentence that is grammatically correct and coherent. In choice A, "waterways," the correct plural form of "waterway," conveys the idea that acid whey could impact multiple bodies of water. Additionally, the compound verb "can pollute" suggests that acid whey presents an ongoing, potential problem.

Choices B and D are incorrect because both use the possessive form of "waterway." Choice C is incorrect because it creates an unnecessary shift in verb tense. The present tense verb "can pollute" should be used instead, as it is consistent with the other verbs in the paragraph.

QUESTION 4

Choice C is the best answer because it utilizes proper punctuation for items listed in a series. In this case those items are nouns: "Yogurt manufacturers, food scientists, and government officials."

Choices A and B are incorrect because both fail to recognize that the items are a part of a series. Since a comma is used after "manufacturers," a semicolon or colon should not be used after "scientists." Choice D is incorrect because the comma after "and" is unnecessary and deviates from grammatical conventions for presenting items in a series.

QUESTION 5

Choice C is the best answer because sentence 5 logically links sentence 2, which explains why Greek yogurt production yields large amounts of acid whey, and sentence 3, which mentions the need to dispose of acid whey properly.

Choices A, B, and D are incorrect because each would result in an illogical progression of sentences for this paragraph. If sentence 5 were left where it is or placed after sentence 3, it would appear illogically after the discussion of "the problem of disposal." If sentence 5 were placed after sentence 1, it would illogically discuss "acid-whey runoff" before the mention of acid whey being "difficult to dispose of."

QUESTION 6

Choice D is the best answer because the paragraph includes several benefits of consuming Greek yogurt, particularly in regard to nutrition and satisfying hunger, to support the sentence's claim that the conservation efforts are "well worth the effort." This transition echoes the passage's earlier claim that "the advantages of Greek yogurt outweigh the potential drawbacks of its production."

Choices A, B, and C are incorrect because they inaccurately describe the sentence in question.

QUESTION 7

Choice B is the best answer because it provides a grammatically standard preposition that connects the verb "serves" and noun "digestive aid" and accurately depicts their relationship.

Choice A is incorrect because the infinitive form "to be" yields a grammatically incorrect verb construction: "serves to be." Choices C and D are incorrect because both present options that deviate from standard English usage.

QUESTION 8

Choice C is the best answer because it presents a verb tense that is consistent in the context of the sentence. The choice is also free of the redundant "it."

Choice A is incorrect because the subject "it" creates a redundancy. Choices B and D are incorrect because they present verb tenses that are inconsistent in the context of the sentence.

QUESTION 9

Choice A is the best answer because it properly introduces an additional health benefit in a series of sentences that list health benefits. "Also" is the logical and coherent choice to communicate an addition.

Choices B, C, and D are incorrect because none of the transitions they offer logically fits the content that precedes or follows the proposed choice.

QUESTION 10

Choice A is the best answer because "satiated" is the only choice that communicates effectively that Greek yogurt will satisfy hunger for a longer period of time.

Choices B, C, and D are incorrect because each is improper usage in this context. A person can be "fulfilled" spiritually or in other ways, but a person who has eaten until he or she is no longer hungry cannot be described as fulfilled. Neither can he or she be described as being "complacent" or "sufficient."

QUESTION 11

Choice B is the best answer because it provides a syntactically coherent and grammatically correct sentence.

Choices A and C are incorrect because the adverbial conjunctions "therefore" and "so," respectively, are unnecessary following "Because." Choice D is incorrect because it results in a grammatically incomplete sentence (the part of the sentence before the colon must be an independent clause).

QUESTION 12

Choice B is the best answer because the graph clearly indicates that, on March 5, average low temperatures are at their lowest point: 12 degrees Fahrenheit.

Choice A is incorrect because the phrase "as low as" suggests that the temperature falls no lower than 20 degrees Fahrenheit, but the chart shows that in January, February, and March, the temperature frequently falls below that point. Choices C and D are incorrect because the information each provides is inconsistent with the information on the chart.

QUESTION 13

Choice A is the best answer because it concisely combines the two sentences while maintaining the original meaning.

Choices B, C, and D are incorrect because each is unnecessarily wordy, thus undermining one purpose of combining two sentences: to make the phrasing more concise.

QUESTION 14

Choice B is the best answer because it provides a conjunctive adverb that accurately represents the relationship between the two sentences. "However" signals an exception to a case stated in the preceding sentence.

Choices A, C, and D are incorrect because each provides a transition that does not accurately represent the relationship between the two sentences, and as a result each compromises the logical coherence of these sentences.

QUESTION 15

Choice C is the best answer because it provides commas to offset the nonrestrictive modifying clause "an associate professor of geology at Ohio State."

Choices A, B, and D are incorrect because each provides punctuation that does not adequately separate the nonrestrictive modifying clause about Jason Box from the main clause.

QUESTION 16

Choice C is the best answer because the colon signals that the other factor that contributed to the early thaw is about to be provided.

Choice A is incorrect because it results in a sentence that deviates from grammatical standards: a semicolon should be used to separate two independent clauses, but in choice A the second clause only has a subject, not a verb. Choice B is incorrect because it is unnecessarily wordy. Choice D is incorrect because "being" is unnecessary and creates an incoherent clause.

QUESTION 17

Choice C is the best answer because it provides the correct preposition ("of") and relative pronoun ("which") that together create a dependent clause following the comma.

Choices A, B, and D are incorrect because each results in a comma splice. Two independent clauses cannot be joined with only a comma.

QUESTION 18

Choice A is the best answer because the verb tense is consistent with the preceding past tense verbs in the sentence, specifically "produced" and "drifted."

Choices B, C, and D are incorrect because each utilizes a verb tense that is not consistent with the preceding past tense verbs in the sentence.

QUESTION 19

Choice D is the best answer because "their" is the possessive form of a plural noun. In this case, the noun is plural: "snow and ice."

Choices A and B are incorrect because the possessive pronoun must refer to a plural noun, "snow and ice," rather than a singular noun. Choice C is incorrect because "there" would result in an incoherent sentence.

QUESTION 20

Choice D is the best answer. The preceding sentences in the paragraph have established that a darker surface of soot-covered snow leads to more melting because this darker surface absorbs heat, whereas a whiter surface, free of soot, would deflect heat. As the passage points out, exposed land and water are also dark and cannot deflect heat the way ice and snow can. Only choice D reflects the self-reinforcing cycle that the preceding sentences already imply.

Choices A, B, and C are incorrect because the information each provides fails to support the previous claim that the "result" of the soot "is a self-reinforcing cycle."

QUESTION 21

Choice B is the best answer because it is free of redundancies.

Choices A, C, and D are incorrect because each of the three presents a redundancy: Choice A uses "repeat" and "again"; Choice C uses "damage" and "harmful effects"; and Choice D uses "may" and "possibly."

QUESTION 22

Choice D is the best answer because sentence 5 describes the information Box seeks: "to determine just how much the soot is contributing to the melting of the ice sheet." Unless sentence 4 comes after sentence 5, readers will not know what the phrase "this crucial information" in sentence 4 refers to.

Choices A, B, and C are incorrect because each results in an illogical sentence progression. None of the sentences that would precede sentence 4 provides details that could be referred to as "this crucial information."

QUESTION 23

Choice D is the best answer because it is free of redundancies and offers the correct form of the verb "wear" in this context.

Choices A, B, and C are incorrect because all three contain a redundancy. Considering that "quickly" is a fixed part of the sentence, choice A's "soon" and choice B and C's "promptly" all result in redundancies. Choices A and B are also incorrect because each uses an incorrect form of the verb.

QUESTION 24

Choice D is the best answer because it is the only choice that provides a grammatically standard and coherent sentence. The participial phrase "Having become frustrated. . ." functions as an adjective modifying "I," the writer.

Choices A, B, and C are incorrect because each results in a dangling modifier. The participial phrase "Having become frustrated . . ." does not refer to choice A's "no colleagues," choice B's "colleagues," or choice C's "ideas." As such, all three choices yield incoherent and grammatically incorrect sentences.

QUESTION 25

Choice B is the best answer because it provides the correct preposition in this context, "about."

Choices A, C, and D are incorrect because each provides a preposition that deviates from correct usage. One might read an article "about" coworking spaces but not an article "into," "upon," or "for" coworking spaces.

QUESTION 26

Choice A is the best answer because it provides the correct punctuation for the dependent clause that begins with the phrase "such as."

Choices B, C, and D are incorrect because each presents punctuation that deviates from the standard way of punctuating the phrase "such as." When "such as" is a part of a nonrestrictive clause, as it is here, only one comma is needed to separate it from the main independent clause.

QUESTION 27

Choice B is the best answer because it provides a transitional phrase, "In addition to equipment," that accurately represents the relationship between the two sentences connected by the transitional phrase. Together, the sentences describe the key features of coworking spaces, focusing on what the spaces offer (equipment and meeting rooms).

Choices A, C, and D are incorrect because each provides a transition that does not accurately represent the relationship between the two sentences.

QUESTION 28

Choice C is the best answer because the sentence is a distraction from the paragraph's focus. Nothing in the paragraph suggests that the cost of setting up a coworking business is relevant here.

Choices A and D are incorrect because neither accurately represents the information in the paragraph. Choice B is incorrect because it does not accurately represent the information in the next paragraph.

QUESTION 29

Choice B is the best answer because it logically follows the writer's preceding statement about creativity and accurately represents the information in the graph.

Choices A, C, and D are incorrect because they present inaccurate and unsupported interpretations of the information in the graph. In addition, none of these choices provides directly relevant support for the main topic of the paragraph.

QUESTION 30

Choice D is the best answer because it provides a relative pronoun and verb that create a standard and coherent sentence. The relative pronoun "who" refers to the subject "the people," and the plural verb "use" corresponds grammatically with the plural noun "people."

Choices A and B are incorrect because "whom" is the relative pronoun used to represent an object. The noun "people" is a subject performing an action (using the coworking space). Choices B and C are also incorrect because they display a form of the verb "to use" that does not correspond to the plural noun "people."

QUESTION 31

Choice C is the best answer because the proposed sentence offers a necessary and logical transition between sentence 2, which introduces the facility the writer chose, and sentence 3, which tells what happened at the facility "Throughout the morning."

Choices A, B, and D are incorrect because each would result in an illogical progression of sentences.

QUESTION 32

Choice A is the best answer because the punctuation it provides results in a grammatically standard and coherent sentence. When an independent clause is followed by a list, a colon is used to link the two.

Choice B is incorrect because the punctuation creates a fragment (a semicolon should be used to link two independent clauses). Choice C is incorrect because its use of the comma creates a series in which "several of my coworking colleagues" are distinguished from the "website developer" and others, although the logic of the sentence would suggest that they are the same. Choice D is incorrect because it lacks the punctuation necessary to link the independent clause and the list.

QUESTION 33

Choice A is the best answer because it provides a phrase that is consistent with standard English usage and also maintains the tone and style of the passage.

Choice B is incorrect because "give some wisdom" deviates from standard English usage and presents a somewhat colloquial phrase in a text that is generally free of colloquialisms. Choices C and D are incorrect because both are inconsistent with the tone of the passage as well as its purpose. The focus of the paragraph is on sharing, not on proclaiming opinions.

QUESTION 34

Choice A is the best answer because it offers a phrase that introduces a basic definition of philosophy and thereby fits the sentence.

Choices B, C, and D are incorrect because each offers a transition that does not suit the purpose of the sentence.

QUESTION 35

Choice A is the best answer because it offers the most succinct comparison between the basic definition of philosophy and the fact that students can gain specific, practical skills from the study of philosophy. There is no need to include the participle "speaking" in this sentence, as it is clear from context that the writer is offering a different perspective.

Choices B, C, and D are incorrect because they provide options that are unnecessarily wordy.

QUESTION 36

Choice B is the best answer because it provides a verb that creates a grammatically complete, standard, and coherent sentence.

Choices A, C, and D are incorrect because each results in a grammatically incomplete and incoherent sentence.

QUESTION 37

Choice D is the best answer because it most effectively sets up the information in the following sentences, which state that (according to information from the 1990s) "only 18 percent of American colleges required at least one philosophy course," and "more than 400 independent philosophy departments were eliminated" from colleges. These details are most logically linked to the claim that "colleges have not always supported the study of philosophy."

Choices A, B, and C are incorrect because none of these effectively sets up the information that follows, which is about colleges' failure to support the study of philosophy.

QUESTION 38

Choice C is the best answer because it provides a transition that logically connects the information in the previous sentence to the information in this one. Both sentences provide evidence of colleges' lack of support of philosophy programs, so the adverb "Moreover," which means "In addition," accurately captures the relationship between the two sentences.

Choices A, B, and D are incorrect because each presents a transition that does not accurately depict or support the relationship between the two sentences. The second sentence is not a result of the first ("Therefore," "Thus"), and the sentences do not provide a contrast ("However").

QUESTION 39

Choice A is the best answer because it succinctly expresses the idea that "students who major in philosophy often do better . . . as measured by standardized test scores."

Choices B and D are incorrect because they introduce a redundancy and a vague term, "results." The first part of the sentence mentions a research finding or conclusion but does not directly address any "results," so it is confusing to refer to "these results" and indicate that they "can be" or "are measured by standardized test scores." The best way to express the idea is simply to say that some students "often do better" than some other students "in both verbal reasoning and analytical writing as measured by standardized test scores." Choice C is incorrect because there is no indication that multiple criteria are used to evaluate students' "verbal reasoning and analytical writing": test scores and something else. Only test scores are mentioned.

QUESTION 40

Choice B is the best answer because it provides subject-verb agreement and thus creates a grammatically correct and coherent sentence.

Choice A is incorrect because the verb "has scored" does not correspond with the plural subject "students." Similarly, Choice C is incorrect because the verb "scores" would correspond with a singular subject, but not the plural subject present in this sentence. Choice D is incorrect because it results in a grammatically incomplete and incoherent sentence.

QUESTION 41

Choice B is the best answer because it provides a coherent and grammatically standard sentence.

Choices A and D are incorrect because both present "students" in the possessive form, whereas the sentence establishes "students" as the subject ("many students . . . have"). Choice C is incorrect because the verb form it proposes results in an incomplete and incoherent sentence.

QUESTION 42

Choice C is the best answer because it accurately depicts how inserting this sentence would affect the overall paragraph. The fact that Plato used the dialogue form has little relevance to the preceding claim about the usefulness of a philosophy background.

Choices A and B are incorrect because the proposed sentence interrupts the progression of reasoning in the paragraph. Choice D is incorrect because, as with Choice A, Plato's works have nothing to do with "the employability of philosophy majors."

QUESTION 43

Choice D is the best answer because it creates a complete and coherent sentence.

Choices A, B, and C are incorrect because each inserts an unnecessary relative pronoun or conjunction, resulting in a sentence without a main verb.

Choice D is the best answer because it provides a possessive pronoun that is consistent with the sentence's plural subject "students," thus creating a grammatically sound sentence.

Choices A, B, and C are incorrect because each proposes a possessive pronoun that is inconsistent with the plural noun "students," the established subject of the sentence.

Section 3: Math Test – No Calculator

QUESTION 1

Choice D is correct. Since $k = 3$, one can substitute 3 for k in the equation $\frac{x-1}{3} = k$, which gives $\frac{x-1}{3} = 3$. Multiplying both sides of $\frac{x-1}{3} = 3$ by 3 gives $x - 1 = 9$ and then adding 1 to both sides of $x - 1 = 9$ gives $x = 10$.

Choices A, B, and C are incorrect because the result of subtracting 1 from the value and dividing by 3 is not the given value of k, which is 3.

QUESTION 2

Choice A is correct. To calculate $(7 + 3i + (-8 + 9i)$, add the real parts of each complex number, $7 + (-8) = -1$, and then add the imaginary parts, $3i + 9i = 12i$. The result is $-1 + 12i$.

Choices B, C, and D are incorrect and likely result from common errors that arise when adding complex numbers. For example, choice B is the result of adding $3i$ and $-9i$, and choice C is the result of adding 7 and 8.

QUESTION 3

Choice C is correct. The total number of text messages sent by Armand can be found by multiplying his rate of texting, in number of text messages sent per hour, by the total number of hours he spent sending them; that is m texts/hour × 5 hours = $5m$ texts. Similarly, the total number of text messages sent by Tyrone is his hourly rate of texting multiplied by the 4 hours he spent texting: p texts/hour × 4 hours = $4p$ texts. The total number of text messages sent by Armand and Tyrone is the sum of the total number of messages sent by Armand and the total number of messages sent by Tyrone: $5m + 4p$.

Choice A is incorrect and arises from adding the coefficients and multiplying the variables of $5m$ and $4p$. Choice B is incorrect and is the result of multiplying $5m$ and $4p$. The total number of messages sent by Armand and Tyrone should be the sum of $5m$ and $4p$, not the product of these terms. Choice D is incorrect because it multiplies Armand's number of hours spent texting by Tyrone's hourly rate of texting, and vice versa. This mix-up results in an expression that does not equal the total number of messages sent by Armand and Tyrone.

QUESTION 4

Choice B is correct. The value 108 in the equation is the value of *P* in $P = 108 - 23d$ when $d = 0$. When $d = 0$, Kathy has worked 0 days that week. In other words, 108 is the number of phones left before Kathy has started work for the week. Therefore, the meaning of the value 108 in the equation is that Kathy starts each week with 108 phones to fix.

Choice A is incorrect because Kathy will complete the repairs when $P = 0$. Since $P = 108 - 23d$, this will occur when $0 = 108 - 23d$ or when $d = \frac{108}{23}$, not when $d = 108$. Therefore, the value 108 in the equation does not represent the number of days it will take Kathy to complete the repairs. Choices C and D are incorrect because the number 23 in $P = 108 - 23d$ indicates that the number of phones left will decrease by 23 for each increase in the value of *d* by 1; in other words, Kathy is repairing phones at a rate of 23 per day, not 108 per hour (choice C) or 108 per day (choice D).

QUESTION 5

Choice C is correct. Only like terms, with the same variables and exponents, can be combined to determine the answer as shown here:

$$(x^2y - 3y^2 + 5xy^2 - (-x^2y + 3xy^2 - 3y^2)$$
$$= (x^2y - (-x^2y + (-3y^2 - (-3y^2)) + (5xy^2 - 3xy^2)$$
$$= 2x^2y + 0 + 2xy^2$$
$$= 2x^2y + 2xy^2$$

Choices A, B, and D are incorrect and are the result of common calculation errors or of incorrectly combining like and unlike terms.

QUESTION 6

Choice A is correct. In the equation $h = 3a + 28.6$, if *a*, the age of the boy, increases by 1, then *h* becomes $h = 3(a + 1) + 28.6 = 3a + 3 + 28.6 = 3a + 28.6) + 3$. Therefore, the model estimates that the boy's height increases by 3 inches each year.

Alternatively: The height, *h*, is a linear function of the age, *a*, of the boy. The coefficient 3 can be interpreted as the rate of change of the function; in this case, the rate of change can be described as a change of 3 inches in height for every additional year in age.

Choices B, C, and D are incorrect and are likely the result of dividing 28.6 by 5, 3, and 2, respectively. The number 28.6 is the estimated height, in inches, of a newborn boy. However, dividing 28.6 by 5, 3, or 2 has no meaning in the context of this question.

QUESTION 7

Choice B is correct. Since the right-hand side of the equation is

P times the expression $\dfrac{\left(\dfrac{r}{1,200}\right)\left(1+\dfrac{r}{1,200}\right)^{N}}{\left(1+\dfrac{r}{1,200}\right)^{N}-1}$, multiplying both

sides of the equation by the reciprocal of this expression results

in $\dfrac{\left(1+\dfrac{r}{1,200}\right)^{N}-1}{\left(\dfrac{r}{1,200}\right)\left(1+\dfrac{r}{1,200}\right)^{N}}\,m=P.$

Choice A is incorrect and is the result of multiplying both sides of the

equation by the rational expression $\dfrac{\left(\dfrac{r}{1,200}\right)\left(1+\dfrac{r}{1,200}\right)^{N}}{\left(1+\dfrac{r}{1,200}\right)^{N}-1}$ rather than

by the reciprocal of this expression $\dfrac{\left(1+\dfrac{r}{1,200}\right)^{N}-1}{\left(\dfrac{r}{1,200}\right)\left(1+\dfrac{r}{1,200}\right)^{N}}$. Choices C

and D are incorrect and are likely the result of errors while trying to solve for P.

QUESTION 8

Choice C is correct. Since $\dfrac{a}{b}=2$, it follows that $\dfrac{b}{a}=\dfrac{1}{2}$. Multiplying both

sides of the equation by 4 gives $4\left(\dfrac{b}{a}\right)=4\left(\dfrac{1}{2}\right)$, or $\dfrac{4b}{a}=2$.

Choice A is incorrect because if $\dfrac{4b}{a}=0$, then $\dfrac{a}{b}$ would be undefined.

Choice B is incorrect because if $\dfrac{4b}{a}=1$, then $\dfrac{a}{b}=4$. Choice D is

incorrect because if $\dfrac{4b}{a}=4$, then $\dfrac{a}{b}=1$.

QUESTION 9

Choice B is correct. Adding x and 19 to both sides of $2y-x=-19$
gives $x=2y+19$. Then, substituting $2y+19$ for x in $3x+4y=-23$ gives
$3(2y+19)+4y=-23$. This last equation is equivalent to $10y+57=-23$.
Solving $10y+57=-23$ gives $y=-8$. Finally, substituting -8 for y in
$2y-x=-19$ gives $2(-8)-x=-19$, or $x=3$. Therefore, the solution (x,y)
to the given system of equations is $(3,-8)$.

Choices A, C, and D are incorrect because when the given values of
x and y are substituted in $2y-x=-19$, the value of the left side of the
equation does not equal -19.

QUESTION 10

Choice A is correct. Since g is an even function, $g-4)=g(4)=8$.

Alternatively: First find the value of a, and then find $g(-4)$.
Since $g(4)=8$, substituting 4 for x and 8 for $g(x)$ gives
$8=a(4)^{2}+24=16a+24$. Solving this last equation gives $a=-1$.
Thus $g(x=-x^{2}+24$, from which it follows that
$g-4)=-(-4)^{2}+24$; $g-4)=-16+24$; and $g-4)=8$.

Choices B, C, and D are incorrect because g is a function and there can only be one value of g −4).

QUESTION 11

Choice D is correct. To determine the price per pound of beef when it was equal to the price per pound of chicken, determine the value of x (the number of weeks after July 1) when the two prices were equal. The prices were equal when $b = c$; that is, when $2.35 + 0.25x = 1.75 + 0.40x$. This last equation is equivalent to $0.60 = 0.15x$, and so $x = \frac{0.60}{0.15} = 4$. Then to determine b, the price per pound of beef, substitute 4 for x in $b = 2.35 + 0.25x$, which gives $b = 2.35 + 0.25(4) = 3.35$ dollars per pound.

Choice A is incorrect. It results from substituting the value 1, not 4, for x in $b = 2.35 + 0.25x$. Choice B is incorrect. It results from substituting the value 2, not 4, for x in $b = 2.35 + 0.25x$. Choice C is incorrect. It results from substituting the value 3, not 4, for x in $c = 1.75 + 0.40x$.

QUESTION 12

Choice D is correct. In the xy-plane, all lines that pass through the origin are of the form $y = mx$, where m is the slope of the line. Therefore, the equation of this line is $y = \frac{1}{7}x$, or $x = 7y$. A point with coordinates (a, b) will lie on the line if and only if $a = 7b$. Of the given choices, only choice D, $(14, 2)$, satisfies this condition: $14 = 7(2)$.

Choice A is incorrect because the line determined by the origin $(0, 0)$ and $(0, 7)$ is the vertical line with equation $x = 0$; that is, the y-axis. The slope of the y-axis is undefined, not $\frac{1}{7}$. Therefore, the point $(0, 7)$ does not lie on the line that passes the origin and has slope $\frac{1}{7}$. Choices B and C are incorrect because neither of the ordered pairs has a y-coordinate that is $\frac{1}{7}$ the value of the corresponding x-coordinate.

QUESTION 13

Choice B is correct. To rewrite $\dfrac{1}{\frac{1}{x+2} + \frac{1}{x+3}}$, multiply by $\dfrac{(x+2)(x+3)}{(x+2)(x+3)}$. This results in the expression $\dfrac{(x+2)(x+3)}{(x+2) + (x+3)}$, which is equivalent to the expression in choice B.

Choices A, C, and D are incorrect and could be the result of common algebraic errors that arise while manipulating a complex fraction.

QUESTION 14

Choice A is correct. One approach is to express $\frac{8^x}{2^y}$ so that the numerator and denominator are expressed with the same base. Since 2 and 8 are both powers of 2, substituting 2^3 for 8 in the numerator of $\frac{8^x}{2^y}$ gives $\frac{(2^3)^x}{2^y}$, which can be rewritten as $\frac{2^{3x}}{2^y}$. Since the numerator and denominator of $\frac{2^{3x}}{2^y}$ have a common base, this expression can be rewritten as 2^{3x-y}. It is given that $3x - y = 12$, so one can substitute 12 for the exponent, $3x - y$, given that the expression $\frac{8^x}{2^y}$ is equal to 2^{12}.

Choice B is incorrect. The expression $\frac{8^x}{2^y}$ can be rewritten as $\frac{2^{3x}}{2^y}$, or 2^{3x-y}. If the value of 2^{3x-y} is 4^4, which can be rewritten as 28, then $2^{3x-y} = 2^8$, which results in $3x - y = 8$, not 12. Choice C is incorrect. If the value of $\frac{8^x}{2^y}$ is 8^2, then $2^{3x-y} = 8^2$, which results in $3x - y = 6$, not 12. Choice D is incorrect because the value of $\frac{8^x}{2^y}$ can be determined.

QUESTION 15

Choice D is correct. One can find the possible values of a and b in $(ax + 2)(bx + 7)$ by using the given equation $a + b = 8$ and finding another equation that relates the variables a and b. Since $(ax + 2)(bx + 7) = 15x^2 + cx + 14$, one can expand the left side of the equation to obtain $abx^2 + 7ax + 2bx + 14 = 15x^2 + cx + 14$. Since ab is the coefficient of x^2 on the left side of the equation and 15 is the coefficient of x^2 on the right side of the equation, it must be true that $ab = 15$. Since $a + b = 8$, it follows that $b = 8 - a$. Thus, $ab = 15$ can be rewritten as $a(8 - a) = 15$, which in turn can be rewritten as $a^2 - 8a + 15 = 0$. Factoring gives $(a - 3)(a - 5) = 0$. Thus, either $a = 3$ and $b = 5$, or $a = 5$ and $b = 3$. If $a = 3$ and $b = 5$, then $(ax + 2)(bx + 7) = (3x + 2)(5x + 7) = 15x^2 + 31x + 14$. Thus, one of the possible values of c is 31. If $a = 5$ and $b = 3$, then $(ax + 2)(bx + 7) = (5x + 2)(3x + 7) = 15x^2 + 41x + 14$. Thus, another possible value for c is 41. Therefore, the two possible values for c are 31 and 41.

Choice A is incorrect; the numbers 3 and 5 are possible values for a and b, but not possible values for c. Choice B is incorrect; if $a = 5$ and $b = 3$, then 6 and 35 are the coefficients of x when the expression $(5x + 2)(3x + 7)$ is expanded as $15x^2 + 35x + 6x + 14$. However, when the coefficients of x are 6 and 35, the value of c is 41 and not 6 and 35. Choice C is incorrect; if $a = 3$ and $b = 5$, then 10 and 21 are the coefficients of x when the expression $(3x + 2)(5x + 7)$ is expanded as $15x^2 + 21x + 10x + 14$. However, when the coefficients of x are 10 and 21, the value of c is 31 and not 10 and 21.

QUESTION 16

The correct answer is 2. To solve for t, factor the left side of $t^2 - 4 = 0$, giving $(t - 2)(t + 2) = 0$. Therefore, either $t - 2 = 0$ or $t + 2 = 0$. If $t - 2 = 0$, then $t = 2$, and if $t + 2 = 0$, then $t = -2$. Since it is given that $t > 0$, the value of t must be 2.

Another way to solve for t is to add 4 to both sides of $t^2 - 4 = 0$, giving $t^2 = 4$. Then, taking the square root of the left and the right side of the equation gives $t = \pm\sqrt{4} = \pm 2$. Since it is given that $t > 0$, the value of t must be 2.

QUESTION 17

The correct answer is 1600. It is given that $\angle AEB$ and $\angle CDB$ have the same measure. Since $\angle ABE$ and $\angle CBD$ are vertical angles, they have the same measure. Therefore, triangle EAB is similar to triangle DCB because the triangles have two pairs of congruent corresponding angles (angle-angle criterion for similarity of triangles). Since the triangles are similar, the corresponding sides are in the same proportion; thus $\frac{CD}{x} = \frac{BD}{EB}$. Substituting the given values of 800 for CD, 700 for BD, and 1400 for EB in $\frac{CD}{x} = \frac{BD}{EB}$ gives $\frac{800}{x} = \frac{700}{1400}$. Therefore, $x = \frac{800)(1400)}{700} = 1600$.

QUESTION 18

The correct answer is 7. Subtracting the left and right sides of $x + y = -9$ from the corresponding sides of $x + 2y = -25$ gives $(x + 2y - (x + y = -25 - (-9)$, which is equivalent to $y = -16$. Substituting -16 for y in $x + y = -9$ gives $x + (-16) = -9$, which is equivalent to $x = -9 - (-16) = 7$.

QUESTION 19

The correct answer is $\frac{4}{5}$ or 0.8. By the complementary angle relationship for sine and cosine, $\sin(x°) = \cos(90° - x°)$. Therefore, $\cos(90° - x°) = \frac{4}{5}$. Either the fraction 4/5 or its decimal equivalent, 0.8, may be gridded as the correct answer.

Alternatively, one can construct a right triangle that has an angle of measure $x°$ such that $\sin(x°) = \frac{4}{5}$, as shown in the figure below, where $\sin(x°)$ is equal to the ratio of the length of the side opposite the angle measuring $x°$ to the length of the hypotenuse, or $\frac{4}{5}$.

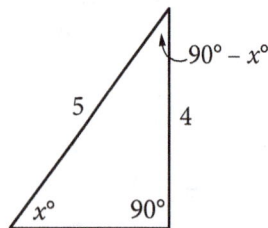

Since two of the angles of the triangle are of measure $x°$ and $90°$, the third angle must have the measure $180° - 90° - x° = 90° - x°$. From the figure, $\cos(90° - x°)$, which is equal to the ratio of the length of the side adjacent to the angle measuring $90° - x°$ to the hypotenuse, is also $\frac{4}{5}$.

QUESTION 20

The correct answer is 100. Since $a = 5\sqrt{2}$, one can substitute $5\sqrt{2}$ for a in $2a = \sqrt{2x}$, giving $10\sqrt{2} = \sqrt{2x}$. Squaring each side of $10\sqrt{2} = \sqrt{2x}$ gives $\left(10\sqrt{2}\right)^2 = \left(\sqrt{2x}\right)^2$, which simplifies to $(10)^2\left(\sqrt{2}\right)^2 = \left(\sqrt{2x}\right)^2$, or $200 = 2x$. This gives $x = 100$. To verify, substitute 100 for x and $5\sqrt{2}$ for a in the equation $2a = \sqrt{2x}$, which yields $2(5\sqrt{2}) = \sqrt{2}(100)$; this is true since $2(5\sqrt{2}) = 10\sqrt{2}$ and $\sqrt{2}(100) = \sqrt{2}\sqrt{100} = 10\sqrt{2}$.

Section 4: Math Test – Calculator

QUESTION 1

Choice B is correct. On the graph, a line segment with a positive slope represents an interval over which the target heart rate is strictly increasing as time passes. A horizontal line segment represents an interval over which there is no change in the target heart rate as time passes, and a line segment with a negative slope represents an interval over which the target heart rate is strictly decreasing as time passes. Over the interval between 40 and 60 minutes, the graph consists of a line segment with a positive slope followed by a line segment with a negative slope, with no horizontal line segment in between, indicating that the target heart rate is strictly increasing then strictly decreasing.

Choice A is incorrect because the graph over the interval between 0 and 30 minutes contains a horizontal line segment, indicating a period in which there was no change in the target heart rate. Choice C is incorrect because the graph over the interval between 50 and 65 minutes consists of a line segment with a negative slope followed by a line segment with a positive slope, indicating that the target heart rate is strictly decreasing then strictly increasing. Choice D is incorrect because the graph over the interval between 70 and 90 minutes contains horizontal line segments and no segment with a negative slope.

QUESTION 2

Choice C is correct. Substituting 6 for x and 24 for y in $y = kx$ gives $24 = (k)(6)$, which gives $k = 4$. Hence, $y = 4x$. Therefore, when $x = 5$, the value of y is $(4)(5) = 20$. None of the other choices for y is correct because y is a function of x, and so there is only one y-value for a given x-value.

Choices A, B, and D are incorrect. Choice A is the result of substituting 6 for y and substituting 5 for x in the equation $y = kx$, when solving for k. Choice B results from substituting 3 for k and 5 for x in the equation $y = kx$, when solving for y. Choice D results from using $y = k + x$ instead of $y = kx$.

QUESTION 3

Choice D is correct. Consider the measures of ∠3 and ∠4 in the figure below.

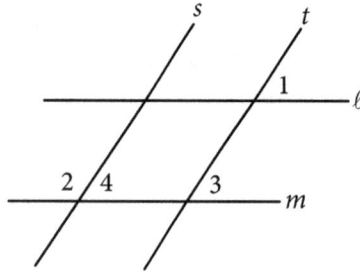

The measure of ∠3 is equal to the measure of ∠1 because they are corresponding angles for the parallel lines ℓ and m intersected by the transversal line t. Similarly, the measure of ∠3 is equal to the measure of ∠4 because they are corresponding angles for the parallel lines s and t intersected by the transversal line m. Since the measure of ∠1 is 35°, the measures of ∠3 and ∠4 are also 35°. Since ∠4 and ∠2 are supplementary angles, the sum of the measures of these two angles is 180°. Therefore, the measure of ∠2 is 180° − 35° = 145°.

Choice A is incorrect because 35° is the measure of ∠1, and ∠1 is not congruent to ∠2. Choice B is incorrect because it is the measure of the complementary angle of ∠1, and ∠1 and ∠2 are not complementary angles. Choice C is incorrect because it is double the measure of ∠1, which cannot be inferred from the information given.

QUESTION 4

Choice C is correct. The description "16 + 4x is 10 more than 14" can be written as the equation 16 + 4x = 10 + 14, which is equivalent to 16 + 4x = 24. Subtracting 16 from each side of 16 + 4x = 24 gives 4x = 8. Since 8x is 2 times 4x, multiplying both sides of 4x = 8 by 2 gives 8x = 16. Therefore, the value of 8x is 16.

Choice A is incorrect because it is the value of x, not 8x. Choices B and D are incorrect and may be the result of errors made when solving the equation 16 + 4x = 10 + 14 for x. For example, choice D could be the result of subtracting 16 from the left side of the equation and adding 16 to the right side of the equation 16 + 4x = 10 + 14, giving 4x = 40 and 8x = 80.

QUESTION 5

Choice D is correct. A graph with a strong negative association between d and t would have the points on the graph closely aligned with a line that has a negative slope. The more closely the points on a graph are aligned with a line, the stronger the association between d and t, and a negative slope indicates a negative association. Of the four graphs, the points on graph D are most closely aligned with a line with a negative slope. Therefore, the graph in choice D has the strongest negative association between d and t.

Choice A is incorrect because the points are more scattered than the points in choice D, indicating a weaker negative association between *d* and *t*. Choice B is incorrect because the points are aligned to either a curve or possibly a line with a small positive slope. Choice C is incorrect because the points are aligned to a line with a positive slope, indicating a positive association between *d* and *t*.

QUESTION 6

Choice D is correct. Since there are 10 grams in 1 decagram, there are 2 × 10 = 20 grams in 2 decagrams. Since there are 1,000 milligrams in 1 gram, there are 20 × 1,000 = 20,000 milligrams in 20 grams. Therefore, 20,000 1-milligram doses of the medicine can be stored in a 2-decagram container.

Choice A is incorrect; 0.002 is the number of grams in 2 milligrams. Choice B is incorrect; it could result from multiplying by 1,000 and dividing by 10 instead of multiplying by both 1,000 and 10 when converting from decagrams to milligrams. Choice C is incorrect; 2,000 is the number of milligrams in 2 grams, not the number of milligrams in 2 decagrams.

QUESTION 7

Choice C is correct. Let *x* represent the number of installations that each unit on the *y*-axis represents. Then $9x$, $5x$, $6x$, $4x$, and $3.5x$ are the number of rooftops with solar panel installations in cities A, B, C, D, and E, respectively. Since the total number of rooftops is 27,500, it follows that $9x + 5x + 6x + 4x + 3.5x = 27,500$, which simplifies to $27.5x = 27,500$. Thus, $x = 1,000$. Therefore, an appropriate label for the *y*-axis is "Number of installations (in thousands)."

Choices A, B, and D are incorrect and may result from errors when setting up and calculating the units for the *y*-axis.

QUESTION 8

Choice D is correct. If the value of $|n - 1| + 1$ is equal to 0, then $|n - 1| + 1 = 0$. Subtracting 1 from both sides of this equation gives $|n - 1| = -1$. The expression $|n - 1|$ on the left side of the equation is the absolute value of $n - 1$, and the absolute value of a quantity can never be negative. Thus $|n - 1| = -1$ has no solution. Therefore, there are no values for *n* for which the value of $|n - 1| + 1$ is equal to 0.

Choice A is incorrect because $|0 - 1| + 1 = 1 + 1 = 2$, not 0. Choice B is incorrect because $|1 - 1| + 1 = 0 + 1 = 1$, not 0. Choice C is incorrect because $|2 - 1| + 1 = 1 + 1 = 2$, not 0.

QUESTION 9

Choice A is correct. Subtracting 1,052 from both sides of the equation $a = 1,052 + 1.08t$ gives $a - 1,052 = 1.08t$. Then dividing both sides of $a - 1,052 = 1.08t$ by 1.08 gives $t = \dfrac{a - 1,052}{1.08}$.

Choices B, C, and D are incorrect and could arise from errors in rewriting $a = 1,052 + 1.08t$. For example, choice B could result if 1,052 is added to the left side of $a = 1,052 + 1.08t$ and subtracted from the right side, and then both sides are divided by 1.08.

QUESTION 10

Choice B is correct. The air temperature at which the speed of a sound wave is closest to 1,000 feet per second can be found by substituting 1,000 for a and then solving for t in the given formula. Substituting 1,000 for a in the equation $a = 1,052 + 1.08t$ gives $1,000 = 1,052 + 1.08t$. Subtracting 1,052 from both sides of the equation $1,000 = 1,052 + 1.08t$ and then dividing both sides of the equation by 1.08 yields $t = \frac{-52}{1.08} \approx -48.15$. Of the choices given, −48°F is closest to −48.15°F.

Choices A, C, and D are incorrect and might arise from errors made when substituting 1,000 for a or solving for t in the equation $a = 1,052 + 1.08t$ or in rounding the result to the nearest integer. For example, choice C could be the result of rounding −48.15 to −49 instead of −48.

QUESTION 11

Choice A is correct. Subtracting $3x$ and adding 3 to both sides of $3x - 5 \geq 4x - 3$ gives $-2 \geq x$. Therefore, x is a solution to $3x - 5 \geq 4x - 3$ if and only if x is less than or equal to −2 and x is NOT a solution to $3x - 5 \geq 4x - 3$ if and only if x is greater than −2. Of the choices given, only −1 is greater than −2 and, therefore, cannot be a value of x.

Choices B, C, and D are incorrect because each is a value of x that is less than or equal to −2 and, therefore, could be a solution to the inequality.

QUESTION 12

Choice C is correct. The average number of seeds per apple is the total number of seeds in the 12 apples divided by the number of apples, which is 12. On the graph, the horizontal axis is the number of seeds per apple and the height of each bar is the number of apples with the corresponding number of seeds. The first bar on the left indicates that 2 apples have 3 seeds each, the second bar indicates that 4 apples have 5 seeds each, the third bar indicates that 1 apple has 6 seeds, the fourth bar indicates that 2 apples have 7 seeds each, and the fifth bar indicates that 3 apples have 9 seeds each. Thus, the total number of seeds for the 12 apples is $2 \times 3) + (4 \times 5) + (1 \times 6) + (2 \times 7) + (3 \times 9) = 73$, and the average number of seeds per apple is $\frac{73}{12} = 6.08$. Of the choices given, 6 is closest to 6.08.

Choice A is incorrect; it is the number of apples represented by the tallest bar but is not the average number of seeds for the 12 apples. Choice B is incorrect; it is the number of seeds per apple corresponding to the tallest bar, but is not the average number of seeds for the 12 apples. Choice D is incorrect; a student might choose this value by correctly calculating the average number of seeds, 6.08, but incorrectly rounding up to 7.

QUESTION 13

Choice C is correct. From the table, there was a total of 310 survey respondents, and 19% of all survey respondents is equivalent to $\frac{19}{100} \times 310 = 58.9$ respondents. Of the choices given, 59, the number of males taking Geometry, is closest to 58.9 respondents.

Choices A, B, and D are incorrect because the number of males taking Geometry is closer to 58.9 (which is 19% of 310) than the number of respondents in each of these categories.

QUESTION 14

Choice C is correct. The range of the lengths of the 21 fish represented in the table is $24 - 8 = 16$ inches, and the range of the remaining 20 lengths after the 24-inch measurement is removed is $16 - 8 = 8$ inches. Therefore, after the 24-inch measurement is removed, the change in range, 8 inches, is much greater than the change in the mean or median.

Choice A is incorrect. Let m be the mean of the lengths, in inches, of the 21 fish. Then the sum of the lengths, in inches, of the 21 fish is $21m$. After the 24-inch measurement is removed, the sum of the lengths, in inches, of the remaining 20 fish is $21m - 24$, and the mean length, in inches, of these 20 fish is $\frac{21m - 24}{20}$, which is a change of $\frac{24 - m}{20}$ inches. Since m must be between the smallest and largest measurements of the 21 fish, it follows that $8 < m < 24$, from which it can be seen that the change in the mean, in inches, is between $\frac{24 - 24}{20} = 0$ and $\frac{24 - 8}{20} = \frac{4}{5}$, and so must be less than the change in the range, 8 inches. Choice B is incorrect because the median length of the 21 fish represented in the table is 12, and after the 24-inch measurement is removed, the median of the remaining 20 lengths is also 12. Therefore, the change in the median (0) is less than the change in the range (8). Choice D is incorrect because the changes in the mean, median, and range of the measurements are different.

QUESTION 15

Choice A is correct. The total cost C of renting a boat is the sum of the initial cost to rent the boat plus the product of the cost per hour and the number of hours, h, that the boat is rented. The C-intercept is the point on the C-axis where h, the number of hours the boat is rented, is 0. Therefore, the C-intercept is the initial cost of renting the boat.

Choice B is incorrect because the graph represents the cost of renting only one boat. Choice C is incorrect because the total number of hours of rental is represented by h-values, each of which corresponds to the first coordinate of a point on the graph not the C-intercept of the graph. Choice D is incorrect because the increase in cost for each additional hour is given by the slope of the line, not by the C-intercept.

QUESTION 16

Choice C is correct. If m is the slope and b is the C-intercept of the line, the relationship between h and C can be represented by $C = mh + b$. The C-intercept of the line is 5. Since the points (0, 5) and (1, 8) lie on the line, the slope of the line is $\frac{8-5}{1-0} = \frac{3}{1} = 3$. Therefore, the relationship between h and C can be represented by $C = 3h + 5$, the slope-intercept equation of the line.

Choices A and D are incorrect because each of these equations represents a line that passes through the origin (0, 0). However, C is not equal to zero when $h = 0$. Choice B is incorrect and may result from errors made when reading the scale on each axis as related to calculating the slope.

QUESTION 17

Choice B is correct. The minimum value of the function corresponds to the y-coordinate of the point on the graph that has the smallest y-coordinate on the graph. Since the smallest y-coordinate belongs to the point with coordinates (−3, −2), the minimum value of the graph is $f(−3) = −2$. Therefore, the minimum value of $f(x)$ is at $x = −3$.

Choice A is incorrect; −5 is the least value for an x-coordinate, not the y-coordinate, of a point on the graph of $y = f(x)$. Choice C is incorrect; it is the minimum value of f, not the value of x that corresponds to the minimum of f. Choice D is incorrect; it is the value of x for which the value of $f(x)$ has its <u>maximum</u>, not minimum.

QUESTION 18

Choice A is correct. Since (0, 0) is a solution to the system of inequalities, substituting 0 for x and 0 for y in the given system must result in two true inequalities. After this substitution, $y < −x + a$ becomes $0 < a$, and $y > x + b$ becomes $0 > b$. Hence, a is positive and b is negative. Therefore, $a > b$.

Choice B is incorrect because $b > a$ cannot be true if b is negative and a is positive. Choice C is incorrect because it is possible to find an example where (0, 0) is a solution to the system, but $|a| < |b|$; for example, if $a = 6$ and $b = −7$. Choice D is incorrect because the equation $a = −b$ doesn't have to be true; for example, (0, 0) is a solution to the system of inequalities if $a = 1$ and $b = −2$.

QUESTION 19

Choice B is correct. To determine the number of salads sold, write and solve a system of two equations. Let x equal the number of salads sold and let y equal the number of drinks sold. Since a total of 209 salads and drinks were sold, the equation $x + y = 209$ must hold. Since salads cost $6.50 each, drinks cost $2.00 each, and the total revenue from selling x salads and y drinks was $836.50, the equation $6.50x + 2.00y = 836.50$ must also hold. The equation $x + y = 209$ is equivalent to $2x + 2y = 418$, and subtracting $(2x + 2y)$ from the left-hand side and subtracting 418 from the right-hand side of $6.50x + 2.00y = 836.50$ gives $4.5x = 418.50$. Therefore, the number of salads sold, x, was $x = \frac{418.50}{4.50} = 93$.

Choices A, C, and D are incorrect and could result from errors in writing the equations and solving the system of equations. For example, choice C could have been obtained by dividing the total revenue, $836.50, by the total price of a salad and a drink, $8.50, and then rounding up.

QUESTION 20

Choice D is correct. Let x be the original price of the computer, in dollars. The discounted price is 20 percent off the original price, so $x - 0.2x = 0.8x$ is the discounted price, in dollars. The sales tax is 8 percent of the discounted price, so $0.08(0.8x)$ represents the sales tax Alma paid. The price p, in dollars, that Alma paid the cashiers is the sum of the discounted price and the tax: $p = 0.8x + (0.08)(0.8x)$ which can be rewritten as $p = 1.08(0.8x)$. Therefore, the original price, x, of the computer, in dollars, can be written as $\frac{p}{0.8)(1.08)}$ in terms of p.

Choices A, B, and C are incorrect. The expression in choice A represents 88% of the amount Alma paid to the cashier, and can be obtained by subtracting the discount of 20% from the original price and adding the sales tax of 8%. However, this is incorrect because 8% of the tax is over the discounted price, not the original one. The expression in choice B is the result of adding the factors associated with the discount and sales tax, 0.8 and .08, rather than multiplying them. The expression in choice C results from assigning p to represent the original price of the laptop, rather than to the amount Alma paid to the cashier.

QUESTION 21

Choice C is correct. The probability that a person from Group Y who recalled at least 1 dream was chosen at random from the group of all people who recalled at least 1 dream is equal to the number of people in Group Y who recalled at least 1 dream divided by the total number of people in the two groups who recalled at least 1 dream. The number of people in Group Y who recalled at least 1 dream is the sum of the 11 people in Group Y who recalled 1 to 4 dreams and the 68 people in Group Y who recalled 5 or more dreams: $11 + 68 = 79$. The total number of people who recalled at least 1 dream is the sum of the 79 people in Group Y who recalled at least 1 dream, the 28 people in Group X who recalled 1 to 4 dreams, and the 57 people in Group X who recalled 5 or more dreams: $79 + 28 + 57 = 164$. Therefore, the probability is $\frac{79}{164}$.

Choice A is incorrect; it is the probability of choosing at random a person from Group Y who recalled 5 or more dreams. Choice B is incorrect; it is the probability of choosing at random a person from Group Y who recalled at least 1 dream. Choice D is incorrect; it is the probability of choosing at random a person from the two groups combined who recalled at least 1 dream.

QUESTION 22

Choice B is correct. The amounts given in the table are in thousands of dollars. Therefore, the amount in the annual budget for agriculture/natural resources is actually $488,106,000 in 2010 and $358,708,000 in 2008. Therefore, the change in the budgeted amount is $488,106,000 − $358,708,000 = $129,398,000. Hence, the average change in the annual budget for agriculture/natural resources from 2008 to 2010 is $\frac{\$129,398,000}{2}$ = $64,699,000 per year. Of the options given, this average rate of change is closest to $65,000,000 per year.

Choices A and C are incorrect and may result from errors in setting up or calculating the average rate of change. Choice D is incorrect; $130,000,000 is the approximate total change in the annual budget for agriculture/natural resources from 2008 to 2010, not the average rate of change from 2008 to 2010.

QUESTION 23

Choice B is correct. The human resources budget in 2007 was 4,051,050 thousand dollars, and the human resources budget in 2010 was 5,921,379 thousand dollars. Therefore, the ratio of the 2007 budget to the 2010 budget is slightly greater than $\frac{4}{6} = \frac{2}{3}$. Similar estimates for agriculture/natural resources give a ratio of the 2007 budget to the 2010 budget of slightly greater than $\frac{3}{4}$; for education, a ratio of slightly greater than $\frac{2}{3}$; for highways and transportation, a ratio of slightly less than $\frac{5}{6}$; and for public safety, a ratio of slightly greater than $\frac{5}{9}$. Therefore, of the given choices, education's ratio of the 2007 budget to the 2010 budget is closest to that of human resources.

Choices A, C, and D are incorrect because the ratio of the 2007 budget to 2010 budget for each of the programs given in these choices is further from the corresponding ratio for human resources than the corresponding ratio for education.

QUESTION 24

Choice A is correct. The equation of a circle can be written as $(x - h)^2 + (y - k)^2 = r^2$ where (h, k) are the coordinates of the center of the circle and r is the radius of the circle. Since the coordinates of the center of the circle are (0, 4), the equation of the circle is $x^2 + (y - 4)^2 = r^2$. The radius of the circle is the distance from the center, 0, 4), to the given endpoint of a radius, $\left(\frac{4}{3}, 5\right)$. By the distance formula, $r^2 = \left(\frac{4}{3} - 0\right)^2 + (5 - 4)^2 = \frac{25}{9}$. Therefore, an equation of the given circle is $x^2 + (y - 4)^2 = \frac{25}{9}$.

Choices B and D are incorrect. The equations given in these choices represent a circle with center (0, −4), not (0, 4). Choice C is incorrect; it results from using r instead of r^2 in the equation for the circle.

QUESTION 25

Choice D is correct. When the ball hits the ground, its height is 0 meters. Substituting 0 for h in $h = -4.9t^2 + 25t$ gives $0 = -4.9t^2 + 25t$, which can be rewritten as $0 = t(-4.9t + 25)$. Thus, the possible values of t are $t = 0$ and $t = \frac{25}{4.9} \approx 5.1$. The time $t = 0$ seconds corresponds to the time the ball is launched from the ground, and the time $t \approx 5.1$ seconds corresponds to the time after launch that the ball hits the ground. Of the given choices, 5.0 seconds is closest to 5.1 seconds, so the ball returns to the ground approximately 5.0 seconds after it is launched.

Choice A, B, and C are incorrect and could arise from conceptual or computation errors while solving $0 = -4.9t^2 + 25t$ for t.

QUESTION 26

Choice B is correct. Let x represent the number of pears produced by the Type B trees. Type A trees produce 20 percent more pears than Type B trees, or x, which can be represented as $x + 0.20x = 1.20x$ pears. Since Type A trees produce 144 pears, it follows that $1.20x = 144$. Thus $x = \frac{144}{1.20} = 120$. Therefore, the Type B trees produced 120 pears.

Choice A is incorrect because while 144 is reduced by approximately 20 percent, increasing 115 by 20 percent gives 138, not 144. Choice C is incorrect; it results from subtracting 20 from the number of pears produced by the Type A trees. Choice D is incorrect; it results from adding 20 percent of the number of pears produced by Type A trees to the number of pears produced by Type A trees.

QUESTION 27

Choice C is correct. The area of the field is 100 square meters. Each 1-meter-by-1-meter square has an area of 1 square meter. Thus, on average, the earthworm counts to a depth of 5 centimeters for each of the regions investigated by the students should be about $\frac{1}{100}$ of the total number of earthworms to a depth of 5 centimeters in the entire field. Since the counts for the smaller regions are from 107 to 176, the estimate for the entire field should be between 10,700 and 17,600. Therefore, of the given choices, 15,000 is a reasonable estimate for the number of earthworms to a depth of 5 centimeters in the entire field.

Choice A is incorrect; 150 is the approximate number of earthworms in 1 square meter. Choice B is incorrect; it results from using 10 square meters as the area of the field. Choice D is incorrect; it results from using 1,000 square meters as the area of the field.

QUESTION 28

Choice C is correct. To determine which quadrant does not contain any solutions to the system of inequalities, graph the inequalities. Graph the inequality $y \geq 2x + 1$ by drawing a line through the y-intercept $(0, 1)$ and the point $(1, 3)$, as shown. The solutions to this inequality are all points contained on and above this line. Graph the inequality $y > \frac{1}{2}x - 1$ by drawing a dashed line through the y-intercept $(0, -1)$ and the point $(2, 0)$, as shown. The solutions to this inequality are all points above this dashed line.

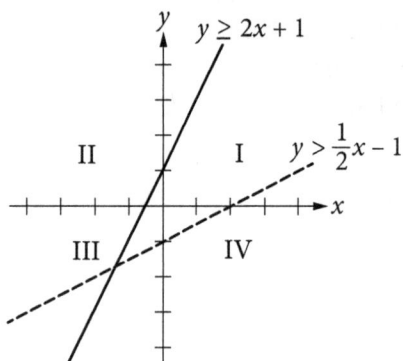

The solution to the system of inequalities is the intersection of the regions above the graphs of both lines. It can be seen that the solutions only include points in quadrants I, II, and III and do not include any points in quadrant IV.

Choices A and B are incorrect because quadrants II and III contain solutions to the system of inequalities, as shown in the figure above. Choice D is incorrect because there are no solutions in quadrant IV.

QUESTION 29

Choice D is correct. If the polynomial $p(x)$ is divided by $x - 3$, the result can be written as $\frac{p(x)}{x-3} = q(x) + \frac{r}{x-3}$, where $q(x)$ is a polynomial and r is the remainder. Since $x - 3$ is a degree 1 polynomial, the remainder is a real number. Hence, $p(x)$ can be written as $p(x) = (x - 3)q(x) + r$, where r is a real number. It is given that $p(3) = -2$ so it must be true that $-2 = p$ 3$) = (3 - 3)q$ 3$) + r = (0)q$ 3$) + r = r$. Therefore, the remainder when $p(x)$ is divided by $x - 3$ is -2.

Choice A is incorrect because p 3$) = -2$ does <u>not</u> imply that $p(5) = 0$. Choices B and C are incorrect because the remainder -2 or its opposite, 2, need not be a root of $p(x)$.

QUESTION 30

Choice D is correct. Any quadratic function q can be written in the form $q(x) = a(x - h)^2 + k$, where a, h, and k are constants and (h, k) is the vertex of the parabola when q is graphed in the coordinate plane. This form can be reached by completing the square in the expression that defines q. The equation of the graph is $y = x^2 - 2x - 15$.

Since the coefficient of x is -2, this equation can be written in terms of $(x-1)^2 = x^2 - 2x + 1$ as follows: $y = x^2 - 2x - 15 = (x^2 - 2x + 1) - 16 = (x-1)^2 - 16$. From this form of the equation, the coefficients of the vertex can be read as $(1, -16)$.

Choices A and C are incorrect because the coordinates of the vertex A do not appear as constants in these equations. Choice B is incorrect because it is not equivalent to the given equation.

QUESTION 31

The correct answer is any number between 4 and 6, inclusive. Since Wyatt can husk at least 12 dozen ears of corn per hour, it will take him no more than $\frac{72}{12} = 6$ hours to husk 72 dozen ears of corn. On the other hand, since Wyatt can husk at most 18 dozen ears of corn per hour, it will take him at least $\frac{72}{18} = 4$ hours to husk 72 dozen ears of corn.

Therefore, the possible times it could take Wyatt to husk 72 dozen ears of corn are 4 hours to 6 hours, inclusive. Any number between 4 and 6, inclusive, can be gridded as the correct answer.

QUESTION 32

The correct answer is 107. Since the weight of the empty truck and its driver is 4500 pounds and each box weighs 14 pounds, the weight, in pounds, of the delivery truck, its driver, and x boxes is $4500 + 14x$. This weight is below the bridge's posted weight limit of 6000 pounds if $4500 + 14x < 6000$. Subtracting 4500 from both sides of this inequality and then dividing both sides by 14 yields $x < \frac{1500}{14}$ or $x < 107\frac{1}{7}$. Since the number of packages must be an integer, the maximum possible value for x that will keep the combined weight of the truck, its driver, and the x identical boxes below the bridge's posted weight limit is 107.

QUESTION 33

The correct answer is $\frac{5}{8}$ or .625. Based on the line graph, the number of portable media players sold in 2008 was 100 million, and the number of portable media players sold in 2011 was 160 million. Therefore, the number of portable media players sold in 2008 is $\frac{100 \text{ million}}{160 \text{ million}}$ of the portable media players sold in 2011. This fraction reduces to $\frac{5}{8}$.

Either 5/8 or its decimal equivalent, .625, may be gridded as the correct answer.

QUESTION 34

The correct answer is 96. Since each day has a total of 24 hours of time slots available for the station to sell, there is a total of 48 hours of time slots available to sell on Tuesday and Wednesday. Each time slot is a 30-minute interval, which is equal to a $\frac{1}{2}$-hour interval. Therefore, there are $\dfrac{48 \text{ hours}}{\frac{1}{2} \text{ hours/time slot}}$ = 96 time slots of 30 minutes for the station to sell on Tuesday and Wednesday.

QUESTION 35

The correct answer is 6. The volume of a cylinder is $\pi r^2 h$, where r is the radius of the base of the cylinder and h is the height of the cylinder. Since the storage silo is a cylinder with volume 72π cubic yards and height 8 yards, it follows that $72\pi = \pi r^2(8)$, where r is the radius of the base of the cylinder, in yards. Dividing both sides of the equation $72\pi = \pi r^2(8)$ by 8π gives $r^2 = 9$, and so the radius of the base of the cylinder is 3 yards. Therefore, the <u>diameter</u> of the base of the cylinder is 6 yards.

QUESTION 36

The correct answer is 3. The function $h(x)$ is undefined when the denominator of $\dfrac{1}{(x-5)^2 + 4(x-5) + 4}$ is equal to zero. The expression $(x-5)^2 + 4(x-5) + 4$ is a perfect square: $(x-5)^2 + 4(x-5) + 4 = ((x-5) + 2)^2$, which can be rewritten as $(x-3)^2$. The expression $(x-3)^2$ is equal to zero if and only if $x = 3$. Therefore, the value of x for which $h(x$ is undefined is 3.

QUESTION 37

The correct answer is 1.02. The initial deposit earns 2 percent interest compounded annually. Thus at the end of 1 year, the new value of the account is the initial deposit of $100 plus 2 percent of the initial deposit: $100 + \dfrac{2}{100}$ ($100) = $100(1.02). Since the interest is compounded annually, the value at the end of each succeeding year is the sum of the previous year's value plus 2 percent of the previous year's value. This is again equivalent to multiplying the previous year's value by 1.02. Thus, after 2 years, the value will be $100(1.02)(1.02) = $100(1.02)^2$; after 3 years, the value will be $100(1.02)^3$; and after t years, the value will be $100(1.02)^t$. Therefore, in the formula for the value for Jessica's account after t years, $100(x)^t$, the value of x must be 1.02.

QUESTION 38

The correct answer is 6.11. Jessica made an initial deposit of $100 into her account. The interest on her account is 2 percent compounded annually, so after 10 years, the value of her initial deposit has been multiplied 10 times by the factor $1 + 0.02 = 1.02$. Hence, after 10 years, Jessica's deposit is worth $100(1.02)^{10} = \$121.899$ to the nearest tenth of a cent. Tyshaun made an initial deposit of $100 into his account. The interest on his account is 2.5 percent compounded annually, so after 10 years, the value of his initial deposit has been multiplied 10 times by the factor $1 + 0.025 = 1.025$. Hence, after 10 years, Tyshaun's deposit is worth $100(1.025)^{10} = \$128.008$ to the nearest tenth of a cent. Hence, Jessica's initial deposit earned $21.899 and Tyshaun's initial deposit earned $28.008. Therefore, to the nearest cent, Tyshaun's initial deposit earned $6.11 more than Jessica's initial deposit.

Answer Explanations

SAT Practice Test #2

Section 1: Reading Test

QUESTION 1

Choice A is the best answer. The narrator admits that his job is "irksome" (line 7) and reflects on the reasons for his dislike. The narrator admits that his work is a "dry and tedious task" (line 9) and that he has a poor relationship with his superior: "the antipathy which had sprung up between myself and my employer striking deeper root and spreading denser shade daily, excluded me from every glimpse of the sunshine of life" (lines 28-31).

Choices B, C, and D are incorrect because the narrator does not become increasingly competitive with his employer, publicly defend his choice of occupation, or exhibit optimism about his job.

QUESTION 2

Choice B is the best answer. The first sentence of the passage explains that people do not like to admit when they've chosen the wrong profession and that they will continue in their profession for a while before admitting their unhappiness. This statement mirrors the narrator's own situation, as the narrator admits he finds his own occupation "irksome" (line 7) but that he might "long have borne with the nuisance" (line 10) if not for his poor relationship with his employer.

Choices A, C, and D are incorrect because the first sentence does not discuss a controversy, focus on the narrator's employer, Edward Crimsworth, or provide any evidence of malicious conduct.

QUESTION 3

Choice C is the best answer. The first paragraph shifts from a general discussion of how people deal with choosing an occupation they later regret (lines 1-6) to the narrator's description of his own dissatisfaction with his occupation (lines 6-33).

Choices A, B, and D are incorrect because the first paragraph does not focus on the narrator's self-doubt, his expectations of life as a tradesman, or his identification of alternatives to his current occupation.

QUESTION 4

Choice A is the best answer. In lines 27-33, the narrator is describing the hostile relationship between him and his superior, Edward Crimsworth. This relationship causes the narrator to feel like he lives in the "shade" and in "humid darkness." These words evoke the narrator's feelings of dismay toward his current occupation and his poor relationship with his superior — factors that cause him to live without "the sunshine of life."

Choices B, C, and D are incorrect because the words "shade" and "darkness" do not reflect the narrator's sinister thoughts, his fear of confinement, or his longing for rest.

QUESTION 5

Choice D is the best answer. The narrator states that Crimsworth dislikes him because the narrator may "one day make a successful tradesman" (line 43). Crimsworth recognizes that the narrator is not "inferior to him" but rather more intelligent, someone who keeps "the padlock of silence on mental wealth in which [Crimsworth] was no sharer" (lines 44-48). Crimsworth feels inferior to the narrator and is jealous of the narrator's intellectual and professional abilities.

Choices A and C are incorrect because the narrator is not described as exhibiting "high spirits" or "rash actions," but "Caution, Tact, [and] Observation" (line 51). Choice B is incorrect because the narrator's "humble background" is not discussed.

QUESTION 6

Choice B is the best answer. Lines 61-62 state that the narrator "had long ceased to regard Mr. Crimsworth as my brother." In these lines, the term "brother" means friend or ally, which suggests that the narrator and Crimsworth were once friendly toward one another.

Choices A, C, and D are incorrect because the narrator originally viewed Crimsworth as a friend, or ally, and later as a hostile superior; he never viewed Crimsworth as a harmless rival, perceptive judge, or demanding mentor.

QUESTION 7

Choice D is the best answer. In lines 61-62, the narrator states that he once regarded Mr. Crimsworth as his "brother." This statement provides evidence that the narrator originally viewed Crimsworth as a sympathetic ally.

Choices A, B, and C do not provide the best evidence for the claim that Crimsworth was a sympathetic ally. Rather, choices A, B, and C provide evidence of the hostile relationship that currently exists between the narrator and Crimsworth.

QUESTION 8

Choice D is the best answer. In lines 48-53, the narrator states that he exhibited "Caution, Tact, [and] Observation" at work and watched Mr. Crimsworth with "lynx-eyes." The narrator acknowledges that Crimsworth was "prepared to steal snake-like" if he caught the narrator acting without tact or being disrespectful toward his superiors (lines 53-56). Thus, Crimsworth was trying to find a reason to place the narrator "in a ridiculous or mortifying position" (lines 49-50) by accusing the narrator of acting unprofessionally. The use of the lynx and snake serve to emphasize the narrator and Crimsworth's adversarial, or hostile, relationship.

Choices A and B are incorrect because the description of the lynx and snake does not contrast two hypothetical courses of action or convey a resolution. Choice C is incorrect because while lines 48-56 suggest that Crimsworth is trying to find a reason to fault the narrator's work, they do not imply that an altercation, or heated dispute, between the narrator and Crimsworth is likely to occur.

QUESTION 9

Choice B is the best answer. Lines 73-74 state that the narrator noticed there was no "cheering red gleam" of fire in his sitting-room fireplace. The lack of a "cheering," or comforting, fire suggests that the narrator sometimes found his lodgings to be dreary or bleak.

Choices A and D are incorrect because the narrator does not find his living quarters to be treacherous or intolerable. Choice C is incorrect because while the narrator is walking home he speculates about the presence of a fire in his sitting-room's fireplace (lines 69-74), which suggests that he could not predict the state of his living quarters.

QUESTION 10

Choice D is the best answer. In lines 68-74, the narrator states that he did not see the "cheering" glow of a fire in his sitting-room fireplace. This statement provides evidence that the narrator views his lodgings as dreary or bleak.

Choices A, B, and C do not provide the best evidence that the narrator views his lodgings as dreary. Choices A and C are incorrect because they do not provide the narrator's opinion of his lodgings, and choice B is incorrect because lines 21-23 describe the narrator's lodgings only as "small."

QUESTION 11

Choice D is the best answer. In lines 11-12, the author introduces the main purpose of the passage, which is to examine the "different views on where ethics should apply when someone makes an economic decision." The passage examines what historical figures Adam Smith, Aristotle, and John Stuart Mill believed about the relationship between ethics and economics.

Choices A, B, and C are incorrect because they identify certain points addressed in the passage (cost-benefit analysis, ethical economic behavior, and the role of the free market), but do not describe the passage's main purpose.

QUESTION 12

Choice D is the best answer. In lines 4-5, the author suggests that people object to criticizing ethics in free markets because they believe free markets are inherently ethical, and therefore, the role of ethics in free markets is unnecessary to study. In the opinion of the critics, free markets are ethical because they allow individuals to make their own choices about which goods to purchase and which goods to sell.

Choices A and B are incorrect because they are not objections that criticize the ethics of free markets. Choice C is incorrect because the author does not present the opinion that free markets depend on devalued currency.

QUESTION 13

Choice A is the best answer. In lines 4-5, the author states that some people believe that free markets are "already ethical" because they "allow for personal choice." This statement provides evidence that some people believe criticizing the ethics of free markets is unnecessary because free markets permit individuals to make their own choices.

Choices B, C, and D are incorrect because they do not provide the best evidence of an objection to a critique of the ethics of free markets.

QUESTION 14

Choice B is the best answer. In lines 6-7, the author states that people "have accepted the ethical critique and embraced corporate social responsibility." In this context, people "embrace," or readily adopt, corporate social responsibility by acting in a certain way.

Choices A, C, and D are incorrect because in this context "embraced" does not mean lovingly held, eagerly hugged, or reluctantly used.

QUESTION 15

Choice C is the best answer. The third and fourth paragraphs of the passage present Adam Smith's and Aristotle's different approaches to defining ethics in economics. The fifth paragraph offers a third approach to defining ethical economics, how "instead of rooting ethics in character or the consequences of actions, we can focus on our actions themselves. From this perspective some things are right, some wrong" (lines 45-48).

Choice A is incorrect because the fifth paragraph does not develop a counterargument. Choices B and D are incorrect because although "character" is briefly mentioned in the fifth paragraph, its relationship to ethics is examined in the fourth paragraph.

QUESTION 16

Choice A is the best answer. In lines 57-59, the author states that "Many moral dilemmas arise when these three versions pull in different directions but clashes are not inevitable." In this context, the three different perspectives on ethical economics may "clash," or conflict, with one another.

Choices B, C, and D are incorrect because in this context "clashes" does not mean mismatches, collisions, or brawls.

QUESTION 17

Choice C is the best answer. In lines 59-64, the author states, "Take fair trade coffee . . . for example: buying it might have good consequences, be virtuous, and also be the right way to act in a flawed market." The author is suggesting that in the example of fair trade coffee, all three perspectives about ethical economics — Adam Smith's belief in consequences dictating action, Aristotle's emphasis on character, and the third approach emphasizing the virtue of good actions — can be applied. These three approaches share "common ground" (line 64), as they all can be applied to the example of fair trade coffee without contradicting one another.

Choices A, B, and D are incorrect because they do not show how the three different approaches to ethical economics share common ground. Choice A simply states that there are "different views on ethics" in economics, choice B explains the third ethical economics approach, and choice D suggests that people "behave like a herd" when considering economics.

QUESTION 18

Choice C is the best answer. In lines 83-88, the author states that psychology can help "define ethics for us," which can help explain why people "react in disgust at economic injustice, or accept a moral law as universal."

Choices A and B are incorrect because they identify topics discussed in the final paragraph (human quirks and people's reaction to economic injustice) but not its main idea. Choice D is incorrect because the final paragraph does not suggest that economists may be responsible for reforming the free market.

QUESTION 19

Choice A is the best answer. The data in the graph show that in Tanzania between the years 2000 and 2008, fair trade coffee profits were around $1.30 per pound, while profits of regular coffee were in the approximate range of 20–60 cents per pound.

Choices B, C, and D are incorrect because they are not supported by information in the graph.

QUESTION 20

Choice B is the best answer. The data in the graph indicate that between 2002 and 2004 the difference in per-pound profits between fair trade and regular coffee was about $1. In this time period, fair trade coffee was valued at around $1.30 per pound and regular coffee was valued at around 20 cents per pound. The graph also shows that regular coffee recorded the lowest profits between the years 2002 and 2004, while fair trade coffee remained relatively stable throughout the entire eight-year span (2000 to 2008).

Choices A, C, and D are incorrect because they do not indicate the greatest difference between per-pound profits for fair trade and regular coffee.

QUESTION 21

Choice C is the best answer. In lines 59-61, the author defines fair trade coffee as "coffee that is sold with a certification that indicates the farmers and workers who produced it were paid a fair wage." This definition suggests that purchasing fair trade coffee is an ethically responsible choice, and the fact that fair trade coffee is being produced and is profitable suggests that ethical economics is still a consideration. The graph's data support this claim by showing how fair trade coffee was more than twice as profitable as regular coffee.

Choice A is incorrect because the graph suggests that people acting on empathy (by buying fair trade coffee) is productive for fair trade coffee farmers and workers. Choices B and D are incorrect because the graph does not provide support for the idea that character or people's fears factor into economic choices.

QUESTION 22

Choice C is the best answer. The author of Passage 1 indicates that people can benefit from using screen-based technologies as these technologies strengthen "certain cognitive skills" (line 3) and the "brain functions related to fast-paced problem solving" (lines 14-15).

Choice A is incorrect because the author of Passage 1 cites numerous studies of screen-based technologies. Choice B is incorrect because it is not supported by Passage 1, and choice D is incorrect because while the author mentions some benefits to screen-based technologies, he does not encourage their use.

QUESTION 23

Choice A is the best answer. In lines 3-4, the author of Passage 1 provides evidence that the use of screen-based technologies has some positive effects: "Certain cognitive skills are strengthened by our use of computers and the Net."

Choices B, C, and D are incorrect because they do not provide the best evidence that the use of screen-based technologies has some positive effects. Choices B, C, and D introduce and describe the author's reservations about screen-based technologies.

QUESTION 24

Choice B is the best answer. The author of Passage 1 cites Patricia Greenfield's study, which found that people's use of screen-based technologies weakened their ability to acquire knowledge, perform "inductive analysis" and "critical thinking," and be imaginative and reflective (lines 34-38). The author of Passage 1 concludes that the use of screen-based technologies interferes with people's ability to think "deeply" (lines 47-50).

Choices A, C, and D are incorrect because the author of Passage 1 does not address how using the Internet affects people's health, social contacts, or self-confidence.

QUESTION 25

Choice C is the best answer. In lines 39-41, the author states, "We know that the human brain is highly plastic; neurons and synapses change as circumstances change." In this context, the brain is "plastic" because it is malleable, or able to change.

Choices A, B, and D are incorrect because in this context "plastic" does not mean creative, artificial, or sculptural.

QUESTION 26

Choice B is the best answer. In lines 60-65, the author of Passage 2 explains how speed-reading does not "revamp," or alter, how the brain processes information. He supports this statement by explaining how Woody Allen's reading of *War and Peace* in one sitting caused him to describe the novel as "about Russia." Woody Allen was not able to comprehend the "famously long" novel by speed-reading it.

Choices A and D are incorrect because Woody Allen's description of *War and Peace* does not suggest he disliked Tolstoy's writing style or that he regretted reading the book. Choice C is incorrect because the anecdote about Woody Allen is unrelated to multitasking.

QUESTION 27

Choice D is the best answer. The author of Passage 2 states that people like novelists and scientists improve in their profession by "immers[ing] themselves in their fields" (line 79). Both novelists and scientists, in other words, become absorbed in their areas of expertise.

Choices A and C are incorrect because the author of Passage 2 does not suggest that novelists and scientists both take risks when they pursue knowledge or are curious about other subjects. Choice B is incorrect because the author of Passage 2 states that "accomplished people" don't perform "intellectual calisthenics," or exercises that improve their minds (lines 77-78).

QUESTION 28

Choice D is the best answer. In lines 83-90, the author of Passage 2 criticizes media critics for their alarmist writing: "Media critics write as if the brain takes on the qualities of whatever it consumes, the informational equivalent of 'you are what you eat.'" The author then compares media critics' "you are what you eat" mentality to ancient people's belief that "eating fierce animals made them fierce." The author uses this analogy to discredit media critics' belief that consumption of electronic media alters the brain.

Choices A, B, and C are incorrect because the final sentence of Passage 2 does not use ornate language, employ humor, or evoke nostalgia for the past.

QUESTION 29

Choice D is the best answer. The author of Passage 1 argues that online and other screen-based technologies affect people's abilities to think deeply (lines 47-50). The author of Passage 2 argues that the effects of consuming electronic media are less drastic than media critics suggest (lines 81-82).

Choices A and B are incorrect because they discuss points made in the passages but not the main purpose of the passages. Choice C is incorrect because neither passage argues in favor of increasing financial support for certain studies.

QUESTION 30

Choice B is the best answer. The author of Passage 1 cites scientific research that suggests online and screen-based technologies have a negative effect on the brain (lines 25-38). The author of Passage 2 is critical of the research highlighted in Passage 1: "Critics of new media sometimes use science itself to press their case, citing research that shows how 'experience can change the brain.' But cognitive neuroscientists roll their eyes at such talk" (lines 51-54).

Choices A, C, and D are incorrect because they do not accurately describe the relationship between the two passages. Passage 1 does not take a clinical approach to the topic. Passage 2 does not take a high-level view of a finding examined in depth in Passage 1, nor does it predict negative reactions to the findings discussed in paragraph 1.

QUESTION 31

Choice C is the best answer. In Passage 1, the author cites psychologist Patricia Greenfield's finding that "'every medium develops some cognitive skills at the expense of others'" (lines 29-31). In Passage 2, the author states "If you train people to do one thing (recognize shapes, solve math puzzles, find hidden words), they get better at doing that thing, but almost nothing else" (lines 71-74). Both authors would agree than an improvement in one cognitive area, such as visual-spatial skills, would not result in improved skills in other areas.

Choice A is incorrect because hand-eye coordination is not discussed in Passage 2. Choice B is incorrect because Passage 1 does not suggest that critics of electronic media tend to overreact. Choice D is incorrect because neither passage discusses whether Internet users prefer reading printed texts or digital texts.

QUESTION 32

Choice B is the best answer. In Passage 1, the author cites Michael Merzenich's claim that when people adapt to a new cultural phenomenon, including the use of a new medium, we end up with a "different brain" (lines 41-43). The author of Passage 2 somewhat agrees with Merzenich's claim by stating, "Yes, every time we learn a fact or skill the wiring of the brain changes" (lines 54-56).

Choices A, C, and D do not provide the best evidence that the author of Passage 2 would agree to some extent with Merzenich's claim. Choices A and D are incorrect because the claims are attributed to critics of new media. Choice C is incorrect because it shows that the author of Passage 2 does not completely agree with Merzenich's claim about brain plasticity.

QUESTION 33

Choice B is the best answer. In lines 15-30, Stanton argues that men make all the decisions in "the church, the state, and the home." This absolute power has led to a disorganized society, a "fragmentary condition of everything." Stanton confirms this claim when she states that society needs women to "lift man up into the higher realms of thought and action" (lines 59-60).

Choices A and D are incorrect because Stanton does not focus on women's lack of equal educational opportunities or inability to hold political positions. Choice C is incorrect because although Stanton implies women are not allowed to vote, she never mentions that "poor candidates" are winning elections.

QUESTION 34

Choice A is the best answer. Stanton argues that women are repressed in society because men hold "high carnival," or have all the power, and make the rules in "the church, the state, and the home" (lines 15-30). Stanton claims that men have total control over women, "overpowering the feminine element everywhere" (line 17).

Choices B, C, and D are incorrect because Stanton does not use the term "high carnival" to emphasize that the time period is freewheeling, or unrestricted; that there has been a scandalous decline in moral values; or that the power of women is growing.

QUESTION 35

Choice D is the best answer. In lines 15-22, Stanton states that men's absolute rule in society is "crushing out all the diviner qualities in human nature," such that society knows very "little of true manhood and womanhood." Stanton argues that society knows less about womanhood than manhood, because womanhood has "scarce been recognized as a power until within the last century." This statement indicates that society's acknowledgment of "womanhood," or women's true character, is a fairly recent historical development.

Choices A, B, and C are incorrect because Stanton describes men's control of society, their domination of the domestic sphere, and the prevalence of war and injustice as long-established realities.

QUESTION 36

Choice B is the best answer. In lines 15-22, Stanton provides evidence for the claim that society's acknowledgment of "womanhood," or women's true character, is a fairly recent historical development: "[womanhood] has scarce been recognized as a power until within the last century."

Choices A, C, and D are incorrect because they do not provide the best evidence that society's acknowledgment of "womanhood," or women's true character, is a fairly recent historical development. Rather, choices A, C, and D discuss men's character, power, and influence.

QUESTION 37

Choice B is the best answer. In lines 22-25, Stanton states, "Society is but the reflection of man himself, untempered by woman's thought; the hard iron rule we feel alike in the church, the state, and the home." In this context, man's "rule" in "the church, the state, and the home" means that men have a controlling force in all areas of society.

Choices A, C, and D are incorrect because in this context "rule" does not mean a general guideline, an established habit, or a procedural method.

QUESTION 38

Choice D is the best answer. In lines 31-34, Stanton argues that people use the term "the strong-minded" to refer to women who advocate for "the right of suffrage," or the right to vote in elections. In this context, people use the term "the strong-minded" to criticize female suffragists, as they believe voting will make women too "masculine."

Choices A and B are incorrect because Stanton does not suggest that people use the term "the strong-minded" as a compliment. Choice C is incorrect because Stanton suggests that "the strong-minded" is a term used to criticize women who want to vote, not those who enter male-dominated professions.

QUESTION 39

Choice C is the best answer. In lines 35-38, Stanton states that society contains hardly any women in the "best sense," and clarifies that too many women are "reflections, varieties, and dilutions of the masculine gender." Stanton is suggesting that there are few "best," or genuine, women who are not completely influenced or controlled by men.

Choices A, B, and D are incorrect because in this context "best" does not mean superior, excellent, or rarest.

QUESTION 40

Choice A is the best answer. In lines 53-55, Stanton argues that man "mourns," or regrets, how his power has caused "falsehood, selfishness, and violence" to become the "law" of society. Stanton is arguing that men are lamenting, or expressing regret about, how their governance has created problems.

Choices B, C, and D are incorrect because Stanton does not suggest that men are advocating for women's right to vote or for female equality, nor are they requesting women's opinions about improving civic life.

QUESTION 41

Choice B is the best answer. In lines 53-55, Stanton provides evidence that men are lamenting the problems they have created, as they recognize that their actions have caused "falsehood, selfishness, and violence [to become] the law of life."

Choices A, C, and D are incorrect because they do not provide the best evidence that men are lamenting the problems they have created. Choice A explains society's current fragmentation. Choices C and D present Stanton's main argument for women's enfranchisement.

QUESTION 42

Choice D is the best answer. In the sixth paragraph, Stanton differentiates between men and masculine traits. Stanton argues that masculine traits or "characteristics," such as a "love of acquisition and conquest," serve to "subjugate one man to another" (lines 67-78). Stanton is suggesting that some masculine traits position men within certain power structures.

Choices A and B are incorrect because the sixth paragraph does not primarily establish a contrast between men and women or between the spiritual and material worlds. Choice C is incorrect because although Stanton argues that not "all men are hard, selfish, and brutal," she does not discuss what constitutes a "good" man.

QUESTION 43

Choice C is the best answer. In the first paragraph, the author identifies the natural phenomenon "internal waves" (line 3), and explains why they are important: "internal waves are fundamental parts of ocean water dynamics, transferring heat to the ocean depths and bringing up cold water from below" (lines 7-9).

Choices A, B, and D are incorrect because they do not identify the main purpose of the first paragraph, as that paragraph does not focus on a scientific device, a common misconception, or a recent study.

QUESTION 44

Choice B is the best answer. In lines 17-19, researcher Tom Peacock argues that in order to create precise global climate models, scientists must be able to "capture processes" such as how internal waves are formed. In this context, to "capture" a process means to record it for scientific study.

Choices A, C, and D are incorrect because in this context "capture" does not mean to control, secure, or absorb.

QUESTION 45

Choice D is the best answer. In lines 17-19, researcher Tom Peacock argues that scientists need to "capture processes" of internal waves to develop "more and more accurate climate models." Peacock is suggesting that studying internal waves will inform the development of scientific models.

Choices A, B, and C are incorrect because Peacock does not state that monitoring internal waves will allow people to verify wave heights, improve satellite image quality, or prevent coastal damage.

QUESTION 46

Choice C is the best answer. In lines 17-19, researcher Tom Peacock provides evidence that studying internal waves will inform the development of key scientific models, such as "more accurate climate models."

Choices A, B, and D are incorrect because they do not provide the best evidence that studying internal waves will inform the development of key scientific models; rather, they provide general information about internal waves.

QUESTION 47

Choice A is the best answer. In lines 65-67, the author notes that Tom Peacock and his team "were able to devise a mathematical model that describes the movement and formation of these waves." In this context, the researchers devised, or created, a mathematical model.

Choices B, C, and D are incorrect because in this context "devise" does not mean to solve, imagine, or begin.

QUESTION 48

Choice B is the best answer. Tom Peacock and his team created a model of the "Luzon's Strait's underwater topography" and determined that its "distinct double-ridge shape . . . [is] responsible for generating the underwater [internal] waves" (lines 53-55). The author notes that this model describes only internal waves in the Luzon Strait but that the team's findings may "help researchers understand how internal waves are generated in other places around the world" (lines 67-70). The author's claim suggests that while internal waves in the Luzon Strait are "some of the largest in the world" (line 25) due to the region's topography, internal waves occurring in other regions may be caused by some similar factors.

Choice A is incorrect because the author notes that the internal waves in the Luzon Strait are "some of the largest in the world" (line 25), which suggests that internal waves reach varying heights. Choices C and D are incorrect because they are not supported by the researchers' findings.

QUESTION 49

Choice D is the best answer. In lines 67-70, the author provides evidence that, while the researchers' findings suggest the internal waves in the Luzon Strait are influenced by the region's topography, the findings may "help researchers understand how internal waves are generated in other places around the world." This statement suggests that all internal waves may be caused by some similar factors.

Choices A, B, and C are incorrect because they do not provide the best evidence that internal waves are caused by similar factors but influenced by the distinct topographies of different regions. Rather, choices A, B, and C reference general information about internal waves or focus solely on those that occur in the Luzon Strait.

QUESTION 50

Choice D is the best answer. During the period 19:12 to 20:24, the graph shows the 13°C isotherm increasing in depth from about 20 to 40 meters.

Choices A, B, and C are incorrect because during the time period 19:12 to 20:24 the 9°C, 10°C, and 11°C isotherms all decreased in depth.

QUESTION 51

Choice D is the best answer. In lines 3-6, the author notes that internal waves "do not ride the ocean surface" but "move underwater, undetectable without the use of satellite imagery or sophisticated monitoring equipment." The graph shows that the isotherms in an internal wave never reach the ocean's surface, as the isotherms do not record a depth of 0.

Choice A is incorrect because the graph provides no information about salinity. Choice B is incorrect because the graph shows layers of less dense water (which, based on the passage, are warmer) riding above layers of denser water (which, based on the passage, are cooler). Choice C is incorrect because the graph shows that internal waves push isotherms of warmer water above bands of colder water.

QUESTION 52

Choice A is the best answer. In lines 7-9, the author notes that internal waves are "fundamental parts of ocean water dynamics" because they transfer "heat to the ocean depths and brin[g] up cold water from below." The graph shows an internal wave forcing the warm isotherms to depths that typically are colder. For example, at 13:12, the internal wave transfers "heat to the ocean depths" by forcing the 10°C, 11°C, and 13°C isotherms to depths that typically are colder.

Choices B, C, and D are incorrect because the graph does not show how internal waves affect the ocean's density, surface temperature, or tide flow.

Section 2: Writing and Language Test

QUESTION 1

Choice B is the best answer because it provides a noun, "reductions," yielding a grammatically complete and coherent sentence.

Choices A, C, and D are incorrect because each provides a verb or gerund, while the underlined portion calls for a noun.

QUESTION 2

Choice B is the best answer because it offers a transitional adverb, "Consequently," that communicates a cause-effect relationship between the funding reduction identified in the previous sentence and the staffing decrease described in this sentence.

Choices A, C, and D are incorrect because each misidentifies the relationship between the preceding sentence and the sentence of which it is a part.

QUESTION 3

Choice A is the best answer because the singular verb "has" agrees with the singular noun "trend" that appears earlier in the sentence.

Choices B, C, and D are incorrect because the plural verb "have" does not agree with the singular subject "trend," and the relative pronoun "which" unnecessarily interrupts the direct relationship between "trend" and the verb.

QUESTION 4

Choice A is the best answer because it states accurately why the proposed clause should be added to the sentence. Without these specific examples, readers have only a vague sense of what "nonprint" formats might be.

Choices B, C, and D are incorrect because each represents a misinterpretation of the relationship between the proposed clause to be added and the surrounding text in the passage.

QUESTION 5

Choice D is the best answer because it includes only the preposition and noun that the sentence requires.

Choices A, B, and C are incorrect because each includes an unnecessary pronoun, either "them" or "their." The sentence contains no referents that would circulate e-books.

QUESTION 6

Choice D is the best answer because the verb form "cataloging" parallels the other verbs in the series.

Choices A, B, and C are incorrect because each interrupts the parallel structure in the verb series, either through an incorrect verb form or with an unnecessary subject.

QUESTION 7

Choice B is the best answer because it consolidates references to the subject, "librarians," by placing the relative pronoun "whose" immediately following "librarians." This results in a logical flow of information within the sentence.

Choices A, C, and D are incorrect because each fails to place "librarians" as the main subject of the sentence without redundancy, resulting in a convoluted sentence whose relevance to the preceding and subsequent sentences is unclear.

QUESTION 8

Choice D is the best answer because no conjunction is necessary to communicate the relationship between the clauses in the sentence. The conjunction "While" at the beginning of the sentence already creates a comparison.

Choices A, B, and C are incorrect because each provides an unnecessary coordinating conjunction.

QUESTION 9

Choice B is the best answer because it mentions time periods when the free services described later in the sentence are particularly useful to library patrons.

Choices A, C, and D are incorrect because each creates redundancy or awkwardness in the remainder of the sentence.

QUESTION 10

Choice B is the best answer because it is concise; it is also consistent with the formal language in the rest of the sentence and the passage overall.

Choices A, C, and D are incorrect because each is either unnecessarily wordy or uses colloquial language that does not correspond with the tone of the passage.

QUESTION 11

Choice C is the best answer because it restates the writer's primary argument, which may be found at the end of the first paragraph: "As public libraries adapt to rapid technological advances in information distribution, librarians' roles are actually expanding."

Choices A, B, and D are incorrect because they do not paraphrase the writer's primary claim.

QUESTION 12

Choice B is the best answer because it clarifies that the sentence, which mentions a specific large-scale painting at the Art Institute of Chicago, is an example supporting the preceding claim about large-scale paintings.

Choices A, C, and D are incorrect because they propose transitional words or phrases that do not accurately represent the relationship between the preceding sentence and the sentence containing the underlined portion.

QUESTION 13

Choice D is the best answer because no punctuation is necessary in the underlined phrase.

Choices A, B, and C are incorrect because each separates parts of the noun phrase "painter Georges Seurat's 10-foot-wide *A Sunday Afternoon on the Island of La Grande Jatte*" from one another with one or more unnecessary commas.

QUESTION 14

Choice C is the best answer because it provides the appropriate possessive form, "its," and a colon to introduce the identifying phrase that follows.

Choices A, B, and D are incorrect because none contains both the appropriate possessive form of "it" and the punctuation that creates a grammatically standard sentence.

QUESTION 15

Choice C is the best answer because an analysis of the consequences of King Louis XV's reign is irrelevant to the paragraph.

Choices A, B, and D are incorrect because each represents a misinterpretation of the relationship between the proposed sentence to be added and the main point of the paragraph.

QUESTION 16

Choice C is the best answer because it provides a coordinating conjunction, "and," to connect the two verb phrases "are characterized" and "are covered."

Choices A, B, and D are incorrect because each lacks the conjunction needed to connect the two verb phrases "are characterized" and "are covered."

QUESTION 17

Choice B is the best answer because it offers an example of an additional household item, a "tea cup," with a specific measurement that is one-twelfth of its actual size.

Choices A, C, D are incorrect because, compared to the example preceding the underlined portion, each is vague and fails to offer a specific measurement of an additional household item.

QUESTION 18

Choice B is the best answer because it provides correct punctuation and the coordinating conjunction "but," which acknowledges the possible contrast between being "sparsely furnished" and displaying "just as true" period details.

Choices A, C, and D are incorrect because each communicates an illogical relationship between the phrases that precede and follow the underlined portion.

QUESTION 19

Choice A is the best answer because it provides a clause that is the most similar to the two preceding clauses, which both end with a reference to a specific wall.

Choices B, C, and D are incorrect because each deviates from the stylistic pattern of the preceding two clauses.

QUESTION 20

Choice D is the best answer because the article "a" requires the singular noun "visitor," and the simple present verb "remark" is the appropriate verb tense in this context.

Choices A, B, and C are incorrect because each contains either a noun or verb that does not fit the context.

QUESTION 21

Choice D is the best answer because it identifies the drawers, rather than the visitor, as being "dotted with pin-sized knobs."

Choices A, B, and C are incorrect because all three contain dangling modifiers that obscure the relationship between the visitor, the drawers, and the pin-sized knobs.

QUESTION 22

Choice B is the best answer because paragraph 3 offers an overview of the exhibit and so serves to introduce the specific aspects of particular miniature rooms described in paragraphs 2 and 4.

Choices A, C, and D are incorrect because each proposes a placement of paragraph 2 that prevents the passage from developing in a logical sequence.

QUESTION 23

Choice A is the best answer because it correctly completes the noun phrase that begins with "sea otters," and directly follows the noun phrase with the verb "help."

Choices B, C, and D are incorrect because each separates the noun "otters" from the verb "help" in a way that results in a grammatically incomplete sentence.

QUESTION 24

Choice B is the best answer because the data in the chart show lower sea urchin density in areas where sea otters have lived for two years or less than in areas where no otters are present.

Choices A, C, and D are incorrect because none accurately describes the data in the chart.

QUESTION 25

Choice B is the best answer because the conjunctive adverb "however" accurately communicates the contrast between an environment shaped by the presence of sea otters, described in the preceding sentence, and an environment shaped by the absence of sea otters, described in this sentence.

Choices A, C, and D are incorrect because each presents a conjunctive adverb that does not accurately depict the relationship between the preceding sentence and the sentence with the underlined word.

QUESTION 26

Choice A is the best answer because the additional information usefully connects the carbon dioxide levels mentioned in this sentence with the global warming mentioned in the previous sentence.

Choices B, C, and D are incorrect because each misinterprets the relationship between the proposed information and the main points of the paragraph and the passage.

QUESTION 27

Choice D is the best answer because it offers the verb "suggests" followed directly by its object, a that-clause, without interruption.

Choices A, B, and C are incorrect because each contains punctuation that unnecessarily separates the study from its findings — that is, separates the verb from its object.

QUESTION 28

Choice A is the best answer because it accurately reflects the fact that sea urchins "graze voraciously on kelp," as stated in the first paragraph, and it also maintains the tone of the passage.

Choices B, C, and D are incorrect because each offers a term that does not accurately describe the behavior of sea otters.

QUESTION 29

Choice C is the best answer because the possessive singular pronoun "its" corresponds with the referent "kelp," which appears later in the sentence, and with the possessive relationship between the pronoun and the "terrestrial plant cousins."

Choices A, B, and D are incorrect because none provides a pronoun that is both singular and possessive.

QUESTION 30

Choice C is the best answer because it provides the noun "sea otters" to identify who or what "played a role."

Choices A, B, and D are incorrect because each provides a pronoun that makes no sense in the context of the paragraph and the passage, which is about the role sea otters play — not the role scientists play or the role kelp plays.

QUESTION 31

Choice D is the best answer because sentence 5 indicates that sea otters' importance in decreasing atmospheric carbon dioxide was not known, and the sentence to be added indicates that a surprise will follow. Sentence 6 provides that surprise: sea otters have a large impact on the amount of carbon dioxide kelp can remove from the atmosphere.

Choices A, B, and C are incorrect because each interrupts the logical flow of ideas in the paragraph.

QUESTION 32

Choice B is the best answer because its clear wording and formal tone correspond with the passage's established style.

Choices A, C, and D are incorrect because each contains vague language that is inconsistent with the passage's clear wording and formal tone.

QUESTION 33

Choice D is the best answer because it provides punctuation that appropriately identifies "removed" as the definition of "sequestered."

Choices A, B, and C are incorrect because each contains punctuation that obscures the relationship between "sequestered," "removed," and the text that follows.

QUESTION 34

Choice D is the best answer because it provides a conjunction that correctly identifies the relationship between "a practice" and the actions involved in the practice.

Choices A, B, and C are incorrect because each contains a conjunction that miscommunicates the relationship between the text that precedes and follows the underlined portion.

QUESTION 35

Choice A is the best answer because it provides a comma to close the appositive clause "a practice whereby products are designed to have a limited period of usefulness," which also begins with a comma.

Choices B, C, and D are incorrect because each provides closing punctuation inconsistent with the punctuation at the beginning of the clause.

QUESTION 36

Choice D is the best answer because it provides an adjective that accurately describes the clear "contrast" between products "designed to have a limited period of usefulness" and those "produced to be durable."

Choices A, B, and C are incorrect because none provides an adjective that appropriately modifies "contrast" in the context of the paragraph.

QUESTION 37

Choice A is the best answer because by mentioning the "specialized" methods used in repair shops, it suggests that repairing goods is seen as a specialty rather than as a common activity. This connects logically with the "rare" repair shops introduced just before the underlined portion.

Choices B, C, and D are incorrect because none provides information that supports the claim made in the sentence.

QUESTION 38

Choice B is the best answer because it provides the correct spelling of the noun "fair," meaning exhibition, and uses the correct word "than" to create the comparison between a "fair" and a "café."

Choices A, C, and D are incorrect because each contains a misspelling of either "fair" or "than."

QUESTION 39

Choice C is the best answer because it offers a relative pronoun that properly links the noun "Martine Postma" with the appropriate verb "wanted."

Choices A, B, and D are incorrect because none contains a pronoun that is appropriate for the referent and placement of the clause.

QUESTION 40

Choice D is the best answer because it provides the most concise phrasing and links the sentence appropriately to the previous sentence.

Choices A, B, and C are incorrect because each provides an unnecessary adverb that obscures the relationship between this sentence and the previous one.

QUESTION 41

Choice D is the best answer because the gerund "waiting" corresponds with the preposition "for" and the present tense used in the rest of the sentence.

Choices A, B, and C are incorrect because each contains a verb form not used with the preposition "for."

QUESTION 42

Choice C is the best answer because it appropriately places sentence 5, which describes the places Repair Cafés can be found today, between a sentence that gives the first Repair Café's location and purpose and a statement about current customers and how they use Repair Cafés.

Choices A, B, and D are incorrect because each creates a paragraph with an inappropriate shift in verb tense and, therefore, an illogical sequence of information.

QUESTION 43

Choice C is the best answer because it accurately states that the issue of "corporate and service-based jobs" is not particularly relevant at this point in the paragraph. The focus here is on repairing objects in a "throwaway culture," not jobs.

Choices A, B, and D are incorrect because each misinterprets the relationship between the proposed text and the information in the paragraph.

QUESTION 44

Choice D is the best answer because the phrase "and other countries" communicates the fact that there are additional items not being named that could be added to the list; no other wording is required to clarify that point.

Choices A, B, and C are incorrect because each presents a word or phrase that results in a redundancy with "and other countries."

Section 3: Math Test – No Calculator

QUESTION 1

Choice C is correct. Subtracting 6 from each side of $5x + 6 = 10$ yields $5x = 4$. Dividing both sides of $5x = 4$ by 5 yields x $\frac{4}{5}$. The value of x can now be substituted into the expression $10x + 3$, giving $10\left(\frac{4}{5}\right) + 3 = 11$.

Alternatively, the expression $10x + 3$ can be rewritten as $2(5x + 6) - 9$, and 10 can be substituted for $5x + 6$, giving $2(10) - 9 = 11$.

Choices A, B, and D are incorrect. Each of these choices leads to $5x + 6 \neq 10$, contradicting the given equation, $5x + 6 = 10$. For example, choice A is incorrect because if the value of $10x + 3$ were 4, then it would follow that $x = 0.1$, and the value of $5x + 6$ would be 6.5, not 10.

QUESTION 2

Choice B is correct. Multiplying each side of $x + y = 0$ by 2 gives $2x + 2y = 0$. Then, adding the corresponding sides of $2x + 2y = 0$ and $3x - 2y = 10$ gives $5x = 10$. Dividing each side of $5x = 10$ by 5 gives $x = 2$. Finally, substituting 2 for x in $x + y = 0$ gives $2 + y = 0$, or $y = -2$. Therefore, the solution to the given system of equations is $(2, -2)$.

Alternatively, the equation $x + y = 0$ can be rewritten as $x = -y$, and substituting x for $-y$ in $3x - 2y = 10$ gives $5x = 10$, or $x = 2$. The value of y can then be found in the same way as before.

Choices A, C, and D are incorrect because when the given values of x and y are substituted into $x + y = 0$ and $3x - 2y = 10$, either one or both of the equations are not true. These answers may result from sign errors or other computational errors.

QUESTION 3

Choice A is correct. The price of the job, in dollars, is calculated using the expression $60 + 12nh$, where 60 is a fixed price and $12nh$ depends on the number of landscapers, n, working the job and the number of hours, h, the job takes those n landscapers. Since nh is the total number of hours of work done when n landscapers work h hours, the cost of the job increases by \$12 for each hour each landscaper works. Therefore, of the choices given, the best interpretation of the number 12 is that the company charges \$12 per hour for each landscaper.

Choice B is incorrect because the number of landscapers that will work each job is represented by n in the equation, not by the number 12. Choice C is incorrect because the price of the job increases by $12n$ dollars each hour, which will not equal 12 dollars unless $n = 1$. Choice D is incorrect because the total number of hours each landscaper works is equal to h. The number of hours each landscaper works in a day is not provided.

QUESTION 4

Choice A is correct. If a polynomial expression is in the form $(x)^2 + 2(x)(y) + (y)^2$, then it is equivalent to $(x + y)^2$. Because $9a^4 + 12a^2b^2 + 4b^4 = (3a^2)^2 + 2(3a^2 (2b^2 + (2b^2)^2$, it can be rewritten as $(3a^2 + 2b^2)^2$.

Choice B is incorrect. The expression $(3a + 2b)^4$ is equivalent to the product $(3a + 2b \ 3a + 2b \ 3a + 2b \ 3a + 2b$. This product will contain the term $4(3a)^3(2b = 216a^3b$. However, the given polynomial, $9a^4 + 12a^2b^2 + 4b^4$, does not contain the term $216a^3b$. Therefore, $9a^4 + 12a^2b^2 + 4b^4 \neq (3a + 2b)^4$. Choice C is incorrect. The expression $(9a^2 + 4b^2)^2$ is equivalent to the product $(9a^2 + 4b^2)(9a^2 + 4b^2$. This product will contain the term $(9a^2)(9a^2 = 81a^4$. However, the given polynomial, $9a^4 + 12a^2b^2 + 4b^4$, does not contain the term $81a^4$. Therefore, $9a^4 + 12a^2b^2 + 4b^4 \neq (9a^2 + 4b^2)^2$. Choice D is incorrect. The expression $(9a + 4b)^4$ is equivalent to the product $(9a + 4b)(9a + 4b)(9a + 4b)(9a + 4b$. This product will contain the term $(9a)(9a)(9a)(9a = 6{,}561a^4$. However, the given polynomial, $9a^4 + 12a^2b^2 + 4b^4$, does not contain the term $6{,}561a^4$. Therefore, $9a^4 + 12a^2b^2 + 4b^4 \neq (9a + 4b)^4$.

QUESTION 5

Choice C is correct. Since $\sqrt{2k^2 + 17} - x = 0$, and $x = 7$, one can substitute 7 for x, which gives $\sqrt{2k^2 + 17} - 7 = 0$. Adding 7 to each side of $\sqrt{2k^2 + 17} - 7 = 0$ gives $\sqrt{2k^2 + 17} = 7$. Squaring each side of $\sqrt{2k^2 + 17} = 7$ will remove the square root symbol: $\left(\sqrt{2k^2 + 17}\right)^2 = (7)^2$, or $2k^2 + 17 = 49$. Then subtracting 17 from each side of $2k^2 + 17 = 49$ gives $2k^2 = 49 - 17 = 32$, and dividing each side of $2k^2 = 32$ by 2 gives $k^2 = 16$. Finally, taking the square root of each side of $k^2 = 16$ gives $k = \pm 4$, and since the problem states that $k > 0$, it follows that $k = 4$.

Since the sides of an equation were squared while solving $\sqrt{2k^2 + 17} - 7 = 0$, it is possible that an extraneous root was produced. However, substituting 4 for k in $\sqrt{2k^2 + 17} - 7 = 0$ confirms that 4 is a solution for k: $\sqrt{2(4)^2 + 17} - 7 = \sqrt{32 + 17} - 7 = \sqrt{49} - 7 = 7 - 7 = 0$.

Choices A, B, and D are incorrect because substituting any of these values for k in $\sqrt{2k^2 + 17} - 7 = 0$ does not yield a true statement.

QUESTION 6

Choice D is correct. Since lines ℓ and k are parallel, the lines have the same slope. The slope m of a line that passes through two points (x_1, y_1) and (x_2, y_2) can be found as $m = \frac{y_2 - y_1}{x_2 - x_1}$. Line ℓ passes through the points $(0, 2)$ and $(-5, 0)$, so its slope is $\frac{0 - 2}{-5 - 0}$, which is $\frac{2}{5}$. The slope of line k must also be $\frac{2}{5}$. Since line k has slope $\frac{2}{5}$ and passes through the points $(p, 0)$ and $(0, -4)$, it follows that $\frac{-4 - 0}{0 - p} = \frac{2}{5}$, or $\frac{4}{p} = \frac{2}{5}$. Multiplying each side of $\frac{4}{p} = \frac{2}{5}$ by $5p$ gives $20 = 2p$, and therefore, $p = 10$.

Choices A, B, and C are incorrect and may result from conceptual or calculation errors.

QUESTION 7

Choice A is correct. Since the numerator and denominator of $\frac{x^{a^2}}{x^{b^2}}$ have a common base, it follows by the laws of exponents that this expression can be rewritten as $x^{a^2 - b^2}$. Thus, the equation $\frac{x^{a^2}}{x^{b^2}} = x^{16}$ can be rewritten as $x^{a^2 - b^2} = x^{16}$. Because the equivalent expressions have the common base x, and $x > 1$, it follows that the exponents of the two expressions must also be equivalent. Hence, the equation $a^2 - b^2 = 16$ must be true. The left-hand side of this new equation is a difference of squares, and so it can be factored: $(a + b)(a - b) = 16$. It is given that $(a + b) = 2$; substituting 2 for the factor $(a + b)$ gives $2(a - b) = 16$. Finally, dividing both sides of $2(a - b) = 16$ by 2 gives $a - b = 8$.

Choices B, C, and D are incorrect and may result from errors in applying the laws of exponents or errors in solving the equation $a^2 - b^2 = 16$.

QUESTION 8

Choice C is correct. The relationship between n and A is given by the equation $nA = 360$. Since n is the number of sides of a polygon, n must be a positive integer, and so $nA = 360$ can be rewritten as $A = \frac{360}{n}$. If the value of A is greater than 50, it follows that $\frac{360}{n} > 50$ is a true statement. Thus, $50n < 360$, or $n < \frac{360}{50}$ 7.2. Since n must be an integer, the greatest possible value of n is 7.

Choices A and B are incorrect. These are possible values for n, the number of sides of a regular polygon, if $A > 50$, but neither is the greatest possible value of n. Choice D is incorrect. If $A < 50$, then $n = 8$ is the least possible value of n, the number of sides of a regular polygon. However, the question asks for the <u>greatest</u> possible value of n if $A > 50$, which is $n = 7$.

QUESTION 9

Choice B is correct. Since the slope of the first line is 2, an equation of this line can be written in the form $y = 2x + c$, where c is the y-intercept of the line. Since the line contains the point $(1, 8)$, one can substitute 1 for x and 8 for y in $y = 2x + c$, which gives $8 = 2(1) + c$, or $c = 6$. Thus, an equation of the first line is $y = 2x + 6$. The slope of the second line is equal to $\frac{1-2}{2-1}$ or -1. Thus, an equation of the second line can be written in the form $y = -x + d$, where d is the y-intercept of the line. Substituting 2 for x and 1 for y gives $1 = -2 + d$, or $d = 3$. Thus, an equation of the second line is $y = -x + 3$.

Since a is the x-coordinate and b is the y-coordinate of the intersection point of the two lines, one can substitute a for x and b for y in the two equations, giving the system $b = 2a + 6$ and $b = -a + 3$. Thus, a can be found by solving the equation $2a + 6 = -a + 3$, which gives $a = -1$. Finally, substituting -1 for a into the equation $b = -a + 3$ gives $b = -(-1) + 3$, or $b = 4$. Therefore, the value of $a + b$ is 3.

Alternatively, since the second line passes through the points $(1, 2)$ and $(2, 1)$, an equation for the second line is $x + y = 3$. Thus, the intersection point of the first line and the second line, (a, b) lies on the line with equation $x + y = 3$. It follows that $a + b = 3$.

Choices A and C are incorrect and may result from finding the value of only a or b, but not calculating the value of $a + b$. Choice D is incorrect and may result from a computation error in finding equations of the two lines or in solving the resulting system of equations.

QUESTION 10

Choice C is correct. Since the square of any real number is nonnegative, every point on the graph of the quadratic equation $y = (x - 2)^2$ in the xy-plane has a nonnegative y-coordinate. Thus, $y \geq 0$ for every point on the graph. Therefore, the equation $y = (x - 2)^2$ has a graph for which y is always greater than or equal to -1.

Choices A, B, and D are incorrect because the graph of each of these equations in the xy-plane has a y-intercept at $(0, -2)$. Therefore, each of these equations contains at least one point where y is less than -1.

QUESTION 11

Choice C is correct. To perform the division $\frac{3 - 5i}{8 + 2i}$, multiply the numerator and denominator of $\frac{3 - 5i}{8 + 2i}$ by the conjugate of the denominator, $8 - 2i$. This gives $\frac{(3 - 5i)(8 - 2i)}{(8 + 2i)(8 - 2i)} = \frac{24 - 6i - 40i + (-5i)(-2i)}{8^2 - (2i)^2}$.

Since $i^2 = -1$, this can be simplified to $\frac{24 - 6i - 40i - 10}{64 + 4} = \frac{14 - 46i}{68}$, which then simplifies to $\frac{7}{34} - \frac{23i}{34}$.

Choices A and B are incorrect and may result from misconceptions about fractions. For example, $\frac{a + b}{c + d}$ is equal to $\frac{a}{c + d} + \frac{b}{c + d}$, not $\frac{a}{c} + \frac{b}{d}$.

Choice D is incorrect and may result from a calculation error.

QUESTION 12

Choice B is correct. Multiplying each side of $R = \frac{F}{N + F}$ by $N + F$ gives $R(N + F) = F$, which can be rewritten as $RN + RF = F$. Subtracting RF from each side of $RN + RF = F$ gives $RN = F - RF$, which can be factored as $RN = F(1 - R)$. Finally, dividing each side of $RN = F(1 - R)$ by $1 - R$, expresses F in terms of the other variables: $F = \frac{RN}{1 - R}$.

Choices A, C, and D are incorrect and may result from calculation errors when rewriting the given equation.

QUESTION 13

Choice D is correct. The problem asks for the sum of the solutions of the quadratic equation $2m^2 - 16m + 8 = 0$. Dividing each side of the equation by 2 gives $m^2 - 8m + 4 = 0$. Applying the quadratic formula to $m^2 - 8m + 4 = 0$ gives $m = \frac{8 \pm \sqrt{(-8)^2 - 4(1)(4)}}{2(1)}$, which simplifies to $m = 4 \pm 2\sqrt{3}$. Thus the two solutions are $4 + 2\sqrt{3}$ and $4 - 2\sqrt{3}$, and the sum of the solutions is 8.

Alternatively, the structure of the equation can be used to solve the problem. Dividing both sides of the equation $2m^2 - 16m + 8 = 0$ by 2 gives $m^2 - 8m + 4 = 0$. If the solutions of $m^2 - 8m + 4 = 0$ are s_1 and s_2, then the expression $m^2 - 8m + 4$ can be rewritten as $(m - s_1)(m - s_2)$. Multiplying the two binomials gives $m^2 - (s_1 + s_2)m + s_1 \cdot s_2$. Since the expressions $m^2 - 8m + 4$ and $m^2 - (s_1 + s_2)m + s_1 \cdot s_2$ are equivalent, it follows that $s_1 + s_2 = 8$.

Choices A, B, and C are incorrect and may result from calculation errors when applying the quadratic formula or a sign error when determining the sum of the roots of a quadratic equation from its coefficients.

QUESTION 14

Choice A is correct. Each year, the amount of the radioactive substance is reduced by 13 percent from the prior year's amount; that is, each year, 87 percent of the previous year's amount remains. Since the initial amount of the radioactive substance was 325 grams, after 1 year, 325(0.87) grams remains; after 2 years 325(0.87)(0.87) = $325(0.87)^2$ grams remains; and after t years, $325(0.87)^t$ grams remains. Therefore, the function $f(t = 325(0.87)^t$ models the remaining amount of the substance, in grams, after t years.

Choice B is incorrect and may result from confusing the amount of the substance remaining with the decay rate. Choices C and D are incorrect and may result from confusing the original amount of the substance and the decay rate.

QUESTION 15

Choice D is correct. The given expression can be rewritten as

$$\frac{5x - 2}{x + 3} = \frac{(5x + 15) - 15 - 2}{x + 3}$$

$$= \frac{5\ x + 3) - 17}{x + 3}$$

$$= \frac{5(x + 3)}{x + 3} - \frac{17}{x + 3}$$

$$= 5 - \frac{17}{x + 3}$$

Therefore, the expression $\frac{5x - 2}{x + 3}$ can be rewritten as $5 - \frac{17}{x + 3}$.

Choices A, B, and C are incorrect and may result from a computation or simplification error such as incorrectly canceling out the x in the expression $\frac{5x - 2}{x + 3}$.

QUESTION 16

The correct answer is 3, 6, or 9. Let x be the number of $250 bonuses awarded, and let y be the number of $750 bonuses awarded. Since $3000 in bonuses were awarded, and this included at least one $250 bonus and one $750 bonus, it follows that $250x + 750y = 3000$, where x and y are positive integers. Dividing each side of $250x + 750y = 3000$ by 250 gives $x + 3y = 12$, where x and y are positive integers. Since 3y and 12 are each divisible by 3, it follows that $x = 12 - 3y$ must also be divisible by 3. If $x = 3$, then $y = 3$; if $x = 6$, then $y = 2$; and if $x = 9$, then $y = 1$. If $x = 12$, then $y = 0$, but this is not possible since there was at least one $750 bonus awarded. Therefore, the possible numbers of $250 bonuses awarded are 3, 6, and 9. Any of the numbers 3, 6, or 9 may be gridded as the correct answer.

QUESTION 17

The correct answer is 19. Since $2x 3x + 5) + 3(3x + 5) = ax^2 + bx + c$ for all values of x, the two sides of the equation are equal, and the value of b can be determined by simplifying the left-hand side of the equation and writing it in the same form as the right-hand side. Using the distributive property, the equation becomes $(6x^2 + 10x) + (9x + 15) = ax^2 + bx + c$. Combining like terms gives $6x^2 + 19x + 15 = ax^2 + bx + c$. The value of b is the coefficient of x, which is 19.

QUESTION 18

The correct answer is 12. Angles ABE and DBC are vertical angles and thus have the same measure. Since segment AE is parallel to segment CD, angles A and D are of the same measure by the alternate interior angle theorem. Thus, by the angle-angle theorem, triangle ABE is similar to triangle DBC, with vertices A, B, and E corresponding to vertices D, B, and C, respectively. Thus, $\frac{AB}{DB} = \frac{EB}{CB}$, or $\frac{10}{5} = \frac{8}{CB}$. It follows that $CB = 4$, and so $CE = CB + BE = 4 + 8 = 12$.

QUESTION 19

The correct answer is 6. By the distance formula, the length of radius OA is $\sqrt{(\sqrt{3})^2 + 1^2} = \sqrt{3 + 1} = 2$. Thus, $\sin(\angle AOB = \frac{1}{2}$. Therefore, the measure of $\angle AOB$ is $30°$, which is equal to $30\left(\frac{\pi}{180}\right) = \frac{\pi}{6}$ radians. Hence, the value of a is 6.

QUESTION 20

The correct answer is $\frac{2}{8}$ or $\frac{1}{4}$ or .25. In order for a system of two linear equations to have infinitely many solutions, the two equations must be equivalent. Thus, the equation $ax + by = 12$ must be equivalent to the equation $2x + 8y = 60$. Multiplying each side of $ax + by = 12$ by 5 gives $5ax + 5by = 60$, which must be equivalent to $2x + 8y = 60$. Since the right-hand sides of $5ax + 5by = 60$ and $2x + 8y = 60$ are the same, equating coefficients gives $5a = 2$, or $a = \frac{2}{5}$, and $5b = 8$, or $b = \frac{8}{5}$. Therefore, the value of $\frac{a}{b} = \left(\frac{2}{5}\right) \div \left(\frac{8}{5}\right)$, which is equal to $\frac{1}{4}$. Either the fraction 1/4 or its equivalent decimal, .25, may be gridded as the correct answer.

Alternatively, since $ax + by = 12$ is equivalent to $2x + 8y = 60$, the equation $ax + by = 12$ is equal to $2x + 8y = 60$ multiplied on each side by the same constant. Since multiplying $2x + 8y = 60$ by a constant does not change the ratio of the coefficient of x to the coefficient of y, it follows that $\frac{a}{b} = \frac{2}{8} = \frac{1}{4}$.

Section 4: Math Test – Calculator

QUESTION 1

Choice C is correct. Since the musician earns $0.09 for each download, the musician earns 0.09d dollars when the song is downloaded d times. Similarly, since the musician earns $0.002 each time the song is streamed, the musician earns 0.002s dollars when the song is streamed s times. Therefore, the musician earns a total of 0.09d + 0.002s dollars when the song is downloaded d times and streamed s times.

Choice A is incorrect because the earnings for each download and the earnings for time streamed are interchanged in the expression. Choices B and D are incorrect because in both answer choices, the musician will lose money when a song is either downloaded or streamed. However, the musician only earns money, not loses money, when the song is downloaded or streamed.

QUESTION 2

Choice B is correct. The quality control manager selects 7 lightbulbs at random for inspection out of every 400 lightbulbs produced.
A quantity of 20,000 lightbulbs is equal to $\frac{20,000}{400}$ = 50 batches of 400 lightbulbs. Therefore, at the rate of 7 lightbulbs per 400 lightbulbs produced, the quality control manager will inspect a total of 50 × 7 = 350 lightbulbs.

Choices A, C, and D are incorrect and may result from calculation errors or misunderstanding of the proportional relationship.

QUESTION 3

Choice A is correct. The value of m when ℓ is 73 can be found by substituting the 73 for ℓ in $\ell = 24 + 3.5m$ and then solving for m. The resulting equation is 73 = 24 + 3.5m; subtracting 24 from each side gives 49 = 3.5m. Then, dividing each side of 49 = 3.5m by 3.5 gives 14 = m. Therefore, when ℓ is 73, m is 14.

Choice B is incorrect and may result from adding 24 to 73, instead of subtracting 24 from 73, when solving 73 = 24 + 3.5m. Choice C is incorrect because 73 is the given value for ℓ, not for m. Choice D is incorrect and may result from substituting 73 for m, instead of for ℓ, in the equation $\ell = 24 + 3.5m$.

QUESTION 4

Choice C is correct. The amount of money the performer earns is directly proportional to the number of people who attend the performance. Thus, by the definition of direct proportionality, $M = kP$, where M is the amount of money the performer earns, in dollars, P is the number of people who attend the performance, and k is a constant.

Since the performer earns $120 when 8 people attend the performance, one can substitute 120 for M and 8 for P, giving $120 = 8k$. Hence, $k = 15$, and the relationship between the number of people who attend the performance and the amount of money, in dollars, the performer earns is $M = 15P$. Therefore, when 20 people attend the performance, the performer earns $15(20) = 300$ dollars.

Choices A, B, and D are incorrect and may result from either misconceptions about proportional relationships or computational errors.

QUESTION 5

Choice C is correct. If 43% of the money earned is used to pay for costs, then the rest, 57%, is profit. A performance where 8 people attend earns the performer $120, and 57% of $120 is $120 × 0.57 = $68.40.

Choice A is incorrect. The amount $51.60 is 43% of the money earned from a performance where 8 people attend, which is the cost of putting on the performance, not the profit from the performance. Choice B is incorrect. It is given that 57% of the money earned is profit, but 57% of $120 is not equal to $57.00. Choice D is incorrect. The profit can be found by subtracting 43% of $120 from $120, but 43% of $120 is $51.60, not $43.00. Thus, the profit is $120 − $51.60 = $68.40, not $120 − $43.00 = $77.00.

QUESTION 6

Choice B is correct. When 4 times the number x is added to 12, the result is $12 + 4x$. Since this result is equal to 8, the equation $12 + 4x = 8$ must be true. Subtracting 12 from each side of $12 + 4x = 8$ gives $4x = -4$, and then dividing both sides of $4x = -4$ by 4 gives $x = -1$. Therefore, 2 times x added to 7, or $7 + 2x$, is equal to $7 + 2(-1) = 5$.

Choice A is incorrect because -1 is the value of x, not the value of $7 + 2x$. Choices C and D are incorrect and may result from calculation errors.

QUESTION 7

Choice D is correct. The x-intercepts of the parabola represented by $y = x^2 - 6x + 8$ in the xy-plane are the values of x for which y is equal to 0. The factored form of the equation, $y = (x - 2)(x - 4)$, shows that y equals 0 if and only if $x = 2$ or $x = 4$. Thus, the factored form, $y = (x - 2)(x - 4)$, displays the x-intercepts of the parabola as the constants 2 and 4.

Choices A, B, and C are incorrect because none of these forms shows the x-intercepts 2 and 4 as constants or coefficients.

QUESTION 8

Choice D is correct. Since a player starts with k points and loses 2 points each time a task is not completed, the player's score will be $k - 2n$ after n tasks are not completed (and no additional points are gained). Since a player who fails to complete 100 tasks has a score of 200 points, the equation $200 = k - 100(2)$ must be true. This equation can be solved by adding 200 to each side, giving $k = 400$.

Choices A, B, and C are incorrect and may result from errors in setting up or solving the equation relating the player's score to the number of tasks the player fails to complete. For example, choice A may result from subtracting 200 from the left-hand side of $200 = k - 100(2)$ and adding 200 to the right-hand side.

QUESTION 9

Choice A is correct. Since x is the number of 40-pound boxes, $40x$ is the total weight, in pounds, of the 40-pound boxes; and since y is the number of 65-pound boxes, $65y$ is the total weight, in pounds, of the 65-pound boxes. The combined weight of the boxes is therefore $40x + 65y$, and the total number of boxes is $x + y$. Since the forklift can carry up to 45 boxes or up to 2,400 pounds, the inequalities that represent these relationships are $40x + 65y \le 2{,}400$ and $x + y \le 45$.

Choice B is incorrect. The second inequality correctly represents the maximum number of boxes on the forklift, but the first inequality divides, rather than multiplies, the number of boxes by their respective weights. Choice C is incorrect. The combined weight of the boxes, $40x + 65y$, must be less than or equal to 2,400 pounds, not 45; the total number of boxes, $x + y$, must be less than or equal to 45, not 2,400. Choice D is incorrect. The second inequality correctly represents the maximum weight, in pounds, of the boxes on the forklift, but the total number of boxes, $x + y$, must be less than or equal to 45, not 2,400.

QUESTION 10

Choice B is correct. It is given that $g(3) = 2$. Therefore, to find the value of $f(g(3))$, substitute 2 for g 3): $f(g$ 3)) = f 2) = 3.

Choices A, C, and D are incorrect and may result from misunderstandings about function notation.

QUESTION 11

Choice B is correct. Tony reads 250 words per minute, and he plans to read for 3 hours, which is 180 minutes, each day. Thus, Tony is planning to read $250 \times 180 = 45{,}000$ words of the novel per day. Since the novel has 349,168 words, it will take Tony $\frac{349{,}168}{45{,}000} \approx 7.76$ days of reading to finish the novel. That is, it will take Tony 7 full days of reading and most of an 8th day of reading to finish the novel. Therefore, it will take Tony 8 days to finish the novel.

Choice A is incorrect and may result from an incorrect calculation or incorrectly using the numbers provided in the table. Choice C is incorrect and may result from taking the total number of words in the novel divided by the rate Tony reads per hour. Choice D is incorrect and may result from taking the total number of words in the novel divided by the number of pages in the novel.

QUESTION 12

Choice D is correct. Since there were 175,000 tons of trash in the landfill on January 1, 2000, and the amount of trash in the landfill increased by 7,500 tons each year after that date, the amount of trash, in tons, in the landfill y years after January 1, 2000, can be expressed as $175{,}000 + 7{,}500y$. The landfill has a capacity of 325,000 tons. Therefore, the set of years where the amount of trash in the landfill is at (equal to) or above (greater than) capacity is described by the inequality $175{,}000 + 7{,}500y \geq 325{,}000$.

Choice A is incorrect. This inequality does not account for the 175,000 tons of trash in the landfill on January 1, 2000, nor does it accurately account for the 7,500 tons of trash that are added to the landfill each <u>year</u> after January 1, 2000. Choice B is incorrect. This inequality does not account for the 175,000 tons of trash in the landfill on January 1, 2000. Choice C is incorrect. This inequality represents the set of years where the amount of trash in the landfill is at or <u>below</u> capacity.

QUESTION 13

Choice D is correct. Survey research is an efficient way to estimate the preferences of a large population. In order to reliably generalize the results of survey research to a larger population, the participants should be randomly selected from all people in that population. Since this survey was conducted with a population that was not randomly selected, the results are not reliably representative of all people in the town. Therefore, of the given factors, where the survey was given makes it least likely that a reliable conclusion can be drawn about the sports-watching preferences of all people in the town.

Choice A is incorrect. In general, larger sample sizes are preferred over smaller sample sizes. However, a sample size of 117 people would have allowed a reliable conclusion about the population if the participants had been selected at random. Choice B is incorrect. Whether the population is large or small, a large enough sample taken from the population is reliably generalizable if the participants are selected at random from that population. Thus, a reliable conclusion could have been drawn about the population if the 117 survey participants had been selected at random. Choice C is incorrect. When giving a survey, participants are not forced to respond. Even though some people refused to respond, a reliable conclusion could have been drawn about the population if the participants had been selected at random.

QUESTION 14

Choice C is correct. According to the graph, the horizontal line that represents 550 billion miles traveled intersects the line of best fit at a point whose horizontal coordinate is between 2000 and 2005, and slightly closer to 2005 than to 2000. Therefore, of the choices given, 2003 best approximates the year in which the number of miles traveled by air passengers in Country X was estimated to be 550 billion.

Choice A is incorrect. According to the line of best fit, in 1997 the estimated number of miles traveled by air passengers in Country X was about 450 billion, not 550 billion. Choice B is incorrect. According to the line of best fit, in 2000 the estimated number of miles traveled by air passengers in Country X was about 500 billion, not 550 billion. Choice D is incorrect. According to the line of best fit, in 2008 the estimated number of miles traveled by air passengers in Country X was about 600 billion, not 550 billion.

QUESTION 15

Choice A is correct. The number of miles Earth travels in its one-year orbit of the Sun is 580,000,000. Because there are about 365 days per year, the number of miles Earth travels per day is $\frac{580,000,000}{365} \approx 1,589,041$. There are 24 hours in one day, so Earth travels at $\frac{1,589,041}{24} \approx 66,210$ miles per hour. Therefore, of the choices given, 66,000 miles per hour is closest to the average speed of Earth as it orbits the Sun.

Choices B, C, and D are incorrect and may result from calculation errors.

QUESTION 16

Choice B is correct. According to the table, there are 18 + 7 = 25 graduates who passed the bar exam, and 7 of them did not take the review course. Therefore, if one of the surveyed graduates who passed the bar exam is chosen at random, the probability that the person chosen did not take the review course is $\frac{7}{25}$.

Choices A, C, and D are incorrect. Each of these choices represents a different probability from the conditional probability that the question asks for. Choice A represents the following probability. If one of the surveyed graduates who passed the bar exam is chosen at random, the probability that the person chosen <u>did</u> take the review course is $\frac{18}{25}$. Choice C represents the following probability. If one of the surveyed graduates is chosen at random, the probability that the person chosen passed the bar exam is $\frac{25}{200}$. Choice D represents the following probability. If one of the surveyed graduates is chosen at random, the probability that the person chosen passed the exam and took the review course is $\frac{7}{200}$.

QUESTION 17

Choice C is correct. To find the atomic weight of an unknown element that is 20% less than the atomic weight of calcium, multiply the atomic weight, in amu, of calcium by (1 − 0.20). This gives 40)(1 − 0.20) = (40)(0.8) = 32.

Choice A is incorrect. This value is 20% of the atomic weight of calcium, not an atomic weight 20% less than that atomic weight of calcium. Choice B is incorrect. This value is 20 amu less, not 20% less, than the atomic weight of calcium. Choice D is incorrect. This value is 20% more, not 20% less, than the atomic weight of calcium.

QUESTION 18

Choice C is correct. The mean and median values of a data set are equal when there is a symmetrical distribution. For example, a normal distribution is symmetrical. If the mean and the median values are not equal, then the distribution is not symmetrical. Outliers are a small group of values that are significantly smaller or larger than the other values in the data. When there are outliers in the data, the mean will be pulled in their direction (either smaller or larger) while the median remains the same. The example in the question has a mean that is larger than the median, and so an appropriate conjecture is that large outliers are present in the data; that is, that there are a few homes that are valued much more than the rest.

Choice A is incorrect because a set of home values that are close to each other will have median and mean values that are also close to each other. Choice B is incorrect because outliers with small values will tend to make the mean lower than the median. Choice D is incorrect because a set of data where many homes are valued between $125,000 and $165,000 will likely have both a mean and a median between $125,000 and $165,000.

QUESTION 19

Choice B is correct. The median of a data set is the middle value when the data points are sorted in either ascending or descending order. There are a total of 600 data points provided, so the median will be the average of the 300th and 301st data points. When the data points are sorted in order:

- Values 1 through 260 will be 0.
- Values 261 through 450 will be 1.
- Values 451 through 540 will be 2.
- Values 541 through 580 will be 3.
- Values 581 through 600 will be 4.

Therefore, both the 300th and 301st values are 1, and hence the median is 1.

Choices A, C, and D are incorrect and may result from either a calculation error or a conceptual error.

QUESTION 20

Choice C is correct. When survey participants are selected at random from a larger population, the sample statistics calculated from the survey can be generalized to the larger population. Since 10 of 300 students surveyed at Lincoln School have 4 siblings, one can estimate that this same ratio holds for all 2,400 students at Lincoln School. Also, since 10 of 300 students surveyed at Washington School have 4 siblings, one can estimate that this same ratio holds for all 3,300 students at Washington School. Therefore, approximately $\frac{10}{300} \times 2,400 = 80$ students at Lincoln School and $\frac{10}{300} \times 3,300 = 110$ students at Washington School are expected to have 4 siblings. Thus, the total number of students with 4 siblings at Washington School is expected to be $110 - 80 = 30$ more than the total number of students with 4 siblings at Lincoln School.

Choices A, B, and D are incorrect and may result from either conceptual or calculation errors. For example, choice A is incorrect; even though there is the same <u>ratio</u> of survey participants from Lincoln School and Washington School with 4 siblings, the two schools have a different <u>total</u> number of students, and thus, a different expected total number of students with 4 siblings.

QUESTION 21

Choice D is correct. The difference between the number of hours the project takes, y, and the number of hours the project was estimated to take, x, is $|y - x|$. If the goal is met, the difference is less than 10, which can be represented as $|y - x| < 10$, or $-10 < y - x < 10$.

Choice A is incorrect. This inequality states that the estimated number of hours plus the actual number of hours is less than 10, which cannot be true because the estimate is greater than 100. Choice B is incorrect. This inequality states that the actual number of hours is greater than the estimated number of hours plus 10, which could be true only if the goal of being within 10 hours of the estimate were not met. Choice C is incorrect. This inequality states that the actual number of hours is less than the estimated number of hours minus 10, which could be true only if the goal of being within 10 hours of the estimate were not met.

QUESTION 22

Choice B is correct. To rearrange the formula $I = \frac{P}{4\pi r^2}$ in terms of r^2, first multiply each side of the equation by r^2. This yields $r^2 I = \frac{P}{4\pi}$. Then dividing each side of $r^2 I = \frac{P}{4\pi}$ by I gives $r^2 = \frac{P}{4\pi I}$.

Choices A, C, and D are incorrect and may result from algebraic errors during the rearrangement of the formula.

QUESTION 23

Choice A is correct. If I_A is the intensity measured by Observer A from a distance of r_A and I_B is the intensity measured by Observer B from a distance of r_B, then $I_A = 16I_B$. Using the formula $I = \dfrac{P}{4\pi^2}$, the intensity measured by Observer A is $I_A = \dfrac{P}{4\pi r_A^2}$, which can also be written in terms of I_B as $I_A = 16I_B = 16\left(\dfrac{P}{4\pi r_B^2}\right)$. Setting the right-hand sides of these two equations equal to each other gives $\dfrac{P}{4\pi r_A^2} = 16\left(\dfrac{P}{4\pi r_B^2}\right)$, which relates the distance of Observer A from the radio antenna to the distance of Observer B from the radio antenna. Canceling the common factor $\dfrac{P}{4\pi}$ and rearranging the equation gives $r_B^2 = 16r_A^2$. Taking the ' square root of each side of $r_B^2 = 16r_A^2$ gives $r_B = 4r_A$, and then dividing each side by 4 yields $r_A = \dfrac{1}{4}r_B$. Therefore, the distance of Observer A from the radio antenna is $\dfrac{1}{4}$ the distance of Observer B from the radio antenna.

Choices B, C, and D are incorrect and may result from errors in deriving or using the formula $\dfrac{P}{4\pi r_A^2} = (16)\left(\dfrac{P}{4\pi r_B^2}\right)$.

QUESTION 24

Choice A is correct. The equation of a circle with center (h, k) and radius r is $(x - h)^2 + (y - k)^2 = r^2$. To put the equation $x^2 + y^2 + 4x - 2y = -1$ in this form, complete the square as follows:

$$x^2 + y^2 + 4x - 2y = -1$$

$$(x^2 + 4x) + (y^2 - 2y) = -1$$

$$(x^2 + 4x + 4) - 4 + (y^2 - 2y + 1) - 1 = -1$$

$$(x + 2)^2 + (y - 1)^2 - 4 - 1 = -1$$

$$(x + 2)^2 + (y - 1)^2 = 4 = 2^2$$

Therefore, the radius of the circle is 2.

Choice C is incorrect because it is the square of the radius, not the radius. Choices B and D are incorrect and may result from errors in rewriting the given equation in standard form.

QUESTION 25

Choice A is correct. In the xy-plane, the slope m of the line that passes through the points (x_1, y_1) and $(x_2, y_2$ is given by the formula $m = \dfrac{y_2 - y_1}{x_2 - x_1}$. Thus, if the graph of the linear function f has intercepts at $(a, 0)$ and $(0, b$, then the slope of the line that is the graph of $y = f(x)$ is $m = \dfrac{0 - b}{a - 0} = -\dfrac{b}{a}$. It is given that $a + b = 0$, and so $a = -b$. Finally, substituting $-b$ for a in $m = -\dfrac{b}{a}$ gives $m = -\dfrac{b}{-b} = 1$, which is positive.

Choices B, C, and D are incorrect and may result from a conceptual misunderstanding or a calculation error.

QUESTION 26

Choice D is correct. The definition of the graph of a function f in the xy-plane is the set of all points $(x, f(x$. Thus, for $-4 \leq a \leq 4$, the value of $f(a$ is 1 if and only if the unique point on the graph of f with x-coordinate a has y-coordinate equal to 1. The points on the graph of f with x-coordinates -4, $\frac{3}{2}$, and 3 are, respectively, $(-4, 1), \left(\frac{3}{2}, 1\right)$, and $3, 1)$. Therefore, all of the values of f given in I, II, and III are equal to 1.

Choices A, B, and C are incorrect because they each omit at least one value of x for which $f(x = 1$.

QUESTION 27

Choice D is correct. According to the graph, in the interval from 0 to 10 minutes, the non-insulated sample decreased in temperature by about 18°C, while the insulated sample decreased by about 8°C; in the interval from 10 to 20 minutes, the non-insulated sample decreased in temperature by about 9°C, while the insulated sample decreased by about 5°C; in the interval from 40 to 50 minutes, the non-insulated sample decreased in temperature by about 1°C, while the insulated sample decreased by about 3°C; and in the interval from 50 to 60 minutes, the non-insulated sample decreased in temperature by about 1°C, while the insulated sample decreased by about 2°C. The description in choice D accurately summarizes these rates of temperature change over the given intervals. (Note that since the two samples of water have equal mass and so must lose the same amount of heat to cool from 60°C to 25°C, the faster cooling of the non-insulated sample at the start of the cooling process must be balanced out by faster cooling of the insulated sample at the end of the cooling process.)

Choices A, B, and C are incorrect. None of these descriptions accurately compares the rates of temperature change shown in the graph for the 10-minute intervals.

QUESTION 28

Choice B is correct. In the xy-plane, the slope m of the line that passes through the points (x_1, y_1) and (x_2, y_2) is $m = \frac{y_2 - y_1}{x_2 - x_1}$. Thus, the slope of the line through the points E 1, 0) and C 7, 2) is $\frac{2 - 0}{7 - 1}$, which simplifies to $\frac{2}{6} = \frac{1}{3}$. Therefore, diagonal AC has a slope of $\frac{1}{3}$. The other diagonal of the square is a segment of the line that passes through points B and D. The diagonals of a square are perpendicular, and so the product of the slopes of the diagonals is equal to -1. Thus, the slope of the line that passes through B and D is -3 because $\frac{1}{3}$ $-3) = -1$.

Hence, an equation of the line that passes through B and D can be written as $y = -3x + b$, where b is the y-intercept of the line. Since diagonal BD will pass through the center of the square, $E(1, 0)$, the equation $0 = -3(1) + b$ holds. Solving this equation for b gives $b = 3$. Therefore, an equation of the line that passes through points B and D is $y = -3x + 3$, which can be rewritten as $y = -3(x - 1)$.

Choices A, C, and D are incorrect and may result from a conceptual error or a calculation error.

QUESTION 29

Choice B is correct. Substituting 3 for y in $y = ax^2 + b$ gives $3 = ax^2 + b$, which can be rewritten as $3 - b = ax^2$. Since $y = 3$ is one of the equations in the given system, any solution x of $3 - b = ax^2$ corresponds to the solution $(x, 3)$ of the given system. Since the square of a real number is always nonnegative, and a positive number has two square roots, the equation $3 - b = ax^2$ will have two solutions for x if and only if (1) $a > 0$ and $b < 3$ or (2) $a < 0$ and $b > 3$. Of the values for a and b given in the choices, only $a = -2$, $b = 4$ satisfy one of these pairs of conditions.

Alternatively, if $a = -2$ and $b = 4$, then the second equation would be $y = -2x^2 + 4$. The graph of this quadratic equation in the xy-plane is a parabola with y-intercept $(0, 4)$ that opens downward. The graph of the first equation, $y = 3$, is the horizontal line that contains the point $(0, 3)$. As shown below, these two graphs have two points of intersection, and therefore, this system of equations has exactly two real solutions. Graphing shows that none of the other three choices produces a system with exactly two real solutions.)

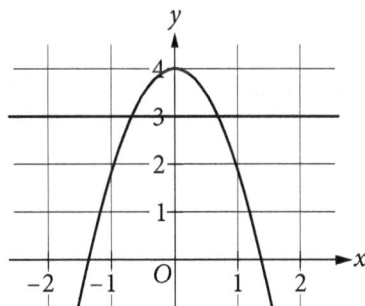

Choices A, C, and D are incorrect and may result from calculation or conceptual errors.

QUESTION 30

Choice A is correct. The regular hexagon can be divided into 6 equilateral triangles of side length a by drawing the six segments from the center of the regular hexagon to each of its 6 vertices. Since the area of the hexagon is $384\sqrt{3}$ square inches, the area of each equilateral triangle will be $\dfrac{384\sqrt{3}}{6} = 64\sqrt{3}$ square inches.

Drawing any altitude of an equilateral triangle divides it into two 30°-60°-90° triangles. If the side length of the equilateral triangle is a, then the hypotenuse of each 30°-60°-90° triangle is a, and the altitude of the equilateral triangle will be the side opposite the 60° angle in each of the 30°-60°-90° triangles. Thus, the altitude of the equilateral triangle is $\dfrac{\sqrt{3}}{2}a$, and the area of the equilateral triangle is $\dfrac{1}{2}(a)\left(\dfrac{\sqrt{3}}{2}a\right) = \dfrac{\sqrt{3}}{4}a^2$. Since the area of each equilateral triangle is $64\sqrt{3}$ square inches, it follows that $a^2 = \dfrac{4}{\sqrt{3}}64\sqrt{3} = 256$ square inches. And since the area of the square with side length a is a^2, it follows that the square has area 256 square inches.

Choices B, C, and D are incorrect and may result from calculation or conceptual errors.

QUESTION 31

The correct answer is 14. Since the coastal geologist estimates that the country's beaches are eroding at a rate of 1.5 feet every year, they will erode by $1.5x$ feet in x years. Thus, if the beaches erode by 21 feet in x years, the equation $1.5x = 21$ must hold. The value of x is then $\dfrac{21}{1.5} = 14$. Therefore, according to the geologist's estimate, it will take 14 years for the country's beaches to erode by 21 feet.

QUESTION 32

The correct answer is 7. There are 60 minutes in each hour, and so there are $60h$ minutes in h hours. Since h hours and 30 minutes is equal to 450 minutes, it follows that $60h + 30 = 450$. This equation can be simplified to $60h = 420$, and so the value of h is $\dfrac{420}{60} = 7$.

QUESTION 33

The correct answer is 11. It is given that the function $f(x)$ passes through the point $(3, 6)$. Thus, if $x = 3$, the value of $f(x)$ is 6 (since the graph of f in the xy-plane is the set of all points $(x, f(x))$. Substituting 3 for x and 6 for $f(x)$ in $f(x = 3x^2 - bx + 12$ gives $6 = 3(3)^2 - b(3) + 12$. Performing the operations on the right-hand side of this equation gives $6 = 3(9) - 3b + 12 = 27 - 3b + 12 = 39 - 3b$. Subtracting 39 from each side of $6 = 39 - 3b$ gives $-33 = -3b$, and then dividing each side of $-3b = -33$ by -3 gives the value of b as 11.

QUESTION 34

The correct answer is 105. Let D be the number of hours Doug spent in the tutoring lab, and let L be the number of hours Laura spent in the tutoring lab. Since Doug and Laura spent a combined total of 250 hours in the tutoring lab, the equation $D + L = 250$ holds. The number of hours Doug spent in the lab is 40 more than the number of hours Laura spent in the lab, and so the equation $D = L + 40$ holds. Substituting $L + 40$ for D in $D + L = 250$ gives $(L + 40) + L = 250$, or $40 + 2L = 250$. Solving this equation gives $L = 105$. Therefore, Laura spent 105 hours in the tutoring lab.

QUESTION 35

The correct answer is 15. The amount, a, that Jane has deposited after t fixed weekly deposits is equal to the initial deposit plus the total amount of money Jane has deposited in the t fixed weekly deposits. This amount a is given to be $a = 18t + 15$. The amount she deposited in the t fixed weekly deposits is the amount of the weekly deposit times t; hence, this amount must be given by the term $18t$ in $a = 18t + 15$ (and so Jane must have deposited 18 dollars each week after the initial deposit). Therefore, the amount of Jane's original deposit, in dollars, is $a - 18t = 15$.

QUESTION 36

The correct answer is 32. Since segments LM and MN are tangent to the circle at points L and N, respectively, angles OLM and ONM are right angles. Thus, in quadrilateral $OLMN$, the measure of angle O is $360° - (90° + 60° + 90°) = 120°$. Thus, in the circle, central angle O cuts off $\frac{120}{360} = \frac{1}{3}$ of the circumference; that is, minor arc LN is $\frac{1}{3}$ of the circumference. Since the circumference is 96, the length of minor arc LN is $\frac{1}{3} \times 96 = 32$.

QUESTION 37

The correct answer is 3284. According to the formula, the number of plants one year from now will be $3000 + 0.2(3000)\left(1 - \frac{3000}{4000}\right)$, which is equal to 3150. Then, using the formula again, the number of plants two years from now will be $3150 + 0.2(3150)\left(1 - \frac{3150}{4000}\right)$, which is 3283.875. Rounding this value to the nearest whole number gives 3284.

QUESTION 38

The correct answer is 7500. If the number of plants is to be increased from 3000 this year to 3360 next year, then the number of plants that the environment can support, K, must satisfy the equation $3360 = 3000 + 0.2(3000)\left(1 - \frac{3000}{K}\right)$. Dividing both sides of this equation by 3000 gives $1.12 = 1 + 0.2\left(1 - \frac{3000}{K}\right)$, and therefore, it must be true that $0.2\left(1 - \frac{3000}{K}\right) = 0.12$, or equivalently, $1 - \frac{3000}{K} = 0.6$. It follows that $\frac{3000}{K} = 0.4$, and so $K = \frac{3000}{0.4} = 7500$.

SAT Practice Test #3

Section 1: Reading Test

QUESTION 1

Choice B is the best answer. In the passage, Lady Carlotta is approached by the "imposingly attired lady" Mrs. Quabarl while standing at a train station (lines 32-35). Mrs. Quabarl assumes Lady Carlotta is her new nanny, Miss Hope: "You must be Miss Hope, the governess I've come to meet" (lines 36-37). Lady Carlotta does not correct Mrs. Quabarl's mistake and replies, "Very well, if I must I must" (line 39).

Choices A, C, and D are incorrect because the passage is not about a woman weighing a job choice, seeking revenge on an acquaintance, or disliking her new employer.

QUESTION 2

Choice C is the best answer. In lines 1-3, the narrator states that Lady Carlotta "stepped out on to the platform of the small wayside station and took a turn or two up and down its uninteresting length" in order to "kill time." In this context, Lady Carlotta was taking a "turn," or a short walk, along the platform while waiting for the train to leave the station.

Choices A, B, and D are incorrect because in this context "turn" does not mean slight movement, change in rotation, or course correction. While Lady Carlotta may have had to rotate her body while moving across the station, "took a turn" implies that Lady Carlotta took a short walk along the platform's length.

QUESTION 3

Choice A is the best answer. In lines 10-14, the narrator states that some of Lady Carlotta's acquaintances would often admonish, or criticize, Lady Carlotta for meddling in or openly expressing her opinion on other people's affairs.

Choices B, C, and D are incorrect because the narrator does not suggest that other people viewed Lady Carlotta as tactful, ambitious, or unfriendly.

QUESTION 4

Choice A is the best answer. In lines 10-14, the narrator states that people often criticized Lady Carlotta and suggested that she not interfere in other people's affairs, which were "none of her business." The fact that people often were critical of Lady Carlotta's behavior provides evidence that Lady Carlotta was outspoken.

Choices B, C, and D do not provide the best evidence that Lady Carlotta was outspoken. Choices B, C, and D mention Lady Carlotta, but do not specify how others view her.

QUESTION 5

Choice C is the best answer. Lines 4-10 establish that Lady Carlotta intervened on the part of a struggling horse, the kind of behavior for which, lines 10-14 indicate, she received "plentiful admonition" from "certain of her acquaintances," who believed that she should mind her own business. Lines 14-22 indicate that Lady Carlotta had "only once . . . put the doctrine of non-interference into practice," and that was when "one of its most eloquent exponents" had been "besieged for nearly three hours in a small and extremely uncomfortable may-tree by an angry boar-pig" while Lady Carlotta blithely ignored the other woman's hypocritical pleas for interference. This incident provides insight into Lady Carlotta's character and also evokes humor through language choice (e.g., the droll understatement of "it is to be feared that [Lady Carlotta] lost the friendship of the ultimately rescued lady"; lines 22-23) and the sense that, narratively speaking, justice has been served.

Choice A is incorrect because nothing about the incident suggests deception on Lady Carlotta's part. Choice B is incorrect because there is nothing subtle about Lady Carlotta leaving another woman stuck in a tree for nearly three hours. Moreover, the passage does not suggest that this was an act of cruelty on Lady Carlotta's part; rather, the passage suggests that Lady Carlotta was justified in giving the woman stuck in a tree exactly what the woman had so often asked for: noninterference. Choice D is incorrect because the passage indicates that Lady Carlotta was acting consistently with her beliefs and only invoked the doctrine to teach a hypocritical person a lesson.

QUESTION 6

Choice A is the best answer. The narrator explains that Mrs. Quabarl told Lady Carlotta about the "nature of the charge" when she gave Lady Carlotta details about the Quabarl children (line 53-61). Since Lady Carlotta is pretending to be a governess, the term "charge" refers to her responsibilities, or job duties, when caring for the Quabarl children.

Choices B, C, and D are incorrect because in this context "charge" does not mean attack, fee, or expense.

QUESTION 7

Choice A is the best answer. Lady Carlotta learns about Mrs. Quabarl's children Claude, Wilfrid, and Irene (lines 53-58). The narrator then describes Mrs. Quabarl's child Viola as "something or other else of a mould equally commonplace among children of that class and type in the twentieth century" (lines 58-61). This statement about Viola implies that all of the Quabarl children have skills typical, or "of a mould equally commonplace," to other peers in their social class.

Choices B, C, and D are incorrect because the narrator does not indicate that all of the Quabarl children are unusually creative and intelligent, hostile to the idea of having a governess, or more educated than their peers.

QUESTION 8

Choice B is the best answer. In lines 62-69, Mrs. Quabarl explains to Lady Carlotta that she wants her children to actively participate in their education, and that Lady Carlotta should not create lessons that require her children to simply memorize historical figures and dates. Mrs. Quabarl emphasizes an education centered on active engagement when she states that her children should "not only be TAUGHT . . . but INTERESTED in what they learn."

Choices A, C, and D are incorrect because the narrator does not suggest that Mrs. Quabarl favors an education that emphasizes traditional values, artistic experimentation, or factual retention.

QUESTION 9

Choice B is the best answer. In lines 77-82, the narrator describes Mrs. Quabarl as appearing "magnificent and autocratic," or outwardly domineering, but easily "cowed and apologetic" when someone challenges, or defies, her authority.

Choices A, C, and D are incorrect because the narrator does not describe Mrs. Quabarl as selfish, bitter, or frequently imprudent.

QUESTION 10

Choice D is the best answer. In lines 77-82, the narrator provides evidence that Mrs. Quabarl appears imposing, or autocratic, but is easily defied, or opposed: "She was one of those imperfectly self-assured individuals who are magnificent and autocratic as long as they are not seriously opposed. The least show of unexpected resistance goes a long way towards rendering them cowed and apologetic."

Choices A, B, and C do not provide the best evidence that Mrs. Quabarl appears imposing but is easily defied. Choices A and B are incorrect because they present Mrs. Quabarl's opinions on railway companies and education, and choice C is incorrect because it focuses on Lady Carlotta, not Mrs. Quabarl.

QUESTION 11

Choice A is the best answer. While the author predominantly supports the use of public transportation, in the third paragraph he recognizes some limitations to the public transportation system: it is a "depressing experience" (lines 25-26) and "underfunded, ill-maintained, and ill-planned" (line 31).

Choices B, C, and D are incorrect because the third paragraph does not expand upon an argument made in the first two paragraphs, provide an overview of a problem, or advocate ending the use of public transportation.

QUESTION 12

Choice C is the best answer. The author notes that in North America "hopping in a car almost always gets you to your destination more quickly" (lines 32-34). This statement suggests that speed is one advantage to driving in North America.

Choices A, B, and D are incorrect because the author does not cite environmental impact, convenience, or cost as advantages of driving in North America.

QUESTION 13

Choice D is the best answer. In lines 32-34, the author provides evidence that speed is one advantage to driving in North America, because driving "almost always gets you to your destination more quickly."

Choices A, B, and C do not provide the best evidence that speed is one advantage to driving in North America. Choices A and B are incorrect because they offer general information about using public transportation. Choice C is incorrect because although these lines mention North America, they focus on the disadvantages of public transportation.

QUESTION 14

Choice B is the best answer. The author argues in the fourth paragraph that public transportation "can be faster, more comfortable, and cheaper than the private automobile" (lines 36-37) and provides examples of fast and convenient public transportation systems.

Choices A, C, and D are incorrect because they focus on points made in the fourth paragraph rather than the paragraph's central idea.

QUESTION 15

Choice B is the best answer. In lines 35-37, the author provides evidence that some public transportation systems are superior to driving, because public transportation "can be faster, more comfortable, and cheaper than the private automobile."

Choices A, C, and D do not provide the best evidence that some public transportation systems are superior to driving, as they highlight points made in the fourth paragraph rather than the paragraph's central idea.

QUESTION 16

Choice C is the best answer. In the last paragraph, the author explains the trend that people who became adults around the end of the twentieth century are more willing to use public transportation than people from older generations. The author notes, "If you credit the demographers, this transit trend has legs" (lines 58-59). In this context, "credit" means to believe the demographers' claims about the trend.

Choices A, B, and D are incorrect because in this context, "credit" does not mean endow, attribute, or honor.

QUESTION 17

Choice B is the best answer. In lines 59-63, the author explains the trend of people who became adults around the end of the twentieth century "tend[ing] to favor cities over suburbs." In this context, these adults "favor," or prefer, cities over suburbs.

Choices A, C, and D are incorrect because in this context "favor" does not mean indulge, resemble, or serve.

QUESTION 18

Choice B is the best answer. In lines 63-67, the author explains that while riding on public transportation, people can use personal electronic devices, such as "iPads, MP3 players, Kindles, and smartphones."

Choices A, C, and D are incorrect because they do not show that public transportation is compatible with the use of personal electronic devices.

QUESTION 19

Choice A is the best answer. Figure 1 shows that 10.7% of public transportation passengers are students and 6.7% of public transportation passengers are retirees. Thus, more students than retirees use public transportation.

Choices B and C are incorrect because figure 1 shows that more employed than unemployed people use public transportation and that more employed people than homemakers use public transportation.

Choice D is incorrect because figure 1 does not explain how frequently passengers use public transportation; it only identifies public transportation passengers by their primary occupation.

QUESTION 20

Choice A is the best answer. Figure 1 shows that 72% of public transportation passengers are "employed outside the home," and figure 2 indicates that 59.1% of public transportation trips are for "work." It can be inferred from these figures that many public transportation passengers take public transportation to their place of employment.

Choices B, C, and D are incorrect because figure 1 and figure 2 do not indicate that public transportation passengers primarily use the system to run errands, use their own car on weekends, or are planning to purchase a car.

QUESTION 21

Choice D is the best answer. The author explains that Ken Dial created an experiment to study the evolution of flight by observing how baby Chukars learn to fly. During the experiment, Dial noticed the unusual way Chukars use their "'wings and legs cooperatively'" to scale hay bales (lines 38-43), and he created "a series of ingenious experiments" (line 46) to study this observation. After his additional experiments, Dial determined that these baby birds angle "their wings differently from birds in flight" (lines 49-50).

Choices A, B, and C are incorrect because they do not accurately reflect the sequence of events in the passage.

QUESTION 22

Choice A is the best answer. In lines 6-9, the author explains that Dial was "challenged," or dared, by graduate students to develop "new data" on a long-standing scientific debate (the "ground-up-tree-down" theory).

Choices B, C, and D are incorrect because in this context "challenged" does not mean required, disputed with, or competed with.

QUESTION 23

Choice A is the best answer. The author explains that Dial created his initial experiment to try and create "new data on the age-old ground-up-tree-down debate," and that he looked for "clues" in "how baby game birds learned to fly" (lines 8-11). The note at the beginning of the passage explains the "age-old ground-up-tree down debate" and offers two different theories on how birds evolved to fly. Finally, the last paragraph of the passage discusses WAIR in an evolutionary context.

Choices B, C, and D are incorrect because they do not identify Dial's central assumption in setting up his research.

QUESTION 24

Choice B is the best answer. In lines 6-11, the author provides evidence that Dial's central assumption in setting up his research is that the acquisition of flight in young birds is linked to the acquisition of flight in their ancestors. The author notes that Dial created a project to "come up with new data on the age-old ground-up-tree-down debate."

Choices A, C, and D do not provide the best evidence that Dial's central assumption in setting up his research is that the acquisition of flight in young birds is linked to the acquisition of flight in their ancestors. Choices A, C, and D are incorrect because they focus on Dial's experiment and his observations on ground birds.

QUESTION 25

Choice C is the best answer. When a rancher observed Dial's laboratory setup, he was "incredulous" that the Chukars were living on the ground, and he advised Dial to give the birds "something to climb on" (lines 16-23). This "key piece of advice" (line 14) led Dial to add hay bales to his laboratory. Dial later noticed that the Chukars were using their legs and wings to scale the hay bales, and this observation became the focal point of his research.

Choices A, B, and D are incorrect because the incident with the local rancher did not serve to reveal Dial's motivation for creating the project, emphasize differences in laboratory and field research, or introduce a contributor to a scientific theory.

QUESTION 26

Choice C is the best answer. The author explains that Dial's "aha moment" came when he determined the Chukars used "their legs and wings cooperatively" to scale the hay bales (lines 40-42). Dial then created additional experiments to study how the birds dealt with gradually steeper inclines: "[he filmed] the birds as they raced up textured ramps tilted at increasing angles" (lines 46-48).

Choices A, B, and D are incorrect because Dial's "aha moment" was not followed by Dial teaching the birds to fly, studying videos to find out why the birds no longer hopped, or consulting with other researchers.

QUESTION 27

Choice B is the best answer. Dial observed that as the Chukars raced up steep ramps, they "began to flap" and "aimed their flapping down and backward, using the force . . . to keep their feet firmly pressed against the ramp" (lines 49-53). Dial determined that the position of their flapping wings facilitated the baby Chukars' traction on the steep ramps.

Choices A, C, and D are incorrect because the passage does not indicate that the Chukars' speed, alternation of wing and foot movement, or continual hopping motions facilitated their traction on steep ramps.

QUESTION 28

Choice B is the best answer. In lines 61-63, the author explains that Dial named his scientific finding "WAIR, for wing-assisted incline running, and went on to document it in a wide range of species." In this context, Dial "documented," or recorded, the existence of WAIR in numerous bird species.

Choices A, C, and D are incorrect because in this context, "document" does not mean to portray, publish, or process.

QUESTION 29

Choice D is the best answer. In lines 70-74, the author explains that gliding animals do not use a "flapping flight stroke," or WAIR, wing-assisted incline running. Since Chukars, a ground bird, use WAIR to help scale steep inclines, it can be reasonably inferred that gliding animals do not use WAIR to aid in climbing slopes.

Choices A, B, and C are incorrect because the passage does not include information on gliding animals' offspring, their method of locomotion, or their feeding habits.

QUESTION 30

Choice D is the best answer. In lines 73-75, the author provides evidence that "the flapping flight stroke" is "something gliding animals don't do."

Choices A, B, and C do not provide the best evidence that gliding animals do not use a flapping stroke to aid in climbing slopes. These choices do not contain information about gliding animals.

QUESTION 31

Choice B is the best answer. In lines 21-24, the authors of Passage 1 state society's "common happiness" is dependent on women never becoming involved in politics. In this context, the authors of Passage 1 are suggesting that all members of society can have a "common," or shared, happiness.

Choices A, C, and D are incorrect because in this context, "common" does not mean average, coarse, or similar.

QUESTION 32

Choice C is the best answer. In lines 25-30, the authors of Passage 1 state that women should seek "gentle occupations and the cares of the home" so they can avoid performing difficult, or "strenuous," and unpleasant, or "onerous," tasks.

Choices A, B, and D are incorrect because the authors of Passage 1 do not suggest that running a household and raising children are rewarding for both sexes, yield less value for society, or require professional or political skills.

QUESTION 33

Choice C is the best answer. In lines 25-30, the authors of Passage 1 provide evidence that women should run households and raise children because these roles do not require "strenuous habits and onerous duties."

Choices A, B, and D do not provide the best evidence that running a household and raising children entail very few activities that are difficult or unpleasant; rather, these lines offer general information about the differences between the sexes.

QUESTION 34

Choice D is the best answer. In lines 41-46, Wollstonecraft argues that if women do not receive an education "to become the companion of man," or one that is comparable to men's education, then society will not progress in "knowledge and virtue."

Choices A, B, and C are incorrect because Wollstonecraft does not suggest that society can progress only if women have happiness and financial security, follow societal rules, or replace men as figures of power.

QUESTION 35

Choice C is the best answer. Wollstonecraft argues that women should be granted an education comparable to men's so that truth is "common to all" (lines 41-46). Wollstonecraft states that education will "strengthen [women's] reason till she comprehend her duty" (lines 49-50). In this context, Wollstonecraft is arguing that education will improve women's "reason," or intellect, and allow women to consider their role in society.

Choices A, B, and D are incorrect because in this context "reason" does not mean motive, sanity, or explanation.

QUESTION 36

Choice A is the best answer. In lines 72-78, Wollstonecraft argues that the laws passed by society's leaders allow men to "contend for their freedom" but serve to "subjugate women." In this context, "subjugate" means to control. Wollstonecraft is arguing that society's leaders grant men freedoms that are denied to women.

Choices B, C, and D are incorrect because Wollstonecraft does not claim that society's leaders have granted freedoms that created a general reduction in individual virtue, caused arguments about happiness, or ensured equality for all people.

QUESTION 37

Choice D is the best answer. In lines 72-75, Wollstonecraft provides evidence that society's leaders grant freedoms that privilege men. She argues that while society's leaders believe they "are acting in the manner best calculated to promote [women's] happiness," their decisions don't allow women to "contend for their freedom."

Choices A, B, and C do not provide the best evidence that society's leaders grant freedoms that privilege men over women.

QUESTION 38

Choice C is the best answer. Wollstonecraft cites the statement made by the authors of Passage 1 that excluding women from political participation is "according to abstract principles . . . impossible to explain" (lines 61-65). Wollstonecraft then states that if the authors of Passage 1 can discuss "the abstract rights of man" they should be able to discuss the abstract rights of women (lines 66-69). In these lines, Wollstonecraft is developing her argument by highlighting a flaw in the reasoning presented by the authors of Passage 1.

Choices A, B, and D are incorrect because Wollstonecraft does not refer to the statement made in Passage 1 to call into question the authors' qualifications, dispute the assertion that women are excluded by their own government (sentence one of Passage 1), or validate the authors' conclusions on gender roles.

QUESTION 39

Choice A is the best answer. The authors of Passage 1 argue that while restricting women's freedoms may be "impossible to explain" (line 7), this restriction is necessary for society's overall happiness (lines 13-17). Wollstonecraft, however, strongly challenges this argument, asking the authors of Passage 1, "Who made man the exclusive judge" of which freedoms are granted to women, and likening society's male leaders to tyrants as they deny women their "civil and political rights" and leave them "groping in the dark" (lines 78-88).

Choices B, C, and D are incorrect because they do not characterize the overall relationship between Passage 1 and Passage 2.

QUESTION 40

Choice D is the best answer. The authors of Passage 1 admit that women are "excluded by the other half [men] from any participation in government" (lines 1-2), and Wollstonecraft states that society's male leaders create laws that deny women "civil and political rights" (line 86).

Choices A, B, and C are incorrect because the authors of both passages would not agree that women had the same preferences as men, required a good education, or were as happy as men.

QUESTION 41

Choice A is the best answer. Wollstonecraft argues in the final paragraph of Passage 2 that society's male leaders are like "tyrants" that deny women "civil and political rights" (lines 81-88). The authors of Passage 1 would most likely argue that allowing women these rights would be "a reversal of [society's] primary destinies" as society's leaders should only seek women's interests as they pertain to the "wishes of nature," such as women's role as mothers (lines 18-30). The authors of Passage 1 clarify that "nature" created two sexes for a particular reason, so while men can exercise civil and political rights, women are not naturally suited to these activities (lines 30-36).

Choices B and C are incorrect because they are not supported by information in Passage 1. Choice D is incorrect because the authors of Passage 1 do not mention "natural law," only the "wishes of nature."

QUESTION 42

Choice C is the best answer. When discussing problems with bee colonies, the authors use phrases like "we suspect" (line 19) and "we postulate" (line 21) to show they are hypothesizing reasons for bee colonies' susceptibility to mite infestations. The use of "can," "may," and "could" creates a tentative tone and provides further evidence that the authors believe, but are not certain, that their hypothesis is correct.

Choices A, B, and D are incorrect because the authors' use of "can," "may," and "could" does not create an optimistic, dubious, or critical tone.

QUESTION 43

Choice C is the best answer. In lines 24-28, the authors hypothesize that bee colonies will be susceptible to mite infestations if they do not occasionally feed on pyrethrum producing plants. In lines 42-46, they suggest creating a trial where a "small number of commercial honey bee colonies are offered a number of pyrethrum producing plants" to test their hypothesis.

Choices A, B, and D are incorrect because the authors do not hypothesize that honeybees' exposure to both pyrethrums and mites will cause the honeybees to develop secondary infections, that beekeepers should increase their use of insecticides, or that humans are more susceptible to varroa mites.

QUESTION 44

Choice D is the best answer. In lines 24-28, the authors provide evidence that a bee colony may be more resistant to mite infections if the bees eat pyrethrums because this diet may help prevent bees from becoming "immunocompromised or nutritionally deficient." In lines 42-50, the authors suggest testing this hypothesis in a trial on honeybees.

Choices A, B, and C do not describe any of the authors' hypotheses.

QUESTION 45

Choice D is the best answer. The authors explain that when beekeepers use commercially produced insecticides to fight mite infections, they may "further weaken" bees that are "immunocompromised or nutritionally deficient" (lines 31-35).

Choices A, B, and C are incorrect because the authors do not suggest that beekeepers' use of commercially produced insecticides increases mite populations, kills bacteria, or destroys bees' primary food source.

QUESTION 46

Choice C is the best answer. In lines 31-35, the authors provide evidence that beekeepers' use of commercially produced insecticides may cause further harm to "immunocompromised or nutritionally deficient bees."

Choices A, B, and D are incorrect because they do not provide the best evidence that beekeepers' use of commercially produced insecticides may be harmful to bees; choices A, B, and D focus on mite infestations' impact on honeybees.

QUESTION 47

Choice B is the best answer. In lines 31-35, the authors argue that beekeepers' use of insecticides to control mite infestations may be harmful to some bees. The authors then state, "We further postulate that the proper dosage necessary to prevent mite infestation may be better left to the bees" (lines 35-37). In this context, the authors "postulate," or put forth the idea that the bees may naturally control mite infestations better than insecticides.

Choices A, C, and D are incorrect because in this context, "postulate" does not mean to make an unfounded assumption, question a belief or theory, or conclude based on firm evidence.

QUESTION 48

Choice B is the best answer. In the fourth paragraph the authors propose a trial to study if honeybees' consumption of pyrethrum producing plants helps the honeybees defend against mite infestations. In the experiment, the authors plan to offer honey bee colonies both pyrethrum producing plants and "a typical bee food source such as clover" to determine if these different diets affect the bees' susceptibility to mite infestations.

Choices A, C, and D are incorrect because the main purpose of the fourth paragraph is not to summarize the results of an experiment, provide a comparative nutritional analysis, or predict an outcome of an unfinished experiment.

QUESTION 49

Choice A is the best answer. In lines 43-45, the authors propose a scientific trial in which honeybees are "offered a number of pyrethrum producing plants, as well as a typical bee food source such as clover." Since the authors contrast the "pyrethrum producing plants" with clover, a "typical bee food source," it can be assumed that clover does not produce pyrethrums.

Choice B is incorrect because it is stated in the passage. Choices C and D are incorrect because they are not assumptions made by the authors.

QUESTION 50

Choice B is the best answer. The table shows that 77 percent of the honeybee colonies with colony collapse disorder were infected by all four pathogens.

Choices A, C, and D are incorrect because they do not identify the percent of honeybee colonies with colony collapse disorder that were infected by all four pathogens as based on data in the table.

QUESTION 51

Choice D is the best answer. The table shows that 81 percent of colonies without colony collapse disorder were affected by the pathogen *Nosema ceranae.*

Choices A, B, and C are incorrect because they do not identify the pathogen that infected the highest percentage of honeybee colonies without colony collapse disorder as based on data in the table.

QUESTION 52

Choice D is the best answer. The table discusses pathogen occurrence in honeybee colonies, but it includes no information as to whether these honeybees were infected with mites. Because the table does not suggest mites infested the honeybee colonies, no conclusions can be made as to whether mites increased the honeybees' "susceptibility to secondary infection with fungi, bacteria or viruses" (lines 4-5).

Choices A, B, and C are incorrect because the table provides no information about whether these honeybees were infected with mites.

Section 2: Writing and Language Test

QUESTION 1

Choice A is the best answer because by providing the comparative adjective "healthier" and the word "more" to make "productive" comparative, it creates a parallel structure within the list that begins with "happier."

Choices B, C, and D are incorrect because none creates a parallel structure within the list of qualities.

QUESTION 2

Choice B is the best answer. The ways in which exposure to natural light affects employees is the main subject of the passage.

Choices A, C, and D are incorrect because none introduces the topic discussed in the remainder of the passage.

QUESTION 3

Choice C is the best answer. It accurately notes that the proposed sentence would be placed directly between the first mention of circadian rhythms and the explanation of the term.

Choices A, B, and D are incorrect because each misinterprets the relationship between the proposed additional text and the ideas in the paragraph.

QUESTION 4

Choice C is the best answer. It provides the correct possessive construction for "body," which must be a singular noun when discussed in general terms as in this sentence. Choice C also provides the correct plural construction for "clocks."

Choices A, B, and D are incorrect because each applies either a possessive or a plural construction in a place where it doesn't belong.

QUESTION 5

Choice A is the best answer. The singular verb "is" agrees with the singular noun "absenteeism."

Choices B, C, and D are incorrect because each provides a verb that either fails to agree with the singular subject "absenteeism" or introduces redundancy.

QUESTION 6

Choice B is the best answer. It contains a direct reference to productivity, the topic introduced in the previous sentence.

Choices A, C, and D are incorrect because none directly addresses employee productivity, the primary subject of the previous sentence.

QUESTION 7

Choice A is the best answer. It opens with a reference to lowered worker productivity, creating a transition from the previous paragraph, and clearly positions the high energy costs of artificial light sources as an additional disadvantage.

Choices B, C, and D are incorrect because none of the choices offers an adequate transition from the previous paragraph: Each awkwardly inserts the issue of lower worker productivity into a statement about the high energy costs of artificial light sources.

QUESTION 8

Choice D is the best answer. The word "annual" is adequate to communicate that the savings occurred every year.

Choices A, B, and C are incorrect because each proposes an option that would result in a redundancy with "annual."

QUESTION 9

Choice C is the best answer. It provides a transitional adverb that accurately communicates that this sentence describes an option that companies could choose ("light tubes") instead of the option described in the previous sentence ("full-pane windows").

Choices A, B, and D are incorrect because each proposes a transitional adverb that does not accurately reflect the relationship between this sentence and the one preceding it.

QUESTION 10

Choice C is the best answer. It provides the correct relative pronoun to correspond with the plural referent "light tubes" and the correct verb to introduce the definition that follows.

Choices A, B, and D are incorrect because each offers a pronoun inappropriate for opening a dependent clause defining "light tubes."

QUESTION 11

Choice B is the best answer. The preposition "of" idiomatically follows the noun "means," particularly as a way to connect it to another noun or verb.

Choices A, C, and D are incorrect because each results in nonstandard phrasing with "means."

QUESTION 12

Choice A is the best answer. The plural reflexive pronoun "themselves" corresponds with the plural noun "settlers."

Choices B, C, and D are incorrect because each provides either a nonstandard phrase or a singular pronoun that does not correspond with "settlers."

QUESTION 13

Choice C is the best answer. It creates a transition from the poor food quality mentioned in the previous sentence to the information about Harvey in the remainder of the sentence.

Choices A, B, and D are incorrect because none offers a transition from the previous sentence or a detail that corresponds precisely with the information in the remainder of the sentence.

QUESTION 14

Choice D is the best answer. It correctly provides a comma to close the modifying clause "an English-born entrepreneur," which opens with a comma.

Choices A, B, and C are incorrect because each proposes punctuation that creates an inappropriately strong separation between the subject "Fred Harvey" and the verb "decided."

QUESTION 15

Choice B is the best answer. It provides the plural verb and plural possessive pronoun that grammatically correspond to the plural referent "Harvey Houses."

Choices A, C, and D are incorrect because each either fails to provide a verb that corresponds with the plural referent "Harvey Houses" or fails to provide the appropriate possessive pronoun.

QUESTION 16

Choice C is the best answer. It accurately echoes an earlier characterization of the food as being of "terrible quality," while maintaining the established tone of the passage.

Choices A, B, and D are incorrect either because the word is less formal than the established tone of the passage ("icky") or because it illogically attributes agency to food ("sinister," "surly").

QUESTION 17

Choice C is the best answer. It accurately interprets "not content to follow conventional business practices" as logically introducing the new practice of "employing women" described in the following sentences.

Choices A, B, and D are incorrect because none recognizes why the sentence is relevant to this particular location in the passage.

QUESTION 18

Choice B is the best answer. It is concise and free of redundancies.

Choices A, C, and D are incorrect because each pairs "overwhelming" and "tremendous," adjectives so close in meaning that together they present a redundancy.

QUESTION 19

Choice D is the best answer. It contains the pronoun "they," a necessary reference to "such regulations" in the previous clause.

Choices A, B, and C are incorrect because each lacks a necessary subject, such as a pronoun or noun.

QUESTION 20

Choice C is the best answer. It refers directly to benefits for the restaurants' female employees, the subject of the previous sentence.

Choices A, B, and D are incorrect because none logically builds upon the sentence that precedes it.

QUESTION 21

Choice D is the best answer. It provides punctuation that indicates that the opening dependent clause modifies the subject "Harvey Girls."

Choices A, B, and C are incorrect because each uses the punctuation for a dependent clause ("Living independently and demonstrating an intense work ethic") as if it were an independent clause.

QUESTION 22

Choice A is the best answer. It recognizes that the new information supports the previous sentence's claim that "the Harvey Girls became known as a transformative force."

Choices B, C, and D are incorrect because each misinterprets the relationship between the proposed text and the passage.

QUESTION 23

Choice A is the best answer. It opens with a clause that identifies how 1-MCP affects apples, which focuses the sentence on 1-MCP as the subject and allows the ideas in the sentence to progress logically.

Choices B, C, and D are incorrect because each displays awkward or flawed modification and progression of ideas or creates redundancy.

QUESTION 24

Choice D is the best answer. Only the comma is necessary to separate "ethylene" from the appositive noun phrase that defines it.

Choices A, B, and C are incorrect because each creates a comma splice and/or adds unnecessary words.

QUESTION 25

Choice B is the best answer. It offers an adjective that accurately describes fresh apples.

Choices A, C, and D are incorrect because each proposes an adjective that does not describe a plausible fruit texture.

QUESTION 26

Choice A is the best answer. The plural possessive pronoun "their" corresponds with the plural referent "apples."

Choices B, C, and D are incorrect because none provides a pronoun that is both possessive and plural.

QUESTION 27

Choice D is the best answer. It provides the pronoun "who," which accurately identifies the referent "consumers" as people and appropriately begins the relative clause.

Choices A, B, and C are incorrect because each contains a pronoun that either does not correspond with the human referent "consumers" or does not correctly begin the relative clause.

QUESTION 28

Choice B is the best answer. It provides the present tense verb "do," which corresponds to the present tense established earlier in the sentence.

Choices A, C, and D are incorrect because each contains a verb that deviates from the simple present tense established in the sentence.

QUESTION 29

Choice B is the best answer. It provides a colon to appropriately introduce the clause that follows, an elaboration on the preceding claim that Bartlett pears are an example of fruit that "do not respond as well to 1-MCP treatment."

Choices A, C, and D are incorrect because each either creates a comma splice or uses a transitional phrase ("For instance") illogically.

QUESTION 30

Choice B is the best answer. Sentence 4 begins with "But," indicating a contrast with a previous idea, and goes on to mention that 1-MCP can have negative effects. Sentence 1 continues the discussion of benefits of 1-MCP, and sentence 2 names the adverse effect of limiting scent production, so the most logical spot for sentence 4 is between these sentences.

Choices A, C, and D are incorrect because each proposes placing the sentence at a point where it would compromise the logical development of ideas in the paragraph.

QUESTION 31

Choice D is the best answer. It most accurately reflects the data in the graph, which shows a steep decrease in percentage of flesh browning when untreated apples are left in the open air for three weeks rather than placed immediately into a controlled atmosphere.

Choices A, B, and C are incorrect because each presents an inaccurate interpretation of the data in the graph.

QUESTION 32

Choice B is the best answer. It accurately interprets the data as indicating that "roughly half of their flesh turns brown" when apples are treated with 1-MCP: both bars representing 1-MCP treatment are near the 50% line.

Choices A, C, and D are incorrect because each proposes an inaccurate interpretation of the data.

QUESTION 33

Choice C is the best answer. It describes an action, weighing the relative values, that fruit sellers must take as a result of 1-MCP's limitations.

Choices A, B, and D are incorrect because none specifically connects the shortcomings of 1-MCP with any action on the part of fruit sellers.

QUESTION 34

Choice D is the best answer. It clearly communicates that the preceding dependent clause modifies "works by human artists."

Choices A, B, and C are incorrect because each fails to link the preceding dependent clause to an independent clause, resulting in an incomplete sentence.

QUESTION 35

Choice B is the best answer. It provides the necessary em dash to close the aside about artist C.M. Coolidge, which opens with an em dash.

Choices A, C, and D are incorrect because each provides closing punctuation for the aside that does not correspond with the opening punctuation.

QUESTION 36

Choice C is the best answer. The plural verb "portray" corresponds with the plural noun "works of art."

Choices A, B, and D are incorrect because none provides the plural verb in the present tense that the sentence requires.

QUESTION 37

Choice D is the best answer. It names a "museum in Russia," which is the subject of the next paragraph.

Choices A, B, and C are incorrect because each provides an overly general phrase that does not specifically link to the paragraph that follows.

QUESTION 38

Choice C is the best answer. It creates parallelism with the verb "could damage" that appears earlier in the clause ("rodents that could damage . . . [and could] scare off visitors").

Choices A, B, and D are incorrect because each presents a verb tense that is inconsistent with the sentence's other present tense verb ("could damage") that shares "mice, rats, and other rodents" as its subject.

QUESTION 39

Choice C is the best answer. Sentence 5, which discusses Peter the Great's daughter continuing his tradition, most logically follows the sentence about Peter the Great.

Choices A, B, and D are incorrect because each presents a placement that would compromise the logical development of the paragraph.

QUESTION 40

Choice B is the best answer. "Commissioned" describes the act of hiring an artist to create a specific work.

Choices A, C, and D are incorrect because each provides a word that does not correspond logically with the context.

QUESTION 41

Choice D is the best answer. It provides punctuation that clearly places the noun phrase "digital artist Eldar Zakirov" as an appositive identifying the person mentioned in the previous phrase, "The person chosen for this task."

Choices A, B, and C are incorrect because each fails to open and close the uninterrupted appositive noun phrase "digital artist Eldar Zakirov" with commas.

QUESTION 42

Choice A is the best answer. The phrase "noble individuals" corresponds with the subsequent examples of portraits where the cats are depicted as "aristocratic," "stately," and like a "trusted royal advisor."

Choices B, C, and D are incorrect because each provides a statement that does not logically connect to the examples that follow.

QUESTION 43

Choice D is the best answer. It accurately states that the information in the proposed additional sentence is not related to formal portraits of cats, the main topic of the paragraph.

Choices A, B, and C are incorrect because each fails to recognize that the proposed sentence interrupts the logical development of the paragraph.

QUESTION 44

Choice D is the best answer. The tone corresponds with that established in the passage, and the phrasing appropriately focuses on the cats' contribution to protecting artwork rather than on simply killing rodents.

Choices A, B, and C are incorrect because none makes explicit the link between the cats' hunting activities and the service to the museum.

Section 3: Math Test – No Calculator

QUESTION 1

Choice C is correct. The painter's fee is given by $nK\ell h$, where n is the number of walls, K is a constant with units of dollars per square foot, ℓ is the length of each wall in feet, and h is the height of each wall in feet. Examining this equation shows that ℓ and h will be used to determine the area of each wall. The variable n is the number of walls, so n times the area of each wall will give the amount of area that will need to be painted. The only remaining variable is K, which represents the cost per square foot and is determined by the painter's time and the price of paint. Therefore, K is the only factor that will change if the customer asks for a more expensive brand of paint.

Choice A is incorrect because a more expensive brand of paint would not cause the height of each wall to change. Choice B is incorrect because a more expensive brand of paint would not cause the length of each wall to change. Choice D is incorrect because a more expensive brand of paint would not cause the number of walls to change.

QUESTION 2

Choice D is correct. Dividing each side of the equation $3r = 18$ by 3 gives $r = 6$. Substituting 6 for r in the expression $6r + 3$ gives $6(6) + 3 = 39$.

Alternatively, the expression $6r + 3$ can be rewritten as $2(3r) + 3$. Substituting 18 for $3r$ in the expression $2(3r) + 3$ yields $2(18) + 3$, or $36 + 3 = 39$.

Choice A is incorrect because 6 is the value of r; however, the question asks for the value of the expression $6r + 3$. Choices B and C are incorrect because if $6r + 3$ were equal to either of these values, then it would not be possible for $3r$ to be equal to 18, as stated in the question.

QUESTION 3

Choice D is correct. By definition, $a^{\frac{m}{n}} = \sqrt[n]{a^m}$ for any positive integers m and n. It follows, therefore, that $a^{\frac{2}{3}} = \sqrt[3]{a^2}$.

Choice A is incorrect. By definition, $a^{\frac{1}{n}} = \sqrt[n]{a}$ for any positive integer n. Applying this definition as well as the power property of exponents to the expression $\sqrt{a^{\frac{1}{3}}}$ yields $\sqrt{a^{\frac{1}{3}}} = \left(a^{\frac{1}{3}}\right)^{\frac{1}{2}} = a^{\frac{1}{6}}$. Because $a^{\frac{1}{6}} \neq a^{\frac{2}{3}}$, $\sqrt{a^{\frac{1}{3}}}$ is not the correct answer. Choice B is incorrect. By definition, $a^{\frac{1}{n}} = \sqrt[n]{a}$ for any positive integer n. Applying this definition as well as the power property of exponents to the expression $\sqrt{a^3}$ yields $\sqrt{a^3} = (a^3)^{\frac{1}{2}} = a^{\frac{3}{2}}$. Because $a^{\frac{3}{2}} \neq a^{\frac{2}{3}}$, $\sqrt{a^3}$ is not the correct answer. Choice C is incorrect. By definition, $a^{\frac{1}{n}} = \sqrt[n]{a}$ for any positive integer n. Applying this definition as well as the power property of exponents to the expression $\sqrt[3]{a^{\frac{1}{2}}}$ yields $\sqrt[3]{a^{\frac{1}{2}}} = \left(a^{\frac{1}{2}}\right)^{\frac{1}{3}} = a^{\frac{1}{6}}$. Because $a^{\frac{1}{6}} \neq a^{\frac{2}{3}}$, $\sqrt[3]{a^{\frac{1}{2}}}$ is not the correct answer.

QUESTION 4

Choice B is correct. To fit the scenario described, 30 must be twice as large as x. This can be written as $2x = 30$.

Choices A, C, and D are incorrect. These equations do not correctly relate the numbers and variables described in the stem. For example, the expression in choice C states that 30 is half as large as x, not twice as large as x.

QUESTION 5

Choice C is correct. Multiplying each side of $\frac{5}{x} = \frac{15}{x+20}$ by $x(x + 20)$ gives $5(x + 20) = 15x$. Using the distributive property to eliminate the parentheses yields $5x + 100 = 15x$, and then subtracting $5x$ from each side of the equation $5x + 100 = 15x$ gives $100 = 10x$. Finally, dividing both sides of the equation $100 = 10x$ by 10 gives $10 = x$. Therefore, the value of $\frac{x}{5}$ is $\frac{10}{5} = 2$.

Choice A is incorrect because it is the value of x, not $\frac{x}{5}$. Choices B and D are incorrect and may be the result of errors in arithmetic operations on the given equation.

QUESTION 6

Choice C is correct. Multiplying each side of the equation $2x - 3y = -14$ by 3 gives $6x - 9y = -42$. Multiplying each side of the equation $3x - 2y = -6$ by 2 gives $6x - 4y = -12$. Then, subtracting the sides of $6x - 4y = -12$ from the corresponding sides of $6x - 9y = -42$ gives $-5y = -30$. Dividing each side of the equation $-5y = -30$ by -5 gives $y = 6$. Finally, substituting 6 for y in $2x - 3y = -14$ gives $2x - 3(6) = -14$, or $x = 2$. Therefore, the value of $x - y$ is $2 - 6 = -4$.

Alternatively, adding the corresponding sides of $2x - 3y = -14$ and $3x - 2y = -6$ gives $5x - 5y = -20$, from which it follows that $x - y = -4$.

Choices A and B are incorrect and may be the result of an arithmetic error when solving the system of equations. Choice D is incorrect and may be the result of finding $x + y$ instead of $x - y$.

QUESTION 7

Choice C is correct. If $x - b$ is a factor of $f(x)$, then $f(b)$ must equal 0. Based on the table, $f(4) = 0$. Therefore, $x - 4$ must be a factor of $f(x)$.

Choice A is incorrect because $f(2) \neq 0$. Choice B is incorrect because no information is given about the value of $f(3)$, so $x - 3$ may or may not be a factor of $f(x)$. Choice D is incorrect because $f(5) \neq 0$.

QUESTION 8

Choice A is correct. The linear equation $y = kx + 4$ is in slope-intercept form, and so the slope of the line is k. Since the line contains the point (c, d), the coordinates of this point satisfy the equation $y = kx + 4$; therefore, $d = kc + 4$. Solving this equation for the slope, k, gives $k = \frac{d - 4}{c}$.

Choices B, C, and D are incorrect and may be the result of errors in substituting the coordinates of (c, d) in $y = kx + 4$ or of errors in solving for k in the resulting equation.

QUESTION 9

Choice A is correct. If a system of two linear equations has no solution, then the lines represented by the equations in the coordinate plane are parallel. The equation $kx - 3y = 4$ can be rewritten as $y = \frac{k}{3}x - \frac{4}{3}$, where $\frac{k}{3}$ is the slope of the line, and the equation $4x - 5y = 7$ can be rewritten as $y = \frac{4}{5}x - \frac{7}{5}$, where $\frac{4}{5}$ is the slope of the line. If two lines are parallel, then the slopes of the line are equal. Therefore, $\frac{4}{5} = \frac{k}{3}$, or $k = \frac{12}{5}$. (Since the y-intercepts of the lines represented by the equations are $-\frac{4}{3}$ and $-\frac{7}{5}$, the lines are parallel, not identical.)

Choices B, C, and D are incorrect and may be the result of a computational error when rewriting the equations or solving the equation representing the equality of the slopes for k.

QUESTION 10

Choice A is correct. Substituting 25 for y in the equation $y = (x - 11)^2$ gives $25 = (x - 11)^2$. It follows that $x - 11 = 5$ or $x - 11 = -5$, so the x-coordinates of the two points of intersection are $x = 16$ and $x = 6$, respectively. Since both points of intersection have a y-coordinate of 25, it follows that the two points are (16, 25) and (6, 25). Since these points lie on the horizontal line $y = 25$, the distance between these points is the positive difference of the x-coordinates: $16 - 6 = 10$.

Alternatively, since a translation is a rigid motion, the distance between points A and B would be the same as the distance between the points of intersection of the line $y = 25$ and the parabola $y = x^2$. Since those graphs intersect at (0, 5) and (0, −5), the distance between the two points, and thus the distance between A and B, is 10.

Choices B, C, and D are incorrect and may be the result of an error in solving the quadratic equation that results when substituting 25 for y in the given quadratic equation.

QUESTION 11

Choice B is correct. Since the angles marked $y°$ and $u°$ are vertical angles, $y = u$. Substituting y for u in the equation $x + y = u + w$ gives $x = w$. Since the angles marked $w°$ and $z°$ are vertical angles, $w = z$. Therefore, by the transitive property, $x = z$, and so I must be true.

The equation in II need not be true. For example, if $x = w = z = t = 70$ and $y = u = 40$, then all three pairs of vertical angles in the figure have equal measure and the given condition $x + y = u + w$ holds. But it is not true in this case that y is equal to w. Therefore, II need not be true.

Since the top three angles in the figure form a straight angle, it follows that $x + y + z = 180$. Similarly, $w + u + t = 180$, and so $x + y + z = w + u + t$. Subtracting the sides of the given equation $x + y = u + w$ from the corresponding sides of $x + y + z = w + u + t$ gives $z = t$. Therefore, III must be true. Since only I and III must be true, the correct answer is choice B.

Choices A, C, and D are incorrect because each of these choices includes II, which need not be true.

QUESTION 12

Choice A is correct. The parabola with equation $y = a(x - 2)(x + 4)$ crosses the x-axis at the points $(-4, 0)$ and $(2, 0)$. By symmetry, the x-coordinate of the vertex of the parabola is halfway between the x-coordinates of $(-4, 0)$ and $(2, 0)$. Thus, the x-coordinate of the vertex is $\frac{-4 + 2}{2} = -1$. This is the value of c. To find the y-coordinate of the vertex, substitute -1 for x in $y = a(x - 2)(x + 4)$:

$$y = a(x - 2)(x + 4) = a(-1 - 2)(-1 + 4) = a(-3)(3) = -9a$$

Therefore, the value of d is $-9a$.

Choice B is incorrect because the value of the constant term in the equation is not the y-coordinate of the vertex, unless there were no linear terms in the quadratic. Choice C is incorrect and may be the result of a sign error in finding the x-coordinate of the vertex. Choice D is incorrect because the negative of the coefficient of the linear term in the quadratic equation is not the y-coordinate of the vertex.

QUESTION 13

Choice B is correct. Since $24x^2 + 25x - 47$ divided by $ax - 2$ is equal to $-8x - 3$ with remainder -53, it is true that $(-8x - 3)(ax - 2) - 53 = 24x^2 + 25x - 47$. (This can be seen by multiplying each side of the given equation by $ax - 2$). This can be rewritten as $-8ax^2 + 16x - 3ax + 6 - 53 = 24x^2 + 25x - 47$. Since the coefficients of the x^2-term have to be equal on both sides of the equation, $-8a = 24$, or $a = -3$.

Choices A, C, and D are incorrect and may be the result of either a conceptual misunderstanding or a computational error when trying to solve for the value of a.

QUESTION 14

Choice A is correct. Dividing each side of the given equation by 3 gives the equivalent equation $x^2 + 4x + 2 = 0$. Then using the quadratic formula, $\frac{-b \pm \sqrt{b^2 - 4ac}}{2a}$ with $a = 1$, $b = 4$, and $c = 2$, gives the solutions $x = -2 \pm \sqrt{2}$.

Choices B, C, and D are incorrect and may be the result of errors when applying the quadratic formula.

QUESTION 15

Choice D is correct. If C is graphed against F, the slope of the line is equal to $\frac{5}{9}$ degrees Celsius/degrees Fahrenheit, which means that for an increase of 1 degree Fahrenheit, the increase is $\frac{5}{9}$ of 1 degree Celsius. Thus, statement I is true. This is the equivalent to saying that an increase of 1 degree Celsius is equal to an increase of $\frac{9}{5}$ degrees Fahrenheit.

Since $\frac{9}{5} = 1.8$, statement II is true. On the other hand, statement III is not true, since a temperature increase of $\frac{9}{5}$ degrees Fahrenheit, not $\frac{5}{9}$ degree Fahrenheit, is equal to a temperature increase of 1 degree Celsius.

Choices A, B, and C are incorrect because each of these choices omits a true statement or includes a false statement.

QUESTION 16

The correct answer is either 1 or 2. The given equation can be rewritten as $x^5 - 5x^3 + 4x = 0$. Since the polynomial expression on the left has no constant term, it has x as a factor: $x(x^4 - 5x^2 + 4) = 0$. The expression in parentheses is a quadratic equation in x^2 that can be factored, giving $x(x^2 - 1)(x^2 - 4) = 0$. This further factors as $x(x - 1)(x + 1)(x - 2)(x + 2) = 0$. The solutions for x are $x = 0$, $x = 1$, $x = -1$, $x = 2$, and $x = -2$. Since it is given that $x > 0$, the possible values of x are $x = 1$ and $x = 2$. Either 1 or 2 may be gridded as the correct answer.

QUESTION 17

The correct answer is 2. First, clear the fractions from the given equation by multiplying each side of the equation by 36 (the least common multiple of 4, 9, and 12). The equation becomes $28x - 16x = 9 + 15$. Combining like terms on each side of the equation yields $12x = 24$. Finally, dividing both sides of the equation by 12 yields $x = 2$.

Alternatively, since $\frac{7}{9}x - \frac{4}{9}x = \frac{3}{9}x = \frac{1}{3}x$ and $\frac{1}{4} + \frac{5}{12} = \frac{3}{12} + \frac{5}{12} = \frac{8}{12} = \frac{2}{3}$, the given equation simplifies to $\frac{1}{3}x = \frac{2}{3}$. Multiplying each side of $\frac{1}{3}x = \frac{2}{3}$ by 3 yields $x = 2$.

QUESTION 18

The correct answer is 105. Since $180 - z = 2y$ and $y = 75$, it follows that $180 - z = 150$, and so $z = 30$. Thus, each of the base angles of the isosceles triangle on the right has measure $\frac{180° - 30°}{2} = 75°$. Therefore, the measure of the angle marked $x°$ is $180° - 75° = 105°$, and so the value of x is 105.

QUESTION 19

The correct answer is 370. A system of equations can be used where h represents the number of calories in a hamburger and f represents the number of calories in an order of fries. The equation $2h + 3f = 1700$ represents the fact that 2 hamburgers and 3 orders of fries contain a total of 1700 calories, and the equation $h = f + 50$ represents the fact that one hamburger contains 50 more calories than an order of fries. Substituting $f + 50$ for h in $2h + 3f = 1700$ gives $2(f + 50) + 3f = 1700$. This equation can be solved as follows:

$$2f + 100 + 3f = 1700$$

$$5f + 100 = 1700$$

$$5f = 1600$$

$$f = 320$$

The number of calories in an order of fries is 320, so the number of calories in a hamburger is 50 more than 320, or 370.

QUESTION 20

The correct answer is $\frac{3}{5}$ or .6. Triangle ABC is a right triangle with its right angle at B. Thus, $\overline{AC}$ is the hypotenuse of right triangle ABC, and $\overline{AB}$ and $\overline{BC}$ are the legs of right triangle ABC. By the Pythagorean theorem, $AB = \sqrt{20^2 - 16^2} = \sqrt{400 - 256} = \sqrt{144} = 12$. Since triangle DEF is similar to triangle ABC, with vertex F corresponding to vertex C, the measure of angle F equals the measure of angle C. Thus, $\sin F = \sin C$. From the side lengths of triangle ABC, $\sin C = \dfrac{\text{opposite side}}{\text{hypotenuse}} = \dfrac{AB}{AC} = \dfrac{12}{20} = \dfrac{3}{5}$. Therefore, $\sin F = \dfrac{3}{5}$. Either 3/5 or its decimal equivalent, .6, may be gridded as the correct answer.

Section 4: Math Test – Calculator

QUESTION 1

Choice C is correct. Marilyn's distance from her campsite remained the same during the time she ate lunch. This is represented by a horizontal segment in the graph. The only horizontal segment in the graph starts at a time of about 1:10 P.M. and ends at about 1:40 P.M. Therefore, Marilyn finished her lunch and continued her hike at about 1:40 P.M.

Choices A, B, and D are incorrect and may be the result of a misinterpretation of the graph. For example, choice B is the time Marilyn started her lunch, and choice D is the time Marilyn was at the maximum distance from her campsite.

QUESTION 2

Choice B is correct. Of the 25 people who entered the contest, there are 8 females under age 40 and 2 males age 40 or older. Because there is no overlap in the categories, the probability that the contest winner will be either a female under age 40 or a male age 40 or older is $\dfrac{8}{25} + \dfrac{2}{25} = \dfrac{10}{25}$.

Choice A is incorrect and may be the result of dividing 8 by 2, instead of adding 8 to 2, to find the probability. Choice C is incorrect; it is the probability that the contest winner will be either a female under age 40 or a female age 40 or older. Choice D is incorrect and may be the result of multiplying 8 and 2, instead of adding 8 and 2, to find the probability.

QUESTION 3

Choice C is correct. Based on the graph, sales increased in the first 3 years since 1997, which is until year 2000, and then generally decreased thereafter.

Choices A, B, and D are incorrect; each of these choices contains inaccuracies in describing the general trend of music album sales from 1997 through 2009.

QUESTION 4

Choice C is correct. The graph of $y = f(n)$ in the coordinate plane is a line that passes through each of the points given in the table. From the table, one can see that an increase of 1 unit in n results in an increase of 3 units in $f(n)$; for example, $f 2) - f(1) = 1 - (-2) = 3$. Therefore, the graph of $y = f(n)$ in the coordinate plane is a line with slope 3. Only choice C is a line with slope 3. The y-intercept of the line is the value of $f(0)$. Since an increase of 1 unit in n results in an increase of 3 units in $f(n)$, it follows that $f 1) - f(0) = 3$. Since $f(1) = -2$, it follows that $f(0) = f(1) - 3 = -5$. Therefore, the y-intercept of the graph of $f(n)$ is -5, and the equation in slope-intercept form that defined f is $f(n) = 3n - 5$.

Choices A, B, and D are incorrect because each equation has the incorrect slope of the line (the y-intercept in each equation is also incorrect).

QUESTION 5

Choice B is correct. Since 7 percent of the 562 juniors is 0.07(562) and 5 percent of the 602 seniors is 0.05(602), the expression 0.07(562) + 0.05(602) can be evaluated to determine the total number of juniors and seniors inducted into the National Honor Society. Of the given choices, 69 is closest to the value of the expression.

Choice A is incorrect and may be the result of adding the number of juniors and seniors and the percentages given and then using the expression (0.07 + 0.05)(562 + 602). Choices C and D are incorrect and may be the result of finding either only the number of juniors inducted or only the number of seniors inducted.

QUESTION 6

Choice A is correct. The sum of the two polynomials is $(3x^2 - 5x + 2) + (5x^2 - 2x - 6)$. This can be rewritten by combining like terms:

$$(3x^2 - 5x + 2) + (5x^2 - 2x - 6 = (3x^2 + 5x^2) + -5x - 2x) + (2 - 6) = 8x^2 - 7x - 4$$

Choice B is incorrect and may be the result of a sign error when combining the coefficients of the x-term. Choice C is incorrect and may be the result of adding the exponents, as well as the coefficients, of like terms. Choice D is incorrect and may be the result of a combination of the errors described in choice B and choice C.

QUESTION 7

Choice D is correct. To solve the equation for w, multiply both sides of the equation by the reciprocal of $\frac{3}{5}$, which is $\frac{5}{3}$. This gives $\left(\frac{5}{3}\right) \cdot \frac{3}{5} w = \frac{4}{3} \cdot \left(\frac{5}{3}\right)$, which simplifies to $w = \frac{20}{9}$.

Choices A, B, and C are incorrect and may be the result of errors in arithmetic when simplifying the given equation.

QUESTION 8

Choice C is correct. In the equation $y = 0.56x + 27.2$, the value of x increases by 1 for each year that passes. Each time x increases by 1, y increases by 0.56 since 0.56 is the slope of the graph of this equation. Since y represents the average number of students per classroom in the year represented by x, it follows that, according to the model, the estimated increase each year in the average number of students per classroom at Central High School is 0.56.

Choice A is incorrect because the total number of students in the school in 2000 is the product of the average number of students per classroom and the total number of classrooms, which would appropriately be approximated by the y-intercept (27.2) times the total number of classrooms, which is not given. Choice B is incorrect because the average number of students per classroom in 2000 is given by the y-intercept of the graph of the equation, but the question is asking for the meaning of the number 0.56, which is the slope. Choice D is incorrect because 0.56 represents the estimated yearly change in the average number of students per classroom. The estimated difference between the average number of students per classroom in 2010 and 2000 is 0.56 times the number of years that have passed between 2000 and 2010, that is, $0.56 \times 10 = 5.6$.

QUESTION 9

Choice B is correct. Because Nate walks 25 meters in 13.7 seconds, and 4 minutes is equal to 240 seconds, the proportion $\frac{25 \text{ meters}}{13.7 \text{ sec}} = \frac{x \text{ meters}}{240 \text{ sec}}$ can be used to find out how many meters, x, Nate walks in 4 minutes. The proportion can be simplified to $\frac{25}{13.7} = \frac{x}{240}$, because the units of meters per second cancel, and then each side of the equation can be multiplied by 240, giving $\frac{(240)(25)}{13.7} = x \approx 438$. Therefore, of the given options, 450 meters is closest to the distance Nate will walk in 4 minutes.

Choice A is incorrect and may be the result of setting up the proportion as $\frac{13.7 \text{ sec}}{25 \text{ meters}} = \frac{x \text{ meters}}{240 \text{ sec}}$ and finding that $x \approx 132$, which is close to 150. Choices C and D are incorrect and may be the result of errors in calculation.

QUESTION 10

Choice D is correct. On Mercury, the acceleration due to gravity is 3.6 m/sec². Substituting 3.6 for g and 90 for m in the formula $W = mg$ gives $W = 90(3.6) = 324$ newtons.

Choice A is incorrect and may be the result of dividing 90 by 3.6. Choice B is incorrect and may be the result of subtracting 3.6 from 90 and rounding to the nearest whole number. Choice C is incorrect because an object with a weight of 101 newtons on Mercury would have a mass of about 28 kilograms, not 90 kilograms.

QUESTION 11

Choice B is correct. On Earth, the acceleration due to gravity is 9.8 m/sec². Thus, for an object with a weight of 150 newtons, the formula $W = mg$ becomes $150 = m(9.8)$, which shows that the mass of an object with a weight of 150 newtons on Earth is about 15.3 kilograms. Substituting this mass into the formula $W = mg$ and now using the weight of 170 newtons gives $170 = 15.3g$, which shows that the second planet's acceleration due to gravity is about 11.1 m/sec². According to the table, this value for the acceleration due to gravity holds on Saturn.

Choices A, C, and D are incorrect. Using the formula $W = mg$ and the values for g in the table shows that an object with a weight of 170 newtons on these planets would not have the same mass as an object with a weight of 150 newtons on Earth.

QUESTION 12

Choice D is correct. A zero of a function corresponds to an x-intercept of the graph of the function in the xy-plane. Therefore, the complete graph of the function f, which has five distinct zeros, must have five x-intercepts. Only the graph in choice D has five x-intercepts, and therefore, this is the only one of the given graphs that could be the complete graph of f in the xy-plane.

Choices A, B, and C are incorrect. The number of x-intercepts of each of these graphs is not equal to five; therefore, none of these graphs could be the complete graph of f, which has five distinct zeros.

QUESTION 13

Choice D is correct. Starting with the original equation, $h = -16t^2 + vt + k$, in order to get v in terms of the other variables, $-16t^2$ and k need to be subtracted from each side. This yields $vt = h + 16t^2 - k$, which when divided by t will give v in terms of the other variables. However, the equation $v = \frac{h + 16t^2 - k}{t}$ is not one of the options, so the right side needs to be further simplified. Another way to write the previous equation is $v = \frac{h - k}{t} + \frac{16t^2}{t}$, which can be simplified to $v = \frac{h - k}{t} + 16t$.

Choices A, B, and C are incorrect and may be the result of arithmetic errors when rewriting the original equation to express v in terms of h, t, and k.

QUESTION 14

Choice A is correct. The hotel charges $0.20 per minute to use the meeting-room phone. This per-minute rate can be converted to the hourly rate using the conversion 1 hour = 60 minutes, as shown below.

$$\frac{\$0.20}{\text{minute}} \times \frac{60 \text{ minutes}}{1 \text{ hour}} = \frac{\$(0.20 \times 60)}{\text{hour}}$$

Thus, the hotel charges $(0.20 × 60) per hour to use the meeting-room phone. Therefore, the cost c, in dollars, for h hours of use is $c = (0.20 \times 60)h$, which is equivalent to $c = 0.20(60h)$.

Choice B is incorrect because in this expression the per-minute rate is multiplied by h, the number of <u>hours</u> of phone use. Furthermore, the equation indicates that there is a flat fee of $60 in addition to the per-minute or per-hour rate. This is not the case. Choice C is incorrect because the expression indicates that the hotel charges $\left(\frac{60}{0.20}\right)$ per hour for use of the meeting-room phone, not $0.20(60) per hour. Choice D is incorrect because the expression indicates that the hourly rate is $\frac{1}{60}$ times the per-minute rate, not 60 times the per-minute rate.

QUESTION 15

Choice A is the correct answer. Experimental research is a method used to study a small group of people and generalize the results to a larger population. However, in order to make a generalization involving cause and effect:

- The population must be well defined.
- The participants must be selected at random.
- The participants must be randomly assigned to treatment groups.

When these conditions are met, the results of the study can be generalized to the population with a conclusion about cause and effect. In this study, all conditions are met and the population from which the participants were selected are people with poor eyesight. Therefore, a general conclusion can be drawn about the effect of Treatment X on the population of people with poor eyesight.

Choice B is incorrect. The study did not include all available treatments, so no conclusion can be made about the relative effectiveness of all available treatments. Choice C is incorrect. The participants were selected at random from a large population of people with poor eyesight. Therefore, the results can be generalized only to that population and not to anyone in general. Also, the conclusion is too strong: an experimental study might show that people are likely to be helped by a treatment, but it cannot show that <u>anyone</u> who takes the treatment will be helped. Choice D is incorrect. This conclusion is too strong. The study shows that Treatment X is <u>likely</u> to improve the eyesight of people with poor eyesight, but it cannot show that the treatment definitely <u>will</u> cause improvement in eyesight for every person. Furthermore, since the people undergoing the treatment in the study were selected from people with poor eyesight, the results can be generalized only to this population, not to all people.

QUESTION 16

Choice B is correct. The graphs of $y = f(x)$ and $y = g(x)$ are given. In order for $f(x) + g(x)$ to be 0, there must be one or more values of x for which the y-coordinates of the graphs are opposites. Looking at the graphs, one can see that this occurs at $x = -2$: the point $(-2, -2)$ lies on the graph of f, and the point $(-2, 2)$ lies on the graph of g. Thus, at $x = -2$, the value of $f(x) + g(x$ is $-2 + 2 = 0$.

Choices A, C, and D are incorrect because none of these x-values satisfies the given equation, $f(x) + g(x) = 0$.

QUESTION 17

Choice B is correct. The quantity of the product supplied to the market is given by the function $S(P) = \frac{1}{2}P + 40$. If the price P of the product increases by \$10, the effect on the quantity of the product supplied can be determined by substituting $P + 10$ for P in the function $S(P) = \frac{1}{2}P + 40$. This gives $S(P + 10) = \frac{1}{2}(P + 10) + 40 = \frac{1}{2}P + 45$, which shows that $S(P + 10) = S(P) + 5$. Therefore, the quantity supplied to the market will increase by 5 units when the price of the product is increased by \$10.

Alternatively, look at the coefficient of P in the linear function S. This is the slope of the graph of the function, where P is on the horizontal axis and $S(P)$ is on the vertical axis. Since the slope is $\frac{1}{2}$, for every increase of 1 in P, there will be an increase of $\frac{1}{2}$ in $S(P)$, and therefore, an increase of 10 in P will yield an increase of 5 in $S(P)$.

Choice A is incorrect. If the quantity supplied decreases as the price of the product increases, the function $S(P)$ would be decreasing, but $S(P) = \frac{1}{2}P + 40$ is an increasing function. Choice C is incorrect and may be the result of assuming the slope of the graph of $S(P)$ is equal to 1. Choice D is incorrect and may be the result of confusing the y-intercept of the graph of $S(P)$ with the slope, and then adding 10 to the y-intercept.

QUESTION 18

Choice B is correct. The quantity of the product supplied to the market will equal the quantity of the product demanded by the market if $S(P)$ is equal to $D(P)$, that is, if $\frac{1}{2}P + 40 = 220 - P$. Solving this equation gives $P = 120$, and so $120 is the price at which the quantity of the product supplied will equal the quantity of the product demanded.

Choices A, C, and D are incorrect. At these dollar amounts, the quantities given by $S(P)$ and $D(P)$ are not equal.

QUESTION 19

Choice C is correct. It is given that 1 ounce of graphene covers 7 football fields. Therefore, 48 ounces can cover $7 \times 48 = 336$ football fields. If each football field has an area of $1\frac{1}{3}$ acres, then 336 football fields have a total area of $336 \times 1\frac{1}{3} = 448$ acres. Therefore, of the choices given, 450 acres is closest to the number of acres 48 ounces of graphene could cover.

Choice A is incorrect and may be the result of dividing, instead of multiplying, the number of football fields by $1\frac{1}{3}$. Choice B is incorrect and may be the result of finding the number of football fields, not the number of acres, that can be covered by 48 ounces of graphene. Choice D is incorrect and may be the result of setting up the expression $\frac{7 \times 48 \times 4}{3}$ and then finding only the numerator of the fraction.

QUESTION 20

Choice B is correct. To answer this question, find the point in the graph that represents Michael's 34-minute swim and then compare the actual heart rate for that swim with the expected heart rate as defined by the line of best fit. To find the point that represents Michael's swim that took 34 minutes, look along the vertical line of the graph that is marked "34" on the horizontal axis. That vertical line intersects only one point in the scatterplot, at 148 beats per minute. On the other hand, the line of best fit intersects the vertical line representing 34 minutes at 150 beats per minute. Therefore, for the swim that took 34 minutes, Michael's actual heart rate was $150 - 148 = 2$ beats per minute less than predicted by the line of best fit.

Choices A, C, and D are incorrect and may be the result of misreading the graph.

QUESTION 21

Choice C is correct. Linear growth is characterized by an increase of a quantity at a constant rate. Exponential growth is characterized by an increase of a quantity at a relative rate; that is, an increase by the same factor over equal increments of time. In choice C, the value of the account increases by 1% each year; that is, the value is multiplied by the same factor, 1.01, each year. Therefore, the value described in choice C grows exponentially.

Choices A and B are incorrect because the rate depends only on the initial value, and thus the value increases by the same amount each year. Both options A and B describe linear growth. Choice D is incorrect; it is is also a description of linear growth, as the increase is constant each year.

QUESTION 22

Choice B is correct. One of the three numbers is x; let the other two numbers be y and z. Since the sum of three numbers is 855, the equation $x + y + z = 855$ is true. The statement that x is 50% more than the sum of the other two numbers can be represented as $x = 1.5(y + z)$, or $x = \frac{3}{2}(y + z)$. Multiplying both sides of the equation $x = \frac{3}{2}(y + z)$ by $\frac{2}{3}$ gives $\frac{2}{3}x = y + z$. Substituting $\frac{2}{3}x$ in $x + y + z = 855$ gives $x + \frac{2}{3}x = 855$, or $\frac{5x}{3} = 855$. Therefore, x equals $\frac{3}{5} \times 855 = 513$.

Choices A, C, and D are incorrect and may be the result of computational errors.

QUESTION 23

Choice C is correct. Since the angles are acute and $\sin(a°) = \cos(b°)$, it follows from the complementary angle property of sines and cosines that $a + b = 90$. Substituting $4k - 22$ for a and $6k - 13$ for b gives $(4k - 22) + (6k - 13) = 90$, which simplifies to $10k - 35 = 90$. Therefore, $10k = 125$, and $k = 12.5$.

Choice A is incorrect and may be the result of mistakenly assuming that $a = b$ and making a sign error. Choices B and D are incorrect because they result in values for a and b such that $\sin(a°) \neq \cos(b°)$.

QUESTION 24

Choice D is correct. Let c be the number of students in Mr. Kohl's class. The conditions described in the question can be represented by the equations $n = 3c + 5$ and $n + 21 = 4c$. Substituting $3c + 5$ for n in the second equation gives $3c + 5 + 21 = 4c$, which can be solved to find $c = 26$.

Choices A, B, and C are incorrect because the values given for the number of students in the class cannot fulfill both conditions given in the question. For example, if there were 16 students in the class, then the first condition would imply that there are $3(16) + 5 = 53$ milliliters of solution in the beaker, but the second condition would imply that there are 4(16) − 21 = 43 milliliters of solution in the beaker. This contradiction shows that there cannot be 16 students in the class.

QUESTION 25

Choice D is correct. The volume of the grain silo can be found by adding the volumes of all the solids of which it is composed. The silo is made up of a cylinder with height 10 feet (ft) and base radius 5 ft and two cones, each having height 5 ft and base radius 5 ft. The formulas $V_{cylinder} = \pi r^2 h$ and $V_{cone} = \frac{1}{3}\pi r^2 h$ can be used to determine the total volume of the silo. Since the two cones have identical dimensions, the total volume, in cubic feet, of the silo is given by $V_{silo} = \pi(5)^2(10) + (2)\left(\frac{1}{3}\right)\pi(5)^2(5) = \left(\frac{4}{3}\right)(250)\pi$, which is approximately equal to 1,047.2 cubic feet.

Choice A is incorrect because this is the volume of only the two cones. Choice B is incorrect because this is the volume of only the cylinder. Choice C is incorrect because this is the volume of only one of the cones plus the cylinder.

QUESTION 26

Choice C is correct. The line passes through the origin, (2, k), and (k, 32). Any two of these points can be used to find the slope of the line. Since the line passes through (0, 0) and (2, k), the slope of the line is equal to $\frac{k-0}{2-0} = \frac{k}{2}$. Similarly, since the line passes through (0, 0) and (k, 32), the slope of the line is equal to $\frac{32-0}{k-0} = \frac{32}{k}$. Since each expression gives the slope of the same line, it must be true that $\frac{k}{2} = \frac{32}{k}$. Multiplying each side of $\frac{k}{2} = \frac{32}{k}$ by 2k gives $k^2 = 64$, from which it follows that $k = 8$ or $k = -8$. Therefore, of the given choices, only 8 could be the value of k.

Choices A, B, and D are incorrect and may be the result of computational errors.

QUESTION 27

Choice C is correct. Let ℓ and w be the length and width, respectively, of the original rectangle. The area of the original rectangle is $A = \ell w$. The rectangle is altered by increasing its length by 10 percent and decreasing its width by p percent; thus, the length of the altered rectangle is 1.1ℓ, and the width of the altered rectangle is $\left(1 - \frac{p}{100}\right)w$. The alterations decrease the area by 12 percent, so the area of the altered rectangle is (1 − 0.12)A = 0.88A. The area of the altered rectangle is the product of its length and width, so 0.88A = (1.1ℓ)$\left(1 - \frac{p}{100}\right)w$. Since $A = \ell w$, this last equation can be rewritten as $0.88A = (1.1)\left(1 - \frac{p}{100}\right)\ell w = (1.1)\left(1 - \frac{p}{100}\right)A$, from

which it follows that $0.88 = (1.1)\left(1 - \frac{p}{100}\right)$, or $0.8 = \left(1 - \frac{p}{100}\right)$.

Therefore, $\frac{p}{100} = 0.2$, and so the value of p is 20.

Choice A is incorrect and may be the result of confusing the 12 percent decrease in area with the percent decrease in width. Choice B is incorrect because decreasing the width by 15 percent results in a 6.5 percent decrease in area, not a 12 percent decrease. Choice D is incorrect and may be the result of adding the percents given in the question (10 + 12).

QUESTION 28

Choice D is correct. For the present population to decrease by 10 percent, it must be multiplied by the factor 0.9. Since the engineer estimates that the population will decrease by 10 percent every 20 years, the present population, 50,000, must be multiplied by $(0.9)^n$, where n is the number of 20-year periods that will have elapsed t years from now. After t years, the number of 20-year periods that

have elapsed is $\frac{t}{20}$. Therefore, $50{,}000(0.9)^{\frac{t}{20}}$ represents the engineer's

estimate of the population of the city t years from now.

Choices A, B, and C are incorrect because each of these choices either confuses the percent decrease with the multiplicative factor that represents the percent decrease or mistakenly multiplies t by 20 to find the number of 20-year periods that will have elapsed in t years.

QUESTION 29

Choice A is correct. Let x be the number of left-handed female students and let y be the number of left-handed male students. Then the number of right-handed female students will be $5x$ and the number of right-handed male students will be $9y$. Since the total number of left-handed students is 18 and the total number of right-handed students is 122, the system of equations below must be satisfied.

$$\begin{cases} x + y = 18 \\ 5x + 9y = 122 \end{cases}$$

Solving this system gives $x = 10$ and $y = 8$. Thus, 50 of the 122 right-handed students are female. Therefore, the probability that a right-

handed student selected at random is female is $\frac{50}{122}$, which to the

nearest thousandth is 0.410.

Choices B, C, and D are incorrect and may be the result of incorrectly calculating the missing values in the table.

QUESTION 30

Choice A is correct. Subtracting the sides of $3y + c = 5y - 7$ from the corresponding sides of $3x + b = 5x - 7$ gives $(3x - 3y) + (b - c) = (5x - 5y + (-7 - (-7)))$. Since $b = c - \frac{1}{2}$, or $b - c = -\frac{1}{2}$, it follows that $(3x - 3y) + \left(-\frac{1}{2}\right) = (5x - 5y)$. Solving this equation for x in terms of y gives $x = y - \frac{1}{4}$. Therefore, x is y minus $\frac{1}{4}$.

Choices B, C, and D are incorrect and may be the result of making a computational error when solving the equations for x in terms of y.

QUESTION 31

The correct answer is either 4 or 5. Because each student ticket costs \$2 and each adult ticket costs \$3, the total amount, in dollars, that Chris spends on x student tickets and 1 adult ticket is $2(x) + 3(1)$. Because Chris spends at least \$11 but no more than \$14 on the tickets, one can write the compound inequality $2x + 3 \geq 11$ and $2x + 3 \leq 14$. Subtracting 3 from each side of both inequalities and then dividing each side of both inequalities by 2 yields $x \geq 4$ and $x \leq 5.5$. Thus, the value of x must be an integer that is both greater than or equal to 4 and less than or equal to 5.5. Therefore, $x = 4$ or $x = 5$. Either 4 or 5 may be gridded as the correct answer.

QUESTION 32

The correct answer is 58.6. The mean of a data set is determined by calculating the sum of the values and dividing by the number of values in the data set. The sum of the ages, in years, in the data set is 703, and the number of values in the data set is 12. Thus, the mean of the ages, in years, of the first 12 United States presidents at the beginning of their terms is $\frac{703}{12}$. The question asks for an answer rounded to the nearest tenth, so the decimal equivalent, rounded to the nearest tenth, is the correct answer. This rounded decimal equivalent is 58.6.

QUESTION 33

The correct answer is 9. To rewrite the difference $(-3x^2 + 5x - 2) - 2(x^2 - 2x - 1)$ in the form $ax^2 + bx + c$, the expression can be simplified by using the distributive property and combining like terms as follows:

$$-3x^2 + 5x - 2) - (2x^2 - 4x - 2)$$

$$-3x^2 - 2x^2) + (5x - (-4x + (-2 - (-2)))$$

$$-5x^2 + 9x + 0$$

The coefficient of x is the value of b, which is 9.

Alternatively, since b is the coefficient of x in the difference $-3x^2 + 5x - 2) - 2(x^2 - 2x - 1)$, one need only compute the x-term in the difference. The x-term is $5x - 2(-2x) = 5x + 4x = 9x$, so the value of b is 9.

QUESTION 34

The correct answer is $\frac{5}{8}$ or .625. A complete rotation around a point is 360° or 2π radians. Since the central angle *AOB* has measure $\frac{5\pi}{4}$ radians, it represents $\frac{\frac{5\pi}{4}}{2\pi} = \frac{5}{8}$ of a complete rotation around point *O*. Therefore, the sector formed by central angle *AOB* has area equal to $\frac{5}{8}$ the area of the entire circle. Either the fraction 5/8 or its decimal equivalent, .625, may be gridded as the correct answer.

QUESTION 35

The correct answer is 50. The mean of a data set is the sum of the values in the data set divided by the number of values in the data set. The mean of 75 is obtained by finding the sum of the first 10 ratings and dividing by 10. Thus, the sum of the first 10 ratings was 750. In order for the mean of the first 20 ratings to be at least 85, the sum of the first 20 ratings must be at least (85)(20) = 1700. Therefore, the sum of the next 10 ratings must be at least 1700 − 750 = 950. The maximum rating is 100, so the maximum possible value of the sum of the 12th through 20th ratings is 9 × 100 = 900. Therefore, for the store to be able to have an average of at least 85 for the first 20 ratings, the least possible value for the 11th rating is 950 − 900 = 50.

QUESTION 36

The correct answer is 750. The inequalities $y \leq -15x + 3000$ and $y \leq 5x$ can be graphed in the *xy*-plane. They are represented by the lower half-planes with the boundary lines $y = -15x + 3000$ and $y = 5x$, respectively. The solution set of the system of inequalities will be the intersection of these half-planes, including the boundary lines, and the solution (*a*, *b*) with the greatest possible value of *b* will be the point of intersection of the boundary lines. The intersection of boundary lines of these inequalities can be found by substituting $5x$ for *y* in the equation for the first line: $5x = -15x + 3000$, which has solution $x = 150$. Thus, the *x*-coordinate of the point of intersection is 150. Therefore, the *y*-coordinate of the point of intersection of the boundary lines is $5(150) = -15(150) + 3000 = 750$. This is the maximum possible value of *b* for a point (*a*, *b*) that is in the solution set of the system of inequalities.

QUESTION 37

The correct answer is 7. The average number of shoppers, *N*, in the checkout line at any time is $N = rt$, where *r* is the number of shoppers entering the checkout line per minute and *T* is the average number of minutes each shopper spends in the checkout line. Since 84 shoppers per hour make a purchase, 84 shoppers per hour enter the checkout line. This needs to be converted to the number of shoppers per minute. Since there are 60 minutes in one hour, the rate is $\frac{84 \text{ shoppers}}{60 \text{ minutes}} = 1.4$ shoppers per minute. Using the given formula with $r = 1.4$ and $t = 5$ yields $N = rt = (1.4)(5) = 7$. Therefore, the average number of shoppers, N, in the checkout line at any time during business hours is 7.

QUESTION 38

The correct answer is 60. The estimated average number of shoppers in the original store at any time is 45. In the new store, the manager estimates that an average of 90 shoppers per <u>hour</u> enter the store, which is equivalent to 1.5 shoppers per minute. The manager also estimates that each shopper stays in the store for an average of 12 minutes. Thus, by Little's law, there are, on average,

$N = rt = (1.5)(12) = 18$ shoppers in the new store at any time. This is $\frac{45 - 18}{45} \times 100 = 60$ percent less than the average number of shoppers in the original store at any time.

Answer Explanations

SAT Practice Test #4

Section 1: Reading Test

QUESTION 1

Choice C is the best answer. The narrator initially expresses uncertainty, or uneasiness, over his decision to set out for the North Pole: "my motives in this undertaking are not entirely clear" (lines 9-10). At the end of the passage, the narrator recognizes that because of this journey he is "on the brink of knowing . . . not an ethereal mathematical spot," the North Pole, but himself (lines 56-57).

Choices A, B, and D are incorrect because the narrator does not suggest that he fears going on the expedition, doubts his own abilities, or feels disdain for the North Pole.

QUESTION 2

Choice D is the best answer. Lines 56-57 provide evidence that the narrator eventually recognizes his motives for traveling to the North Pole: "What I am on the brink of knowing, I now see, is not an ephemeral mathematical spot but myself." The narrator initially was unsure of why he was traveling to the North Pole, but realizes that he has embarked on a journey to find himself.

Choices A, B, and C are incorrect because they do not provide the best evidence that the narrator eventually recognizes his motives for traveling to the North Pole. Rather, choices A, B, and C all focus on the narrator's preparations and expectations for the journey.

QUESTION 3

Choice D is the best answer. In lines 1-6, the narrator says that he feels a "vast yearning" and that his emotions are "complicated." He explains that he does "not understand quite what it is that the yearning desires." In this context, his emotions are "not readily verifiable," or not completely understood.

Choices A, B, and C are incorrect because in this context, "not readily verifiable" does not mean unable to be authenticated, likely to be contradicted, or without empirical support.

QUESTION 4

Choice C is the best answer. In lines 10-13, the narrator explains that "the machinery of [his] destiny has worked in secret" to prepare him for this journey, as "its clockwork" has propelled him to "this time and place." By using the phrases "the machinery" and "its clockwork," the narrator is showing that powerful and independent forces are causing him to journey to the North Pole.

Choices A, B, and D are incorrect because they do not indicate the main purpose of lines 10-13. While lines 10-13 mention that these powerful and independent forces have been working "for years, for a lifetime" to convince the narrator to journey to the North Pole, they do not expose a hidden side of the narrator, demonstrate the narrator's manner, or explain the amount of time the narrator has spent preparing for his expedition.

QUESTION 5

Choice A is the best answer. In lines 20-21, the narrator states that many people have perished while journeying to the North Pole: "Nobody has succeeded in this thing, and many have died."

Choices B, C, and D are incorrect because the narrator does not indicate that previous explorers have made surprising discoveries, have failed to determine the exact location of the North Pole, or had different motivations than his own.

QUESTION 6

Choice A is the best answer. In lines 20-21, the narrator provides evidence that many previous explorers seeking the North Pole have perished in the attempt: "Nobody has succeeded in this thing, and many have died."

Choices B, C, and D do not mention previous explorers; therefore, these lines do not provide the best evidence that explorers died while seeking the North Pole.

QUESTION 7

Choice B is the best answer. In lines 27-39, the narrator states that he is "intent" on traveling to the North Pole but acknowledges that the journey is absurd: "Who wants the North Pole! What good is it! Can you eat it! Will it carry you from Gothenburg to Malmö like a railway?" By asking these questions, the narrator recognizes that the North Pole has no practical value. Still, the narrator admits that finding the North Pole is necessary, as it "must nevertheless be sought for."

Choices A, C, and D are incorrect because the narrator does not view his expedition to the North Pole as immoral, socially beneficial, or scientifically important.

QUESTION 8

Choice D is the best answer. In lines 27-31, the narrator asks a series of rhetorical questions about the North Pole: "Who wants the North Pole! What good is it! Can you eat it? Will it carry you from Gothenburg to Malmö like a railway?" In this context, the narrator is suggesting that reaching the North Pole has no foreseeable benefit or value to humanity; unlike trains that bring travelers to specific destinations, the North Pole does not provide humans with a specific benefit or form of convenience.

Choices A, B, and C are incorrect because the question posed in lines 30-31 does not debate modes of travel, examine the proximity of cities that can be reached by trains, or question how often people travel.

QUESTION 9

Choice D is the best answer. In lines 48-49, the narrator states that the North Pole "is an abstraction, a mathematical fiction" and that "no one but a Swedish madman could take the slightest interest in it." In this context, the narrator is stating that people would not "take the slightest interest in," or be curious about, the North Pole.

Choices A, B, and C are incorrect because in this context, "take the slightest interest in" does not mean to accept responsibility for, to possess little regard for, or to pay no attention to something.

QUESTION 10

Choice A is the best answer. In lines 49-51, the narrator describes his balloon journey toward the North Pole: "The wind is still from the south, bearing us steadily northward at the speed of a trotting dog." In this context, the wind is "bearing," or carrying, the narrator in a direction to the North.

Choices B, C, and D are incorrect because in this context, "bearing" does not mean affecting, yielding, or enduring.

QUESTION 11

Choice C is the best answer. The author states that "demographic inversion is not a proxy for population growth" (lines 32-33). In other words, demographic inversion is distinct from population growth. The author also notes that demographic inversion is evident in many American cities, as it "can occur in cities that are growing, those whose numbers are flat, and even in those undergoing a modest decline in size" (lines 33-35).

Choices A, B, and D are incorrect because they do not summarize the first paragraph.

QUESTION 12

Choice D is the best answer. The author notes that one of "the most powerful demographic events of the past decade [was] the movement of African Americans out of central cities" (lines 14-17).

Choices A, B, and C are incorrect because the author does not state that the unemployed, immigrants, or young professionals moved away from central-city areas in large numbers in the early 2000s.

QUESTION 13

Choice A is the best answer. The author states that democratic inversion "can occur in cities that are growing, those whose numbers are flat, and even in those undergoing a modest decline in size" (lines 33-35). In this context, cities whose "numbers," or population size, are "flat" have static, or unchanging, populations.

Choices B, C, and D are incorrect because in this context, "flat" does not mean deflated, featureless, or obscure.

QUESTION 14

Choice B is the best answer. The author states that many major American cities are currently experiencing economic hardship, or "enormous fiscal problems," because of "public pension obligations they incurred in the more prosperous years of the past two decades" (lines 36-39). The author then provides the example of Chicago, a city that can no longer afford to pay the "public services to which most of [its] citizens have grown to feel entitled" (lines 41-43). The author is arguing that many major American cities face economic hardship due to past promises (such as public services) they made to their constituents.

Choices A, C, and D are incorrect because the passage does not discuss expected tax increases, an inner-city tax base, or manufacturing production as they relate to the financial status of many major American cities.

QUESTION 15

Choice A is the best answer. In lines 36-39, the author provides evidence that many major American cities are currently experiencing economic hardship due to promises made in past years: "America's major cities face enormous fiscal problems, many of them the result of public pension obligations they incurred in the more prosperous years of the past two decades." America's major cities made past promises, such as "public pension obligations," to their citizens, which caused their current financial situation.

Choices B, C, and D are incorrect because they do not provide evidence that many major American cities are currently experiencing economic hardship due to promises made in past years.

QUESTION 16

Choice C is the best answer. The author explains how sociologist Ernest W. Burgess determined that urban areas have a traditional four-zone structure (lines 54-63). He then states that Burgess was "right about the urban America of 1974" (line 65) as it also followed the traditional four-zone structure: "Virtually every city in the country had a downtown, where the commercial life of the metropolis was conducted; it had a factory district just beyond; it had districts of working-class residences just beyond that; and it had residential suburbs for the wealthy and the upper middle class at the far end of the continuum" (lines 66-71).

Choices A, B, and D are incorrect because the passage does not imply that American cities in 1974 were witnessing the flight of minority populations to the suburbs, had begun to lose their manufacturing sectors, or were already experiencing demographic inversion.

QUESTION 17

Choice C is the best answer. In lines 66-71, the author provides evidence that American cities in 1974 had a traditional four-zone structure: "Virtually every city in the country had a downtown, where the commercial life of the metropolis was conducted; it had a factory district just beyond; it had districts of working-class residences just beyond that; and it had residential suburbs for the wealthy and the upper middle class at the far end of the continuum."

Choices A, B, and D are incorrect because they do not provide evidence that American urban cities in 1974 had a traditional four-zone structure. Choice A references a seminal paper on the layout of American cities, choice B identifies Burgess's original theory, and choice D focuses on movement to the suburbs.

QUESTION 18

Choice A is the best answer. In lines 66-68, the author notes that American cities in 1974 each had a "downtown, where the commercial life of the metropolis was conducted." In this context, the author is stating that these cities "conducted," or carried out, business, the "commercial life," in downtown areas.

Choices B, C, and D are incorrect because in this context, "conducted" does not mean supervised, regulated, or inhibited.

QUESTION 19

Choice B is the best answer. Chart 1 shows the percentage of the US population in 2010 that lived in non-metro, small metro, and large metro areas. While the author cites census numbers, he notes that "when it comes to measuring demographic inversion, raw census numbers are an ineffective blunt instrument" (lines 11-13). Census data refer to the number of people living in a specific area and the demographic information that's been collected on them. The author would most likely consider the information in chart 1 to be possibly accurate but an "ineffective blunt instrument" that's not truly informative.

Choices A and C are incorrect because the author would not consider census data to be excellent or compelling. Choice D is incorrect because while the author does not believe the census completely explains demographic inversion, he would be unlikely to disagree with the census data.

QUESTION 20

Choice A is the best answer. Chart 2 shows that the growth of all metropolitan areas in the 1990s was higher than the growth in all metropolitan areas in the 2000s: large metro areas experienced a growth of 14.3% in the 1990s versus a growth of 10.9% in the 2000s, small metro areas experienced a growth of 13.1% in the 1990s versus a growth of 10.3% in the 2000s, and non-metro areas experienced a growth of 9.0% in the 1990s versus a growth of 4.5% in the 2000s.

Choices B, C, and D are incorrect because they do not accurately characterize the US growth rate by metro size from 2000-2010 as illustrated in chart 2.

QUESTION 21

Choice D is the best answer. Chart 2 shows that in the 1990s the US population increased in large metro, small metro, and non-metro areas when compared to the population growth experienced in the 1980s. Large metro areas experienced a growth of 12.5% in the 1980s versus a growth of 14.3% in the 1990s, small metro areas experienced a growth of 8.8% in the 1980s versus a growth of 13.1% in the 1990s, and non-metro areas experienced a growth of 1.8% in the 1980s versus a growth of 9.0% in the 1990s. Given this information, the population grew more in all metro areas in the 1990s when compared to the growth of those areas in the 1980s.

Choices A, B, and C are incorrect because they do not draw an accurate conclusion about the US growth rate in the 1990s.

QUESTION 22

Choice A is the best answer. Lines 9-11 introduce the focus of the passage: "Welcome to the world of 'pharming,' in which simple genetic tweaks turn animals into living pharmaceutical factories." The passage then discusses the chronological development of "pharming," and describes ATryn, a useful drug produced after decades of laboratory experiments.

Choices B and C are incorrect because the passage does not primarily evaluate research or summarize long-term research findings. Choice D is incorrect because "pharming" is not a branch of scientific study.

QUESTION 23

Choice C is the best answer. The author is appreciative of pharming and describes it as turning "animals into living pharmaceutical factories" (lines 10-11). She expresses a positive view of pharming in line 70, when she describes its end result: "*Et voilà* — human medicine!"

Choices A, B, and D are incorrect because the author's attitude about pharming is not accurately characterized as one of fear, disinterest, or surprise.

QUESTION 24

Choice C is the best answer. In lines 19-21, the author explains that dairy animals are "expert," or capable, "protein producers."

Choices A, B, and D are incorrect because in this context "expert" does not mean knowledgeable, professional, or trained.

QUESTION 25

Choice B is the best answer. In line 36, the author explains that the initial transgenic studies were "lab-bound thought experiments come true." Those first studies, in other words, were considered to be of theoretical value only. They were not expected to yield products ready for human use.

Choices A and D are incorrect because the cost of animal research and the molecular properties of certain animals are not discussed in the passage. Choice C is incorrect because the passage does not suggest that all of the transgenic studies were focused on anticoagulants.

QUESTION 26

Choice C is the best answer. In lines 35-36, the author provides evidence that the transgenic studies done in the 1980s and 1990s were not expected to yield products ready for human use. The author explains that the initial transgenic studies were "merely gee-whiz, scientific geekery, lab-bound thought experiments come true."

Choices A, B, and D are incorrect because they do not provide evidence that the transgenic studies done in the 1980s and 1990s were not expected to yield products ready for human use. Choices A and B do not address the transgenic studies, and choice D focuses on ATryn, a drug that was intended for human use.

QUESTION 27

Choice A is the best answer. Lines 42-44 explain that ATryn "acts as a molecular bouncer, sidling up to clot-forming compounds and escorting them out of the bloodstream." Antithrombin can thus be seen as an agent that reduces the amount of dangerous clots in the bloodstream.

Choices B, C, and D are incorrect because the passage does not suggest that antithrombin stems from a rare genetic mutation, is a sequence of DNA, or occurs naturally in goats' mammary glands.

QUESTION 28

Choice B is the best answer. Lines 42-44 provide evidence that antithrombin reduces compounds that lead to blood clots, as it acts as a "molecular bouncer, sidling up to clot-forming compounds and escorting them out of the bloodstream."

Choices A, C, and D do not provide evidence that antithrombin reduces compounds that lead to blood clots; these lines describe proteins, people unable to produce antithrombin, and the production of ATryn.

QUESTION 29

Choice B is the best answer. In lines 60-62, the description of female goats' kids mentions that "some of them proved to be transgenic, the human gene nestled safely in their cells." The statement "some of them" indicates that while a number of the newborn goats were transgenic, others were not.

Choices A, C, and D are incorrect because the passage does not suggest that the female goats used in the initial experiment secreted antithrombin in their milk after giving birth, were the first animals to receive the microinjections, or had cells that contained genes usually found in humans.

QUESTION 30

Choice D is the best answer. In lines 63-64, the parenthetical is added after the phrase "a promoter," which is "(. . . a sequence of DNA that controls gene activity)." The parenthetical's purpose is to define the term "promoter."

Choices A, B, and C are incorrect because they do not correctly identify the purpose of the parenthetical information in lines 63-64.

QUESTION 31

Choice D is the best answer. Gold is a valuable element that commands high prices, so calling something "liquid gold" implies that it has great value. Because the pharmaceutical company GTC was producing the drug in order to sell it, it can be inferred that describing ATryn as "liquid gold" means it proved to be a lucrative product for GTC.

Choices A, B, and C are incorrect because the phrase "liquid gold" does not refer to the microinjection technique, efficiency in dairy production, or transgenic goats being beneficial to dairy farmers.

QUESTION 32

Choice D is the best answer. In lines 25-29, Burke describes the contract between a person and society as one that is "not a partnership in things subservient only to the gross animal existence of a temporary and perishable nature. It is a partnership in all science; a partnership in all art; a partnership in every virtue, and in all perfection." Describing that contract as a partnership in all things indicates its seriousness, while describing it as not being a "temporary and perishable nature" implies its permanence.

Choice A is incorrect because line 27 states that the contract between a person and society is not "temporary or perishable," meaning it is not brief. Choices B and C are incorrect because the passage does not compare the contracts in terms of complexity or precision.

QUESTION 33

Choice D is the best answer. In lines 1-9, Burke explains that people have "consecrated the state" to "avoid . . . the evils of inconstancy and versatility," and that people should examine "the faults of the state . . . with pious awe and trembling solitude." Burke then explains that society is taught to "look with horror on those children of their country who want to hack that aged parent in pieces" (lines 10-12). Burke is arguing that children want to revise the state, or "this aged parent," by amending its faults. In this context, "state" refers to a political entity, or government, that attempts to protect its citizens from "the evils of inconstancy and versatility."

Choices A, B, and C are incorrect because in this context, "state" does not mean style of living, position in life, or temporary condition.

QUESTION 34

Choice A is the best answer. In lines 17-29, Burke argues that "subordinate contracts," are simply business agreements over traded goods, while the state is not merely "a partnership agreement in a trade . . . or some other such low concern . . . but a partnership in all science; a partnership in all art; a partnership in every virtue, and in all perfection." In this context, Burke is stating that the state is not a contract consisting of "low" or petty concerns.

Choices B, C, and D are incorrect because in this context, "low" does not mean weak, inadequate, or depleted.

QUESTION 35

Choice D is the best answer. In lines 41-43, Paine asserts that "Every age and generation must be as free to act for itself, *in all cases*, as the ages and generations which preceded it." He later states that deceased citizens of a state should no longer have "any authority in directing who shall be its governors, or how its government shall be organized, or how administered" (lines 61-63). Paine doesn't believe, in other words, that the decisions of previous generations should dictate the conditions of modern life and government.

Choices A, B, and C are incorrect because they do not accurately characterize the way Paine views historical precedents.

QUESTION 36

Choice B is the best answer. In lines 30-34, Burke describes societal contracts as long-term agreements that preserve the interests of past generations and link the living and the dead into a "partnership." Paine, however, states that past generations have no "control" over the decisions made by living (line 71) because the dead have "no longer any participation in the concerns of this world" (lines 59-60).

Choices A, C, and D are incorrect because they do not accurately characterize how Paine would respond to Burke's claim that societal contracts link past and current generations.

QUESTION 37

Choice D is the best answer. Lines 67-72 provide the best evidence that Paine would respond to Burke's statement that society is a "partnership" between past and current generations (lines 30-34) with the explanation that the current generation cannot know what judgments the dead would make about contemporary issues. In these lines Paine explains: "What possible obligation, then, can exist between them; what rule or principle can be laid down, that two nonentities, the one out of existence, and the other not in, and who never can meet in this world, that the one should control the other to the end of time?"

Choices A, B, and C are incorrect because the lines cited do not provide the best evidence that Paine would respond to Burke's statement that society is a "partnership" between past and current generations (lines 30-34) by arguing that the current generation cannot know what judgments the dead would make about contemporary issues.

QUESTION 38

Choice D is the best answer. Paine concludes Passage 2 with the argument that because social issues change over time, the living should not try to adhere to decisions made by former generations (lines 73-80). Burke, however, states that living citizens exist within a "universal kingdom" (line 35) comprised of the living, the dead, and those who are not yet born. Burke argues that the living do not have the right to change their government based on "their speculations of a contingent improvement" (lines 36-37). Therefore, Burke would disapprove of Paine's concluding argument, as he believes the living do not have sufficient justification for changing the existing governmental structure.

Choices A, B, and C are incorrect because they do not accurately describe how Burke would likely have responded to Paine's remarks in the final paragraph of Passage 2.

QUESTION 39

Choice D is the best answer. Lines 34-38 provide the best evidence that Burke would disapprove of Paine's remarks in the final paragraph of Passage 2: "The municipal corporations of that universal kingdom are not morally at liberty at [the living's] pleasure, and on their speculations of a contingent improvement, wholly to separate and tear asunder the bands of their subordinate community." In these lines, Burke is arguing that the living do not have sufficient justification to change the existing governmental structure.

Choices A, B, and C do not provide the best evidence that Burke would disapprove of Paine's remarks in the final paragraph of Passage 2, as Burke believes the living do not have sufficient justification for changing the existing governmental structure.

QUESTION 40

Choice A is the best answer. The primary argument of Passage 1 is that an inviolable contract exists between a people and its government, one that is to be "looked on with other reverence" (lines 24-25). Passage 1 suggests that this contract exists between past and future generations as well; in effect, current and future generations should be governed by decisions made in the past. Passage 2 challenges these points, as it argues that current and future generations are not obligated to preserve past generations' beliefs: "The Parliament or the people of 1688, or of any other period, had no more right to dispose of the people of the present day, or to bind or to control them in any shape whatever, than the parliament or the people of the present day have to dispose of, bind, or control those who are to live a hundred or a thousand years hence" (lines 48-54).

Choices B, C, and D are incorrect because Passage 2 does not offer an alternative approach to Passage 1, support an idea introduced in Passage 1, or exemplify an attitude promoted in Passage 1.

QUESTION 41

Choice B is the best answer. Passage 1 argues that the government is sacred (lines 3-6) and that no person should interfere with it (lines 6-9). Passage 2 argues that people have the right to make changes to their government: "The circumstances of the world are continually changing, and the opinions of men change also; and as government is for the living, and not for the dead, it is the living only that has any right in it" (lines 73-76).

Choices A, C, and D are incorrect because they do not identify the main purpose of both passages.

QUESTION 42

Choice C is the best answer. The author explains that a "powerful volcano" erupted around 750 years ago and caused "a centuries-long cold snap known as the Little Ice Age" (lines 1-3). The author then states that a group of scientists believe the volcano Samalas was this "powerful volcano," and she explains how the scientists' research supports this claim (lines 17-78).

Choices A, B, and D are incorrect because they do not identify the main purpose of the passage.

QUESTION 43

Choice B is the best answer. The author begins the passage by explaining how the Little Ice Age was a "centuries-long cold snap" that was likely caused by a volcanic eruption (lines 1-3). The author then explains how scientists used radiocarbon analysis to determine when the Little Ice Age began and how a volcanic eruption triggered the cooling temperatures (lines 17-25).

Choices A, C, and D are incorrect because the passage does not criticize a scientific model, offer a new method of measuring sulfates, or shift from the use of radiocarbon dating to an examination of volcanic glass.

QUESTION 44

Choice A is the best answer. In lines 17-25, the passage shifts focus from describing a recorded event to providing evidence that the Little Ice Age was likely caused by a volcanic eruption. The passage states that scientists used "radiocarbon dating of dead plant material from beneath the ice caps on Baffin Island and Iceland, as well as ice and sediment core data" to determine when the Little Ice Age began and how it was connected to the "mystery" volcanic eruption.

Choices B, C, and D are incorrect because they do not provide the best evidence that the passage shifts focus from a description of a recorded event to its likely cause. Choices B, C, and D all focus on the scientists' research but do not explain what caused the Little Ice Age.

QUESTION 45

Choice D is the best answer. According to lines 5-8, "That a powerful volcano erupted somewhere in the world, sometime in the Middle Ages, is written in polar ice cores in the form of layers of sulfate deposits and tiny shards of volcanic glass." The phrase "is written in" reinforces the idea that the polar ice caps contain evidence of the volcanic eruption, and that scientists can interpret this evidence by examining the "sulfate deposits and tiny shards of volcanic glass."

Choices A, B, and C are incorrect because the author does not use the phrase "is written in" to demonstrate the concept of the hands-on nature of the scientists' work, highlight the fact that scientists often write about their work, or underscore the sense of importance scientists have about their work.

QUESTION 46

Choice A is the best answer. The scientists believe the volcano Samalas, located in Indonesia, was most likely the medieval volcanic eruption (lines 33-35). The eruption likely occurred near the equator because an equatorial location is "consistent with the apparent climate impacts" the scientists observed (lines 61-67).

Choices B, C, and D are incorrect because the scientists do not suggest that the medieval volcanic eruption was located in the Arctic region, the Antarctic region, or Ecuador.

QUESTION 47

Choice D is the best answer. In lines 61-64, the author cites geochemist Gifford Miller's findings that provide evidence that the medieval volcanic eruption most likely occurred in Indonesia near the equator: "It's not a total surprise that an Indonesian volcano might be the source of the eruption, Miller says. 'An equatorial eruption is more consistent with the apparent climate impacts.'"

Choices A, B, and C are incorrect because they do not provide evidence that the medieval volcanic eruption most likely occurred in Indonesia near the equator. Rather, choices A, B, and C focus on the medieval volcano's power, impact, and magnitude.

QUESTION 48

Choice C is the best answer. In lines 68-71, the author states, "Another possible candidate — both in terms of timing and geographical location — is Ecuador's Quilotoa, estimated to have last erupted between 1147 and 1320 C.E." The phrase "another possible candidate" implies that the scientists believe that in the Middle Ages a different volcanic eruption, such as an eruption from the volcano Quilotoa, could have been responsible for the onset of the Little Ice Age.

Choices A, B, and D are incorrect because the phrase "another possible candidate" does not imply the frequency or effects of volcanic eruptions, or that some volcanoes have large calderas.

QUESTION 49

Choice D is the best answer. In lines 71-75, the author explains how Lavigne's team proved that Quilotoa's eruption did not cause the Little Ice Age:

"But when Lavigne's team examined shards of volcanic glass from this volcano, they found that they didn't match the chemical composition of the glass found in polar ice cores, whereas the Samalas glass is a much closer match." These findings show that Samalas, not Quilotoa, was responsible for the onset of the Little Ice Age.

Choices A, B, and C are incorrect because they focus on the difficulty of identifying the volcano responsible for the Little Ice Age, the magnitude of the volcanic eruption, and the researchers' experiment.

QUESTION 50

Choice C is the best answer. The data in the figure show the greatest below-average temperature variation occurred in 1675 CE, as the temperature reached a variation of −1.0° Celsius.

Choice A is incorrect because the figure shows that the temperature in 1200 CE was above average (+0.25° Celsius). Choices B and D are incorrect because the below-average temperature variation reported in 1675 CE (at −1.0° Celsius) was greater than the below-average temperature variation reported for 1375 CE (around −0.25° Celsius) and 1750 CE (around (−0.5° Celsius).

QUESTION 51

Choice B is the best answer. The passage says that the Little Ice Age began "about 750 years ago" (line 1) and that "the cold summers and ice growth began abruptly between 1275 and 1300 C.E." (lines 23-24). The figure indicates that average temperatures in central England began to drop around 1275 CE, and this drop in temperatures continued "through the 1700s" (line 32).

Choices A, C, and D are incorrect because the passage and figure do not indicate that the Little Ice Again began around 1150 CE, just before 1500 CE, or around 1650 CE.

QUESTION 52

Choice A is the best answer. The figure shows that the greatest cooling period of the Little Ice Age occurred between 1500 and 1700 CE; it also shows that the greatest warming period of the Medieval Warm Period occurred between 1150 and 1250 CE. Therefore, the Little Ice Age's greatest cooling occurred a couple of centuries, or "hundreds of years," after the temperature peaks of the Medieval Warm Period.

Choices B, C, and D are incorrect because the figure does not focus on equatorial volcanic eruptions, pyroclastic flows, or radiocarbon analysis.

Section 2: Writing and Language Test

QUESTION 1

Choice B is the best answer because the relative clause appropriately modifies the noun "work" in the preceding independent clause.

Choices A, C, and D are incorrect because each creates a comma splice.

QUESTION 2

Choice B is the best answer because it creates the appropriate contrasting transition from the fact that the first two panels were painted during the day to the fact that the third panel was painted at night.

Choices A, C, and D are incorrect because each creates an inappropriate transition from the previous sentence. Choice A and choice D imply addition rather than contrast. Choice C results in an incomplete sentence.

QUESTION 3

Choice B is the best answer because it creates an appropriate appositive to the subject "mural," and is correctly set off by commas on both sides.

Choices A, C, and D are incorrect because each is incorrectly punctuated. Choice A lacks a comma after "centerpiece," choice C unnecessarily introduces an independent clause, and choice D contains an em dash that has no parallel earlier in the sentence.

QUESTION 4

Choice A is the best answer because it explicitly introduces the explanation for the behavior (painting at night) described in the previous paragraph.

Choices B, C, and D are incorrect because none alludes to the artist's painting at night, which is described at the end of the previous paragraph and explained in this paragraph.

QUESTION 5

Choice D is the best answer because it refers to an action that can be performed on a physical object such as a mural.

Choices A, B, and C are incorrect because each refers to an action that is performed on information rather than on a physical object.

QUESTION 6

Choice B is the best answer because it creates a past tense construction consistent with the verb "was dominated."

Choices A, C, and D are incorrect because none is consistent with the verb tense established earlier in the sentence.

QUESTION 7

Choice D is the best answer because it is the most precise choice, specifying the noun that the demonstrative pronoun "this" refers to.

Choices A, B, and C are incorrect because each provides a vague, nonspecific pronoun that does not concretely define a referent.

QUESTION 8

Choice B is the best answer because it correctly places and punctuates the appositive phrase that describes the "Chicano mural movement."

Choices A, C, and D are incorrect because each contains awkward syntax that obscures the relationship between the key noun phrases "an explosion of mural painting" and "the Chicano mural movement."

QUESTION 9

Choice C is the best answer because it creates parallel construction within the list of locations ("*in* abandoned lots, *on* unused buildings, or *on* infrastructure").

Choices A, B, and D are incorrect because none follows the construction established within the list of locations.

QUESTION 10

Choice A is the best answer because it alludes to the uniquely high level of investment, described in the next sentence, that the new group of artists is making in restoring and publicizing "América Tropical."

Choices B, C, and D are incorrect because each fails to express the connection between the general restoration efforts mentioned in the previous sentence and the specific role of "América Tropical" in these efforts, which is described in the next sentence.

QUESTION 11

Choice C is the best answer because details of the initial reaction to Siqueiros's mural and its subsequent rediscovery are given previously in the passage and are not needed to set up the forward-looking sentence that follows.

Choices A, B, and D are incorrect because each provides an inaccurate interpretation of the sentence that the writer is considering adding.

QUESTION 12

Choice D is the best answer because without the underlined portion, the sentence contains an appropriate parallel contrast between the phrases "organically grown crops" and "conventionally grown counterparts," each of which describes crops.

Choices A, B, and C are incorrect because each creates an illogical comparison: crops to "people," crops to "purchase," and crops to "purchasing."

QUESTION 13

Choice B is the best answer because it provides the subject "consumers," creating a complete sentence and providing a referent for the pronoun "they" that appears later in the sentence.

Choices A, C, and D are incorrect because each lacks the subject that the sentence requires and none provide a referent for "they."

QUESTION 14

Choice D is the best answer because it efficiently creates a contrast with "organically grown."

Choices A, B, and C are incorrect because they are unnecessarily wordy and repeat information given in previous sentences.

QUESTION 15

Choice C is the best answer because it sets up the contrast between the added expense of organic food and the evidence that suggests a lack of benefits from eating organic food.

Choices A, B, and D are incorrect because each fails to acknowledge the contrast between the last sentence in the paragraph and the previous sentences.

QUESTION 16

Choice C is the best answer because "maintain" is commonly used to describe advocating a position in an argument.

Choices A, B, and D are incorrect because none is appropriate in the context of describing an opinion advocated by a group of people.

QUESTION 17

Choice A is the best answer because the transitional phrase "For instance" sets up an example supporting the point, made in the previous sentence, that organic food may not contain more vitamins and minerals than conventionally grown food.

Choices B, C, and D are incorrect because none indicates that the sentence is providing an example supporting the point made in the previous sentence.

QUESTION 18

Choice C is the best answer because it accurately identifies the reason that the writer should not add the proposed sentence: the paragraph is about evidence of nutritional content, not the availability of organic food.

Choices A, B, and D are incorrect because each provides an inaccurate interpretation of the proposed sentence's relationship to the passage.

QUESTION 19

Choice A is the best answer because the plural verb "have" is consistent with the plural subject "amounts."

Choices B, C, and D are incorrect because each is a singular verb, which is inconsistent with the plural subject "amounts."

QUESTION 20

Choice C is the best answer because the example it supplies, that pesticides can be minimized by washing or peeling produce, supports the claim that nonorganic food is safe.

Choices A, B, and D are incorrect because none supports the paragraph's claim about the safety of nonorganic food.

QUESTION 21

Choice B is the best answer because the plural noun phrase "numerous other reasons" must be preceded by a plural verb and a pronoun that does not indicate possession: "there are."

Choices A, C, and D are incorrect because each contains the singular verb "is," the possessive pronoun "their," or both.

QUESTION 22

Choice D is the best answer because a nonrestrictive clause must be preceded by a comma; in addition, "such as" is never followed by a comma. In this case, the list of reasons supporting the claim that there are benefits to buying organic food is nonrestrictive; the list tells the reader something about organic food but does not restrict or place limits on organic food.

Choices A, B, and C are incorrect because each places erroneous punctuation after the phrase "such as." Choices B and C also lack the necessary comma preceding "such as."

QUESTION 23

Choice C is the best answer because "intriguing" conveys a realistic level of interest for the entertaining but ultimately inconsequential question of regional differences in words for carbonated beverages.

Choices A, B, and D are incorrect because each mocks the topic of regional words for carbonated beverages.

QUESTION 24

Choice C is the best answer because "but also" is the appropriate transition to complete the correlative pair "not only . . . but also," which begins earlier in the sentence.

Choices A, B, and D are incorrect because each fails to complete the phrase "not only . . . but also."

QUESTION 25

Choice B is the best answer because it is consistent with the fact that there remains a "veritable army of trained volunteers traveling the country" and because it uses "still" to contrast this method with the "new avenues."

Choices A, C, and D are incorrect because none is consistent with the information contained later in the passage.

QUESTION 26

Choice D is the best answer because it uses the relative pronoun "who" to avoid needless repetition of the word "scholars."

Choices A, B, and C are incorrect because each unnecessarily repeats the word "scholars."

QUESTION 27

Choice C is the best answer because the new sentence provides a logical transition from sentences 3 and 4, which describe the data collection, to sentence 5, which explains that completing the dictionary took far longer than expected.

Choices A, B, and D are incorrect because each fails to create a logical transition between the preceding and subsequent sentences.

QUESTION 28

Choice A is the best answer because the singular verb "requires" agrees with the singular subject "research."

Choices B, C, and D are incorrect because they do not create subject-verb agreement.

QUESTION 29

Choice D is the best answer because a colon is the correct punctuation to introduce the elaborating phrase that follows the word "army."

Choices A, B, and C are incorrect because none provides the appropriate punctuation.

QUESTION 30

Choice B is the best answer because it contains both the correct word to refer to an Internet location — "site" — and the correct preposition to complete the collocation "in search of."

Choices A, C, and D are incorrect because each contains a word that does not refer to an Internet location, and choices C and D contain the wrong preposition.

QUESTION 31

Choice C is the best answer because it correctly associates each beverage term with the region described in the sentence according to the information contained in the map.

Choices A, B, and D are incorrect because each contradicts the information contained in the map.

QUESTION 32

Choice B is the best answer because it contains the two plural possessive pronouns needed to refer to the subject "findings" — "their" and "their."

Choices A, C, and D are incorrect because each contains a word frequently confused with "their."

QUESTION 33

Choice A is the best answer because it provides a summary and evaluation of gathering data from the Internet, which is the focus of the paragraph.

Choices B, C, and D are incorrect because each is either irrelevant to the main point of the paragraph or unnecessarily repeats information.

QUESTION 34

Choice C is the best answer because it uses the present tense, which is consistent with the verbs that appear later in the sentence.

Choices A, B, and D are incorrect because they create awkward shifts in tense.

QUESTION 35

Choice C is the best answer because the em dashes correctly bracket the examples of the types of elements.

Choices A, B, and D are incorrect because each uses either inconsistent or incorrect punctuation to set off the types of elements.

QUESTION 36

Choice B is the best answer because a period is an appropriate way to separate the two independent clauses that meet at the underlined text.

Choices A, C, and D are incorrect because each either creates a comma splice or lacks necessary punctuation.

QUESTION 37

Choice D is the best answer because the proposed sentence to be added is a paraphrase of the sentence before it, containing the same ideas.

Choices A, B, and C are incorrect because none fully acknowledges the relationship between the proposed sentence to be added and the other sentences in the paragraph.

QUESTION 38

Choice A is the best answer because it highlights the importance of the game designer's communication with others, which is the paragraph's main point.

Choices B, C, and D are incorrect because none describes communication originating with the game designer, which is the main focus of the paragraph.

QUESTION 39

Choice C is the best answer because the importance of communication is established in the previous sentences. The transition "consequently" best captures the fact that the designer must be skilled in this area.

Choices A, B, and D are incorrect because each contains a transition that either repeats information or creates an illogical relationship between this sentence and the previous sentences.

QUESTION 40

Choice B is the best answer because it provides the singular nouns "writer" and "speaker" to agree with the singular pronoun "anyone."

Choices A, C, and D are incorrect because none creates pronoun-referent agreement.

QUESTION 41

Choice D is the best answer because it expresses in the clearest, simplest way the idea that many game designers start out as programmers.

Choices A, B, and C are incorrect because each is unnecessarily wordy and obscures meaning.

QUESTION 42

Choice D is the best answer because it logically and appropriately modifies the phrase "collaboration skills."

Choices A, B, and C are incorrect because none appropriately describes the value of collaboration skills.

QUESTION 43

Choice A is the best answer because it provides a logical subject for the modifying phrase "demanding and deadline driven."

Choices B, C, and D are incorrect because each creates a dangling modifier.

QUESTION 44

Choice B is the best answer because sentence 5 expresses the main point upon which the paragraph elaborates.

Choices A, C, and D are incorrect because none places sentence 5 in the appropriate position to set up the details contained in the paragraph.

Section 3: Math Test – No Calculator

QUESTION 1

Choice A is correct. The expression $|x - 1| - 1$ will equal 0 if $|x - 1| = 1$. This is true for $x = 2$ and for $x = 0$. For example, substituting $x = 2$ into the expression $|x - 1| - 1$ and simplifying the result yields $|2 - 1| - 1 = |1| - 1 = 1 - 1 = 0$. Therefore, there is a value of x for which $|x - 1| - 1$ is equal to 0.

Choices B, C, and D are incorrect. By definition, the absolute value of any expression is a nonnegative number. For example, in answer choice B, substituting any value for x into the expression $|x + 1|$ will yield a nonnegative number. Because the sum of a nonnegative number and a positive number is positive, $|x + 1| + 1$ will be a positive number for any value of x. Therefore, $|x + 1| + 1 \neq 0$ for any value of x. Similarly, the expressions given in answer choices C and D are not equivalent to zero for any value of x.

QUESTION 2

Choice A is correct. Since $f(x) = \frac{3}{2}x + b$ and $f(6) = 7$, substituting 6 for x in $f(x) = \frac{3}{2}x + b$ gives $f(6) = \frac{3}{2}(6) + b = 7$. Then, solving the equation $\frac{3}{2}(6) + b = 7$ for b gives $\frac{18}{2} + b = 7$, or $9 + b = 7$. Thus, $b = 7 - 9 = -2$. Substituting -2 for the constant b gives $f(x) = \frac{3}{2}x - 2$; therefore, one can evaluate $f(-2)$ by substituting -2 for x: $\frac{3}{2}(-2) - 2 = -\frac{6}{2} - 2 = -3 - 2 = -5$.

Choice B is incorrect as it is the value of b, not of $f(-2)$. Choice C is incorrect as it is the value of $f(2)$, not of $f(-2)$. Choice D is incorrect as it is the value of $f(6)$, not of $f(-2)$.

QUESTION 3

Choice A is correct. The first equation can be rewritten as $x = 6y$. Substituting $6y$ for x in the second equation gives $4(y + 1) = 6y$. The left-hand side can be rewritten as $4y + 4$, giving $4y + 4 = 6y$. Subtracting $4y$ from both sides of the equation gives $4 = 2y$, or $y = 2$.

Choices B, C, and D are incorrect and may be the result of a computational or conceptual error when solving the system of equations.

QUESTION 4

Choice B is correct. If $f(x = -2x + 5$, then one can evaluate $f -3x$ by substituting $-3x$ for every instance of x. This yields $f -3x = -2(-3x + 5$, which simplifies to $6x + 5$.

Choices A, C, and D are incorrect and may be the result of miscalculations in the substitution or of misunderstandings of how to evaluate $f -3x$).

QUESTION 5

Choice C is correct. The expression $3(2x + 1)(4x + 1)$ can be simplified by first distributing the 3 to yield $(6x + 3)(4x + 1)$, and then multiplying the binomials together to obtain $24x^2 + 12x + 6x + 3$. Combining like terms gives $24x^2 + 18x + 3$.

Choice A is incorrect and may be the result of performing the multiplication of $3(2x + 1)(4x + 1)$ to result in $24x^2 + 18x + 3$, then incorrectly combining terms to result in $45x$. Choice B is incorrect and may be the result of correctly finding $(6x + 3)(4x + 1)$, but then multiplying only the first terms, $(6x)(4x)$, and the last terms, $(3)(1)$, but not the outer or inner terms, $(6x)(1)$ and $(3)(4x)$. Choice D is incorrect and may be the result of incorrectly distributing the 3 to both $(2x + 1)$ and $(4x + 1)$ to obtain $(6x + 3)(12x + 3)$, and then adding $3 + 3$ and $6x + 12x$ and incorrectly adding the exponents of x.

QUESTION 6

Choice B is correct. The equation $\frac{a-b}{b} = \frac{3}{7}$ can be rewritten as $\frac{a}{b} - \frac{b}{b} = \frac{3}{7}$, from which it follows that $\frac{a}{b} - 1 = \frac{3}{7}$, or $\frac{a}{b} = \frac{3}{7} + 1 = \frac{10}{7}$.

Choices A, C, and D are incorrect and may be the result of calculation errors in rewriting $\frac{a-b}{b} = \frac{3}{7}$. For example, choice A may be the result of a sign error in rewriting $\frac{a-b}{b}$ as $\frac{a}{b} + \frac{b}{b} = \frac{a}{b} + 1$.

QUESTION 7

Choice D is correct. In Amelia's training schedule, her longest run in week 16 will be 26 miles and her longest run in week 4 will be 8 miles. Thus, Amelia increases the distance of her longest run by 18 miles over the course of 12 weeks. Since Amelia increases the distance of her longest run each week by a constant amount, her rate of increase is $\frac{26-8}{16-4} = \frac{18}{12}$ miles per week, which is equal to 1.5 miles per week. So each week she increases the distance of her longest run by 1.5 miles.

Choices A, B, and C are incorrect because none of these training schedules would result in increasing Amelia's longest run from 8 miles in week 4 to 26 miles in week 16. For example, choice A is incorrect because if Amelia increases the distance of her longest run by 0.5 miles each week and has her longest run of 8 miles in week 4, her longest run in week 16 would be $8 + 0.5 \cdot 12 = 14$ miles, not 26 miles.

QUESTION 8

Choice A is correct. For an equation of a line in the form $y = mx + b$, the constant m is the slope of the line. Thus, the line represented by $y = -3x + 4$ has slope -3. Lines that are parallel have the same slope. To determine which of the given equations represents a line with the same slope as the line represented by $y = -3x + 4$, one can rewrite each equation in the form $y = mx + b$, that is, solve each equation for y. Choice A, $6x + 2y = 15$, can be rewritten as $2y = -6x + 15$ by subtracting $6x$ from each side of the equation. Then, dividing each side of $2y = -6x + 15$ by 2 gives $y = -\frac{6}{2}x + \frac{15}{2}$, which simplifies to y -3 $x + \frac{15}{2}$. Therefore, this line has slope -3 and is parallel to the line represented by $y = -3x + 4$. (The lines are parallel, not coincident, because they have different y-intercepts.)

Choices B, C, and D are incorrect and may be the result of common misunderstandings about which value in the equation of a line represents the slope of the line.

QUESTION 9

Choice D is correct. The question states that $\sqrt{x - a} = x - 4$ and that $a = 2$, so substituting 2 for a in the equation yields $\sqrt{x - 2} = x - 4$. To solve for x, square each side of the equation, which gives $\left(\sqrt{x - 2}\right)^2 = x - 4)^2$, or $x - 2 = x - 4)^2$. Then, expanding $(x - 4)^2$ yields $x - 2 = x^2 - 8x + 16$, or $0 = x^2 - 9x + 18$. Factoring the right-hand side gives $0 = (x - 3)(x - 6)$, and so $x = 3$ or $x = 6$. However, for $x = 3$, the original equation becomes $\sqrt{3 - 2} = 3 - 4$, which yields $1 = -1$, which is not true. Hence, $x = 3$ is an extraneous solution that arose from squaring each side of the equation. For $x = 6$, the original equation becomes $\sqrt{6 - 2} = 6 - 4$, which yields $\sqrt{4}$ 2, or $2 = 2$. Since this is true, the solution set of $\sqrt{x - 2} = x - 4$ is $\{6\}$.

Choice A is incorrect because it includes the extraneous solution in the solution set. Choice B is incorrect and may be the result of a calculation or factoring error. Choice C is incorrect because it includes only the extraneous solution, and not the correct solution, in the solution set.

QUESTION 10

Choice D is correct. Multiplying each side of $\frac{t + 5}{t - 5} = 10$ by $t - 5$ gives $t + 5 = 10(t - 5)$. Distributing the 10 to the binomial $(t - 5)$ yields $t + 5 = 10t - 50$. Subtracting t from each side of this equation gives $5 = 9t - 50$, and then adding 50 to each side gives $55 = 9t$. Finally, dividing each side of the equation $55 = 9t$ by 9 yields $t = \frac{55}{9}$.

Choices A, B, and C are incorrect and may be the result of calculation errors or incorrectly applying the distribution property.

QUESTION 11

Choice C is correct. It is given that $x = 2y + 5$ and $y = (2x - 3)(x + 9)$. To solve the system of equations, the quantity $(2x - 3)(x + 9)$ can be substituted for y in the first equation to yield $x = 2((2x - 3)(x + 9)) + 5$, which simplifies to $x = 4x^2 + 30x - 49$ and can be rewritten as $4x^2 + 29x - 49 = 0$. The discriminant of a quadratic equation in the form $ax^2 + bx + c = 0$, where a, b, and c are constants, is $b^2 - 4ac$. The discriminant for this quadratic equation is $29^2 - 4(4)(-49)$. This is a positive number which indicates that this quadratic equation has 2 distinct roots. The roots to the quadratic equation are the two x-coordinates of the ordered pairs which satisfy the system of equations. Since no other value of x satisfies $4x^2 + 29x - 49 = 0$, there are no other ordered pairs that satisfy the given system. Therefore, there are 2 ordered pairs (x, y) that satisfy the given system of equations.

Choices A and B are incorrect and may be the result of either a miscalculation or a conceptual error. Choice D is incorrect because a system of one quadratic equation and one linear equation cannot have infinitely many solutions.

QUESTION 12

Choice C is correct. Since the price of Ken's sandwich was x dollars, and Paul's sandwich was \$1 more, the price of Paul's sandwich was $x + 1$ dollars. Thus, the total cost of the sandwiches was $2x + 1$ dollars. Since this cost was split evenly between two people, Ken and Paul each paid $\frac{2x + 1}{2} = x + 0.5$ dollars plus a 20% tip. After adding the 20% tip, each of them paid $(x + 0.5) + 0.2(x + 0.5) = 1.2(x + 0.5)$ $1.2x + 0.6$ dollars.

Choices A, B, and D are incorrect. These expressions do not model the given context. They may be the result of errors in setting up the expression or of calculation errors.

QUESTION 13

Choice B is correct. The points where the two graphs intersect can be found by setting the functions $f(x)$ and $g(x)$ equal to one another and then solving for x. This yields $8x^2 - 2 = -8x^2 + 2$. Adding $8x^2$ and 2 to each side of the equation gives $16x^2 = 4$. Then dividing each side by 16 gives $x^2 = \frac{1}{4}$; therefore, x must be either $\frac{1}{2}$ or $-\frac{1}{2}$. From the graph, the value of k is the x-coordinate of the point of intersection on the positive x-axis. Therefore, $k = \frac{1}{2}$.

Alternatively, since $(k, 0)$ lies on the graph of both f and g, it follows that $f(k = g(k = 0$. Thus, evaluating $f(x = 8x^2 - 2$ at $x = k$ gives $0 = 8k^2 - 2$. Adding 2 to each side yields $2 = 8k^2$ and then dividing each side by 8 gives $\frac{1}{4} = k^2$. Therefore, the value of k must be $\frac{1}{2}$ or $-\frac{1}{2}$. From the graph, k is positive, so $k = \frac{1}{2}$.

Choices A, C, and D are incorrect and may be the result of calculation errors in solving for x or k.

QUESTION 14

Choice A is correct. To rewrite $\frac{8-i}{3-2i}$ in the standard form $a + bi$,

multiply the numerator and denominator of $\frac{8-i}{3-2i}$ by the conjugate of the

denominator, $3 + 2i$. This gives $\left(\frac{8-i}{3-2i}\right)\left(\frac{3+2i}{3+2i}\right) = \frac{24 + 16i - 3i + (-i)(2i)}{3^2 - 6i + 6i - (2i)^2}$.

Since $i^2 = -1$, this can be rewritten as $\frac{24 + 16i - 3i + 2}{9 - (-4)} = \frac{26 + 13i}{13}$, which

simplifies to $2 + i$. Therefore, when $\frac{8-i}{3-2i}$ is rewritten in the standard

form $a + bi$, the value of a is 2.

Choices B, C, and D are incorrect and may be the result of errors in symbolic manipulation. For example, choice B could be the result of

mistakenly rewriting $\frac{8-i}{3-2i}$ as $\frac{8}{3} + \frac{1}{2}i$.

QUESTION 15

Choice B is correct. The given quadratic equation can

be rewritten as $2x^2 - kx - 4p = 0$. Applying the quadratic

formula, $\frac{-b \pm \sqrt{b^2 - 4ac}}{2a}$, to this equation with $a = 2$, $b = -k$, and $c = -4p$

gives the solutions $\frac{k}{4} \pm \frac{\sqrt{k^2 + 32p}}{4}$.

Choices A, C, and D are incorrect and may be the result of errors in applying the quadratic formula.

QUESTION 16

The correct answer is 9. Since the three shelves of the triangular shelf system are parallel, the three triangles in the figure are similar. Since the shelves divide the left side of the largest triangle in the ratio 2 to 3 to 1, the similarity ratios of the triangles are as follows.

- Smallest to middle: 2 to 5

- Smallest to largest: 2 to 6, or 1 to 3

- Middle to largest: 5 to 6

The height of the largest shampoo bottle that can stand upright on the middle shelf is equal to the height of the middle shelf. The height of the entire triangular shelf system is 18 inches. This is the height of the largest triangle. The height of the middle shelf is the height of the middle triangle minus the height of the smallest triangle. Since the similarity ratio of the middle triangle to the largest triangle is 5 to 6, the height of the middle triangle is $\frac{5}{6}(18) = 15$ inches. Since the similarity ratio of the smallest triangle to the largest triangle is 1 to 3, the height of the smallest triangle is $\frac{1}{3}(18)$ = 6 inches. Therefore the height of the largest shampoo bottle that can fit on the middle shelf is 15 − 6 = 9 inches.

Alternatively, in the diagram below, the altitude of the largest triangle has been drawn and is a line segment that intersects and is perpendicular to each of the parallel lines.

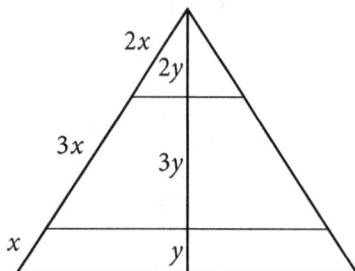

Using the proportional segment theorem, it follows that the lengths of the three segments formed by the altitude are in the ratio 2:3:1 (from top to bottom). If y is the length of the shortest segment, then the lengths of the three segments are 2y, 3y, and y, with 3y being the height of the middle shelf. Since 2y + 3y + y = 18, it follows that 3y = 9.

QUESTION 17

The correct answer is .6 or $\frac{3}{5}$. The angles marked $x°$ and $y°$ are acute angles in a right triangle. Thus, they are complementary angles. By the complementary angle relationship between sine and cosine, it follows that $\sin(x°) = \cos(y°)$. Therefore, the cosine of $y°$ is .6. Either .6 or the equivalent fraction 3/5 may be gridded as the correct answer.

Alternatively, since the sine of $x°$ is .6, the ratio of the side opposite the $x°$ angle to the hypotenuse is .6. The side opposite the $x°$ angle is the side adjacent to the $y°$ angle. Thus, the ratio of the side adjacent to the $y°$ angle to the hypotenuse, which is equal to the cosine of $y°$, is equal to .6.

QUESTION 18

The correct answer is 5. The four-term polynomial expression can be factored completely, by grouping, as follows:

$$(x^3 - 5x^2) + (2x - 10) = 0$$

$$x^2(x - 5) + 2(x - 5) = 0$$

$$(x - 5)(x^2 + 2) = 0$$

By the zero product property, set each factor of the polynomial equal to 0 and solve each resulting equation for x. This gives $x = 5$ or $x = \pm i\sqrt{2}$, respectively. Because the question asks for the real value of x that satisfies the equation, the correct answer is 5.

QUESTION 19

The correct answer is 0. Multiplying each side of $-3x + 4y = 20$ by 2 gives $-6x + 8y = 40$. Adding each side of $-6x + 8y = 40$ to the corresponding side of $6x + 3y = 15$ gives $11y = 55$, or $y = 5$. Finally, substituting 5 for y in $6x + 3y = 15$ gives $6x + 3(5) = 15$, or $x = 0$.

QUESTION 20

The correct answer is 25. In the mesosphere, an increase of 10 kilometers in the distance above Earth results in a decrease in the temperature by $k°$ Celsius where k is a constant. Thus, the temperature in the mesosphere is linearly dependent on the distance above Earth. Using the values provided, one can calculate the unit rate of change for the temperature in the mesosphere to be $\frac{-80 - (-5)}{80 - 50} = \frac{-75}{30} = \frac{-25}{10}$.

Therefore, within the mesosphere, if the distance above Earth increases by 1 kilometer, the temperature decreases by 2.5° Celsius. Therefore, if the distance above Earth increases by $(1 \times 10) = 10$ kilometers, the temperature will decrease by $(2.5 \times 10) = 25°$ Celsius. Thus, the value of k is 25.

Section 4: Math Test – Calculator

QUESTION 1

Choice B is correct. Let m be the number of movies Jill rented online during the month. Since the monthly membership fee is $9.80 and there is an additional fee of $1.50 to rent each movie online, the total of the membership fee and the movie rental fees, in dollars, can be written as $9.80 + 1.50m$. Since the total of these fees for the month was $12.80, the equation $9.80 + 1.50m = 12.80$ must be true. Subtracting 9.80 from each side and then dividing each side by 1.50 yields $m = 2$.

Choices A, C, and D are incorrect and may be the result of errors in setting up or solving the equation that represents the context.

QUESTION 2

Choice C is correct. Donald believes he can increase his typing speed by 5 words per minute each month. Therefore, in m months, he believes he can increase his typing speed by $5m$ words per minute. Because he is currently able to type at a speed of 180 words per minute, he believes that in m months, he will be able to increase his typing speed to $180 + 5m$ words per minute.

Choice A is incorrect because the expression indicates that Donald currently types 5 words per minute and will increase his typing speed by 180 words per minute each month. Choice B is incorrect because the expression indicates that Donald currently types 225 words per minute, not 180 words per minute. Choice D is incorrect because the expression indicates that Donald will decrease, not increase, his typing speed by 5 words per minute each month.

QUESTION 3

Choice C is correct. Because there are 16 ounces in 1 pound, a 3-pound pizza weighs 3 × 16 = 48 ounces. One half of the pizza weighs $\frac{1}{2}$ × 48 = 24 ounces, and one-third of the half weighs $\frac{1}{3}$ × 24 = 8 ounces.

Alternatively, since $\frac{1}{2}$ × $\frac{1}{3}$ = $\frac{1}{6}$, cutting the pizza into halves and then into thirds results in a pizza that is cut into sixths. Therefore, each slice of the 48-ounce pizza weighs $\frac{1}{6}$ × 48 = 8 ounces.

Choice A is incorrect and is the result of cutting each half into sixths rather than thirds. Choice B is incorrect and is the result of cutting each half into fourths rather than thirds. Choice D is incorrect and is the result of cutting the whole pizza into thirds.

QUESTION 4

Choice B is correct. Because Nick surveyed a random sample of the freshman class, his sample was representative of the entire freshman class. Thus, the percent of students in the entire freshman class expected to prefer the Fall Festival in October is appropriately estimated by the percent of students who preferred it in the sample, 25.6%. Thus, of the 225 students in the freshman class, approximately 225 × 0.256 = 57.6 or about 60 students would be expected to prefer having the Fall Festival in October.

Choices A, C, and D are incorrect. These choices may be the result of misapplying the concept of percent or of calculation errors.

QUESTION 5

Choice B is correct. The density of an object is equal to the mass of the object divided by the volume of the object, which can be expressed as density = $\frac{\text{mass}}{\text{volume}}$. Thus, if an object has a density of 3 grams per milliliter and a mass of 24 grams, the equation becomes 3 grams/milliliter = $\frac{24 \text{ grams}}{\text{volume}}$. This can be rewritten as volume = $\frac{24 \text{ grams}}{3 \text{ grams/milliliter}}$ = 8 milliliters.

Choice A is incorrect and be may be the result of confusing the density and the volume and setting up the density equation as 24 = $\frac{3}{\text{volume}}$. Choice C is incorrect and may be the result of a conceptual error that leads to subtracting 3 from 24. Choice D is incorrect and may be the result of confusing the mass and the volume and setting up the density equation as 24 = $\frac{\text{volume}}{3}$.

QUESTION 6

Choice A is correct. Let a be the number of hours Angelica worked last week. Since Raul worked 11 more hours than Angelica, Raul worked $a + 11$ hours last week. Since they worked a combined total of 59 hours, the equation $a + (a + 11) = 59$ can represent this situation This equation can be simplified to $2a + 11 = 59$, or $2a = 48$. Therefore, $a = 24$, and Angelica worked 24 hours last week.

Choice B is incorrect because it is the number of hours Raul worked last week. Choice C is incorrect. If Angelica worked 40 hours and Raul worked 11 hours more, Raul would have worked 51 hours, and the combined total number of hours they worked would be 91, not 59. Choice D is incorrect and may be the result of solving the equation $a + 11 = 59$ rather than $a + (a + 11) = 59$.

QUESTION 7

Choice A is correct. According to the table, of the 50 movies with the greatest ticket sales in 2012, 4 are comedy movies with a PG-13 rating. Therefore, the proportion of the 50 movies with the greatest ticket sales in 2012 that are comedy movies with a PG-13 rating is $\frac{4}{50}$, or equivalently, $\frac{2}{25}$.

Choice B is incorrect; $\frac{9}{50}$ is the proportion of the 50 movies with the greatest ticket sales in 2012 that are comedy movies, regardless of rating. Choice C is incorrect; $\frac{2}{11} = \frac{4}{22}$ is the proportion of movies with a PG-13 rating that are comedy movies. Choice D is incorrect; $\frac{11}{25} = \frac{22}{50}$ is the proportion of the 50 movies with the greatest ticket sales in 2012 that have a rating of PG-13.

QUESTION 8

Choice D is correct. The quadrants of the xy-plane are defined as follows: Quadrant I is above the x-axis and to the right of the y-axis; Quadrant II is above the x-axis and to the left of the y-axis; Quadrant III is below the x-axis and to the left of the y-axis; and Quadrant IV is below the x-axis and to the right of the y-axis. It is possible for line ℓ to pass through Quadrants II, III, and IV, but not Quadrant I, only if line ℓ has negative x- and y-intercepts. This implies that line ℓ has a negative slope, since between the negative x-intercept and the negative y-intercept the value of x increases (from negative to zero) and the value of y decreases (from zero to negative); so the quotient of the change in y over the change in x, that is, the slope of line ℓ, must be negative.

Choice A is incorrect because a line with an undefined slope is a vertical line, and if a vertical line passes through Quadrant IV, it must pass through Quadrant I as well. Choice B is incorrect because a line with a slope of zero is a horizontal line and, if a horizontal line passes through Quadrant II, it must pass through Quadrant I as well. Choice C is incorrect because if a line with a positive slope passes through Quadrant IV, it must pass through Quadrant I as well.

QUESTION 9

Choice B is correct. According to the table, in 2012 there was a total of 14,766 + 47,896 = 62,662 registered voters between 18 and 44 years old, and 3,453 + 11,237 = 14,690 of them were from the Midwest region. Therefore, the probability that a randomly chosen registered voter who was between 18 and 44 years old in 2012 was from the Midwest region is $\frac{14,690}{62,662} \approx 0.234$. Of the given choices, 0.25 is closest to this value.

Choice A is incorrect; this is the probability of selecting at random a registered voter from the Midwest who is 18 to 24 years old. Choice C is incorrect; this is the probability of selecting at random a registered voter from the Midwest who is 18 to 44 years old. Choice D is incorrect and may be the result of errors made when choosing the correct proportion or in calculating the probability.

QUESTION 10

Choice A is correct. According to the graph, the animal with the longest gestation period (60 days) has a life expectancy of 3 years.

Choices B, C, and D are incorrect. All the animals that have a life expectancy of 4, 8, or 10 years have a gestation period that is shorter than 60 days, which is the longest gestation period.

QUESTION 11

Choice A is correct. The ratio of life expectancy to gestation period for the animal represented by point A is approximately $\frac{7 \text{ years}}{23 \text{ days}}$, or about 0.3 years/day, which is greater than the ratio for the animals represented by the other labeled points (the ratios for points B, C, and D, in units of years of life expectancy per day of gestation, are approximately $\frac{8}{44}$, $\frac{8}{51}$, and $\frac{10}{51}$ respectively, each of which is less than 0.2 years/day).

Choices B, C, and D are incorrect and may be the result of errors in calculating the ratio or in reading the graph.

QUESTION 12

Choice C is correct. All of the given choices are polynomials. If the graph of a polynomial function f in the xy-plane has an x-intercept at b, then $(x - b)$ must be a factor of $f(x)$. Since −3, −1, and 1 are each x-intercepts of the graph of f, it follows that $(x + 3)$, $(x + 1)$, and $(x - 1)$ must each be a factor of $f(x)$. Of the given equations, only the equation in choice C has these 3 factors. Therefore, only the equation in choice C could define the function f.

Choices A, B, and D are incorrect because these equations do not contain all three factors necessary in order for the graph of the polynomial function f to have x-intercepts at –3, –1, and 1.

QUESTION 13

Choice C is correct. The mosquito population starts at 100 in week 0 and then is multiplied by a factor of 10 every 5 weeks. Thus, if $P(t)$ is the mosquito population after t weeks, then based on the table, $P(t) = 100\,(10)^{\frac{t}{5}}$, which indicates an exponential growth relationship.

Choice A is incorrect. Increasing linearly means that the estimated population grows by the same amount every 5 weeks. According to the table, from week 0 to week 5, the estimated population grows by 900 mosquitoes, and from week 5 to week 10, it grows by 9,900 mosquitoes. Therefore, the estimated population is not increasing linearly. Choices B and C are incorrect because according to the table, the estimated population is increasing, not decreasing.

QUESTION 14

Choice D is correct. According to the given formula, the amount of money generated for a year at 5% interest, compounded monthly, is $1{,}000\left(1 + \dfrac{5}{1{,}200}\right)^{12}$, whereas the amount of money generated at 3% interest, compounded monthly, is $1{,}000\left(1 + \dfrac{3}{1{,}200}\right)^{12}$. Therefore, the difference between these two amounts, $1{,}000\left(1 + \dfrac{5}{1{,}200}\right)^{12} - 1{,}000\left(1 + \dfrac{3}{1{,}200}\right)^{12}$, shows how much additional money is generated at an interest rate of 5% than at an interest rate of 3%.

Choices A, B, and C are incorrect and may be the result of misinterpreting the given formula. For example, the expression in choice C gives how many times as much money, not how much additional money, is generated at an interest rate of 5% than at an interest rate of 3%.

QUESTION 15

Choice B is correct. The graph of $y = ax^b$, where a is positive and b is negative, would show a trend that is decreasing, but with a rate of decrease that slows as x increases. Of the scatterplots shown, only the one in choice B would be appropriately modeled by such a function.

Choice A is incorrect, as this scatterplot is appropriately modeled by a linear function. Choice C is incorrect, as this scatterplot is appropriately modeled by an increasing function. Choice D is incorrect, as this scatterplot shows no clear relationship between x and y.

QUESTION 16

Choice A is correct. The total cost y, in dollars, of buying the materials and renting the tools for x days from Store A and Store B is found by substituting the respective values for these stores from the table into the given equation, $y \quad M + (W + K)x$, as shown below.

Store A: $y = 750 + (15 + 65)x = 750 + 80x$

Store B: $y = 600 + (25 + 80)x = 600 + 105x$

Thus, the number of days, x, for which the total cost of buying the materials and renting the tools from Store B is less than or equal to the total cost of buying the materials and renting the tools from Store A can be found by solving the inequality $600 + 105x \le 750 + 80x$. Subtracting $80x$ and 600 from each side of $600 + 105x \le 750 + 80x$ and combining like terms yields $25x \le 150$. Dividing each side of $25x \le 150$ by 25 yields $x \le 6$.

Choice B is incorrect. The inequality $x \ge 6$ is the number of days for which the total cost of buying the materials and renting the tools from Store B is <u>greater than</u> or equal to the total cost of buying the materials and renting the tools from Store A. Choices C and D are incorrect and may be the result of an error in setting up or simplifying the inequality.

QUESTION 17

Choice D is correct. The total cost, y, of buying the materials and renting the tools in terms of the number of days, x, is given as $y = M + (W + K)x$. If this relationship is graphed in the xy-plane, the slope of the graph is equal to $W + K$, which is the daily rental cost of the wheelbarrow plus the daily rental cost of the concrete mixer, that is, the total daily rental costs of the tools.

Choice A is incorrect because the total cost of the project is y. Choice B is incorrect because the total cost of the materials is M, which is the y-intercept of the graph of $y = M + (W + K)x$. Choice C is incorrect because the total daily cost of the project is the total cost of the project divided by the total number of days the project took and, since materials cost more than 0 dollars, this is not the same as the total daily rental costs.

QUESTION 18

Choice C is correct. The volume V of a right circular cylinder is given by the formula $V = \pi r^2 h$, where r is the base radius of the cylinder and h is the height of the cylinder. Since each glass has an internal diameter of 3 inches, each glass has a base radius of $\frac{3}{2}$ inches. Since the height of the milk in each glass is 6 inches, the volume of milk in each glass is $V = \pi \left(\frac{3}{2}\right)^2 6) \approx 42.41$ cubic inches. The total number of glasses Jim can pour from 1 gallon is equal to $\frac{\text{number of cubic inches in 1 gallon}}{\text{number of cubic inches in 1 glass}} = \frac{231}{42.41}$, which is approximately 5.45 glasses. Since the question asks for the largest number of <u>full</u> glasses Jim can pour, the number of glasses needs to be rounded down to 5.

Choices A, B, and D are incorrect and may be the result of conceptual errors or calculation errors. For example, choice D is incorrect because even though Jim can pour more than 5 full glasses, he will not have enough milk to pour a full 6th glass.

QUESTION 19

Choice A is correct. Adding 4 to each side of the inequality $3p - 2 \geq 1$ yields the inequality $3p + 2 \geq 5$. Therefore, the least possible value of $3p + 2$ is 5.

Choice B is incorrect because it gives the least possible value of $3p$, not of $3p + 2$. Choice C is incorrect. If the least possible value of $3p + 2$ were 2, then it would follow that $3p + 2 \geq 2$. Subtracting 4 from each side of this inequality would yield $3p - 2 \geq -2$. This contradicts the given inequality, $3p - 2 \geq 1$. Therefore, the least possible value of $3p + 2$ cannot be 2. Choice D is incorrect because it gives the least possible value of p, not of $3p + 2$.

QUESTION 20

Choice C is correct. Since the biomass of the lake doubles each year, the biomass starts at a positive value and then increases exponentially over time. Of the graphs shown, only the graph in choice C is of an increasing exponential function.

Choice A is incorrect because the biomass of the lake must start at a positive value, not zero. Furthermore, this graph shows linear growth, not exponential growth. Choice B is incorrect because the biomass of the lake must start at a positive value, not zero. Furthermore, this graph has vertical segments and is not a function. Choice D is incorrect because the biomass of the lake does not remain the same over time.

QUESTION 21

Choice C is correct. For a data point to be above the line $y = x$, the value of y must be greater than the value of x. That is, the consumption in 2010 must be greater than the consumption in 2000. This occurs for 3 types of energy sources shown in the bar graph: biofuels, geothermal, and wind.

Choices A, B, and D are incorrect and may be the result of a conceptual error in presenting the data shown in a scatterplot. For example, choice B is incorrect because there are 2 data points in the scatterplot that lie <u>below</u> the line $y = x$.

QUESTION 22

Choice B is correct. Reading the graph, the amount of wood power used in 2000 was 2.25 quadrillion BTUs and the amount used in 2010 was 2.00 quadrillion BTUs. To find the percent decrease, find the positive difference between the two amounts, divide by the earlier amount (from 2000), and then multiply by 100: $\frac{2.25 - 2.00}{2.25} \times 100 = \frac{0.25}{2.25} \times 100 \approx 11.1$ percent. Of the choices given, 11% is closest to the percent decrease in the consumption of wood power from 2000 to 2010.

Choices A, C, and D are incorrect and may be the result of errors in reading the bar graph or in calculating the percent decrease.

QUESTION 23

Choice B is correct. The standard deviation is a measure of how far the data set values are from the mean. In the data set for City A, the large majority of the data are in three of the five possible values, which are the three values closest to the mean. In the data set for City B, the data are more spread out, with many values at the minimum and maximum values. Therefore, by observation, the data for City B have a larger standard deviation.

Alternatively, one can calculate the mean and visually inspect the difference between the data values and the mean. For City A the mean is $\frac{1,655}{21} \approx 78.8$, and for City B the mean is $\frac{1,637}{21} \approx 78.0$. The data for City A are closely clustered near 79, which indicates a small standard deviation. The data for City B are spread out away from 78, which indicates a larger standard deviation.

Choices A, C, and D are incorrect and may be the result of misconceptions about the standard deviation.

QUESTION 24

Choice C is correct. Since segment AB is a diameter of the circle, it follows that arc ADB is a semicircle. Thus, the circumference of the circle is twice the length of arc ADB which is $2(8\pi = 16\pi$. Since the circumference of a circle is 2π times the radius of the circle, the radius of this circle is 16π divided by 2π, which is equal to 8.

Choice A is incorrect. If the radius of the circle is 2, the circumference of the circle would be $2(2\pi)$ and the length of arc ADB would be 2π, not 8π. Choice B is incorrect. If the radius of the circle is 4, the circumference of the circle would be $2(4\pi)$ and the length of arc ADB would be 4π, not 8π. Choice D is incorrect; 16 is the length of the diameter of the circle, not of the radius.

QUESTION 25

Choice B is correct. In $f(x)$, factoring out the greatest common factor, $2x$, yields $f(x) = 2x(x^2 + 3x + 2)$. It is given that $g(x = x^2 + 3x + 2$, so using substitution, $f(x)$ can be rewritten as $f(x) = 2x \cdot g(x)$. In the equation $p(x = f(x) + 3g(x)$, substituting $2x \cdot g(x)$ for $f(x)$ yields $p(x) = 2x \cdot g(x) + 3 \cdot g(x)$. In $p(x)$, factoring out the greatest common factor, $g(x)$, yields $p(x = g(x))(2x + 3)$. Because $2x + 3$ is a factor of $p(x)$, it follows that $p(x)$ is divisible by $2x + 3$.

Choices A, C, and D are incorrect because $2x + 3$ is not a factor of the polynomials $h(x)$, $r(x)$, or $s(x)$. Using the substitution $f(x = 2x \cdot g(x)$, and factoring further, $h(x)$, $r(x)$, and $s(x)$ can be rewritten as follows:

$$h(x = (x + 1)(x + 2)(2x + 1)$$

$$r(x = (x + 1)(x + 2)(4x + 3)$$

$$s(x = 2(x + 1)(x + 2)(3x + 1)$$

Because $2x + 3$ is not a factor of $h(x)$, $r(x)$, or $s(x)$, it follows that $h(x)$, $r(x)$, and $s(x)$ are each not divisible by $2x + 3$.

QUESTION 26

Choice C is correct. If $-y < x < y$, the value of x is either 0 or between $-y$ and 0 or between 0 and y, so statement I, $|x| < y$ is true. It is possible that the value of x is greater than zero, but x could be negative. For example, a counterexample to statement II, $x > 0$, is $x = -2$ and $y = 3$, yielding $-3 < -2 < 3$, so the given condition is satisfied. Statement III must be true since $-y < x < y$ implies that $-y < y$, so y must be greater than 0. Therefore, statements I and III are the only statements that must be true.

Choices A, B, and D are incorrect because each of these choices either omits a statement that must be true or includes a statement that could be false.

QUESTION 27

Choice D is correct. To interpret what the number 61 in the equation of the line of best fit represents, one must first understand what the data in the scatterplot represent. Each of the points in the scatterplot represents a large US city, graphed according to its population density (along the horizontal axis) and its relative housing cost (along the vertical axis). The line of best fit for this data represents the expected relative housing cost for a certain population density, based on the data points in the graph. Thus, one might say, on average, a city of population density x is expected to have a relative housing cost of y%, where $y = 0.0125x + 61$. The number 61 in the equation represents the y-intercept of the line of best fit, in that when the population density, x, is 0, there is an expected relative housing cost of 61%. This might not have meaning within the context of the problem, in that when the population density is 0, the population is 0, so there probably wouldn't be any housing costs. However, it could be interpreted that for cities with low population densities, housing costs were likely around or above 61% (since below 61% would be for cities with negative population densities, which is impossible).

Choice A is incorrect because it interprets the values of the vertical axis as dollars and not percentages. Choice B is incorrect because the lowest housing cost is about 61% of the national average, not 61% of the highest housing cost. Choice C is incorrect because one cannot absolutely assert that no city with a low population density had housing costs below 61% of the national average, as the model shows that it is unlikely, but not impossible.

QUESTION 28

Choice D is correct. The minimum value of a quadratic function appears as a constant in the vertex form of its equation, which can be found from the standard form by completing the square. Rewriting $f(x = (x + 6)(x - 4)$ in standard form gives $f(x = x^2 + 2x - 24$. Since the coefficient of the linear term is 2, the equation for $f(x)$ can be rewritten in terms of $(x + 1)^2$ as follows:

$$f(x = x^2 + 2x - 24 = (x^2 + 2x + 1) - 1 - 24 = (x + 1)^2 - 25$$

The vertex form $f(x = (x + 1)^2 - 25$ shows that the minimum value of f is -25 (and occurs at $x = -1$).

Alternatively, since $f -6) = f(4) = 0$, by symmetry the vertex must have an x-coordinate at the midpoint between -6 and 4, which is -1. Since $f(-1) = (5)(-5) = -25$, the vertex must be at $(-1, -25)$. Finally since the coefficient of x^2 is 1, the vertex form must be $f(x = (x + 1)^2 - 25$.

Choices A and C are incorrect because they are not equivalent to the given equation for f. Choice B is incorrect because the minimum value of f, which is -25, does not appear as a constant or a coefficient.

QUESTION 29

Choice B is correct. Since the average of 2 numbers is the sum of the 2 numbers divided by 2, the equations $x = \frac{m + 9}{2}$, $y = \frac{2m + 15}{2}$ and $z = \frac{3m + 18}{2}$ are true. The average of x, y, and z is given by $\frac{x + y + z}{3}$. Because x, y, and z are defined in terms of m, the expressions in terms of m can be substituted for each variable to give $\frac{\frac{m + 9}{2} + \frac{2m + 15}{2} + \frac{3m + 18}{2}}{3}$. This fraction can be simplified to $\frac{6m + 42}{6}$, or $m + 7$.

Choices A, C, and D are incorrect and may be the result of conceptual errors or calculation errors. For example, choice D is the sum of x, y, and z, not the average.

QUESTION 30

Choice D is correct. The equation $f(x = k$ gives the solutions to the system of equations $y = f(x) = x^3 - x^2 - x - \frac{11}{4}$ and $y = k$. A real solution of a system of two equations corresponds to a point of intersection of the graphs of the two equations in the xy-plane. The graph of $y = k$ is a horizontal line that contains the point $(0, k)$. Thus, the line with equation $y = -3$ is a horizontal line that intersects the graph of the cubic equation three times, and it follows that the equation $f(x = x^3 - x^2 - x - \frac{11}{4} = -3$ has three real solutions.

Choices A, B, and C are incorrect because the graphs of $y = 2$, $y = 0$, and $y = -2$ are horizontal lines that do not intersect the graph of the cubic equation three times.

QUESTION 31

The correct answer is 1160. The pool contains 600 gallons of water before the hose is turned on, and water flows from the hose into the pool at a rate of 8 gallons per minute. Thus, the number of gallons of water in the pool m minutes after the hose is turned on is given by the expression $600 + 8m$. Therefore, after 70 minutes, there will be $600 + 8(70) = 1160$ gallons of water in the pool.

QUESTION 32

The correct answer is $\frac{1}{2}$ or .5. The equation that models the normal systolic blood pressure P, in millimeters of mercury, for a male x years old, $P = \frac{x + 220}{2}$, can be rewritten as $P = \frac{1}{2}x + 110$. For each increase of 1 year in age, the value of x increases by 1; hence, P becomes $\frac{1}{2}(x + 1) + 110 = \left(\frac{1}{2}x + 110\right) + \frac{1}{2}$. That is, P increases by $\frac{1}{2}$ millimeter of mercury. Either the fraction 1/2 or its decimal equivalent, .5, may be gridded as the correct answer.

QUESTION 33

The correct answer is 4.55. Since there are 16 Roman digits in a Roman pes, 75 digits is equal to $\frac{75}{16}$ pes. Since 1 pes is equal to 11.65 inches, $\frac{75}{16}$ pes is equal to $\frac{75}{16}(11.65)$ inches. Since 12 inches is equal to 1 foot, $\frac{75}{16}(11.65)$ inches is equal to $\frac{75}{16}(11.65)\left(\frac{1}{12}\right) = 4.55078125$ feet. Therefore, 75 digits is equal to $\frac{75}{16}(11.65)\left(\frac{1}{12}\right) = 4.55078125$ feet. Rounded to the nearest hundredth of a foot, 75 Roman digits is equal to 4.55 feet.

QUESTION 34

The correct answer is 150. In the study, 240 male and 160 plus another 100 female bats have been tagged, so that 500 bats have been tagged altogether. If x more male bats must be tagged for $\frac{3}{5}$ of the total number of bats to be male, the proportion $\frac{\text{male bats}}{\text{total bats}} = \frac{240 + x}{500 + x} = \frac{3}{5}$ must be true. Multiplying each side of $\frac{240 + x}{500 + x} = \frac{3}{5}$ by $5(500 + x)$ gives $5(240 + x = 3(500 + x$, which simplifies to $1200 + 5x = 1500 + 3x$. Subtracting 1200 from both sides and subtracting $3x$ from both sides yields $2x = 300$, and dividing both sides by 2 gives $x = 150$. Therefore, 150 more male bats must be tagged; this will bring the total to 390 male bats out of 650 bats, which is equal to $\frac{3}{5}$.

QUESTION 35

The correct answer is 2.25 or $\frac{9}{4}$. Let q_s be the dynamic pressure of the slower fluid moving with velocity v_s, and let q_f be the dynamic pressure of the faster fluid moving with velocity v_f. Then $v_f = 1.5v_s$.

Given the equation $q = \frac{1}{2}nv^2$, substituting the dynamic pressure and velocity of the faster fluid gives $q_f = \frac{1}{2}nv_f^2$. Since $v_f = 1.5v_s$, the expression $1.5v_s$ can be substituted for v_f in this equation, giving $q_t = \frac{1}{2}n(1.5v_s)^2$. This can be rewritten as $q_f = (2.25)\frac{1}{2}nv_s^2 = (2.25)q_s$.

Therefore, the ratio of the dynamic pressure of the faster fluid is $\frac{q_f}{q_s} = \frac{2.25q_s}{q_s} = 2.25$. Either 2.25 or the equivalent improper fraction 9/4 may be gridded as the correct answer.

Alternatively, since q is directly proportional to the square of v, scaling v by 1.5 should scale q by $(1.5)^2 = 2.25$.

QUESTION 36

The correct answer is 29, 30, 31, 32, 33, or 34. Since the radius of the circle is 10, its circumference is 20π. The full circumference of a circle is $360°$. Thus, an arc of length s on the circle corresponds to a central angle of $x°$, where $\frac{x}{360} = \frac{s}{20\pi}$, or $x = \frac{360}{20\pi}(s)$. Since $5 < s < 6$, it follows that $\frac{360}{20\pi}(5) < x < \frac{360}{20\pi}(6)$, which becomes, to the nearest tenth, $28.6 < x < 34.4$. Therefore, the possible integer values of x are 29, 30, 31, 32, 33, and 34. Any one of these numbers may be gridded as the correct answer.

QUESTION 37

The correct answer is .72. According to the analyst's estimate, the value V, in dollars, of the stock will decrease by 28% each week for t weeks, where $t = 1, 2,$ or 3, with its value being given by the formula $V = 360(r)^t$. This equation is an example of exponential decay. A stock losing 28% of its value each week is the same as the stock's value decreasing to 72% of its value from the previous week, since $V - (.28)V = (.72)V$. Using this information, after 1 week the value, in dollars, of the stock will be V $360(.72)$; aft er 2 weeks the value of the stock will be $V = 360(.72)(.72) = 360(.72)^2$; and after 3 weeks the value of the stock will be $V = 360(.72)(.72)(.72) = 360(.72)^3$. For all of the values of t in question, namely $t = 1, 2,$ and 3, the equation $V = 360(.72)^t$ is true. Therefore, the analyst should use .72 as the value of r.

QUESTION 38

The correct answer is 134. The analyst's prediction is that the stock will lose 28 percent of its value for each of the next three weeks. Thus, the predicted value of the stock after 1 week is $360 − (.28)$360 = $259.20; after 2 weeks, $259.20 − (.28)$259.20 ≈ $186.62; and after 3 weeks, $186.62 − (.28)$186.62 ≈ $134.37. Therefore, to the nearest dollar, the stock analyst believes the stock will be worth 134 dollars after three weeks.

Answer Explanations
SAT® Practice Test #5

K-5MSA04

Answer Explanations

SAT Practice Test #5

Section 1: Reading Test

QUESTION 1

Choice D is the best answer. The passage begins with the main character, Lymie, sitting in a restaurant and reading a history book. The first paragraph describes the book in front of him ("Blank pages front and back were filled in with maps, drawings, dates, comic cartoons, and organs of the body," lines 11-13). The second paragraph reveals what Lymie is reading about (the Peace of Paris and the Congress of Vienna) and suggests his intense concentration on the book ("sometimes he swallowed whole the food that he had no idea he was eating," lines 23-24). In the third paragraph, the focus of the passage shifts to a description and discussion of others in the restaurant, namely "A party of four, two men and two women . . . " (lines 42-43).

Choice A is incorrect because the passage does not provide observations made by other characters, only offering Lymie's and the narrator's observations. Choice B is incorrect because the beginning of the passage focuses on Lymie as he reads by himself and the end of the passage focuses on the arrival of Lymie's father, with whom Lymie's relationship seems somewhat strained. Choice C is incorrect because the setting is described in the beginning of the first paragraph but is never the main focus of the passage.

QUESTION 2

Choice C is the best answer. The main purpose of the first paragraph is to establish the passage's setting by describing a place and an object. The place is the Alcazar Restaurant, which is described as being "long and narrow" and decorated with "*art moderne*," murals, and plants (lines 2-6), and the object is the history book Lymie is reading.

Choice A is incorrect because rather than establishing what Lymie does every night, the first paragraph describes what Lymie is doing on *one* night. Choice B is incorrect because nothing in the first paragraph indicates when the passage takes place, as the details provided (such as the restaurant and the book) are not specific to one era. Choice D is incorrect because nothing in the first paragraph clearly foreshadows a later event.

QUESTION 3

Choice C is the best answer. The passage states that "when Lymie put down his fork and began to count . . . the waitress, whose name was Irma, thought he was through eating and tried to take his plate away" (lines 34-38). It is reasonable to assume that Irma thinks Lymie is finished eating because he is no longer holding his fork.

Choice A is incorrect because Lymie has already been reading his book while eating for some time before Irma thinks he is finished eating. Choice B is incorrect because the passage doesn't state that Lymie's plate is empty, and the fact that Lymie stops Irma from taking his plate suggests that it is not empty. Choice D is incorrect because the passage gives no indication that Lymie asks Irma to clear the table.

QUESTION 4

Choice A is the best answer. The passage makes it clear that Lymie finds the party of four who enter the restaurant to be loud and bothersome, as their entrance means he is no longer able to concentrate on his book: "They laughed more than there seemed any occasion for . . . and their laughter was too loud. But it was the women's voices . . . which caused Lymie to skim over two whole pages without knowing what was on them" (lines 52-59).

Choices B, C, and D are incorrect because lines 55-59 make clear that Lymie is annoyed by the party of four, not that he finds their presence refreshing (choice B), thinks they resemble the people he is reading about (choice C), or thinks they represent glamour and youth (choice D).

QUESTION 5

Choice C is the best answer. The previous question asks about Lymie's impression of the party of four who enter the restaurant, with the correct answer being that he finds them noisy and distracting. This is supported in lines 55-59: "But it was the women's voices, the terrible not quite sober pitch of the women's voices, which caused Lymie to skim over two whole pages without knowing what was on them."

Choices A, B, and D are incorrect because the lines cited do not support the answer to the previous question about Lymie's impression of the party of four who enter the restaurant. Rather than showing that Lymie finds the group of strangers noisy and distracting, the lines simply describe how two of the four people look (choices A and B) and indicate what Lymie does when his father joins him in the restaurant (choice D).

QUESTION 6

Choice A is the best answer. In the passage, Lymie closes his book only after "a coat that he recognized as his father's was hung on the hook next to his chair" (lines 67-68). It is Lymie's father's arrival that causes him to close the book.

Choices B, C, and D are incorrect because lines 67-70 of the passage clearly establish that Lymie closes his book because his father has arrived, not that he does so because the party of four is too loud (choice B), because he has finished reading a section of the book (choice C), or because he is getting ready to leave (choice D).

QUESTION 7

Choice D is the best answer. In lines 74-79, the narrator describes Mr. Peters as "gray" and balding, noting that he has "lost weight" and his color is "poor." This description suggests Mr. Peters is aging and losing strength and vigor.

Choices A, B, and C are incorrect because the description of Mr. Peters in lines 74-79 suggests he is a person who is wan and losing vitality, not someone who is healthy and in good shape (choice A), angry and intimidating (choice B), or emotionally anxious (choice C).

QUESTION 8

Choice B is the best answer. In the last paragraph of the passage, Mr. Peters is described as being unaware "that there had been any change" in his appearance since he was younger (lines 80-81). Later in the paragraph, the passage states that "the young man" Mr. Peters once was "had never for one second deserted" him (lines 90-91). The main idea of the last paragraph is that Mr. Peters still thinks of himself as young, or at least acts as if he is a younger version of himself.

Choice A is incorrect because Mr. Peters is spending time with Lymie, his son, and there is no indication that he generally does not spend time with his family. Choice C is incorrect because although there are brief mentions of a diamond ring and manicured fingers, the paragraph focuses on Mr. Peters's overall appearance, not on his awareness of status symbols. Choice D is incorrect because the last paragraph clearly states that Mr. Peters is "not aware that there had been any change" and thinks of himself as young.

QUESTION 9

Choice B is the best answer. In lines 81-85, Mr. Peters is described as having "straightened his tie self-consciously" and gestured with a menu "so that the two women at the next table would notice the diamond ring on the fourth finger of his right hand." Mr. Peters's actions are those of someone who wants to attract attention and be noticed.

Choices A, C, and D are incorrect because the lines cited do not support the idea Mr. Peters wants to attract attention to himself. Choices A and C address Mr. Peters's view of himself. Choice D indicates that Mr. Peters's view of himself affects his behavior but does not reveal that he acts in a way meant to draw attention.

QUESTION 10

Choice B is the best answer. The last sentence of the passage states that Mr. Peters's mischaracterization of himself makes him act in ways that are not "becoming" for a man of his age. In this context, "becoming" suggests behavior that is appropriate or fitting.

Choices A, C, and D are incorrect because in the context of describing one's behavior, "becoming" means appropriate or fitting, not becoming known (choice A), becoming more advanced (choice C), or simply occurring (choice D).

QUESTION 11

Choice B is the best answer. In Passage 1, Beecher makes the point that even if women in her society are perceived as being inferior to men, they are still able to effect considerable influence on that society: "But while woman holds a subordinate relation in society to the other sex, it is not because it was designed that her duties or her influence should be any the less important, or all-pervading" (lines 6-10).

Choice A is incorrect because Beecher describes the dynamic between men and women in terms of the way they can change society, not in terms of security and physical safety. Choice C is incorrect because even though Beecher implies that women have fewer rights in society than men do, she doesn't say that women have fewer responsibilities. Choice D is incorrect because Beecher does not assert that women are superior to men.

QUESTION 12

Choice A is the best answer. The previous question asks what point Beecher makes regarding the relationship between men and women in her society, with the answer being that women are considered inferior but can still have influence. This is supported in lines 6-10: "But while woman holds a subordinate relation in society to the other sex, it is not because it was designed that her duties or her influence should be any the less important, or all-pervading."

Choices B, C, and D are incorrect because the lines cited do not support the answer to the previous question about the point Beecher makes regarding the relationship between men and women in her society. Instead, they describe ways men can affect society (choices B and C) and explain how certain actions undertaken by a woman can be viewed negatively (choice D).

QUESTION 13

Choice B is the best answer. In the third paragraph (lines 22-37), Beecher suggests that women can be "so much respected, esteemed and loved" by those around them that men will accede to their wishes: "then, the fathers, the husbands, and the sons, will find an influence thrown around them, to which they will yield not only willingly but proudly . . . ." These lines show that Beecher believes women can influence society by influencing the men around them; in other words, women have an indirect influence on public life.

Choices A, C, and D are incorrect because lines 34-37 make it clear that Beecher believes women do have an effect on society, even if it is an indirect effect. Beecher does not indicate that women's effect on public life is ignored because most men are not interested (choice A), unnecessary because men do not need help governing society (choice C), or merely symbolic because women tend to be idealistic (choice D).

QUESTION 14

Choice D is the best answer. Regarding the dynamic of men and women in society, Beecher says that one sex is given "the subordinate station" while the other is given the "superior" station (lines 1-2). In the context of how one gender exists in comparison to the other, the word "station" suggests a standing or rank.

Choices A, B, and C are incorrect because in the context of the relative standing of men and women in Beecher's society, the word "station" suggests a standing or rank, not a physical location or area (choices A, B, and C).

QUESTION 15

Choice C is the best answer. When describing how men and women can influence society, Beecher says the ways they can do so "should be altogether different and peculiar" (lines 11-12). In the context of the "altogether different" ways men and women can influence society, the word "peculiar" implies being unique or distinctive.

Choices A, B, and D are incorrect because in the context of the "altogether different" ways men and women can influence society, the word "peculiar" suggests something unique or distinctive, not something unusual and odd (choice A), unexpected (choice B), or rare (choice D).

QUESTION 16

Choice A is the best answer. In Passage 2, Grimké makes the main point that people have rights because they are human, not because of their gender or race. This is clear in lines 58-60, when Grimké states that "human beings have *rights*, because they are *moral* beings: the rights of *all* men grow out of their moral nature" and lines 65-68, when Grimké writes, "Now if rights are founded in the nature of our moral being, then the *mere circumstance of sex* does not give to man higher rights and responsibilities, than to woman."

Choices B, C, and D are incorrect because Grimké primarily emphasizes that all men and women inherently have the same rights ("rights are founded in the nature of our moral being," lines 65-66). Her central claim is not that men and women need to work together to change society (choice B), that moral rights are the distinguishing characteristic separating humans from animals (choice C), or that there should be equal opportunities for men and women to advance and succeed.

QUESTION 17

Choice B is the best answer. In Passage 2, Grimké makes the point that human rights are not fleeting or changeable but things that remain, regardless of the circumstances, because they are tied to humans' moral nature. She emphasizes that human rights exist even if societal laws attempt to contradict or override them, citing slavery as an example: "These rights may be wrested from the slave, but they cannot be alienated: his title to himself is as perfect now, as is that of Lyman Beecher: it is stamped on his moral being, and is, like it, imperishable" (lines 61-65).

Choices A and D are incorrect because in Passage 2, Grimké makes the point that human rights are inherent and unchanging, not that they are viewed differently in different societies (choice A) or that they have changed and developed over time (choice D). Choice C is incorrect because Grimké doesn't describe a clash between human rights and moral responsibilities; instead, she says that humans have rights "because they are *moral* beings" (lines 58-59).

QUESTION 18

Choice B is the best answer. The previous question asks what point Grimké makes about human rights in Passage 2, with the answer being that they exist and have moral authority whether or not they are established by societal law. This is supported in lines 61-65: "These rights may be wrested from the slave, but they cannot be alienated: his title to himself is as perfect now, as is that of Lyman Beecher: it is stamped on his moral being, and is, like it, imperishable."

Choices A, C, and D are incorrect because the lines cited do not support the answer to the previous question about the point Grimké makes about human rights in Passage 2. Instead, they explain the source of all people's human rights (choice A), indicate what would happen if rights were determined by gender (choice C), and discuss why gender is irrelevant to rights (choice D).

QUESTION 19

Choice B is the best answer. In Passage 1, Beecher asserts that men and women naturally have different positions in society: "Heaven has appointed to one sex the superior, and to the other the subordinate station" (lines 1-2). She goes on to argue that a woman should act within her subordinate role to influence men but should not "exert coercive influences" that would put her "out of her appropriate sphere" (lines 44-46). In Passage 2, Grimké takes issue with the idea that men and women have different rights and roles. She asserts that as moral beings all people have the same inherent rights and states that "the *mere circumstance of sex* does not give to man higher rights and responsibilities, than to woman" (lines 66-68).

Choice A is incorrect because Passage 2 does not discuss the practical difficulties of something that is proposed in Passage 1 but rather argues against the main point of Passage 1. Choice C is incorrect because Passage 2 does not provide historical context for the view expressed in Passage 1; the passages were published at around the same time and both discuss contemporary society. Choice D is incorrect because Passage 2 does not elaborate on implications found in Passage 1 as much as it disputes the ideas explicitly expressed in Passage 1.

QUESTION 20

Choice A is the best answer. While Beecher and Grimké clearly disagree regarding a woman's role in society, the passages suggest that both authors share the belief that women do have moral duties and responsibilities in society. In Passage 1, Beecher writes that "while woman holds a subordinate relation in society to the other sex, it is not because it was designed that her duties or her influence should be any the less important, or all-pervading" (lines 6-10). She suggests that women do have an obligation to use their influence to bring about beneficial changes in society. In Passage 2, Grimké asserts that all people "are *moral* beings" (lines 58-59) and that both men and women have "rights and responsibilities" (line 68). She concludes that "whatever it is morally right for man to do, it is morally right for woman to do" (lines 81-83).

Choice B is incorrect because neither author suggests that when men work to bring about political changes, they often do so out of consideration for others rather than considerations for themselves. Choice C is incorrect because neither passage discusses the value given to women's ethical obligations, although both authors suggest that women do have ethical and moral obligations. Choice D is incorrect because in Passage 1 Beecher argues that women should avoid direct political activism, cautioning against actions that would put them outside their "appropriate sphere" (line 46).

QUESTION 21

Choice D is the best answer. In lines 65-68 of Passage 2, Grimké writes, "Now if rights are founded in the nature of our moral being, then the *mere circumstance of sex* does not give to man higher rights and responsibilities, than to woman." In other words, gender does not make men's rights and duties superior to women's. Beecher, on the other hand, begins Passage 1 by stating that "heaven has appointed to one sex the superior, and to the other the subordinate station," suggesting that men and women have fundamentally different natures. Therefore, Beecher most likely would have disagreed with Grimké's assertion.

Choices A and B are incorrect because Beecher fundamentally disagrees with Grimké regarding the basic nature and societal roles of men and women, making it very unlikely that she would have viewed Grimké's statement in lines 65-68 with either sympathy or agreement. Choice C is incorrect because Beecher wouldn't necessarily have been dismayed by Grimké's belief as much as she would have simply disagreed with it, and she does not indicate that the role of women in society is more difficult to play than is that of men.

QUESTION 22

Choice A is the best answer. In line 14, the passage states that industrial agriculture has become "incredibly efficient on a simple land to food basis." In this context, "simple" suggests something basic or straightforward.

Choices B, C, and D are incorrect because in the context of a land to food dynamic, the word "simple" suggests something basic or straightforward, not something humble (choice B), something without any decoration or ornamentation (choice C), or something that requires little effort (choice D).

QUESTION 23

Choice B is the best answer. The passage clearly states that conventional agriculture is very efficient, especially when compared to organic farming: "organic farming yields 25% fewer crops on average than conventional agriculture" (lines 40-42) and in a study "organic farming delivered a lower yield for every crop type" (lines 51-52). It can therefore be understood from the passage that conventional agriculture does a good job maximizing the output of the land that is farmed.

Choice A is incorrect because the passage states how efficient conventional agriculture is in regard to the amount of food it can produce but does not indicate that it produces a significantly wide variety of fruits and vegetables. Choice C is incorrect because even if the passage does say that each American farmer can produce crops to feed "over 155 people worldwide" (lines 16-17), it never claims that conventional agriculture can satisfactorily feed everyone in the world. Choice D is incorrect because the passage states that conventional agriculture uses a great deal of nitrogen, not that it changes the need for nitrogen in plant growth one way or the other.

QUESTION 24

Choice A is the best answer. The passage makes it clear that "most environmentalists" (line 27) believe conventional agriculture produces food that is not as healthy as food produced through organic farming and that it is more harmful to the environment than organic farming is: many environmentalists "have embraced organic food as better for the planet—and healthier and tastier, too—than the stuff produced by agricultural corporations" (lines 28-31).

Choices B, C, and D are incorrect because they are not supported by the passage. The passage never states that many environmentalists believe that conventional farming reduces the need to convert wilderness to farmland (choice B), is in any way good for the environment (choice C), or protects wildlife habitats (choice D).

QUESTION 25

Choice B is the best answer. The previous question asks how environmentalists perceive conventional agriculture, with the answer being that they believe it produces a product that is less healthy and more environmentally destructive than that produced by organic farming. This is supported in lines 28-31: "They have embraced organic food as better for the planet—and healthier and tastier, too—than the stuff produced by agricultural corporations."

Choices A, C, and D are incorrect because the lines cited do not support the answer to the previous question about how environmentalists perceive the efforts of conventional agriculture. Although the lines in choice A do touch on environmentalists' views, they indicate only that most environmentalists don't view conventional agriculture's ability to "produce more food on less land" (line 25) as beneficial to the environment. Choice C is incorrect because these lines address environmentalists' view of the environmental effects of conventional and organic farming but not the taste or nutritional value of the food produced. Choice D is incorrect because these lines focus on a drawback to organic farming.

QUESTION 26

Choice C is the best answer. The passage makes it clear that while both conventional and organic farming need nitrogen for plant growth, conventional farming uses synthetic fertilizers and organic does not: "Conventional agriculture makes use of 171 million metric tons of synthetic fertilizer each year, and all that nitrogen enables much faster plant growth than the slower release of nitrogen from the compost or cover crops used in organic farming" (lines 61-65).

Choice A is incorrect because the passage does not state that conventional and organic farming are equally sustainable and does state that organic farming needs "more land" to produce "fewer crops" (lines 42-43) but does not indicate that it always requires dramatically more land. Choice B is incorrect because the passage does not state that organic farming uses artificial chemicals. Choice D is incorrect because the passage mentions nitrogen runoff only as a product of conventional farming, not organic farming, and does not indicate that only the nitrogen in conventional fertilizers is dangerous.

QUESTION 27

Choice D is the best answer. The previous question asks about the relationship between conventional agriculture and organic farming, with the answer being that unlike organic farms, conventional farms use synthetic fertilizers. This is supported in lines 61-65: "Conventional agriculture makes use of 171 million metric tons of synthetic fertilizer each year, and all that nitrogen enables much faster plant growth than the slower release of nitrogen from the compost or cover crops used in organic farming."

Choices A, B, and C are incorrect because the lines cited do not support the answer to the previous question about the relationship between conventional and organic farming, instead describing the efficiency only of conventional agriculture (choice A), discussing one perceived positive aspect of conventional agriculture (choice B), and highlighting a drawback of organic farming (choice C).

QUESTION 28

Choice B is the best answer. The passage states that the authors of the study comparing conventional and organic farming have come to the conclusion that an "ideal global agriculture system" would "borrow the best from both systems" (lines 80-82). The quote from Jonathan Foley in lines 84-97 indicates that this ideal system would take into consideration many different factors, including the nutrition and calories offered by specific types of foods as well as different geographic, economic, and social needs.

Choices A and D are incorrect because the passage makes it clear that the "ideal global agriculture system" would give consideration to multiple factors, not that it would focus mainly on productivity (choice A) or nutritional value (choice D). Choice C is incorrect because Foley states that the ideal system would take economics into consideration but does not indicate that farmers' economic interests would be weighed against consumers' needs.

QUESTION 29

Choice D is the best answer. The passage states that conventional agriculture can be superior to organic farming in terms of producing "sheer calories" (line 88). In this context, "sheer" most nearly means pure; the passage is referring to the pure number of calories delivered by foods.

Choices A, B, and C are incorrect because in the context of discussing the calories foods can provide, "sheer" suggests the pure number of calories. Also, it does not make sense to say that calories can be seen through (choice A), are somehow sudden or happen unexpectedly (choice B), or are at a very sharp angle (choice C).

QUESTION 30

Choice B is the best answer. Figure 1 shows that the organic yield as a percentage of conventional yield is similar for cereals and all crops, with both yielding roughly 75%.

Choice A is incorrect because figure 1 shows that the organic yield as a percentage of conventional yield is higher for fruits (just under 100%) than for vegetables (just under 70%). Choice C is incorrect because figure 1 shows there were only 28 observations for oilseed crops. Choice D is incorrect because figure 1 shows that the organic yield as a percentage of conventional yield is higher for oilseed crops (approximately 90%) than for vegetables (just under 70%).

QUESTION 31

Choice D is the best answer. Every organically grown species represented in figure 2 produces a smaller yield than do their conventional counterparts. All of the organically grown species are within a range of approximately 60–90% of the conventional yield.

Choice A is incorrect because figure 2 shows that soybeans have the highest yield (approximately 90%), not the lowest. Choice B is incorrect because figure 2 shows that organically grown barley and maize are produced at a lower yield than the conventionally grown species (just below 70% and just below 90%, respectively), not a comparable one. Choice C is incorrect because figure 2 shows that soybeans, not tomatoes, have the highest yield of the organically grown species.

QUESTION 32

Choice B is the best answer. The majority of the passage focuses on the experiment concerning "how much the crowd influences the individual, and whether it can be controlled from outside" (lines 42-44). After explaining the experiment and the results it produced, the passage moves on to consider questions raised by the results, such as whether the findings are site specific or "true in general" (lines

75-76), why different findings are observed, and whether companies can "boost their products by manipulating online ratings on a massive scale" (lines 85-86).

Choice A is incorrect because the passage does not conclude by explaining the practical ways the experiment's findings have been applied but rather by considering questions the findings raise. Choices C and D are incorrect because the passage does not indicate that there were any flaws in the experiment's findings and does not include statements from anyone who disputes the findings.

QUESTION 33

Choice C is the best answer. The author of the passage suggests that a group of people can be "wiser" and more effective than a single person at assessing a quantitative answer, or a measurement, versus producing a valid qualitative judgment, or a judgment of the quality of something. This is most clear in lines 11-14, which state that when guessing a bull's weight or how many gumballs are in a jar, "your guess is probably going to be far from the mark, whereas the average of many people's choices is remarkably close to the true number."

Choices A, B, and D are incorrect because lines 11-14 indicate that the author believes that crowds may be more effective than individuals when arriving at quantitative answers rather than qualitative results. Nothing in the passage suggests that the author believes that crowds are better at starting disagreements than studying an issue in depth (choice A), supporting ideas rather than challenging them (choice B), or ranking opinions rather than coming up with new ideas (choice D).

QUESTION 34

Choice B is the best answer. The previous question asks what the author of the passage suggests about the wisdom of crowds, with the answer being that crowds can be more effective at producing quantitative answers than qualitative results. This is supported in lines 11-14: when it comes to guessing a bull's weight or how many gumballs are in a jar, "your guess is probably going to be far from the mark, whereas the average of many people's choices is remarkably close to the true number."

Choices A, C, and D are incorrect because the lines cited do not support the answer to the previous question about the author's belief about when the wisdom of a crowd is effective. Instead, they simply state that crowds are sometimes wiser than individuals, without explaining when (choice A), put forth a theory held by someone other than the author (choice C), and explain how hypotheses about the wisdom of crowds could be tested (choice D).

QUESTION 35

Choice A is the best answer. In the passage, the author explains that those who are skeptical of the theory that "measuring the aggregate of people's opinions produces a stable, reliable value" (lines 18-20) believe that "people's opinions are easily swayed by those of others" (lines 20-21). This idea is best supported in lines 55-58, which describe a finding from a study of opinions in crowds: "Comments that received fake positive votes from the researchers were 32% more likely to receive more positive votes compared with a control, the team reports." In other words, people were more likely to give a positive vote when they thought other people had given positive votes.

Choices B, C, and D are incorrect because the lines cited do not provide support for the skeptics' idea that people's opinions are easily influenced by the thoughts of others. Instead, they cite findings concerning people giving ratings *different* from those already given (choices B and C) and share an observation that the degree to which others can be influenced depends in part on the context of the situation (choice D).

QUESTION 36

Choice B is the best answer. One question Watts asks in regard to the experiment is whether the results would hold true on a larger scale. The passage quotes him in lines 74-76: "'[But] one question is whether the positive [herding] bias is specific to this site' or true in general." Doing the experiment again but collecting ratings on multiple websites would address Watts's question, as it would show whether or not the same results occur on other sites.

Choices A, C, and D are incorrect. Providing fewer fake positive comments during the experiment (choice A), requiring users to be registered on the website (choice C), or telling users that their answers will be studied (choice D) are actions that likely would affect the results of the experiment involving users voting on comments about stories on one news website, but they would not address Watts's questions about whether the study would produce the same results on *other* websites or why different categories of news items had different effects on the news website.

QUESTION 37

Choice C is the best answer. In lines 85-86 the author asks, "Will companies be able to boost their products by manipulating online ratings on a massive scale?" In the context of selling products by manipulating user reviews, "boost" most nearly means promote.

Choices A, B, and D are incorrect because in the context of selling products by manipulating user reviews, the word "boost" refers to promoting the products, not making them larger or bigger (choice A), faster (choice B), or safe (choice D).

QUESTION 38

Choice A is the best answer. In lines 85-86 the author asks, "Will companies be able to boost their products by manipulating online ratings on a massive scale?" In the context of selling products by manipulating user reviews on a massive scale, the word "scale" most nearly means level or size.

Choices B, C, and D are incorrect because in the context of selling products by manipulating user reviews, a massive "scale" refers to a great level or size, not to a payment (choice B), an interval or space between things (choice C), or a plan (choice D).

QUESTION 39

Choice B is the best answer. The figure shows that while the mean score of the control comments in the politics category is below 2.0, the artificially up-voted mean score for that category is exactly 2.5.

Choice A is incorrect because the artificially up-voted mean score of comments in the business category is higher than 3.0. Choice C is incorrect because the artificially up-voted mean score of comments in the fun category is less than 2.5. Choice D is incorrect because the artificially up-voted mean score of the comments in the general news category is just over 2.0.

QUESTION 40

Choice D is the best answer. The figure shows that the mean score for both control comments and artificially up-voted comments in the general news category is just above 2.0.

Choice A is incorrect because the mean score for the control comments in the culture and society category is a little below 2.5 while the mean score for the artificially up-voted comments is over 3.0. Choice B is incorrect because the mean score for the control comments in the information technology category is a little above 1.5 while the mean score for the artificially up-voted comments is above 2.0. Choice C is incorrect because the mean score for the control comments in the fun category is exactly 2.0 while the mean score for the artificially up-voted comments is nearly 2.5.

QUESTION 41

Choice D is the best answer. In the passage Watts notes that "the category of the news items . . . had a strong effect on how much people could be manipulated" (lines 76-79). That idea is directly supported by the data in the figure, which show that the difference in mean score between the control comments and the artificially up-voted comments varies by subject (for example, in the general news category there is virtually no difference between the mean scores of the two types of comments, while for the business category there is almost a 1.0-point difference between the mean scores).

Choices A and B are incorrect because the passage provides no data for artificially down-voted comments or negative social influence. Choice C is incorrect because the figure applies only to one context (mean score of control comments versus mean score of artificially up-voted comments on the news site); there is no way to tell what patterns would be observed in other contexts.

QUESTION 42

Choice C is the best answer. According to the passage, Maguire found that taxi drivers' hippocampi are "7 percent larger than normal," which is evidence that "way-finding around London had physically altered the gross structure of their brains" (lines 10-14). In lines 20-26, the passage indicates that this finding challenges an earlier consensus: "It had long been thought that the adult brain was incapable of spawning new neurons—that . . . the brain's basic anatomical structure was more or less static. Maguire's study suggested the old inherited wisdom was simply not true."

Choice A is incorrect because the passage does not indicate that Maguire used a new method in her study or that her findings demonstrate the validity of a method. Choice B is incorrect because lines 20-26 show that Maguire's findings disprove a popular viewpoint, not that they support one. Choice D is incorrect because although Maguire's findings call into question a previous idea, there is no indication that they challenge the authenticity of any previous data.

QUESTION 43

Choice D is the best answer. The previous question asks about the significance of Maguire's findings, with the answer being that her findings call into question a previous belief. This is supported in lines 20-26: "It had long been thought that the adult brain was incapable of spawning new neurons—that . . . the brain's basic anatomical structure was more or less static. Maguire's study suggested the old inherited wisdom was simply not true."

Choices A, B, and C are incorrect because the lines cited do not support the answer to the previous question about the significance of Maguire's findings. Choices A and B are incorrect because these lines present Maguire's observation and her conclusion but do not indicate that her findings call into question a previous belief. Choice C is incorrect because these lines simply explain one capability of the human brain.

QUESTION 44

Choice D is the best answer. In line 24, the passage discusses the "brain's basic anatomical structure." In this context, the word "basic" most nearly means fundamental.

Choices A, B, and C are incorrect because in the context of discussing the brain's structure, the word "basic" most nearly means fundamental, not first (choice A), uncomplicated (choice B), or required (choice C).

QUESTION 45

Choice C is the best answer. The purpose of Maguire's study of the mental athletes was to try to determine what it is that makes them so good at memorization, and in particular if they have structurally different brains than people without such extraordinary memorization skills or if they have normal brain structures but use them in unusual ways. This is supported in lines 33-37, which state that Maguire and her team "wanted to find out if the memorizers' brains were—like the London cabbies'—structurally different from the rest of ours, or if they were somehow just making better use of memory abilities that we all possess."

Choice A is incorrect because the study was an attempt to compare the brains of mental athletes to the brains of the general population, not to compare the use of different brain structures in memorization and navigation. Choices B and D are incorrect because the passage makes it clear that it was not known if mental athletes have unusual brain structures; finding out if they do was actually one of the goals of the study.

QUESTION 46

Choice B is the best answer. The previous question asks what Maguire's study of mental athletes attempted to answer, with the answer being the question of whether it is brain structure or an unusual use of the brain that gives certain people extraordinary memorization skills. This is supported in lines 33-37: "They wanted to find out if the memorizers' brains were—like the London cabbies'—structurally different from the rest of ours, or if they were somehow just making better use of memory abilities that we all possess."

Choices A, C, and D are incorrect because the lines cited do not support the answer to the previous question about what Maguire's study of mental athletes was investigating. Instead they simply identify the subject of the study (choice A), explain what the study involved (choice C), and state a finding concerning the cognitive ability of the mental athletes (choice D).

QUESTION 47

Choice A is the best answer. In lines 38-39, the passage describes part of Maguire's study by stating that "the researchers put both the mental athletes and a group of matched control subjects into MRI scanners." In the context of a study that has two groups of subjects, the word "matched" suggests subjects that are similar or comparable.

Choices B, C, and D are incorrect because in the context of a study with two groups of subjects, the word "matched" suggests subjects that are similar or comparable, not ones that are exactly the same (choice B), ones that are recognizably different (choice C), or ones that are rivals (choice D).

QUESTION 48

Choice C is the best answer. The main purpose of the fifth paragraph (lines 57-65) is to relate what Maguire discovered about the mental athletes, namely that their brain structures are not different from those of the control group but that the mental athletes use their brains differently: "there was one telling difference . . . regions of the brain that were less active in the control subjects seemed to be working in overdrive for the mental athletes."

Choice A is incorrect because the fifth paragraph does not mention the taxi drivers or the study involving them. Choice B is incorrect because the fifth paragraph describes some of the unexpected results of Maguire's study but does not address the possible reasons for those results. Choice D is incorrect because the fifth paragraph describes only Maguire's findings, not her methods.

QUESTION 49

Choice C is the best answer. The passage indicates that Maguire's second study revealed that people in the control group don't have different brain structures than the mental athletes but that they use their brains differently. In particular, the two groups use different pathways in the brain: "regions of the brain that were less active in the control subjects seemed to be working in overdrive for the mental athletes" (lines 63-65).

Choices A and D are incorrect because the passage states that there was only "one telling difference between the brains of the mental athletes and the control subjects" (lines 57-58); there is no indication that the control group showed less total brain activity or had smaller hippocampal regions. Choice B is incorrect because the passage mentions only the general cognitive ability of the mental athletes, noting that their scores were "within the normal range" (line 54).

QUESTION 50

Choice A is the best answer. After establishing in lines 50-51 that the brains of the control group and the mental athletes seemed to be "indistinguishable," the passage suggests that the reason mental athletes are so good at memorization is that they use parts of their brains that most other people don't use when memorizing: "Surprisingly, when the mental athletes were learning new information, they were engaging several regions of the brain known to be involved in two specific tasks: visual memory and spatial navigation, including the same right posterior hippocampal region that the London cabbies had enlarged with all their daily way-finding" (lines 66-72).

Choices B and C are incorrect because the passage explains that the mental athletes were converting information into images, not abstract symbols or numerical lists. Choice D is incorrect because it is not supported by the passage, as the author discusses the mental athletes' actions while memorizing but not any brain exercises the mental athletes regularly do.

QUESTION 51

Choice A is the best answer. The previous question asks what the passage suggests about the mental athletes' success with memorization, with the answer being that they use parts of the brain that most other people don't use when memorizing. This is supported in lines 66-72: "Surprisingly, when the mental athletes were learning new information, they were engaging several regions of the brain known to be involved in two specific tasks: visual memory and spatial navigation, including the same right posterior hippocampal region that the London cabbies had enlarged with all their daily way-finding."

Choices B, C, and D are incorrect because the lines cited do not support the answer to the previous question about what the passage suggests about the mental athletes' success with memorization. Instead, they acknowledge that Maguire's findings seem odd (choice B), describe how Maguire first responded to the results (choice C), and explain things that *don't* account for the mental athletes' ability (choice D).

QUESTION 52

Choice B is the best answer. According to the passage, Maguire's study revealed that the mental athletes were using the same parts of the brain for memorization as were the London cabbies from the first study, a result that was initially puzzling. The questions in lines 74-78 highlight and expand on that result, making it clear that it is surprising to find that the mental athletes use images to remember numbers or use a part of the brain associated with navigation when trying to remember shapes. Although it became clear *how* the mental athletes were memorizing things, it was not clear why they were doing it that way.

Choice A is incorrect because the questions in lines 74-78 seem to reflect additional questions Maguire and others had based on their result and do not suggest that Maguire's conclusions may not be reliable. Choice C is incorrect because the passage makes no mention of any earlier studies of the phenomenon of using images to remember numbers or to use a part of the brain associated with navigation when trying to remember shapes. Choice D is incorrect because the questions in lines 74-78 specifically address Maguire's two studies but not her earlier work.

Section 2: Writing Test

QUESTION 1

Choice C is the best answer because the sentence is not directly related to the main point of the paragraph and should not be added. The main idea of the paragraph is that new high-tech fossil models help expand scientists' knowledge of ancient species. There is no indication in the paragraph that these scientists are concerned about the age of the rocks in which fossils are found.

Choices A and B are incorrect because the sentence should not be added. It neither adds support to an argument nor provides a transition from one sentence to another. Choice D is incorrect because the sentence does not undermine any claim made in the paragraph.

QUESTION 2

Choice D is the best answer because "promise" suggests the hope of good things to come. The models offer the possibility of advancing the field of paleontology in the future.

Choices A, B, and C are incorrect because they do not make sense in the context of the passage.

QUESTION 3

Choice B is the best answer because the sentence should be kept: it provides a brief but useful explanation of how a 3-D printer works.

Choice A is incorrect. The sentence should be kept because it provides important information about 3-D printers, not because it explains why X-rays are used in CT scanners. Choices C and D are incorrect because the sentence is neither contradictory nor confusing and should not be deleted.

QUESTION 4

Choice C is the best answer because the relative pronoun "which" appropriately follows the independent clause "The plastic hardens quickly." It introduces the relative clause explaining what the fact that the plastic hardens quickly allows the printer to do.

Choices A, B, and D are incorrect because each results in a comma splice (the joining of two independent clauses with only a comma).

QUESTION 5

Choice A is the best answer because no change is needed. The prepositional phrase "in order" and the infinitive "to learn" are appropriately used in conjunction to create an idiomatic phrase.

Choices B and D are incorrect because the phrases "in order for learning" and "so to learn" are not idiomatic. Choice C is incorrect because the pronoun "one" is inconsistent with the noun "team," which identifies a specific team.

QUESTION 6

Choice C is the best answer because the personal plural pronoun "their" agrees in number with its antecedent, the plural noun "fossils."

Choice A is incorrect because the pronoun "its" is singular and doesn't agree with the plural antecedent "fossils." Choices B and D are incorrect because a personal pronoun is needed in the sentence. Neither "it's" (the contraction of "it is") nor "there" is a personal pronoun.

QUESTION 7

Choice D is the best answer because sentence 2 should be placed after sentence 5 to make the paragraph most logical. Sentence 2 begins "But now," signaling a contrast with the past. Sentences 4 and 5 tell what scientists did in the past, so it makes sense for sentence 2 to follow sentence 5.

Choices A, B, and C are incorrect because they result in a paragraph that does not proceed logically. Keeping sentence 2, which begins "But now," where it is now (choice A) or placing it at the beginning of the paragraph (choice B) signals a contrast with the past that doesn't make sense in context. Placing sentence 2 after sentence 4 (choice C) appropriately signals a contrast with the past but creates problems for sentence 5, which needs to be placed directly after sentence 4 to continue the discussion of past research limitations.

QUESTION 8

Choice D is the best answer because the phrase "for example" indicates that an example will follow. In this paragraph, the sentence that follows the phrase provides a relevant example of the use of technology to "reproduce fossils that scientists cannot observe firsthand."

Choices A, B, and C are incorrect because they set up expectations that are not carried out in the paragraph. "By contrast" in choice A and "nonetheless" in choice B suggest that contrary information will follow. "Besides" in choice C suggests that additional information will follow. None of these choices indicates what should be indicated: that an example will follow.

QUESTION 9

Choice B is the best answer because the simple past tense verb "relied" is consistent with the other past tense verbs in the National Museum of Brazil example, such as "dug" and "determined."

Choices A and D are incorrect because they provide singular verbs that don't agree in number with the plural subject "researchers." Choice C is incorrect because the future tense helping verb "will" is inconsistent with the other past tense verbs in the National Museum of Brazil example.

QUESTION 10

Choice C is the best answer because it clearly and concisely combines the sentences in a way that shows the cause-effect relationship between the condition of the fossil and the decision by the research team.

Choices A, B, and D are incorrect because they do not effectively combine the sentences. In each of these choices, the sentence mischaracterizes the relationship between the condition of the fossil and the decision by the research team.

QUESTION 11

Choice C is the best answer because the plural pronoun "they" correctly refers to its plural antecedent "researchers."

Choices A, B, and D are incorrect because "one," "he or she," and "it" are singular pronouns. A plural pronoun is needed to agree in number with the plural antecedent "researchers."

QUESTION 12

Choice D is the best answer because no transitional phrase is needed between the two sentences. The first sentence indicates that Tweed wanted to silence Nast, and the second sentence simply states what happened next: that his attempt to do so failed.

Choices A, B, and C are incorrect because no transitional phrase or conjunctive adverb such as "therefore" or "furthermore" is needed between the sentences. The information in the second sentence neither results from information in the first nor is in addition to it. Rather, it tells what happened next: the first sentence indicates that Tweed wanted to silence Nast, and the second states that his attempt to do so failed.

QUESTION 13

Choice D is the best answer because it is the only choice that clearly and concisely conveys the key information that "in the 1860s and the 1870s, . . . organizations known as 'political machines' started taking control of city governments."

Choices A, B, and C are incorrect because they all contain unnecessary words or invert the logical order of words in ways that lead to vagueness and redundancy. In choice A, it is unclear if the pronoun "they" refers to "organizations" or "governments." In choices B and C, word order is inverted, creating a lack of concision ("political organizations that were powerful" is used instead of "powerful political organizations"; "governments were taken control of" and "organizations . . . did so" are used instead of "organizations . . . started taking control of governments").

QUESTION 14

Choice A is the best answer because no words are needed between the noun phrase "purchasing votes" and the explanatory appositive phrase that follows it ("a form of . . .").

Choices B, C, and D are incorrect because the participle "being" and the pronouns "that" and "which" are not needed to introduce the appositive phrase "a form of . . .," which explains the concept of "purchasing votes."

QUESTION 15

Choice B is the best answer because the comma after "1860s" is used correctly with the comma after "group" to set off the inessential (nonrestrictive) clause "which controlled New York City in the 1860s."

Choice A is incorrect because a dash cannot be used in conjunction with a comma to set off a nonessential clause. Either two commas or two dashes may be used, but not one of each. Choice C is incorrect because a comma is not needed after "City." Choice D is incorrect because a comma is necessary to separate the nonessential clause from the rest of the sentence.

QUESTION 16

Choice C is the best answer because the sentence should be deleted. Although the information is true, it is not essential to the paragraph, which is focused on political machines in general and the Tammany Hall group in particular, not on Tweed himself.

Choices A and B are incorrect because the sentence should not be kept. Choice D is incorrect because, while the sentence should be deleted, it does not undermine or challenge the main claim of the passage.

QUESTION 17

Choice C is the best answer because no comma is needed before "commented," and the comma after "commented" correctly separates the first part of the sentence from the quotation it introduces.

Choices A, B, and D are incorrect because each includes one or more unnecessary commas.

QUESTION 18

Choice A is the best answer because the adjective "famous," which means widely known, clearly and concisely describes "images."

Choices B, C, and D are incorrect because "well-known" and "commonly known" are repetitive when used with the adjective "famous," which means widely known.

QUESTION 19

Choice D is the best answer because it adds the most relevant supporting information. The paragraph is focused on the cartoons' depictions of Tweed as a thief, so making an explicit connection between one cartoon and "Tweed's greedy nature" is extremely relevant to the paragraph.

Choices A, B, and C are incorrect because they all contain irrelevant information. Information about Nast's other cartoons, Tweed's prison escape, and Tweed's hat is not important to add to the paragraph, which is focused on the cartoons' depictions of Tweed as a thief.

QUESTION 20

Choice D is the best answer because the word "prosecuted" correctly indicates that Tweed was charged and tried for his crimes. The preposition "on" is idiomatic when used with the verb "prosecuted."

Choices A, B, and C are incorrect because the word "persecuted" means that someone is harassed or oppressed, not that he or she is charged with a crime. "Persecuted" doesn't fit into the context of this sentence, which is about the legal troubles of Tweed and his gang.

QUESTION 21

Choice A is the best answer because the past tense verb "brought" is consistent with the other past tense verbs in the sentence, such as "escaped" and "fled."

Choices B, C, and D are incorrect because the participle "bringing," the present tense verb "brings," and the present perfect tense verb "has brought" are not consistent with the other verbs in the sentence.

QUESTION 22

Choice B is the best answer because "triumph" indicates victory. It could be considered a victory for political cartoons that Tweed was recaptured because he was recognized from a Nast cartoon.

Choices A, C, and D are incorrect because "pinnacle," "culmination," and "apex" all suggest the highest point or end of something. None of these words indicates the appropriate relationship between the recapture of Tweed and the impact of Nast's cartoons.

QUESTION 23

Choice B is the best answer because the singular possessive pronoun "its" is used correctly to refer to the singular noun "system."

Choice A is incorrect because the contraction "it's" cannot be used to show possession. Choice C is incorrect because "its" is already possessive; an apostrophe is unnecessary. Choice D is incorrect because "their" is a plural possessive pronoun that does not agree in number with the singular noun "system."

QUESTION 24

Choice B is the best answer because it clearly and concisely combines the sentences to show the relationship between the claim ("the idea is obviously very attractive") and the supporting information about the cameras' cost.

Choices A, C, and D are incorrect because they mischaracterize the relationship between the claim ("the idea is obviously very attractive") and the supporting information about the cameras' cost. The claim about the idea's attractiveness is not *in addition to* the information about the cost; rather, the information about the cameras' cost supports the claim that the idea is very attractive.

QUESTION 25

Choice A is the best answer because "however" is used correctly to indicate contrast. Some people consider the art space vital, but that group of people may be too small to generate necessary funding for the project.

Choices B, C, and D are incorrect because neither "therefore," "in effect," nor "as a rule" indicates the appropriate relationship between the two sentences being connected. The two sentences form a contrast: some people consider the art space vital, but that group of people may be too small to generate necessary funding for the project.

QUESTION 26

Choice B is the best answer because no commas are needed to set off the restrictive clause ("that is easily understood and appreciated") that follows the subject.

Choices A and D are incorrect because the clause that describes "work" is essential and should not be set off with punctuation. Setting off a clause with two commas or dashes indicates that it is nonessential to the sentence (nonrestrictive). Choice C is incorrect because no comma is needed between the two verbs.

QUESTION 27

Choice D is the best answer because the sentence should not be added. The general information it contains is not relevant to this paragraph's discussion of crowdfunding for the arts.

Choices A and B are incorrect because the sentence should not be added. Information about crowdfunding in general is not relevant to the discussion of the arts in this paragraph. Additionally, the sentence doesn't support the writer's point about funding of artistic projects.

Choice C is incorrect because, while the sentence should not be added, "funding received from public institutions" is not an idea that is developed in the passage.

QUESTION 28

Choice A is the best answer because "in addition" appropriately introduces an additional problem with crowdfunding in the arts.

Choices B, C, and D are incorrect because "conversely," "however," and "thus" do not indicate the appropriate relationship between what is said earlier in the paragraph about problems with crowdfunding in the arts and the additional problem that follows.

QUESTION 29

Choice C is the best answer because the pronoun "who" appropriately introduces a dependent clause defining "free riders."

Choice A is incorrect because it results in a comma splice (two independent clauses cannot be joined by only a comma). Choice B is incorrect because it is not clear which people don't contribute: "audiences" or "free riders." Choice D is incorrect because the infinitive phrase "to not make" doesn't make sense in the sentence.

QUESTION 30

Choice B is the best answer because the plural pronoun "they" agrees in number with the plural noun "people" and results in a clear, straightforward clause: "if people begin to feel that paying for the art they love is someone else's responsibility."

Choice A is incorrect because the passive voice is unnecessary and adds some confusion about which antecedent the pronoun "them" is referring to: "arts" or "people." Choices C and D are incorrect because the pronouns "him" and "her" and "he" and "she" are singular and do not agree in number with the plural antecedent "people."

QUESTION 31

Choice C is the best answer because the singular pronoun "her" is consistent with the pronoun "her" that is used earlier in the sentence to refer to the playwright.

Choices A and B are incorrect because they are plural pronouns that are not consistent with the singular pronoun "her" used earlier in the sentence to refer to the singular noun "playwright." Choice D is incorrect because the singular pronoun "its" is not consistent with "her" and is not used to refer to a person.

QUESTION 32

Choice D is the best answer because sentence 2, which mentions the high price of the playwright's tickets, logically follows sentence 5, which addresses how the price of tickets was determined.

Choices A, B, and C are incorrect because sentence 2 does not logically follow sentences 1, 3, or 4. Sentences 3, 4, and 5 present a logical sequence of activities that establish the ticket price: first the playwright presents the total cost of her production, then she projects the attendance, and then she sets a per-person cost and prices tickets accordingly. Sentence 2, which addresses the ticket price, must come after the completion of this sequence; it can't come before the sequence (choice A) or interrupt the sequence (choices B and C).

QUESTION 33

Choice A is the best answer because it accurately interprets data in the graph. The category "dance" had the lowest amount of money raised but also had the highest percentage of projects fully funded.

Choices B, C, and D are incorrect because they do not accurately interpret the information provided in the graph.

QUESTION 34

Choice C is the best answer because sentence 3 needs to be placed before sentence 2 for the paragraph to be cohesive. Sentence 3 presents a cause ("newspapers . . . have been hit especially hard by the widespread availability of free news online") and sentence 2 presents an effect of that cause ("newspapers have reduced or eliminated investigative resources").

Choice A is incorrect because sentence 3 needs to precede sentence 2, not follow it: sentence 3 presents a cause ("newspapers . . . have been hit especially hard"), and sentence 2 presents an effect ("newspapers have reduced or eliminated investigative resources"). Choice B is incorrect because sentence 1 needs to precede sentence 3, not follow it: sentence 1 offers a general assessment of "print journalism as a viable profession," and sentence 3 offers information about one form of print journalism (newspapers). Choice D is incorrect because sentence 3 is needed to provide an explanation for the "lower print circulation and diminished advertising revenue" noted in sentence 2.

QUESTION 35

Choice B is the best answer because the plural noun "reporters" is used correctly as the object of the preposition "of" and because the colon appropriately joins two independent clauses, indicating that the second clause ("their work is expensive and time-consuming") follows logically from the first ("It is not difficult . . . reporters").

Choices A and D are incorrect because the singular possessive "reporter's" does not provide an object for the preposition "of." Choice C is incorrect because the comma after "reporters" creates a comma splice (the comma is used without a conjunction to join two independent clauses).

QUESTION 36

Choice B is the best answer because the phrase "undertaken in" appropriately identifies why and for whom investigative journalism is conducted ("in the public interest"—that is, to serve the interests of all of the people instead of only a few).

Choice A is incorrect because "taking on the public interest" implies that investigative journalism is the adversary of the public interest (that is, it "takes on," or confronts, the interests of ordinary people). Choice C is incorrect because it implies that investigative journalism overpowers or takes control of the public interest. Choice D is incorrect because it is unclear what "taking off from the public interest" might mean in this context.

QUESTION 37

Choice D is the best answer because the general term "illegal activities" creates redundancy with the specific examples provided in the sentence and should be deleted. "Street crime," "corporate wrongdoing," and "political corruption" are all specific examples of "illegal activities," so it is unnecessary to mention "illegal activities" as a separate item in the list.

Choice A is incorrect because the general term "illegal activities" creates redundancy with the specific examples of illegal activities provided in the sentence. Choices B and C are incorrect because they repeat ideas that are already in the sentence: "corporate wrongdoing" is a type of "business scandal," and "political corruption" is a type of "abuse of government power."

QUESTION 38

Choice C is the best answer because the sentence is out of place in the paragraph: the year 1954 breaks the chronology of the other examples (1974, 2004), and the example is about television news instead of print journalism.

Choices A and B are incorrect because the sentence is out of place in the paragraph and should not be added. Choice D is incorrect because, while the passage should not be added, the reason is not the one specified. The example of journalists reporting a story that exposes a person in power is consistent with the passage's definition of investigative journalism.

QUESTION 39

Choice D is the best answer because "deterrent" and "rebuke to" appropriately indicate the effect that exposure by reporters has had on "malfeasance" (misconduct).

Choices A, B, and C are incorrect because they do not appropriately indicate the effect that exposure by reporters has had on "malfeasance" (misconduct). It is unclear how journalism would act as a "blockade" to misconduct, and it is not idiomatic to say that these reports have acted as an important "interference to" or "drag on" misconduct.

QUESTION 40

Choice B is the best answer because the verb phrase "need not entail"—an inverted form of "does not need to entail"—appropriately conveys the writer's point that the decline in traditional print media does not *necessarily* mean "the end of investigative journalism." In other words, this possibility is real but can be prevented.

Choices A and C are incorrect because "could not" and "will not" indicate certainty—in other words, that there is no possibility of an end to investigative journalism. Choice D is incorrect because "must not" suggests a call to action by the writer ("this *must* be prevented") that is inconsistent with the approach taken in the paragraph.

QUESTION 41

Choice D is the best answer because the noun phrase "innovative adjustments" sets up the examples that follow. The examples of the Organized Crime and Corruption Reporting Project, blogs and Twitter, and Help Me Investigate all refer to innovative projects and media that enable investigative journalism to thrive outside of traditional newspapers and magazines.

Choices A, B, and C are incorrect because they do not set up the specific examples of innovative projects and media that are helping fill the void left by the decline of investigative journalism in traditional newspapers and magazines.

QUESTION 42

Choice A is the best answer because no punctuation is needed to separate the subject of the sentence, "enterprises," from the adjective phrase beginning "such as."

Choices B and C are incorrect because placing a colon before or after "such as" would create an error in sentence structure: a colon must be preceded by an independent clause. Choice D is incorrect because no comma is necessary here.

QUESTION 43

Choice A is the best answer because the transitional phrase "for example" appropriately indicates that the Help Me Investigate project discussed in the sentence is an example of the use of social media mentioned in the previous sentence.

Choices B, C, and D are incorrect because neither "therefore," "however," nor "in any case" indicates the true relationship between this and the previous sentence. The Help Me Investigate project discussed in the current sentence is an example of the use of social media mentioned in the previous sentence.

QUESTION 44

Choice C is the best answer because the full subject of the independent clause, "the advent of the digital age," directly follows the dependent clause that introduces it.

Choices A, B, and D are incorrect because the subjects of their independent clauses do not directly follow the introductory dependent clause. "Far from marking the end of investigative journalism" refers to the "advent of the digital age," not to "cooperation among journalists" (choice A) or "the number of potential investigators" (choice B). In choice D, an interrupting phrase ("by facilitating cooperation among journalists and ordinary citizens") separates the subject from the dependent clause that modifies it.

Section 3: Math Test - No Calculator

QUESTION 1

Choice D is correct. From the graph, the y-intercept of line ℓ is (0, 1). The line also passes through the point (1, 2). Therefore the slope of the line is $\frac{2-1}{1-0} = \frac{1}{1} = 1$, and in slope-intercept form, the equation for line ℓ is $y = x + 1$.

Choice A is incorrect. It is the equation of the vertical line that passes through the point (1, 0). Choice B is incorrect. It is the equation of the horizontal line that passes through the point (0, 1). Choice C is incorrect. The line defined by this equation has y-intercept (0, 0), whereas line ℓ has y-intercept (0, 1).

QUESTION 2

Choice A is correct. A circle has 360 degrees of arc. In the circle shown, O is the center of the circle and angle AOC is a central angle of the circle. From the figure, the two diameters that meet to form angle AOC are perpendicular, so the measure of angle AOC is 90°. This central angle intercepts minor arc AC, meaning minor arc AC has 90° of arc. Since the circumference (length) of the entire circle is 36, the length of minor arc AC is $\frac{90}{360} \times 36 = 9$.

Choices B, C, and D are incorrect. The perpendicular diameters divide the circumference of the circle into four equal arcs; therefore, minor arc AC is $\frac{1}{4}$ of the circumference. However, the lengths in choices B and C are, respectively, $\frac{1}{3}$ and $\frac{1}{2}$ the circumference of the circle, and the length in choice D is the length of the entire circumference. None of these lengths is $\frac{1}{4}$ the circumference.

QUESTION 3

Choice B is correct. Dividing both sides of the quadratic equation $4x^2 - 8x - 12 = 0$ by 4 yields $x^2 - 2x - 3 = 0$. The equation $x^2 - 2x - 3 = 0$ can be factored as $(x + 1)(x - 3) = 0$. This equation is true when $x + 1 = 0$ or $x - 3 = 0$. Solving for x gives the solutions to the original quadratic equation: $x = -1$ and $x = 3$.

Choices A and C are incorrect because -3 is not a solution of $4x^2 - 8x - 12 = 0$: $4(-3)^2 - 8(-3) - 12 = 36 + 24 - 12 \neq 0$. Choice D is incorrect because 1 is not a solution of $4x^2 - 8x - 12 = 0$: $4(1)^2 - 8(1) - 12 = 4 - 8 - 12 \neq 0$.

QUESTION 4

Choice C is correct. If f is a function of x, then the graph of f in the xy-plane consists of all points $(x, f(x))$. An x-intercept is where the graph intersects the x-axis; since all points on the x-axis have y-coordinate 0, the graph of f will cross the x-axis at values of x such that $f(x) = 0$. Therefore, the graph of a function f will have no x-intercepts if and only if f has no real zeros. Likewise, the graph of a quadratic function with no real zeros will have no x-intercepts.

Choice A is incorrect. The graph of a linear function in the xy-plane whose rate of change is not zero is a line with a nonzero slope. The x-axis is a horizontal line and thus has slope 0, so the graph of the linear function whose rate of change is not zero is a line that is not parallel to the x-axis. Thus, the graph must intersect the x-axis at some point, and this point is an x-intercept of the graph. Choices B and D are incorrect because the graph of any function with a real zero must have an x-intercept.

QUESTION 5

Choice D is correct. If $x = 9$ in the equation $\sqrt{k+2} - x = 0$, this equation becomes $\sqrt{k+2} - 9 = 0$, which can be rewritten as $\sqrt{k+2} = 9$. Squaring each side of $\sqrt{k+2} = 9$ gives $k + 2 = 81$, or $k = 79$. Substituting $k = 79$ into the equation $\sqrt{k+2} - 9 = 0$ confirms this is the correct value for k.

Choices A, B, and C are incorrect because substituting any of these values for k in the equation $\sqrt{k+2} - 9 = 0$ gives a false statement. For example, if $k = 7$, the equation becomes $\sqrt{7+2} - 9 = \sqrt{9} - 9 = 3 - 9 = 0$, which is false.

QUESTION 6

Choice A is correct. The sum of $(a^2 - 1)$ and $(a + 1)$ can be rewritten as $(a^2 - 1) + (a + 1)$, or $a^2 - 1 + a + 1$, which is equal to $a^2 + a + 0$. Therefore, the sum of the two expressions is equal to $a^2 + a$.

Choices B and D are incorrect. Since neither of the two expressions has a term with a^3, the sum of the two expressions cannot have the term a^3 when simplified. Choice C is incorrect. This choice may result from mistakenly adding the terms a^2 and a to get $2a^2$.

QUESTION 7

Choice C is correct. If Jackie works x hours as a tutor, which pays $12 per hour, she earns $12x$ dollars. If Jackie works y hours as a lifeguard, which pays $9.50 per hour, she earns $9.5y$ dollars. Thus the total, in dollars, Jackie earns in a week that she works x hours as a tutor and y hours as a lifeguard is $12x + 9.5y$. Therefore, the condition that Jackie wants to earn at least $220 is represented by the inequality $12x + 9.5y \geq 220$. The condition that Jackie can work no more than 20 hours per week is represented by the inequality $x + y \leq 20$. These two inequalities form the system shown in choice C.

Choice A is incorrect. This system represents the conditions that Jackie earns no more than $220 and works at least 20 hours. Choice B is incorrect. The first inequality in this system represents the condition that Jackie earns no more than $220. Choice D is incorrect. The second inequality in this system represents the condition that Jackie works at least 20 hours.

QUESTION 8

Choice A is correct. The constant term 331.4 in $S(T) = 0.6T + 331.4$ is the value of S when $T = 0$. The value $T = 0$ corresponds to a temperature of 0°C. Since $S(T)$ represents the speed of sound, 331.4 is the speed of sound, in meters per second, when the temperature is 0°C.

Choice B is incorrect. When $T = 0.6$°C, $S(T) = 0.6(0.6) + 331.4 = 331.76$, not 331.4, meters per second. Choice C is incorrect. Based on the given formula, the speed of sound increases by 0.6 meters per second for every increase of temperature by 1°C, as shown by the equation $0.6(T + 1) + 331.4 = (0.6T + 331.4) + 0.6$. Choice D is incorrect. An increase in the speed of sound, in meters per second, that corresponds to an increase of 0.6°C is $0.6(0.6) = 0.36$.

QUESTION 9

Choice A is correct. Substituting x^2 for y in the second equation gives $2(x^2) + 6 = 2(x + 3)$. This equation can be solved as follows:

$2x^2 + 6 = 2x + 6$ (Apply the distributive property.)

$2x^2 + 6 - 2x - 6 = 0$ (Subtract $2x$ and 6 from both sides of the equation.)

$2x^2 - 2x = 0$ (Combine like terms.)

$2x(x - 1) = 0$ (Factor both terms on the left side of the equation by $2x$.)

Thus, $x = 0$ and $x = 1$ are the solutions to the system. Since $x > 0$, only $x = 1$ needs to be considered. The value of y when $x = 1$ is $y = x^2 = 1^2 = 1$. Therefore, the value of xy is $(1)(1) = 1$.

Choices B, C, and D are incorrect and likely result from a computational or conceptual error when solving this system of equations.

QUESTION 10

Choice B is correct. Substituting $a^2 + b^2$ for z and ab for y into the expression $4z + 8y$ gives $4(a^2 + b^2) + 8ab$. Multiplying $a^2 + b^2$ by 4 gives $4a^2 + 4b^2 + 8ab$, or equivalently $4(a^2 + 2ab + b^2)$. Since $(a^2 + 2ab + b^2) = (a + b)^2$, it follows that $4z + 8y$ is equivalent to $(2a + 2b)^2$.

Choices A, C, and D are incorrect and likely result from errors made when substituting or factoring.

QUESTION 11

Choice C is correct. The volume of right circular cylinder A is given by the expression $\pi r^2 h$, where r is the radius of its circular base and h is its height. The volume of a cylinder with twice the radius and half the height of cylinder A is given by $\pi(2r)^2(\frac{1}{2})h$, which is equivalent to $4\pi r^2(\frac{1}{2})h = 2\pi r^2 h$. Therefore, the volume is twice the volume of cylinder A, or $2 \times 22 = 44$.

Choice A is incorrect and likely results from not multiplying the radius of cylinder A by 2. Choice B is incorrect and likely results from not squaring the 2 in $2r$ when applying the volume formula. Choice D is incorrect and likely results from a conceptual error.

QUESTION 12

Choice D is correct. Since 9 can be rewritten as 3^2, $9^{\frac{3}{4}}$ is equivalent to $3^{2(\frac{3}{4})}$. Applying the properties of exponents, this can be written as $3^{\frac{3}{2}}$, which can further be rewritten as $3^{\frac{2}{2}}(3^{\frac{1}{2}})$, an expression that is equivalent to $3\sqrt{3}$.

Choices A is incorrect; it is equivalent to $9^{\frac{1}{3}}$. Choice B is incorrect; it is equivalent to $9^{\frac{1}{4}}$. Choice C is incorrect; it is equivalent to $3^{\frac{1}{2}}$.

QUESTION 13

Choice B is correct. When n is increased by 1, t increases by the coefficient of n, which is 1.

Choices A, C, and D are incorrect and likely result from a conceptual error when interpreting the equation.

QUESTION 14

Choice C is correct. The graph of $y = -f(x)$ is the graph of the equation $y = -(2^x + 1)$, or $y = -2^x - 1$. This should be the graph of a decreasing exponential function. The y-intercept of the graph can be found by substituting the value $x = 0$ into the equation, as follows: $y = -2^0 - 1 = -1 - 1 = -2$. Therefore, the graph should pass through the point $(0, -2)$. Choice C is the only function that passes through this point.

Choices A and B are incorrect because the graphed functions are increasing instead of decreasing. Choice D is incorrect because the function passes through the point $(0, -1)$ instead of $(0, -2)$.

QUESTION 15

Choice D is correct. Since gasoline costs $4 per gallon, and since Alan's car travels an average of 25 miles per gallon, the expression $\frac{4}{25}$ gives the cost, in dollars per mile, to drive the car. Multiplying $\frac{4}{25}$ by m gives the cost for Alan to drive m miles in his car. Alan wants to reduce his weekly spending by $5, so setting $\frac{4}{25}m$ equal to 5 gives the number of miles, m, by which he must reduce his driving.

Choices A, B, and C are incorrect. Choices A and B transpose the numerator and the denominator in the fraction. The fraction $\frac{25}{4}$ would result in the unit miles per dollar, but the question requires a unit of dollars per mile. Choices A and C set the expression equal to 95 instead of 5, a mistake that may result from a misconception that Alan wants to reduce his driving by 5 miles each week; instead, the question says he wants to reduce his weekly expenditure by $5.

QUESTION 16

The correct answer is 4. The equation $60h + 10 \leq 280$, where h is the number of hours the boat has been rented, can be written to represent the situation. Subtracting 10 from both sides and then dividing by 60 yields $h \leq 4.5$. Since the boat can be rented only for whole numbers of hours, the maximum number of hours for which Maria can rent the boat is 4.

QUESTION 17

The correct answer is $\frac{6}{5}$, or 1.2. To solve the equation $2(p + 1) + 8(p - 1) = 5p$, first distribute the terms outside the parentheses to the terms inside the parentheses: $2p + 2 + 8p - 8 = 5p$. Next, combine like terms on the left side of the equal sign: $10p - 6 = 5p$. Subtracting $10p$ from both sides yields $-6 = -5p$. Finally, dividing both sides by -5 gives $p = \frac{6}{5} = 1.2$. Either 6/5 or 1.2 can be gridded as the correct answer.

QUESTION 18

The correct answer is $\frac{21}{4}$, or 5.25. Use substitution to create a one-variable equation that can be solved for x. The second equation gives that $y = 2x$. Substituting $2x$ for y in the first equation gives $\frac{1}{2}(2x + 2x) = \frac{21}{2}$. Dividing both sides of this equation by $\frac{1}{2}$ yields $(2x + 2x) = 21$. Combining like terms results in $4x = 21$. Finally, dividing both sides by 4 gives $x = \dfrac{21}{4} = 5.25$. Either 21/4 or 5.25 can be gridded as the correct answer.

QUESTION 19

The correct answer is 2. The given expression can be rewritten as $\dfrac{2x+6}{(x+2)^2} - \dfrac{2x+4}{(x+2)^2}$, which is equivalent to $\dfrac{2x+6-2x-4}{(x+2)^2}$, or $\dfrac{2}{(x+2)^2}$. This is in the form $\dfrac{a}{(x+2)^2}$; therefore, $a = 2$.

QUESTION 20

The correct answer is 97. The intersecting lines form a triangle, and the angle with measure of $x°$ is an exterior angle of this triangle. The measure of an exterior angle of a triangle is equal to the sum of the measures of the two nonadjacent interior angles of the triangle. One of these angles has measure of 23° and the other, which is supplementary to the angle with measure 106°, has measure of 180° − 106° = 74°. Therefore, the value of x is 23 + 74 = 97.

Section 4: Math Test - Calculator

QUESTION 1

Choice D is correct. The change in the number of 3-D movies released between any two consecutive years can be found by first estimating the number of 3-D movies released for each of the two years and then finding the positive difference between these two estimates. Between 2003 and 2004, this change is approximately 2 − 2 = 0 movies; between 2008 and 2009, this change is approximately 20 − 8 = 12 movies; between 2009 and 2010, this change is approximately 26 − 20 = 6 movies; and between 2010 and 2011, this change is approximately 46 − 26 = 20 movies. Therefore, of the pairs of consecutive years in the choices, the greatest increase in the number of 3-D movies released occurred during the time period between 2010 and 2011.

Choices A, B, and C are incorrect. Between 2010 and 2011, approximately 20 more 3-D movies were released. The change in the number of 3-D movies released between any of the other pairs of consecutive years is significantly smaller than 20.

QUESTION 2

Choice C is correct. Because f is a linear function of x, the equation $f(x) = mx + b$, where m and b are constants, can be used to define the relationship between x and $f(x)$. In this equation, m represents the increase in the value of $f(x)$ for every increase in the value of x by 1. From the table, it can be determined that the value of $f(x)$ increases by 8 for every increase in the value of x by 2. In other words, for the function f the value of m is $\dfrac{8}{2}$, or 4. The value of b can be found by substituting the values of x and $f(x)$ from any row of the table and the value of m into the equation $f(x) = mx + b$ and solving for b. For example, using $x = 1$, $f(x) = 5$, and $m = 4$ yields $5 = 4(1) + b$. Solving for b yields $b = 1$. Therefore, the equation defining the function f can be written in the form $f(x) = 4x + 1$.

Choices A, B, and D are incorrect. Any equation defining the linear function f must give values of $f(x)$ for corresponding values of x, as shown in each row of the table. According to the table, if $x = 3$, $f(x) = 13$. However, substituting $x = 3$ into the equation given in choice A gives $f(3) = 2(3) + 3$, or $f(3) = 9$, not 13. Similarly, substituting $x = 3$ into the equation given in choice B gives $f(3) = 3(3) + 2$, or $f(3) = 11$, not 13. Lastly, substituting $x = 3$ into the equation given in choice D gives $f(3) = 5(3)$, or $f(3) = 15$, not 13. Therefore, the equations in choices A, B, and D cannot define f.

QUESTION 3

Choice A is correct. If 2.5 ounces of chocolate are needed for each muffin, then the number of ounces of chocolate needed to make 48 muffins is $48 \times 2.5 = 120$ ounces. Since 1 pound = 16 ounces, the number of pounds that is equivalent to 120 ounces is $\dfrac{120}{16} = 7.5$ pounds. Therefore, 7.5 pounds of chocolate are needed to make the 48 muffins.

Choice B is incorrect. If 10 pounds of chocolate were needed to make 48 muffins, then the total number of ounces of chocolate needed would be $10 \times 16 = 160$ ounces. The number of ounces of chocolate per muffin would then be $\dfrac{160}{48} = 3.33$ ounces per muffin, not 2.5 ounces per muffin. Choices C and D are also incorrect. Following the same procedures as used to test choice B gives 16.8 ounces per muffin for choice C and 40 ounces per muffin for choice D, not 2.5 ounces per muffin. Therefore, 50.5 and 120 pounds cannot be the number of pounds needed to make 48 signature chocolate muffins.

QUESTION 4

Choice B is correct. The value of $c + d$ can be found by dividing both sides of the given equation by 3. This yields $c + d = \dfrac{5}{3}$.

Choice A is incorrect. If the value of $c + d$ is $\frac{3}{5}$, then $3 \times \frac{3}{5} = 5$; however, $\frac{9}{5}$ is not equal to 5.

Choice C is incorrect. If the value of $c + d$ is 3, then $3 \times 3 = 5$; however, 9 is not equal to 5.

Choice D is incorrect. If the value of $c + d$ is 5, then $3 \times 5 = 5$; however, 15 is not equal to 5.

QUESTION 5

Choice C is correct. The weight of an object on Venus is approximately $\frac{9}{10}$ of its weight on Earth. If an object weighs 100 pounds on Earth, then the object's weight on Venus is given by $\frac{9}{10}(100)$ = 90 pounds. The same object's weight on Jupiter is approximately $\frac{23}{10}$ of its weight on Earth; therefore, the object weighs $\frac{23}{10}(100)$ = 230 pounds on Jupiter. The difference between the object's weight on Jupiter and the object's weight on Venus is 230 – 90 = 140 pounds. Therefore, an object that weighs 100 pounds on Earth weighs 140 more pounds on Jupiter than it weighs on Venus.

Choice A is incorrect because it is the weight, in pounds, of the object on Venus. Choice B is incorrect because it is the weight, in pounds, of an object on Earth if it weighs 100 pounds on Venus. Choice D is incorrect because it is the weight, in pounds, of the object on Jupiter.

QUESTION 6

Choice B is correct. Let n be the number of novels and m be the number of magazines that Sadie purchased. If Sadie purchased a total of 11 novels and magazines, then $n + m = 11$. It is given that the combined price of 11 novels and magazines is $20. Since each novel sells for $4 and each magazine sells for $1, it follows that $4n + m = 20$. So the system of equations below must hold.

$$4n + m = 20$$
$$n + m = 11$$

Subtracting side by side the second equation from the first equation yields $3n = 9$, so $n = 3$. Therefore, Sadie purchased 3 novels.

Choice A is incorrect. If 2 novels were purchased, then a total of $8 was spent on novels. That leaves $12 to be spent on magazines, which means that 12 magazines would have been purchased. However, Sadie purchased a total of 11 novels and magazines. Choices C and D are incorrect. If 4 novels were purchased, then a total of $16 was spent on novels. That leaves $4 to be spent on magazines, which means that 4 magazines would have been purchased. By the same logic, if Sadie purchased 5 novels, she would have no money at all ($0) to buy magazines. However, Sadie purchased a total of 11 novels and magazines.

QUESTION 7

Choice A is correct. The DBA plans to increase its membership by n businesses each year, so x years from now, the association plans to have increased its membership by nx businesses. Since there are already b businesses at the beginning of this year, the total number of businesses, y, the DBA plans to have as members x years from now is modeled by $y = nx + b$.

Choice B is incorrect. The equation given in choice B correctly represents the increase in membership x years from now as nx. However, the number of businesses at the beginning of the year, b, has been subtracted from this amount of increase, not added to it. Choices C and D are incorrect because they use exponential models to represent the increase in membership. Since the membership increases by n businesses each year, this situation is correctly modeled by a linear relationship.

QUESTION 8

Choice C is correct. The first expression $(1.5x - 2.4)^2$ can be rewritten as $(1.5x - 2.4)(1.5x - 2.4)$. Applying the distributive property to this product yields $(2.25x^2 - 3.6x - 3.6x + 5.76) - (5.2x^2 - 6.4)$. This difference can be rewritten as $(2.25x^2 - 3.6x - 3.6x + 5.76) + (-1)(5.2x^2 - 6.4)$. Distributing the factor of -1 through the second expression yields $2.25x^2 - 3.6x - 3.6x + 5.76 - 5.2x^2 + 6.4$. Regrouping like terms, the expression becomes $(2.25x^2 - 5.2x^2) + (-3.6x - 3.6x) + (5.76 + 6.4)$. Combining like terms yields $-2.95x^2 - 7.2x + 12.16$.

Choices A, B, and D are incorrect and likely result from errors made when applying the distributive property or combining the resulting like terms.

QUESTION 9

Choice B is correct. In 1908, the marathon was lengthened by $42 - 40 = 2$ kilometers. Since 1 mile is approximately 1.6 kilometers, the increase of 2 kilometers can be converted to miles by multiplying as shown: $2\,\text{kilometers} \times \dfrac{1\,\text{mile}}{1.6\,\text{kilometers}} = 1.25\,\text{miles}$.

Choices A, C, and D are incorrect and may result from errors made when applying the conversion rate or other computational errors.

QUESTION 10

Choice A is correct. The density d of an object can be found by dividing the mass m of the object by its volume V. Symbolically this is expressed by the equation $d = \dfrac{m}{V}$. Solving this equation for m yields $m = dV$.

Choices B, C, and D are incorrect and are likely the result of errors made when translating the definition of density into an algebraic equation and errors made when solving this equation for m. If the equations given in choices B, C, and D are each solved for density d, none of the resulting equations are equivalent to $d = \dfrac{m}{V}$.

QUESTION 11

Choice A is correct. The equation $-2x + 3y = 6$ can be rewritten in the slope-intercept form as follows: $y = \dfrac{2}{3}x + 2$. So the slope of the graph of the given equation is $\dfrac{2}{3}$. In the xy-plane, when two nonvertical lines are perpendicular, the product of their slopes is -1. So, if m is the slope of a line perpendicular to the line with equation $y = \dfrac{2}{3}x + 2$, then $m \times \dfrac{2}{3} = -1$, which yields $m = -\dfrac{3}{2}$. Of the given choices, only the equation in choice A can be rewritten in the form $y = -\dfrac{3}{2}x + b$, for some constant b. Therefore, the graph of the equation in choice A is perpendicular to the graph of the given equation.

Choices B, C, and D are incorrect because the graphs of the equations in these choices have slopes, respectively, of $-\dfrac{3}{4}$, $-\dfrac{1}{2}$, and $-\dfrac{1}{3}$, not $-\dfrac{3}{2}$.

QUESTION 12

Choice D is correct. Adding the two equations side by side eliminates y and yields $x = 6$, as shown.

$$\frac{1}{2}y = 4$$
$$x - \frac{1}{2}y = 2$$
$$\overline{\rule{0pt}{0pt}\hspace{2cm}}$$
$$x + 0 = 6$$

If (x, y) is a solution to the system, then (x, y) satisfies both equations in the system and any equation derived from them. Therefore, $x = 6$.

Choices A, B, and C are incorrect and may be the result of errors when solving the system.

QUESTION 13

Choice D is correct. Any point (x, y) that is a solution to the given system of inequalities must satisfy both inequalities in the system. Since the second inequality in the system can be rewritten as $y < x - 1$, the system is equivalent to the following system.

$$y \leq 3x + 1$$
$$y < x - 1$$

Since $3x + 1 > x - 1$ for $x > -1$ and $3x + 1 \leq x - 1$ for $x \leq -1$, it follows that $y < x - 1$ for $x > -1$ and $y \leq 3x + 1$ for $x \leq -1$. Of the given choices, only $(2, -1)$ satisfies these conditions because $-1 < 2 - 1 = 1$.

Alternate approach: Substituting $(2, -1)$ into the first inequality gives $-1 \leq 3(2) + 1$, or $-1 \leq 7$, which is a true statement. Substituting $(2, -1)$ into the second inequality gives $2 - (-1) > 1$, or $3 > 1$, which is a true statement. Therefore, since $(2, -1)$ satisfies both inequalities, it is a solution to the system.

Choice A is incorrect because substituting -2 for x and -1 for y in the first inequality gives $-1 \leq 3(-2) + 1$, or $-1 \leq -5$, which is false. Choice B is incorrect because substituting -1 for x and 3 for y in the first inequality gives $3 \leq 3(-1) + 1$, or $3 \leq -2$, which is false. Choice C is incorrect because substituting 1 for x and 5 for y in the first inequality gives $5 \leq 3(1) + 1$, or $5 \leq 4$, which is false.

QUESTION 14

Choice A is correct. According to the table, 74 orthopedic surgeons indicated that research is their major professional activity. Since a total of 607 surgeons completed the survey, it follows that the probability that the randomly selected surgeon is an orthopedic surgeon whose indicated major professional activity is research is 74 out of 607, or 74/607, which is ≈ 0.122.

Choices B, C, and D are incorrect and may be the result of finding the probability that the randomly selected surgeon is an orthopedic surgeon whose major professional activity is teaching (choice B), an orthopedic surgeon whose major professional activity is either teaching or research (choice C), or a general surgeon or orthopedic surgeon whose major professional activity is research (choice D).

QUESTION 15

Choice A is correct. Statement I need not be true. The fact that 78% of the 1,000 adults who were surveyed responded that they were satisfied with the air quality in the city does not mean that the exact same percentage of all adults in the city will be satisfied with the air quality in the city. Statement II need not be true because random samples, even when they are of the same size, are not necessarily identical with regard to percentages of people in them who have a certain opinion. Statement III need not be true for the same reason that statement II need not be true: results from different samples can vary. The variation may be even bigger for this sample since it would be selected from a different city. Therefore, none of the statements must be true.

Choices B, C, and D are incorrect because none of the statements must be true.

QUESTION 16

Choice D is correct. According to the given information, multiplying a tree species' growth factor by the tree's diameter is a method to approximate the age of the tree. Multiplying the growth factor, 4.0, of the American elm given in the table by the given diameter of 12 inches yields an approximate age of 48 years.

Choices A, B, and C are incorrect because they do not result from multiplying the given diameter of an American elm tree with that tree species' growth factor..

QUESTION 17

Choice D is correct. The growth factor of a tree species is approximated by the slope of a line of best fit that models the relationship between diameter and age. A line of best fit can be visually estimated by identifying a line that goes in the same direction of the data and where roughly half the given data points fall above and half the given data points fall below the line. Two points that fall on the line can be used to estimate the slope and y-intercept of the equation of a line of best fit. Estimating a line of best fit for the given scatterplot could give the points (11, 80) and (15, 110). Using these two points, the slope of the equation of the line of best fit can be calculated as $\frac{110-80}{15-11}$, or 7.5. The slope of the equation is interpreted as the growth factor for a species of tree. According to the table, the species of tree with a growth factor of 7.5 is shagbark hickory.

Choices A, B, and C are incorrect and likely result from errors made when estimating a line of best fit for the given scatterplot and its slope.

QUESTION 18

Choice C is correct. According to the given information, multiplying a tree species' growth factor by the tree's diameter is a method to approximate the age of the tree. A white birch with a diameter of 12 inches (or 1 foot) has a given growth factor of 5 and is approximately 60 years old. A pin oak with a diameter of 12 inches (or 1 foot) has a given growth factor of 3 and is approximately 36 years old. The diameters of the two trees 10 years from now can be found by dividing each tree's age in 10 years, 70 years, and 46 years, by its respective growth factor. This yields 14 inches and $15\frac{1}{3}$ inches. The difference between $15\frac{1}{3}$ and 14 is $1\frac{1}{3}$, or approximately 1.3 inches.

Choices A, B, and D are incorrect and a result of incorrectly calculating the diameters of the two trees in 10 years.

QUESTION 19

Choice B is correct. Triangles *ADB* and *CDB* are congruent to each other because they are both 30°-60°-90° triangles and share the side $\overline{BD}$. In triangle *ADB*, side $\overline{AD}$ is opposite to the angle 30°; therefore, the length of $\overline{AD}$ is half the length of hypotenuse $\overline{AB}$. Since the triangles are congruent, *AB* = *BC* = 12. So the length of $\overline{AD}$ is $\frac{12}{2}$ = 6.

Choice A is incorrect. If the length of $\overline{AD}$ were 4, then the length of $\overline{AB}$ would be 8. However, this is incorrect because $\overline{AB}$ is congruent to $\overline{BC}$, which has a length of 12. Choices C and D are also incorrect. Following the same procedures as used to test choice A gives $\overline{AB}$ a length of $12\sqrt{2}$ for choice C and $12\sqrt{3}$ for choice D. However, these results cannot be true because $\overline{AB}$ is congruent to $\overline{BC}$, which has a length of 12.

QUESTION 20

Choice D is correct. The graph on the right shows the change in distance from the ground of the mark on the rim over time. The y-intercept of the graph corresponds to the mark's position at the start of the motion ($t = 0$); at this moment, the mark is at its highest point from the ground. As the wheel rolls, the mark approaches the ground, its distance from the ground decreasing until it reaches 0—the point where it touches the ground. After that, the mark moves up and away from the ground, its distance from the ground increasing until it reaches its maximum height from the ground. This is the moment when the wheel has completed a full rotation. The remaining part of the graph shows the distance of the mark from the ground during the second rotation of the wheel. Therefore, of the given choices, only choice D is in agreement with the given information.

Choice A is incorrect because the speed at which the wheel is rolling does not change over time, meaning the graph representing the speed would be a horizontal line. Choice B is incorrect because the distance of the wheel from its starting point to its ending point increases continuously; the graph shows a quantity that changes periodically over time, alternately decreasing and increasing. Choice C is incorrect because the distance of the mark from the center of the wheel is constant and equals the radius of the wheel. The graph representing this distance would be a horizontal line, not the curved line of the graph shown.

QUESTION 21

Choice A is correct. The equation can be rewritten as $1 - \dfrac{b}{a} = c$, or equivalently $1 - c = \dfrac{b}{a}$. Since a < 0 and b > 0, it follows that $\dfrac{b}{a} < 0$, and so $1 - c < 0$, or equivalently $c > 1$.

Choice B is incorrect. If $c = 1$, then $a - b = a$, or $b = 0$. But it is given that $b > 0$, so $c = 1$ cannot be true. Choice C is incorrect. If $c = -1$, then $a - b = -a$, or $2a = b$. But this equation contradicts the premise that $a < 0$ and $b > 0$, so $c = -1$ cannot be true. Choice D is incorrect. For example, if $c = -2$, then $a - b = -2a$, or $3a = b$. But this contradicts the fact that a and b have opposite signs, so $c < -1$ cannot be true.

QUESTION 22

Choice C is correct. It is given that 34.6% of 26 students in Mr. Camp's class reported that they had at least two siblings. Since 34.6% of 26 is 8.996, there must have been 9 students in the class who reported having at least two siblings and 17 students who reported that they had fewer than two siblings. It is also given that the average eighth-grade class size in the state is 26 and that Mr. Camp's class is representative of all eighth-grade classes in the state. This means that in each eighth-grade class in the state there are about 17 students who have fewer than two siblings. Therefore, the best estimate of the number of eighth-grade students in the state who have fewer than two siblings is 17 × (number of eighth-grade classes in the state), or 17 × 1,800 = 30,600.

Choice A is incorrect because 16,200 is the best estimate for the number of eighth-grade students in the state who have at least, not fewer than, two siblings. Choice B is incorrect because 23,400 is half of the estimated total number of eighth-grade students in the state; however, since the students in Mr. Camp's class are representative of students in the eighth-grade classes in the state and more than half of the students in Mr. Camp's class have fewer than two siblings, more than half of the students in each eighth-grade class in the state have fewer than two siblings, too. Choice D is incorrect because 46,800 is the estimated total number of eighth-grade students in the state.

QUESTION 23

Choice D is correct. The linear function that represents the relationship will be in the form $r(p)$ = $ap + b$, where a and b are constants and $r(p)$ is the monthly rental price, in dollars, of a property that was purchased with p thousands of dollars. According to the table, (70, 515) and (450, 3,365) are ordered pairs that should satisfy the function, which leads to the system of equations below.

$$\begin{cases} 70a + b = 515 \\ 450a + b = 3,365 \end{cases}$$

Subtracting side by side the first equation from the second eliminates b and gives $380a = 2,850$; solving for a gives $a = \dfrac{2,850}{380} = 7.5$. Substituting 7.5 for a in the first equation of the system gives $525 + b = 515$; solving for b gives $b = -10$. Therefore, the linear function that represents the relationship is $r(p) = 7.5p - 10$.

Choices A, B, and C are incorrect because the coefficient of p, or the rate at which the rental price, in dollars, increases for every thousand-dollar increase of the purchase price is different from what is suggested by these choices. For example, the Glenview Street property was purchased for $140,000, but the rental price that each of the functions in these choices provides is significantly off from the rental price given in the table, $1,040.

QUESTION 24

Choice B is correct. Let x be the original price, in dollars, of the Glenview Street property. After the 40% discount, the price of the property became $0.6x$ dollars, and after the additional 20% off the discounted price, the price of the property became $0.8(0.6x)$. Thus, in terms of the original price of the property, x, the purchase price of the property is $0.48x$. It follows that $0.48x$ = 140,000. Solving this equation for x gives $x = 291,666.\overline{6}$. Therefore, of the given choices, $291,700 best approximates the original price of the Glenview Street property.

Choice A is incorrect because it is the result of dividing the purchase price of the property by 0.4, as though the purchase price were 40% of the original price. Choice C is incorrect because it is the closest to dividing the purchase price of the property by 0.6, as though the purchase price were 60% of the original price. Choice D is incorrect because it is the result of dividing the purchase price of the property by 0.8, as though the purchase price were 80% of the original price.

QUESTION 25

Choice D is correct. Of the first 150 participants, 36 chose the first picture in the set, and of the 150 remaining participants, p chose the first picture in the set. Hence, the proportion of the participants who chose the first picture in the set is $\dfrac{36 + p}{300}$. Since more than 20% of all the participants chose the first picture, it follows that $\dfrac{36 + p}{300} > 0.20$. This inequality can be rewritten as $p + 36 > 0.20(300)$. Since p is a number of people among the remaining 150 participants, $p \le 150$.

Choices A, B, and C are incorrect and may be the result of some incorrect interpretations of the given information or of computational errors.

QUESTION 26

Choice B is correct. A cube has 6 faces of equal area, so if the total surface area of a cube is $6\left(\dfrac{a}{4}\right)^2$, then the area of one face is $\left(\dfrac{a}{4}\right)^2$. Likewise, the area of one face of a cube is the square of one of its sides; therefore, if the area of one face is $\left(\dfrac{a}{4}\right)^2$, then the length of one side of the cube is $\dfrac{a}{4}$. Since the perimeter of one face of a cube is four times the length of one side, the perimeter is $4\left(\dfrac{a}{4}\right) = a$.

Choice A is incorrect because if the perimeter of one face of the cube is $\dfrac{a}{4}$, then the total surface area of the cube is $6\left(\dfrac{\frac{a}{4}}{4}\right)^2 = 6\left(\dfrac{a}{16}\right)^2$, which is not $6\left(\dfrac{a}{4}\right)^2$. Choice C is incorrect because if the perimeter of one face of the cube is $4a$, then the total surface area of the cube is $6\left(\dfrac{4a}{4}\right)^2 = 6a^2$, which is not $6\left(\dfrac{a}{4}\right)^2$. Choice D is incorrect because if the perimeter of one face of the cube is $6a$, then the total surface area of the cube is $6\left(\dfrac{6a}{4}\right)^2 = 6\left(\dfrac{3a}{2}\right)^2$, which is not $6\left(\dfrac{a}{4}\right)^2$.

QUESTION 27

Choice C is correct. If the mean score of 8 players is 14.5, then the total of all 8 scores is 14.5 × 8 = 116. If the mean of 7 scores is 12, then the total of all 7 scores is 12 × 7 = 84. Since the set of 7 scores was made by removing the highest score of the set of 8 scores, then the difference between the total of all 8 scores and the total of all 7 scores is equal to the removed score: 116 − 84 = 32.

Choice A is incorrect because if 20 is removed from the group of 8 scores, then the mean score of the remaining 7 players is $\frac{(14.5 \cdot 8) - 20}{7} \approx 13.71$, not 12. Choice B is incorrect because if 24 is removed from the group of 8 scores, then the mean score of the remaining 7 players is $\frac{(14.5 \cdot 8) - 24}{7} \approx 13.14$, not 12. Choice D is incorrect because if 36 is removed from the group of 8 scores, then the mean score of the remaining 7 players is $\frac{(14.5 \cdot 8) - 36}{7} \approx 11.43$, not 12.

QUESTION 28

Choice C is correct. The slope of a line is $\frac{\text{rise}}{\text{run}}$ and can be calculated using the coordinates of any two points on the line. For example, the graph of f passes through the points (0, 3) and (2, 4), so the slope of the graph of f is $\frac{4-3}{2-0} = \frac{1}{2}$. The slope of the graph of function g is 4 times the slope of the graph of f, so the slope of the graph of g is $4\left(\frac{1}{2}\right) = 2$. Since the point (0, −4) is the y-intercept of g, g is defined as $g(x) = 2x - 4$. It follows that $g(9) = 2(9) - 4 = 14$.

Choice A is incorrect because if $g(9) = 5$, then the slope of the graph of function g is $\frac{-4-5}{0-9} = 1$, which is not 4 times the slope of the graph of f. Choices B and D are also incorrect. The same procedures used to test choice A yields $\frac{-4-9}{0-9} = \frac{13}{9}$ and $\frac{-4-18}{0-9} = \frac{22}{9}$ for the slope of the graph of g for choices B and D, respectively. Neither of these slopes is 4 times the slope of the graph of f.

QUESTION 29

Choice B is correct. The standard equation of a circle in the xy-plane is of the form $(x - h)^2 + (y - k)^2 = r^2$, where (h, k) are the coordinates of the center of the circle and r is the radius. To convert the given equation to the standard form, complete the squares. The first two terms need a 100 to complete the square, and the second two terms need a 64. Adding 100 and 64 to both sides of the given equation yields $(x^2 + 20x + 100) + (y^2 + 16y + 64) = -20 + 100 + 64$, which is equivalent to $(x + 10)^2 + (y + 8)^2 = 144$. Therefore, the coordinates of the center of the circle are (−10, −8).

Choice A is incorrect and is likely the result of not properly dividing when attempting to complete the square. Choice C is incorrect and is likely the result of making a sign error when evaluating the coordinates of the center. Choice D is incorrect and is likely the result of not properly dividing when attempting to complete the square and making a sign error when evaluating the coordinates of the center.

QUESTION 30

Choice B is correct. The given equation can be thought of as the difference of two squares, where one square is x^2 and the other square is $\left(\sqrt{a}\right)^2$. Using the difference of squares formula, the equation can be rewritten as $y = \left(x + \sqrt{a}\right)\left(x - \sqrt{a}\right)$.

Choices A, C, and D are incorrect because they are not equivalent to the given equation. Choice A is incorrect because it is equivalent to $y = x^2 - a^2$. Choice C is incorrect because it is equivalent to $y = x^2 - \dfrac{a^2}{4}$. Choice D is incorrect because it is equivalent to $y = x^2 + 2ax + a^2$.

QUESTION 31

The correct answer is 1492. Let x be the number of watts that is equal to 2 horsepower. Since 5 horsepower is equal to 3730 watts, it follows that $\dfrac{2}{5} = \dfrac{x}{3730}$. Solving this proportion for x yields $5x = 7460$, or $x = \dfrac{7460}{5} = 1492$.

QUESTION 32

The correct answer is $\dfrac{29}{3}$. It is given that the height of the original painting is 29 inches and the reproduction's height is $\dfrac{1}{3}$ the original height. One-third of 29 is $\dfrac{29}{3}$, or $9.\overline{6}$. Either the fraction 29/3 or the decimals 9.66 or 9.67 can be gridded as the correct answer.

QUESTION 33

The correct answer is 7. It is given that $PQ = RS$, and the diagram shows that $PQ = x − 1$ and $RS = 3x − 7$. Therefore, the equation $x − 1 = 3x − 7$ must be true. Solving this equation for x leads to

2x = 6, so x = 3. The length of segment *PS* is the sum of the lengths of *PQ*, *QR*, and *RS*, which is (*x* − 1) + *x* + (3*x* − 7), or equivalently 5*x* − 8. Substituting 3 for *x* in this expression gives 5(3) − 8 = 7.

QUESTION 34

The correct answer is 9. Since the point (2, 5) lies on the graph of *y* = *f*(*x*) in the *xy*-plane, the ordered pair (2, 5) must satisfy the equation *y* = *f*(*x*). That is, 5 = *f*(2), or $5 = k - 2^2$. This equation simplifies to 5 = *k* − 4. Therefore, the value of the constant *k* is 9.

QUESTION 35

The correct answer is 13. Let *w* represent the width of the rectangular garden, in feet. Since the length of the garden will be 5 feet longer than the width of the garden, the length of the garden will be *w* + 5 feet. Thus the area of the garden will be *w*(*w* + 5). It is also given that the area of the garden will be 104 square feet. Therefore, *w*(*w* + 5) = 104, which is equivalent to $w^2 + 5w - 104 = 0$. The quadratic formula can be used or the equation above can be factored to result in (*w* + 13)(*w* − 8) = 0. Therefore, *w* = 8 and *w* = −13. Because width cannot be negative, the width of the garden must be 8 feet. This means the length of the garden must be 8 + 5 = 13 feet.

QUESTION 36

The correct answer is 80. The measure of an angle inscribed in a circle is half the measure of the central angle that intercepts the same arc. That is, $\text{m}ÐA = \dfrac{x°}{2}$. Also, the sum of the interior angles of quadrilateral *ABCP* is 360°, and the measure of the obtuse angle *P* is 360° − *x*°. Hence, $\dfrac{x°}{2} + 20° + (360° - x°) + 20° = 360°$. Simplifying this equation gives $\dfrac{x°}{2} = 40°$, and so *x* = 80.

Alternate approach: If points *A* and *P* are joined, then the triangles that will be formed, *APB* and *APC*, are isosceles because *PA* = *PB* = *PC*. It follows that the base angles on both triangles each have measure of 20°. Angle *A* consists of two base angles, and therefore, $\text{m}\angle A = 40°$. Since the measure of an angle inscribed in a circle is half the measure of the central angle that intercepts the same arc, it follows that the value of *x* is 80°.

QUESTION 37

The correct answer is 43.5, 43, or 44. The distance from Ms. Simon's home to her workplace is 0.6 + 15.4 + 1.4 = 17.4 miles. Ms. Simon took 24 minutes to drive this distance. Since there are 60 minutes in one hour, her average speed, in miles per hour, for this trip is $\dfrac{17.4}{24} \times 60$ = 43.5 miles per hour. Based on the directions, 87/2 or 43.5 can be gridded as the correct answer. We are accepting 43 and 44 as additional correct answers because the precision of the measurements provided does not support an answer with three significant digits.

QUESTION 38

The correct answer is 6. Ms. Simon travels 15.4 miles on the freeway, and her average speed for this portion of the trip is 50 miles per hour when there is no traffic delay. Therefore, when there is no traffic delay, Ms. Simon spends $\dfrac{15.4\,\text{miles}}{50\,\text{mph}} = 0.308$ hours on the freeway. Since there are 60 minutes in one hour, she spends $(0.308)(60) = 18.48$ minutes on the freeway when there is no delay. Leaving at 7:00 a.m. results in a trip that is 33% longer, and 33% of 18.48 minutes is 6.16; the travel time for each of the other two segments does not change. Therefore, rounded to the nearest minute, it takes Ms. Simon 6 more minutes to drive to her workplace when she leaves at 7:00 a.m.

CollegeBoard

Answer Explanations
SAT® Practice Test #6

5MSA05

Answer Explanations

SAT Practice Test #6

Section 1: Reading Test

QUESTION 1

Choice C is the best answer. In the first paragraph the reader is introduced to Nawab, a father of twelve daughters who feels compelled to make more money to care for his family: "he must proliferate his sources of revenue" (lines 6-7). The remainder of the paragraph focuses on the way Nawab attempts to "proliferate" those income sources by identifying some of the moneymaking schemes Nawab undertakes, including setting up a flour mill and a fish farm and attempting to fix both radios and watches.

Choice A is incorrect because even if the first paragraph does indicate that Nawab is willing to work hard to take care of his family, it does not specifically address how he interacts with his daughters emotionally. Choice B is incorrect because the first paragraph describes some of Nawab's activities but not the specifics of his schedule. Choice D is incorrect because the first paragraph introduces Harouni as Nawab's employer but does not describe his lifestyle.

QUESTION 2

Choice B is the best answer. The passage states that Nawab earned "more kicks than kudos" (line 16) for his failed attempts at fixing watches. In the context of not doing a job well, this means Nawab was not given compliments ("kudos") for his efforts but complaints ("kicks") about them.

Choices A and D are incorrect because the passage clearly states that Nawab was not successful fixing watches, which earned him a negative response ("kicks," or complaints). In this context it would be illogical to suggest that Nawab's unsuccessful efforts at fixing watches would result in the sort of positive response implied by choice A ("thrills") or choice D ("interests"). Choice C is incorrect because even though "jolts" might be unpleasant, they're not the kind of negative response one would get instead of compliments.

QUESTION 3

Choice D is the best answer. The passage states that Nawab works "like an engineer tending the boilers on a foundering steamer in an Atlantic gale" (lines 26-28) in his attempts to keep his employer comfortable. The author likely uses this image because it highlights the challenging nature of Nawab's work—work that is described in the next sentence as requiring "superhuman efforts" (line 28).

Choices A, B, and C are incorrect because the author's use of the image of an engineer working hard on a "foundering steamer" describes the effort Nawab is making in keeping his employer comfortable, not what Nawab might be dreaming about, anything to do with tube wells (which are not mentioned in the second paragraph), or that Nawab has had many different jobs in his life.

QUESTION 4

Choice A is the best answer because lines 28-32 show that Nawab is an efficient employee, stating that due to his "superhuman efforts," Nawab is able to keep his employer comfortable, or in almost "the same mechanical cocoon . . . that the landowner enjoyed in Lahore."

Choice B is incorrect because lines 40-42 describe the actions of Nawab's employer only and do not address the employer's feelings about Nawab's work. Choice C is incorrect because lines 46-49 show Nawab characterizing himself as an old and ineffective employee, not one who performs his job well. Choice D is incorrect because line 58 addresses the fact Nawab had always lived in his employer's household but not his effectiveness as an employee.

QUESTION 5

Choice C is the best answer. The main purpose of Nawab's comments in lines 43-52 is to highlight the labor and service he has provided for Harouni over the years. Nawab says "there is but one man, me, your servant" to take care of the tube wells on all Harouni's vast lands and that the extensive work has resulted in Nawab earning gray hairs on his employer's behalf.

Choice A is incorrect because even though lines 43-52 initially highlight the vastness of Harouni's lands, those lines primarily focus on Nawab's dedication and service to Harouni. Choice B is incorrect because lines 43-52 emphasize not that Nawab is competent and reliable but that Nawab feels he is no longer able to adequately fulfill his duties. Choice D is incorrect because in lines 43-52, Nawab doesn't say he intends to quit his job, asking instead only for help doing it.

QUESTION 6

Choice D is the best answer. In lines 61-62, Nawab says to his employer that he "cannot any longer bicycle about like a bridegroom from farm to farm." In this context, Nawab uses the word "bridegroom" to imply he is no longer a young man who can easily travel such great distances on his bike.

Choices A, B, and C are incorrect because in the context of Nawab not being able to bike so far, he uses the word "bridegroom" to imply that he is no longer young, not that he is no longer in love (choice A), naive (choice B), or busy (choice C).

QUESTION 7

Choice B is the best answer. Harouni's reaction to Nawab's request for a new motorcycle can be found in lines 66-68, where the employer is said not to "particularly care one way or the other, except that it touched on his comfort—a matter of great interest to him." For Harouni, in other words, the issue of Nawab getting a new motorcycle came down to what was best for Harouni, not what was best for Nawab.

Choice A is incorrect because in the passage Harouni is said not to be particularly impressed with how hard Nawab works; he cares about the issue of the motorcycle only in regard to its effect on his own comfort. Choice C is incorrect because Harouni is said to find Nawab's speech not eloquent but "florid" (line 54), meaning flamboyant or ostentatious. Choice D is incorrect because Nawab does not threaten to quit his job but politely asks his employer to "let me go" (line 64).

QUESTION 8

Choice B is the best answer. The previous question asks why Harouni purchases his employee Nawab a new motorcycle, with the correct answer (that Harouni did so because it was in his own best interest) supported in lines 66-68: "He didn't particularly care one way or the other, except that it touched on his comfort—a matter of great interest to him."

Choices A, C, and D are incorrect because the lines cited do not support the answer to the previous question about why Harouni buys Nawab a new motorcycle. Instead, they simply identify the issue (choice A), note that Harouni also gave Nawab money for gas (choice C), and show how the motorcycle affects Nawab's side businesses (choice D).

QUESTION 9

Choice A is the best answer. The passage states that Nawab's new motorcycle leads to the "disgust of the farm managers" (line 74).

Choices B, C, and D are incorrect because the passage specifically says Nawab's new motorcycle leads to the "disgust of the farm managers," not their happiness (choice B), envy (choice C), or indifference (choice D).

QUESTION 10

Choice D is the best answer. The passage specifically states what Nawab considers the greatest part of his getting a new motorcycle: "Best of all, now he could spend every night with his wife" (lines 81-82).

Choices A, B, and C are incorrect because the passage explicitly states that Nawab believes the best thing about his new motorcycle is that he can "spend every night with his wife," not that people start calling him "Uncle" (choice A), that he is able to expand his business (choice B), or that he is able to educate his daughters (choice C).

QUESTION 11

Choice B is the best answer. The passage states that historically, "newspapers such as *The Times* and broadcasters such as the BBC were widely regarded as the trusted shapers of authoritative agendas and conventional wisdom" (lines 27-30). But it goes on to say that "there is a growing feeling . . . that the news media should be 'informative rather than authoritative'" (lines 70-73). Together these lines indicate the main purpose of the passage, which is to discuss how people's perception of the news media is changing from its being an authoritative voice to simply an informative one.

Choice A is incorrect because the passage deals with changes in the way news is perceived but does not primarily focus on the technological changes that may have resulted in those or other changes. Choice C is incorrect because even if the passage implies that viewers might increasingly believe a journalist's values can affect the news stories being produced, it does not provide specific examples of that happening. Choice D is incorrect because the passage begins with the simple sentence "The news is a form of public knowledge" (line 1) and makes no attempt to refute that claim.

QUESTION 12

Choice D is the best answer. Although the passage initially states that traditional news authorities were once implicitly "trusted" (line 29) regarding the content they produced, it goes on to note that "as part of the general process of the transformation of authority . . . the demand has been for all authority to make explicit the frames of value which determine their decisions" (lines 33-38). The modern audience, in other words, wants to hear not only the stories a news organization produces but also the values that form the foundation of that organization's beliefs.

Choices A, B, and C are incorrect because lines 33-38 make clear that the expectation traditional authorities now face is the need to "make explicit the frames of value which determine their decisions," not that they shouldn't be affected by commercial interests (choice A), that they should work for the common good (choice B), or that they should consider the context of public versus private knowledge (choice C).

QUESTION 13

Choice C is the best answer. The previous question asks what expectation traditional authorities now face, with the answer being that they must make their perspectives or beliefs clear to the audience. This is supported in lines 33-38: "As part of the general process of the transformation of authority . . . the demand has been for all authority to make explicit the frames of value which determine their decisions."

Choices A, B, and D are incorrect because the lines cited do not support the answer to the previous question about what expectation traditional authorities now face, instead contrasting private and public knowledge (choice A), explaining the complexity of news dissemination (choice B), and providing one way news has changed in modern times (choice D).

QUESTION 14

Choice C is the best answer. In lines 23-25, the passage states that "there is not always common agreement about what the public needs to know." In this context, a "common" agreement is a widespread one shared by many people.

Choices A, B, and D are incorrect because in the context of something shared by many people, the word "common" implies that it is widespread, not that it is plentiful or abundant (choice A), recognizable to others (choice B), or normal (choice D).

QUESTION 15

Choice B is the best answer. Two quotes are provided in lines 43-53, one highlighting the way editors work differently in modern times due to the demands of the audience and one offering an opinion about the perceived negative effects of that new reality of news. Those extended quotations were added by the authors most likely because they provide concrete examples of how some journalists feel about modern news dissemination.

Choice A is incorrect because the two quotations provided in lines 43-53 are not contradictory: the first offers a description of how news editors work differently in modern times, and the second describes how certain changes might affect news stories or the audience. Choices C and D are incorrect because the two quotations illustrate how some feel about the way the dissemination of news might be changing and are not used to either criticize or make suggestions.

QUESTION 16

Choice A is the best answer. The passage explains that although the major news organizations were once considered "trusted shapers" (line 29) of public knowledge, that perception is changing due to the "growing feeling . . . that the news media should be 'informative rather than authoritative'; the job of journalists should be to 'give the news as raw as it is, without putting their slant on it'; and people should be given 'sufficient information' from which 'we would be able to form opinions of our own'" (lines 70-77). In other words, the audience now wants raw facts about the world, not facts constructed in support of a certain opinion.

Choice B is incorrect because the passage presents the public as wanting information without any slant on it, not as wanting only a limited amount of information. Choices C and D are incorrect because the passage does not specifically identify the public's feelings about including quotations from authorities in news stories or how they would want journalists to handle private details that the subjects of news stories do not want revealed.

QUESTION 17

Choice D is the best answer. The previous question asks what the public is beginning to believe should be avoided in news stories, with the answer being the personal opinions or feelings of journalists. This is supported in lines 70-77: "There is a growing feeling . . . that the news media should be 'informative rather than authoritative'; the job of journalists should be to 'give the news as raw as it is, without putting their slant on it'; and people should be given 'sufficient information' from which 'we would be able to form opinions of our own.'"

Choices A, B, and C are incorrect because the lines cited do not support the answer that the modern public wants journalists to avoid personal judgments when telling news stories, instead contrasting personal or private knowledge with public knowledge (choice A), characterizing how trusted broadcasters were once viewed (choice B), and explaining how some professional journalists feel about the new reality of the news (choice C).

QUESTION 18

Choice A is the best answer. In lines 73-75, the passage states the modern belief that "the job of journalists should be to 'give the news as raw as it is, without putting their slant on it.'" In this context, the word "raw" means unfiltered or in its most basic state.

Choices B, C, and D are incorrect because in the context of news without any "slant on it," the word "raw" implies something unfiltered, not something unprotected or uncovered (choice B), severe (choice C), or untried or unproven (choice D).

QUESTION 19

Choice A is the best answer. The table shows that in 1985, 55% of respondents believed news organizations "get the facts straight," which was the highest percentage for that choice for any of the years provided.

Choices B, C, and D are incorrect because the table shows that the percentage of respondents who believed news organizations "get the facts straight" was smaller in 1992 (49%), 2003 (36%), and 2011 (25%) than in 1985 (55%).

QUESTION 20

Choice C is the best answer. The table shows that from 2003 to 2007, the percentage of people who believed news organizations "get the facts straight" rose only minimally, from 36 to 39%, while their perception of the independence and fairness of those organizations changed not at all, remaining at 23% and 26%, respectively.

Choice A is incorrect because the table indicates viewers' perceptions of the accuracy of news organizations but does not identify how many inaccurate news stories there were in any of the years listed. Choice B is incorrect because the number of people who believe news organizations "tend to favor one side" did not double between 1992 and 2003, rising only from 63% to 66%. Choice D is incorrect because the table shows that between 2007 and 2011, people's perception of the accuracy of news organizations decreased rather than increased, dropping from 39% to 25%.

QUESTION 21

Choice C is the best answer. The 2011 data in the table indicate that only 25% of respondents believed news organizations were accurate, 15% believed they were independent, and 16% believed they were fair. Combined, these data support the idea put forth in lines 69-70 that modern audiences are becoming skeptical of the authority of experts.

Choices A, B, and D are incorrect because the 2011 data in the table show the public's lack of faith in the accuracy, independence, and fairness of news organizations but do not indicate how politically involved that public was (choice A), demonstrate the claims of experts (choice B), or reveal the importance of viewer mouse clicks in modern news (choice D).

QUESTION 22

Choice B is the best answer. The first paragraph of the passage identifies and describes "Texas gourd vines" (line 1), but the primary focus of the passage is introduced in the first sentence of the second paragraph: "In one recent study, Nina Theis and Lynn Adler took on the specific problem of the Texas gourd—how to attract enough pollinators but not too many beetles" (lines 17-20). The remainder of the passage focuses on describing the purpose, process, and results of the recent research done on those Texas gourd vines.

Choice A is incorrect because the passage doesn't focus on the assumptions behind a theory but rather on the way in which that theory was tested. Choice C is incorrect because the passage does not present much conflicting data; most of it supports the idea there can be too much fragrance for the Texas gourd vine. Choice D is incorrect because the passage explains the procedures used in a study were "'very labor intensive'" (line 58) but does not present them as particularly innovative.

QUESTION 23

Choice A is the best answer. The passage says that to test their hypothesis, the scientists "planted 168 Texas gourd vines in an Iowa field" (lines 33-34) and then ultimately walked "from flower to flower, observing each for two-minute intervals" (lines 62-63). Because they gathered data by looking at and studying the plants in question, the scientists' research is best characterized as relying on direct observation.

Choices B, C, and D are incorrect because lines 62-63 make clear that the research emphasized direct observation, not historical data (choice B), expert testimony (choice C), or random sampling (choice D).

QUESTION 24

Choice D is the best answer. The passage states that by using the smell of their nectar to lure pollinators like bees, Texas gourd vines are employing an "'open communication network'" that attracts "'not just the good guys, but . . . also . . . the bad guys'" (lines 7-10). Because cucumber beetles are then identified as some of "the very bad guys" (line 12) as far as the Texas gourd plant is concerned, it can be inferred that both the beetles and the bees are attracted to the same scent.

Choices A and C are incorrect because they are not supported by the text; the passage states that cucumber beetles "chew up pollen and petals" (lines 12-13) from the Texas gourd vines but not that those vines are their "primary" food source, and the passage does not address any effects, positive or negative, that cucumber beetles experience as a result of carrying bacterial wilt disease. Choice B is incorrect because the passage states that treating the Texas gourd vines with dimethoxybenzene led to "double the normal number of beetles" (lines 65-66) but that pollinators like bees "did not prefer" (line 67) the treated flowers, which implies that cucumber beetles are not less attracted but more attracted to dimethoxybenzene than honey bees are.

QUESTION 25

Choice C is the best answer. The author indicates that it is reasonable to think that the Texas gourd plants might lure more pollinators if their smell was stronger. This is clear from lines 26-27, which state that "intuition suggests that more of that aroma should be even more appealing to bees."

Choices A and D are incorrect because lines 26-27 support the idea that it was initially thought that Texas gourd vines could lure more pollinators through "more of that aroma," not by lacking an aroma (choice A) or giving off a more varied aroma (choice D). Choice B is incorrect because bees are the only pollinators specifically discussed in the passage, and there is no suggestion that targeting other insects would attract more bees.

QUESTION 26

Choice A is the best answer. The passage explains that as part of their research the scientists "made half the plants more fragrant by tucking dimethoxybenzene-treated swabs deep inside their flowers. Each treated flower emitted about 45 times more fragrance than a normal one" (lines 35-39). In this context, a flower that was "treated" would be one that was changed or altered.

Choices B, C, and D are incorrect because in the context of a flower having a compound like dimethoxybenzene added to it, the word "treated" means changed or altered, not returned to normal (choice B), given (choice C), or kept for future use (choice D).

QUESTION 27

Choice D is the best answer. In the passage Theis surmises that honey bees were likely repelled not by the enhanced fragrance of the dimethoxybenzene-treated flowers but "by the abundance of beetles" (lines 71-72) found on them. She was able to make that assumption because the honey bees were able to choose between both normal flowers and fragrance-enhanced flowers without any beetles on them, because one of the parameters of the research was that "every half hour throughout the experiments, the team plucked all the beetles off of half the fragrance-enhanced flowers and half the control flowers, allowing bees to respond to the blossoms with and without interference by beetles" (lines 45-50).

Choice A is incorrect because the passage states only that the scientists observed the bees and beetles on the flowers as soon as they opened (lines 59-61), not both before and after they opened. Choice B is incorrect because although the passage does state that the experiment only took place during the "August flowering season" (line 35), it doesn't state that this was a variable in the experiment or had any effect on it. Choice C is incorrect because comparing gourds based on the type of pollination is not related to the issue of what repelled bees from the fragrance-enhanced plants.

QUESTION 28

Choice A is the best answer. The previous question asks what Theis and Adler did to allow Theis to theorize that the bees were repelled not by the enhanced fragrance of certain flowers but by the excessive number of beetles on them, with the answer (they give the bees the chance to visit both normal and fragrance-enhanced flowers that did not have beetles on them) being supported in lines 45-50: "So every half hour throughout the experiments, the team plucked all the beetles off of half the fragrance-enhanced flowers and half the control flowers, allowing bees to respond to the blossoms with and without interference by beetles."

Choices B, C, and D are incorrect because the lines cited do not support the answer to the previous question about what allowed Theis and Adler to theorize that the bees were repelled not by fragrance but by insects, instead highlighting a variable that didn't directly address the effect of fragrance on bees (choice B), describing the timing of one of the steps undertaken in the experiment (choice C), and discussing an aspect of gourd growth that was not related to the question of why bees may or may not have wanted to visit fragrance-enhanced flowers (choice D).

QUESTION 29

Choice A is the best answer. The first six paragraphs (lines 1-64) of the passage introduce a plant (the Texas gourd vine) and its problem (luring enough insects to pollinate it but not too many of those that will harm it) and then describe a study undertaken to deal with "the specific problem of the Texas gourd—how to attract enough pollinators but not too many beetles" (lines 18-20). After the specifics of that experiment are described in detail, the results are explained and summarized in the seventh and eighth paragraphs (lines 65-84): "What they saw was double the normal number of beetles. . . . Squash bees were indifferent, and honey bees visited enhanced flowers less often. . . . That added up to less reproduction for fragrance-enhanced flowers" (lines 65-76).

Choice B is incorrect because Theis and Adler's hypothesis (that more fragrance would make the flowers "even more appealing to bees," line 27) is found in the third paragraph (lines 26-40). Choice C is incorrect because Theis and Adler's methods are described in the third through sixth paragraphs (lines 26-64), not the seventh and eighth (lines 65-84). Choice D is incorrect because the seventh and eighth paragraphs detail the results in an experiment but do not focus on the researchers' reasoning.

QUESTION 30

Choice B is the best answer. To be "indifferent" is to be apathetic, or without care or concern. In the context of an experiment that tested whether or not insects preferred normally scented flowers or ones with enhanced fragrance, describing the squash bees as "indifferent" implies they did not care about the scents and were equally drawn to both types of flowers.

Choice A is incorrect because "indifference" suggests the amount of concern one has about something but not anything to do with physical capabilities (such as being able to distinguish between the flowers). Choice C is incorrect because "indifference" suggests that one has no preference. Choice D is incorrect because the squash bees are said to be "indifferent" to certain flowers based on their fragrance, not on the number of beetles that may or may not be on them.

QUESTION 31

Choice B is the best answer. Theis and Adler's research clearly provided an answer to the question of why there is an upper limit on the intensity of the aroma emitted by Texas gourd plants, as their experiment was described as being able to "provide a reason that Texas gourd plants never evolved to produce a stronger scent" (lines 85-86).

Choice A is incorrect because Theis and Adler's research was not able to show how to increase pollinator visits to the Texas gourd vine, as the results of their experiment showed that "pollinators, to their surprise, did not prefer the highly scented flowers" (lines 67-68). Choice C is incorrect because Theis and Adler's research was not able to explain how hand pollination rescued fruit weight, a finding the passage describes as "a hard-to-interpret result" (line 83). Choice D is incorrect because the passage never indicates that the flowers stop producing fragrance when beetles are present.

QUESTION 32

Choice D is the best answer. The previous question asks what question from among the answer choices Theis and Adler's research was able to answer regarding Texas gourd vines. The answer (they determined why there was an upper limit to the amount of fragrance produced) is supported in lines 85-86: "The new results provide a reason that Texas gourd plants never evolved to produce a stronger scent."

Choices A, B, and C are incorrect because the lines cited do not support the answer to the previous question about what Theis and Adler's research revealed about Texas gourd vines, instead explaining the goal of the experiment undertaken (choice A), identifying some of the fragrance compounds found in the plant's aroma (choice B), and describing results related to hand pollination rather than fragrance (choice C).

QUESTION 33

Choice B is the best answer. In Passage 1, Lincoln asserts that citizens of the United States should never break the laws of their land, for any reason, because to do so undermines the nation's values. This is clearly demonstrated when he says, "let every man remember that to violate the law, is to trample on the blood of his father, and to tear the character of his own, and his children's liberty" (lines 9-12).

Choice A is incorrect because Lincoln says that bad laws "should be repealed as soon as possible" (line 30), not that breaking the law would slow their repeals. Choice C is incorrect because Lincoln says that "there is no grievance that is a fit object of redress by mob law" (lines 36-37) but doesn't argue that breaking the law will lead to mob rule. Choice D is incorrect because in his speech Lincoln doesn't discuss divisions between social groups.

QUESTION 34

Choice A is the best answer. The previous question asks what Lincoln believes is the result of breaking the laws, with the answer being that such actions undermine a nation's values. This is supported in lines 9-12: "let every man remember that to violate the law, is to trample on the blood of his father, and to tear the character of his own, and his children's liberty."

Choices B, C, and D are incorrect because the lines cited do not support the answer to the previous question regarding what Lincoln contends happens when citizens break the law, instead explaining exactly which groups Lincoln believes should vow to follow the laws (choice B), illustrating how Lincoln believes unjust laws should be dealt with (choice C), and stating Lincoln's belief that no law is ever improved through mob rule (choice D).

QUESTION 35

Choice D is the best answer. In lines 24-25, Lincoln says, "I so pressingly urge a strict observance of all the laws." In this context, the word "urge" most nearly means advocate, because when Lincoln urges people to obey the laws, he is pleading in favor of them doing so.

Choices A and C are incorrect because in the context of lines 24-25 ("I so pressingly urge a strict observance of all the laws"), to urge that laws be followed is to advocate for them to be obeyed, not to speed up such adherence (choice A) or make such adherence necessary (choice C). Choice B is incorrect because Lincoln is asking people to follow the laws but not directly causing people to obey them.

QUESTION 36

Choice D is the best answer. After advocating for citizens "never to violate in the least particular, the laws of the country" (lines 3-4), Lincoln begins the second paragraph by making another point: "When I so pressingly urge a strict observance of all the laws, let me not be understood as saying there are no bad laws, nor that grievances may not arise, for the redress of which, no legal provisions have been made" (lines 24-28). This sentence is an attempt on Lincoln's part to make clear what could be a misunderstanding of his position ("let me not be understood") and to correct that possible misunderstanding. Lincoln doesn't want people to believe he is saying all laws are always good, but rather that those laws need to be followed as long as they are on the books.

Choices A and B are incorrect because the sentence in lines 24-28 does not raise and refute a possible counterargument to Lincoln's argument or identify a shortcoming of his argument, but rather it is an attempt on Lincoln's part to make sure he is not misunderstood. Choice C is incorrect because that sentence does not acknowledge and provide support for a central assumption of Lincoln's argument but looks at a different aspect of the issue.

QUESTION 37

Choice A is the best answer. In the passage Lincoln states his belief that any laws that "continue in force, for the sake of example, they should be religiously observed" (lines 31-32). In this context, "observed" most nearly means followed, as Lincoln is urging citizens to heed or follow the country's laws.

Choices B, C, and D are incorrect because in the context of Lincoln advocating that laws be religiously "observed," he means those laws should be followed, not that they should be studied closely (choice B), considered at length (choice C), or merely recognized (choice D).

QUESTION 38

Choice D is the best answer. Passage 2 begins with Thoreau's statement that "unjust laws exist" (line 45). His philosophy regarding how to deal with those unjust laws is evident in lines 58-59: "If the injustice is part of the necessary friction of the machine of government, let it go, let it go." Thoreau believes, in other words, that some injustices are an unfortunate part of normal governance and just need to be endured ("let it go, let it go").

Choice A is incorrect because Thoreau does not say some unjust aspects of government can be fixed easily or that they are merely superficial. Choice B is incorrect because Thoreau does not argue that such injustices are subtle and should be studied, but rather that in certain cases it is best to "let it go, let it go" (line 59), while in other cases one should act or "break the law" (line 66). Choice C is incorrect because Thoreau does not say that any such unjust aspects of government are beneficial or helpful.

QUESTION 39

Choice C is the best answer. The previous question asks what Thoreau feels about some unjust aspects of government, with the answer being that he finds them inevitable and something that needs to be endured. This is supported in lines 58-59: "If the injustice is part of the necessary friction of the machine of government, let it go, let it go."

Choices A, B, and D are incorrect because the lines cited do not support the answer to the previous question about Thoreau's thoughts regarding certain injustices in government, instead asking a theoretical question about how one should respond to unjust laws (choice A), providing an observation about how some view acting out against unjust laws (choice B), and acknowledging that in some questions of conscience, one may or may not choose to act (choice D).

QUESTION 40

Choice C is the best answer. In Passage 1, Lincoln makes clear his belief that individuals should always heed the laws: "Let every American . . . swear . . . never to violate in the least particular, the laws of the country" (lines 1-4). Even bad laws, he states, "while they continue in force, for the sake of example, they should be religiously observed" (lines 30-32). In Passage 2, Thoreau is less rigid in his beliefs regarding the need for individuals to heed the laws of the country, arguing at times that some laws should be broken: "but if it is of such a nature that it requires you to be the agent of injustice to another, then, I say, break the law" (lines 64-66). While Lincoln and Thoreau can therefore be said to disagree about the moral imperative to follow existing laws, both passages advance an opinion regarding the need to follow or not follow all of the country's laws.

Choice A is incorrect because the passages are not making arguments about differences between legal duties and moral imperatives but rather are addressing the need to follow (or not) the laws of a land. Choice B is incorrect. Both passages address the question of changing existing laws in the United States, but that is only a minor part of what is a greater debate about the need to follow or not follow existing laws. Choice D is incorrect because neither passage addresses the standards for determining whether or not laws are just, only whether laws should be heeded or not.

QUESTION 41

Choice B is the best answer. In Passage 2, Thoreau says that if a law "is of such a nature that it requires you to be the agent of injustice to another, then, I say, break the law" (lines 64-66). It is clear from Passage 1 that Lincoln would reject this stance, as he says individuals should never break the law ("Let every American . . . swear . . . never to violate in the least particular, the laws of the country," lines 1-4) and should wait for a bad law to be repealed ("bad laws, if they exist, should be repealed . . . still while they continue . . . they should be religiously observed," lines 29-32).

Choices A and C are incorrect because in Passage 1, Lincoln is absolutely clear that all laws "should be religiously observed" (line 32); he does not describe anyone's suggestion to break the law as either excusable (choice A) or honorable (choice C). Choice D is incorrect because it is not supported by the passage, as Lincoln does not discuss the core principles of the Constitution in Passage 1.

QUESTION 42

Choice D is the best answer. In Passage 1, Lincoln uses abolitionism solely as an example to illustrate the argument he is making about heeding the law: "In any case that arises, as for instance, the promulgation of abolitionism, one of two positions is necessarily true" (lines 37-39). In Passage 2, Thoreau does the same thing by noting that "those who call themselves Abolitionists should at once effectually withdraw their support . . . from the government" (lines 79-82). Although Lincoln and Thoreau use the cause of abolitionism to argue different points, a commonality they share is that neither embraces the cause personally in the passage; Lincoln simply uses it as an example ("as for instance") while Thoreau specifically talks of *other people* "who call themselves Abolitionists."

Choice A is incorrect because in Passage 1, Lincoln argues against drastic action, saying that even in the case of abolitionism, such a response is not "necessary, justifiable, or excusable" (line 44). Choice B is incorrect because it's not accurate to say abolitionism was central to the arguments, only that each used that subject as an example. Choice C is incorrect because neither Lincoln nor Thoreau offers an opinion about whether or not abolitionism will gain widespread acceptance, instead they incorporate it only as an example in their discussions of just and unjust laws.

QUESTION 43

Choice C is the best answer. In lines 10-17, the passage illustrates how the cost of solar energy has dropped in recent years: "A few years ago, silicon solar panels cost $4 per watt. . . . 'Now it's down to something like 50 cents a watt, and there's talk of hitting 36 cents per watt.'" In lines 44-47, the passage describes some of the new technology that exists in the field: "Meanwhile, researchers at the National Renewable Energy Laboratory have made flexible solar cells on a new type of glass from Corning called Willow Glass, which is thin and can be rolled up." Overall, the passage can be regarded as an objective overview of the solar panel industry delivered by a journalist covering the field.

Choices A and D are incorrect because the author does not present himself as either a consumer who plans to buy solar panels or a hobbyist with a personal interest in solar panel technology. Rather, the author focuses on developments in solar technology. Choice B is incorrect because the passage does not discuss research methods used in the solar panel field but rather the technologies that exist in the field.

QUESTION 44

Choice A is the best answer. In the context of describing the solar panel manufacturing industry as being "in the doldrums because supply far exceeds demand" (lines 2-3), saying it is currently a "poor" market implies it is a weak, or slow, market.

Choices B, C, and D are incorrect because in the context of describing the solar panel manufacturing industry as being "in the doldrums," saying it is a poor market implies it is a weak market, not a modest one (choice B), a pathetic one (choice C), or an outdated one (choice D).

QUESTION 45

Choice C is the best answer. It can reasonably be inferred that much of the solar panel industry believes current solar technology is too expensive and inefficient because the passage states that the industry has been working to improve those two things: "All parts of the silicon solar panel industry have been looking for ways to cut costs and improve the power output of solar panels, and that's led to steady cost reductions" (lines 27-30).

Choice A is incorrect because the passage explains how solar panels work but never states or implies that consumers do not understand the technology. Choice B is incorrect because while the passage explains how two-sided solar cells can increase solar electric output, it does not suggest that they have any existing or possible weaknesses. Choice D is incorrect because the passage characterizes Willow Glass as entirely promising and doesn't imply that it is not efficient enough to be marketed.

QUESTION 46

Choice D is the best answer. The previous question asks what can be inferred from the passage about beliefs in the solar panel industry, with the answer being that many in the industry believe current solar technology is too expensive and too inefficient. This is supported in lines 27-30: "All parts of the silicon solar panel industry have been looking for ways to cut costs and improve the power output of solar panels, and that's led to steady cost reductions."

Choices A, B, and C are incorrect because the lines cited do not support the answer to the previous question, which is that much of the solar panel industry believes current solar technology is too expensive and inefficient. Choice A highlights the industry's current limited sales. Choice B addresses the high cost of solar panels but not their inefficiency. Choice C addresses a potential decrease in the cost of solar panels and does not mention efficiency.

QUESTION 47

Choice B is the best answer. The passage clearly states how two-sided solar panels will increase the efficiency of solar electricity units, explaining that they will be able to absorb excess reflected light, especially if those panels are built on sand: "That light reflects onto the back of the panels and could be harvested to increase the power output" (lines 61-62).

Choices A, C, and D are incorrect because the passage explains only that two-sided solar panels can raise efficiency by harvesting reflected light, not that they can raise efficiency because they take little energy to operate (choice A), are cost-effective (choice C), or keep sunlight from reaching the ground (choice D).

QUESTION 48

Choice B is the best answer. The previous question asks how two-sided solar panels can raise the efficiency of solar electricity units, with the answer being they can increase solar power input by catching excess reflected light. This is supported in lines 61-62: "That light reflects onto the back of the panels and could be harvested to increase the power output."

Choices A, C, and D are incorrect because the lines cited do not support the answer to the previous question about how two-sided solar panels can raise the efficiency of solar electricity units, instead highlighting that some sunlight is missed by current units (choice A), explaining why two-sided solar panels work well in sand (choice C), and projecting how much more effective those two-sided solar panels could be (choice D).

QUESTION 49

Choice D is the best answer. In lines 69-71, the passage states that "even longer-term, Green is betting on silicon, aiming to take advantage of the huge reductions in cost already seen with the technology." In this context, the phrase "betting on" most nearly means "optimistic about," as the sentence implies that Green has positive expectations for silicon use now and in the future.

Choice A is incorrect because "dabbling in" a subject implies being only minimally involved with it, but in lines 69-71, Green is shown to be committed to silicon use. Choice B is incorrect because in this context the phrase "betting on" is figurative and implies believing in something, not actually being involved with games of chance. Choice C is incorrect because Green is said to want to "take advantage" of silicon use, meaning he does not intend to switch from it.

QUESTION 50

Choice B is the best answer. The passage concludes by stating that "the challenge is to produce good connections between these semiconductors, something made challenging by the arrangement of silicon atoms in crystalline silicon" (lines 81-84). As this last sentence identifies an issue the solar panel industry still faces, and describes it as a "challenging" one at that, it mainly serves to identify a problem or hurdle that must be dealt with by the industry.

Choices A, C, and D are incorrect because the main point of the passage's last sentence is that there is a "challenge" or hurdle that the solar panel industry has to deal with; it doesn't express concerns about what a material won't be able to do (choice A), make predictions (choice C), or introduce a new idea for study (choice D).

QUESTION 51

Choice D is the best answer. Figure 2 shows that in 2009, the US average electricity cost per megawatt-hour (MWh) was $120. Of the projected 2017 energy costs for fuels listed in figure 1, the one closest to the 2009 US average electricity cost 120 dollars per megawatt-hour is the projected cost of advanced nuclear energy, estimated at just below 125 dollars per megawatt-hour.

Choices A, B, and C are incorrect because figure 1 shows the projected energy costs of natural gas, wind (onshore), and conventional coal as just below 75 dollars per megawatt-hour, 100 dollars per megawatt-hour, and approximately 105 dollars per megawatt-hour, respectively. None of these costs is as close to the 2009 US average electricity cost of 120 dollars per megawatt-hour as the projected 2017 cost of advanced nuclear energy, which is just below 125 dollars per megawatt-hour.

QUESTION 52

Choice B is the best answer. Figure 2 shows that the dropping cost of solar photovoltaic power per megawatt-hour is projected to intersect with the 2009 US average electricity cost of 120 dollars per megawatt-hour in the year 2020.

Choice A is incorrect because figure 2 projects that the solar photovoltaic cost per megawatt-hour in 2018 will be approximately $140, which is more than the 2009 US average electricity cost of 120 dollars per megawatt-hour. Choices C and D are incorrect because figure 2 projects that the solar photovoltaic cost per megawatt-hour will be around $90 in 2025 and $70 in 2027, both of which are less than the 2009 US average electricity cost of 120 dollars per megawatt-hour.

Section 2: Writing Test

QUESTION 1

Choice D is the best answer because a comma is needed to separate the main independent clause ("In the winter . . . Lake 227") from the dependent clause that describes the lake. The pronoun "one" is used correctly to refer to its antecedent "Lake 227."

Choice A is incorrect because it creates a comma splice (two independent clauses joined by only a comma). Choices B and C are incorrect because in both choices the information that follows the period is not in the form of a complete sentence.

QUESTION 2

Choice A is the best answer because the comma is used correctly to separate the introductory dependent clause ("While . . . irresponsible") from the independent clause that follows it.

Choices B, C, and D are incorrect because the comma in each is misplaced. Choices B and D lack a comma where one is needed after the dependent clause ("While . . . irresponsible"). In choice C, while a comma is provided after "irresponsible," there is an unnecessary comma after "and."

QUESTION 3

Choice D is the best answer because it most clearly and concisely combines the sentences using the correct punctuation. This choice eliminates unnecessary words, and the commas are placed correctly between the clauses.

Choice A is incorrect because the phrase "the result being that it" is wordy and could be replaced with the single word "which." Choice B is incorrect because the words "algal blooms cause oxygen depletion" need not be repeated. Choice C is incorrect because there is unnecessary repetition of the words "oxygen depletion" and "algal blooms."

QUESTION 4

Choice B is the best answer because the colon is used properly to introduce an independent clause ("it was . . . Erie") that explains or elaborates on the information that came before in the sentence.

Choice A is incorrect because the colon is misplaced. It should be placed after the word "green," not after "with." Choice C is incorrect because the dash is not placed correctly. If it were placed after the word "green," it could be used. Choice D is incorrect because the comma creates a comma splice. A comma cannot be used without a conjunction to join two independent clauses.

QUESTION 5

Choice C is the best answer because it contains the best transition between the two paragraphs. The previous paragraphs describe an experiment that Schindler and Brunskill conducted in Lake 227. This paragraph is about an experiment they performed in Lake 226. Only choice C provides a transition that introduces the new experiment performed in Lake 226.

Choice A is incorrect because it contains no specific reference to the previous paragraph and is too general to be tied to this paragraph. Choices B and D are incorrect because they contain unnecessary details that do not connect the ideas in the paragraphs.

QUESTION 6

Choice B is the best answer because it is concise. It does not repeat the idea of addition.

Choices A, C, and D are incorrect because they are repetitive. The conjunction "and" is sufficient after "they added just nitrates" to indicate that "a source of carbon" was also added. Choice A needlessly contains "was added." In choice C "plus also" and in choice D "also adding" are similarly repetitive.

QUESTION 7

Choice A is the best answer because the singular past tense verb "was teeming" agrees in number with the singular subject "half" and is consistent with the other past tense verbs in the paragraph.

Choices B and C are incorrect because they contain plural verbs instead of the singular one that is needed to agree with the singular subject "half." Choice D is incorrect because it contains a present tense verb that is inconsistent with the past tense verbs in the paragraph.

QUESTION 8

Choice C is the best answer because the verb "published" most effectively indicates the relationship between research findings and a journal, *Science*. Scientific research is published in scientific journals.

Choices A, B, and D are incorrect because they don't feature the specific vocabulary required, and the tone of the answer choices is too informal for the content of the passage.

QUESTION 9

Choice D is the best answer because "subsequently" logically indicates that after the research demonstrated a clear correlation between the growth of blue-green algae and the introduction of phosphates into the water, Canadian legislators passed laws banning phosphates in laundry detergent.

Choices A, B, and C are incorrect because the transitional phrase "for example" and the conjunctive adverbs "similarly" and "however" do not indicate a logical relationship between what the research demonstrated and what the Canadian legislators did with that knowledge.

QUESTION 10

Choice B is the best answer because it deals with a "policy outcome" related to the research. The adoption of legislation to reduce or eliminate phosphates in detergents is a policy outcome (a change in official policy concerning detergents) that was clearly informed by Schindler and Brunskill's research.

Choices A, C, and D are incorrect because they do not mention legislation or policies that were adopted as a result of Schindler and Brunskill's research on the effects of phosphates in laundry detergents.

QUESTION 11

Choice C is the best answer because it offers a counterargument to the previous sentence's claim in favor of "experiments like these." Acknowledging that "scientists should not be allowed to randomly perform experiments on just any body of water" shows that the writer is aware of the potential problems with these experiments.

Choices A, B, and D are incorrect because none of them offers a counterargument. They all make factual statements.

QUESTION 12

Choice D is the best answer because it correctly provides the plural noun "stages" and the singular possessive pronoun "its" (no apostrophe).

Choices A and C are incorrect because a possessive pronoun is needed to replace the proper noun "Tower of Pisa," not the contraction "it's." Choices B and C are incorrect because there is no reason to make "stage" possessive; nothing belongs to it.

QUESTION 13

Choice A is the best answer because the conjunctive adverb "indeed" appropriately points back to and elaborates on the fact provided in the previous sentence (that the Tower has been leaning from the very beginning).

Choices B, C, and D are incorrect because they do not accurately present the relationship between the first and second sentences. Choice B, "therefore," indicates that what follows is a consequence of what came before. Choice C, "nevertheless," and choice D, "however," suggest that what follows contrasts with what was stated previously.

QUESTION 14

Choice B is the best answer because the participle "attracting" introduces a dependent clause ("attracting . . . world") that appropriately modifies the noun "icon."

Choice A is incorrect because it creates a comma splice. A comma cannot be used without a conjunction to separate two independent clauses. Choice C is incorrect because the possessive pronoun "its" makes no sense in the context of the sentence. Choice D is incorrect because a semicolon is used to join two independent clauses, not an independent and a dependent clause.

QUESTION 15

Choice C is the best answer because it would be appropriate to characterize a famous and unusual building like the Tower of Pisa as "one of the greatest architectural oddities in the world."

Choices A, B, and D are incorrect. The words "weirdnesses," "deviations," and "abnormalities" would all result in inappropriate characterizations. The Tower is a beloved icon and tourist magnet; as such, it is more fitting to describe it as an architectural oddity than as an architectural weirdness, architectural deviation, or architectural abnormality.

QUESTION 16

Choice B is the best answer because it confirms that the sentence should be added and provides the appropriate reason: it establishes a key shift in the passage between the introduction of the tower and the discussion of recent attempts to save it.

Choice A is incorrect because the suggested sentence does not repeat a previous idea. Choices C and D are incorrect because the sentence should be added. The suggested sentence does not contain irrelevant information that interrupts the flow of the paragraph, nor does it repeat information.

QUESTION 17

Choice A is the best answer because the comma is used correctly after the prepositional phrase "in 1990" to introduce the independent clause "Italy's government closed the tower. . . ."

Choices B and C are incorrect because each places a comma between the subject "government" and the verb "closed." Choice D is incorrect because a comma can be used, but not a colon, after an introductory prepositional phrase.

QUESTION 18

Choice C is the best answer because it supports the main point of the paragraph. The paragraph suggests that the committee's goal was to maintain the tower's "aesthetic" by reducing (but not eliminating) the tilt without ruining the tower's appearance or causing it to fall.

Choices A, B, and D are incorrect because none of the choices supports the main point of the paragraph—the need to both keep the tower from falling and maintain its charming appearance. Choice A repeats an idea from earlier in the passage. Choices B and D provide information that is only loosely related to the paragraph's discussion of efforts to save the tower.

QUESTION 19

Choice D is the best answer because deleting "he is" eliminates the comma splice that exists in the original sentence. Two independent clauses cannot be joined by only a comma.

Choice A is incorrect because two independent clauses cannot be joined by only a comma. Choice B is incorrect because it creates a comma splice and also needlessly repeats Burland's name. Choice C is incorrect because "his being" is unnecessary and unidiomatic in this context.

QUESTION 20

Choice D is the best answer because the earlier phrase "a years-long process" is sufficient to indicate that Burland's work spanned several years.

Choices A, B, and C are incorrect because they all repeat information provided in the earlier phrase "a years-long process."

QUESTION 21

Choice A is the best answer because the verb "advocated" and the participle "using" are appropriate in this context: "advocated" functions as the main verb and "using" introduces the clause that tells what Burland advocated.

Choices B and C are incorrect because they are unidiomatic. Choice D doesn't provide a main verb necessary to create an independent clause before the semicolon.

QUESTION 22

Choice A is the best answer because sentence 5 introduces Burland's plan for using gravity to straighten the tower—a plan that is presented in detail in the subsequent sentences 2, 3, and 4.

Choices B and C are incorrect because if sentence 5 were to be placed after either sentence 2 or sentence 3, the sequencing and logic of the paragraph would be impaired. Choice D is incorrect because if sentence 5 were to be deleted, a key aspect of the plan—its use of gravity to straighten the tower—would never be mentioned. The reader would then have to infer what Burland was doing by "drilling out small amounts of soil from under the tower."

QUESTION 23

Choice B is the best answer because the main point of the paragraph is that the supply of physicians in the United States is not expected to keep up with the demand or need for them in the future. Choice B introduces the idea that it may become increasingly difficult for Americans to find a physician.

Choice A is not correct because it discusses "paramedics," health care workers who are not mentioned elsewhere in the paragraph. Choice C is incorrect because it does not introduce the doctor shortage problem that is the main topic of the paragraph. Choice D is incorrect because the paragraph is not focused on the costs of health care.

QUESTION 24

Choice A is the best answer because "keep pace" is an appropriate idiomatic expression that clearly indicates the writer's concern that the supply of doctors won't be able to match the growing demand for them.

Choices B, C, and D are incorrect because they are unidiomatic in the context of the sentence. The sentence discusses the mismatch between the "increased demand for care" and the limited "supply of physicians." The writer is concerned with the extent to which supply can grow to meet the growth in demand—or, in other words, "keep pace" with increased demand. The phrases "maintain the tempo," "get in line," and "move along" are inappropriate to convey this idea.

QUESTION 25

Choice B is the best answer because "bolstering" means supporting, which is appropriate in the context of "medical-college enrollments." It makes sense in a discussion of a doctor shortage to mention the idea of providing support for enrollments—that is, maintaining and perhaps increasing the numbers of students enrolled in medical colleges.

Choices A and D are incorrect because they are excessively casual and unclear in context: it is not clear what it would mean for "medical-college enrollments" (the numbers of students enrolled in medical colleges) to be amped or revved up. Choice C is incorrect because it would be inappropriate to describe enrollments as being aroused.

QUESTION 26

Choice B is the best answer because it provides an appropriate reason for adding the sentence. In context, the sentence sets up the "several factors" that follow in the paragraph: the services that a PA can provide, the monetary advantages associated with employing a PA, and the short training period required for becoming a PA.

Choice A is incorrect because the sentence does not introduce a counterargument; rather, it supports the claim made in the previous sentence. Choices C and D are incorrect because the sentence should be added.

QUESTION 27

Choice C is the best answer because the plural possessive pronoun "their" correctly refers to its plural antecedent "PAs."

Choice A is incorrect because the word "there" does not show possession and does not make sense in the context of the sentence. Choice B is incorrect because the contraction "they're" does not show possession and does not make sense in the context of the sentence. Choice D is incorrect because the singular pronoun phrase "his or her" does not agree in number with the plural antecedent "PAs."

QUESTION 28

Choice D is the best answer because the comma is used correctly to separate the items in the list of jobs that PAs can perform.

Choice A is incorrect because a colon should not be used to separate items in a list. Choice B is incorrect because, while semicolons may be used to separate items in a list, they must be used consistently (that is, after "conditions" as well as after "surgeries"). Choice C is incorrect because a comma should not be used after the conjunction "and" in a list of items.

QUESTION 29

Choice B is the best answer because the parentheses are used correctly to enclose information that is interesting but not essential to the sentence. If the parenthetical information were to be deleted, the sentence would still make sense.

Choice A is incorrect because a comma or other punctuation is necessary to separate "well compensated" from the nonessential clause "earning in 2012 a median annual salary of $90,930." Choice C is incorrect because a comma is necessary after "$90,930" to set off the clause from the rest of the sentence. Choice D is incorrect because a colon is typically preceded by an independent clause and because a nonessential clause should be set off from the sentence by matching punctuation, such as two commas or parentheses.

QUESTION 30

Choice C is the best answer because "that for" agrees with the singular antecedent "period" and compares two similar things: the training period for PAs and that (the training period) for physicians.

Choice A is incorrect because the plural pronoun "those" doesn't agree with the singular antecedent "period." Choice B is incorrect because "compared with" repeats the idea of comparison already provided in the word "shorter." Choice D is incorrect because the underlined portion cannot be deleted without eliminating a necessary element in the comparison. A "training period" can't be compared to "physicians."

QUESTION 31

Choice A is the best answer because the transitional phrase "in addition" correctly introduces another example of PAs' "extraordinary contribution to rural health care."

Choices B, C, and D are incorrect because they do not convey the appropriate relationship between ideas. In choice B, "Thus" does not make sense because the claim that PAs "provide a broader spectrum of such services" is not a result or consequence of the claim that they provide "cost-efficient, widely appreciated services." Choices C and D, "despite this" and "on the other hand," incorrectly indicate that the claim about the "broader spectrum of such services" is in contrast to the previous claim rather than in addition to it.

QUESTION 32

Choice C is the best answer because it gives an appropriate explanation for why the sentence should not be added. While relevant, the sentence does not accurately interpret the data in the table, which indicates that the number of physicians in 2025 will be 216,000 and the number of physician assistants will be 42,000.

Choices A and B are incorrect because the sentence incorrectly interprets the data in the table and should not be added. Choice D is incorrect because the sentence contains false information, not irrelevant information.

QUESTION 33

Choice D is the best answer because the word "patients" correctly identifies the people served by PAs. Additionally, the comparative conjunction "than" is used correctly in the comparison introduced by the adverb "more."

Choices A and B are incorrect because the noun "patience" refers to a human quality of tolerance or perseverance. It cannot be used to refer to people served by PAs. Choice C is incorrect because the word "then" refers to a time sequence or tells when something happened.

QUESTION 34

Choice B is the best answer because it most effectively combines the underlined sentences. The introductory dependent clause clearly and concisely sets up the comparison between the "rebooting" of films and the reworking of comic books. It also provides a clear and logical referent for the phrase "This practice" in the second sentence.

Choices A, C, and D are incorrect because the combinations do not connect the two sentences logically and concisely to demonstrate the comparison between the "rebooting" of films and the reworking of comic books. In addition, none provides a clear and logical referent for the phrase "This practice" in the second sentence.

QUESTION 35

Choice B is the best answer because the adjective "old" is used appropriately to describe a longstanding practice.

Choices A and D, "elderly" and "geriatric," are incorrect in this context because they are generally used to refer to people, not to a practice. Choice C, "mature," is incorrect because it does not fit the context of the sentence, which is about a longstanding practice, not a fully developed one.

QUESTION 36

Choice D is the best answer because no punctuation is needed to set off the prepositional phrase "of publishers."

Choices A and B are incorrect because neither a colon nor a comma is needed to separate the noun "example" from the prepositional phrase that describes it. Choice C is incorrect because no comma is needed to separate the noun "publishers" from the participle "responding" that describes it.

QUESTION 37

Choice A is the best answer because the phrase "lift a car over his head" is consistent with the other examples of Superman's superhuman physical abilities: "hurdle skyscrapers," "leap an eighth of a mile," etc.

Choices B, C, and D are incorrect because they are inconsistent with the other examples in the sentence of Superman's superhuman physical abilities. Holding a job, wearing a costume, and living in a city describe the original Superman but do not characterize his physical abilities.

QUESTION 38

Choice D is the best answer because it most effectively sets up the following sentences, which describe the "realistic" nature of superheroes in the Silver Age. According to these sentences, Silver Age superheroes dealt with everyday problems and had richer interior lives and more complex motivations than their Golden Age counterparts.

Choices A, B, and C are incorrect because neither "scientific experiments gone wrong," conservatism in the United States in the 1950s, nor the influence of science fiction on comics is addressed in the following two sentences.

QUESTION 39

Choice D is the best answer because it uses punctuation correctly. Because there is a dash between "them" and the verb "had," another dash is required before "Spider-Man" to set off the nonessential clause "Spider-Man, the Fantastic Four, and the Hulk among them." A nonessential clause should be set off from the sentence by matching punctuation, such as two dashes or commas.

Choice A is incorrect because a colon needs to be preceded by an independent clause. Choice B is incorrect because, when used in this way, a semicolon needs to be preceded and followed by independent clauses. Choice C is incorrect because a comma and a dash cannot be used to enclose a nonessential clause. Two dashes or two commas should be used instead.

QUESTION 40

Choice C is the best answer because, as the only choice that focuses on Silver Age characters ("the upstarts"), it most logically completes the discussion of the Silver Age. It also provides an effective transition to the next paragraph: by indicating that "the Silver Age drew to a close," it sets up the next paragraph's discussion of the Bronze and other ages.

Choices A and D are incorrect because each focuses on Golden Age characters and thus fails to logically complete the discussion of the Silver Age. Choice B is incorrect because it prematurely discusses a topic that would be better addressed in the next paragraph.

QUESTION 41

Choice A is the best answer because the present perfect verb "have yielded" is used correctly to indicate that the action of the sentence began in the past and is ongoing in the present. In this case, the transformation of comics from the Silver Age to subsequent ages began in the past and continues today.

Choice B is incorrect because the verb "would have yielded" indicates that an action was possible but never happened. Choice C is incorrect because the past tense verb "were yielding" indicates that the action happened and ended in the past. Choice D is incorrect because the verb "will yield" means that the action will happen in the future, which is not necessarily true.

QUESTION 42

Choice D is the best answer because the possessive plural noun "Comics'" and adjective "superhero" appropriately indicate that the "superhero line" is a feature of the comics.

Choices A, B, and C are incorrect because the possessive singular noun "superhero's" is not correctly used in the sentence. Nothing belongs to a singular "superhero" in the sentence. Furthermore, in choice B, the singular possessive noun "Comic's" is used incorrectly since more than one comic is being referred to. In choice C, "Comics" is plural, but it needs to be possessive, too.

QUESTION 43

Choice A is the best answer because the conjunctive adverb "then" correctly shows that given previously stated information, the conclusion that can be drawn is that the transition between the Golden and Silver Ages of comic books was more successful than others.

Choices B, C, and D are incorrect because they do not indicate the correct relationship between the information presented earlier and conclusions that can be drawn from the information. "However," "nevertheless," and "yet" are ordinarily used to indicate that in spite of some action, a different or unexpected result occurs.

QUESTION 44

Choice C is the best answer because the singular pronoun "that" agrees in number with its singular antecedent "transition."

Choices A and B are incorrect because the plural pronouns "those" and "these" do not agree with the singular antecedent "transition." Additionally, choice B is incorrect because "these" implies that whatever is being referred to is at hand, not in the past. Choice D is incorrect because a pronoun is needed to complete the comparison of transitions between comic book ages.

Section 3: Math Test - No Calculator

QUESTION 1

Choice B is correct. The total amount T, in dollars, Salim will pay for n tickets is given by $T = 15n + 12$, which consists of both a per-ticket charge and a one-time service fee. Since n represents the number of tickets that Salim purchases, it follows that $15n$ represents the price, in dollars, of n tickets. Therefore, 15 must represent the per-ticket charge. At the same time, no matter how many tickets Salim purchases, he will be charged the $12 fee only once. Therefore, 12 must represent the amount of the service fee, in dollars.

Choice A is incorrect. Since n represents the total number of tickets that Salim purchases, it follows that $15n$ represents the price, in dollars, of n tickets, excluding the service fee. Therefore, 15, not 12, must represent the price of 1 ticket. Choice C is incorrect. If Salim purchases only 1 ticket, the total amount, in dollars, Salim will pay can be found by substituting $n = 1$ into the equation for T. If $n = 1$, $T = 15(1) + 12 = 27$. Therefore, the total amount Salim will pay for one ticket is $27, not $12. Choice D is incorrect. The total amount, in dollars, Salim will pay for *n* tickets is given by $15n + 12$. The value 12 represents only a portion of this total amount. Therefore, the value 12 does not represent the total amount, in dollars, for any number of tickets.

QUESTION 2

Choice B is correct. Since Fertilizer A contains 60% filler materials by weight, it follows that *x* pounds of Fertilizer A consists of $0.6x$ pounds of filler materials. Similarly, *y* pounds of Fertilizer B consists of $0.4y$ pounds of filler materials. When *x* pounds of Fertilizer A and *y* pounds of Fertilizer B are combined, the result is 240 pounds of filler materials. Therefore, the total amount, in pounds, of filler materials in a mixture of *x* pounds of Fertilizer A and *y* pounds of Fertilizer B can be expressed as $0.6x + 0.4y = 240$.

Choice A is incorrect. This choice transposes the percentages of filler materials for Fertilizer A and Fertilizer B. Fertilizer A consists of $0.6x$ pounds of filler materials and Fertilizer B consists of $0.4y$ pounds of filler materials. Therefore, $0.6x + 0.4y$ is equal to 240, not $0.4x + 0.6y$. Choice C is incorrect. This choice incorrectly represents how to take the percentage of a value mathematically. Fertilizer A consists of $0.6x$ pounds of filler materials, not $60x$ pounds of filler materials, and Fertilizer B consists of $0.4y$ pounds of filler materials, not $40y$ pounds of filler materials. Choice D is incorrect. This choice transposes the percentages of filler materials for Fertilizer A and Fertilizer B and incorrectly represents how to take the percentage of a value mathematically.

QUESTION 3

Choice C is correct. For a complex number written in the form $a + bi$, *a* is called the real part of the complex number and *b* is called the imaginary part. The sum of two complex numbers, $a + bi$ and $c + di$, is found by adding real parts and imaginary parts, respectively; that is, $(a + bi) + (c + di) = (a + c) + (b + d)i$. Therefore, the sum of $2 + 3i$ and $4 + 8i$ is $(2 + 4) + (3 + 8)i = 6 + 11i$.

Choice A is incorrect and is the result of disregarding *i* and adding all parts of the two complex numbers together, $2 + 3 + 4 + 8 = 17$. Choice B is incorrect and is the result of adding all parts of the two complex numbers together and multiplying the sum by *i*. Choice D is incorrect and is the result of multiplying the real parts and imaginary parts of the two complex numbers, $(2)(4) = 8$ and $(3)(8) = 24$, instead of adding those parts together.

QUESTION 4

Choice A is correct. The right side of the equation can be multiplied using the distributive property: $(px + t)(px - t) = p^2x^2 - ptx + ptx - t^2$. Combining like terms gives $p^2x^2 - t^2$. Substituting this expression for the right side of the equation gives $4x^2 - 9 = p^2x^2 - t^2$, where *p* and *t* are constants. This equation is true for all values of x only when $4 = p^2$ and $9 = t^2$. If $4 = p^2$, then $p = 2$ or $p = -2$. Therefore, of the given answer choices, only 2 could be the value of p.

Choices B, C, and D are incorrect. For the equation to be true for all values of x, the coefficients of x^2 on both sides of the equation must be equal; that is, $4 = p^2$. Therefore, the value of p cannot be 3, 4, or 9.

QUESTION 5

Choice D is correct. In the xy-plane, the graph of the equation $y = mx + b$, where m and b are constants, is a line with slope m and y-intercept $(0, b)$. Therefore, the graph of $y = 2x - 5$ in the xy-plane is a line with slope 2 and a y-intercept $(0, -5)$. Having a slope of 2 means that for each increase in x by 1, the value of y increases by 2. Only the graph in choice D has a slope of 2 and crosses the y-axis at $(0, -5)$. Therefore, the graph shown in choice D must be the correct answer.

Choices A, B, and C are incorrect. The graph of $y = 2x - 5$ in the xy-plane is a line with slope 2 and a y-intercept at $(0, -5)$. The graph in choice A crosses the y-axis at the point $(0, 2.5)$, not $(0, -5)$, and it has a slope of $\frac{1}{2}$, not 2. The graph in choice B crosses the y-axis at $(0, -5)$; however, the slope of this line is -2, not 2. The graph in choice C has a slope of 2; however, the graph crosses the y-axis at $(0, 5)$, not $(0, -5)$.

QUESTION 6

Choice A is correct. Substituting the given value of $y = 18$ into the equation $x = \frac{2}{3}y$ yields $x = \left(\frac{2}{3}\right)(18)$, or $x = 12$. The value of the expression $2x - 3$ when $x = 12$ is $2(12) - 3 = 21$.

Choice B is incorrect. If $2x - 3 = 15$, then adding 3 to both sides of the equation and then dividing both sides of the equation by 2 yields $x = 9$. Substituting 9 for x and 18 for y into the equation $x = \frac{2}{3}y$ yields $9 = \frac{2}{3}18 = 12$, which is false. Therefore, the value of $2x - 3$ cannot be 15. Choices C and D are also incorrect. As with choice B, assuming the value of $2x - 3$ is 12 or 10 will lead to a false statement.

QUESTION 7

Choice C is correct. By properties of multiplication, the formula $n = 7\ell h$ can be rewritten as $n = (7h)\ell$. To solve for ℓ in terms of n and h, divide both sides of the equation by the factor $7h$.

Solving this equation for ℓ gives $\ell = \dfrac{n}{7h}$.

Choices A, B, and D are incorrect and may result from algebraic errors when rewriting the given equation.

QUESTION 8

Choice B is correct. This question can be answered by making a connection between the table and the algebraic equation. Each row of the table gives a value of x and its corresponding values in both $w(x)$ and $t(x)$. For instance, the first row gives $x = 1$ and the corresponding values $w(1) =$ −1 and $t(1) = -3$. The row in the table where $x = 2$ is the only row that has the property $x = w(x) + t(x)$: $2 = 3 + (-1)$. Therefore, choice B is the correct answer.

Choice A is incorrect because when $x = 1$, the equation $w(x) + t(x) = x$ is not true. According to the table, $w(1) = -1$ and $t(1) = -3$. Substituting the values of each term when $x = 1$ gives −1 + (−3) = 1, an equation that is not true. Choice C is incorrect because when $x = 3$, the equation $w(x) + t(x) = x$ is not true. According to the table, $w(3) = 4$ and $t(3) = 1$. Substituting the values of each term when $x = 3$ gives 4 + 1 = 3, an equation that is not true. Choice D is incorrect because when $x = 4$, the equation $w(x) + t(x) = x$ is not true. According to the table, $w(4) = 3$ and $t(4) = 3$. Substituting the values of each term when $x = 4$ gives 3 + 3 = 4, an equation that is not true.

QUESTION 9

Choice C is correct. The two numerical expressions in the given equation can be simplified as $\sqrt{9} = 3$ and $\sqrt{64} = 8$, so the equation can be rewritten as $\sqrt{x} + 3 = 8$, or $\sqrt{x} = 5$. Squaring both sides of the equation gives $x = 25$.

Choice A is incorrect and may result from a misconception about how to square both sides of $\sqrt{x} = 5$ to determine the value of x. Choice B is incorrect. The value of $\sqrt{x}$, not x, is 5. Choice D is incorrect and represents a misconception about the properties of radicals. While it is true that 55 + 9 = 64, it is not true that $\sqrt{55} + \sqrt{9} = \sqrt{64}$.

QUESTION 10

Choice D is correct. Jaime's goal is to average at least 280 miles per week for 4 weeks. If T is the total number of miles Jamie will bicycle for 4 weeks, then his goal can be represented symbolically by the inequality: $\dfrac{T}{4} \geq 280$, or equivalently $T \geq 4(280)$. The total number of miles

Jamie will bicycle during this time is the sum of the distances he has completed and has yet to complete. Thus $T = 240 + 310 + 320 + x$. Substituting this expression into the inequality $T \geq 4(280)$ gives $240 + 310 + 320 + x \geq 4(280)$. Therefore, choice D is the correct answer.

Choices A, B, and C are incorrect because they do not correctly capture the relationships between the total number of miles Jaime will ride his bicycle ($240 + 310 + 320 + x$) and the minimum number of miles he is attempting to bicycle for the four weeks ($280 + 280 + 280 + 280$).

QUESTION 11

Choice B is correct. Since the shown parabola opens upward, the coefficient of x^2 in the equation $y = ax^2 + c$ must be positive. Given that a is positive, $-a$ is negative, and therefore the graph of the equation $y = -a(x - b)^2 + c$ will be a parabola that opens downward. The vertex of this parabola is (b, c), because the maximum value of y, c, is reached when $x = b$. Therefore, the answer must be choice B.

Choices A and C are incorrect. The coefficient of x^2 in the equation $y = -a(x - b)^2 + c$ is negative. Therefore, the parabola with this equation opens downward, not upward. Choice D is incorrect because the vertex of this parabola is (b, c), not $(-b, c)$, because the maximum value of y, c, is reached when $x = b$.

QUESTION 12
Choice D is correct. Dividing $4x^2 + 6x$ by $4x + 2$ gives:

$$
\begin{array}{r}
x + 1 \\
4x + 2 \overline{\smash{\big)}\ 4x^2 + 6x} \\
-(4x \ \ +2x) \\
\hline
4x \\
-(4x + 2) \\
\hline
-2
\end{array}
$$

Therefore, the expression $\dfrac{4x^2 + 6x}{4x + 2}$ is equivalent to $x + 1 - \dfrac{2}{4x + 2}$.

Alternate approach: The numerator of the given expression, $4x^2 + 6x$, can be rewritten in terms of the denominator, $4x + 2$, as follows: $4x^2 + 2x + 4x + 2 - 2$, or $x(4x + 2) + (4x + 2) - 2$. So the given expression can be rewritten as

$$
\frac{x(4x+2)+(4x+2)-2}{4x+2} = x+1-\frac{2}{4x+2}.
$$

Choices A and B are incorrect and may result from incorrectly factoring the numerator and denominator of the expression $\frac{4x^2 + 6x}{4x + 2}$ and then incorrectly identifying common factors in the two factored expressions. Choice C is incorrect and may result from a variety of mistakes made when performing long division.

QUESTION 13

Choice A is correct. The number of solutions to any quadratic equation in the form $ax^2 + bx + c = 0$, where a, b, and c are constants, can be found by evaluating the expression $b^2 - 4ac$, which is called the discriminant. If the value of $b^2 - 4ac$ is a positive number, then there will be exactly two real solutions to the equation. If the value of $b^2 - 4ac$ is zero, then there will be exactly one real solution to the equation. Finally, if the value of $b^2 - 4ac$ is negative, then there will be no real solutions to the equation.

The given equation $2x^2 - 4x = t$ is a quadratic equation in one variable, where t is a constant. Subtracting t from both sides of the equation gives $2x^2 - 4x - t = 0$. In this form, $a = 2$, $b = -4$, and $c = -t$. The values of t for which the equation has no real solutions are the same values of t for which the discriminant of this equation is a negative value. The discriminant is equal to $(-4)^2 - 4(2)(-t)$; therefore, $(-4)^2 - 4(2)(-t) < 0$. Simplifying the left side of the inequality gives $16 + 8t < 0$. Subtracting 16 from both sides of the inequality and then dividing both sides by 8 gives $t < -2$. Of the values given in the options, -3 is the only value that is less than -2. Therefore, choice A must be the correct answer.

Choices B, C, and D are incorrect and may result from a misconception about how to use the discriminant to determine the number of solutions of a quadratic equation in one variable.

QUESTION 14

Choice A is correct. The number of containers in a shipment must have a weight less than 300 pounds. The total weight, in pounds, of detergent and fabric softener that the supplier delivers can be expressed as the weight of each container multiplied by the number of each type of container, which is $7.35d$ for detergent and $6.2s$ for fabric softener. Since this total cannot exceed 300 pounds, it follows that $7.35d + 6.2s \le 300$. Also, since the laundry service wants to buy at least twice as many containers of detergent as containers of fabric softener, the number of containers of detergent should be greater than or equal to two times the number of containers of fabric softener. This can be expressed by the inequality $d \ge 2s$.

Choice B is incorrect because it misrepresents the relationship between the numbers of each container that the laundry service wants to buy. Choice C is incorrect because the first inequality of the system incorrectly doubles the weight per container of detergent. The weight of each container of detergent is 7.35, not 14.7 pounds. Choice D is incorrect because it doubles the weight per container of detergent and transposes the relationship between the numbers of containers.

QUESTION 15

Choice D is correct. The expression can be rewritten as $\left(a + \frac{b}{2}\right)\left(a + \frac{b}{2}\right)$. Using the distributive property, the expression yields $\left(a + \frac{b}{2}\right)\left(a + \frac{b}{2}\right) = a^2 + \frac{ab}{2} + \frac{ab}{2} + \frac{b^2}{4}$. Combining like terms gives $a^2 + ab + \frac{b^2}{4}$.

Choices A, B, and C are incorrect and may result from errors using the distributive property on the given expression or combining like terms.

QUESTION 16

The correct answers are 1, 2, 4, 8, or 16. Number 16 can be written in exponential form $a^{\frac{b}{4}}$, where a and b are positive integers as follows: 2^4, 4^2, 16^1, $\left(16^2\right)^{\frac{1}{2}}$, $\left(16^4\right)^{\frac{1}{4}}$. Hence, if $a^{\frac{b}{4}} = 16$, where a and b are positive integers, then $\frac{b}{4}$ can be 4, 2, 1, $\frac{1}{2}$, or $\frac{1}{4}$. So the value of b can be 16, 8, 4, 2, or 1. Any of these values may be gridded as the correct answer.

QUESTION 17

The correct answer is $\frac{15}{4}$ or 3.75. Multiplying both sides of the equation $\frac{2}{3}t = \frac{5}{2}$ by $\frac{3}{2}$ results in $t = \frac{15}{4}$, or $t = 3.75$.

QUESTION 18

The correct answer is 30. In the figure given, since $\overline{BD}$ is parallel to $\overline{AE}$ and both segments are intersected by $\overline{CE}$, then angle BDC and angle AEC are corresponding angles and therefore congruent. Angle BCD and angle ACE are also congruent because they are the same angle. Triangle BCD and triangle ACE are similar because if two angles of one triangle are congruent to two angles of another triangle, the triangles are similar. Since triangle BCD and triangle ACE are similar, their corresponding sides are proportional. So in triangle BCD and triangle ACE, $\overline{BD}$ corresponds to $\overline{AE}$ and $\overline{CD}$ corresponds to $\overline{CE}$. Therefore, $\frac{BD}{CD} = \frac{AE}{CE}$. Since triangle BCD is a right triangle, the Pythagorean theorem can be used to give the value of CD: $6^2 + 8^2 = CD^2$. Taking the square root of each side gives $CD = 10$. Substituting the values in the proportion $\frac{BD}{CD} = \frac{AE}{CE}$ yields

$\frac{6}{10} = \frac{18}{CE}$. Multiplying each side by CE, and then multiplying by $\frac{10}{6}$ yields CE = 30. Therefore, the length of $\overline{CE}$ is 30.

QUESTION 19

The correct answer is 1.5 or $\frac{3}{2}$. The total amount, in liters, of a saline solution can be expressed as the liters of each type of saline solution multiplied by the percent of the saline solution. This gives 3(0.10), x(0.25), and (x + 3)(0.15), where x is the amount, in liters, of a 25% saline solution and 10%, 15%, and 25% are represented as 0.10, 0.15, and 0.25, respectively. Thus, the equation 3(0.10) + 0.25x = 0.15(x + 3) must be true. Multiplying 3 by 0.10 and distributing 0.15 to (x + 3) yields 0.30 + 0.25x = 0.15x + 0.45. Subtracting 0.15x and 0.30 from each side of the equation gives 0.10x = 0.15. Dividing each side of the equation by 0.10 yields x = 1.5, or $x = \frac{3}{2}$.

QUESTION 20

The correct answer is $\frac{1}{6}$, .166, or .167. The circumference, C, of a circle is $C = 2\pi r$, where r is the radius of the circle. For the given circle with a radius of 1, the circumference is $C = 2(\pi)(1)$, or $C = 2\pi$. To find what fraction of the circumference the length of arc AB is, divide the length of the arc by the circumference, which gives $\frac{\pi}{3} \div 2\pi$. This division can be represented by $\frac{\pi}{3} \cdot \frac{1}{2\pi} = \frac{1}{6}$. The fraction $\frac{1}{6}$ can also be rewritten as .166 or .167.

Section 4: Math Test - Calculator

QUESTION 1

Choice A is correct. The given expression $(2x^2 - 4) - (-3x^2 + 2x - 7)$ can be rewritten as $2x^2 - 4 + 3x^2 - 2x + 7$. Combining like terms yields $5x^2 - 2x + 3$.

Choices B, C, and D are incorrect because they are the result of errors when applying the distributive property.

QUESTION 2

Choice C is correct. The lines shown on the graph give the positions of Paul and Mark during the race. At the start of the race, 0 seconds have elapsed, so the y-intercept of the line that represents Mark's position during the race represents the number of yards Mark was from Paul's position (at 0 yards) at the start of the race. Because the y-intercept of the line that represents Mark's position is at the grid line that is halfway between 12 and 24, Mark had a head start of 18 yards.

Choices A, B, and D are incorrect. The *y*-intercept of the line that represents Mark's position shows that he was 18 yards from Paul's position at the start of the race, so he did not have a head start of 3, 12, or 24 yards.

QUESTION 3

Choice A is correct. The leftmost segment in choice A, which represents the first time period, shows that the snow accumulated at a certain rate; the middle segment, which represents the second time period, is horizontal, showing that the snow stopped accumulating; and the rightmost segment, which represents the third time period, is steeper than the first segment, indicating that the snow accumulated at a faster rate than it did during the first time period.

Choice B is incorrect. This graph shows snow accumulating faster during the first time period than during the third time period; however, the question says that the rate of snow accumulation in the third time period is higher than in the first time period. Choice C is incorrect. This graph shows snow accumulation increasing during the first time period, not accumulating during the second time period, and then decreasing during the third time period; however, the question says that no snow melted (accumulation did not decrease) during this time. Choice D is incorrect. This graph shows snow accumulating at a constant rate, not stopping for a period of time or accumulating at a faster rate during a third time period.

QUESTION 4

Choice D is correct. The equation $12d + 350 = 1{,}010$ can be used to determine d, the number of dollars charged per month. Subtracting 350 from both sides of this equation yields $12d = 660$, and then dividing both sides of the equation by 12 yields $d = 55$.

Choice A is incorrect. If d were equal to 25, the first 12 months would cost $350 + (12)(25) = 650$ dollars, not $1,010. Choice B is incorrect. If d were equal to 35, the first 12 months would cost $350 + (12)(35) = 770$ dollars, not $1,010. Choice C is incorrect. If d were equal to 45, the first 12 months would cost $350 + (12)(45) = 890$ dollars, not $1,010.

QUESTION 5

Choice B is correct. Both sides of the given inequality can be divided by 3 to yield $2x - 3y > 4$.

Choices A, C, and D are incorrect because they are not equivalent to (do not have the same solution set as) the given inequality. For example, the ordered pair $(0, -1.5)$ is a solution to the given inequality, but it is not a solution to any of the inequalities in choices A, C, or D.

QUESTION 6

Choice C is correct. According to the table, 63% of survey respondents get most of their medical information from a doctor and 13% get most of their medical information from the Internet. Therefore, 76% of the 1,200 survey respondents get their information from either a doctor or the Internet, and 76% of 1,200 is 912.

Choices A, B, and D are incorrect. According to the table, 76% of survey respondents get their information from either a doctor or the Internet. Choice A is incorrect because 865 is about 72% (the percent of survey respondents who get most of their medical information from a doctor or from magazines/brochures), not 76%, of 1,200. Choice B is incorrect because 887 is about 74%, not 76%, of 1,200. Choice D is incorrect because 926 is about 77%, not 76%, of 1,200.

QUESTION 7

Choice D is correct. The members of the city council wanted to assess opinions of all city residents. To gather an unbiased sample, the council should have used a random sampling design to select subjects from all city residents. The given survey introduced a sampling bias because the 500 city residents surveyed were all dog owners. This sample is not representative of all city residents.

Choice A is incorrect because when the sampling method isn't random, there is no guarantee that the survey results will be reliable; hence, they cannot be generalized to the entire population. Choice B is incorrect because a larger sample size would not correct the sampling bias. Choice C is incorrect because a survey sample of non–dog owners would likely have a biased opinion, just as a sample of dog owners would likely have a biased opinion.

QUESTION 8

Choice D is correct. According to the table, 13 people chose vanilla ice cream. Of those people, 8 chose hot fudge as a topping. Therefore, of the people who chose vanilla ice cream, the fraction who chose hot fudge as a topping is $\dfrac{8}{13}$.

Choice A is incorrect because it represents the fraction of people at the party who chose hot fudge as a topping. Choice B is incorrect because it represents the fraction of people who chose vanilla ice cream with caramel as a topping. Choice C is incorrect because it represents the fraction of people at the party who chose vanilla ice cream.

QUESTION 9

Choice B is correct. The land area of the coastal city can be found by subtracting the area of the water from the total area of the coastal city; that is, 92.1 − 11.3 = 80.8 square miles. The population density is the population divided by the land area, or $\frac{621,000}{80.8} = 7,685$, which is closest to 7,690 people per square mile.

Choice A is incorrect and may be the result of dividing the population by the total area, instead of the land area. Choice C is incorrect and may be the result of dividing the population by the area of water. Choice D is incorrect and may be the result of making a computational error with the decimal place.

QUESTION 10

Choice B is correct. Let x represent the number of days the second voyage lasted. The number of days the first voyage lasted is then $x + 43$. Since the two voyages combined lasted a total of 1,003 days, the equation $x + (x + 43) = 1,003$ must hold. Combining like terms yields $2x + 43 = 1,003$, and solving for x gives $x = 480$.

Choice A is incorrect because 460 + (460 + 43) = 963, not 1,003 days. Choice C is incorrect because 520 + (520 + 43) = 1,083, not 1,003 days. Choice D is incorrect because 540 + (540 + 43) = 1,123, not 1,003 days.

QUESTION 11

Choice B is correct. Adding the equations side-by-side eliminates y, as shown below.

$$
\begin{array}{l}
7x + 3y = 8 \\
6x - 3y = 5 \\
\hline
13x + 0 = 13
\end{array}
$$

Solving the obtained equation for x gives $x = 1$. Substituting 1 for x in the first equation gives $7(1) + 3y = 8$. Subtracting 7 from both sides of the equation yields $3y = 1$, so $y = \frac{1}{3}$. Therefore, the value of $x - y$ is $1 - \frac{1}{3}$, or $\frac{2}{3}$.

Choice C is incorrect because $1 + \frac{1}{3} = \frac{4}{3}$ is the value of $x + y$, not $x - y$. Choices A and D are incorrect and may be the result of some computational errors.

QUESTION 12

Choice D is correct. The average growth rate of the sunflower over a certain time period is the increase in height of the sunflower over the period divided by the time. Symbolically, this rate is $\frac{h(b)-h(a)}{b-a}$, where a and b are the first and the last day of the time period, respectively. Since the time period for each option is the same (21 days), the total growth over the period can be used to evaluate in which time period the sunflower grew the least. According to the graph, the sunflower grew the least over the period from day 63 to day 84. Therefore, the sunflower's average growth rate was the least from day 63 to day 84.

Alternate approach: The average growth rate of the sunflower over a certain time period is the slope of the line segment that joins the point on the graph at the beginning of the time period with the point on the graph at the end of the time period. Based on the graph, of the four time periods, the slope of the line segment is least between the sunflower's height on day 63 and its height on day 84.

Choices A, B, and C are incorrect. On the graph, the line segment from day 63 to 84 is less steep than each of the three other line segments representing other periods. Therefore, the average growth rate of the sunflower is the least from day 63 to 84.

QUESTION 13

Choice A is correct. Based on the definition and contextual interpretation of the function h, when the value of t increases by 1, the height of the sunflower increases by a centimeters. Therefore, a represents the predicted amount, in centimeters, by which the sunflower grows each day during the period the function models.

Choice B is incorrect. In the given model, the beginning of the period corresponds to $t = 0$, and since $h(0) = b$, the predicted height, in centimeters, of the sunflower at the beginning of the period is represented by b, not by a. Choice C is incorrect. If the period of time modeled by the function is c days long, then the predicted height, in centimeters, of the sunflower at the end of the period is represented by $ac + b$, not by a. Choice D is incorrect. If the period of time modeled by the function is c days long, the predicted total increase in the height of the sunflower, in centimeters, during that period is represented by the difference $h(c) - h(0) = (ac + b) - (a \cdot 0 + b)$, which is equivalent to ac, not a.

QUESTION 14

Choice B is correct. According to the table, the height of the sunflower is 36.36 cm on day 14 and 131.00 cm on day 35. Since the height of the sunflower between day 14 and day 35 changes at a nearly constant rate, the height of the sunflower increases by approximately

$\dfrac{131.00-36.36}{35-14} \approx 4.5$ cm per day. Therefore, the equation that models the height of the sunflower t days after it begins to grow is of the form $h = 4.5t + b$. Any ordered pair (t, h) from the table between day 14 and day 35 can be used to estimate the value of b. For example, substituting the ordered pair (14, 36.36) for (t, h) into the equation $h = 4.5t + b$ gives 36.36 = 4.5(14) + b. Solving this for b yields $b = -26.64$. Therefore, of the given choices, the equation $h = 4.5t - 27$ best models the height h, in centimeters, of the sunflower t days after it begins to grow.

Choices A, C, and D are incorrect because the growth rates of the sunflower from day 14 to day 35 in these choices are significantly higher or lower than the true growth rate of the sunflower as shown in the graph or the table. These choices may result from considering time periods different from the period indicated in the question or from calculation errors.

QUESTION 15

Choice D is correct. According to the table, the value of y increases by $\dfrac{14}{4} = \dfrac{7}{2}$ every time the value of x increases by 1. It follows that the simplest equation relating y to x is linear and of the form $y = \dfrac{7}{2}x + b$ for some constant b. Furthermore, the ordered pair $\left(1, \dfrac{11}{4}\right)$ from the table must satisfy this equation. Substituting 1 for x and $\dfrac{11}{4}$ for y in the equation $y = \dfrac{7}{2}x + b$ gives $\dfrac{11}{4} = \dfrac{7}{2}(1) + b$. Solving this equation for b gives $b = -\dfrac{3}{4}$. Therefore, the equation in choice D correctly relates y to x.

Choices A and B are incorrect. The relationship between x and y cannot be exponential because the differences, not the ratios, of y-values are the same every time the x-values change by the same amount. Choice C is incorrect because the ordered pair $\left(2, \dfrac{25}{4}\right)$ is not a solution to the equation $y = \dfrac{3}{4}x + 2$. Substituting 2 for x and $\dfrac{25}{4}$ for y in this equation gives $\dfrac{25}{4} = \dfrac{3}{2} + 2$, which is false.

QUESTION 16

Choice B is correct. In right triangle ABC, the measure of angle B must be 58° because the sum of the measure of angle A, which is 32°, and the measure of angle B is 90°. Angle D in the right triangle DEF has measure 58°. Hence, triangles ABC and DEF are similar. Since BC is the side opposite to the angle with measure 32° and *AB* is the hypotenuse in right triangle *ABC*, the ratio $\dfrac{BC}{AB}$ is equal to $\dfrac{DF}{DE}$.

Alternate approach: The trigonometric ratios can be used to answer this question. In right triangle *ABC*, the ratio $\dfrac{BC}{AB} = \sin(32°)$. The angle *E* in triangle *DEF* has measure 32° because $m(\angle D) + m(\angle E) = 90°$. In triangle *DEF*, the ratio $\dfrac{DF}{DE} = \sin(32°)$. Therefore, $\dfrac{DF}{DE} = \dfrac{BC}{AB}$.

Choice A is incorrect because $\dfrac{DE}{DF}$ is the inverse of the ratio $\dfrac{BC}{AB}$. Choice C is incorrect because $\dfrac{DF}{EF} = \dfrac{BC}{AC}$, not $\dfrac{BC}{AB}$. Choice D is incorrect because $\dfrac{EF}{DE} = \dfrac{AC}{AB}$, not $\dfrac{BC}{AB}$.

QUESTION 17

Choice B is correct. Isolating the term that contains the riser height, *h*, in the formula 2*h* + *d* = 25 gives 2*h* = 25 – *d*. Dividing both sides of this equation by 2 yields $h = \dfrac{25 - d}{2}$, or

$$h = \dfrac{1}{2}(25 - d).$$

Choices A, C, and D are incorrect and may result from incorrect transformations of the riser-tread formula 2*h* + *d* = 25 when expressing *h* in terms of *d*.

QUESTION 18

Choice C is correct. Since the tread depth, *d*, must be at least 9 inches, and the riser height, *h*, must be at least 5 inches, it follows that *d* ≥ 9 and *h* ≥ 5, respectively. Solving for *d* in the riser-tread formula 2*h* + *d* = 25 gives *d* = 25 – 2*h*. Thus the first inequality, *d* ≥ 9, is equivalent to 25 – 2*h* ≥ 9. This inequality can be solved for *h* as follows:

$$-2h \geq 9 - 25$$

$$2h \leq 25 - 9$$

$$2h \leq 16$$

$$h \leq 8$$

Therefore, the inequality $5 \leq h \leq 8$, derived from combining the inequalities $h \geq 5$ and $h \leq 8$, represents the set of all possible values for the riser height that meets the code requirement.

Choice A is incorrect because the riser height, h, cannot be less than 5 inches. Choices B and D are incorrect because the riser height, h, cannot be greater than 8. For example, if $h = 10$, then according to the riser-tread formula $2h + d = 25$, it follows that $d = 5$ inches. However, d must be at least 9 inches according to the building codes, so h cannot be 10.

QUESTION 19

Choice C is correct. Let h be the riser height, in inches, and n be the number of the steps in the stairway. According to the architect's design, the total rise of the stairway is 9 feet, or $9 \times 12 = 108$ inches. Hence, $nh = 108$, and solving for n gives $n = \dfrac{108}{h}$. It is given that $7 < h < 8$. It follows that $\dfrac{108}{8} < \dfrac{108}{h} < \dfrac{108}{7}$, or equivalently, $\dfrac{108}{8} < n < \dfrac{108}{7}$. Since $\dfrac{108}{8} < 14$ and $\dfrac{108}{7} > 15$ and n is an integer, it follows that $14 \leq n \leq 15$. Since n can be an odd number, n can only be 15; therefore, $h = \dfrac{108}{15} = 7.2$ inches. Substituting 7.2 for h in the riser-tread formula $2h + d = 25$ gives $14.4 + d = 25$. Solving for d gives $d = 10.6$ inches.

Choice A is incorrect because 7.2 inches is the riser height, not the tread depth of the stairs. Choice B is incorrect and may be the result of calculation errors. Choice D is incorrect because 15 is the number of steps, not the tread depth of the stairs.

QUESTION 20

Choice C is correct. Since the product of $x - 6$ and $x + 0.7$ equals 0, by the zero product property either $x - 6 = 0$ or $x + 0.7 = 0$. Therefore, the solutions to the equation are 6 and −0.7. The sum of 6 and −0.7 is 5.3.

Choice A is incorrect and is the result of subtracting 6 from −0.7 instead of adding. Choice B is incorrect and may be the result of erroneously calculating the sum of −6 and 0.7 instead of 6 and −0.7. Choice D is incorrect and is the sum of 6 and 0.7, not 6 and −0.7.

QUESTION 21

Choice D is correct. The sample of 150 largemouth bass was selected at random from all the largemouth bass in the pond, and since 30% of them weighed more than 2 pounds, it can be concluded that approximately 30% of all largemouth bass in the pond weigh more than 2 pounds.

Choices A, B, and C are incorrect. Since the sample contained 150 largemouth bass, of which 30% weighed more than 2 pounds, the largest population to which this result can be generalized is the population of the largemouth bass in the pond.

QUESTION 22

Choice B is correct. The median of a list of numbers is the middle value when the numbers are listed in order from least to greatest. For the electoral votes shown in the table, their frequency should also be taken into account. Since there are 21 states represented in the table, the middle number will be the eleventh number in the ordered list. Counting the frequencies from the top of the table (4 + 4 + 1 + 1 + 3 = 13) shows that the median number of electoral votes for the 21 states is 15.

Choice A is incorrect. If the electoral votes are ordered from least to greatest taking into account the frequency, 13 will be in the tenth position, not the middle. Choice C is incorrect because 17 is in the fourteenth position, not in the middle, of the ordered list. D is incorrect because 20 is in the fifteenth position, not in the middle, of the ordered list.

QUESTION 23

Choice C is correct. Since the graph shows the height of the ball above the ground after it was dropped, the number of times the ball was at a height of 2 feet is equal to the number of times the graph crosses the horizontal grid line that corresponds to a height of 2 feet. The graph crosses this grid line three times.

Choices A, B, and D are incorrect. According to the graph, the ball was at a height of 2 feet three times, not one, two, or four times.

QUESTION 24

Choice D is correct. To find the percent increase of the customer's water bill, the absolute increase of the bill, in dollars, is divided by the original amount of the bill, and the result is multiplied by 100%, as follows: $\frac{79.86 - 75.74}{75.74} \approx 0.054$; $0.054 \times 100\% = 5.4\%$.

Choice A is incorrect. This choice is the difference 79.86 − 75.74 rounded to the nearest tenth, which is the (absolute) increase of the bill's amount, not its percent increase. Choice B is incorrect and may be the result of some calculation errors. Choice C is incorrect and is the result of dividing the difference between the two bill amounts by the new bill amount instead of the original bill amount.

QUESTION 25

Choice B is correct. A linear function has a constant rate of change, and any two rows of the shown table can be used to calculate this rate. From the first row to the second, the value of x is increased by 2 and the value of $f(x)$ is increased by $6 = 4 - (-2)$. So the values of $f(x)$ increase by 3 for every increase by 1 in the value of x. Since $f(2) = 4$, it follows that $f(2 + 1) = 4 + 3 = 7$. Therefore, $f(3) = 7$.

Choice A is incorrect. This is the third x-value in the table, not $f(3)$. Choices C and D are incorrect and may result from errors when calculating the function's rate of change.

QUESTION 26

Choice C is correct. Since Gear A has 20 teeth and Gear B has 60 teeth, the gear ratio for Gears A and B is 20:60. Thus the ratio of the number of revolutions per minute (rpm) for the two gears is 60:20, or 3:1. That is, when Gear A turns at 3 rpm, Gear B turns at 1 rpm. Similarly, since Gear B has 60 teeth and Gear C has 10 teeth, the gear ratio for Gears B and C is 60:10, and the ratio of the rpms for the two gears is 10:60. That is, when Gear B turns at 1 rpm, Gear C turns at 6 rpm. Therefore, if Gear A turns at 100 rpm, then Gear B turns at $\dfrac{100}{3}$ rpm, and Gear C turns at $\dfrac{100}{3} \times 6 = 200$ rpm.

Alternate approach: Gear A and Gear C can be considered as directly connected since their "contact" speeds are the same. Gear A has twice as many teeth as Gear C, and since the ratios of the number of teeth are equal to the reverse of the ratios of rotation speeds, in rpm, Gear C would be rotated at a rate that is twice the rate of Gear A. Therefore, Gear C will be rotated at a rate of 200 rpm since Gear A is rotated at 100 rpm.

Choice A is incorrect and may result from using the gear ratio instead of the ratio of the rpm when calculating the rotational speed of Gear C. **Choice B is incorrect** and may result from comparing the rpm of the gears using addition instead of multiplication. **Choice D is incorrect** and may be the result of multiplying the 100 rpm for Gear A by the number of teeth in Gear C.

QUESTION 27

Choice A is correct. One way to find the radius of the circle is to put the given equation in standard form, $(x - h)^2 + (y - k)^2 = r^2$, where (h, k) is the center of the circle and the radius of the circle is r. To do this, divide the original equation, $2x^2 - 6x + 2y^2 + 2y = 45$, by 2 to make the leading coefficients of x^2 and y^2 each equal to 1: $x^2 - 3x + y^2 + y = 22.5$. Then complete the square to put the equation in standard form. To do so, first rewrite $x^2 - 3x + y^2 + y = 22.5$ as $(x^2 - 3x + 2.25) - 2.25 + (y^2 + y + 0.25) - 0.25 = 22.5$. Second, add 2.25 and 0.25 to both sides of the equation: $(x^2 - 3x + 2.25) + (y^2 + y + 0.25) = 25$. Since $x^2 - 3x + 2.25 = (x - 1.5)^2$, $y^2 - x + 0.25 = (y$

$- 0.5)^2$, and $25 = 5^2$, it follows that $(x - 1.5)^2 + (y - 0.5)^2 = 5^2$. Therefore, the radius of the circle is 5.

Choices B, C, and D are incorrect and may be the result of errors in manipulating the equation or of a misconception about the standard form of the equation of a circle in the *xy*-plane.

QUESTION 28

Choice A is correct. The coordinates of the points at a distance *d* units from the point with coordinate *a* on the number line are the solutions to the equation $|x - a| = d$. Therefore, the coordinates of the points at a distance of 3 units from the point with coordinate −4 on the number line are the solutions to the equation $|x - (-4)| = 3$, which is equivalent to $|x + 4| = 3$.

Choice B is incorrect. The solutions of $|x - 4| = 3$ are the coordinates of the points on the number line at a distance of 3 units from the point with coordinate 4. Choice C is incorrect. The solutions of $|x + 3| = 4$ are the coordinates of the points on the number line at a distance of 4 units from the point with coordinate −3. Choice D is incorrect. The solutions of $|x - 3| = 4$ are the coordinates of the points on the number line at a distance of 4 units from the point with coordinate 3.

QUESTION 29

Choice B is correct. The average speed of the model car is found by dividing the total distance traveled by the car by the total time the car traveled. In the first *t* seconds after the car starts, the time changes from 0 to *t* seconds. So the total distance the car traveled is the distance it traveled at *t* seconds minus the distance it traveled at 0 seconds. At 0 seconds, the car has traveled $16(0)\sqrt{0}$ inches, which is equal to 0 inches. According to the equation given, after *t* seconds, the car has traveled $16t\sqrt{t}$ inches. In other words, after the car starts, it travels a total of $16t\sqrt{t}$ inches in *t* seconds. Dividing this total distance traveled by the total time shows the

car's average speed: $\dfrac{16t\sqrt{t}}{t} = 16\sqrt{t}$ inches per second.

Choices A, C, and D are incorrect and may result from misconceptions about how average speed is calculated.

QUESTION 30

Choice D is correct. The data in the scatterplot roughly fall in the shape of a downward-opening parabola; therefore, the coefficient for the x^2 term must be negative. Based on the location of the data points, the y-intercept of the parabola should be somewhere between 740 and 760. Therefore, of the equations given, the best model is $y = -1.674x^2 + 19.76x + 745.73$.

Choices A and C are incorrect. The positive coefficient of the x^2 term means that these these equations each define upward-opening parabolas, whereas a parabola that fits the data in the scatterplot must open downward. Choice B is incorrect because it defines a parabola with a y-intercept that has a negative y-coordinate, whereas a parabola that fits the data in the scatterplot must have a y-intercept with a positive y-coordinate.

QUESTION 31

The correct answer is 10. Let n be the number of friends originally in the group. Since the cost of the trip was \$800, the share, in dollars, for each friend was originally $\dfrac{800}{n}$. When two friends decided not to go on the trip, the number of friends who split the \$800 cost became $n - 2$, and each friend's cost became $\dfrac{800}{n-2}$. Since this share represented a \$20 increase over the original share, the equation $\dfrac{800}{n} + 20 = \dfrac{800}{n-2}$ must be true. Multiplying each side of $\dfrac{800}{n} + 20 = \dfrac{800}{n-2}$ by $n(n - 2)$ to clear all the denominators gives

$$800(n - 2) + 20n(n - 2) = 800n$$

This is a quadratic equation and can be rewritten in the standard form by expanding, simplifying, and then collecting like terms on one side, as shown below:

$$800n - 1600 + 20n^2 - 40n = 800n$$

$$40n - 80 + n^2 - 2n = 40n$$

$$n^2 - 2n - 80 = 0$$

After factoring, this becomes $(n + 8)(n - 10) = 0$.

The solutions of this equation are -8 and 10. Since a negative solution makes no sense for the number of people in a group, the number of friends originally in the group was 10.

QUESTION 32

The correct answer is 31. The equation can be solved using the steps shown below.

$2(5x - 20) - 15 - 8x = 7$

$2(5x) - 2(20) - 15 - 8x = 7$ (Apply the distributive property.)

$10x - 40 - 15 - 8x = 7$ (Multiply.)

$2x - 55 = 7$ (Combine like terms.)

$2x = 62$ (Add 55 to both sides of the equation.)

$x = 31$ (Divide both sides of the equation by 2.)

QUESTION 33

The possible correct answers are 97, 98, 99, 100, and 101. The volume of a cylinder can be found by using the formula $V = \pi r^2 h$, where r is the radius of the circular base and h is the height of the cylinder. The smallest possible volume, in cubic inches, of a graduated cylinder produced by the laboratory supply company can be found by substituting 2 for r and 7.75 for h, giving $V = \pi(2^2)(7.75)$. This gives a volume of approximately 97.39 cubic inches, which rounds to 97 cubic inches. The largest possible volume, in cubic inches, can be found by substituting 2 for r and 8 for h, giving $V = \pi(2^2)(8)$. This gives a volume of approximately 100.53 cubic inches, which rounds to 101 cubic inches. Therefore, the possible volumes are all the integers greater than or equal to 97 and less than or equal to 101, which are 97, 98, 99, 100, and 101. Any of these numbers may be gridded as the correct answer.

QUESTION 34

The correct answer is 5. The intersection points of the graphs of $y = 3x^2 - 14x$ and $y = x$ can be found by solving the system consisting of these two equations. To solve the system, substitute x for y in the first equation. This gives $x = 3x^2 - 14x$. Subtracting x from both sides of the equation gives $0 = 3x^2 - 15x$. Factoring $3x$ out of each term on the left-hand side of the equation gives $0 = 3x(x - 5)$. Therefore, the possible values for x are 0 and 5. Since $y = x$, the two intersection points are (0, 0) and (5, 5). Therefore, $a = 5$.

QUESTION 35

The correct answer is 1.25 or $\dfrac{5}{4}$. The y-coordinate of the x-intercept is 0, so 0 can be substituted for y, giving $\dfrac{4}{5}x + \dfrac{1}{3}(0) = 1$. This simplifies to $\dfrac{4}{5}x = 1$. Multiplying both sides of $\dfrac{4}{5}x$

= 1 by 5 gives $4x = 5$. Dividing both sides of $4x = 5$ by 4 gives $x = \dfrac{5}{4}$, which is equivalent to 1.25. Either 5/4 or 1.25 may be gridded as the correct answer.

QUESTION 36

The correct answer is 2.6 or $\dfrac{13}{5}$. Since the mean of a set of numbers can be found by adding the numbers together and dividing by how many numbers there are in the set, the mean mass, in kilograms, of the rocks Andrew collected is $\dfrac{2.4+2.5+3.6+3.1+2.5+2.7}{6} = \dfrac{16.8}{6} = 2.8$. Since the mean mass of the rocks Maria collected is 0.1 kilogram greater than the mean mass of rocks Andrew collected, the mean mass of the rocks Maria collected is 2.8 + 0.1 = 2.9 kilograms. The value of x can be found by using the algorithm for finding the mean: $\dfrac{x+3.1+2.7+2.9+3.3+2.8}{6} = 2.9$. Solving this equation gives $x = 2.6$, which is equivalent to $\dfrac{13}{5}$. Either 2.6 or 13/5 may be gridded as the correct answer.

QUESTION 37

The correct answer is 30. The situation can be represented by the equation $x(2^4) = 480$, where the 2 represents the fact that the amount of money in the account doubled each year and the 4 represents the fact that there are 4 years between January 1, 2001, and January 1, 2005. Simplifying $x(2^4) = 480$ gives $16x = 480$. Therefore, $x = 30$.

QUESTION 38

The correct answer is 8. The 6 students represent $(100 - 15 - 45 - 25)\% = 15\%$ of those invited to join the committee. If x people were invited to join the committee, then $0.15x = 6$. Thus, there were $\dfrac{6}{0.15} = 40$ people invited to join the committee. It follows that there were $0.45(40) = 18$ teachers and $0.25(40) = 10$ school and district administrators invited to join the committee. Therefore, there were 8 more teachers than school and district administrators invited to join the committee.